Better Homes and Gardens®

NEW Dieter's COOKBOOK

EAT WELL

FEEL GREAT

LOSE WEIGHT

Meredith® Books
Des Moines, Iowa

New Dieter's Cookbook

Editor: Kristi M. Thomas, R.D.
Senior Associate Design Director: Doug Samuelson
Contributing Editors: Marcia Stanley, R.D.; Joyce Trollope; Spectrum Communication Services, Inc.
Contributing Writer: Diane Quagliani, R.D.
Copy Chief: Terri Fredrickson
Copy and Production Editor: Victoria Forlini
Editorial Operations Manager: Karen Schirm
Managers, Book Production: Pam Kvitne, Marjorie J. Schenkelberg, Rick von Holdt
Contributing Copy Editor: Kim Catanzarite
Contributing Proofreaders: Maria Duryée, Gretchen Kauffman, Susan J. Kling
Photographers: Marty Baldwin, Mike Dieter, Scott Little, Jay Wilde
Food Stylists: Jill Lust, Dianna Nolin, Charles Worthington
Prop Stylist: Susan Strelecki
Indexer: Kathleen Poole
Electronic Production Coordinator: Paula Forest
Editorial and Design Assistants: Karen McFadden, Mary Lee Gavin
Test Kitchen Director: Lynn Blanchard
Test Kitchen Product Supervisors: Marilyn Cornelius, Jennifer Kalinowski, R.D.
Test Kitchen Home Economists: Juliana Hale; Laura Harms, R.D.; Maryellyn Krantz; Jill Moberly;
    Colleen Weeden; Lori Wilson

Meredith® Books

Editor in Chief: Linda Raglan Cunningham
Design Director: Matt Strelecki
Executive Editor, Food and Crafts: Jennifer Dorland Darling

Publisher: James D. Blume
Executive Director, Marketing: Jeffrey Myers
Executive Director, New Business Development: Todd M. Davis
Executive Director, Sales: Ken Zagor
Director, Operations: George A. Susral
Director, Production: Douglas M. Johnston
Business Director: Jim Leonard

Vice President and General Manager: Douglas J. Guendel

Better Homes and Gardens® Magazine

Editor in Chief: Karol DeWulf Nickell
Deputy Editor, Food and Entertaining: Nancy Hopkins

Meredith Publishing Group

President, Publishing Group: Stephen M. Lacy
Vice President-Publishing Director: Bob Mate

Meredith Corporation

Chairman and Chief Executive Officer: William T. Kerr

In Memoriam: E. T. Meredith III (1933-2003)

All of us at Better Homes and Gardens® Books are dedicated to providing you with the information and ideas you need to create delicious foods. We welcome your comments and suggestions. Write to us at: Better Homes and Gardens Books, Cookbook Editorial Department, 1716 Locust St., Des Moines, IA 50309-3023.

If you would like to purchase any of our cooking, crafts, gardening, home improvement, or home decorating and design books, check wherever quality books are sold. Or visit us at: bhgbooks.com

* Reviews on back cover for *New Dieter's Cookbook,* 2nd edition, from Amazon. com.

Our seal assures you that every recipe in *New Dieter's Cookbook* has been tested in the Better Homes and Gardens® Test Kitchen. This means that each recipe is practical and reliable, and meets our high standards of taste appeal. We guarantee your satisfaction with this book for as long as you own it.

Pictured on the cover: Spicy Chicken with Fruit (recipe on page 308)

CHAPTER 1

WEIGHT LOSS GUIDE

CONTENTS

Taco Pizza
Kids' Favorites, page 144

**Rosemary-Rubbed
Lamb Chops**
Pork, Ham & Lamb, page 290

Mocha Cake
Desserts, page 501

INTRODUCTION

New and Improved

This edition of *Better Homes and Gardens*® *New Dieter's Cookbook* is new in every sense of the word. Of course, all of the recipes and photography are new, and more than that, this cookbook takes a surprisingly new approach to dieting, which is not dieting at all.

We're not suggesting that you should not worry about reaching your optimal weight. Maintaining a desirable weight enhances your appearance, boosts your energy level, and helps you stay healthy. The alarming number of overweight and obese Americans (including children) is proof enough that the problem must be addressed. To help with this effort, we've compiled hundreds of good-for-you recipes, weight loss tips, inspiration, and encouragement to help anyone lose weight—without severely restricting food intake. Join the owners of previous editions of *New Dieter's Cookbook* who've written to thank us for helping them lose weight. Great-tasting recipes are the hallmark of all *Better Homes and Gardens* cookbooks, and that premise holds for this edition. We invite you to taste for yourself!

At any given time, millions of Americans claim to be "on a diet." Because there are almost as many diets as there are people who want to lose weight, this can mean almost anything, but the method dieters choose could be the difference between successful or unsuccessful weight loss. When deciding on which route to take in an effort to lose those extra pounds, don't be fooled. The typical strict and restrictive weight loss diets are unlikely to help you reach and maintain a healthy weight. Why? Consider these points:

- An estimated 95 percent of people who lose weight by restrictive dieting gain back the weight—and often a few additional pounds—within five years.

- People often view dieting as a temporary situation to endure until they lose weight. After that, they resume their old way of eating, which caused them to gain weight to begin with.

- With dieting comes the false hope that losing weight is magically life changing. Many people believe that if they lose weight, they will look like a fashion model, find true love, or receive a promotion. The reality is that they'll still be the same people living the same lives. The only difference is that they will wear a smaller size.

- Because diets dictate when, what, and how much to eat, they undermine a person's inborn signals of hunger and fullness. Listening to these signals is the best gauge for how much food your body needs.

- Some diets are hazardous to your health because they forbid consumption of certain foods or food groups, making it difficult to get the nutrients you need.

If the old-fashioned, restrictive diets don't work, then what does? The surest route to a healthy weight is to take gradual, permanent steps toward changing the way you eat and how much physical activity you get. In this introduction, you'll find the information and tools you need to do just that.

You'll learn how to determine your readiness to embark on a weight loss plan, assess the healthfulness of your weight, set reasonable goals, and calculate your daily calorie needs for weight loss. You'll also find lots of strategies and tips to help you and your family make healthful eating and physical activity a permanent part of your lives. Most importantly, you'll discover that a "no-diet" way to lose pounds and maintain a healthful weight is possible.

What's Causing America's Weight Problem?

According to the latest government surveys, nearly two out of three (64.5 percent) American adults age 20 years and older were classified as overweight or obese, and this number is rising steadily.

In the simplest terms, human beings gain weight when they eat more calories than they burn off. Consuming just 100 extra calories per day—the amount in a cookie, a handful of potato chips, or an 8-ounce soft drink—can add up to a 10-pound weight gain in a year. That's a simple calculation, but the factors fueling caloric imbalance are complex and specific to each individual.

Some factors are as basic as being surrounded by bountiful food portions, cleaning plates when over full, and living sedentary lifestyles. Nowadays people drive short distances that are more appropriate for walking and use laborsaving devices, such as elevators or escalators, power lawn mowers, and leaf blowers, that eliminate many calorie-burning activities.

Individual differences in metabolism and genetic makeup also influence the tendency to gain weight. In addition, researchers are examining the body's complex system of hormones that control appetite to determine their roles in making weight loss more difficult for some people.

Are You Ready to Lose Weight?

This may seem like a silly question, but the fact is many people don't stay motivated because their reasons for losing weight aren't clear in their minds or because they're trying to lose for the wrong reasons. If you answer "no" to one or more of these questions, reconsider whether this is the right time to attempt a weight loss plan.

● Are your reasons specific and meaningful? A vague reason such as "I know I should" is not as motivating as one that improves your quality of life, such as "I want to feel more energetic" or "I want to lower my blood pressure in hopes of reducing my medication."

● Are you doing it just for you? Losing weight to please someone else probably won't be enough motivation to reach your goal.

● Are you ready to do the work? Succeeding at weight loss requires a firm commitment to changing your eating and exercise habits. You must be willing to develop and carry out an action plan.

● Is your life basically in order? Now is probably not the right time if you're in the midst of a family, work, or health crisis or major life event. Wait until things calm down.

● Are you in it for the long haul? Losing weight for an upcoming wedding or class reunion is motivating until the big event. Consider how you'll stick with your plan afterwards.

What's Your Healthy Weight?

Are you overweight or obese? The answer to this question is not as clear-cut as you might think. Perhaps a better question to ask is "Are you 'over fat'?" Extra body weight from fat increases your risk for developing health problems, such as high blood pressure, heart disease, diabetes, and some cancers.

How do you know if you are over fat? The number you see on the scale provides only one piece of the puzzle because it doesn't tell you how much of your weight is fat, muscle, bone, or fluid. Consulting a weight chart offers another clue, but most charts don't account for individual characteristics such as your age and frame size. In addition, like the scale, charts can't tell you whether you are carrying a less-than-healthful amount of fat. It's best to use these tools as general guidelines only.

Two reliable guidelines for assessing your weight are the Body Mass Index (BMI) and your waist measurement. Health experts say the higher your BMI and your waist measurement, the higher your potential for developing weight-related health problems, especially if you exhibit one or more risk factors.

For instance, your risk may be greater if close relatives have suffered from heart disease or type 2 diabetes. If you already have a health condition associated with obesity, such as high cholesterol, high blood pressure, diabetes, or heart disease, your risk of a heart attack or stroke is increased, particularly if you are overweight or obese. Being sedentary and a smoker also increase your risk.

To calculate your BMI and waist measurement, and evaluate whether your weight is putting your health at risk, see "Evaluate Your Weight," below.

Setting a Goal Weight

If your BMI or waist measurement suggests you need to lose weight, the next step is to set a realistic and healthful goal weight.

The best weight for you is as individual as your fingerprints. To make sure your goal is reasonable and realistic, ask yourself these questions:

EVALUATE YOUR WEIGHT

Grab a calculator and a tape measure, and follow the steps below to evaluate whether your weight is putting your health at risk.

To calculate your BMI:
The Body Mass Index (BMI) measures weight in relation to height. People with a high BMI tend to have a high risk of developing long-term health problems. (One discrepancy is if you are muscular, because you may have a high BMI without any additional health risks.) Use the formula below to calculate your BMI.

BMI = [Weight in pounds ÷ Height in inches ÷ Height in inches] x 703

For example, a 145-pound woman who stands 5'6" (66") tall has a BMI of 23, which falls into the "healthy weight" category.

BMI = [145 pounds ÷ 66" ÷ 66"] x 703 = 23

Once you calculate your BMI, check the chart below to see which category it falls into.

Body Mass Index (BMI)	Category
18.5 to 25	Healthy weight
25 to 30	Overweight
30 or higher	Obese

Source: Report of the Dietary Guidelines Advisory Committee on the Dietary Guidelines for Americans, 2000, page 3.

To calculate your waist measurement:
Excess abdominal fat may increase your risk for health problems, even if your BMI is in the "healthy weight" range. While standing, measure around your waist, just above your hipbones. A measurement of greater than 35 inches for women or 40 inches for men indicates greater risk for health problems.

• Am I relying on a weight chart to find the best weight for me? Because weight charts offer general guidelines only, the best weight for you may be higher or lower than the chart indicates.

• Is my goal weight realistic for me? Most people don't have the build of a tall, willowy fashion model. Set a goal that suits your particular build.

• Can I comfortably maintain my goal weight without constant dieting and exercising? A healthful weight is one you can maintain by eating moderate portions of a wide variety of foods and by getting moderate amounts of physical activity. To start, set your goal at the lowest adult weight you've comfortably maintained for a year or more. When you reach this goal, re-evaluate whether you are happy with this weight or want to set a lower goal weight.

Have your doctor or a registered dietitian help you assess your need to lose weight and set the most healthful goal weight for you.

How Many Calories Do You Need?

How many calories do you need each day to reach your healthy goal weight? It depends on several factors including your age, body size, and activity level. Although obsessive calorie counting is not the goal, knowing the approximate number of calories your body requires throughout the day is helpful in determining why you weigh more than you should. To get an idea of how many calories you need a day, see "Calculate Your Calorie Needs," page 11.

A pound of body fat contains approximately 3,500 calories (about the same as a pound of butter or margarine). Think of it this way: If, over time, you eat 3,500 fewer calories than your body uses, you will shed about 1 pound. Take in 7,000 fewer calories—or use up 7,000 extra calories—and you will lose about 2 pounds. (Most nutrition experts do not recommend losing more than 2 pounds per week.) Remember, if you eat too few calories, you'll risk slowing down your metabolism, which will make losing weight more difficult. To lose weight faster, follow an exercise program and you'll burn both body fat and calories.

How does all of this translate into everyday living? By eating 500 fewer calories each day, you should lose about 1 pound a week. Or cut only 250 calories each day and lose ½ pound a week. (Better yet, perform some kind of physical activity to burn the other half of the calories.)

To lose ½ to 1 pound a week, subtract 250 to 500 calories a day from the figure you came up with for maintenance calories. Create a daily deficit of 500 calories per day by eating fewer calories, burning off extra calories with physical activity, or by doing both. You can actually do this in different ways. For example, each day you could eat 400 fewer calories and burn off 100 extra calories with physical activity, or eat 300 fewer calories and burn off 200 extra calories. Choose whatever combination works for you.

CALCULATE YOUR CALORIE NEEDS

Women

1 Begin with a base of 655 calories

2 Multiply your weight (in pounds) by 4.3

3 Multiply your height (in inches) by 4.7

4 Add numbers from #1, #2, and #3

5 Multiply your age by 4.7

6 Subtract the total of #5 from the results of #4 to get your **Resting Metabolic Rate (RMR)** in calories. (This is what you need just to maintain your bodily functions.)

7 To determine your daily maintenance calories, use your RMR (#6) and multiply it by one of the following:

1.2 if you don't exercise

1.3 if you exercise 2 to 3 hours a week

1.4 if you exercise 4 to 6 hours a week

1.6 if you exercise 7 hours or more a week

Men

1 Begin with a base of 66 calories

2 Multiply your weight (in pounds) by 6.3

3 Multiply your height (in inches) by 12.7

4 Add numbers from #1, #2, and #3

5 Multiply your age by 6.8

6 Subtract the total of #5 from the results of #4 to get your **Resting Metabolic Rate (RMR)** in calories. (This is what you need just to maintain your bodily functions.)

7 To determine your daily maintenance calories, use your RMR (#6) and multiply it by one of the following:

1.2 if you don't exercise

1.3 if you exercise 2 to 3 hours a week

1.4 if you exercise 4 to 6 hours a week

1.6 if you exercise 7 hours or more a week

Do not cut calories severely! It is very difficult to get all the nutrients you need when you eat fewer than 1,200 calories per day. Most nutrition experts warn that your calorie intake should never go below your Resting Metabolic Rate (RMR) and, ideally, should be at least 150 calories above it. If you do delve lower than 1,200 calories, enlist the supervision of your doctor.

The Food Factor

Now that you have your goal weight and an estimate of your calorie needs for weight loss, what foods should you eat? The chart "What to Eat" on page 12 recommends daily food choices for good health. The following help you put these guidelines into practice.

Be calorie conscious. It isn't recommended that you obsess about every calorie down to the last digit, but educating yourself about the calories and other nutrients in foods helps you abide by a set calorie level and make informed, healthful food choices. To learn how many calories are in the foods you eat, check food labels for serving sizes and the number of calories per serving. Weigh and measure foods until you have learned what a serving looks like (you will probably be surprised). The Nutrition Facts included with all recipes in this book and the "Calorie Tally" on page 28 also provide useful information.

Use easy calorie-trimming tricks. This allows you more leeway to include

WHAT TO EAT? A DAILY FOOD GUIDE

An eating plan that promotes good health is built on a foundation of whole grains, fruits, vegetables, lean meats, and low-fat dairy products. This chart outlines a healthful daily eating plan and highlights some super-nutritious choices.

- To get the nutrients you need, choose a wide variety of foods from within each food group.
- To lose weight, choose a lower number of servings from the ranges given.
- Go easy on extras such as chips, desserts, sweets, soft drinks, butter, margarine, and regular salad dressing or mayonnaise. They provide calories but few nutrients.
- For heart health, choose a cooking oil that's high in unsaturated fat, such as olive, canola, sunflower, peanut, soybean, or corn oil. All oils contain 120 calories per tablespoon, so use them sparingly.

What to Eat	Serving Sizes	Best Picks for Good Health
6 to 11 servings of breads, cereals, rice, and pasta	1 slice bread; 1 cup ready-to-eat cereal; $1/2$ cup cooked cereal, rice, or pasta	3 or more daily servings of whole grains: whole wheat bread and pasta, oatmeal, shredded wheat, brown rice, popcorn, pearl barley, bulgur, quinoa. Whole grains may reduce risk for heart disease, certain cancers, and type 2 diabetes.
3 to 5 servings of vegetables	1 cup raw leafy vegetables; $1/2$ cup other cooked or raw vegetables; $3/4$ cup vegetable juice	Vivid veggies such as tomatoes, red peppers, carrots, sweet potatoes, winter squash, broccoli, any type of greens. These may reduce risk for heart disease and certain cancers.
2 to 4 servings of fruit	1 medium piece whole fruit; $1/2$ cup chopped, cooked, frozen, or canned fruit; $3/4$ cup fruit juice; $1/2$ cup berries or cut-up fruit; $1/4$ cup dried fruit	Bright-colored fruits, such as oranges, pink grapefruit, cantaloupe, mangoes, apricots, peaches, may reduce risk for heart disease and certain cancers. Choose whole fruit more often than juice for its fiber and fullness factor.
2 to 3 servings of milk, yogurt, and cheese	1 cup milk or yogurt; $1\frac{1}{2}$ ounces natural cheese; 2 ounces processed cheese	Low-fat or fat-free versions skim fat and calories while providing all the calcium, vitamin D, protein, and other nutrients regular versions boast.
2 to 3 servings of meat, poultry, fish, dry beans, eggs, nuts, and soy foods	One serving is 2 to 3 ounces cooked meat, poultry, fish. Count the following as 1 ounce: $1/2$ cup cooked dry beans; 1 egg; 2 tablespoons peanut butter; $1/3$ cup nuts; $1/2$ cup tofu; one $2\frac{1}{2}$-ounce soy burger	Pick lean meats, skinless poultry, omega-3-rich fish such as salmon and tuna (may reduce risk for heart disease), dry beans (their soluble fiber helps fill you up), nuts (they're high in healthful unsaturated fats), soy foods (eating 25 grams of soy protein daily may help lower blood cholesterol levels).

other foods within your calorie budget. Some ideas: Grill, bake, or broil foods instead of frying. Trim fat off of meat and the skin off of poultry; use half the usual amount of butter or margarine on your toast. Choose reduced-fat milk and cheese; reduced-calorie versions of salad dressing, mayonnaise, and sour cream; fruit canned in water or juice instead of syrup; and diet soft drinks or water instead of regular soft drinks.

Conquer mountainous portions. Spoon reasonable portions onto plates rather than putting serving bowls on the table. Family members can always request seconds if their hunger persists. Put snacks into a small bowl instead of eating out of the box or bag. At fast-food restaurants, shun super sizes in favor of smaller options. In sit-down restaurants, ask for a take-home container before you start eating so you can immediately put half of your meal away for tomorrow.

Tackle trouble spots. Develop tactics to deal with situations in which you repeatedly overeat. For instance, if every afternoon your sweet tooth sends you to the office vending machine for a candy bar, stock your desk or the office fridge with smaller, fun size candy bars (if you can stop at just one) or mini boxes of raisins, small cartons of fruit yogurt, or single-serving pudding cups.

Snack to your advantage. A healthy snack between meals keeps you fueled up, energizes you for a late afternoon workout, and prevents the munchies while you prepare dinner after work.

The key is to include your snacks within your daily calorie total and plan ahead. Keep a piece of fruit, a cheese stick, a few whole-grain crackers, a small handful of nuts, or a carton of yogurt available. (See pages 163 to 192 for healthy snack recipes.)

Enjoy your favorite foods. An eating plan you enjoy is an eating plan you'll stick with. Saying "never again" to favorites such as cake, cookies, or chocolate is unrealistic and often backfires, spurring an all-out binge. Occasionally include treats in reasonable portions—and savor every bite.

Learn to trust your inner signals. Rather than eating by the clock or automatically cleaning your plate, tune in to your body's signals of hunger and fullness, your natural gauges for when and how much to eat. It may take some practice, but with patience and gentle persistence, listening and responding to your inner signals will become second nature in guiding you to eat the right amount of food for achieving a weight that is healthful and easy to maintain.

List strategies to stop emotional eating. In this hectic and stressful world, it's not uncommon for people to turn to food to soothe them, comfort them, or cheer them up. Rather than using food to cope, write a list of 10 things you like to do and keep it in your purse or wallet. When your emotions unravel, take out this list and do one of the activities instead of eating. Journaling, taking a quick nap, reading, or deep breathing can get you centered again without food.

Enlist support. Support and encouragement from family and friends help strengthen your motivation and reinforce the positive changes you make. Involve loved ones in planning and preparing healthful meals and in enjoyable physical activities. It's good for them too!

Eat, enjoy, and savor good food! Eating is something everyone has to do, and most find pleasure in doing so. By choosing foods wisely, you can be slimmer and healthier. The recipes in *New Dieter's Cookbook* are tools to help you reach that goal. Restrictive dieting creates an ongoing battle between the dieter and food in general, but a relationship between you and food has to exist in order for you to live! Why not make it a peaceful relationship?

Are You Fat Phobic? Get Over It!

Remember the fat-free craze of the 1990s? Not long ago many people thought the surest route to good health and weight loss was to drastically reduce the amount of fat they ate. As a result, a whole population of people embraced the plethora of fat-free (and sometimes flavor-free) products, such as chips, cake, and ice cream, without realizing that fat-free did not mean calorie-free. In fact, because of their increased sugar content, some reduced-fat and fat-free foods contain as many or more calories than regular versions.

Thank goodness those days are over. Dietary guidelines recommend a diet that is moderate in total fat (no more than 30 percent of your daily caloric intake). The good news is that the inclusion of some fat in your meals and snacks actually may help you lose weight because fat is digested more slowly, so you feel full longer. Fat also brings its delicious flavor to foods, making those foods more satisfying.

The type of fats you choose is important because some fats are more healthful than others. The unsaturated fats found in olive, canola, peanut, corn, safflower, and soybean oils help lower blood cholesterol levels. The omega-3 fatty acids found in fatty fish such as salmon and tuna, nuts, seeds, and canola, soybean, and flaxseed oils may reduce risk for heart attacks and hardening of the arteries.

Eating too much saturated fat (found in fatty meats, poultry skin, butter, and full-fat cheese, milk, and ice cream) and trans fatty acids (found in foods containing partially hydrogenated oils, such as hard margarines and some fried and baked foods) may raise blood cholesterol and increase risk for heart disease. "Too much" translates to more than 10 percent of your total caloric intake (18 grams for an 1,800 calorie diet). Eating too much of any type of fat is linked to increased risk for various types of cancers and may promote weight gain because all fats and oils are calorie-dense.

The bottom line: It's fine to enjoy some fats, oils, and high-fat foods in your eating plan because they add to the enjoyment of eating—just don't go overboard. (You will note that many recipes in this book include ingredients such as butter or cream that typically have been "forbidden" in other traditional reduction diets. Used in moderation, these foods are not harmful.)

Living the Active Life Leads to a Healthy Weight—and Much More

How much would you pay for an elixir that could…

- Help you lose weight and keep it off
- Increase physical fitness
- Strengthen bones, muscles, and joints
- Build endurance and strength
- Reduce the risk for heart disease, high blood pressure, colon cancer, and type 2 diabetes
- Promote a sense of well-being and reduce feelings of depression or anxiety

Most people would be willing to pay a lot, but you don't have to. The fact is, these benefits are yours free of charge when you live a physically active lifestyle.

To reap these benefits, you don't have to spend numerous hours sweating in the gym or huffing and puffing around a track. The Dietary Guidelines for Americans recommend physical activity levels that are a lot less stern than most people think. They say adults should accumulate at least 30 minutes of moderate physical activity most days of the week, preferably every day. You can even break that 30 minutes into shorter chunks of time—10 minutes here, 20 minutes there. What could be easier? Moreover, your health is worth taking just 30 minutes out of your day.

A moderate physical activity is one that requires about as much energy as walking two miles in 30 minutes. In addition to walking, activities such as jogging, swimming, biking, and exercise classes are a terrific way to meet your daily physical activity quota. But everyday activities count toward your quota too. If you're new to exercise, daily activities (including chores) are a great way to get started or to rely on when you're especially strapped for time. Here's a sampling of what counts.

- Taking short walks to the corner store, from the bus stop to work, or around the mall
- Climbing the stairs instead of riding the elevator or escalator
- Housecleaning such as washing windows, mopping, scrubbing, and vacuuming
- Outdoor tasks such as gardening, mowing the lawn, raking leaves, and shoveling snow
- Actively playing, romping, dancing, wrestling, jumping, and running with the kids

The Triple Crown of Fitness

Ready to step up the pace? Once you get hooked on how great 30 minutes of daily physical activity makes you feel, you might want to begin a more structured, consistent program. People who maintain a healthy weight tend to get at least one hour of moderate-intensity physical activity daily, according to the Institute of Medicine of the National Academies.

No Time for Healthy Eating and Exercise?

Why aren't you doing more to eat better and get more exercise? If you said you don't have time, you're not alone. A shortage of time is one of the top reasons cited by respondents in the American Dietetic Association's nutrition trends survey. These tactics can help you tackle the time challenge.

Enlist the supermarket as your kitchen assistant. A wealth of washed, chopped, sliced, and diced fruits and vegetables is available for the picking. The salad bar is a source of ready-to-use recipe ingredients, such as chopped veggies for a stir-fry or a fruit salad for dessert. Swing by the deli for a roasted chicken and some salads or other premade side dishes. And remember, it doesn't take extra time to pick up good-for-you whole grain bread, cereal, and pasta, lean cuts of meat, skinless and boneless chicken breasts, or reduced-fat dairy products.

Don't be caught shorthanded. When you're trying to eat right, the last thing you want to do is run out of food and have to resort to a fast, fat-laden meal. Instead, stock up on quick fixings for healthy meals and snacks. You can combine precooked chicken strips, canned beans, a variety of pastas, quick-cooking brown rice, prewashed bagged salad mixes, frozen vegetables, and canned and dried fruit in a variety of ways. On weekends, cook up a big casserole or pot of hearty soup or chili so you'll have several meals for the week and some to freeze too.

Search out quick-and-easy recipes such as the ones on pages 119 to 140. These recipes help you get a healthful meal on the table when you're short on time.

When there's no getting around fast food, choose small burgers, grilled chicken sandwiches, baked potatoes, salads with reduced-calorie dressing, low-fat milk, bottled water, or diet soft drinks. To save about 100 calories per serving, ask to have the mayo or sauce left off of your sandwich. If you simply can't resist french fries, share an order or two with the whole family.

Schedule exercise classes or walking dates with a friend into your calendar or appointment book just as you would any other important appointment. Pedal an exercise bike, lift light hand weights, or do stretches while watching TV. Pop in an exercise video whenever you have a few free minutes. It all adds up, so use short snatches of time to take a quick walk or put on some favorite music and move!

The American Council on Exercise (ACE) says that a complete fitness program includes three components: aerobic exercise, strength training, and flexibility training. (For more ACE information and safety guidelines, go to the ACE website at acefitness.org.)

Aerobic exercise promotes a healthy cardiovascular system and a healthy weight. Examples include any activity that gets your heart pumping faster, such as brisk walking, jogging, jumping rope, dancing, kickboxing, cycling (both outdoors and indoors on a stationary bike), and swimming. For good health, do aerobic exercise three to four days each week for 20 minutes or more. To promote weight loss, gradually build up to four or more weekly sessions (with at least one day off) of 45 minutes or more. If you have bad knees or other delicate joints, choose low-impact activities such as walking, swimming, or cycling performed at a low intensity.

Strength training (also called weight training or muscular conditioning) strengthens muscles, reduces risk for injury, and aids weight control. With all the benefits attributed to weight training, it is worth including it in any serious weight control plan. Weight training:

- Increases bone strength and reduces the risk of osteoporosis
- Prevents joint injuries by strengthening connective tissues
- Increases lean muscle mass and decreases body fat
- Increases your metabolism so you burn more calories (a huge bonus!)

• Improves recreational sports performance, which means more fun

Strength training programs utilize weight machines, free weights, exercise tubing and bands, and calisthenics. A good program covers all major muscle groups. Do strength training at least twice a week, with at least 1 day off between workouts.

Flexibility training maintains the range of motion in the joints, improves posture, promotes relaxation, and reduces risk of injury and muscle soreness. Examples include stretching exercises, yoga, Pilates, and tai chi. Do flexibility exercises for at least 30 minutes, three times a week. At minimum, stretch for a few minutes before and after aerobic exercise or strength training.

Note: If you have health problems, are a man over age 40, or a woman over age 50, consult your doctor before you begin a new physical activity program.

Q: Instead of exercising, why can't I simply keep cutting back on calories to lose weight?
A: Severely cutting calories may seem like an easy route to take. And it may work initially. But over time this strategy backfires. When you restrict calories too severely, your body kicks into starvation mode, triggering a slower metabolism so your body burns fewer and fewer calories. Eating a reasonable number of calories each day (at least 1,200) and physical activity is the safest and surest route to weight loss and keeping it off.

Q: As a woman, won't lifting weights make me bulk up too much and look masculine?
A: This is a common worry among women, but it needn't be. The only women who build huge muscles are female body builders who lift superheavy weights, follow special diets, and often take steroids. For the average woman, strengthening muscles by lifting weights actually provides a leaner appearance. That's because muscle is more compact than fat, so women who strength train look more toned and less flabby. More good news: The more muscle you have, the more calories your body burns.

Q: My doctor says I should lose weight to improve my health, but I have a lot to lose and I feel overwhelmed! How much do I have to lose before my overall health benefits?
A: Even modest weight loss yields big benefits. Losing just 5 to 10 percent of your initial body weight reduces risk for heart disease, high blood pressure, and type 2 diabetes. If your starting weight is 200 pounds, losing 10 to 20 pounds and keeping them off puts you on the path to better health right away.

Making Change Permanent
These ideas can help you stick to your new hard-earned, healthful habits.
• Break it down into small steps. Rather than trying to change everything

at once, change your eating and physical activity habits gradually. You're more likely to maintain new habits when you adopt them one or two at a time. Similarly, set short-term goals for weight loss in addition to your long-term goal. As you reach each short-term goal, you'll feel motivated to continue.

• Be specific. Rather than setting vague goals such as eating more fruit or walking more each day, take concrete action, such as packing an apple for an afternoon snack or scheduling a class after work or a 30-minute walk over your lunch hour.

• Help yourself succeed. Reaching goals takes forethought and preparation. Stock up on the foods you need to carry out your eating plan. Pack your gym bag or walking shoes the night before so you can get to the gym on your lunch hour.

• Make it noteworthy. Keep a journal to outline your goals, track your progress, devise solutions to difficult situations, and highlight your successes.

• Celebrate your successes. Reward your progress with something other than food. Treat yourself to flowers, new walking shoes, or a manicure when you reach a short-term goal. Splurge on a new outfit or a complete makeover when you reach a long-term goal.

• Think progress, not perfection. It can take three to six months to establish a new habit. Don't be discouraged if you eat a bit too much or skip your walk one day. Just make sure you get right back on track.

Keeping It Off: Lessons from Successful Losers

For many people, losing weight is the easy part. Keeping it off is another story. If you can identify with this problem, take heart, because there are plenty of long-term success stories out there. A collection of nearly 3,000 of them resides in the National Weight Control Registry, a database established in 1993 by researchers at the University of Colorado and University of Pittsburgh.

Registry members have maintained a weight loss of at least 30 pounds for at least one year. The average member has lost more than 60 pounds and kept it off for about five years. How they reached their weight goals varies. Some created their own eating and exercise plan; others used methods such as joining a weight-loss group, following a liquid diet, or receiving counseling from a doctor or registered dietitian. Though they reached their goals in different ways, their techniques for keeping off the weight are strikingly similar. Registry members tend to:

• Modify fat intake and keep calories in check. On average, members get 24 percent of their calories from fat and consume 1,400 calories per day.

• Keep a watchful eye on their weight.

• Prepare for action. If their weight creeps up, they immediately take steps to return to their goal weight. This usually means trimming food intake or increasing exercise.

• Make exercise a daily habit. Members burn about 2,800 calories per week by exercising one hour per day. Walking is the top favorite activity.

- Eat breakfast. Nearly 8 out of 10 members eat breakfast every day. Researchers speculate that eating breakfast helps stave off overeating later in the day and provides the necessary energy to be physically active.
- Enjoy their new healthy lifestyle. In fact, the longer members maintain their weight loss, the less effort it seems to take.

What's New in the Weight Loss World?

While eating fewer calories and being more physically active make up the foundation for a successful weight management plan, researchers are continually unearthing clues about how to tweak plans for better success. Stay tuned as research continues to unfold.

High or low protein? Middle-of-the-road may be the way to go. Researchers from the University of Illinois compared overweight women who consumed a balanced, higher protein diet (10 ounces of meat daily) to overweight women who consumed a balanced, high-carbohydrate, lower-protein diet (about 5 ounces of meat daily). Both groups ate about 1,700 calories per day. After 10 weeks, both groups lost about 16 pounds, but the higher protein group lost more body fat and retained more muscle mass. Researchers think the amino acid leucine, found in high-quality protein foods such as beef, poultry, fish, eggs, and dairy products, is responsible for the beneficial effect.

Very High-Protein, Low-Carb Diets Still under Scrutiny

High-protein, low-carbohydrate diets sound appealing because they promise easy weight loss while you eat unlimited amounts of high-protein (and often high-fat) foods such as steak, cheese, butter, and eggs. A recent study showed that people who followed a popular high-protein, low-carbohydrate diet lost more weight than people who followed a high-carbohydrate, low-fat diet recommended by current dietary guidelines. It's important to note, however, that this study involved a small number of people (120 total participants, with just 60 following the high-protein diet) over a period of only six months.

More research is needed to determine whether people who follow a high-protein diet keep off the weight long-term and whether there are any health consequences from following such a diet. Expect more definitive answers from a large, multiyear government-sponsored study that's currently being conducted. It will compare results of overweight subjects who followed a high-protein, low-carbohydrate diet with subjects who followed a high-carbohydrate, low-fat diet.

Until then, keep in mind that if you lose weight on a high-protein, low-carbohydrate diet, it's probably because you're cutting calories.

If you choose to try this type of diet, it's important to be aware that very high-protein diets tax the kidneys and may bring about bad breath, fatigue, headaches, nausea, and constipation. Major health organizations, including the American Heart Association and the American Dietetic Association, discourage high-protein diets because these diets often are high in saturated fat (a cause of heart disease) and low in or devoid of whole grains, fruits, and vegetables, which are proven to prevent heart disease and cancer.

Calcium flicks the fat-burning switch. Extensive research in humans and animals shows that consuming more calcium as part of a calorie-controlled weight-management plan helps the body burn more fat. It seems calcium turns on cells' fat-burning machinery. Consuming 1,000 mg calcium per day from dairy foods such as milk, yogurt, and cheese is more effective than getting calcium from pills. Choose two to three daily servings of fat-free or reduced-fat dairy products.

Go for oats. Research shows that people who eat oatmeal for breakfast experience less hunger during the morning and eat less at lunchtime than people who eat sugared cornflakes for breakfast. The fiber in oatmeal seems to slow down the digestion process, so you feel full longer.

Watery foods help cut calories and soup up satisfaction. Research done at Pennsylvania State University shows that humans tend to eat the same weight of food each day, regardless of calories. Eating more "watery" foods such as fruits, vegetables, cooked cereal, pasta, and other grains, stews, and soups may aid weight loss because these foods are filling and the high water content makes them less calorie dense than some other foods. Take note: Drinking a glass of water with your meal doesn't seem to have the same effect. Therefore, for best results, choose watery foods.

Kids and Weight: Cause for Alarm

More than 15 percent of American children and adolescents are overweight, according to the latest government surveys. Alarmingly, that means about twice as many children and three times as many adolescents are overweight today compared to the number who tipped the scale only two decades ago.

Along with these sharp increases come worrisome signs of chronic diseases once common only among adults. Nearly 6 in 10 overweight children exhibit one risk factor for heart disease, such as high blood cholesterol or high blood pressure; 20 percent exhibit two or more risk factors. Even type 2 diabetes (formerly called "adult onset" diabetes) is appearing more frequently in children.

Like adults, children are carrying around excess weight because they're burning off fewer calories than they consume. While experts can't point to one particular reason for this caloric imbalance, frequent fast-food meals and high-calorie snacks and soft drink consumption often are cited as culprits. Certainly the immobile lifestyle of many children is a huge contributor. Though the Dietary Guidelines for Americans recommends children get at least 60 minutes of moderate physical activity daily, many get far less. What's keeping the kids from exercising? Some blame little or no physical education at school, while others fault too many hours spent on daily "screen time." According to the National Institute on Media and the Family, kids ages 2 to 17 watch TV, play video games, and use the computer an average of nearly 4½ hours daily.

Is It OK to Put Kids on a Diet?

Restrictive diets generally are not recommended for overweight children. Children need sufficient calories and nutrients to grow and develop. Instead, experts usually recommend the promotion of healthful eating and physical activity. Good eating habits and exercise will help your child "grow into" his or her weight.

To determine the extent of your child's weight problem, your child's doctor can calculate his or her BMI (see page 9) and plot the result on a sex-specific growth chart for children ages 2 to 20. If your child is seriously overweight, the doctor may recommend a treatment program that includes lifestyle counseling from a pediatrician, a registered dietitian, an exercise physiologist, and a psychologist.

What's a Parent to Do?
10 Food and Fitness Tips for a Healthy Family

Children see, children do, say health experts. A parent's job as a role model is the most important influence on children's eating and exercise habits. In other words, if you eat wisely and exercise, they'll be more likely to as well. Consider these tips to help you and your family.

1. Don't forbid favorite foods; doing so will backfire. Face it, kids like fast food, ice cream, candy, and soft drinks. If you forbid foods like these, your kids will most likely find another way to get them, and they may binge on them when they do. It's fine for children to enjoy these foods occasionally, as long as the portion size is not excessive and the frequency isn't daily.

2. Don't go to the opposite extreme and allow a food free-for-all. Provide well-balanced meals and snacks that include a variety of nutrient-dense foods. Be the one who decides whether it's OK to have ice cream for dessert or whether it's fresh fruit night.

3. Make fruits and veggies available. Stock a wide array of easy-to-eat produce for snack time. Baby carrots, red pepper strips, zucchini or cucumber slices, and broccoli florets are colorful and crunchy options for dipping into reduced-fat salad dressing. Young children love the sweetness and novelty of frozen grapes or banana slices. Keep a bowl of their favorite fruits in plain sight on the kitchen counter.

4. Get kids cooking. Children love to help out in the kitchen. They take pride in their creations and are more likely to eat what they prepare. It's fun to cook together too. The Kids' Favorites recipes, on pages 141 to 162, are a great place to start.

5. Make yours an active family. Have fun together by practicing the latest dance steps, riding bikes, playing touch football, shooting hoops, swimming, or simply taking a walk after dinner. Treat kids to a trip to the zoo, museum, or a guided nature hike where they can learn, have fun, and be active.

6. Encourage foot and pedal power. Instead of driving your kids everywhere they need to go, encourage them to walk or bike to school, to a friend's house, or to the convenience store if it's a safe, reasonable distance.

7. Assign kids active household chores such as vacuuming, mopping, sweeping, dusting, pulling weeds, raking leaves, and walking the dog.

8. Strive to "out step" each other. Fitness experts say that for good health, individuals should take 10,000 steps every day. Kids and adults alike enjoy tracking their steps by wearing a step counter on their waistband throughout the day. Step counters are available at sporting goods stores in a variety of price ranges. Get one for each family member and have a friendly competition to out step each other.

9. Slash screen time. The American Academy of Pediatrics recommends that parents limit children's time spent watching TV, playing video games, and using the computer to one to two hours daily. Allow your child to decide how to divvy up the time.

10. Most people, including kids, don't like change, so start small. Even one change per month amounts to many healthful new habits over time.

Resources

These books and websites provide more information about weight management.

Books

Better Homes and Gardens® *The Smart Diet* and *3 Steps to Weight Loss*

Websites

cdc.gov Access extensive information about weight management and other health issues at the Centers for Disease Control and Prevention (CDC) website.

eatright.org For customized weight-management counseling, you can find a registered dietitian (RD) near you at the American Dietetic Association website.

acefitness.org The American Council on Exercise (ACE) website helps you find an ACE-certified personal trainer or fitness instructor in your area. Also check out the Fit Facts section for articles on safe and effective exercise.

bam.gov This CDC sponsored website answers kids' questions about healthy eating, physical activity, and other health topics.

kidnetic.com This interactive, educational website for children and parents promotes healthful eating and physical activity in fun ways. It is sponsored by the International Food Information Council.

niddk.nih.gov/health/nutrition.htm The Weight-Control Information Network (WIN) is a service of the National Institutes of Health. WIN was established in 1994 to raise awareness and provide up-to-date, science-based information on obesity, physical activity, weight control, and related nutritional issues.

obesity.org The American Obesity Association focuses on changing public policy and perceptions about obesity and stresses education, research, and prevention of obesity.

dietitian.com/ibw/ibw.html Healthy Body Calculator helps you determine whether you are overweight based on your personal data (such as daily activity, frame size, body fat, etc.).

14-Day Menu Plans

When you or your dietitian determine your calorie level, use these helpful menus as a guide for planning your meals. If you require 1,200 calories, the first set of foods for each day adds up to that calorie amount. The next two sets of foods should be added for a meal or snack to total either 1,500 or 1,800 calories.

	Breakfast	Lunch	Dinner	Snack
Day 1 For 1,200 calories:	Fruit and Caramel Oatmeal (p. 213) ½ of a whole wheat English muffin, toasted 2 teaspoons sugar-free jam 1 cup fat-free milk	Chicken-Vegetable Soup (p. 322) Old-Fashioned Corn Bread (p. 478)	Spinach-Feta Bake (p. 417) 1 soft breadstick 1 cup fresh red raspberries	2 cups popped popcorn (no added fat) ½ cup orange juice
For 1,500 calories add:	½ of a whole wheat English muffin 1 teaspoon butter or margarine	1 cup raw celery sticks and carrot sticks	1 soft breadstick 1 teaspoon butter or margarine	no additions
For 1,800 calories also add:	no additions	1 small unfrosted brownie	no additions	½ cup orange juice 2 cups popped popcorn (no added fat) 1 ounce reduced-fat cheese
Day 2 For 1,200 calories:	1 bagel (2 ounces) 1 tablespoon peanut butter ½ of a large grapefruit	Deli-Style Pasta Salad (p. 441) ½ cup canned sweet cherries	Beef Loin with Tarragon Sauce (p. 233) ½ cup wilted spinach ½ baked potato (3 ounces) 1 teaspoon butter or margarine 1 tablespoon fat-free sour cream	1 low-fat fruit yogurt with nonnutritive sweetener 1 tablespoon granola
For 1,500 calories add:	no additions	no additions	½ baked potato (3 ounces) 1 teaspoon butter or margarine	1 tablespoon granola 1 Fruit-Filled Muffin (p. 471)
For 1,800 calories also add	1 cup fat-free milk	½ cup canned sweet cherries	½ cup wilted spinach ½ cup low-fat frozen yogurt	no additions

	Breakfast	Lunch	Dinner	Snack
Day 3 For 1,200 calories:	2 slices English Muffin Bread, toasted (p. 486) 2 teaspoons sugar-free jam 1 teaspoon butter or margarine 1 small banana 1 cup fat-free milk	Turkey sandwich (2 slices whole wheat bread, 2 ounces sliced turkey breast, 2 slices tomato, 2 lettuce leaves, and 1 teaspoon mustard) Cranberry Coleslaw (p. 446)	Pacific Rim Shrimp and Snow Peas (p. 364) 1/2 of a small mango, sliced	3/4 ounce whole wheat crackers (no added fat) 1/2 cup low-fat cottage cheese 1/2 cup vegetable juice cocktail
For 1,500 calories add:	1 teaspoon butter or margarine	1 ounce reduced-fat provolone cheese 1/2 cup sorbet	no additions	no additions
For 1,800 calories also add	no additions	1 ounce sliced turkey breast 3/4 ounce baked tortilla chips	1/2 of a small mango, sliced	1/2 cup vegetable juice cocktail 3/4 ounce whole wheat crackers (no added fat)
Day 4 For 1,200 calories:	1½ cups unsweetened cereal 1 cup fat-free milk 1 cup fresh strawberries	Peppery Artichoke Pitas (p. 429) 2 Mocha Meringue Kisses (p. 497) 1/2 cup canned peach slices (juice pack)	Coriander Pork Chops (p. 273) 2/3 cup hot cooked rice 1/2 cup steamed green beans 1 teaspoon butter or margarine	Veggies with Mustard Dipping Sauce (p. 167)
For 1,500 calories add:	1 slice whole wheat bread, toasted 1 teaspoon butter or margarine	no additions	no additions	1 fat-free granola bar
For 1,800 calories also add	no additions	1/2 cup canned peach slices (juice pack) 1 low-fat fruit yogurt with nonnutritive sweetener	1/3 cup hot cooked rice 1/2 cup steamed green beans 1 teaspoon butter or margarine	no additions
Day 5 For 1,200 calories:	1 scrambled egg 1 slice unfrosted cinnamon bread, toasted 1 teaspoon butter or margarine 1 orange 1 cup fat-free milk	Tossed salad (1½ cups torn romaine, 2 ounces smoked turkey, 1/3 cup chopped tomato, and 1/4 cup sliced cucumber) 2 tablespoons fat-free ranch salad dressing 4 Cumin Caraway Crackers (p. 475)	Ginger Beef Stir-Fry (p. 121) Minted Fruit Compote (p. 514) 5 vanilla wafers	1/2 cup frozen fat-free, sugar-free yogurt
For 1,500 calories add:	1 slice unfrosted raisin-cinnamon bread, toasted 1 teaspoon butter or margarine	1 ounce smoked turkey 3/4 cup fresh blueberries	no additions	1/2 cup frozen fat-free, sugar-free yogurt
For 1,800 calories also add	1 scrambled egg	1 ounce reduced-fat cheese 2 Cumin Caraway Crackers (p. 475)	1/3 cup hot cooked rice	no additions

	Breakfast	Lunch	Dinner	Snack
Day 6 For 1,200 calories:	Blueberry-Cornmeal Pancakes (p. 207); 2 tablespoons sugar-free syrup; 1 cup fat-free milk	Beef Goulash Soup (p. 247); 1 soft breadstick; 3/4 cup mandarin orange segments	Cuban Broiled Snapper (p. 341); 2/3 cup hot cooked brown rice; 1 teaspoon butter or margarine; 1/2 cup steamed broccoli	Maple-Mustard Crunch (p. 183)
For 1,500 calories add:	no additions	1 soft breadstick	no additions	1/3 cup hummus; 1/2 of a small pita bread
For 1,800 calories also add:	2 ounces Canadian-style bacon	1 teaspoon butter or margarine	1/3 cup hot cooked brown rice; 1 teaspoon butter or margarine; 1/2 cup steamed broccoli	no additions
Day 7 For 1,200 calories:	Stuffed French Toast (p. 212); 1/4 cup canned apricot halves; 1 cup fat-free milk	Eggplant Panini (p. 430); 1 cup cauliflower florets and cucumber slices	Filet Mignon with Cognac Sauce (p. 379); Four-Veggie Roast (p. 456); 2/3 cup hot cooked wild rice; 1 teaspoon butter or margarine	3/4 cup cubed cantaloupe
For 1,500 calories add:	1/4 cup canned apricot halves	1 almond granola bar	1/3 cup hot cooked wild rice; 1 teaspoon butter or margarine	no additions
For 1,800 calories also add:	no additions	1/2 of a fresh pear	1/2 cup sherbet	3 gingersnaps
Day 8 For 1,200 calories:	Honey Granola with Yogurt (p. 215)	1 cup tomato soup (prepared with water or broth); Cottage Cheese-Chive Biscuits (p. 476); 1 ounce reduced-fat cheese; 1 cup fat-free milk	Whitefish with Roasted Asparagus (p. 351); 1 whole wheat dinner roll; 1 teaspoon butter or margarine; Poached Tangerines and Oranges (p. 512)	Antipasto Kabobs (p. 165)
For 1,500 calories add:	1/2 bagel, toasted (1 ounce); 1 tablespoon low-fat cream cheese	1/2 cup tomato soup (prepared with water or broth)	no additions	1 1/2 ounces baked tortilla chips; 1/4 cup salsa
For 1,800 calories also add:	1/2 bagel, toasted (1 ounce); 1 tablespoon low-fat cream cheese	1 small nectarine	1 whole wheat dinner roll; 1 teaspoon butter or margarine	no additions

	Breakfast	Lunch	Dinner	Snack
Day 9 For 1,200 calories:	Melon Smoothie (p. 222) 1 slice seven-grain bread, toasted 1 teaspoon butter or margarine	Chicken and Feta Salad-Stuffed Pitas (p. 330) 1 cup honeydew melon	Peachy Pork Tenderloin (p. 385) 2 cups tossed salad 2 tablespoons fat-free salad dressing 2 crisp breadsticks (2/3 ounce)	2 small low-fat oatmeal cookies 1 cup fat-free milk
For 1,500 calories add:	1 slice seven-grain bread, toasted 1 teaspoon butter or margarine	1 small unfrosted brownie	1 cup cubed papaya	no additions
For 1,800 calories also add	no additions	no additions	1 small slice angel food cake	Pretzels and Fruit Snack Mix (p. 184)
Day 10 For 1,200 calories:	Ham and Potato Scramble (p. 202) 1/2 cinnamon-raisin bagel, toasted (1 ounce) 1 tablespoon low-fat cream cheese 1 cup fat-free milk	Crab and Pasta Gazpacho (p. 375) 7 multigrain crackers (no added fat) 3 tablespoons dried tart cherries or raisins	Asian Flank Steak Roll-Ups (p. 41) 1 sliced kiwifruit	Spicy Broccoli Spread (p. 170)
For 1,500 calories add:	1/2 cinnamon-raisin bagel, toasted (1 ounce) 1 tablespoon low-fat cream cheese	no additions	no additions	4 teaspoons peanut butter 8 saltine crackers
For 1,800 calories also add	1/2 cup apple juice	1/2 cup low-fat cottage cheese 7 multigrain crackers (no added fat) 3 tablespoons dried tart cherries or raisins	no additions	no additions
Day 11 For 1,200 calories:	Date-Nut Bread (p. 483) 1 cup low-fat fruit yogurt with nonnutritive sweetener	Beef and Garlic Pita Roll-Ups (p. 259) 25 small red grapes	Spicy Chicken with Fruit (p. 308) 2/3 cup hot cooked rice 1/2 cup cooked Brussels sprouts	2 cups cucumber slices and carrot sticks 3 tablespoons low-fat sour cream dip
For 1,500 calories add:	no additions	no additions	1/3 cup hot cooked rice 1 teaspoon butter or margarine 1/2 cup low-fat pudding	no additions
For 1,800 calories also add	no additions	1 granola bar	1/2 cup cooked Brussels sprouts	1 ounce reduced-fat cheese 7 whole wheat crackers (no added fat)

	Breakfast	Lunch	Dinner	Snack
Day 12 For 1,200 calories:	Fruit and Grain Cereal (p. 214)	Turkey and Rice Soup (p. 324) 1 cup raw cauliflower florets 1 cup low-fat fruit yogurt with nonnutritive sweetener 8 animal crackers	Taco Pizza (p. 144) Mixed Citrus Salad (p. 449)	1/2 cup low-fat ice cream
For 1,500 calories add:	1/2 cup pineapple juice	1/2 ham sandwich (1 slice rye bread, 1 1/2 ounces thinly sliced ham, 1 lettuce leaf, and 1 teaspoon mustard)	no additions	3/4 ounce pretzels
For 1,800 calories also add	1/2 cup pineapple juice	1/2 ham sandwich (same as above)	2 small fat-free cookies	no additions
Day 13 For 1,200 calories:	Baked Brie Strata (p. 203) 1 cup fat-free milk	Roast beef sandwich (2 slices multigrain bread, 2 ounces lean roast beef, 2 slices tomato, 2 lettuce leaves, and 1 teaspoon prepared horseradish) Honeydew and Apple Salad (p. 448)	Chipotle Chicken (p. 396) 1 cup tossed salad 1 tablespoon low-fat salad dressing 1 medium ear corn on the cob 1 teaspoon butter or margarine	3 cups popped popcorn (with no added fat)
For 1,500 calories add:	no additions	1 cup vegetarian vegetable soup 3/4 ounce slice Swiss cheese	1 cup tossed salad 1 tablespoon low-fat salad dressing	Mixed-Fruit Smoothies (p. 190)
For 1,800 calories also add	no additions	no additions	1 medium ear corn on the cob 1 teaspoon butter or margarine 1 frosted cupcake	no additions
Day 14 For 1,200 calories:	Southwest Skillet (p. 197) 1/2 English muffin, toasted 1 teaspoon butter or margarine 1 cup fat-free milk	Asian Chicken Salad (p. 129) 1 fresh plum 2 fortune cookies	Steak with Chutney-Rum Sauce (p. 383) Orzo-Broccoli Pilaf (p. 453)	Caramel Corn (p. 185)
For 1,500 calories add:	1/2 English muffin, toasted 1 teaspoon butter or margarine	1 fresh plum	1/2 cup sherbet	no additions
For 1,800 calories also add	no additions	1 dinner roll 1 teaspoon butter or margarine	no additions	1 low-fat fruit yogurt with nonnutritive sweetener 1/4 cup low-fat granola

Calorie Tally

A

American cheese, processed, 1 ounce 106
Angel food cake, 1 piece 161
Animal crackers, 10 112
Apple juice, 8 ounces 116
Apples, 1 medium 81
Applesauce, sweetened, 1/2 cup 97
Applesauce, unsweetened, 1/2 cup 53
Apricots, 3 medium 51
Apricots, canned in light syrup, 3 halves 54
Apricots, dried, 10 halves 83
Artichoke hearts, cooked, 1/2 cup 37
Artichokes, 1 medium 60
Asparagus, cooked, 1/2 cup or 6 spears 22
Avocados, 1 medium 339

B

Bacon, Canadian-style, cooked, 2 slices 86
Bacon, cooked, 3 slices .109
Bagel, 1 (2-ounce) 163
Baked beans (canned), 1/2 cup 282
Bananas, 1 medium 105
Barbecue sauce, 1 tablespoon 12
Barley, cooked, 1 cup 193
Beans (dried), cooked, 1 cup
    Black 227
    Garbanzo 269
    Great Northern 210
    Kidney 225
    Navy 259
    Pinto 235
Beans, refried (canned), 1/2 cup 270
Beef, cooked, 3 ounces
    Flank steak, lean only 194
    Ground beef, lean .240
    Ground beef, regular 250
    Pot roast, chuck, lean only 188
    Rib roast, lean only 208
    Round steak, lean only 162
    Sirloin steak, lean only 171
Beef bouillon cubes, 1 14
Beef broth, 1 cup 16
Beer, 12 fluid ounces
    Light 99
    Regular 146
Biscuits, 1 103
Blueberries, 1 cup 82

Blue cheese, 1 ounce 100
Bran raisin muffins, 1 142
Bread, 1 slice
    French 81
    Italian 78
    Pumpernickel 82
    Raisin 70
    Rye 66
    White 64
    Whole wheat 65
Breadsticks, 2 77
Broccoli
    Cooked, 1/2 cup 22
    Raw, 1 cup 24
Brownie with nuts, 3x1 inches 97
Brussels sprouts, cooked, 1/2 cup 30
Bulgur, cooked, 1 cup 152
Butter, 1 tablespoon 108

C

Cabbage, raw, shredded, 1/2 cup 8
Candy, hard, 1 ounce 106
Candy corn, 1/4 cup 182
Cantaloupe, 1 cup 57
Carrots
    Cooked, 1/2 cup 35
    Raw, 1 medium 31
Catsup, 1 tablespoon 16
Cauliflower, cooked, 1/2 cup 15
Celery, raw, 1 stalk 6
Cheddar cheese, 1 ounce
    Fat-free 41
    Reduced-fat 90
    Regular-fat, ...114
Cheesecake, 1/16 of pie 257
Cherries, sweet, 10 49
Chicken
    Breast, without skin, roasted, 1/2 breast 142
    Dark meat, without skin, roasted, 3 ounces . . .176
    Drumstick, without skin, roasted, 1 76
    Light meat, without skin, roasted, 3 ounces . . .148
Chicken bouillon cubes, 1 9
Chicken broth, 1 cup 24
Chocolate
    Milk, 1.55 ounce bar 226
    Semisweet, 1 ounce 134
    Semisweet pieces, 6 ounces (1 cup) 812
    Unsweetened, 1 ounce 148
Chocolate chip cookies, 1 46
Chocolate syrup, 2 tablespoons 82
Clams, cooked, 3 ounces 126

Club soda, 12 fluid ounces 0
Cocoa powder, unsweetened, 1 tablespoon 11
Coconut, flaked and sweetened, 1 tablespoon . . .22
Cola, 12 fluid ounces
    Diet 0
    Regular 152
Colby cheese, 1 ounce 112
Corn, cream-style, cooked, 1/2 cup 110
Corn, whole kernel, cooked, 1/2 cup 67
Cornbread, 1 piece 198
Corn chips, 1 ounce 153
Cottage cheese, 1 cup
    Creamed 217
    Dry curd 123
    1% fat 164
    2% fat 203
Couscous, 1/2 cup cooked 88
Crab, cooked, 3 ounces 82
Crab-flavored fish, 3 ounces 87
Cranberries, 1 cup 46
Cranberry juice cocktail, 6 ounces 108
Cream, half-and-half, 1 tablespoon 20
Cream, whipping, 1 tablespoon 52
Cream cheese, 1 ounce
    Fat-free 25
    Reduced fat (Neufchâtel) 74
    Regular 100
Cucumber, 1/2 cup slices 7
Cupcakes with icing 173

D–F

Danish pastries, 1 piece .161
Doughnuts, cake, 1 105
Doughnuts, yeast, 1 176
Edam cheese, 1 ounce 101
Eggplant, cooked, 1/2 cup 13
Eggs
    Fried, 1 91
    Poached, 1 74
    Raw, white, 1 17
    Raw, whole, 1 75
    Raw, yolk, 1 59
    Scrambled, 1 egg with milk 101
Egg substitute, refrigerated or frozen, 1/4 cup . .25
English muffins, 1 135
Fennel, raw, 1 cup sliced .27
Feta cheese, 1 ounce 75
Fig bars, 1 53
Fish, cooked, 3 ounces
    Cod 89
    Flounder/sole 99

    Haddock 95
    Halibut 119
    Orange roughy 75
    Salmon (canned) 130
    Salmon (fresh) 183
    Swordfish 132
    Tuna (fresh) 157
    Tuna, light (canned in oil), drained 169
    Tuna, light (canned in water), drained 111
Fish sticks, frozen, 4×2 inches, 1 76
Flour, all-purpose, 1 cup 455
Flour, whole wheat, 1 cup 407
Frankfurters, 1
    Beef 180
    Turkey 100
French toast, 1 slice 153
Fruit cocktail, canned (juice pack), 1/2 cup 56

G

Gelatin, fruit-flavored, 1/2 cup 80
Gelatin, fruit-flavored, low-calorie, 1/2 cup 8
Ginger ale, 12 fluid ounces 124
Gingersnaps, 1 cookie 34
Goat cheese, soft, 1 ounce 76
Graham crackers, 2 1/2-inch square 30
Grapefruit, 1/2 medium 37
Grapefruit juice, 1/2 cup .47
Grape juice, 8 ounces 155
Grapes, 1/2 cup 94
Green beans, cooked, 1/2 cup 22
Gruyère cheese, 1 ounce 117
Gumdrops, 10 small 135

H–L

Ham, fully cooked, lean only, 3 ounces 124
Hoisin sauce, 1 tablespoon 35
Honey, 1 tablespoon 64
Honeydew melons, 1 cup 60
Horseradish, prepared, 1 tablespoon 6
Ice cream, 1/2 cup
    Chocolate 143
    Low-fat 92
    Strawberry 127
    Vanilla 132
Jam, 1 tablespoon 48
Jelly, 1 tablespoon 52
Jelly beans, 10 large (1 ounce) 104
Kiwifruit, 1 medium 46
Ladyfingers, 2 79

Lamb, cooked
Leg, lean only, 3 ounces 158
Loin chop, 1 91
Lemonade (from frozen concentrate),
8 ounces 100
Lemon-lime soda, 12 fluid ounces 149
Lemon or lime juice, 1 tablespoon 4
Lentils, cooked, 1 cup 231
Lettuce, iceberg, 1 leaf 3
Lettuce, leaf, 1/2 cup shredded 5
Lima beans, cooked, 1/2 cup 85
Lobster, cooked, 3 ounces 83

M

Macaroni, cooked, 1 cup 197
Macaroons, 2 cookies 181
Mandarin oranges, canned
(juice pack), 1/2 cup 46
Mangoes, 1 medium 135
Maple syrup, 1 tablespoon 52
Margarine, 1 tablespoon 100
Marshmallow cream, 1 ounce 88
Marshmallows, miniature, 1 cup 147
Marshmallows, 1 regular 23
Mayonnaise, 1 tablespoon
Fat-free 12
Reduced-fat 50
Regular 100
Milk, 8 ounces
Fat-free 86
Light 102
Reduced-fat 121
Whole 150
Molasses cookies, 1 137
Monterey Jack cheese, 1 ounce 106
Mozzarella cheese, part skim, 1 ounce 72
Muenster cheese, 1 ounce 104
Muffins, 1
Blueberry 112
Bran 112
Corn 115
Mushrooms, raw, 1/2 cup pieces 9
Mussels, cooked, 3 ounces 147
Mustard, brown, 1 teaspoon 5
Mustard, yellow, 1 teaspoon 4

N–O

Nectarines, 1 medium 67
Noodles, 1 cup, cooked 212

Nuts, 1 ounce
Almonds 167
Cashews 163
Hazelnuts 188
Macadamia 200
Peanuts 164
Pecans 187
Pine nuts 146
Walnuts 182
Oatmeal, regular or quick, cooked, 1 cup 145
Oatmeal cookies, 1 62
Oil, 1 tablespoon
Cooking (corn oil) 120
Olive oil 119
Omelet, made from 1 egg 92
Onions, green, 1 4
Onions, raw, 1/2 cup chopped 30
Orange juice, 1/2 cup 56
Orange marmalade, 1 tablespoon 49
Oranges, 1 medium 65
Orange soda, 12 fluid ounces 177
Oysters, cooked, 3 ounces 117

P

Pancakes, 1 62
with 1 tablespoon reduced-calorie syrup 46
with 1 tablespoon regular syrup 57
Papayas, 1 medium, ...117
Parmesan cheese, grated, 1 tablespoon 23
Parmesan cheese, 1 ounce 111
Parsnips, cooked, 1/2 cup 63
Peaches, canned (juice pack), 1 cup 109
Peaches, 1 medium 37
Peanut brittle, 1 ounce 128
Peanut butter, 2 tablespoons 188
Peanut butter cookies, 1 cookie 50
Pears, canned (juice pack) 1 cup 123
Pears, 1 medium 98
Peas, cooked, 1/2 cup 67
Peppers, hot chile, 1 18
Peppers, sweet, 1/2 cup chopped 13
Pesto, 1 ounce 155
Pickle relish, 1 tablespoon 19
Pickles, dill, 1 large 12
Pies, 1/8 of pie
Apple 282
Blueberry 286
Cherry 308
Lemon meringue 350
Peach 301

Pecan 431
Pumpkin 241
Rhubarb 299
Pimientos, 1 tablespoon 3
Pineapple, canned (juice pack), 1 cup 150
Pineapple, fresh, 1 cup 77
Pineapple juice, 1/2 cup 70
Pita bread, 1 (6-inch) 165
Plums, 1 medium 36
Popcorn, air-popped, 3 1/2 cups (1 ounce) ...108
Popcorn, oil-popped, 2 1/2 cups (1 ounce) 142
Pork, loin, cooked, 3 ounces 206
Potatoes
  Baked without skin, 1 145
  Baked with skin, 1.....................220
  Boiled without skin, 1 116
  Mashed, 1/2 cup 111
Potato chips, 1 ounce
  Barbecue 139
  Fat-Free 75
  Light 134
  Regular 152
Pretzels, 1 ounce 108
Prunes, dried, 10 201
Pudding (regular mix prepared with reduced-fat
  milk), 1/2 cup
  Chocolate 150
  Vanilla 141

R

Radishes, 10 3
Raisins, 2/3 cup 300
Raspberries, 1 cup 61
Rhubarb, 1 cup pieces 29
Rice, cooked, 1 cup
  Brown 216
  White 205
  Wild 166
Ricotta cheese, 1/2 cup
  Part skim 171
  Whole 216
Rolls, 1
  Dinner 84
  Hamburger or hot dog 123
  Hard, kaiser 167
  Whole wheat 105
Rye bread, 1 slice 83

S

Salad dressings (low-calorie), 1 tablespoon
  Blue cheese 15
  French 22
  Italian 16
  Mayonnaise-type 49
  Thousand Island 24
Salad dressings (regular), 1 tablespoon
  Blue cheese 77
  French 67
  Italian 69
  Mayonnaise-type 99
  Thousand Island 59
Salsa, 1/2 cup 29
Saltine crackers, 2 26
Sauerkraut, canned, 1/2 cup 22
Sausage, pork, cooked, 1 link 48
Scallops, raw, 3 ounces 75
Sherbet, orange, 1/2 cup 132
Shortbread cookies, 1 42
Shortening, 1 tablespoon 106
Shrimp, cooked, 3 ounces 84
Soup, condensed (prepared with reduced-fat
  milk), 1 cup
  Cream of celery 165
  Cream of chicken 191
  Cream of mushroom 203
  Tomato 160
Soup, condensed (prepared with water), 1 cup
  Chicken noodle 75
  Split pea with ham 189
  Tomato 86
Sour cream, 1 tablespoon
  Fat-free 12
  Light 20
  Regular 26
Sour cream dip, 1 tablespoon 30
Soy sauce, 1 tablespoon 10
Soy sauce, light, 1 tablespoon 11
Spaghetti, cooked, 1 cup 197
Spaghetti sauce, 1 cup 272
Spinach, 1/2 cup chopped
  Boiled 21
  Raw 6
Star fruit (carambola), 1 medium 42
Strawberries, 1 cup sliced 50

Squash, 1/2 cup
  Acorn, baked .... .57
  Butternut, cooked .... .41
  Spaghetti squash, cooked .... .23
  Yellow summer, raw .... .12
  Zucchini, raw 9
Succotash, cooked, 1/2 cup .... .111
Sugar, 1 tablespoon
  Brown .... .52
  Granulated .... .48
  Powdered .... .31
Sugar cookies, 2 .... .71
Sweet potatoes
  Baked with skin, 1 .... .118
  Mashed, 1/2 cup .... .172
Swiss cheese, 1 ounce .... .107

T

Toaster pastries, brown sugar cinnamon,
  1 pastry .... .206
Tomato, 1 .... .26
Tomato, dried, 1 piece 5
Tomato, dried and packed in oil, 1 piece 6
Tomatoes, stewed, 1 cup .... .71
Tomato juice, 1/2 cup .... .21
Tomato paste, 1/2 cup .... .107
Tomato sauce, 1/2 cup .... .37
Tortilla chips, regular, 1 ounce .... .142
Tortilla chips, baked, 10 chips .... .54
Tortilla, corn, 1 .... .58
Tortilla, flour, 1 .... .104
Turkey
  Dark meat, without skin, roasted, 3 ounces ...159
  Ground, cooked, 3 ounces .... .193
  Light meat, without skin, roasted, 3 ounces ...133

V–Y

Vanilla wafers, 5 .... .92
Veal, round, cooked, 3 ounces .... .129
Vegetable juice cocktail, 1/2 cup .... .23
Waffles, 1 (4-inch diameter) .... .87
Watermelon, 1 cup pieces .... .50
Wheat germ, toasted, 1/4 cup .... .108
Whipped dessert topping, frozen, 1 tablespoon
  Light .... .10
  Regular .... .15
Whipped topping mix (prepared), 1 tablespoon
  Reduced-calorie 5
  Regular .... .10

Whole-grain rye wafers, 1 .... .37
Whole wheat crackers, 4 .... .71
Wine, 3.5 fluid ounces
  Red .... .74
  White .... .70
Worcestershire sauce, 1 tablespoon ..... .11
Yogurt
  Frozen, soft-serve, 1/2 cup .... .115
  Fruit-flavored, fat-free .... .213
  Fruit-flavored, fat-free, with nonnutritive sweetener,
  8 ounces .... .98
  Fruit-flavored, low-fat, 8 ounces .... .231
  Plain, low-fat, 8 ounces .... .144

fast foods

Biscuit with egg and sausage .... .581
Burrito, bean and cheese .... .189
Cheeseburger, single patty, with condiments ..295
Chicken
  Breast, breaded and fried .... .283
  6 boneless pieces, breaded and fried .... .290
  Chicken fillet sandwich, plain .... .515
Cookies, animal crackers, 1 box .... .299
Eggs, scrambled, 1 serving .... .140
Enchilada with cheese .... .319
English muffin
  with egg, cheese, and Canadian bacon ...289
Fish sandwich
  With tartar sauce .... .431
  With tartar sauce and cheese .... .523
French fries
  Small .... .291
  Large .... .578
Hamburger, regular size, with condiments 272
Hot ham sandwich with Swiss cheese ...... .340
Hot dog, plain .... .242
Ice milk
  Vanilla, soft-serve, with cone .... .164
Pizza, 1 slice
  With cheese .... .140
  With cheese, meat, and vegetables ...... .184
Roast beef sandwich, plain .... .346
Shake (16-ounce)
  Chocolate .... .423
  Vanilla .... .370
Sundae, hot fudge .... .284
Taco, beef
  1 small .... .369
  1 large .... .568
Tostada with beans, beef, and cheese .... .333

On the divider: **Peachy Baked Beans** (see recipe, page 57)

4 chicken breast halves or thighs (about 1¹/₂ pounds total)

2¹/₂ cups water

1 medium onion, sliced and separated into rings

1 teaspoon instant chicken bouillon granules

1 teaspoon snipped fresh thyme or ¹/₄ teaspoon dried thyme, crushed

¹/₄ teaspoon black pepper

2 cups sliced carrots (4 medium)

1 medium bulb fennel, cut into bite-size strips (1¹/₂ cups)

¹/₄ cup cold water

2 tablespoons cornstarch

1 recipe Dumplings

Fresh herb sprigs (optional)

1 Remove the skin from the chicken. In a large saucepan combine the chicken pieces, the 2¹/₂ cups water, the onion, bouillon granules, dried thyme (if using), and pepper. Bring to boiling; reduce heat. Simmer, covered, for 25 minutes. Add the carrots and fennel. Return to boiling and reduce heat. Simmer, covered, for 10 minutes more.

2 Remove chicken pieces from saucepan; set aside. Skim fat from broth in pan. In a small bowl stir together the ¹/₄ cup cold water and the cornstarch; stir into broth in saucepan. Cook and stir until thickened and bubbly. Return chicken to pan; add fresh thyme (if using).

3 Drop Dumplings batter from a tablespoon into 8 mounds onto the hot chicken mixture. Cover; simmer about 10 minutes or until a wooden toothpick inserted into a dumpling comes out clean. If desired, garnish with herb sprigs.

Dumplings: In a small bowl stir together 1 cup all-purpose flour, 1¹/₂ teaspoons baking powder, ¹/₈ teaspoon salt, and ¹/₈ teaspoon coarsely ground black pepper. In another small bowl stir together 1 beaten egg, ¹/₄ cup fat-free milk, and 1 tablespoon cooking oil. Pour into flour mixture; stir with a fork until combined.

327 CALORIES

Chicken and Dumplings

Fennel lends this homey dish its mild anise flavor. During the chillier months of winter, your family will ask for it again and again.

Prep: 20 minutes   **Cook:** 50 minutes
Makes: 4 servings

Nutrition Facts per serving:
327 cal., 6 g total fat (1 g sat. fat), 110 mg chol., 558 mg sodium, 37 g carbo., 12 g fiber, 29 g pro.
Daily Values:
310% vit. A, 18% vit. C, 17% calcium, 15% iron
Exchanges:
1¹/₂ Vegetable, 2 Starch, 3 Meat, ¹/₂ Fat

234 CALORIES

Chicken with Basil Cream Sauce

If you grow basil or can find it fresh at your local supermarket, use it. Fresh always makes a bigger impact than dried.

Prep: 15 minutes **Bake:** 20 minutes
Oven: 400°F **Makes:** 4 servings

¼ cup fine dry bread crumbs

1 tablespoon snipped fresh basil or
    ¾ teaspoon dried basil, crushed

⅛ teaspoon black pepper

⅛ teaspoon paprika

1 tablespoon butter or margarine,
    melted

4 skinless, boneless chicken breast
    halves (about 1¼ pounds total)

⅔ cup reduced-fat milk

2 teaspoons all-purpose flour

¾ teaspoon instant chicken bouillon
    granules

1 In a small bowl stir together the bread crumbs, 2 teaspoons of the fresh basil or ½ teaspoon of the dried basil, the pepper, and paprika. Add melted butter; toss to coat.

2 Arrange chicken in a 2-quart rectangular baking dish. Sprinkle chicken pieces with the crumb mixture, pressing onto the chicken to coat. Bake in a 400° oven for 20 to 25 minutes or until no longer pink (170°F).

3 Meanwhile, in a small saucepan stir together milk, flour, bouillon granules, and remaining dried herb (if using) until combined. Cook and stir until thickened and bubbly. Cook and stir for 1 minute more. Stir in remaining fresh herb (if using). Serve over chicken.

Nutrition Facts per serving:
234 cal., 6 g total fat (3 g sat. fat), 94 mg chol.,
443 mg sodium, 7 g carbo., 0 g fiber, 35 g pro.
Daily Values:
5% vit. A, 4% vit. C, 8% calcium, 8% iron
Exchanges:
½ Starch, 1½ Meat

6 ounces dried spaghetti

1½ cups sliced fresh mushrooms

¾ cup chopped red or green sweet pepper

½ cup cold water

¼ cup all-purpose flour

1 12-ounce can (1½ cups) evaporated low-fat milk

1 teaspoon instant chicken bouillon granules

¼ teaspoon black pepper

⅛ teaspoon salt

1 cup chopped cooked chicken or turkey (5 ounces)

¼ cup finely shredded Parmesan cheese (1 ounce)

2 tablespoons dry sherry or milk

Nonstick cooking spray

1 tablespoon sliced almonds

1 Cook the spaghetti according to package directions, except omit the cooking oil and lightly salt the water. Drain well.

2 Meanwhile, in a large covered saucepan cook the mushrooms and sweet pepper in a small amount of boiling water until tender. Drain well; return to saucepan.

3 In a screw-top jar combine ½ cup cold water and flour; cover and shake well. Stir into the vegetable mixture in saucepan. Stir in the evaporated milk, bouillon granules, black pepper, and salt. Cook and stir until thickened and bubbly. Stir in the cooked spaghetti, chicken, Parmesan cheese, and dry sherry.

4 Lightly coat a 2-quart square baking dish with nonstick cooking spray. Spoon spaghetti mixture into dish. Sprinkle with almonds. Bake, uncovered, in a 400° oven about 10 minutes or until heated through and nuts are lightly toasted.

Chicken Tetrazzini

Made the original way, this dish has the potential to be astronomically high in calories and fat. This healthier alternative tastes just as great. Serve it with a side salad tossed with reduced-calorie Italian dressing.

Prep: 30 minutes   **Bake:** 10 minutes
Oven: 400°F   **Makes:** 4 servings

394 CALORIES

Nutrition Facts per serving:
394 cal., 9 g total fat (4 g sat. fat), 44 mg chol., 492 mg sodium, 50 g carbo., 2 g fiber, 26 g pro.
Daily Values:
32% vit. A, 76% vit. C, 30% calcium, 14% iron
Exchanges:
1 Vegetable, 3 Starch, 2 Meat, ½ Fat

Chicken and Corn Chowder

A south-of-the-border flavor dominates this thick, savory chowder. Green chile peppers provide a kick, and cilantro, a prominent herb in Mexican foods, adds the air of authenticity.

Start to Finish: 40 minutes

Makes: 4 main-dish servings (6½ cups)

300 CALORIES

½ cup chopped onion (1 medium)

1 tablespoon butter or margarine

1½ cups reduced-sodium chicken broth

1½ cups chopped, peeled potato (1 large)

2 cups fresh or frozen whole kernel corn (4 ears)

1 4-ounce can chopped green chile peppers, drained

¼ teaspoon coarsely ground black pepper

2 cups light or low-fat milk

2 tablespoons all-purpose flour

5 ounces cooked chicken, cut into thin strips

2 tablespoons snipped fresh cilantro or 2 teaspoons snipped fresh oregano

1 In a large saucepan cook onion in hot butter for 3 to 4 minutes or until tender. Add broth, potato, corn, chile peppers, and black pepper. Bring to boiling; reduce heat. Simmer, covered, about 15 minutes or until potatoes are tender, stirring occasionally.

2 In a screw-top jar combine milk and flour; cover and shake well. Add to potato mixture. Cook and stir until thickened and bubbly. Add chicken and cilantro or oregano. Heat through.

Nutrition Facts per serving:
300 cal., 8 g total fat (4 g sat. fat), 44 mg chol., 486 mg sodium, 39 g carbo., 4 g fiber, 20 g pro.
Daily Values:
13% vit. A, 43% vit. C, 18% calcium, 11% iron
Exchanges:
½ Milk, ½ Vegetable, 2 Starch, 1 Meat, 1 Fat

8 ounces uncooked bulk turkey sausage

½ cup chopped onion (1 medium)

2 cups purchased spaghetti sauce

1 cup water

2 cups dried wide noodles

1½ cups coarsely chopped zucchini

½ cup fat-free ricotta cheese

2 tablespoons grated Parmesan or Romano cheese

1 tablespoon snipped fresh parsley

½ cup shredded reduced-fat mozzarella cheese (2 ounces)

1 In a large skillet cook sausage and onion until meat is brown and onion is tender, breaking up the meat during cooking. Drain off fat. Stir in spaghetti sauce and the water. Bring to boiling. Stir in uncooked noodles and zucchini. Return to boiling; reduce heat. Simmer, covered, about 12 minutes or until noodles are tender, stirring occasionally.

2 Meanwhile, in a small bowl stir together ricotta cheese, Parmesan cheese, and parsley. Drop cheese mixture by spoonfuls into 6 mounds over the sausage-noodle mixture in the skillet. Sprinkle each mound with mozzarella. Cover and cook on low heat for 4 to 5 minutes or until cheese mixture is heated through. Let stand for 10 minutes before serving.

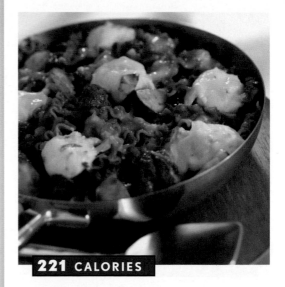

221 CALORIES

Slimmed Skillet Lasagna

When you think of lasagna, the words quick and easy don't normally come to mind. But then again, neither do low calorie and low fat, and this version is all of the above.

Prep: 20 minutes   **Cook:** 16 minutes
Stand: 10 minutes   **Makes:** 6 servings

Nutrition Facts per serving:
221 cal., 8 g total fat (3 g sat. fat), 35 mg chol., 805 mg sodium, 22 g carbo., 3 g fiber, 17 g pro.
Daily Values:
5% vit. A, 16% vit. C, 21% calcium, 13% iron
Exchanges:
1 Vegetable, 1 Starch, 2 Meat

284 CALORIES

Brats with Onion-Pepper Relish

Brats and diets don't normally go together, but rules are meant to be broken. Here you'll get all the flavor you expect, with a lot fewer calories than the concession stand variety.

Prep: 15 minutes **Cook:** 15 minutes
Makes: 4 servings

- 4 uncooked turkey bratwurst
- 1/2 cup water
- 1 small onion, thinly sliced
- 1 small red or green sweet pepper, cut into thin strips
- 1/4 teaspoon black pepper
- 1/8 teaspoon salt
- 2 teaspoons butter or margarine
- 4 bratwurst buns, split and toasted
- 3 tablespoons spicy brown mustard

1 In a large nonstick skillet cook bratwurst over medium heat about 5 minutes or until brown, turning frequently. Carefully add the water. Bring to boiling; reduce heat. Simmer, covered, for 15 to 20 minutes or until internal temperature registers 165°F on an instant-read thermometer. Drain on paper towels.

2 Meanwhile, in a covered medium saucepan cook onion, sweet pepper, black pepper, and salt in hot butter for 3 minutes. Stir onion mixture. Cook, covered, for 3 to 4 minutes more or until onion is golden.

3 Spread cut sides of toasted buns with the mustard. Serve bratwurst in buns topped with onion mixture.

Grill method: Prepare as above, except arrange medium-hot coals around a drip pan in a covered grill. Test for medium heat above the pan. Place bratwurst on grill over the pan. Cover and grill for 20 to 25 minutes or until internal temperature registers 165°F on an instant-read thermometer, turning bratwurst once halfway through grilling. Cook onion mixture and serve as above.

Nutrition Facts per serving:
284 cal., 12 g total fat (4 g sat. fat), 43 mg chol., 1,100 mg sodium, 27 g carbo., 2 g fiber, 17 g pro.
Daily Values:
22% vit. A, 51% vit. C, 10% calcium, 14% iron
Exchanges:
1 Vegetable, 1 1/2 Starch, 1 1/2 Meat, 1/2 Fat

12 ounces beef flank steak

3 tablespoons frozen orange juice concentrate, thawed

3 tablespoons water

2 tablespoons lime juice

1 teaspoon grated fresh ginger

1/2 teaspoon dried oregano, crushed

1/8 teaspoon salt

1/8 teaspoon cayenne pepper

1 clove garlic, minced

4 8- to 10-inch garden vegetable flour tortillas

3/4 cup red and/or yellow sweet pepper strips

1 small onion, sliced and separated into rings

1/4 cup hoisin or plum sauce

1 cup shredded napa cabbage

1 Score meat by making shallow cuts at 1-inch intervals diagonally across steak in a diamond pattern. Repeat on the other side. Place meat in a plastic bag set in a shallow dish. For marinade, in a small bowl combine orange juice concentrate, the water, lime juice, ginger, oregano, salt, cayenne pepper, and garlic. Pour over meat; seal bag. Marinate in the refrigerator for at least 30 minutes or up to 4 hours, turning bag occasionally.

2 Preheat broiler. Drain meat, reserving marinade. Place meat on the unheated rack of a broiler pan. Broil 3 to 4 inches from the heat for 15 to 18 minutes or until medium doneness (160°F), turning once. Thinly slice meat diagonally across the grain.

3 Wrap tortillas in foil. Place beside the broiler pan for the last 8 minutes of broiling meat. Meanwhile, pour reserved marinade into a medium saucepan. Stir in sweet pepper and onion. Bring to boiling; reduce heat. Simmer, covered, for 5 to 8 minutes or until vegetables are tender. To serve, spread each tortilla with some of the hoisin sauce. Top with napa cabbage and beef. Using a slotted spoon, spoon pepper mixture over beef. Roll up.

Asian Flank Steak Roll-Ups

It's easy to tenderize flank steak, a naturally lean cut of meat. Simply score it and let it rest in an orange, lime, and ginger-flavor marinade.

Prep: 15 minutes   **Broil:** 15 minutes

Marinate: 30 minutes to 4 hours

Makes: 4 servings

411 CALORIES

Nutrition Facts per serving:
411 cal., 11 g total fat (4 g sat. fat), 34 mg chol., 673 mg sodium, 50 g carbo., 5 g fiber, 26 g pro.
Daily Values:
42% vit. A, 142% vit. C, 17% calcium, 15% iron
Exchanges:
1 Vegetable, 1 Fruit, 2 Starch, 3 Meat

Garden Pot Roast

Adapt this recipe to whatever fresh vegetables are in season for a different variation all year long.

Prep: 25 minutes   **Bake:** 2½ hours
Oven: 325°F   **Makes:** 8 servings

250 CALORIES

1   **3-pound boneless beef bottom round roast**
    Salt
    Black pepper
1   **tablespoon cooking oil**
1   **14-ounce can beef broth**
½   **cup coarsely chopped onion (1 medium)**
½   **teaspoon dried marjoram, crushed**
½   **teaspoon dried thyme, crushed**
2   **cloves garlic, minced**
4   **cups cut-up vegetables (such as 2-inch pieces of peeled winter squash, carrots, parsnips, and/or green beans)**
2   **tablespoons cold water**
1   **tablespoon cornstarch**

1 Trim fat from meat. Sprinkle meat lightly with salt and pepper. In a 4- to 6-quart Dutch oven brown meat on all sides in hot oil for 5 minutes, turning to brown evenly. Drain off fat. Carefully pour broth over meat. Add onion, marjoram, thyme, and garlic. Bake, covered, in a 325° oven for 2 hours.

2 Add vegetables. Cover and bake for 30 to 40 minutes more or until tender. Transfer meat and vegetables to a serving platter; reserve cooking liquid in Dutch oven. Cover platter with foil to keep warm.

3 For gravy, strain juices into a glass measuring cup. Skim fat from juices; return 1¼ cups of the juices to Dutch oven (discard remaining juices). In a small bowl stir together the cold water and cornstarch. Stir into juices in Dutch oven. Cook and stir until thickened and bubbly. Cook and stir for 2 minutes more. Season to taste with salt and pepper. Slice meat. Spoon some of the gravy over meat and vegetables. Pass remaining gravy.

Nutrition Facts per serving:
250 cal., 8 g total fat (2 g sat. fat), 83 mg chol., 337 mg sodium, 9 g carbo., 2 g fiber, 33 g pro.
Daily Values:
90% vit. A, 12% vit. C, 3% calcium, 22% iron
Exchanges:
1½ Vegetable, 4 Meat

Nonstick cooking spray

1/3 cup sliced green onions

1/4 cup finely chopped red and/or yellow sweet pepper

1/4 cup finely chopped carrot

2 slightly beaten egg whites

1/2 cup finely crushed saltine crackers (14 crackers)

2 tablespoons fat-free milk

1/3 cup bottled chili sauce

1 tablespoon snipped fresh basil or oregano or 1/2 teaspoon dried basil or oregano, crushed

1/4 teaspoon black pepper

1 pound extra-lean ground beef

1 tablespoon brown sugar

1 teaspoon vinegar

Fresh herb sprigs (optional)

1 Coat an unheated small skillet with nonstick cooking spray. Preheat over medium heat. Add the green onions, sweet pepper, and carrot. Cook for 5 to 8 minutes or until vegetables are tender, stirring occasionally. Remove from heat; cool slightly.

2 In a large bowl stir together the egg whites, crushed crackers, milk, 2 tablespoons of the chili sauce, the basil or oregano, and black pepper. Add the cooked vegetables and the ground beef; mix well.

3 Firmly pat the meat mixture into a 7½×3½×2-inch loaf pan. Invert pan with meat mixture into a shallow baking pan; remove loaf pan. Bake the meat loaf in a 350° oven for 30 minutes.

4 Meanwhile, in a small bowl combine remaining chili sauce, brown sugar, and vinegar; spoon over meat loaf. Bake for 15 to 20 minutes more or until internal temperature registers 160°F on an instant-read thermometer. Let stand for 10 minutes. Transfer meat loaf to a platter. To serve, cut into slices. If desired, garnish with herb sprigs.

189 CALORIES

Mom's Meat Loaf

Mom's meat loaf—only better (but don't tell her that!). This mix contains more vegetables than Mom's, a few snips of basil, and chili sauce instead of catsup.

Prep: 30 minutes **Bake:** 45 minutes
Stand: 10 minutes **Oven:** 350°F
Makes: 6 servings

Nutrition Facts per serving:
189 cal., 8 g total fat (3 g sat. fat), 48 mg chol., 319 mg sodium, 12 g carbo., 1 g fiber, 16 g pro.
Daily Values:
35% vit. A, 23% vit. C, 3% calcium, 11% iron
Exchanges:
1 Vegetable, 1/2 Starch, 2 Meat

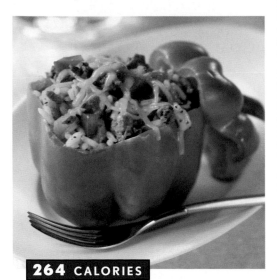

264 CALORIES

Stuffed Green Peppers

Stuffed green peppers have always been good for you, but this version is new and improved. The key is the extra-lean ground beef and just a sprinkling of cheddar cheese.

Prep: 35 minutes **Bake:** 15 minutes
Stand: 2 minutes **Oven:** 375°F
Makes: 4 servings

- 4 small green sweet peppers
  Salt (optional)
- 12 ounces extra-lean ground beef
- 1/3 cup chopped onion (1 small)
- 1 cup water
- 1/3 cup long grain rice
- 1 tablespoon Worcestershire sauce
- 1 tablespoon snipped fresh basil or oregano or 1/2 teaspoon dried basil or oregano, crushed
- 1/4 teaspoon salt
- 1/4 teaspoon black pepper
- 2 medium tomatoes, peeled and chopped
- 1/4 cup shredded cheddar or Monterey Jack cheese (1 ounce)

1 Cut tops off sweet peppers; remove seeds and membranes. Immerse sweet peppers in boiling water for 3 minutes. If desired, sprinkle insides with salt. Invert on paper towels to drain well.

2 In a large skillet cook meat and onion until meat is brown and onion is tender. Drain off fat. Stir in the water, uncooked rice, Worcestershire sauce, dried basil or oregano (if using), the 1/4 teaspoon salt, and the black pepper. Bring to boiling; reduce heat. Simmer, covered, for 15 to 18 minutes or until rice is tender. Stir in tomatoes and the fresh herb (if using).

3 Spoon meat mixture into sweet peppers. Place in a 2-quart square baking dish along with any remaining meat mixture. Bake, uncovered, in a 375° oven for 15 to 20 minutes or until heated through. Sprinkle with cheese. Let stand about 2 minutes or until cheese is melted.

Nutrition Facts per serving:
264 cal., 11 g total fat (5 g sat. fat), 61 mg chol., 278 mg sodium, 22 g carbo., 3 g fiber, 19 g pro.
Daily Values:
18% vit. A, 110% vit. C, 7% calcium, 18% iron
Exchanges:
2 Vegetable, 1 Starch, 2 1/2 Meat

- **1 pound veal leg round steak or veal sirloin steak, or 4 skinless, boneless chicken breast halves (about 1 pound)**
- **3 cups fresh mushrooms (such as crimini, porcini, baby portobello, or button), quartered, halved, or sliced**
- **4 teaspoons olive oil or cooking oil**
- **1/4 teaspoon salt**
- **1/4 teaspoon black pepper**
- **3/4 cup dry Marsala**
- **1/2 cup sliced green onions (4)**
- **1 tablespoon snipped fresh sage or 1/2 teaspoon dried sage, crushed**
- **1 tablespoon cold water**
- **1 teaspoon cornstarch**
- **1/8 teaspoon salt**
- **Fresh herb sprigs (optional)**

Veal Marsala

Though veal is the traditional meat of choice here, chicken makes an inexpensive substitute. If you don't want to pound the chicken, look for breasts that have been tenderized by your supermarket's meat department.

Start to Finish: 35 minutes
Makes: 4 servings

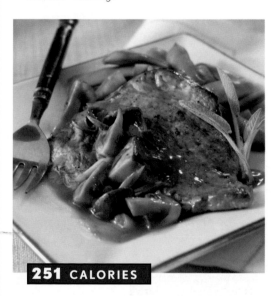

251 CALORIES

1 Cut veal into 4 serving-size pieces. Place each veal piece or chicken breast half between 2 sheets of plastic wrap. Working from center to edges, pound lightly with the flat side of a meat mallet to about 1/8-inch thickness. Remove the plastic wrap. Set meat aside.

2 In a 12-inch skillet cook the mushrooms in 2 teaspoons of the hot oil for 4 to 5 minutes or until tender. Remove from skillet. Set aside.

3 Sprinkle meat with the 1/4 teaspoon salt and the pepper. In the same skillet cook veal or chicken, half at a time, in the remaining 2 teaspoons hot oil over medium-high heat for 2 to 3 minutes or until no longer pink, turning once. Transfer to dinner plates. Keep warm.

4 Add Marsala to drippings in skillet. Bring to boiling. Boil mixture gently, uncovered, for 1 minute, scraping up any browned bits. Return mushrooms to skillet; add green onions and sage. In a small bowl stir together the cold water, the cornstarch, and the 1/8 teaspoon salt; add to skillet. Cook and stir until slightly thickened and bubbly; cook and stir 1 minute more. To serve, spoon the mushroom mixture over meat. Serve immediately. If desired, garnish with herb sprigs.

Nutrition Facts per serving:
251 cal., 8 g total fat (1 g sat. fat), 88 mg chol., 283 mg sodium, 7 g carbo., 1 g fiber, 27 g pro.
Daily Values:
1% vit. A, 4% vit. C, 2% calcium, 9% iron
Exchanges:
1 Vegetable, 3 Meat, 1 Fat

Scalloped Potatoes and Ham

No need for dieters to abandon well-loved side dishes like this one. Grilled chicken and steak wouldn't be the same without a potato partner.

Prep: 25 minutes   **Bake:** 65 minutes
Stand: 10 minutes   **Oven:** 350°F
Makes: 8 side-dish servings

145 CALORIES

1/2   cup chopped onion (1 medium)
 2   cloves garlic, minced
 2   tablespoons butter or margarine
 3   tablespoons all-purpose flour
1/2   teaspoon salt
1/4   teaspoon black pepper
1 1/2   cups reduced-fat milk
 2   teaspoons snipped fresh thyme or
      1/2 teaspoon dried thyme, crushed
1 1/2   pounds potatoes (4 to 5 medium)
 5   ounces low-fat, reduced-sodium
      cooked ham, cut into thin strips

1 For sauce, in a medium saucepan cook onion and garlic in hot butter over medium heat until tender. Stir in flour, salt, and pepper. Add milk all at once. Cook and stir over medium heat until thickened and bubbly. Stir in thyme.

2 Scrub and thinly slice potatoes. Arrange two-thirds of the potato slices in a 2-quart casserole; cover with two-thirds of the sauce. Top with ham. Top with remaining potatoes and remaining sauce.

3 Bake, covered, in a 350° oven for 55 minutes. Uncover and bake for 10 to 15 minutes more or until the potatoes are tender. Let potatoes stand 10 minutes before serving.

Nutrition Facts per serving:
145 cal., 5 g total fat (3 g sat. fat), 19 mg chol., 399 mg sodium, 20 g carbo., 2 g fiber, 7 g pro.
Daily Values:
4% vit. A, 32% vit. C, 7% calcium, 8% iron
Exchanges:
1 1/2 Starch, 1/2 Meat

4 slices firm white bread or sourdough bread

4 teaspoons cranberry or raspberry mustard

2 ounces very thinly sliced reduced-sodium cooked ham

2 slices reduced-fat Swiss cheese (2 ounces)

¼ cup reduced-fat milk

1 egg white

Butter-flavor nonstick cooking spray

1 teaspoon butter or margarine

Sifted powdered sugar (optional)

Raspberry preserves (optional)

1 Spread 1 side of each bread slice lightly with mustard. Layer ham and cheese between the mustard-spread sides of the bread slices. In a shallow bowl or pie plate beat together milk and egg white.

2 Coat an unheated nonstick griddle or large skillet with nonstick cooking spray. Preheat griddle over medium heat. Melt butter on griddle. Dip each sandwich in milk mixture, turning to coat. Place in skillet; cook for 1 to 2 minutes per side or until golden and cheese is melted. If desired, sprinkle with powdered sugar and serve with preserves.

314 CALORIES

Classic Monte Cristo Sandwiches

This hall-of-fame sandwich, known for its crisp egg-batter coating outside and melty perfection inside, gets an extra dose of opulence from sweet-tart cranberry mustard. Sound indulgent? Not this slimmed-down version.

Start to Finish: 15 minutes
Makes: 2 servings

Nutrition Facts per serving:
314 cal., 10 g total fat (4 g sat. fat), 41 mg chol., 606 mg sodium, 33 g carbo., 0 g fiber, 21 g pro.
Daily Values:
12% vit. A, 1% vit. C, 37% calcium, 9% iron
Exchanges:
2 Starch, 2 Meat, ½ Fat

251 CALORIES

Vegetable Lasagna

You won't miss the meat (or the calories) in this tasty lasagna. A sprinkling of tomatoes adds a fresh appeal. To cut calories further, use a light pasta sauce.

Prep: 30 minutes **Bake:** 35 minutes

Oven: 375°F **Stand:** 10 minutes

Makes: 6 servings

Nutrition Facts per serving:
251 cal., 9 g total fat (4 g sat. fat), 25 mg chol., 572 mg sodium, 30 g carbo., 4 g fiber, 15 g pro.
Daily Values:
10% vit. A, 22% vit. C, 26% calcium, 10% iron
Exchanges:
1½ Vegetable, 1½ Starch, 1 Meat, ½ Fat

---

  6 dried lasagna noodles

2½ cups zucchini and/or yellow summer squash halved lengthwise and sliced (2 medium)

  2 cups sliced fresh mushrooms

⅓ cup chopped onion (1 small)

  2 teaspoons olive oil

  1 cup light ricotta cheese

  3 tablespoons finely shredded Parmesan cheese (1 ounce)

¼ teaspoon black pepper

  2 cups purchased pasta sauce

  1 cup shredded part-skim mozzarella cheese (4 ounces)

½ cup chopped, seeded tomato (1 medium)

1 Cook noodles according to package directions; drain and rinse with cold water. Drain well.

2 Meanwhile, in large nonstick skillet cook and stir squash, mushrooms, and onion in hot oil over medium-high heat about 5 minutes or until tender; remove from heat and set aside. In a small bowl combine ricotta cheese, Parmesan cheese, and pepper.

3 To assemble, place 3 lasagna noodles in the bottom of a 2-quart rectangular baking dish, trimming to fit as necessary. Spoon half of the ricotta cheese mixture over the noodles. Top with half of the vegetable mixture, half of the sauce, and half of the mozzarella cheese. Layer with remaining noodles, ricotta cheese mixture, vegetable mixture, and sauce.

4 Bake, uncovered, in a 375° oven for 30 minutes. Sprinkle with tomato and the remaining mozzarella cheese. Bake 5 minutes more or until heated through. Let stand for 10 minutes before serving.

1 **pound fresh or frozen skinless cod, orange roughy, or catfish fillets**

¼ **cup reduced-fat milk**

⅓ **cup all-purpose flour**

½ **cup fine dry bread crumbs**

2 **tablespoons grated Parmesan cheese**

¼ **teaspoon lemon-pepper seasoning**

2 **tablespoons butter or margarine, melted**

Fresh parsley sprigs (optional)

Lemon wedges (optional)

1 Thaw fish, if frozen. Rinse fish; pat dry with paper towels. If necessary, cut into 4 serving-size pieces. Measure the thickness of each piece. Place milk in a shallow dish. Place flour in another shallow dish. In a third shallow dish combine bread crumbs, Parmesan cheese, and lemon-pepper seasoning. Add melted butter to bread crumb mixture; stir until well mixed.

2 Grease a shallow baking pan; set aside. Dip fish in the milk; coat with flour. Dip again in the milk; dip in the crumb mixture, turning to coat all sides. Place fish in a single layer in prepared baking pan. Bake, uncovered, in a 450° oven for 4 to 6 minutes per ½-inch thickness or until fish flakes easily when tested with a fork. If desired, garnish with parsley and lemon.

Oven-Fried Fish

Fried food is a waist-whittler's foe—too many calories, too much fat. Bake this fried fish to reduce both and you needn't avoid it again.

Prep: 10 minutes
Bake: 4 to 6 minutes per ½-inch thickness
Oven: 450°F
Makes: 4 servings

254 CALORIES

Nutrition Facts per serving:
254 cal., 9 g total fat (5 g sat. fat), 75 mg chol., 565 mg sodium, 15 g carbo., 1 g fiber, 26 g pro.
Daily Values:
6% vit. A, 3% vit. C, 12% calcium, 8% iron
Exchanges:
1 Starch, 3 Meat, 1½ Fat

Tuna-Noodle Casserole

Make an old standby new again: Add green beans and mushrooms and breathe new life into everyday tuna-noodle casserole.

Prep: 25 minutes   **Bake:** 20 minutes
Oven: 375°F   **Makes:** 6 servings

258 CALORIES

2	cups dried medium noodles (4 ounces)
2	cups loose-pack frozen cut green beans
$^1/_3$	cup fine dry bread crumbs
2	teaspoons butter or margarine, melted
	Nonstick cooking spray
1	cup sliced fresh mushrooms
$^3/_4$	cup coarsely chopped red sweet pepper
$^1/_2$	cup chopped onion (1 medium)
1	$10^3/_4$-ounce can reduced-fat and reduced-sodium condensed cream of mushroom or celery soup
$^1/_2$	cup reduced-fat milk
$^1/_2$	cup shredded American or process Swiss cheese (2 ounces)
1	$9^1/_4$-ounce can tuna (water pack), drained and flaked

1 Cook noodles according to package directions, adding the green beans for the last 3 minutes of cooking. Drain; set aside.

2 Meanwhile, toss the bread crumbs with melted butter; set aside.

3 Lightly coat an unheated large nonstick skillet with nonstick cooking spray. Preheat over medium heat. Add mushrooms, sweet pepper, and onion. Cook and stir until vegetables are tender. Add soup, milk, and cheese, stirring until cheese is melted. Stir in cooked noodle-green bean mixture and tuna.

4 Spoon noodle mixture into a 1½-quart casserole. Sprinkle bread crumb mixture over noodle mixture. Bake, uncovered, in a 375° oven for 20 to 25 minutes or until heated through and bread crumbs are golden.

Nutrition Facts per serving:
258 cal., 8 g total fat (4 g sat. fat), 52 mg chol., 651 mg sodium, 28 g carbo., 3 g fiber, 18 g pro.
Daily Values:
28% vit. A, 59% vit. C, 13% calcium, 11% iron
Exchanges:
1½ Vegetable, 1½ Starch, 1½ Meat, 1 Fat

- $^{1}/_{3}$ cup bottled reduced-calorie or fat-free Caesar salad dressing
- 2 teaspoons snipped fresh tarragon or $^{1}/_{4}$ teaspoon dried tarragon, crushed
- 1 10-ounce package torn mixed salad greens (8 cups)
- 1 large tomato, cut into thin wedges
- 1 $6^{1}/_{2}$-ounce can chunk white tuna (water pack), drained

1 In a small bowl stir together salad dressing and tarragon; set aside. To serve, arrange greens on 4 salad plates. Top with tomato and tuna. Drizzle each serving with dressing mixture.

121 CALORIES

Light-Style Tuna Salad

You don't need a year-round herb garden to enjoy the diversity of herbs. Simply stock fresh-cut herbs from the produce aisle in your fridge or keep dried herbs on hand in the cupboard.

Start to Finish: 15 minutes

Makes: 4 main-dish servings

Nutrition Facts per serving:
121 cal., 5 g total fat (0 g sat. fat), 22 mg chol., 557 mg sodium, 6 g carbo., 2 g fiber, 13 g pro.
Daily Values:
13% vit. A, 21% vit. C, 3% calcium, 8% iron
Exchanges:
1 Vegetable, $1^{1}/_{2}$ Meat, $^{1}/_{2}$ Fat

267 CALORIES

Paella

Paella (pi-AY-yuh) hails from Spain and boasts a saffron-spiced rice. Harvested from the purple crocus flower, saffron is costly, but a little goes a long way.

Prep: 20 minutes   **Cook:** 40 minutes
Makes: 6 servings

Nutrition Facts per serving:
267 cal., 4 g total fat (1 g sat. fat), 100 mg chol., 400 mg sodium, 33 g carbo., 3 g fiber, 24 g pro.
Daily Values:
28% vit. A, 68% vit. C, 4% calcium, 17% iron
Exchanges:
1 Vegetable, 2 Starch, 2 Meat, 1/2 Fat

8 ounces fresh or frozen medium shrimp in shells
   Nonstick cooking spray
1 cup coarsely chopped onion (1 large)
1 clove garlic, minced
6 chicken thighs (about 1 1/2 pounds)
1 14-ounce can reduced-sodium chicken broth
1 teaspoon snipped fresh thyme or 1/4 teaspoon dried thyme, crushed
1/4 teaspoon salt
1/4 teaspoon ground saffron
1/8 to 1/4 teaspoon cayenne pepper
1 cup long grain rice
1 medium red or green sweet pepper, coarsely chopped
1 cup loose-pack frozen peas
1/2 cup chopped, seeded tomato (1 medium)

1 Thaw shrimp, if frozen. Peel and devein shrimp, leaving tails intact. Rinse shrimp; pat dry with paper towels. Cover and refrigerate until needed.

2 Lightly coat an unheated Dutch oven with nonstick cooking spray. Preheat over medium heat. Add onion and garlic. Cook until onion is tender.

3 Remove skin from the chicken thighs. Add chicken thighs, broth, dried thyme (if using), salt, saffron, and cayenne pepper to Dutch oven. Bring to boiling and reduce heat. Simmer, covered, for 15 minutes.

4 Stir in uncooked rice. Return to boiling; reduce heat. Simmer, covered, about 15 minutes more or until rice is almost tender. Stir shrimp, sweet pepper, peas, tomato, and fresh thyme (if using) into the rice mixture. Simmer, covered, for 5 to 8 minutes more or until the rice and chicken are tender and the shrimp turn opaque.

- **1** pint shucked clams or two 6½-ounce cans minced clams
- **1** cup chopped celery (2 stalks)
- **⅓** cup chopped onion (1 small)
- **¼** cup chopped carrot (1 small)
- **2** tablespoons olive oil or cooking oil
- **1** 8-ounce bottle clam juice or 1 cup chicken broth
- **2** cups red potatoes cut into bite size pieces
- **1** teaspoon dried thyme, crushed
- **⅛** teaspoon cayenne pepper
- **⅛** teaspoon black pepper
- **1** 14½-ounce can diced tomatoes, undrained
- **2** tablespoons purchased cooked bacon pieces or cooked crumbled bacon*

1 Chop fresh clams, if using, reserving juice; set clams aside. Strain clam juice to remove bits of shell. (Or drain canned clams, reserving juice.) If necessary, add enough water to reserved clam juice to equal 1½ cups liquid. Set juice aside.

2 In a large saucepan cook celery, onion, and carrot in hot oil until tender. Stir in the reserved 1½ cups clam juice and the bottled clam juice or chicken broth. Stir in potatoes, thyme, cayenne pepper, and black pepper. Bring to boiling; reduce heat. Simmer, covered, for 10 minutes. Stir in tomatoes, clams, and bacon. Return to boiling; reduce heat. Cook for 1 to 2 minutes more or until heated through.

*Note: If using bacon, cook 2 slices, reserving 2 tablespoons drippings. Omit the oil and cook the celery, onion, and carrot in the reserved drippings.

Manhattan Clam Chowder

Normally creamy chowders are loaded with calories, but Manhattan clam chowder traditionally features tomatoes rather than cream. It's a satisfying soup that needs only a wedge of bread to sop up every last drop in your bowl.

Start to Finish: 40 minutes
Makes: 4 main-dish servings (about 6½ cups)

264 CALORIES

Nutrition Facts per serving:
264 cal., 10 g total fat (2 g sat. fat), 43 mg chol., 375 mg sodium, 23 g carbo., 3 g fiber, 18 g pro.
Daily Values:
47% vit. A, 64% vit. C, 12% calcium, 90% iron
Exchanges:
1 Vegetable, 1 Starch, 2 Meat, 1 Fat

Buttermilk Pancakes

The tangy flavor of buttermilk makes butter unnecessary. With pancakes as tender and light as these, just a little fruit syrup or maple syrup goes a long way.

Prep: 10 minutes **Cook:** 4 minutes per batch
Makes: 4 servings (8 pancakes)

177 CALORIES

1 cup all-purpose flour
2 teaspoons sugar
1 teaspoon baking powder
¼ teaspoon baking soda
¼ teaspoon salt
1 cup buttermilk
2 egg whites
1 tablespoon cooking oil
½ teaspoon vanilla
  Nonstick cooking spray

1 In a medium bowl combine the flour, sugar, baking powder, baking soda, and salt. Make a well in the center of flour mixture; set aside. In a small bowl combine buttermilk, egg whites, oil, and vanilla; add all at once to flour mixture. Stir just until moistened (batter should be slightly lumpy).

2 Lightly coat an unheated griddle or heavy skillet with nonstick cooking spray. Preheat over medium heat. For each pancake, pour a scant ¼ cup of the batter onto the hot griddle or skillet. Cook over medium heat about 2 minutes on each side or until pancakes are golden, turning to second sides when pancakes have bubbly surfaces and edges are slightly dry. Serve warm.

Serving suggestions: Serve pancakes with fruit syrup, light maple-flavored syrup, spreadable fruit, or sprinkle with powdered sugar.

Nutrition Facts per serving:
177 cal., 4 g total fat (1 g sat. fat), 2 mg chol., 416 mg sodium, 27 g carbo., 1 g fiber, 7 g pro.
Daily Values:
1% vit. C, 14% calcium, 8% iron
Exchanges:
2 Starch, ½ Fat

2 **cups all-purpose flour**

4 **teaspoons baking powder**

$1/2$ **teaspoon cream of tartar**

$1/4$ **teaspoon salt**

$1/4$ **cup shortening**

$3/4$ **cup fat-free milk**

2 **tablespoons sugar**

1 **teaspoon ground cinnamon**

1 Grease twelve 2½-inch muffin cups; set aside. In a large bowl stir together flour, baking powder, cream of tartar, and salt. Using a pastry blender, cut in shortening until mixture resembles coarse crumbs. Make a well in the center; add milk. Stir just until dough clings together.

2 Turn dough out onto a lightly floured surface. Knead by folding and gently pressing dough for 10 to 12 strokes or until dough is nearly smooth. Divide dough in half. Roll one portion into a 12×10-inch rectangle. In a small bowl combine the sugar and cinnamon. Sprinkle some of the sugar mixture over the rectangle.

3 Cut rectangle into five 12×2-inch strips. Stack the strips on top of each other Cut into six 2-inch-square stacks. Place each stack, cut side down, in a prepared muffin cup. Repeat with remaining dough and sugar mixture.

4 Bake in a 450° oven for 10 to 12 minutes or until golden. Serve warm.

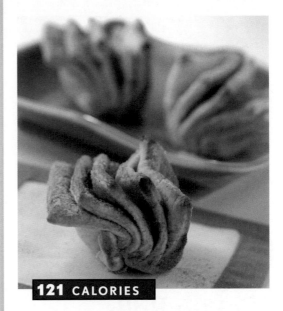

121 CALORIES

Sugar and Spice Biscuits

These biscuits have an interesting fan shape that's surprisingly easy to achieve. Expect them to inspire lively conversation at your next breakfast or brunch.

Prep: 15 minutes   **Bake:** 10 minutes
Oven: 450°F   **Makes:** 12 biscuits

Nutrition Facts per biscuit:
121 cal., 4 g total fat (1 g sat. fat), 0 mg chol., 190 mg sodium, 18 g carbo., 1 g fiber, 3 g pro.
Daily Values:
1% vit. A, 10% calcium, 5% iron
Exchanges:
1 Starch, 1 Fat

104 CALORIES

Potato Rolls

Reserve these yeast rolls for special occasions and holidays. For an elegant presentation, decorate each roll with a sage leaf: Lightly dip the top of each dough ball into flour or brush with egg white. Top each with a sage leaf, brush with egg white, and place on prepared baking sheets.

Prep: 45 minutes **Rise:** 1¼ hours
Bake: 12 minutes **Oven:** 350°F
Makes: 24 rolls

Nutrition Facts per roll:
104 cal., 1 g total fat (1 g sat. fat), 3 mg chol., 174 mg sodium, 20 g carbo., 1 g fiber, 3 g pro.
Daily Values:
1% vit. A, 2% vit. C, 2% calcium, 6% iron
Exchanges:
1½ Starch

1½ cups buttermilk
⅔ cup water
¼ cup sugar
2 tablespoons butter or margarine
1½ teaspoons salt
¾ cup instant mashed potato flakes
2 tablespoons snipped fresh sage or
    2 teaspoons dried sage, crushed
4¼ to 4¾ cups all-purpose flour
2 packages active dry yeast

1 In a medium saucepan bring buttermilk, water, sugar, butter, and salt just to boiling. (Mixture may appear curdled.) Remove from heat. Stir in potato flakes; let stand until temperature is 120°F to 130°F (about 15 minutes). Stir in sage.

2 In a large mixing bowl stir together 1½ cups of the all-purpose flour and the yeast. Add potato mixture. Beat with an electric mixer on low to medium speed for 30 seconds, scraping side of bowl constantly. Beat on high speed for 3 minutes. Using a wooden spoon, stir in as much of the remaining flour as you can.

3 Turn out dough onto a lightly floured surface. Knead in enough of the remaining flour to make a moderately stiff dough that is smooth and elastic (6 to 8 minutes total). Shape into a ball. Place in a lightly greased bowl; turn once to grease the surface of dough. Cover and let rise in a warm place until double in size (45 to 60 minutes).

4 Punch down dough. Turn out onto a lightly floured surface. Divide in half. Cover and let rest for 10 minutes. Grease 2 large baking sheets; set aside. Divide each half of the dough into 12 pieces. Shape pieces into balls. Arrange on prepared baking sheets about 2 inches apart. Loosely cover; let rise until nearly double in size (about 30 minutes).

5 Bake rolls in a 350° oven about 12 minutes or until golden. Remove rolls from baking sheets; cool slightly on wire racks. Serve warm.

1   **pound dry white beans (such as Great Northern, cannellini, or navy beans) (about 2⅓ cups)**

8   **cups water**

1   **to 1½ pounds meaty smoked pork hocks**

8   **cups water**

3   **medium peaches, pitted and cut into wedges (about 3 cups)**

1   **cup chopped onion (1 large)**

1   **cup peach nectar or apple juice**

¼   **cup packed brown sugar**

2   **tablespoons snipped fresh sage or 2 teaspoons dried sage, crushed**

½   **teaspoon salt**

½   **teaspoon black pepper**

1   **or 2 medium peaches, peeled, pitted, and sliced**

   Fresh herb leaves (optional)

1 Rinse beans. In a large Dutch oven combine beans and 8 cups water. Bring to boiling; reduce heat. Simmer for 2 minutes. Remove from heat. Cover and let stand for 1 hour. (Or place beans in water in Dutch oven. Cover and let soak in a cool place overnight.)

2 Drain and rinse beans. Return beans to Dutch oven. Add pork hocks. Stir in 8 cups fresh water. Bring to boiling; reduce heat. Simmer, covered for 1 to 1½ hours or until beans are tender, stirring occasionally. Remove hocks; set aside. Drain beans. When cool enough to handle, cut meat off bones; coarsely chop meat.

3 In a 2½- to 3-quart casserole combine the beans, meat, the peach wedges, and the onion. Stir in peach nectar, brown sugar, sage, salt, and pepper.

4 Bake, covered, in a 300° oven for 1 hour. Uncover and bake about 15 minutes more or until desired consistency, stirring occasionally. Before serving, top with the peach slices. If desired, garnish with herb leaves.

Peachy Baked Beans

With side dishes this good, you don't need much of an entrée. These peachy beans make a hearty dish with a small serving of broiled chicken or fish.

Stand: 1 hour   **Oven:** 300°F
Prep: 20 minutes   **Bake:** 1¼ hours
Cook: 1 hour   **Makes:** 12 side-dish servings

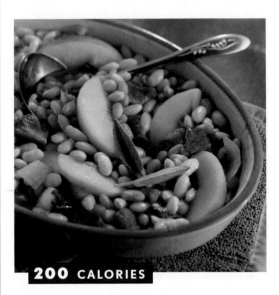

200 CALORIES

Nutrition Facts per serving:
200 cal., 2 g total fat (1 g sat. fat), 6 mg chol., 252 mg sodium, 37 g carbo., 9 g fiber, 11 g pro.
Daily Values:
4% vit. A, 11% vit. C, 7% calcium, 10% iron
Exchanges:
1 Fruit, 1 Starch, 1 Meat

Skinny Mashed Potatoes

These are not your ordinary mashed potatoes. Ranch-flavor sour cream dip, available in light or regular versions, adds pizzazz to these easy spuds.

Prep: 15 minutes   **Cook:** 20 minutes

Bake: 20 minutes   **Oven:** 350°F

Makes: 4 side-dish servings

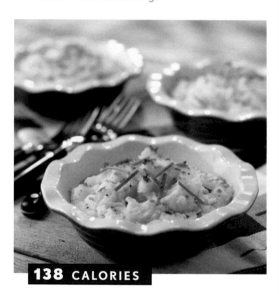

138 CALORIES

4   medium baking potatoes (such as russet, round white, or yellow) (about 1¼ pounds)

⅓   cup light dairy sour cream ranch dip

⅛   teaspoon salt

⅛   teaspoon freshly ground black pepper

1   tablespoons snipped fresh chives or parsley

1   tablespoons butter or margarine, melted

    Snipped fresh chives or parsley (optional)

1   If desired, peel potatoes. Cut up potatoes. In a medium covered saucepan cook potatoes in boiling salted water for 20 to 25 minutes or until tender; drain. Transfer potatoes to a large mixing bowl. Beat potatoes with an electric mixer on low speed until mashed. Add sour cream ranch dip, salt, and pepper; beat until well mixed. Fold in the 1 tablespoon snipped chives.

2   Spoon mixture into four 8-ounce casseroles. Drizzle with melted butter. Bake, uncovered, in a 350° oven for 20 to 25 minutes until heated through. To serve, if desired, garnish with additional snipped chives.

Nutrition Facts per serving:
138 cal., 5 g total fat (3 g sat. fat), 15 mg chol., 216 mg sodium, 21 g carbo., 2 g fiber, 4 g pro.
Daily Values:
5% vit. A, 27% vit. C, 5% calcium, 5% iron
Exchanges:
1½ Starch, ½ Fat

1/3 cup chopped onion (1 small)

1 tablespoon butter or margarine

3 tablespoons fine dry bread crumbs

1 10³/₄-ounce can reduced-fat and reduced-sodium condensed cream of mushroom soup

1/4 cup fat-free plain yogurt

1 2-ounce jar sliced pimiento, drained

1/8 teaspoon black pepper

2 9-ounce packages frozen French-style green beans, thawed and drained*

1 In a small saucepan cook onion in hot butter over medium heat about 4 minutes or until tender. Stir in bread crumbs; set aside.

2 In a large bowl combine soup, yogurt, pimiento, and pepper. Stir in the beans. Transfer mixture to a 1-quart casserole or baking dish. Sprinkle bread crumb mixture on top.

3 Bake, uncovered, in a 350° oven for 25 to 30 minutes or until heated through.

*Note: If you prefer thoroughly cooked beans rather than crisp-tender ones, precook them in boiling water for 5 minutes before adding to the soup mixture. Drain well.

92 CALORIES

Green Bean Casserole

In lieu of the traditional high-fat fried onions, bread crumbs with tender, sweet onion top this casserole. Pimiento adds delightful color and flavor.

Prep: 15 minutes   **Bake:** 25 minutes
Oven: 350°F   **Makes:** 6 side-dish servings

Nutrition Facts per serving:
92 cal., 3 g total fat (1 g sat. fat), 7 mg chol., 313 mg sodium, 12 g carbo., 3 g fiber, 3 g pro.
Daily Values:
11% vit. A, 16% vit. C, 5% calcium, 5% iron
Exchanges:
1 Vegetable, 1/2 Starch, 1/2 Fat

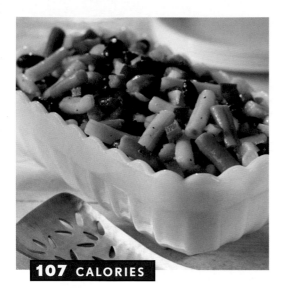

107 CALORIES

Three-Bean Salad

The typical three-bean salad suffers from a drenching in oil. This version gets a light coating, so you can better enjoy the bean flavor and a significant reduction in calories as well.

Prep: 15 minutes   **Chill:** 4 to 24 hours
Makes: 6 side-dish servings

1 cup loose-pack frozen cut green beans or lima beans

1 15- or 16-ounce can cut wax beans, black beans, or chickpeas (garbanzo beans), rinsed and drained

1/2 of a 15-ounce can lower-sodium red kidney beans, rinsed and drained

1/2 cup chopped red or green sweet pepper

1/3 cup chopped red onion (1 small)

1/4 cup cider vinegar or white vinegar

2 tablespoons sugar

2 tablespoons salad oil

1/2 teaspoon celery seeds

1/2 teaspoon dry mustard

1 clove garlic, minced

1 Cook frozen beans according to package directions; drain. Meanwhile, in a large bowl combine wax beans, red kidney beans, sweet pepper, and onion. Add green beans.

2 For dressing, in a screw-top jar combine the vinegar, sugar, salad oil, celery seeds, dry mustard, and garlic. Cover and shake well. Pour over vegetables; stir lightly. Cover and chill for at least 4 hours or up to 24 hours, stirring occasionally. Serve with a slotted spoon.

Nutrition Facts per serving:
107 cal., 5 g total fat (1 g sat. fat), 0 mg chol., 148 mg sodium, 16 g carbo., 3 g fiber, 3 g pro.
Daily Values:
16% vit. A, 42% vit. C, 4% calcium, 7% iron
Exchanges:
1 1/2 Vegetable, 1/2 Starch, 1 Fat

2 cups cubed fresh pineapple or one
15¼-ounce can pineapple chunks
(juice pack), drained

1⅓ cups coarsely chopped apples and/or
pears (2 medium)

½ cup thinly sliced celery

½ cup halved seedless red grapes

2 kiwifruits, peeled, halved lengthwise,
and sliced

⅓ cup fat-free mayonnaise dressing or
salad dressing

⅓ cup fat-free or low-fat lemon yogurt

1 tablespoon honey

2 tablespoons walnut pieces, toasted*

1 In a large bowl toss together pineapple,
apples or pears, celery, grapes, and
kiwifruits. In a small bowl stir together
the mayonnaise dressing, yogurt, and
honey; fold gently into fruit mixture. To
serve, stir in walnuts.

Make-ahead directions: Prepare as above,
except do not stir in walnuts. Cover
and chill for up to 6 hours. To serve, stir
in walnuts.

*Note: To toast walnuts, place them in a small
skillet and cook over medium heat, stirring
often, for 5 to 7 minutes or until golden.

Lightened Waldorf Salad

You won't believe this delicious salad fits
into your slim-down plan. The lemon
yogurt is key to the refreshing dressing.
So much flavor, so few calories.

Start to Finish: 25 minutes

Makes: 6 to 8 side-dish servings

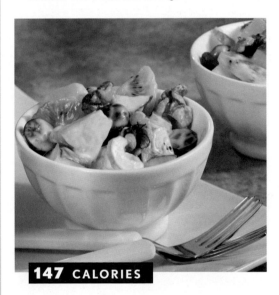

147 CALORIES

Nutrition Facts per serving:
147 cal., 3 g total fat (1 g sat. fat), 4 mg chol.,
142 mg sodium, 29 g carbo., 3 g fiber, 2 g pro.
Daily Values:
2% vit. A, 62% vit. C, 6% calcium, 3% iron
Exchanges:
2 Fruit, ½ Fat

Creamy Potato Salad

When summer rolls around, it's hard to beat potato salad for a picnic. Thanks to lighter dairy products that help bring down the calories, now you don't have to miss out.

Prep: 20 minutes   **Cook:** 20 minutes
Chill: 4 to 24 hours
Makes: 8 side-dish servings

111 CALORIES

- 4   **medium potatoes* (1¼ pounds total)**
- 1   **cup sliced celery (2 stalks)**
- ¼   **cup thinly sliced green onions (2)**
- ½   **cup low-fat mayonnaise dressing**
- ½   **cup light dairy sour cream**
- 2   **tablespoons fat-free milk**
- 2   **teaspoons prepared mustard**
- 1   **teaspoon snipped fresh dill or**
     ¼ teaspoon dried dill
- ¼   **teaspoon salt**
- 1   **hard-cooked egg, chopped**
     Lettuce leaves (optional)

1 Scrub potatoes. In a large covered saucepan cook potatoes in boiling water for 20 to 25 minutes or just until tender. Drain well; cool slightly. Peel and cube potatoes. Transfer to a large bowl. Stir in celery and green onions.

2 In a small bowl stir together the mayonnaise dressing, sour cream, milk, mustard, dill, and salt. Pour over potatoes. Toss lightly to coat. Carefully fold in chopped egg.

3 Cover and chill for at least 4 hours or up to 24 hours. If desired, spoon potato mixture into a lettuce-lined bowl.

*Note: Waxy potatoes, such as long whites and round reds, have a moist, smooth texture and hold their shape after cooking. Tiny new potatoes, which are usually young round reds, also work well in salads.

Nutrition Facts per serving:
111 cal., 3 g total fat (1 g sat. fat), 35 mg chol., 259 mg sodium, 18 g carbo., 2 g fiber, 4 g pro.
Daily Values:
4% vit. A, 21% vit. C, 6% calcium, 7% iron
Exchanges:
1 Starch, ½ Fat

- **1** cup dried elbow or medium shell macaroni or rotini
- **⅓** cup light dairy sour cream
- **¼** cup low-fat mayonnaise dressing or light salad dressing
- **2** teaspoons Dijon-style mustard
- **1** to 2 teaspoons fat-free milk
- **⅛** teaspoon black pepper
- **½** cup chopped green sweet pepper
- **¼** cup shredded carrot
- **2** tablespoons sliced green onion (1)
- **¼** cup diced cheddar cheese (1 ounce) (optional)

1 Cook macaroni according to package directions, except omit the oil and cook in lightly salted water. Drain well. Rinse with cold water; drain again.

2 For dressing, in a salad bowl stir together sour cream, mayonnaise dressing, mustard, 1 teaspoon of the milk, and the black pepper.

3 Stir the cooked macaroni, sweet pepper, carrot, and green onion into the dressing. Toss lightly to coat. If desired, gently stir in cheese. Cover and chill for at least 3 hours or up to 24 hours. Before serving, stir in the remaining milk if necessary to moisten salad.

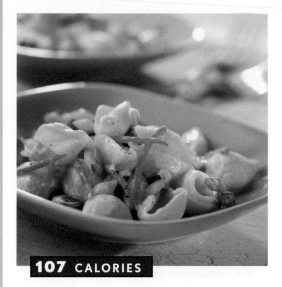

107 CALORIES

Macaroni Salad

This is not your local supermarket's salad. With mustard, sour cream, and chopped veggies, this version takes on a sophisticated flair.

Prep: 20 minutes **Chill:** 3 to 24 hours
Makes: 6 side-dish servings

Nutrition Facts per serving:
107 cal., 2 g total fat (1 g sat. fat), 6 mg chol., 143 mg sodium, 18 g carbo., 1 g fiber, 3 g pro.
Daily Values:
33% vit. A, 18% vit. C, 4% calcium, 4% iron
Exchanges:
½ Vegetable, 1 Starch, ½ Fat

163 CALORIES

Gingerbread

A mere three tablespoons of butter goes into this flavorful dessert. Served warm with light whipped topping, it makes you forget you're keeping tabs on calories.

Prep: 15 minutes   **Bake:** 20 minutes
Oven: 350°F   **Cool:** 10 minutes
Makes: 9 servings

Nonstick cooking spray
1½ cups all-purpose flour
¼ cup sugar
1 teaspoon ground ginger
1 teaspoon ground cinnamon
½ teaspoon baking powder
½ teaspoon baking soda
¼ teaspoon salt
½ cup water
⅓ cup full-flavored molasses
3 tablespoons butter or margarine, melted
2 egg whites
Frozen light whipped dessert topping, thawed (optional)

1 Lightly coat an 8×8×2-inch baking pan with nonstick cooking spray; dust lightly with flour. Set aside.

2 In a large mixing bowl combine the 1½ cups flour, the sugar, ginger, cinnamon, baking powder, baking soda, and salt. Add the water, molasses, butter, and egg whites. Beat with an electric mixer on low to medium speed until combined. Beat on high speed for 2 minutes. Spread into prepared pan.

3 Bake in a 350° oven about 20 minutes or until a wooden toothpick inserted near the center comes out clean. Cool in the pan on a wire rack for 10 minutes. Remove cake from pan. Serve warm and, if desired, with dessert topping.

Nutrition Facts per serving:
163 cal., 4 g total fat (3 g sat. fat), 11 mg chol., 216 mg sodium, 28 g carbo., 1 g fiber, 3 g pro.
Daily Values:
3% vit. A, 5% calcium, 9% iron
Exchanges:
2 Other Carbo., ½ Fat

Nonstick cooking spray

1 cup all-purpose flour

¾ cup granulated sugar

1½ teaspoons apple pie spice

½ teaspoon baking powder

½ teaspoon baking soda

⅛ teaspoon salt

1 cup finely shredded carrot

⅓ cup cooking oil

¼ cup reduced-fat milk

3 egg whites

1 teaspoon sifted powdered sugar

1 Lightly coat an 8×8×2-inch baking pan with nonstick cooking spray. Set aside.

2 In a large bowl combine the flour, granulated sugar, apple pie spice, baking powder, baking soda, and salt. Add carrot, oil, and milk. Stir to moisten. In a medium mixing bowl beat egg whites with an electric mixer on medium to high speed until stiff peaks form (tips stand straight). Fold whites into carrot mixture.

3 Pour the batter into the prepared pan. Bake in a 350° oven for 30 to 35 minutes or until a wooden toothpick inserted near the center comes out clean. Cool completely in pan on a wire rack.

4 To serve, sprinkle with powdered sugar.

Carrot Snack Cake

Usually you find carrot cake under a slathering of cream cheese frosting. Here powdered sugar steps in, which cuts back on fat and calories. It satisfies your sweet tooth, while getting you closer to your weight-loss goal.

Prep: 15 minutes   **Bake:** 30 minutes
Oven: 350°F   **Makes:** 12 servings

147 CALORIES

Nutrition Facts per serving:
147 cal., 6 g total fat (1 g sat. fat), 0 mg chol., 114 mg sodium, 21 g carbo., 1 g fiber, 2 g pro.
Daily Values:
57% vit. A, 2% vit. C, 3% calcium, 4% iron
Exchanges:
1½ Other Carbo., 1 Fat

Cherry-Apple Cobbler

Make sure the fruit filling is hot when you spoon the biscuit batter over it. That way, the bottom of the "cobbled biscuit" will be thoroughly cooked.

Prep: 20 minutes   **Bake:** 18 minutes
Oven: 400°F   **Makes:** 9 servings

172 CALORIES

1 cup all-purpose flour
1/4 cup granulated sugar
1 1/2 teaspoons baking powder
1 teaspoon finely shredded orange peel
1 teaspoon ground cinnamon
3 tablespoons butter or margarine
1/4 cup cold water
4 teaspoons cornstarch
1 16-ounce package frozen unsweetened pitted tart red cherries
3 cups thinly sliced apples (1 pound)
1 egg
1/3 cup fat-free milk

1 For biscuit topping, in a medium bowl stir together flour, 2 tablespoons of the granulated sugar, the baking powder, orange peel, and 1/2 teaspoon of the cinnamon. Using a pastry blender, cut in butter until mixture resembles coarse crumbs. Set aside.

2 For filling, in a medium saucepan stir together the cold water, cornstarch, the remaining 2 tablespoons granulated sugar, and the remaining 1/2 teaspoon cinnamon; add frozen cherries. Cook and stir until thickened and bubbly. Stir in apple slices; heat through. Reduce heat; keep filling hot.

3 In a small bowl stir together egg and milk. Add to biscuit topping mixture, stirring just until moistened. Transfer hot filling to a 2-quart square baking dish. Immediately spoon topping into 9 small mounds on filling. Bake in a 400° oven for 18 to 20 minutes or until a wooden toothpick inserted near the center of a biscuit comes out clean. Serve warm.

Nutrition Facts per serving:
172 cal., 5 g total fat (3 g sat. fat), 35 mg chol., 122 mg sodium, 30 g carbo., 3 g fiber, 3 g pro.
Daily Values:
18% vit. A, 14% vit. C, 7% calcium, 6% iron
Exchanges:
1 Fruit, 1 Other Carbo., 1 Fat

On the divider: Cheese-Stuffed Mushrooms (see recipe, page 72)

16 ³/₈-inch slices baguette-style French
    bread

4   ounces Gorgonzola cheese or other
    blue cheese, crumbled

1   small ripe pear, halved, cored, and
    very thinly sliced

2   tablespoons flavored honey (such
    as French lavender honey) or
    regular honey

    Fresh mint sprigs (optional)

1 Preheat broiler. Place bread slices on a
large baking sheet. Broil 4 to 5 inches
from the heat for 30 to 60 seconds or
until bread is toasted. Turn bread slices
over; top bread slices with Gorgonzola.
Broil for 30 to 60 seconds more or until
cheese is bubbly and bread is toasted.

2 Top bread slices with pear slices. Lightly
drizzle pear slices with honey. Arrange
bread slices on a serving platter. If
desired, garnish with fresh mint sprigs.
Serve immediately.

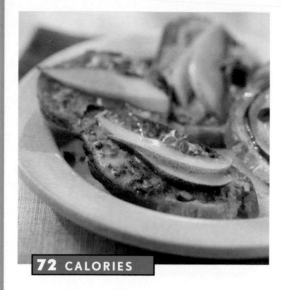

72 CALORIES

Sweet Pear and Cheese Crostini

Blue cheese and pears make a dynamic
duo. Prepare this flavorful appetizer in just
15 minutes for a spur-of-the-moment
dinner party.

Start to Finish: 15 minutes
Makes: 16 appetizers

Nutrition Facts per appetizer:
72 cal., 2 g total fat (1 g sat. fat), 5 mg chol., 175 mg sodium,
10 g carbo., 1 g fiber, 3 g pro.
Daily Values:
1% vit. A, 1% vit. C, 5% calcium, 2% iron
Exchanges:
1 Starch

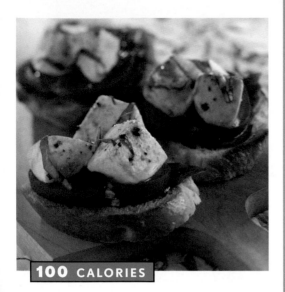

Fresh Mozzarella with Basil

Reinvent this recipe every time you make it by varying the cheese and herb. Try feta with oregano or dill, or queso fresco with cumin or red pepper flakes.

Prep: 15 minutes **Chill:** 1 hour
Makes: 14 to 16 servings

1 **pound fresh mozzarella cheese**
¼ **cup roasted garlic oil or olive oil**
1 **to 2 teaspoons balsamic vinegar**
2 **tablespoons snipped fresh basil or 1 teaspoon dried basil, crushed**
1 **tablespoon freshly cracked black pepper**
Tomato slices (optional)
Fresh basil strips (optional)
Baguette-style French bread slices, toasted (optional)

1 Cut mozzarella into ½-inch pieces. Place pieces in a medium bowl. In a small bowl combine oil, vinegar, snipped basil, and pepper. Pour over cheese; toss gently until cheese is well coated. Cover and chill for 1 hour.

2 If desired, serve with tomato, basil strips, and bread slices.

Make-ahead directions: Prepare as above through step 1. Store, covered, in the refrigerator up to 3 days. To serve, let stand at room temperature until olive oil liquefies. If desired, serve with tomato, basil strips, and bread slices.

Nutrition Facts per serving:
100 cal., 8 g total fat (4 g sat. fat), 25 mg chol., 120 mg sodium, 1 g carbo., 0 g fiber, 6 g pro.
Daily Values:
5% vit. A, 17% calcium, 1% iron
Exchanges:
1 Meat, ½ Fat

1   **3-ounce package cream cheese,**
    softened

¼   **cup coarsely chopped macadamia nuts**

2   **to 3 medium heads Belgian endive,**
    separated into individual leaves

1   **large mango or papaya, cut into thin**
    strips

1 In a small bowl combine the cream
cheese and macadamia nuts. Spoon
about 1 teaspoon of the cream cheese
mixture onto each endive leaf.

2 Top with the mango strips. Arrange on a
serving platter.

Make-ahead directions: Prepare as above
through step 1. Loosely cover with plastic
wrap; chill for up to 2 hours. Before
serving, top with mango strips.

Endive-Mango Appetizers

Served individually, endive leaves make
stunning appetizers; served as a group,
they make an irresistible salad.

Start to Finish: 20 minutes
Makes: about 24 appetizers

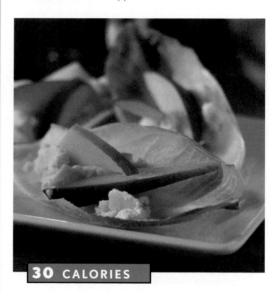

30 CALORIES

Nutrition Facts per appetizer:
30 cal., 2 g total fat (1 g sat. fat), 4 mg chol.,
11 mg sodium, 2 g carbo., 0 g fiber, 0 g pro.
Daily Values:
9% vit. A, 6% vit. C, 1% iron
Exchanges:
½ Fat

Cheese-Stuffed Mushrooms

A savory blend of spinach, fresh basil, dried tomatoes, and four cheeses fills these elegant first-course mushrooms.

Prep: 20 minutes **Bake:** 8 minutes
Oven: 350°F/450°F **Makes:** 24 appetizers

43 CALORIES

24 large fresh mushrooms (1¹/₂ to 2 inches in diameter)
   Olive oil
8 dried tomatoes (not oil-packed)
1 cup ricotta cheese
¹/₂ cup finely chopped fresh spinach
¹/₂ cup shredded Monterey Jack cheese (2 ounces)
3 tablespoons freshly grated Parmesan cheese
1 tablespoon snipped fresh basil
¹/₄ teaspoon salt
¹/₄ teaspoon black pepper
2 cloves garlic, minced
¹/₂ cup crumbled feta cheese (2 ounces)
   Fresh basil leaves (optional)

1 Remove and discard mushroom stems. Brush mushroom caps with oil. Arrange in a shallow baking pan, stem sides down. Bake in a 350° oven for 12 minutes. Drain off any liquid.

2 Meanwhile, cover tomatoes with boiling water; let stand for 10 minutes. Drain; coarsely chop tomatoes. In a medium bowl combine tomatoes, ricotta cheese, spinach, Monterey Jack cheese, Parmesan cheese, snipped basil, salt, pepper, and garlic. Turn mushroom caps stem sides up; fill caps with ricotta mixture. Sprinkle feta cheese over tops.

3 Bake filled caps in a 450° oven for 8 to 10 minutes or until heated through and lightly browned. If desired, garnish with basil leaves.

Make-ahead directions: Prepare as above through step 2. Cover and chill for up to 24 hours. Bake in a 450° oven for 8 to 10 minutes or until heated through and lightly browned. If desired, garnish with basil leaves.

Nutrition Facts per appetizer:
43 cal., 3 g total fat (2 g sat. fat), 10 mg chol., 98 mg sodium, 1 g carbo., 0 g fiber, 3 g pro.
Daily Values:
3% vit. A, 1% vit. C, 6% calcium, 2% iron
Exchanges:
¹/₂ Meat

- ¹/₃ cup light mayonnaise dressing or salad dressing
- 2 tablespoons dairy sour cream
- ¹/₂ teaspoon finely shredded lemon peel
- 1 teaspoon lemon juice
- 2 teaspoons snipped fresh thyme
- 1 8-ounce piece smoked salmon
- 1 lemon, halved and sliced
- 1 tablespoon finely chopped red onion
- 1 tablespoon capers, rinsed and drained
  Fresh thyme sprigs (optional)

1 For sauce, in a small bowl stir together mayonnaise dressing, sour cream, lemon peel, lemon juice, and snipped thyme. Cover and chill for at least 1 hour or up to 6 hours.

2 To serve, arrange salmon and lemon on platter. Sprinkle with red onion and capers. Serve with sauce. If desired, garnish with thyme sprigs.

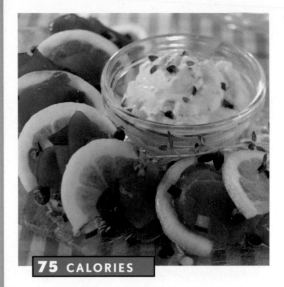

75 CALORIES

Smoked Salmon with Lemon-Thyme Dipping Sauce

Guests love this appetizer, especially because they can garnish the salmon as they please. A sprightly squeeze of lemon and/or a spoonful of the mayonnaise dressing mixture makes all the difference.

Prep: 10 minutes   **Chill:** 1 to 6 hours
Makes: 8 appetizer servings

Nutrition Facts per serving:
75 cal., 5 g total fat (1 g sat. fat), 11 mg chol., 315 mg sodium, 2 g carbo., 0 g fiber, 5 g pro.
Daily Values:
1% vit. A, 4% vit. C, 1% calcium, 2% iron
Exchanges:
¹/₂ Meat, ¹/₂ Fat

250 CALORIES

Roasted Chicken with Citrus Salsa

Gather friends together for this delightful "social" chicken dinner. Because you can prepare the salsa ahead of time and the chicken roasts long enough for you to have a cocktail and hors d'oeuvres before dinner, you can throw the party and enjoy it too.

Prep: 25 minutes   **Roast:** 1¼ hours
Stand: 15 minutes   **Oven:** 375°F
Makes: 6 servings

Nutrition Facts per serving:
250 cal., 6 g total fat (1 g sat. fat), 76 mg chol., 262 mg sodium, 26 g carbo., 3 g fiber, 25 g pro.
Daily Values:
11% vit. A, 50% vit. C, 5% calcium, 8% iron
Exchanges:
1½ Fruit, 3 Meat

1	**3-pound whole broiler-fryer chicken**
1	**tablespoon cooking oil**
2	**cloves garlic, minced**
2	**teaspoons ground cinnamon**
½	**teaspoon salt**
½	**teaspoon ground nutmeg**
¼	**teaspoon black pepper**
3	**tablespoons honey**
⅓	**cup dried tart red cherries**
1⅓	**cups orange sections, halved (about 4 oranges)**
2	**nectarines, pitted and chopped**
2	**tablespoons snipped fresh cilantro**
1	**fresh jalapeño chile pepper, seeded and chopped (see note on page 76)**
1	**tablespoon lime juice**
	Fresh cilantro sprigs (optional)

1 Remove skin from chicken (except for wings). Tie legs to tail. Twist wing tips under back. Place chicken, breast side up, on a rack in a roasting pan. In a bowl combine oil and garlic; brush onto chicken. In another small bowl combine cinnamon, salt, nutmeg, and black pepper. Sprinkle spice mixture evenly over chicken. Insert an oven-going meat thermometer into center of an inside thigh muscle.

2 Roast chicken, uncovered, in a 375° oven for 1 hour. Remove string from legs. Brush honey over chicken. Roast about 15 minutes more or until drumsticks move easily in their sockets, chicken is no longer pink, and meat thermometer registers 180°F. Remove chicken from oven. Cover; let stand for 15 minutes.

3 Meanwhile, for salsa, place cherries in a small saucepan; cover with water. Bring to boiling; remove from heat. Cover; let stand 5 minutes. Drain well. In a bowl combine cherries, orange sections, nectarines, snipped cilantro, jalapeño pepper, and lime juice. Cover; chill until ready to serve. Serve with chicken. If desired, garnish with cilantro sprigs.

12 skinless, boneless chicken thighs
   (2 to 2½ pounds total)

   Salt

   Black pepper

2 tablespoons olive oil

1 large onion, chopped

1 medium red sweet pepper, cut into
   thin strips

3 cloves garlic, minced

1 cup long grain rice

¼ teaspoon thread saffron, crushed,
   or ⅛ teaspoon ground saffron

1½ cups water

½ cup pimiento-stuffed green olives,
   halved

½ cup dry white wine, dry vermouth,
   or chicken broth

   Lemon wedges

   Fresh herb sprigs (optional)

1 Sprinkle chicken with salt and black pepper. In a 12-inch skillet cook chicken in hot oil over medium-high heat about 10 minutes or until browned, turning once. Remove chicken from skillet; reserve 1 tablespoon drippings in skillet.

2 Add onion, sweet pepper, and garlic to skillet; cook and stir for 4 to 5 minutes or until vegetables are tender. Stir in uncooked rice and saffron; add the water, olives, and wine, vermouth, or chicken broth. Bring to boiling. Return chicken to skillet; reduce heat. Simmer, covered, about 25 minutes or until chicken is no longer pink (180°F) and rice is tender. Serve with lemon wedges. If desired, garnish with herb sprigs.

Chicken Thighs with Peppers

This sunny yellow Spanish dish gets its color—and an exotic flavor—from saffron. The world's most expensive spice, saffron is actually the dried stigmas of a small crocus. Luckily, a little bit of saffron goes a long way.

Prep: 25 minutes   **Cook:** 25 minutes
Makes: 6 servings

380 CALORIES

Nutrition Facts per serving:
380 cal., 12 g total fat (2 g sat. fat), 121 mg chol., 410 mg sodium, 29 g carbo., 1 g fiber, 33 g pro.
Daily Values:
25% vit. A, 65% vit. C, 5% calcium, 17% iron
Exchanges:
1 Vegetable, 1½ Starch, 3½ Meat, ½ Fat

Grilled Chicken with Pineapple Relish

Indian cuisine influences this refreshingly different chicken dish. If you have access to an Indian grocery, take the opportunity to try unfamiliar ingredients. Hint: The crisp pepper-and-lentil crackers called pappadam make a terrific appetizer when served with your favorite spread.

Prep: 20 minutes **Grill:** 12 minutes
Makes: 4 servings

228 CALORIES

Nutrition Facts per serving:
228 cal., 5 g total fat (1 g sat. fat), 82 mg chol., 373 mg sodium, 12 g carbo., 2 g fiber, 34 g pro.
Daily Values:
20% vit. A, 77% vit. C, 3% calcium, 8% iron
Exchanges:
1 Fruit, 4½ Meat

$^3/_4$ teaspoon ground cardamom
$^1/_2$ teaspoon salt
$^1/_2$ to 1 teaspoon coarsely ground black pepper
4 skinless, boneless chicken breast halves (about 1¼ pounds total)
2 teaspoons olive oil
$^1/_2$ of a medium fresh pineapple, peeled, cored, and coarsely chopped (about 1²/₃ cups)
$^1/_2$ of a medium red sweet pepper, finely chopped
2 tablespoons snipped fresh cilantro or fresh parsley
2 tablespoons lime juice
2 tablespoons thinly sliced green onion (1)
1 fresh jalapeño chile pepper, seeded and finely chopped*
Fresh herb sprigs (optional)

1 In a small bowl combine ½ teaspoon of the cardamom, the salt, and black pepper. Rub both sides of chicken with oil; sprinkle evenly with spice mixture.

2 Grill chicken on the rack of an uncovered grill directly over medium coals for 12 to 15 minutes or until chicken is no longer pink (170°F), turning once.

3 For relish, in a medium bowl combine pineapple, sweet pepper, cilantro, lime juice, green onion, jalapeño pepper, and the remaining ¼ teaspoon cardamom. Serve chicken with relish. If desired, garnish with herb sprigs.

*Note: Because chile peppers contain volatile oils that can burn your skin and eyes, avoid direct contact with them as much as possible. When working with chile peppers, wear plastic or rubber gloves. If your bare hands do touch the peppers, wash your hands and nails well with soap and warm water.

6 beef tenderloin steaks or 3 beef top sirloin steaks, cut 1 inch thick (about 1½ pounds total)

1½ teaspoons dried whole green peppercorns, crushed, or ½ teaspoon coarsely ground black pepper

1½ teaspoons dried Italian seasoning, crushed

¼ teaspoon salt

Nonstick cooking spray

⅓ cup water

½ teaspoon instant beef bouillon granules

1 3-ounce package fresh shiitake mushrooms or 3 ounces other fresh mushrooms, sliced (about 1¼ cups)

1 cup reduced-fat milk

2 tablespoons all-purpose flour

½ cup light dairy sour cream

3 cups hot cooked noodles

1 Trim fat from meat. For rub, in a small bowl combine peppercorns, 1 teaspoon of the Italian seasoning, and the salt. Sprinkle rub evenly over both sides of meat; press in with your fingers.

2 Coat an unheated large nonstick skillet with nonstick cooking spray. Preheat skillet over medium heat. Add meat; cook for 10 to 12 minutes or until medium doneness (160°F), turning once. Remove from skillet. Cover and keep warm.

3 Add the water and bouillon granules to skillet. Bring to boiling. Add mushrooms. Cook about 2 minutes or until tender. In a small bowl stir together the milk, flour, and remaining ½ teaspoon Italian seasoning. Add to skillet. Cook and stir until thickened and bubbly. Stir in sour cream; heat through, but do not boil. Serve meat with noodles. Spoon the sauce over meat and noodles.

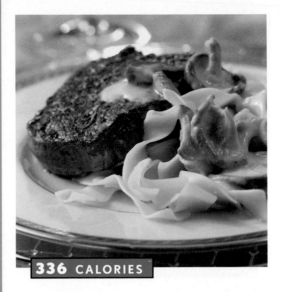

336 CALORIES

Peppered Steak with Mushroom Sauce

A recipe fit for entertaining yet enjoyed without regret is a rare gem indeed. The sour cream is the key, giving the sauce a richness that belies its slim number of calories.

Start to Finish: 40 minutes
Makes: 6 servings

Nutrition Facts per serving:
336 cal., 11 g total fat (4 g sat. fat), 93 mg chol., 262 mg sodium, 26 g carbo., 1 g fiber, 31 g pro.
Daily Values:
5% vit. A, 1% vit. C, 11% calcium, 26% iron
Exchanges:
½ Vegetable, 1½ Starch, 3½ Meat

166 CALORIES

Pork Tenderloin with Plum Salsa

A medley of diverse flavors comes together to produce this sweet and zesty salsa. Unlike most others, this one is served warm.

Prep: 20 minutes **Roast:** 25 minutes
Oven: 425°F **Makes:** 4 servings

1 **12-ounce pork tenderloin**
2 **teaspoons olive oil**
¼ **teaspoon salt**
2 **cloves garlic, minced**
3 **fresh plums, pitted and coarsely chopped (1½ cups)**
3 **tablespoons orange juice**
1 **tablespoon sugar**
1 **whole pickled or fresh jalapeño chile pepper, seeded (see note on page 76)**
1½ **teaspoons lemon juice**
½ **teaspoon grated fresh ginger**
   Fresh oregano sprigs (optional)

1 Brush tenderloin with oil. Rub salt and garlic onto meat. Place meat on rack in a shallow roasting pan. Roast in a 425° oven for 25 to 35 minutes or until internal temperature registers 160°F on an instant-read thermometer.

2 Meanwhile, for salsa, in a food processor bowl combine plums, orange juice, sugar, jalapeño pepper, lemon juice, and ginger. Process with on/off turns until chopped. Transfer to a small saucepan. Cook, uncovered, over medium heat until heated through.

3 To serve, slice meat. Serve with warm salsa. If desired, garnish with oregano.

Nutrition Facts per serving:
166 cal., 5 g total fat (1 g sat. fat), 55 mg chol., 227 mg sodium, 11 g carbo., 1 g fiber, 18 g pro.
Daily Values:
4% vit. A, 21% vit. C, 1% calcium, 6% iron
Exchanges:
½ Fruit, 2½ Meat

- **½** teaspoon black pepper
- **¼** teaspoon celery salt
- **4** boneless pork rib chops (about 1 pound total)
- **1** large onion, thinly sliced and separated into rings
- **2** teaspoons cooking oil
- **2** tablespoons water
- **¾** cup fresh cranberries
- **¼** cup sugar
- **3** tablespoons water
- **2** tablespoons frozen orange juice concentrate, thawed
- **2** teaspoons finely shredded orange peel
- **½** teaspoon ground sage
- **¼** teaspoon salt

1 For rub, in a small bowl stir together pepper and celery salt. Sprinkle rub evenly onto both sides of chops; rub in with your fingers. In a medium skillet cook chops and onion rings in hot oil until chops are brown, turning once. Carefully add the 2 tablespoons water to skillet. Cover and cook over medium heat for 15 to 20 minutes more or until pork is done and juices run clear (160°F). Transfer chops to serving plates; keep warm. Using a slotted spoon, remove onions from juices; set aside.

2 Meanwhile, for the sauce, in a medium saucepan combine the cranberries, sugar, the 3 tablespoons water, the orange juice concentrate, orange peel, sage, and salt. Cook and stir over medium heat about 10 minutes or until the cranberry skins pop and mixture thickens. Remove from heat.

3 To serve, spoon sauce and onions over pork chops.

Cranberry-Onion Pork Chops

For a holiday or a special everyday dinner, the combination of tart cranberries and succulent pork chops is a winner worth celebrating. Complement this main dish with cooked rice sprinkled with snipped fresh herb or sliced green onions.

Start to Finish: 30 minutes
Makes: 4 servings

277 CALORIES

Nutrition Facts per serving:
277 cal., 9 g total fat (3 g sat. fat), 62 mg chol., 288 mg sodium, 22 g carbo., 2 g fiber, 26 g pro.
Daily Values:
1% vit. A, 33% vit. C, 2% calcium, 7% iron
Exchanges:
1 Vegetable, 1 Fruit, 3 Meat

Pan-Seared Salmon with Vegetables

Give salmon a Pan-Asian treatment with a trio of vegetables and a homemade teriyaki sauce fired up with five-spice powder—a mix of star anise, ginger, cinnamon, cloves, and Szechwan peppercorns.

Start to Finish: 35 minutes

Makes: 4 servings

228 CALORIES

Nutrition Facts per serving:
228 cal., 9 g total fat (1 g sat. fat), 59 mg chol., 385 mg sodium, 10 g carbo., 3 g fiber, 25 g pro.
Daily Values:
239% vit. A, 19% vit. C, 7% calcium, 11% iron
Exchanges:
2 Vegetable, 3 Mcat

- 1 **pound fresh or frozen skinless salmon fillets, about ³/₄ inch thick**
- 3 **tablespoons water**
- 2 **tablespoons dry sherry**
- 2 **tablespoons reduced-sodium soy sauce**
- 1 **teaspoon toasted sesame oil**
- ¹/₂ **teaspoon cornstarch**
- ¹/₂ **teaspoon five-spice powder**
- ¹/₄ **teaspoon sugar**
- 1 **tablespoon cooking oil**
- 3 **medium carrots, cut lengthwise into thin ribbons***
- 2 **teaspoons grated fresh ginger**
- 2 **cloves garlic, minced**
- 1 **medium zucchini, sliced lengthwise**
- 6 **medium green onions, bias-sliced into 1-inch lengths**

1 Thaw fish, if frozen. Rinse fish; pat dry with paper towels. Cut the fish into 4 serving-size pieces. Set aside. In a small bowl combine the water, 1 tablespoon of the sherry, 1 tablespoon of the soy sauce, the sesame oil, cornstarch, ¼ teaspoon of the five-spice powder, and the sugar. Set aside.

2 In another small bowl combine the remaining 1 tablespoon sherry, 1 tablespoon soy sauce, and ¼ teaspoon five-spice powder. Brush over both sides of the salmon pieces. In a large nonstick skillet heat oil over medium heat. Add salmon; cook for 6 to 9 minutes or until fish flakes easily when tested with a fork, turning once. Remove from skillet; cover and keep warm.

3 In the same skillet stir-fry carrots, ginger, and garlic for 3 minutes. Add zucchini and green onions and stir-fry for 1 minute more or until vegetables are crisp-tender. Stir cornstarch mixture and add to skillet. Cook and stir 1 minute more.

4 To serve, spoon the vegetable mixture onto dinner plates. Top with the salmon.

***Note:** Use a vegetable peeler to cut the carrots lengthwise into thin ribbons.

1 **pound fresh or frozen sea scallops**

8 **ounces dried angel hair pasta, linguine, or spaghetti**

1/2 **teaspoon finely shredded lemon peel**

1/4 **teaspoon crushed red pepper**

3 **cloves garlic, minced**

2 **tablespoons butter or margarine**

2 **tablespoons lemon juice**

2 **cups fresh baby spinach**

1 **cup coarsely shredded carrot**

Lemon slices (optional)

1 Thaw scallops, if frozen. Rinse scallops; pat dry with paper towels. Halve any large scallops. Cook pasta in lightly salted water according to package directions. Drain and return pasta to hot pan.

2 Meanwhile, in a large skillet cook scallops, lemon peel, red pepper, and garlic in hot butter over medium heat for 3 to 4 minutes or until scallops turn opaque. Add lemon juice, tossing to coat. Add scallop mixture, spinach, and carrot to cooked pasta, tossing lightly to combine. If desired, garnish with lemon slices.

385 CALORIES

Lemony Scallop and Spinach Pasta

Impress a casual gathering of friends with this fresh scallop dish that gets a spark from lemon. The spinach and carrot add color and freshness.

Start to Finish: 25 minutes

Makes: 4 servings

Nutrition Facts per serving:
385 cal., 8 g total fat (4 g sat. fat), 54 mg chol., 277 mg sodium, 50 g carbo., 4 g fiber, 27 g pro.
Daily Values:
194% vit. A, 23% vit. C, 6% calcium, 18% iron
Exchanges:
1 Vegetable, 3 Starch, 2 Meat

95 CALORIES

Parmesan and Pine Nut Focaccia

Focaccia (foh-KAH-chee-ah) is an Italian yeast bread usually topped with onions, herbs, olive oil, or cheese. This easy version takes advantage of hot roll mix. Serve it with pasta or enjoy a slice as a midafternoon snack.

Prep: 20 minutes   **Rise:** 30 minutes

Bake: 15 minutes   **Cool:** 10 minutes

Oven: 375°F   **Makes:** 24 servings

Nonstick cooking spray

1 **16-ounce package hot roll mix**

1 **egg**

2 **tablespoons olive oil**

1 **beaten egg white**

2 **tablespoons water**

¼ **cup pine nuts**

2 **tablespoons finely shredded Parmesan cheese**

1 Coat a 15×10×1-inch baking pan or a 12- to 14-inch pizza pan with nonstick cooking spray. Set aside.

2 Prepare the hot roll mix according to package directions for the basic dough, except use the 1 egg and substitute the olive oil for the margarine. Knead dough; allow to rest as directed. If using the baking pan, roll dough into a 15×10-inch rectangle and carefully transfer to prepared pan. If using the pizza pan, roll dough into a 12-inch circle and carefully transfer to prepared pan.

3 With fingertips, press indentations every inch or so in dough. In a small bowl stir together egg white and the water; brush over dough. Sprinkle with pine nuts, pressing lightly into dough; sprinkle with Parmesan cheese. Cover; let rise in a warm place until nearly double (about 30 minutes).

4 Bake in a 375° oven for 15 to 20 minutes or until golden. Cool 10 minutes on a wire rack. Remove focaccia from pan; cool completely on rack.

Nutrition Facts per serving:
95 cal., 3 g total fat (0 g sat. fat), 9 mg chol.,
121 mg sodium, 15 g carbo., 0 g fiber, 4 g pro.
Daily Values:
1% calcium, 4% iron
Exchanges:
1 Starch, ½ Fat

3 ripe red Bartlett pears, Bosc pears, and/or apples, cored and thinly sliced

2 tablespoons water

1 tablespoon lemon juice

12 ounces Belgian endive, leaves separated (3 medium heads)

2 tablespoons coarsely chopped walnuts, toasted

Dash salt

Dash black pepper

2 tablespoons olive oil or salad oil

2 tablespoons sherry vinegar or white wine vinegar

1 shallot, finely chopped, or 1 tablespoon finely chopped onion

1 tablespoon honey

1 teaspoon Dijon-style mustard

Black peppercorns (optional)

1 In a medium bowl gently toss pear and/or apple slices with 1 tablespoon of the water and the lemon juice. Arrange the endive leaves on 6 salad plates. Using a slotted spoon, spoon the sliced pears or apples onto the endive. Sprinkle with walnuts, salt, and the dash pepper.

2 For vinaigrette, in a small bowl combine oil, vinegar, the remaining 1 tablespoon water, the shallot, honey, and mustard. Whisk until thoroughly mixed.

3 Drizzle the vinaigrette over the salads. If desired, grind peppercorns over salads.

Pear and Endive Salad

Always elegant, this endive and pear salad—and its bold vinaigrette—is worthy of your most impressive company. If you have walnut oil on your shelf, substitute it for the olive oil for a nuttier flavor.

Start to Finish: 20 minutes

Makes: 6 side-dish servings

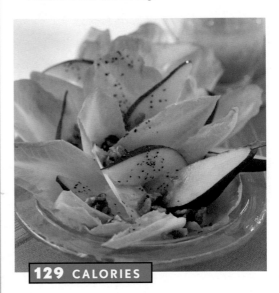

129 CALORIES

Nutrition Facts per serving:
129 cal., 7 g total fat (1 g sat. fat), 0 mg chol., 48 mg sodium, 18 g carbo., 2 g fiber, 1 g pro.
Daily Values:
1% vit. A, 17% vit. C, 1% calcium, 4% iron
Exchanges:
1 Vegetable, 1 Fruit, 1 Fat

Artichoke Salad

You can heighten the flavors of this Provence-inspired salad simply by serving it at room temperature. It's a wonderful accompaniment to grilled chicken or fresh pasta.

Prep: 30 minutes   **Chill:** 2 to 4 hours
Makes: 6 side-dish servings

59 CALORIES

- 10 baby artichokes or two 8-ounce packages frozen artichoke hearts
- 2 tablespoons lemon juice
- 2 tablespoons snipped fresh mint
- 1 teaspoon finely shredded lemon peel
- 2 tablespoons lemon juice
- 4 teaspoons olive oil
- 1/4 teaspoon salt
- 1/8 teaspoon black pepper
- 2 large cloves garlic, minced
- 1 small bulb fennel, halved and cored
- 1/2 of a small red onion
- 1 cup halved cherry tomatoes
  Fresh fennel leaves (optional)

1 To prepare artichokes, trim stems; cut off top one-fourth of each artichoke. Remove outer leaves until you reach the pale green parts. Halve or cut artichokes into wedges. Brush cut edges with some of the 2 tablespoons lemon juice; add remaining juice to cooking water. In a large saucepan cook artichokes in a large amount of boiling water for 12 to 15 minutes or until tender; drain. (Or cook frozen artichoke hearts according to package directions; drain.) Rinse with cold water. Drain and place in a large bowl.

2 Meanwhile, for dressing, in a small bowl combine mint, lemon peel, lemon juice, oil, salt, pepper, and garlic.

3 Thinly slice fennel and red onion. Add to artichokes along with tomatoes. Pour dressing over; toss to coat.

4 Cover and chill for at least 2 hours or up to 4 hours. Serve chilled or at room temperature. If desired, garnish with fennel leaves.

Nutrition Facts per serving:
59 cal., 3 g total fat (0 g sat. fat), 0 mg chol., 135 mg sodium, 8 g carbo., 6 g fiber, 2 g pro.
Daily Values:
5% vit. A, 28% vit. C, 3% calcium, 5% iron
Exchanges:
1 Vegetable, 1/2 Fat

2 cups water

1¹/₂ cups sliced fresh mushrooms

¹/₂ cup shredded carrot

¹/₃ cup thinly sliced green onions

1 tablespoon butter or margarine

2 teaspoons instant chicken bouillon granules

2 teaspoons snipped fresh basil or thyme or ¹/₂ teaspoon dried basil or thyme, crushed

1 10-ounce package quick-cooking couscous

1 In a medium saucepan heat water, mushrooms, carrot, green onions, butter, bouillon granules, and dried herb (if using) to boiling. Stir in couscous and fresh herb (if using). Remove from heat.

2 Cover; let stand about 5 minutes or until liquid is absorbed. Fluff with fork before serving.

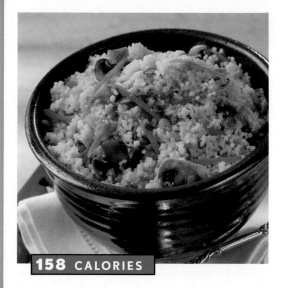

158 CALORIES

Savory Couscous

Jazz up plain couscous with a few added ingredients and it becomes a side dish special enough for company.

Start to Finish: 20 minutes
Makes: 8 side-dish servings

Nutrition Facts per serving:
158 cal., 2 g total fat (1 g sat. fat), 4 mg chol., 241 mg sodium, 29 g carbo., 2 g fiber, 5 g pro.
Daily Values:
44% vit. A, 3% vit. C, 2% calcium, 3% iron
Exchanges:
2 Starch

95 CALORIES

Roasted Vegetables with Balsamic Vinegar

Roasting brings out the natural sweetness of vegetables. These earthy roasted green beans and summer squash balance just about any entrée—steaks, chicken, pork chops, or fish.

Start to Finish: 25 minutes   **Oven:** 450°F

Makes: 4 to 6 side-dish servings

8   ounces fresh green beans, ends trimmed
1   small onion, cut into thin wedges
1   clove garlic, minced
1   tablespoon olive oil
     Dash salt
     Dash black pepper
2   medium yellow summer squash, halved lengthwise and cut into ¼-inch slices
⅓   cup balsamic vinegar

1 In a shallow roasting pan combine beans, onion, and garlic. Drizzle with oil; sprinkle with salt and pepper. Toss mixture until beans are evenly coated. Spread into a single layer.

2 Roast in a 450° oven for 8 minutes. Stir in squash; roast for 5 to 7 minutes more or until vegetables are tender and slightly browned.

3 Meanwhile, in a small saucepan bring the balsamic vinegar to boiling over medium-high heat; reduce heat. Boil gently about 5 minutes or until reduced by half (vinegar will thicken slightly).

4 Drizzle the vinegar over roasted vegetables; toss until vegetables are evenly coated.

Nutrition Facts per serving:
95 cal., 4 g total fat (1 g sat. fat), 0 mg chol., 44 mg sodium, 14 g carbo., 4 g fiber, 2 g pro.
Daily Values:
10% vit. A, 30% vit. C, 4% calcium, 6% iron
Exchanges:
3 Vegetable, ½ Fat

2 tablespoons water

1 tablespoon olive oil

¹/₂ teaspoon finely shredded lemon peel

2 tablespoons lemon juice

2 teaspoons snipped fresh basil or oregano

1 teaspoon Dijon-style mustard

1 clove garlic, minced

2 pounds tiny whole vegetables (such as baby carrots, zucchini, and/or pattypan squash)

8 ounces fresh sugar snap peas, tips and stems removed

12 cherry tomatoes

1 For dressing, in a screw-top jar combine the water, oil, lemon peel, lemon juice, basil, mustard, and garlic.

2 In a large covered saucepan cook tiny whole vegetables in a small amount of boiling water for 3 minutes. Add sugar snap peas; cook for 2 to 3 minutes or until vegetables are crisp-tender. Drain. Rinse vegetables with cold water; drain vegetables again.

3 In a large bowl combine cooked vegetables and tomatoes. Pour dressing over; toss gently to coat. Cover and chill for at least 2 hours or up to 24 hours.

Lemon-Marinated Baby Vegetables

Brighten up your summer gatherings with these colorful diminutive fresh veggies that double as a side-dish salad or an appetizer.

Prep: 20 minutes   **Chill:** 2 to 24 hours
Makes: 8 side-dish servings

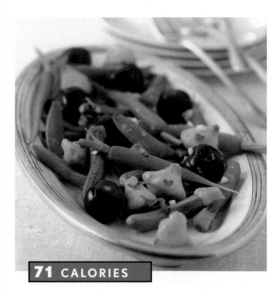

71 CALORIES

Nutrition Facts per serving:
71 cal., 2 g total fat (0 g sat. fat), 0 mg chol., 41 mg sodium, 12 g carbo., 4 g fiber, 2 g pro.
Daily Values:
293% vit. A, 35% vit. C, 4% calcium, 5% iron
Exchanges:
2 Vegetable, ¹/₂ Fat

Autumn Vegetable Medley

Fall brings with it chilly nights and a bountiful harvest. Take advantage with this winning combo of fruits and veggies.

Start to Finish: 35 minutes
Makes: 6 side-dish servings

148 CALORIES

8 ounces parsnips, thinly sliced (about 2¼ cups)

8 ounces carrots, thinly sliced (about 2¼ cups)

2 medium, firm ripe pears, peeled and cut into ½-inch slices

¾ cup orange juice

⅓ cup dried cranberries

1 teaspoon grated fresh ginger or ½ teaspoon ground ginger

2 tablespoons brown sugar

1 tablespoon butter or margarine

1 In a large nonstick skillet combine parsnips, carrots, pears, orange juice, dried cranberries, and ginger. Bring to boiling; reduce heat to medium. Cook, uncovered, for 7 to 8 minutes or until vegetables are crisp-tender and most of the liquid has evaporated, stirring occasionally.

2 Add brown sugar and butter, stirring until butter melts. Cook, uncovered, for 2 to 3 minutes more or until vegetables are glazed.

Nutrition Facts per serving:
148 cal., 3 g total fat (1 g sat. fat), 5 mg chol., 41 mg sodium, 32 g carbo., 5 g fiber, 1 g pro.
Daily Values:
194% vit. A, 43% vit. C, 4% calcium, 4% iron
Exchanges:
1 Vegetable, 1 Fruit, ½ Starch, ½ Fat

2 egg whites

1/4 teaspoon cream of tartar

1/8 teaspoon salt

1/2 cup sugar

1 6-ounce carton piña colada, pineapple, or other tropical fruit-flavor low-fat yogurt

1/2 cup light dairy sour cream

4 cups cut-up, peeled fresh tropical fruit (such as pineapple, mango, papaya, star fruit [carambola], and/or kiwifruit)

2 teaspoons snipped crystallized ginger or 1 tablespoon coconut, toasted (optional)

1 Let egg whites stand at room temperature for 30 minutes. Meanwhile, line a baking sheet with parchment paper or foil. Draw a 7-inch circle on the paper or foil.

2 In a medium mixing bowl combine egg whites, cream of tartar, and salt. Beat with an electric mixer on medium speed until soft peaks form (tips curl).

3 Add the sugar, 1 tablespoon at a time, beating on high speed until very stiff peaks form (tips stand straight) and sugar is almost dissolved (about 4 minutes).

4 Gently spoon egg white mixture into a pastry bag fitted with a pastry tube. Pipe egg white mixture onto the circle on the paper or foil, building up the side to form a shell. (Or use the back of a spoon to spread the egg white mixture over circle, building up side.)

5 Bake in a 300° oven for 40 minutes. Turn off oven. Let shell dry in oven, with door closed, for at least 1 hour. Remove from paper or foil; cool completely on a wire rack.

6 To serve, in a small bowl fold yogurt into sour cream. Spread about two-thirds of the mixture in the shell. Fill with fresh fruit. Pass remaining sour cream mixture. If desired, sprinkle with crystallized ginger or coconut.

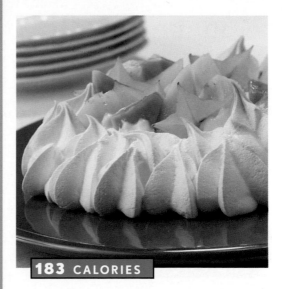

183 CALORIES

Tropical Fruit Pavlova

Named after the famous Russian ballerina Anna Pavlova, this dessert customarily features a baked crisp meringue topped with whipped cream and fruit. Lower-fat sour cream and yogurt pinch-hit for the whipped cream.

Stand: 30 minutes **Prep:** 20 minutes
Bake: 40 minutes **Oven:** 300°F
Cool: 1 hour **Makes:** 6 servings

Nutrition Facts per serving:
183 cal., 2 g total fat (1 g sat. fat), 8 mg chol., 102 mg sodium, 37 g carbo., 1 g fiber, 4 g pro.
Daily Values:
3% vit. A, 25% vit. C, 10% calcium, 1% iron
Exchanges:
1 Fruit, 1 1/2 Other Carbo., 1/2 Fat

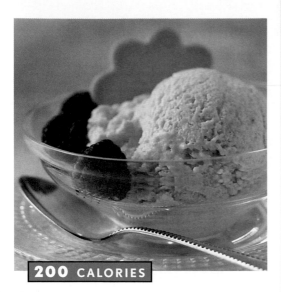

200 CALORIES

Peach Freeze

Don't worry if fresh peaches aren't in season; frozen peaches work just as well. Aren't convenience foods grand?

Prep: 20 minutes   **Stand:** 15 minutes
Freeze: 4 to 24 hours   **Makes:** 6 servings

4   cups sliced, peeled fresh peaches
     or one 16-ounce package frozen
     unsweetened peach slices, thawed
1/3   cup sugar
2   teaspoons finely shredded lemon peel
3   tablespoons lemon juice
1/2   of an 8-ounce container frozen fat-free
     whipped dessert topping, thawed
1/2   cup light dairy sour cream
     Fresh raspberries (optional)
     Purchased sugar cookies (optional)

1 In a large food processor bowl combine peaches, sugar, lemon peel, and lemon juice. Cover and process until smooth. Transfer to a large bowl. Fold in whipped topping and sour cream.

2 Transfer to a freezer container. Cover and freeze for at least 4 hours or up to 24 hours. Before serving, let stand at room temperature for 15 to 20 minutes to soften slightly. If desired, garnish with raspberries and serve with cookies.

Nutrition Facts per serving:
200 cal., 2 g total fat (1 g sat. fat), 7 mg chol., 24 mg sodium, 44 g carbo., 5 g fiber, 3 g pro.
Daily Values:
27% vit. A, 32% vit. C, 5% calcium, 1% iron
Exchanges:
1 Fruit, 2 Other Carbo., 1/2 Fat

Nonstick cooking spray

1 cup all-purpose flour

3/4 cup granulated sugar

1/4 cup unsweetened cocoa powder

2 teaspoons baking powder

1/2 teaspoon salt

1/2 cup fat-free milk

1/2 cup applesauce

1 teaspoon vanilla

1 3/4 cups hot water

3/4 cup packed brown sugar

1/4 cup unsweetened cocoa powder

1 teaspoon instant coffee granules

1 cup cappuccino chunk low-fat
  ice cream

1 Lightly coat an 8×8×2-inch baking pan with nonstick cooking spray.

2 In a large bowl combine flour, granulated sugar, 1/4 cup cocoa powder, the baking powder, and salt. Stir in milk, applesauce, and vanilla until thoroughly mixed. Pour into prepared pan.

3 In a small bowl combine the hot water, brown sugar, 1/4 cup cocoa powder, and the coffee granules. Carefully pour water mixture over cake batter. Bake in a 350° oven for 45 minutes. Spoon warm cake and pudding into dessert dishes. Serve with cappuccino chunk ice cream.

Mocha Pudding Cake

Some simple modifications keep this dessert in check. Applesauce substitutes for the cake's butter, while cocoa powder keeps the pudding slim and trim. Serve it with cappuccino ice cream (yes, it's low-cal) for a winning combo.

Prep: 15 minutes **Bake:** 45 minutes
Oven: 350°F **Makes:** 10 servings

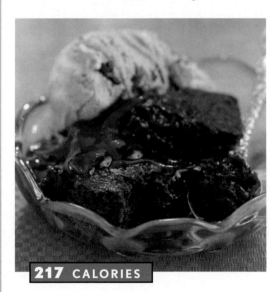

217 CALORIES

Nutrition Facts per serving:
217 cal., 1 g total fat (0 g sat. fat), 2 mg chol., 226 mg sodium, 48 g carbo., 1 g fiber, 3 g pro.
Daily Values:
1% vit. A, 15% calcium, 8% iron
Exchanges:
1/2 Fruit, 2 1/2 Other Carbo.

Baked Red Pears

Tuck tender dried fruits inside a pear and drape it with a sauce of sugar and spice. You'll want to plan on serving this dessert warm from the oven because you won't be able to resist the sweet aromas emanating from your kitchen.

Prep: 15 minutes   **Bake:** 40 minutes
Oven: 350°F   **Makes:** 4 servings

206 CALORIES

1¼   **cups apricot nectar**
⅓   **cup snipped dried apricots**
2   **tablespoons dried tart red cherries or dried cranberries**
4   **medium, firm red pears**
2   **tablespoons sugar**
¼   **teaspoon ground nutmeg**
½   **teaspoon vanilla**
⅛   **teaspoon ground cardamom**

1 In a small saucepan combine apricot nectar, apricots, and cherries or cranberries. Bring to boiling. Remove from heat; let stand for 5 minutes. Drain fruit, reserving liquid.

2 Meanwhile, cut off tops of pears; set aside. Core pears almost through to bottom. Place pears and pear tops in a 2-quart square baking dish. In a small bowl combine drained fruit mixture, sugar, and nutmeg. Spoon into centers of pears. In another small bowl combine reserved liquid, vanilla, and cardamom; pour over and around pears.

3 Cover and bake in a 350° oven for 20 minutes. Uncover; bake for 20 to 25 minutes more or until pears are tender, basting pears occasionally with cooking liquid.

4 To serve, place tops on pears; spoon liquid over pears. Serve warm.

Nutrition Facts per serving:
206 cal., 1 g total fat (0 g sat. fat), 0 mg chol., 4 mg sodium, 52 g carbo., 6 g fiber, 1 g pro.
Daily Values:
37% vit. A, 12% vit. C, 3% calcium, 7% iron
Exchanges:
1 Fruit, 2½ Other Carbo.

On the divider: Beef Tenderloin with Onion-Cherry Chutney (see recipe, page 98)

2 pounds fresh or frozen large shrimp in shells

¼ cup finely chopped fresh Anaheim chile pepper (see note on page 76)

½ teaspoon finely shredded lime peel

¼ cup lime juice

2 tablespoons olive oil

2 tablespoons finely chopped green onion

1 to 2 tablespoons snipped fresh cilantro or parsley

½ teaspoon sugar

½ teaspoon salt

¼ teaspoon black pepper

2 cloves garlic, minced

Crushed ice or lettuce leaves (optional)

Lime wedges (optional)

1 Thaw shrimp, if frozen. Peel and devein shrimp, leaving tails intact, if desired. In a large saucepan bring 4 cups water to boiling. Add shrimp. Simmer, uncovered, for 1 to 3 minutes or until shrimp turn opaque, stirring occasionally. Drain; rinse under cold running water and drain again. Set aside.

2 In a heavy plastic bag set in a medium bowl combine chile pepper, lime peel, lime juice, olive oil, onion, cilantro, sugar, salt, black pepper, and garlic; mix well. Place cooked shrimp in the bag; seal bag. Turn bag to coat shrimp with marinade mixture. Marinate in the refrigerator for 2 to 3 hours, turning the bag occasionally.

3 To serve, drain the shrimp, discarding the marinade. If desired, serve shrimp in ice-filled glasses or on a lettuce-lined platter and accompany with lime wedges.

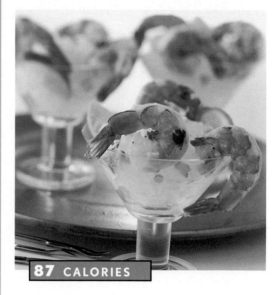

87 CALORIES

Fiesta Shrimp Appetizers

For even more delectable heat, substitute 2 to 4 tablespoons chopped jalapeño chile pepper for the Anaheim pepper.

Prep: 40 minutes   **Marinate:** 2 to 3 hours
Makes: 10 appetizer servings

Nutrition Facts per serving:
87 cal., 3 g total fat (0 g sat. fat), 103 mg chol., 159 mg sodium, 1 g carbo., 0 g fiber, 14 g pro.
Daily Values:
3% vit. A, 12% vit. C, 4% calcium, 9% iron
Exchanges:
2 Meat, ½ Fat

97 CALORIES

Chicken Quesadilla

Short on time? Use purchased roasted chicken breasts from your supermarket deli for the cooked chicken.

Prep: 15 minutes   **Cook:** 2 to 4 minutes
Makes: 6 appetizer servings

1   **10-inch plain or spinach flour tortilla**
    Nonstick cooking spray
¹/₂ **cup shredded cheddar cheese**
    (2 ounces)
¹/₂ **cup shredded cooked chicken or**
    turkey
¹/₄ **cup chopped avocado**
2   **to 3 fresh small jalapeño chile**
    peppers, seeded and thinly sliced
    (see note on page 76)
¹/₂ **cup bottled salsa**

1 Lightly coat one side of tortilla with cooking spray. Sprinkle half of the cheese evenly on half the surface of the unsprayed side of the tortilla. Top with chicken, avocado, and jalapeño. Add a little salsa and sprinkle with remaining cheese. Fold tortilla over filling.

2 Heat a heavy skillet or griddle over medium heat. Cook quesadilla about 1 to 2 minutes per side or until cheese melts and tortilla is lightly browned. Cut into 6 wedges. Serve warm with remaining salsa.

Nutrition Facts per serving:
97 cal., 6 g total fat (3 g sat. fat), 20 mg chol.,
145 mg sodium, 5 g carbo., 1 g fiber, 7 g pro.
Daily Values:
4% vit. A, 7% vit. C, 8% calcium, 4% iron
Exchanges:
¹/₂ Starch, ¹/₂ Meat, ¹/₂ Fat

30 cherry tomatoes (1-inch diameter)
1 cup firmly packed fresh basil leaves
½ cup firmly packed fresh flat-leaf parsley leaves
¼ cup pine nuts, toasted
1 large clove garlic, quartered
⅛ teaspoon black pepper
2 tablespoons olive oil
4 ounces goat cheese (chèvre), crumbled (1 cup)
  Fresh basil leaves (optional)

1 Slice off the top of each tomato. Cut a thin slice off the bottom of each tomato so they stand level. Scoop out tomatoes from the top using a small, narrow spoon or melon baller. Turn upside down on paper towels to drain.

2 For pesto, in a blender container or food processor bowl combine 1 cup basil, the parsley, pine nuts, garlic, and pepper. Cover and blend or process with several on/off turns until a paste forms, stopping machine several times and scraping the sides. With the machine running slowly, gradually add oil and blend or process to the consistency of soft butter. Transfer to a small bowl and stir in the goat cheese.

3 Spoon pesto mixture into a small self-sealing plastic bag. Snip a small hole in one corner of the bag. Seal bag. Squeeze pesto into the tomato shells. Place filled tomatoes on a serving plate. If desired, garnish with small basil leaves.

Make-ahead directions: Prepare as above through step 3. Cover and chill up to 4 hours.

Stuffed Cherry Tomatoes

Pretty as can be, these bite-size tomatoes make a festive red and green contribution to your holiday table. They always taste great, so don't hesitate to make them any time of year.

Prep: 45 minutes   **Makes:** 30 appetizers

29 CALORIES

Nutrition Facts per appetizer:
29 cal., 2 g total fat (1 g sat. fat), 2 mg chol., 16 mg sodium, 1 g carbo., 0 g fiber, 1 g pro.
Daily Values:
4% vit. A, 8% vit. C, 1% calcium, 2% iron
Exchanges:
½ Fat

Beef Tenderloin with Onion-Cherry Chutney

Here is a dish that's more than fit for a holiday feast. Apples, sweet pepper, cherries, and onion add up to a flavorful accompaniment.

Prep: 20 minutes   **Roast:** 35 minutes
Oven: 425°F   **Stand:** 30 minutes
Makes: 10 servings

212 CALORIES

Nutrition Facts per serving:
212 cal., 8 g total fat (2 g sat. fat), 54 mg chol.,
169 mg sodium, 15 g carbo., 2 g fiber, 20 g pro.
Daily Values:
18% vit. A, 44% vit. C, 2% calcium, 17% iron
Exchanges:
1 Fruit, 2½ Meat

1   **2- to 2½-pound beef tenderloin roast**
2   **teaspoons dried thyme, crushed**
3   **cloves garlic, minced**
½   **teaspoon salt**
¼   **teaspoon black pepper**
1   **cup chopped onion (1 large)**
1   **cup chopped red and/or yellow sweet pepper (1 large)**
1   **tablespoon olive oil or cooking oil**
2   **medium apples, cored and chopped (about 1⅓ cups)**
⅓   **cup dried tart cherries**
¼   **cup red wine vinegar**
3   **tablespoons packed brown sugar**

1 Place roast on a rack in a shallow roasting pan. In a small bowl stir together 1½ teaspoons of the thyme, 2 of the minced garlic cloves (1 teaspoon), salt, and black pepper. Rub onto surface of the meat. Insert an oven-going meat thermometer into thickest portion of roast. Roast, uncovered, in a 425° oven; for medium rare, allow 35 to 40 minutes or until the thermometer registers 140°F. Remove the roast from the oven; cover with foil and let stand 15 minutes before carving. The meat's temperature will rise 5° during the time it stands for a final doneness temperature of 145°F.

2 Meanwhile, for chutney, in a medium saucepan cook the onion, sweet pepper, and remaining garlic in hot oil until onion is tender. Add apples and cherries; cook and stir for 2 minutes. Add vinegar, brown sugar, and remaining thyme; boil gently, uncovered, for 10 to 12 minutes or until most of the liquid is evaporated. Remove from heat; cover and let stand for 30 minutes. Slice meat and serve with chutney.

1 8-pound cooked ham (shank portion)
  Whole cloves
1/2 cup packed brown sugar
1/4 cup chutney
1/4 cup plum jam
1 tablespoon Dijon-style mustard
1 clove garlic, minced
1 teaspoon rice vinegar
1/8 teaspoon bottled hot pepper sauce

1 Score ham by making shallow diagonal cuts in a diamond pattern. Stud with cloves. Place on a rack in a shallow roasting pan. Insert an oven-going meat thermometer in meat, making sure it does not touch bone. Bake in a 325° oven about 1¾ hours.

2 For glaze, in medium saucepan combine brown sugar, chutney, jam, mustard, garlic, vinegar, and hot pepper sauce. Cook and stir over medium heat until mixture is bubbly.

3 Brush ham with some of the glaze. Bake about 30 minutes more or until thermometer registers 140°F. Reheat the remaining glaze, if necessary. Pass glaze with ham.

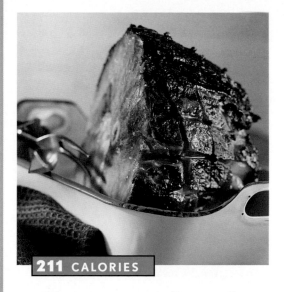

211 CALORIES

Chutney-Glazed Ham

The prep time for this spectacular ham is just 15 minutes, leaving you plenty of time to get the rest of the holiday meal together.

Prep: 15 minutes   **Bake:** 2¼ hours
Oven: 325°F   **Makes:** 20 servings

Nutrition Facts per serving:
211 cal., 6 g total fat (2 g sat. fat), 59 mg chol., 1,410 mg sodium, 11 g carbo., 0 g fiber, 26 g pro.
Daily Values:
3% vit. A, 3% vit. C, 1% calcium, 6% iron
Exchanges:
½ Fruit, 3½ Meat

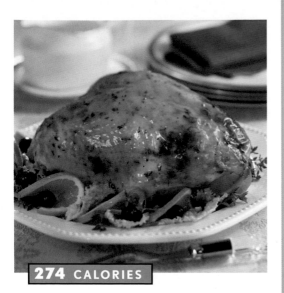

274 CALORIES

Orange Roasted Turkey

Orange, honey, and thyme star in this holiday turkey's special glaze. A matching orange sauce is served for an additional splash of citrus.

Prep: 20 minutes   **Roast:** 1½ hours
Oven: 325°F   **Stand:** 10 minutes
Makes: 10 servings

Nutrition Facts per serving:
274 cal., 11 g total fat (3 g sat. fat), 105 mg chol., 193 mg sodium, 6 g carbo., 0 g fiber, 36 g pro.
Daily Values:
1% vit. A, 14% vit. C, 3% calcium, 11% iron
Exchanges:
½ Fruit, 5 Meat

- 1 4- to 5-pound whole turkey breast
- ¼ teaspoon salt
- ⅛ teaspoon black pepper
- 3 tablespoons frozen orange juice concentrate, thawed
- 2 tablespoons honey
- 2 teaspoons snipped fresh thyme
- 2 teaspoons cornstarch
- 2 teaspoons cold water
- 1 cup reduced-sodium chicken broth
    Orange slices, fresh cranberries, fresh thyme, and leaf lettuce (optional)

1 Sprinkle turkey with the salt and pepper. Place turkey, bone side down, on rack in shallow roasting pan. Insert an oven-going meat thermometer into thickest portion of turkey breast, making sure it does not touch bone.

2 In a small bowl combine 2 tablespoons of the orange juice concentrate, the honey, and thyme. Set aside.

3 Roast turkey, uncovered, in a 325° oven for 1½ to 2¼ hours or until juices run clear and turkey is no longer pink (170°F), brushing with the orange juice concentrate mixture the last 15 minutes of roasting. Transfer turkey to a cutting board; cover with foil and let stand 10 to 15 minutes before carving.

4 Meanwhile, in a small saucepan stir together cornstarch and water until smooth; stir in broth and remaining 1 tablespoon orange juice concentrate. Cook and stir until slightly thickened and bubbly; cook and stir for 2 minutes more. Season to taste with additional salt and pepper. Serve sauce with turkey. If desired, garnish with orange slices, cranberries, fresh thyme sprigs, and lettuce.

4 skinless, boneless chicken breast halves (about 1¼ pounds total)

Black pepper

2 to 3 ounces fontina cheese, crumbled or sliced

½ cup canned roasted red sweet peppers cut into strips

12 fresh sage leaves

¼ cup all-purpose flour

1 tablespoon olive oil

2 cups dry white wine

Fresh sage leaves (optional)

1 Place each chicken breast half, boned side up, between 2 pieces of plastic wrap. Working from the center to the edges, pound lightly with the flat side of a meat mallet to ¼-inch thickness. Remove plastic wrap. Sprinkle chicken lightly with black pepper. Layer cheese, sweet pepper strips, and sage in the center of each breast. Fold in sides; roll up into a spiral, pressing the edges to seal. Roll in flour.

2 In a medium nonstick skillet heat the oil over medium heat. Cook chicken about 5 minutes, turning to brown all sides. Remove chicken from skillet. Drain off any fat.

3 In the same skillet bring wine to boiling; reduce heat. Simmer, uncovered, about 4 minutes or until 1 cup liquid remains. Return chicken to skillet. Cover and simmer for 7 to 8 minutes or until internal temperature of chicken registers 170°F using an instant-read thermometer.

4 Transfer chicken to a serving plate; cover to keep warm. Strain remaining cooking liquid; return to skillet. Bring to boiling; reduce heat. Simmer, uncovered, until mixture measures ½ cup. Serve over stuffed chicken breasts. If desired, garnish with fresh sage leaves.

Tuscany Stuffed Chicken Breasts

These elegant chicken breasts are stuffed with roasted red sweet pepper, sage, and cheese and topped with a wine-based sauce. Simply delicious.

Prep: 30 minutes   **Cook:** 16 minutes
Makes: 4 servings

359 CALORIES

Nutrition Facts per serving:
359 cal., 10 g total fat (4 g sat. fat), 98 mg chol., 196 mg sodium, 8 g carbo., 1 g fiber, 38 g pro.
Daily Values:
5% vit. A, 87% vit. C, 12% calcium, 11% iron
Exchanges:
½ Starch, 5 Meat

Maple-Glazed Pears and Cereal

Serve this fruit and cereal combination at your next holiday brunch. For a family breakfast, the hot cereal can be served in a bowl with the pear set on top.

Prep: 15 minutes   **Bake:** 20 minutes
Oven: 350°F   **Makes:** 8 servings

213 CALORIES

4   **medium, ripe pears, peeled, if desired**
³/₄   **cup desired dried fruit, such as dried cranberries, cherries, apricots, or raisins**
3   **tablespoons chopped walnuts, toasted**
3   **tablespoons maple syrup**
³/₄   **cup pear nectar or apple juice**
3   **cups cooked multigrain cereal**

1 Cut pears into halves, leaving stems intact on 4 of the halves. Remove cores. Arrange pears, cut sides up, in a 3-quart baking dish. Top pears with desired dried fruit and walnuts. Drizzle pears with maple syrup. Add the pear nectar to the baking dish.

2 Bake, uncovered, in a 350° oven for 20 to 25 minutes or until pears are tender, basting occasionally with the cooking liquid. Serve warm pear halves with hot cereal. Drizzle with any remaining cooking liquid.

Nutrition Facts per serving:
213 cal., 3 g total fat (0 g sat. fat), 0 mg chol., 286 mg sodium, 46 g carbo., 4 g fiber, 3 g pro.
Daily Values:
9% vit. A, 12% vit. C, 4% calcium, 13% iron
Exchanges:
1 Fruit, 1 Other Carbo., 1 Starch

3½ to 4 cups all-purpose flour

1 package active dry yeast

1 teaspoon salt

1¼ cups warm water (120°F to 130°F)

2 tablespoons olive oil

⅔ cup shredded Swiss cheese

⅓ cup finely chopped almonds

½ teaspoon cracked black pepper

½ teaspoon coarse sea salt

1 In a large bowl stir together 1¼ cups of the flour, the yeast, and salt. Add the warm water and 1 tablespoon of the oil. Beat with an electric mixer on low to medium speed for 30 seconds, scraping sides of bowl. Beat on high speed for 3 minutes. Stir in as much of the remaining flour as you can with a wooden spoon.

2 Turn out dough onto a lightly floured surface. Knead in enough remaining flour to make a stiff dough that is smooth and elastic (8 to 10 minutes total). Shape dough into a ball. Place in a lightly greased bowl; turn once to grease surface. Cover; let rise in a warm place until double in size (about 1 hour).

3 Punch down dough. Turn out onto a lightly floured surface. Divide in half. Lightly oil 2 baking sheets. Shape each half into a ball. Place on prepared baking sheets. Cover and let rest for 10 minutes. Flatten each ball into a circle about 9 inches in diameter. Press ½-inch-deep indentations about 2 inches apart into the surface with your fingers. Brush with the remaining 1 tablespoon olive oil. Sprinkle with cheese, nuts, pepper, and coarse salt. Cover; let rise in a warm place until nearly double (about 20 minutes).

4 Bake in a 375° oven for 25 to 30 minutes or until golden. Remove from baking sheets; cool on wire racks.

96 CALORIES

Swiss Cheese-Almond Flatbread

When you need a special bread for your holiday gathering, this one is perfect. With Swiss cheese and almonds, it's substantial enough to be served as an appetizer.

Prep: 40 minutes   **Rise:** 1⅓ hours
Bake: 25 minutes   **Oven:** 375°F
Makes: 2 rounds (12 servings per round)

Nutrition Facts per serving:
96 cal., 3 g total fat (1 g sat. fat), 3 mg chol., 141 mg sodium, 13 g carbo., 1 g fiber, 3 g pro.
Daily Values:
1% vit. A, 4% calcium, 5% iron
Exchanges:
1 Starch, ½ Fat

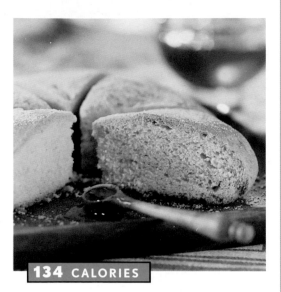

134 CALORIES

Country-Style Semolina Loaves

Semolina is a coarsely ground durum wheat flour. While it's more likely to show up in pasta than in baked goods, here it brings a pleasantly rustic touch to the loaves.

Prep: 40 minutes   **Rise:** 1½ hours
Bake: 25 minutes   **Oven:** 375°F
Makes: 2 loaves (8 servings per loaf)

Nutrition Facts per serving:
134 cal., 5 g total fat (1 g sat. fat), 0 mg chol.,
146 mg sodium, 20 g carbo., 1 g fiber, 3 g pro.
Daily Values:
7% iron
Exchanges:
½ Starch, ½ Fat

1³/₄ **to 2¹/₄ cups all-purpose flour**
   1 **package active dry yeast**
   1 **teaspoon sugar**
   1 **teaspoon salt**
   1 **cup warm water (120°F to 130°F)**
 ¹/₃ **cup olive oil**
1¹/₄ **cups semolina**
      Semolina

1 In a large mixing bowl stir together 1¼ cups of the all-purpose flour, the yeast, sugar, and salt. Add warm water and oil. Beat with an electric mixer on low speed for 30 seconds, scraping sides of bowl. Beat on high speed for 3 minutes. Stir in the 1¼ cups semolina and as much of the remaining all-purpose flour as you can with a wooden spoon.

2 Turn out dough onto a lightly floured surface. Knead in enough remaining all-purpose flour to make a moderately stiff dough that is smooth and elastic (6 to 8 minutes total). Shape dough into a ball. Place in a greased bowl; turn once to grease surface. Cover; let rise in a warm place until double in size (about 1 hour).

3 Punch down dough. Turn out onto a lightly floured surface. Divide in half. Cover and let rest 10 minutes. Grease 2 baking sheets. Shape each half into a ball. Place on the prepared baking sheets. Flatten each ball to about 6½ inches in diameter. Cover and let rise until nearly double (30 to 45 minutes).

4 Rub loaves lightly with additional semolina. Cut a crisscross in the top of each loaf. Bake in a 375° oven about 25 minutes or until golden and the bread sounds hollow when lightly tapped. Remove from baking sheets; cool on wire racks.

2¾ to 3 cups all-purpose flour

1 package active dry yeast

¾ cup milk

⅓ cup granulated sugar

2 tablespoons butter or margarine

1 egg

½ cup finely chopped fresh cranberries

2 tablespoons finely chopped pecans

1½ teaspoons finely shredded orange peel

½ teaspoon pumpkin pie spice

1½ teaspoons butter or margarine, melted

1 recipe Orange Icing

1 In large bowl stir together 1 cup of the flour and yeast; set aside. In small saucepan heat and stir milk, 2 tablespoons of the sugar, the 2 tablespoons butter, and ½ teaspoon salt until warm (120°F to 130°F). Add milk mixture to flour mixture; add egg. Beat with an electric mixer on low to medium speed for 30 seconds, scraping bowl. Beat on high speed 3 minutes. Stir in as much remaining flour as you can.

2 Turn out dough onto a floured surface. Knead in enough remaining flour to make a soft dough that is smooth and elastic (3 to 5 minutes). Shape dough into a ball. Place in a lightly greased bowl; turn once. Cover; let rise until double (1 to 1½ hours). For filling, in small bowl stir together cranberries, remaining sugar, pecans, peel, and spice; set aside.

3 Punch down dough. Turn out onto lightly floured surface. Cover; let rest 10 minutes. Roll dough into a 14×10-inch rectangle. Brush with melted butter. Spread filling over dough. Starting from a long side, roll dough into a spiral. Seal seam. Place seam side down and cut roll in half lengthwise. Place cut sides up, side by side, on greased baking sheet. Loosely twist halves together, keeping cut sides up. Pinch ends to seal. Cover; let rise in a warm place until nearly double (about 30 minutes).

4 Bake in a 375° oven about 25 minutes or until golden brown. Cool on wire rack. Drizzle with Orange Icing.

Orange Icing: Stir together ½ cup sifted powdered sugar and enough orange juice (2 to 3 teaspoons) for drizzling consistency.

Cranberry Twist Bread

Although the orange-flavored drizzle makes a stunning addition to this holiday bread, you can omit it to further reduce the calories.

Prep: 30 minutes **Rise:** 1½ hours
Bake: 25 minutes **Oven:** 375°F
Makes: 16 servings

136 CALORIES

Nutrition Facts per serving:
136 cal., 3 g total fat (2 g sat. fat), 19 mg chol., 102 mg sodium, 24 g carbo., 1 g fiber, 3 g pro.
Daily Values:
2% vit. A, 2% vit. C, 2% calcium, 6% iron
Exchanges:
1½ Starch, ½ Fat

Cherry-Nut Muffins

Break up the hectic holiday time hustle-bustle by having a few friends over for a relaxing tea. Serve these cherry-studded muffins during your well-deserved break.

Prep: 15 minutes   **Bake:** 18 minutes
Oven: 400°F   **Stand:** 5 minutes
Makes: 12 muffins

154 CALORIES

1³/₄   **cups all-purpose flour**
¹/₂   **cup sugar**
2   **teaspoons baking powder**
¹/₄   **teaspoon salt**
1   **slightly beaten egg white**
³/₄   **cup fat-free milk**
3   **tablespoons cooking oil**
1   **teaspoon finely shredded orange peel**
¹/₂   **cup snipped dried tart cherries**
2   **tablespoons chopped walnuts**

1 Line twelve 2½-inch muffin pans with paper bake cups; set aside. In a medium bowl stir together flour, sugar, baking powder, and salt. Make a well in center of flour mixture; set aside.

2 In another bowl combine egg white, milk, oil, and orange peel. Add milk mixture all at once to flour mixture. Stir just until moistened (batter should be lumpy). Gently fold in cherries and nuts.

3 Spoon batter into prepared muffin cups, filling each two-thirds full. Bake in a 400° oven for 18 to 20 minutes or until golden and a wooden toothpick inserted in centers comes out clean. Cool in muffin cups on wire rack for 5 minutes. Remove from muffin cups; serve warm.

Nutrition Facts per muffin:
154 cal., 4 g total fat (1 g sat. fat), 0 mg chol., 128 mg sodium, 26 g carbo., 1 g fiber, 3 g pro.
Daily Values:
1% vit. A, 1% vit. C, 6% calcium, 5% iron
Exchanges:
1½ Starch, ½ Fat

1 **12-ounce package fresh cranberries (3 cups)**

³/₄ cup apple juice

¹/₂ cup sugar

1 tablespoon lemon juice

1 teaspoon dried minced onion

¹/₂ teaspoon dried rosemary, crushed

2 medium pears, cored and chopped (2 cups)

Fresh rosemary sprig (optional)

1 In a medium saucepan combine cranberries, apple juice, sugar, lemon juice, onion, and rosemary. Bring to boiling; reduce heat. Cook, uncovered, over medium heat about 5 minutes or until cranberries pop.

2 Add pears and cook, uncovered, 2 minutes more or just until pears are tender. Serve warm with turkey, ham, or roast pork. If desired, garnish with a rosemary sprig.

Make-ahead directions: Prepare as above. Cool, cover, and chill relish up to 1 day.

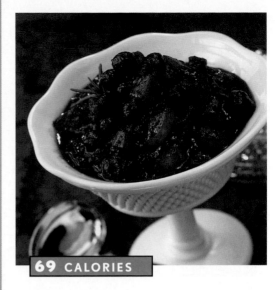

69 CALORIES

Cranberry-Pear Relish

Pears, cranberries, onion, and rosemary? This unexpected mix results in one sophisticated relish.

Start to Finish: 20 minutes
Makes: 12 (about ¹/₄-cup) servings

Nutrition Facts per serving:
69 cal., 0 g total fat (0 g sat. fat), 0 mg chol., 1 mg sodium, 18 g carbo., 2 g fiber, 0 g pro.
Daily Values:
10% vit. C, 1% calcium, 1% iron
Exchanges:
1 Other Carbo.

66 CALORIES

Star Fruit Salad with Raspberry Vinaigrette

Glossy, golden-yellow star fruit needn't be peeled; simply rinse it thoroughly. When ripe, this showy warm-climate fruit is exceedingly juicy and fragrant.

Start to Finish: 15 minutes
Makes: 6 servings

- 3 **tablespoons raspberry vinegar**
- 2 **tablespoons salad oil**
- 1 **tablespoon honey**
- 1 **10-ounce package torn mixed Italian blend salad greens**
- 1 **medium star fruit (carambola), thinly sliced**
- 1/2 **small red onion, thinly sliced**
   Fresh raspberries (optional)

1 In a screw-top jar combine vinegar, oil, and honey. Cover and shake well.

2 In a large bowl toss salad greens with star fruit and onion. Shake dressing well and pour over salad mixture. Toss lightly to coat. If desired, garnish with a few fresh raspberries.

Nutrition Facts per serving:
66 cal., 5 g total fat (1 g sat. fat), 0 mg chol., 5 mg sodium, 6 g carbo., 1 g fiber, 1 g pro.
Daily Values:
5% vit. A, 9% vit. C, 1% calcium, 2% iron
Exchanges:
1/2 Fruit, 1 Fat

Romaine leaves

9 cups torn mixed salad greens

**1 small tart green apple, cored and cut
    into thin wedges**

**1 small red apple, cored and cut into
    thin wedges**

3 tablespoons cider vinegar

3 tablespoons olive oil

¼ teaspoon black pepper

⅛ teaspoon salt

¼ cup mixed nuts, toasted

1 Place several romaine leaves on each salad
plate. Top with the torn greens and apples.

2 In a small screw-top jar combine vinegar,
oil, pepper, and salt. Cover and shake
well. Drizzle dressing over salad. Sprinkle
with nuts.

Nutty Apple Salad

Red and green apple skins add holiday
color to ordinary salad greens. The simple
cider vinegar dressing packs a lot of flavor
without adding a lot of calories.

Start to Finish: 20 minutes
Makes: 8 to 10 servings

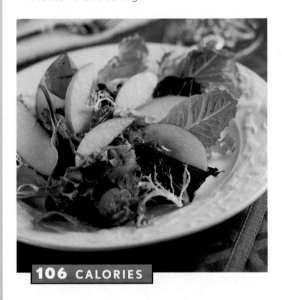

106 CALORIES

Nutrition Facts per serving:
106 cal., 8 g total fat (1 g sat. fat), 0 mg chol.,
73 mg sodium, 9 g carbo., 3 g fiber, 2 g pro.
Daily Values:
15% vit. A, 16% vit. C, 4% calcium, 5% iron
Exchanges:
1 Vegetable, ½ Fruit, 1½ Fat

Warm Beet Salad with Garlic Dressing

If you're a garlic groupie, this stellar salad has your name on it. You'll savor the garlic-spiked dressing over succulent beets and crunchy green beans. Serve the vegetables warm so they absorb the dressing to the fullest.

Start to Finish: 30 minutes

Makes: 4 servings

132 CALORIES

- 1 pound fresh green beans, trimmed
- 1 16-ounce can sliced beets, well drained and cut into thin bite-size strips
- 2 tablespoons orange juice
- 2 tablespoons olive oil
- 1 tablespoon balsamic vinegar
- 2 teaspoons bottled roasted minced garlic
- 1/8 teaspoon salt
  Purchased mixed salad greens
  Coarsely ground black pepper (optional)

1 In a large covered saucepan cook green beans in a small amount of lightly salted boiling water about 15 minutes or until almost tender. Add beets; cook for 2 to 3 minutes more or until beets are heated through. Drain and keep warm.

2 Meanwhile, for dressing*, in a screw-top jar combine orange juice, oil, balsamic vinegar, garlic, and salt. Cover and shake well. Pour dressing over warm beans and beets. To serve, arrange beans, beets, and salad greens on 4 plates. If desired, sprinkle salads with pepper.

*Note: In place of the homemade dressing, you can substitute a bottled garlic salad dressing or stir the roasted minced garlic into an Italian salad dressing.

Nutrition Facts per serving:
132 cal., 7 g total fat (1 g sat. fat), 0 mg chol., 223 mg sodium, 16 g carbo., 6 g fiber, 3 g pro.
Daily Values:
16% vit. A, 40% vit. C, 6% calcium, 15% iron
Exchanges:
3 Vegetable, 1 1/2 Fat

2 **pounds sweet potatoes (4 to 6 medium)**

¹⁄₃ **cup pure maple syrup or maple-flavored syrup**

3 **tablespoons coarse-grain Dijon-style mustard**

2 **tablespoons cooking oil**

¹⁄₂ **teaspoon salt**

¹⁄₂ **teaspoon freshly ground black pepper**

¹⁄₂ **cup fresh cranberries**

1 Peel and cut the sweet potatoes into 1- to 1½-inch chunks. In a large bowl combine the maple syrup, mustard, oil, salt, and pepper; add sweet potatoes and cranberries. Toss to coat. Transfer the mixture to a 3-quart baking dish, spreading mixture evenly.

2 Bake, uncovered, in a 400° oven for 30 to 35 minutes or until potatoes are glazed and tender, stirring twice.

160 CALORIES

Maple-Glazed Sweet Potatoes

Dijon mustard and fresh cranberries are the unique ingredients in this holiday side-dish favorite..

Prep: 20 minutes   **Bake:** 30 minutes
Oven: 400°F   **Makes:** 8 servings

Nutrition Facts per serving:
160 cal., 4 g total fat (1 g sat. fat), 0 mg chol., 287 mg sodium, 30 g carbo., 3 g fiber, 1 g pro.
Daily Values:
311% vit. A, 25% vit. C, 3% calcium, 4% iron
Exchanges:
2 Starch, ¹⁄₂ Fat

155 CALORIES

Sage and Onion Mashed Potatoes

They may seem unobtrusive and downright ordinary, but buttermilk and sage are just the things that make these mashed potatoes shine.

Prep: 25 minutes   **Bake:** 40 minutes
Oven: 450°F   **Makes:** 8 servings

- **6** medium baking potatoes (2 pounds total), peeled and cut into eighths
- **1** cup coarsely chopped onion (1 large)
- **¹/₂** cup water
- **2** tablespoons olive oil or cooking oil
- **2** teaspoons snipped fresh sage or 1 teaspoon ground sage
- **¹/₂** teaspoon salt
- **¹/₄** teaspoon black pepper
- **1** to 1¹/₄ cups buttermilk
  Salt and black pepper

1 In a greased 3-quart rectangular baking dish combine potatoes and onions. In a small bowl combine water, oil, sage, the ¹/₂ teaspoon salt, and ¹/₄ teaspoon pepper; drizzle over potatoes and onions.

2 Bake, uncovered, in a 450° oven for 40 to 45 minutes or until the vegetables are tender and browned, stirring twice.

3 Transfer to a large mixing bowl. Mash with a potato masher or beat with an electric mixer on low speed. Gradually beat in enough buttermilk to make smooth and fluffy. Season to taste with additional salt and pepper.

Nutrition Facts per serving:
155 cal., 5 g total fat (1 g sat. fat), 1 mg chol., 185 mg sodium, 24 g carbo., 2 g fiber, 4 g pro.
Daily Values:
29% vit. C, 5% calcium, 5% iron
Exchanges:
1¹/₂ Starch, ¹/₂ Fat

Nonstick cooking spray

1 **cup chopped onion (1 large)**

1 **cup chopped green or red sweet pepper**

2 **tablespoons butter or margarine**

3 **tablespoons all-purpose flour**

2 **cups reduced-fat milk**

2 **slightly beaten eggs**

2 **16-ounce packages frozen whole kernel corn, thawed and drained**

2 **cups soft bread crumbs**

³/₄ **teaspoon salt**

¹/₄ **teaspoon black pepper**

1 Lightly coat a 2-quart rectangular baking dish with cooking spray; set aside. In a medium saucepan cook onion and sweet pepper in 4 teaspoons of the butter about 5 minutes or until tender. Stir in flour until vegetables are coated. Add milk all at once. Cook and stir until thickened and bubbly; remove from heat and set aside.

2 In a large bowl stir together the eggs, thawed corn, 1 cup of the bread crumbs, the salt, and pepper. Stir in the thickened mixture. Transfer mixture to the prepared baking dish. In a small saucepan melt the remaining butter. Stir in the remaining bread crumbs to coat. Sprinkle over corn mixture.

3 Bake, uncovered, in a 325° oven for 40 to 45 minutes or just until center appears set. Let stand 10 minutes before serving.

Scalloped Corn

This is a good old-fashioned dish that's destined to become an instant classic in your household.

Prep: 25 minutes   **Bake:** 40 minutes
Oven: 325°F   **Stand:** 10 minutes
Makes: 12 servings

153 CALORIES

Nutrition Facts per serving:
153 cal., 5 g total fat (2 g sat. fat), 44 mg chol., 240 mg sodium, 25 g carbo., 2 g fiber, 6 g pro.
Daily Values:
6% vit. A, 24% vit. C, 7% calcium, 5% iron
Exchanges:
1¹/₂ Starch, 1 Fat

Golden Vegetable Gratin

Can't get your children to eat their veggies? This side dish, with Swiss cheese and maple syrup, tastes so good, they'll be asking for seconds.

Prep: 30 minutes   **Bake:** 45 minutes
Oven: 375°F   **Makes:** 8 servings

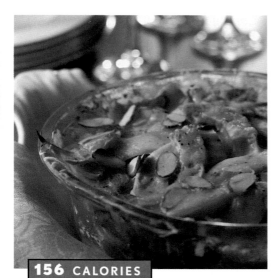

156 CALORIES

1   cup peeled and thinly bias-sliced carrots (2 medium)

3   cups peeled, quartered, and thinly sliced rutabaga (1 small)

3/4   cup finely shredded Swiss cheese (3 ounces)

2 1/2   cups peeled and thinly sliced sweet potatoes (2 medium)

2   cups peeled, quartered lengthwise, and thinly sliced butternut squash (half of a small)

2   tablespoons water

2   tablespoons maple syrup or honey

1/2   teaspoon instant chicken bouillon granules

1/2   teaspoon salt

1/4   teaspoon black pepper

2   tablespoons sliced almonds

1 In a 2-quart baking dish layer in order the carrots, rutabaga, 1/4 cup of the cheese, sweet potatoes, and squash. Combine water, maple syrup, bouillon granules, salt, and pepper; pour over vegetables.

2 Bake, covered, in a 375° oven about 35 minutes or just until vegetables are tender. Uncover vegetables; sprinkle with remaining 1/2 cup cheese and sliced almonds. Bake, uncovered, 10 to 15 minutes more or until almonds are light brown.

Nutrition Facts per serving:
156 cal., 5 g total fat (2 g sat. fat), 11 mg chol., 255 mg sodium, 24 g carbo., 3 g fiber, 6 g pro.
Daily Values:
295% vit. A, 40% vit. C, 18% calcium, 6% iron
Exchanges:
1 1/2 Starch, 1/2 Fat

2 cups 1-inch bias-sliced carrots
   (4 medium)

2 cups 1-inch bias-sliced parsnips
   (4 medium)

2 tablespoons snipped fresh parsley

2 teaspoons snipped fresh marjoram,
   thyme, or rosemary, or $^1/_2$ teaspoon
   dried marjoram, thyme, or rosemary,
   crushed

$^1/_4$ teaspoon salt

1 tablespoon olive oil or cooking oil

2 cups $1^1/_2$-inch pieces peeled, seeded
   winter squash (about $1^1/_4$ pounds
   before trimming)

$^1/_4$ cup packed brown sugar

   Fresh thyme sprigs (optional)

1 In a large saucepan cook carrots and
parsnips in a small amount of water,
covered, for 3 minutes. Drain.

2 Transfer the partially cooked carrots and
parsnips to a 13×9×2-inch baking pan.
Sprinkle with parsley, desired herb, and
salt. Drizzle with oil. Toss gently to coat
vegetables. Cover the pan with foil.

3 Bake in a 375° oven for 30 minutes,
stirring vegetables once. Stir in squash
pieces. Cover and bake about 20 minutes
more or just until vegetables are barely
done. Remove vegetables from oven.

4 Increase oven temperature to 450°. Stir
the brown sugar into vegetables until
thoroughly combined. Return vegetables
to oven and bake, uncovered, for 15 to
20 minutes more or until vegetables are
tender and glazed. Transfer to a serving
dish. If desired, garnish with fresh thyme.

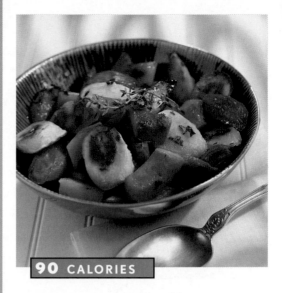

90 CALORIES

Roasted Fall Vegetables

At holiday times, special side dishes are
definitely warranted. These tender fall
vegetables glazed with brown sugar dress
up any festive meal.

Prep: 30 minutes   **Roast:** 65 minutes
Oven: 375°F/450°F   **Makes:** 8 servings

Nutrition Facts per serving:
90 cal., 2 g total fat (0 g sat. fat), 0 mg chol., 91 mg sodium,
18 g carbo., 3 g fiber, 1 g pro.
Daily Values:
177% vit. A, 19% vit. C, 4% calcium, 4% iron
Exchanges:
1 Starch

181 CALORIES

Blue Cheese-Stuffed Figs

Yes, you can eat foods you assumed were off limits—if you eat small servings. These delightful little bites boast so much flavor, you'll be satisfied with just one.

Start to Finish: 25 minutes

Makes: 6 servings

1 cup sweet Marsala wine

1/3 cup orange juice

2 tablespoons packed brown sugar

3 ounces reduced-fat cream cheese (Neufchâtel), softened (about 1/3 cup)

1 ounce blue cheese, crumbled (1/4 cup)

1 tablespoon milk

6 fresh figs or 3 pears

1 tablespoon sliced almonds, chopped and toasted

1 In a medium saucepan combine wine, orange juice, and sugar. Bring to boiling; reduce heat. Boil gently, uncovered, about 15 minutes or until reduced to about 1/3 cup.

2 Meanwhile, in a small bowl stir together cream cheese, blue cheese, and milk. Cut each fig into quarters, leaving fig attached at the bottom. (Or cut pears in half and core.) Drizzle some Marsala mixture onto each of 6 dessert plates. Top each plate with a fig. Spread fig open slightly. Spoon some of the cheese mixture into each fig and sprinkle with almonds. (Or spoon some cheese mixture onto each pear half and sprinkle with almonds.)

Nutrition Facts per serving:
181 cal., 6 g total fat (3 g sat. fat), 14 mg chol., 144 mg sodium, 19 g carbo., 2 g fiber, 4 g pro.
Daily Values:
6% vit. A, 13% vit. C, 7% calcium, 3% iron
Exchanges:
1 1/2 Fruit, 1 Fat

1 recipe Single-Crust Pastry
⅓ cup sugar
2 tablespoons cornstarch
1¾ cups fat-free milk
2 beaten eggs
2 tablespoons chopped crystallized ginger
1 teaspoon vanilla
⅔ cup pear nectar
1½ teaspoons cornstarch
2 small ripe pears, peeled and cored
½ cup fresh raspberries

1 Prepare Single-Crust Pastry. For vanilla cream, in a medium heavy saucepan combine sugar and 2 tablespoons cornstarch. Stir in milk. Cook and stir over medium heat until thickened and bubbly. Cook and stir 2 minutes. Remove from heat. Gradually stir about 1 cup of hot mixture into eggs. Return all of the egg mixture to saucepan. Stir in ginger. Reduce heat. Cook and stir 2 minutes more. Remove from heat. Stir in vanilla. Pour vanilla cream into baked pastry shell. Chill for 1 hour. Cover; chill until ready to assemble.

2 For glaze, in a small saucepan combine pear nectar and 1½ teaspoons cornstarch. Cook and stir until thickened and bubbly. Cook and stir for 2 minutes more. Remove from heat. Cover; cool to room temperature.

3 To assemble, thinly slice pears. Arrange in a concentric pattern over vanilla cream. Spoon glaze over pears, spreading evenly. Cover; chill 1 to 4 hours. Top with berries. Remove side of pan; transfer tart to platter.

Single-Crust Pastry: In bowl combine 1¼ cups all-purpose flour and ¼ teaspoon salt. Cut in ⅓ cup shortening until pieces are pea-size. Sprinkle 1 tablespoon water over part of flour mixture; gently toss with a fork. Push moistened dough to side of bowl. Repeat, using 1 tablespoon water at a time, until all mixture is moistened (4 to 5 tablespoons total). Form into a ball. On a lightly floured surface, flatten ball of dough. Roll from center to edge, forming a circle about 13 inches in diameter. Ease pastry into an 11-inch tart pan with removable bottom; do not stretch pastry. Trim pastry to edge of tart pan. Prick bottom, sides, and corners of pastry generously with fork. Bake in a 450° oven for 10 to 12 minutes until golden. Cool in pan on rack.

Fresh Pear Custard Tart

Expect this elegant dish to turn some heads at your holiday table. Fresh raspberries sparkle like jewels against the creamy-colored pears, and the taste is nothing short of divine.

Prep: 40 minutes   **Cook:** 20 minutes

Bake: 10 minutes   **Oven:** 450°F

Chill: 2 hours   **Makes:** 12 servings

175 CALORIES

Nutrition Facts per serving:
175 cal., 6 g total fat (2 g sat. fat), 36 mg chol., 79 mg sodium, 25 g carbo., 1 g fiber, 4 g pro.
Daily Values:
3% vit. A, 5% vit. C, 6% calcium, 5% iron
Exchanges:
½ Fruit, 1 Other Carbo., 1 Fat

Cherry Puff

What's under the puffy topping? Why, it's a cherry filling. Serve this treat for those special family events.

Prep: 25 minutes   **Bake:** 30 minutes
Oven: 325°F   **Makes:** 6 servings

192 CALORIES

1   **16-ounce can pitted tart red cherries (water pack)**
½   **cup sugar**
2   **tablespoons quick-cooking tapioca**
2   **egg whites**
¼   **teaspoon cream of tartar**
⅛   **teaspoon salt**
2   **egg yolks**
⅓   **cup sugar**
⅓   **cup all-purpose flour**

1 Drain cherries, reserving ½ cup liquid. Transfer cherries to a medium saucepan. Add reserved cherry liquid, the ½ cup sugar, and the tapioca. Cook and stir over medium heat until mixture boils; reduce heat. Simmer, uncovered, for 5 minutes, stirring constantly. Keep the cherry mixture warm while preparing the batter for the topping.

2 In a medium mixing bowl beat egg whites, cream of tartar, and salt with an electric mixer on medium speed until stiff peaks form (tips stand straight); set aside. In a small mixing bowl beat egg yolks for 2 to 3 minutes or until thick and lemon colored; add the ⅓ cup sugar. Beat 1 minute more. Stir a small amount of egg white mixture into egg yolk mixture to lighten. Fold remaining egg yolk mixture into egg white mixture. Sprinkle flour over egg mixture; fold in.

3 Pour hot cherry mixture into six 6- to 8-ounce oven-safe mugs, casseroles, or custard cups or one 1½-quart casserole. Pour batter over cherry mixture. Bake in a 325° oven about 30 minutes for the small cups or casseroles or 35 to 40 minutes for the 1½-quart casserole or until top springs back when lightly touched. Serve warm.

Nutrition Facts per serving:
192 cal., 2 g total fat (1 g sat. fat), 71 mg chol., 75 mg sodium, 42 g carbo., 1 g fiber, 4 g pro.
Daily Values:
14% vit. A, 3% vit. C, 2% calcium, 9% iron
Exchanges:
1 Fruit, 2 Other Carbo.

On the divider: Asian Spring Rolls (see recipe, page 139)

- 8 ounces beef top round steak
- 1/2 cup reduced-sodium beef broth
- 3 tablespoons reduced-sodium soy sauce
- 2 1/2 teaspoons cornstarch
- 1 teaspoon sugar
- 1 teaspoon grated fresh ginger
- Nonstick cooking spray
- 1 1/4 pounds fresh asparagus spears, trimmed and cut into 2-inch pieces (3 cups), or 3 cups small broccoli florets
- 1 1/2 cups sliced fresh mushrooms
- 4 green onions, bias-sliced into 2-inch lengths (1/2 cup)
- 1 tablespoon cooking oil
- 2 cups hot cooked rice

1 If desired, partially freeze beef for easier slicing. Trim fat from beef. Thinly slice beef across the grain into bite-size strips. Set aside. For the sauce, in a small bowl stir together the beef broth, soy sauce, cornstarch, sugar, and ginger; set aside.

2 Lightly coat an unheated wok or large skillet with nonstick cooking spray. Preheat over medium-high heat. Add asparagus or broccoli, mushrooms, and green onions. Stir-fry for 3 to 4 minutes or until vegetables are crisp-tender. Remove from wok or skillet.

3 Carefully add the oil to wok or skillet. Add beef; stir-fry for 2 to 3 minutes or until brown. Push the beef from center of the wok or skillet. Stir sauce. Add sauce to center of wok or skillet. Cook and stir until thickened and bubbly.

4 Return vegetables to wok or skillet. Stir all ingredients together to coat with sauce; heat through. Serve immediately over hot cooked rice.

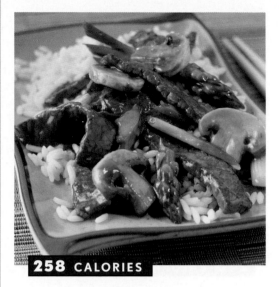

258 CALORIES

Ginger Beef Stir-Fry

When you crave steak but not the high fat and calories that go with it, try this stir-fry. Lean beef and crispy spring vegetables make up a full-flavored dinner you can toss together in minutes.

Start to Finish: 30 minutes
Makes: 4 servings

Nutrition Facts per serving:
258 cal., 7 g total fat (2 g sat. fat), 25 mg chol., 523 mg sodium, 31 g carbo., 3 g fiber, 19 g pro.
Daily Values:
10% vit. A, 20% vit. C, 5% calcium, 18% iron
Exchanges:
1 1/2 Vegetable, 1 1/2 Starch, 1 1/2 Meat, 1/2 Fat

240 CALORIES

Pork Soft Shell Tacos

These tacos get their pizzazz from chipotle chili powder. If you can't find it at your supermarket, you can use a crushed chipotle pepper. In a real pinch, regular chili powder will do.

Start to Finish: 25 minutes

Makes: 4 servings

8   ounces boneless pork loin

2   teaspoons cooking oil

¼   cup light dairy sour cream

¼   teaspoon chipotle chili powder, crushed dried chipotle chile pepper, or chili powder

4   6-inch flour tortillas, warmed, if desired*

½   cup shredded lettuce

½   cup diced tomato

½   cup shredded reduced-fat cheddar cheese (2 ounces)

     Bottled salsa

1 If desired, partially freeze pork for easier slicing. Trim fat from pork. Thinly slice pork across the grain into bite-size strips. In a large skillet cook pork strips in hot oil over medium-high heat until cooked through; set aside.

2 In a small bowl combine sour cream and chipotle chili powder, chipotle pepper, or chili powder; set aside.

3 Spoon one-quarter of the pork onto each tortilla just below the center. Top pork with lettuce, tomato, and cheese. Fold top half of each tortilla over filling. Serve with sour cream mixture and salsa.

*Note: To warm tortillas, wrap them in foil. Place in a 350°F oven for 10 to 15 minutes or until warmed.

Nutrition Facts per serving:
240 cal., 11 g total fat (4 g sat. fat), 48 mg chol., 263 mg sodium, 14 g carbo., 1 g fiber, 19 g pro.
Daily Values:
11% vit. A, 12% vit. C, 17% calcium, 8% iron
Exchanges:
½ Vegetable, 1 Starch, 2 Meat, 1½ Fat

- 1 16-ounce loaf frozen wheat or white bread dough, thawed
- 8 ounces lean ham, thinly sliced
- ¼ cup pitted ripe olives, coarsely chopped
- ¼ cup pimiento-stuffed green olives, coarsely chopped
- ¼ cup shredded mozzarella cheese (1 ounce)
- ⅛ teaspoon crushed red pepper flakes
- 1 tablespoon reduced-fat milk
- 1 tablespoon shredded Parmesan cheese (optional)

1 Line a 15×10×1-inch baking pan with foil; grease foil. Set aside. On a lightly floured surface, roll bread dough to a 15×8-inch rectangle. (If dough is difficult to roll out, cover and let rest a few minutes.) Top dough rectangle with ham to within ½ inch of the edges. Top ham with olives, mozzarella cheese, and crushed red pepper flakes. Brush edges with water.

2 Starting with a long end, roll into a spiral, pinching edges to seal. Pinch ends and tuck under. Place, seam side down, on prepared baking pan. Brush surface with milk. Using a sharp knife, make shallow cuts diagonally at 2-inch intervals along the top to allow steam to escape. If desired, sprinkle with Parmesan cheese.

3 Bake in a 375° oven for 25 to 30 minutes or until brown. (If necessary, cover loosely with foil after 20 minutes of baking to prevent overbrowning.)

Quick Stromboli

Frozen bread dough cuts down on preparation time. Be sure, however, to allow time to thoroughly thaw the dough in the refrigerator before using it. (For easier eating, slice this hearty sandwich spiral into 16 slices and serve two slices per serving.)

Prep: 20 minutes **Bake:** 25 minutes
Oven: 375°F **Makes:** 8 servings

206 CALORIES

Nutrition Facts per serving:
206 cal., 5 g total fat (1 g sat. fat), 16 mg chol., 878 mg sodium, 28 g carbo., 2 g fiber, 14 g pro.
Daily Values:
2% vit. A, 1% vit. C, 4% calcium, 3% iron
Exchanges:
2 Starch, 1 Meat

Sausage and Vegetables with Polenta

The key to lightening up this hearty dish is light smoked turkey sausage. The polenta, already cooked, browns up in less than 15 minutes.

Start to Finish: 35 minutes

Makes: 4 servings

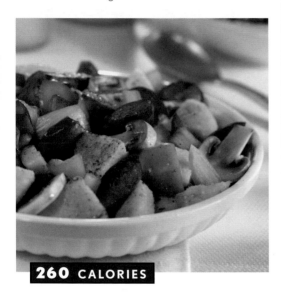

260 CALORIES

- 1 tablespoon olive oil
- 1 1-pound tube refrigerated cooked polenta, cut into 12 slices and quartered
- 8 ounces light smoked turkey sausage, halved lengthwise and cut into 1/2-inch slices
- 2 medium red, green, and/or yellow sweet peppers, cut into bite-size pieces
- 1 medium onion, cut into bite-size pieces
- 1 cup sliced fresh mushrooms
- 1/2 cup purchased pasta sauce

1 In a 12-inch nonstick skillet heat the oil over medium heat. Add polenta in a single layer; cook for 10 to 12 minutes or until lightly browned, stirring occasionally. Remove polenta from skillet; keep warm.

2 Add sausage, sweet peppers, onion, and mushrooms to skillet. Cook and stir until sausage is brown and vegetables are crisp-tender. Stir in pasta sauce. Add polenta; gently toss ingredients to combine. Heat through.

Nutrition Facts per serving:
260 cal., 9 g total fat (2 g sat. fat), 38 mg chol., 1,088 mg sodium, 32 g carbo., 5 g fiber, 14 g pro.
Daily Values:
61% vit. A, 156% vit. C, 2% calcium, 8% iron
Exchanges:
2 Vegetable, 1 1/2 Starch, 1 Meat, 1 Fat

1/4 cup crumbled basil-and-tomato feta cheese (1 ounce)*

2 tablespoons fat-free cream cheese (1 ounce)

4 skinless, boneless chicken breast halves (about 1 1/4 pounds total)

1/4 to 1/2 teaspoon black pepper
Dash salt

1 teaspoon olive oil or cooking oil

1/4 cup chicken broth

1 10-ounce package prewashed fresh spinach, trimmed (8 cups)

2 tablespoons walnut or pecan pieces, toasted

1 tablespoon lemon juice
Lemon slices, halved (optional)

1 In a small bowl combine feta cheese and cream cheese; set aside. Using a sharp knife, cut a horizontal slit through the thickest portion of each chicken breast half to form a pocket. Stuff pockets with the cheese mixture. If necessary, secure openings with wooden toothpicks. Sprinkle chicken with pepper and salt.

2 In a large nonstick skillet cook chicken in hot oil over medium-high heat about 12 minutes or until tender and no longer pink, turning once (reduce heat to medium if chicken browns too quickly). Remove chicken from skillet. Cover and keep warm.

3 Carefully add chicken broth to skillet. Bring to boiling; add half of the spinach. Cover and cook about 3 minutes or just until spinach is wilted. Remove spinach from skillet, reserving liquid in pan. Repeat with remaining spinach. Return all spinach to skillet. Stir in the nuts and lemon juice.

4 To serve, divide spinach mixture among 4 dinner plates. Top with chicken breasts. If desired, garnish with lemon slices.

*Note: If basil-and-tomato feta cheese is not available, stir 1 teaspoon finely snipped fresh basil and 1 teaspoon snipped oil-packed dried tomatoes, drained, into 1/4 cup plain feta cheese.

231 CALORIES

Feta-Stuffed Chicken

Feta is a full-flavored cheese that can be used in small amounts. Here it's mixed with a little fat-free cream cheese (lowering the calorie content even more) and used as a stuffing for chicken.

Start to Finish: 30 minutes
Makes: 4 servings

Nutrition Facts per serving:
231 cal., 8 g total fat (2 g sat. fat), 90 mg chol., 334 mg sodium, 2 g carbo., 6 g fiber, 38 g pro.
Daily Values:
69% vit. A, 31% vit. C, 13% calcium, 31% iron
Exchanges:
1 Vegetable, 4 1/2 Meat

305 CALORIES

Spicy Chicken Pizza

This pizza with a Mexican twist features picante sauce—that's Spanish for spicy! A short list of the ingredients includes chicken, sweet pepper, onion, and cheese.

Prep: 25 minutes **Bake:** 13 minutes
Oven: 400°F **Makes:** 6 servings

- 12 ounces skinless, boneless chicken breasts, cut into thin strips
- 2 teaspoons cooking oil
- 1 medium red sweet pepper, cut into thin strips
- 1/2 of a medium red onion, thinly sliced
  Nonstick cooking spray
- 1 10-ounce package refrigerated pizza dough
- 1/2 cup bottled mild picante sauce
- 1/2 cup shredded sharp cheddar cheese (2 ounces)

1 In a large nonstick skillet cook chicken strips in hot oil over medium-high heat about 5 minutes or until no longer pink. Remove from skillet. Add sweet pepper and onion to skillet; cook about 5 minutes or until tender. Remove from skillet; set aside.

2 Coat a 15×10×1-inch baking pan with nonstick cooking spray. Unroll pizza dough into pan; press with fingers to form a 12×8-inch rectangle. Pinch edges of dough to form a crust.

3 Spread crust with picante sauce. Top with chicken and vegetables; sprinkle with cheddar cheese. Bake in a 400° oven for 13 to 18 minutes or until crust is brown and cheese is melted.

Nutrition Facts per serving:
305 cal., 9 g total fat (3 g sat. fat), 43 mg chol., 527 mg sodium, 34 g carbo., 2 g fiber, 21 g pro.
Daily Values:
25% vit. A, 56% vit. C, 10% calcium, 15% iron
Exchanges:
1/2 Vegetable, 2 Starch, 2 Meat, 1/2 Fat

6 ounces dried fettuccine or linguine

2 cups broccoli or cauliflower florets

1/2 cup reduced-sodium chicken broth

3 tablespoons lemon juice

1 tablespoon honey

2 teaspoons cornstarch

1/4 teaspoon ground white pepper

12 ounces skinless, boneless chicken breasts, cut into bite-size strips

2 teaspoons olive oil or cooking oil

1/2 cup shredded carrot

1 tablespoon snipped fresh tarragon or 1/2 teaspoon dried tarragon, crushed

Lemon slices, halved (optional)

1 Cook pasta according to package directions, adding the broccoli or cauliflower for the last 4 minutes of cooking. Drain.

2 Meanwhile, in a small bowl combine broth, lemon juice, honey, cornstarch, and white pepper; set aside.

3 In a large nonstick skillet stir-fry chicken in hot oil for 3 to 4 minutes or until no longer pink. Stir cornstarch mixture; add to skillet. Cook and stir until thickened and bubbly. Add carrot and tarragon; cook 1 minute more.

4 To serve, spoon chicken mixture over pasta. If desired, garnish with lemon slices. Serve immediately.

Lemon-Tarragon Chicken Toss

A small amount of honey adds a sweet dimension to this lemon-spiked chicken dish.

Start to Finish: 20 minutes

Makes: 4 servings

320 CALORIES

Nutrition Facts per serving:
320 cal., 4 g total fat (1 g sat. fat), 49 mg chol., 143 mg sodium, 43 g carbo., 3 g fiber, 27 g pro.
Daily Values:
90% vit. A, 70% vit. C, 4% calcium, 13% iron
Exchanges:
1 Vegetable, 2 1/2 Starch, 2 1/2 Meat

Chicken Tossed Salad

Personalize this simple salad with your favorite salad dressing. For extra flavor, use the dressing to marinate the chicken as well.

Start to Finish: 20 minutes
Makes: 4 main-dish servings

277 CALORIES

4 skinless, boneless chicken breast halves (about 1 pound total)
1 tablespoon olive oil
¼ teaspoon garlic-pepper blend
8 cups torn mixed salad greens
1 medium yellow or red sweet pepper, cut into bite-size strips
1 medium tomato, cut into wedges
½ cup bottled reduced-calorie salad dressing (such as a berry or roasted garlic vinaigrette or Parmesan-basil Italian)
¼ cup crumbled feta cheese
¼ cup purchased croutons

1 Brush chicken breasts with olive oil; sprinkle with garlic-pepper blend. In a medium nonstick skillet cook chicken over medium heat for 12 to 15 minutes or until no longer pink (170°F). Slice the chicken into bite-size strips. Set aside.

2 In a large serving bowl toss greens, sweet pepper, and tomato; add dressing and toss to coat. Top with chicken, feta cheese, and croutons.

Nutrition Facts per serving:
277 cal., 12 g total fat (2 g sat. fat), 74 mg chol., 536 mg sodium, 12 g carbo., 3 g fiber, 29 g pro.
Daily Values:
44% vit. A, 107% vit. C, 8% calcium, 9% iron
Exchanges:
2 Vegetable, 3½ Meat, ½ Fat

- **1** 10-ounce package torn mixed salad greens
- **8** ounces cooked chicken, cut into bite-size pieces
- **⅓** cup bottled Asian vinaigrette salad dressing
- **1** 11-ounce can mandarin orange sections, drained
- **3** tablespoons sliced almonds, toasted

1 In a large bowl combine greens and chicken. Add salad dressing; toss to coat. Divide greens mixture among 4 salad plates. Top with mandarin orange sections and almonds. Serve immediately.

218 CALORIES

Asian Chicken Salad

When you need something quick and healthy for lunch, this salad is it. The greens are torn and ready to use. The dressing and oranges add a distinctly Asian flavor.

Start to Finish: 15 minutes
Makes: 4 main-dish servings

Nutrition Facts per serving:
218 cal., 9 g total fat (1 g sat. fat), 50 mg chol., 502 mg sodium, 15 g carbo., 2 g fiber, 19 g pro.
Daily Values:
5% vit. A, 15% vit. C, 4% calcium, 9% iron
Exchanges:
1½ Vegetable, ½ Fruit, 2½ Meat, ½ Fat

362 CALORIES

Ginger Noodle Bowl

Thanks to bottled stir-fry sauce, this is a quick meal you can whip up during the busy work week. If you like, substitute regular button mushrooms for shiitakes. Many supermarkets sell button mushrooms already washed and sliced.

Start to Finish: 25 minutes

Makes: 3 servings

2 cups dried Chinese egg noodles or fine egg noodles (4 ounces)

1/4 teaspoon ground ginger

1/3 cup bottled stir-fry sauce

1 cup fresh sugar snap peas or pea pods, tips and stems removed and cut up

1 cup sliced fresh shiitake mushrooms

1 small red sweet pepper, cut into bite-size strips

2 teaspoons peanut oil or cooking oil

5 ounces cooked chicken breast, cut into strips (about 1 cup)

2 tablespoons broken cashews

1 Cook noodles according to package directions. Drain; set aside. Stir ginger into the bottled stir-fry sauce; set aside.

2 In a large skillet cook and stir peas, mushrooms, and sweet pepper in hot oil over medium-high heat for 3 to 5 minutes or until crisp-tender. Add cooked noodles, chicken, stir-fry sauce, and cashews; heat through.

Nutrition Facts per serving:
362 cal., 10 g total fat (2 g sat. fat), 77 mg chol., 734 mg sodium, 42 g carbo., 4 g fiber, 25 g pro.
Daily Values:
29% vit. A, 99% vit. C, 5% calcium, 17% iron
Exchanges:
2 Vegetable, 2 Starch, 2 Meat, 1 1/2 Fat

1 6.2-ounce package quick-cooking
   long grain and wild rice mix
2 14-ounce cans reduced-sodium
   chicken broth
1 tablespoon snipped fresh thyme or
   1 teaspoon dried thyme, crushed
4 cloves garlic, minced
4 cups chopped tomatoes
1 9-ounce package frozen, chopped
   cooked chicken
1 cup finely chopped zucchini
¼ teaspoon freshly ground black pepper
1 tablespoon Madeira or dry sherry

1 Prepare rice mix according to package
directions, except omit the seasoning
packet and the margarine.

2 Meanwhile, in a Dutch oven combine
chicken broth, dried thyme (if using),
and garlic; bring to boiling. Stir in the
tomatoes, chicken, zucchini, pepper, and
fresh thyme (if using). Return to boiling;
reduce heat. Simmer, covered, for
5 minutes. Stir in cooked rice and Madeira
or sherry. Heat through.

Wild Rice
Chicken Soup

The flavors of the Mediterranean shine in
this combination of zucchini, garlic, fresh
herbs, and Madeira. It's a sunny twist on
old-fashioned chicken and rice soup.

Start to Finish: 25 minutes

Makes: 6 main-dish servings (about 10 cups)

223 CALORIES

Nutrition Facts per serving:
223 cal., 4 g total fat (1 g sat. fat), 38 mg chol.,
793 mg sodium, 30 g carbo., 3 g fiber, 18 g pro.
Daily Values:
17% vit. A, 45% vit. C, 5% calcium, 9% iron
Exchanges:
2 Vegetable, 1 Starch, 1½ Meat

Turkey Ravioli Soup

Need a quick meal? This soup is a creative way to use leftover turkey. The ravioli is both unexpected and filling.

Start to Finish: 25 minutes

Makes: 6 main-dish servings (about 8 cups)

246 CALORIES

6	cups reduced-sodium chicken broth
3/4	cup chopped red sweet pepper (1 medium)
1/2	cup chopped onion (1 medium)
1 1/2	teaspoons dried Italian seasoning, crushed
1 1/2	cups cooked turkey, cut into bite-size pieces (about 8 ounces)
1	9-ounce package refrigerated light cheese ravioli
2	cups shredded fresh spinach
	Finely shredded Parmesan cheese (optional)

1 In a Dutch oven combine chicken broth, sweet pepper, onion, and Italian seasoning. Bring to boiling; reduce heat. Simmer, covered, for 5 minutes. Add turkey and ravioli. Return to boiling; reduce heat. Simmer, uncovered, about 6 minutes or just until ravioli is tender. Stir in spinach. If desired, sprinkle with Parmesan cheese.

Nutrition Facts per serving:
246 cal., 7 g total fat (3 g sat. fat), 48 mg chol., 879 mg sodium, 24 g carbo., 2 g fiber, 22 g pro.
Daily Values:
31% vit. A, 56% vit. C, 23% calcium, 16% iron
Exchanges:
1 1/2 Vegetable, 1 Starch, 2 1/2 Meat

- ⅓ cup fine dry bread crumbs
- 2 teaspoons dried Italian seasoning, crushed
- 2 turkey tenderloins (about 1 pound total)
- 2 teaspoons olive oil
- 2 tablespoons snipped fresh basil
- ¼ cup light mayonnaise dressing or salad dressing
- 8 ½-inch slices Italian bread, toasted
- 1 cup bottled roasted red and/or yellow sweet peppers, cut into thin strips
- Fresh basil leaves (optional)

1 In a large plastic bag combine the bread crumbs and Italian seasoning. Slice each turkey tenderloin in half horizontally to make ½-inch steaks. Place a turkey tenderloin steak in bag; seal and shake to coat. Repeat with remaining steaks.

2 In a 12-inch nonstick skillet cook steaks in hot oil over medium heat about 10 minutes or until tender and no longer pink (170°F); turn once.

3 In a small bowl stir 1 tablespoon of the snipped basil into the mayonnaise dressing. Spread dressing mixture on 1 side of 4 bread slices. Top bread slices with turkey steaks, sweet pepper strips, and the remaining snipped basil. If desired, garnish with basil leaves. Top with remaining bread slices.

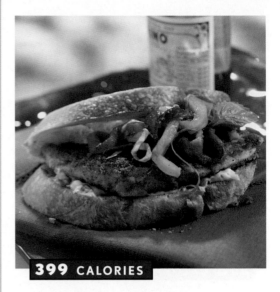

399 CALORIES

Italian Turkey Sandwiches

An aromatic basil-flavored spread takes these sandwiches out of an ordinary realm and puts them into an extraordinary one. Fresh basil is the key here; dried simply doesn't taste as good.

Start to Finish: 20 minutes
Makes: 4 sandwiches

Nutrition Facts per sandwich:
399 cal., 11 g total fat (2 g sat. fat), 73 mg chol., 671 mg sodium, 40 g carbo., 3 g fiber, 33 g pro.
Daily Values:
1% vit. A, 171% vit. C, 9% calcium, 24% iron
Exchanges:
½ Vegetable, 1½ Starch, 3½ Meat, 1½ Fat

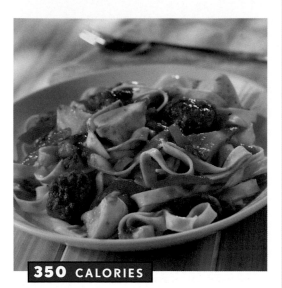

350 CALORIES

Spicy Turkey Pasta Sauce

Use your favorite pasta sauce for this dish, which is quick, easy, low-fat, and best of all, tastes great.

Start to Finish: 25 minutes

Makes: 4 servings

1 9-ounce package refrigerated fettuccine or linguine

8 ounces uncooked turkey Italian sausage (remove casings, if present)

1 cup cut-up pattypan squash or yellow summer squash

1 small red sweet pepper, cut into thin strips

¼ cup chopped red onion

1 14-ounce jar pasta sauce

2 tablespoons shredded Parmesan cheese (optional)

1 Cook pasta according to package directions; drain.

2 Meanwhile, in a large skillet cook the sausage, squash, sweet pepper, and onion over medium heat until sausage is brown; drain off fat. Stir in the pasta sauce; heat through.

3 Serve sausage mixture over pasta. If desired, sprinkle with Parmesan cheese.

Nutrition Facts per serving:
350 cal., 10 g total fat (3 g sat. fat), 115 mg chol., 866 mg sodium, 49 g carbo., 5 g fiber, 20 g pro.
Daily Values:
23% vit. A, 67% vit. C, 11% calcium, 19% iron
Exchanges:
1 Vegetable, 3 Starch, 1½ Meat

¹/₃ cup herb-seasoned stuffing mix,
     crushed (¹/₄ cup)

  2 tablespoons reduced-fat milk

  1 tablespoon snipped fresh sage
     or ¹/₂ teaspoon dried sage, crushed

¹/₄ teaspoon salt

  1 pound uncooked ground turkey

  1 cup torn mixed salad greens,
     watercress leaves, or shredded
     fresh spinach

  4 whole wheat hamburger buns,
     split and toasted

¹/₂ cup whole cranberry sauce

1 Preheat broiler. In a large bowl combine stuffing mix, milk, sage, and salt. Add ground turkey; mix well. Shape into four ½-inch patties. Place patties on unheated rack of a broiler pan. Broil 4 to 5 inches from the heat for 11 to 13 minutes or until internal temperature registers 165°F on an instant-read thermometer; turn once.

2 Divide greens among buns; top with patties and cranberry sauce.

Turkey Burgers with Cranberry Sauce

All the goodness of Thanksgiving dinner comes together in this healthful meal. Cranberry sauce, turkey, stuffing, and sage—without the overeating!

Prep: 12 minutes   **Broil:** 11 minutes
Makes: 4 servings

350 CALORIES

Nutrition Facts per serving:
350 cal., 11 g total fat (3 g sat. fat), 71 mg chol.,
503 mg sodium, 37 g carbo., 3 g fiber, 28 g pro.
Daily Values:
2% vit. A, 2% vit. C, 10% calcium, 17% iron
Exchanges:
2 Starch, ½ Other Carbo., 3 Meat

Turkey-Pear Salad

You'll want to save some leftovers for this special salad. Fruit, turkey, and nuts are a tasty trio, especially when combined with a tangy buttermilk dressing.

Start to Finish: 25 minutes
Makes: 4 main-dish servings

188 CALORIES

$^{1}/_{2}$ cup buttermilk
  2 tablespoons low-fat mayonnaise
     dressing
  1 tablespoon frozen apple juice
     concentrate or frozen orange juice
     concentrate, thawed
  1 teaspoon Dijon-style mustard
  6 cups torn mixed salad greens
  2 medium pears and/or apples, sliced
  8 ounces cooked turkey or chicken,
     cut into bite-size strips (1$^{1}/_{2}$ cups)
$^{1}/_{4}$ cup broken walnuts, toasted (optional)

1 For dressing, in a small bowl stir together buttermilk, mayonnaise dressing, apple juice concentrate, and mustard.

2 In a salad bowl combine salad greens, pear and/or apple slices, and turkey. Drizzle with dressing; toss to coat. If desired, sprinkle with walnuts.

Nutrition Facts per serving:
188 cal., 4 g total fat (1 g sat. fat), 46 mg chol.,
179 mg sodium, 20 g carbo., 3 g fiber, 19 g pro.
Daily Values:
6% vit. A, 12% vit. C, 8% calcium, 10% iron
Exchanges:
1 Vegetable, 1 Fruit, 2 Meat

4 **fresh or frozen fish fillets (such as cod, orange roughy, or pike), about 1/2 inch thick (about 1 pound)**

  Nonstick cooking spray

1/4 **cup fine dry bread crumbs**

1/4 **teaspoon ground ginger**

1/8 **teaspoon salt**

1/8 **teaspoon cayenne pepper**

2 **tablespoons butter or margarine, melted**

4 **lettuce leaves**

4 **baguette-style rolls, hamburger buns, or kaiser rolls, split and toasted**

1 **recipe Ginger Topper**

1 Thaw fish, if frozen. Rinse fish; pat dry with paper towels.

2 Lightly coat a shallow baking pan with nonstick cooking spray; set aside. In a small bowl combine bread crumbs, ginger, salt, and cayenne pepper; set aside. Place fish fillets on waxed paper. Brush tops and sides of the fish with melted butter; coat tops and sides with crumb mixture.

3 Arrange the fish fillets in a single layer, crumb sides up, in prepared baking pan. Bake, uncovered, in a 450° oven for 4 to 6 minutes or until fish flakes easily when tested with a fork.

4 To serve, top bottoms of rolls with lettuce, fish, and Ginger Topper. Add roll tops.

Ginger Topper: In a small bowl stir together 1/4 cup low-fat mayonnaise dressing, 1 teaspoon orange marmalade, and 1/4 teaspoon ground ginger.

319 CALORIES

Fish Sandwich with Ginger Mayonnaise

A fast-food fish sandwich contains more fat than you probably think. This tasty alternative cuts the calories and fat, and takes only 15 minutes to make.

Start to Finish: 15 minutes **Oven:** 450°F
Makes: 4 servings

Nutrition Facts per serving:
319 cal., 10 g total fat (5 g sat. fat), 68 mg chol., 711 mg sodium, 31 g carbo., 2 g fiber, 25 g pro.
Daily Values:
14% vit. A, 9% vit. C, 11% calcium, 14% iron
Exchanges:
2 Starch, 3 Meat

292 CALORIES

Mediterranean Shrimp Packets

You'll treasure these tasty weeknight wonders. Because you fold up the ingredients in parchment or foil, cleanup is a snap. Twenty-five minutes to make, 25 minutes to relax. Ahhh . . .

Prep: 25 minutes   **Bake:** 25 minutes
Oven: 425°F   **Makes:** 4 servings

Nutrition Facts per serving:
292 cal., 3 g total fat (0 g sat. fat), 88 mg chol., 696 mg sodium, 46 g carbo., 7 g fiber, 20 g pro.
Daily Values:
29% vit. A, 67% vit. C, 9% calcium, 14% iron
Exchanges:
2 Vegetable, 2 Starch, 1 1/2 Meat

8   ounces fresh or frozen peeled and deveined medium shrimp
1   cup quick-cooking couscous
1   cup boiling water
2   small zucchini and/or yellow summer squash, halved lengthwise and thinly sliced
1   small red, yellow, or green sweet pepper, cut into thin bite-size strips
1   9-ounce package frozen artichoke hearts, thawed
1/4   teaspoon coarsely ground black pepper
1/8   teaspoon salt
1/2   cup bottled reduced-calorie Italian salad dressing
1/4   cup thinly sliced fresh basil or fresh spinach

1 Thaw shrimp, if frozen. Rinse shrimp; pat dry with paper towels. Set aside. Cut four 16×12-inch pieces of parchment or use precut sheets. (Or tear off four 24×18-inch pieces of heavy foil. Fold each piece in half to make four 18×12-inch pieces.)

2 In a small saucepan combine couscous and boiling water; cover and let stand for 5 minutes. Divide couscous mixture, shrimp, squash, sweet pepper, and artichokes evenly among the 4 pieces of parchment or foil. Sprinkle with black pepper and salt. Drizzle with salad dressing.

3 Bring together 2 opposite edges of parchment or foil; seal with a double fold. Fold remaining ends to completely enclose the food, allowing space for steam to build. Place the packets in a single layer on a baking pan.

4 Bake in a 425° oven about 25 minutes or until shrimp turn opaque (carefully open a packet to check). Carefully open packets and sprinkle each with 1 tablespoon of the basil or spinach.

8   8-inch round spring roll wrappers

8   ounces fresh or frozen cooked, peeled,
    and deveined shrimp, coarsely
    chopped (1¹/₃ cups)

1   small head Bibb lettuce, cored and
    shredded (2 cups)

1   cup shredded carrots (2 medium)

¹/₄ cup sliced green onions (2)

2   tablespoons snipped fresh cilantro

5   tablespoons purchased peanut
    dipping sauce

2   tablespoons seasoned rice vinegar

1 Place some warm water in a shallow dish. Dip each spring roll wrapper in warm water; place between damp paper towels for 10 minutes.

2 Meanwhile, for filling, in a large bowl combine shrimp, lettuce, carrots, green onions, and cilantro. Add 2 tablespoons of the peanut dipping sauce and 1 tablespoon of the rice vinegar. Toss ingredients to coat.

3 For the dipping sauce, in a small bowl stir together the remaining 3 tablespoons peanut sauce and 1 tablespoon rice vinegar; set aside.

4 Place about ½ cup of the filling about ½ inch from the bottom edge of 1 of the moistened spring roll wrappers. Fold the bottom edge of the wrapper over the filling. Fold in sides. Roll up. Repeat with remaining filling and spring roll wrappers. Cut in half. Serve with dipping sauce.

Asian Spring Rolls

When you want a quick dinner that stays far away from run-of-the-mill, try these spring rolls. Here shrimp and vegetables make up the filling. Serve the rolls with peanut sauce for dipping.

Start to Finish: 30 minutes

Makes: 4 servings (8 rolls)

214 CALORIES

Nutrition Facts per serving:
214 cal., 4 g total fat (1 g sat. fat), 111 mg chol., 524 mg sodium, 29 g carbo., 2 g fiber, 15 g pro.
Daily Values:
181% vit. A, 17% vit. C, 5% calcium, 15% iron
Exchanges:
2 Vegetable, 1 Starch, 1½ Meat

Broccoli and Tomato Penne

Broccoli brightens this quick-and-easy entrée. Classic Italian ingredients—garlic, basil, mushrooms, tomato, and Parmesan cheese—dominate the flavor.

Start to Finish: 25 minutes

Makes: 4 servings

275 CALORIES

2¼ cups dried penne or cut ziti (about 8 ounces)

 4 cups broccoli florets

½ cup oil-packed dried tomatoes

 1 cup sliced fresh shiitake mushrooms

¼ teaspoon crushed red pepper

 3 cloves garlic, minced

½ cup shredded fresh basil

Shaved Parmesan cheese (optional)

1 Cook pasta according to package directions, adding broccoli to the pasta for the last 2 minutes of cooking. Drain. Return pasta and broccoli to hot pan.

2 Meanwhile, drain the tomatoes, reserving 2 tablespoons of the oil. Cut tomatoes into strips.

3 In a medium saucepan cook mushrooms, crushed red pepper, and garlic in the hot reserved oil for 3 to 4 minutes or until the mushrooms are tender. Stir in basil. Add to pasta along with tomato strips; toss gently to combine. If desired, top with Parmesan cheese.

Nutrition Facts per serving:
275 cal., 4 g total fat (0 g sat. fat), 0 mg chol., 63 mg sodium, 52 g carbo., 6 g fiber, 12 g pro.
Daily Values:
32% vit. A, 129% vit. C, 7% calcium, 17% iron
Exchanges:
1½ Vegetable, 3 Starch

On the divider: Egg Salad Sandwiches (see recipe, page 152)

1½   **pounds lean ground beef**

½   **cup chopped onion (1 medium)**

⅓   **cup chopped green sweet pepper**

1   **10³⁄₄-ounce can reduced-fat and reduced-sodium condensed tomato soup**

1   **tablespoon Worcestershire sauce**

1   **tablespoon prepared mustard**

   Dill pickle slices (optional)

8   **whole wheat or white hamburger buns, split and toasted**

1 In a large skillet cook ground beef, onion, and sweet pepper until beef is brown. Drain off fat. Stir in the soup, Worcestershire sauce, and mustard. Bring to boiling; reduce heat. Simmer, covered, for 5 minutes. Serve, topped with pickles (if desired), on toasted hamburger buns.

289 CALORIES

Sloppy Beef Burgers

You've probably had soup and a burger as a meal, but did you ever have soup in a burger? It's the soup that makes these loose-meat burgers so good and saucy. Simply add dill pickles and buns, and dinner is ready in less than half an hour.

Start to Finish: 25 minutes
Makes: 8 servings

Nutrition Facts per serving:
289 cal., 11 g total fat (4 g sat. fat), 54 mg chol., 417 mg sodium, 27 g carbo., 2 g fiber, 20 g pro.
Daily Values:
1% vit. A, 16% vit. C, 5% calcium, 19% iron
Exchanges:
2 Starch, 2 Meat

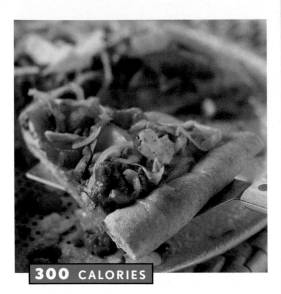

300 CALORIES

Taco Pizza

Intermingle pizza and tacos and what do you get? An instant kid classic. Why didn't you think of it sooner?

Prep: 30 minutes   **Bake:** 16 minutes
Oven: 425°F   **Makes:** 8 servings

Nonstick cooking spray

1   1-pound loaf frozen whole wheat bread dough, thawed

1   cup shredded cheddar cheese (4 ounces)

12   ounces lean ground beef

½   cup chopped onion (1 medium)

⅔   cup bottled salsa

1½   cups chopped tomatoes (2 medium)

½   to 1 cup shredded lettuce and/or spinach

1   cup baked tortilla chips, coarsely crushed, or ½ cup tortilla chips, coarsely crushed

Light dairy sour cream (optional)

Bottled salsa (optional)

1 Lightly coat a 12- to 13-inch pizza pan with nonstick cooking spray. Pat dough evenly into prepared pan, extending edges over pan slightly. (If dough is hard to pat out, allow to rest for 10 minutes.) Sprinkle half of the cheese in a thin strip around the edge of the dough. Moisten edge of dough. Fold down edge over cheese and seal tightly to enclose the cheese. Prick crust all over with a fork. Bake in a 425° oven for 10 minutes.

2 Meanwhile, in a large skillet cook the ground beef and onion until meat is brown and onion is tender. Drain off fat. Stir in the ⅔ cup salsa. Top partially baked crust with meat mixture. Bake for 5 minutes more. Sprinkle with tomatoes and remaining cheese. Bake for 1 to 2 minutes more or until cheese melts.

3 To serve, top with lettuce and tortilla chips. If desired, serve with sour cream and additional salsa.

Nutrition Facts per serving:
300 cal., 11 g total fat (5 g sat. fat), 42 mg chol., 477 mg sodium, 32 g carbo., 3 g fiber, 19 g pro.
Daily Values:
10% vit. A, 16% vit. C, 12% calcium, 7% iron
Exchanges:
1 Vegetable, 2 Starch, 1½ Meat

6 8-inch fat-free flour tortillas

12 ounces extra-lean ground beef

½ cup chopped onion (1 medium)

2 cloves garlic, minced

½ cup chopped green sweet pepper
   (1 small)

½ cup bottled salsa or picante sauce

2 teaspoons dried Mexican seasoning

1½ cups shredded lettuce

1 cup chopped tomatoes (2 medium)

½ cup shredded reduced-fat cheddar or
   Monterey Jack cheese (2 ounces)

   Shredded reduced-fat cheddar or
   Monterey Jack cheese (optional)

   Bottled salsa or picante sauce
   (optional)

1 Wrap tortillas in foil; bake in a 350° oven about 10 minutes or until warmed.

2 Meanwhile, in a large skillet cook the ground beef, onion, and garlic over medium-high heat until meat is brown and onion is tender. Drain off fat. Stir in sweet pepper, the ½ cup salsa or picante sauce, and the Mexican seasoning. Bring to boiling; reduce heat. Simmer, covered, for 10 minutes.

3 Place tortillas on work surface. Top each tortilla with about ½ cup of the meat mixture and some of the lettuce and tomatoes. Sprinkle with the ½ cup cheese. Fold in sides; roll up. Cut in half to serve. If desired, sprinkle with additional cheese and pass additional salsa or picante sauce.

Soft-Shell Burritos

When you have picky eaters at your table, turn to these soft burritos. Wrapped in flour tortillas, they're not only tasty, you also can pick them up to eat them.

Start to Finish: 35 minutes
Oven: 350°F   **Makes:** 6 servings

252 CALORIES

Nutrition Facts per serving:
252 cal., 7 g total fat (3 g sat. fat), 42 mg chol., 532 mg sodium, 29 g carbo., 2 g fiber, 16 g pro.
Daily Values:
14% vit. A, 38% vit. C, 9% calcium, 14% iron
Exchanges:
1 Vegetable, 1½ Starch, 2 Meat

Chicken Fingers

Skip the fast-food chicken fingers. These homemade nuggets are crunchy, juicy, and delicious. Plus, they're baked, instead of fried. Hint: Honey mustard, reduced-calorie buttermilk dressing, or sweet-and-sour sauce is great for dipping.

Prep: 15 minutes **Bake:** 12 minutes
Oven: 450°F **Makes:** 4 servings

12 **ounces skinless, boneless chicken breasts**
 1 **slightly beaten egg**
 1 **tablespoon honey**
 1 **teaspoon prepared mustard**
 1 **cup packaged cornflake crumbs or 2 cups cornflakes, finely crushed**
    Dash black pepper
    Purchased dipping sauce (optional)

1 Cut chicken into 3×¾-inch strips. In a shallow dish combine the egg, honey, and mustard. In another shallow dish stir together cornflake crumbs and pepper. Dip chicken strips into the egg mixture; roll in crumb mixture to coat.

2 Arrange chicken strips on an ungreased baking sheet. Bake in a 450° oven about 12 minutes or until golden and chicken is tender and no longer pink. If desired, serve with your favorite dipping sauce.

212 CALORIES

Nutrition Facts per serving:
212 cal., 3 g total fat (1 g sat. fat), 102 mg chol., 236 mg sodium, 23 g carbo., 0 g fiber, 23 g pro.
Daily Values:
2% vit. A, 1% vit. C, 2% calcium, 24% iron
Exchanges:
1¹⁄₂ Starch, 2¹⁄₂ Meat

- **1** 8-ounce can pineapple chunks (juice-pack)
- **1/2** cup bottled sweet-and-sour sauce
- **12** ounces skinless, boneless chicken breasts, cut into 1-inch pieces
- **1** tablespoon reduced-sodium soy sauce
- **1** medium red sweet pepper, cut into bite-size strips (1 cup)
- **1/2** cup thinly sliced carrot (1)
- **4** teaspoons cooking oil
- **1** cup fresh pea pods, tips and stems removed
- **2** cups hot cooked rice

1 Drain pineapple, reserving 2 tablespoons of the juice; set pineapple chunks aside. In a small bowl stir together the reserved pineapple juice and the sweet-and-sour sauce; set aside. In a medium bowl toss chicken with soy sauce; set aside.

2 In a large nonstick skillet cook and stir sweet pepper and carrot in 3 teaspoons of the hot oil over medium-high heat for 3 minutes. Add pea pods. Cook and stir about 1 minute more or until vegetables are crisp-tender. Remove from skillet; set aside.

3 Add remaining 1 teaspoon oil to skillet. Using a slotted spoon, add chicken to skillet. Cook and stir for 3 to 4 minutes or until chicken is no longer pink. Add sweet-and-sour sauce mixture, vegetable mixture, and pineapple chunks; heat through. Serve chicken mixture with hot cooked rice.

337 CALORIES

Sweet-and-Sour Chicken

A perennial favorite of all ages, sweet-and-sour chicken can be made quickly—without deep frying.

Start to Finish: 25 minutes
Makes: 4 or 5 servings

Nutrition Facts per serving:
337 cal., 6 g total fat (1 g sat. fat), 49 mg chol., 297 mg sodium, 46 g carbo., 3 g fiber, 23 g pro.
Daily Values:
121% vit. A, 129% vit. C, 5% calcium, 13% iron
Exchanges:
1 1/2 Vegetable, 1 Fruit, 1 1/2 Starch, 2 1/2 Meat, 1 Fat

172 CALORIES

Choose-a-Vegetable Chicken and Pasta Soup

Let the kids choose which vegetables to add; the more variety, the more colorful the soup will be. Every time you include kids in the act of cooking, they become more comfortable working in the kitchen.

Start to Finish: 40 minutes

Makes: 6 main-dish servings (about 7½ cups)

2   **14-ounce cans reduced-sodium chicken broth**

2   **cups water**

¼   **teaspoon black pepper**

1   **cup dried twisted spaghetti or broken fusilli**

3   **cups vegetable pieces (such as thinly sliced carrots, small broccoli florets, chopped green or red sweet pepper, and/or fresh or frozen whole kernel corn)**

1½   **cups cubed cooked chicken (about 8 ounces)**

1   **tablespoon snipped fresh basil**

¼   **cup finely shredded Parmesan cheese (1 ounce)**

1 In a Dutch oven combine the broth, the water, and black pepper; bring to boiling. Stir in the pasta. Return to boiling; reduce heat. Simmer, covered, for 5 minutes. Stir in vegetables. Return to boiling; reduce heat. Simmer, covered, for 5 to 8 minutes more or until vegetables and pasta are tender. Stir in chicken and basil; heat through. To serve, top with Parmesan cheese.

Nutrition Facts per serving:
172 cal., 4 g total fat (2 g sat. fat), 35 mg chol., 447 mg sodium, 18 g carbo., 2 g fiber, 16 g pro.
Daily Values:
309% vit. A, 7% vit. C, 7% calcium, 7% iron
Exchanges:
1 Vegetable, 1 Starch, 1½ Meat

Chef's Salad

1 small head iceberg lettuce, cored and cut crosswise into 4 slices

4 ounces cooked lower-fat ham or turkey, cut into bite-size pieces

1/2 cup shredded reduced-fat cheddar cheese (2 ounces)

1 hard-cooked egg, sliced

8 cherry tomatoes, halved

1 small yellow or red sweet pepper, cut into bite-size strips*

1/2 cup purchased croutons

1/2 cup bottled reduced-fat ranch salad dressing

1 Place one slice of lettuce on each of 4 large salad plates. Arrange meat, cheese, egg, tomatoes, and sweet pepper on the greens. Sprinkle with croutons. Drizzle with dressing.

*Note: For a decorative touch, use tiny cookie or hors d'oeuvre cutters to cut the sweet pepper into shapes.

Introduce your kids to main-dish salads with this tasty classic. Ham, cheese, egg, and croutons will fill them up the nutritious way.

Start to Finish: 30 minutes

Makes: 4 main-dish servings

197 CALORIES

Nutrition Facts per serving:
197 cal., 12 g total fat (2 g sat. fat), 86 mg chol., 883 mg sodium, 11 g carbo., 2 g fiber, 13 g pro.
Daily Values:
12% vit. A, 109% vit. C, 13% calcium, 7% iron
Exchanges:
2 Vegetable, 1½ Meat, 1½ Fat

Lunch Box Sub Sandwiches

It's a good idea to keep these ingredients on hand for your little ones' lunches. They'll love the sweet surprise of cherries or raisins in the spread.

Start to Finish: 15 minutes
Makes: 4 sandwiches

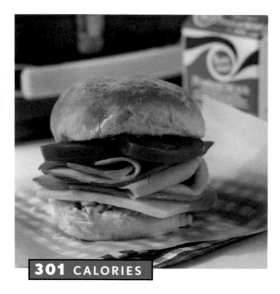

301 CALORIES

¼ cup low-fat mayonnaise dressing
1 teaspoon Dijon-style mustard
¼ cup finely snipped dried tart cherries or raisins
4 hamburger buns, split
4 ³⁄₄-ounce slices mozzarella cheese
6 ounces thinly sliced cooked turkey breast
1 medium tomato, thinly sliced

1 In a small bowl stir together the mayonnaise dressing, mustard, and cherries or raisins. Spread the bottoms of the buns with the dressing mixture. Top with cheese, turkey, and tomato. Add bun tops.

Make-ahead directions: Prepare as above. Wrap each sandwich in plastic wrap. Chill for up to 24 hours. To tote, place in insulated lunch bags with an ice pack.

Nutrition Facts per sandwich:
301 cal., 8 g total fat (3 g sat. fat), 45 mg chol., 515 mg sodium, 34 g carbo., 2 g fiber, 22 g pro.
Daily Values:
7% vit. A, 11% vit. C, 22% calcium, 13% iron
Exchanges:
2 Starch, 2½ Meat

2½ cups dried radiatore, rotelle, or elbow macaroni (8 ounces)

2 cups reduced-fat milk

2 tablespoons all-purpose flour

½ teaspoon dry mustard

¼ teaspoon salt

⅛ teaspoon black pepper

½ cup shredded cheddar cheese (2 ounces)

2 ounces American cheese, cubed (½ cup)

½ cup coarsely crushed purchased seasoned croutons

2 tablespoons finely shredded Parmesan cheese

Cheese shapes* (optional)

1 Cook pasta according to package directions; drain and return to pan.

2 Meanwhile, in a large screw-top jar combine 1 cup of the milk, the flour, mustard, salt, and pepper; cover and shake until combined. Pour into a medium saucepan. Stir in the remaining 1 cup milk. Cook and stir over medium heat just until bubbly. Reduce heat to low. Add cheddar cheese and American cheese, stirring until melted. Pour sauce over pasta, stirring until combined. Spoon into a 1½-quart casserole.

3 Bake, covered, in a 350° oven for 15 minutes. In a small bowl stir together the croutons and Parmesan cheese; sprinkle over casserole. Bake, uncovered, about 5 minutes more or until heated through. Let stand 5 minutes before serving. If desired, garnish each serving with a cheese shape.

*Note: To make cheese shapes, cut ½-inch slices of American cheese; use 1-inch cookie or hors d'oeuvre cutters to cut cheese into shapes.

346 CALORIES

Macaroni and Cheese

Kids love macaroni and cheese from the box, but do you wonder what's really in it? This homemade version tastes great and is nutritious too. It might take more effort than the boxed variety, but it is worth it.

Prep: 30 minutes   **Bake:** 20 minutes
Stand: 5 minutes   **Oven:** 350°F
Makes: 5 servings

Nutrition Facts per serving:
346 cal., 11 g total fat (7 g sat. fat), 33 mg chol., 479 mg sodium, 44 g carbo., 2 g fiber, 16 g pro.
Daily Values:
10% vit. A, 2% vit. C, 31% calcium, 10% iron
Exchanges:
3 Starch, 1 Meat

365 CALORIES

Egg Salad Sandwiches

What would moms do without egg salad sandwiches? Low-fat mayonnaise dressing cuts the calories, while shredded cheese adds a new kick kids will love.

Start to Finish: 20 minutes

Makes: 5 sandwiches

4	hard-cooked eggs, chopped
1/4	cup shredded reduced-fat Colby Jack cheese (1 ounce)
2	tablespoons sweet or dill pickle relish
2	tablespoons finely chopped red sweet pepper
1/4	cup low-fat mayonnaise dressing
1	tablespoon prepared mustard
10	slices whole wheat and/or white bread
5	small romaine leaves
	Halved cherry tomatoes and/or thin, bite-size carrot strips

1 In a medium bowl stir together the eggs, cheese, relish, sweet pepper, mayonnaise dressing, and mustard.

2 If desired, use large cookie cutters to cut bread slices into shapes. Line 5 bread slices with lettuce. Spread on the egg mixture. Top with the remaining bread slices. If desired, garnish sandwiches with cherry tomatoes and/or carrots, using wooden toothpicks to secure.

Nutrition Facts per sandwich:
365 cal., 11 g total fat (3 g sat. fat), 176 mg chol., 599 mg sodium, 54 g carbo., 6 g fiber, 15 g pro.
Daily Values:
12% vit. A, 14% vit. C, 10% calcium, 20% iron
Exchanges:
3 1/2 Starch, 1 Meat, 1/2 Fat

¼ cup canned fat-free refried beans

4 6- to 8-inch flour tortillas

¾ cup shredded reduced-fat sharp cheddar cheese (3 ounces)

Bottled salsa (optional)

1 Spread 1 tablespoon of the refried beans on one half of a tortilla.

2 Place bean-topped tortilla, bean side up, in a medium skillet or on a griddle. Sprinkle one-quarter of the cheese over the bean-topped tortilla.

3 Cook over medium heat about 3 minutes or until cheese begins to melt. Fold tortilla in half. Turn and cook 1 to 2 minutes more or until golden brown. Repeat with remaining refried beans, tortillas, and cheese.

4 To serve, cut each quesadilla into thirds. If desired, serve with salsa.

Cheese and Bean Quesadillas

Dinner is fiesta time, not siesta time, with these tasty tortillas filled with cheese and refried beans.

Start to Finish: 20 minutes

Makes: 4 servings

148 CALORIES

Nutrition Facts per serving:
148 cal., 5 g total fat (3 g sat. fat), 15 mg chol., 300 mg sodium, 14 g carbo., 1 g fiber, 8 g pro.
Daily Values:
18% calcium, 5% iron
Exchanges:
1 Starch, ½ Meat, ½ Fat

Banana Waffle Stacks

Dare your kids to claim they're not hungry. This breakfast looks and tastes like dessert. Make either the mini waffles (shown) or the regular size waffles (instructions follow recipe).

Prep: 15 minutes
Bake: per waffle baker directions
Makes: 24 miniwaffles (8 servings) or 12 four-inch waffles (6 servings)

228 CALORIES

Nonstick cooking spray
1³/₄ **cups all-purpose flour**
  1 **tablespoon sugar**
  1 **tablespoon baking powder**
¹/₄ **teaspoon salt**
¹/₄ **teaspoon ground cinnamon**
1¹/₂ **cups fat-free milk**
²/₃ **cup mashed ripe bananas (2 medium)**
  1 **slightly beaten egg**
  2 **tablespoons cooking oil**
  2 **cups bias-sliced banana**
¹/₂ **cup frozen light whipped dessert topping**
  8 **maraschino cherries**

1 Lightly coat the grids of a waffle baker with nonstick cooking spray. Preheat waffle baker according to manufacturer's directions. Meanwhile, in a large bowl stir together the flour, sugar, baking powder, salt, and cinnamon; set aside. In a medium bowl stir together the milk, mashed bananas, egg, and oil. Add to flour mixture and stir until combined (batter should be slightly lumpy).

2 Spoon about 2 tablespoons batter onto each quarter of the waffle baker. Close lid quickly; do not open until done. Bake according to manufacturer's directions. When done, use a fork to lift waffle off grids. Repeat with remaining batter. Serve waffles warm with banana slices. Top with dessert topping and a cherry.

Banana Waffles: Prepare as above through step 1. Pour about 1 cup of the batter onto grids of the prepared waffle baker. Bake and serve as above. Makes 6 servings (two 4-inch waffles per serving).

Nutrition Facts per serving (miniwaffles):
228 cal., 5 g total fat (1 g sat. fat), 27 mg chol., 257 mg sodium, 41 g carbo., 2 g fiber, 6 g pro.
Daily Values:
4% vit. A, 11% vit. C, 16% calcium, 8% iron
Exchanges:
1 Fruit, 1¹/₂ Starch, 1 Fat

Nutrition Facts per serving (4-inch waffles):
304 cal., 7 g total fat (1 g sat. fat), 36 mg chol., 343 mg sodium, 55 g carbo., 3 g fiber, 8 g pro.
Daily Values:
5% vit. A, 15% vit. C, 21% calcium, 11% iron
Exchanges:
1¹/₂ Fruit, 2¹/₂ Starch, 1 Fat

2 **cups packaged peeled baby carrots**

1 **tablespoon butter or margarine**

2 **tablespoons orange marmalade**

1 In a covered medium saucepan cook the carrots in lightly salted boiling water for 5 minutes. Drain; set carrots aside.

2 In the same saucepan melt the butter over medium heat. Add the carrots and orange marmalade. Cook and stir for 2 to 3 minutes or until carrots are tender and glazed.

77 CALORIES

Orange-Glazed Baby Carrots

How do you get kids to eat their carrots? Toss them with orange marmalade. A dab of butter not only helps the marmalade stick to the carrots, but it also adds body.

Start to Finish: 15 minutes

Makes: 4 side-dish servings

Nutrition Facts per serving:
77 cal., 3 g total fat (2 g sat. fat), 8 mg chol., 57 mg sodium, 13 g carbo., 2 g fiber, 1 g pro.
Daily Values:
310% vit. A, 8% vit. C, 2% calcium, 2% iron
Exchanges:
1 Vegetable, 1/2 Fat

105 CALORIES

Oven-Roasted Fries

French fries have become a mainstay in the diets of the young and old. These oven-roasted fries taste just as good as the fast-food variety and are much better for you. Grated Parmesan supplies an unconventional extra.

Prep: 10 minutes **Bake:** 22 minutes
Oven: 450°F **Makes:** 6 side-dish servings

4   teaspoons olive oil
4   medium baking potatoes (1¹/₂ pounds total), scrubbed
¹/₂ teaspoon salt
¹/₈ to ¹/₄ teaspoon freshly ground black pepper
¹/₄ cup grated Parmesan cheese (1 ounce)

1 Line a 15×10×1-inch baking pan with heavy-duty foil; brush with 2 teaspoons of the oil. Set aside.

2 Cut the potatoes lengthwise into ¹/₂-inch wedges. Transfer to a large bowl. Add remaining 2 teaspoons oil; toss to coat. Sprinkle potato wedges with salt and pepper, tossing to coat. Arrange potato wedges in a single layer in prepared baking pan.

3 Bake in a 450° oven for 12 minutes. Carefully turn potato wedges; sprinkle with cheese. Bake for 10 to 12 minutes more or until potatoes are tender and golden. Serve immediately.

Nutrition Facts per serving:
105 cal., 4 g total fat (1 g sat. fat), 3 mg chol., 262 mg sodium, 14 g carbo., 1 g fiber, 3 g pro.
Daily Values:
22% vit. C, 6% calcium, 7% iron
Exchanges:
1 Starch, ¹/₂ Fat

1 **8-ounce can pineapple tidbits (juice-pack)**

1 **cup shredded carrots (2 medium)**

1 **11-ounce can mandarin orange sections, drained**

²/₃ **cup chopped apple (1 medium)**

¹/₂ **cup raisins and/or dried tart cherries**

¹/₃ **cup apple-cinnamon-flavored low-fat yogurt**

2 **tablespoons peanut butter**

1 **tablespoon shelled sunflower seeds**

1 Drain the pineapple tidbits, reserving 1 tablespoon of the juice; set juice aside. If desired, set aside some of the shredded carrots for garnish. In a medium bowl stir together the pineapple tidbits, the remaining carrots, oranges, apple, and raisins and/or cherries.

2 In a small bowl stir together the yogurt, peanut butter, and reserved pineapple juice. Add to fruit mixture; stir to coat.

3 To serve, sprinkle with sunflower seeds and, if desired, reserved carrots.

Make-ahead directions: Prepare as above through step 2. Cover and chill up to 1 hour. To serve, sprinkle with the sunflower seeds.

Peanut Butter-Fruit Salad

This tastes so good, kids will have no idea how nutritious it is. Serve it as a side dish or snack.

Start to Finish: 15 minutes
Makes: 6 side-dish servings

152 CALORIES

Nutrition Facts per serving:
152 cal., 4 g total fat (1 g sat. fat), 1 mg chol., 44 mg sodium, 29 g carbo., 3 g fiber, 3 g pro.
Daily Values:
121% vit. A, 36% vit. C, 5% calcium, 5% iron
Exchanges:
2 Fruit, 1 Fat

Tropical Trail Mix

Even the little ones can stir together a batch of this high-energy snack mix. Thrown into a self-sealing plastic bag, it's perfect for hiking, biking, or backyard munching.

Start to Finish: 10 minutes

Makes: about 4¹/₂ cups

180 CALORIES

1 cup chopped dried pineapple (6 ounces)

1 cup chopped dried mango (4¹/₂ ounces)

1 cup honey-roasted peanuts

1 6- or 7-ounce package mixed dried fruit bits (1¹/₄ to 1¹/₂ cups)

1 In a large bowl combine pineapple, mango, peanuts, and fruit bits.

Make-ahead directions: Prepare as above. Transfer to a self-sealing plastic bag or an airtight storage container. Seal and store in a cool, dry place up to 1 week.

Nutrition Facts per ¹/₄ cup:
180 cal., 5 g total fat (1 g sat. fat), 0 mg chol., 58 mg sodium, 34 g carbo., 1 g fiber, 4 g pro.
Daily Values:
12% vit. A, 4% vit. C, 1% calcium, 3% iron
Exchanges:
2 Fruit, 1 Fat

2 cups frozen unsweetened peach slices

1³/₄ cups milk

1 to 2 tablespoons honey

1 teaspoon vanilla

1 In a blender container combine frozen peach slices, milk, honey, and vanilla. Cover and blend until smooth. Pour into glasses.

145 CALORIES

Peach Shakes

A mere 10 minutes is all it takes to make this delightful fruit shake. Keep the ingredients on hand for nutritious after-school snacks.

Start to Finish: 10 minutes
Makes: 3 (about 10-ounce) servings

Nutrition Facts per serving:
145 cal., 3 g total fat (2 g sat. fat), 11 mg chol., 72 mg sodium, 25 g carbo., 2 g fiber, 5 g pro.
Daily Values:
18% vit. A, 15% vit. C, 18% calcium, 1% iron
Exchanges:
¹/₂ Milk, 1 Fruit

196 CALORIES

Fruit-Filled Waffle Bowls

These waffle bowls are a great way to get your kids to eat more fruit. Let them choose their favorite pudding flavor and their favorite fruits, and you're sure to please them.

Start to Finish: 10 minutes

Makes: 4 servings

1 **4-serving-size package instant lemon or white chocolate pudding mix**

1⅓ **cups milk**

4 **waffle ice cream bowls or large waffle ice cream cones**

1 **cup fresh fruit (such as blueberries, sliced kiwifruit, sliced strawberries, sliced bananas, or raspberries)**

Fresh mint leaves (optional)

1 Prepare pudding according to package directions using the 1⅓ cups milk. Spoon fruit into waffle bowls or cones. Top with pudding. If desired, garnish with fresh mint leaves. Serve immediately.

Nutrition Facts per serving:
196 cal., 3 g total fat (1 g sat. fat), 6 mg chol., 399 mg sodium, 40 g carbo., 1 g fiber, 3 g pro.
Daily Values:
4% vit. A, 35% vit. C, 10% calcium, 5% iron
Exchanges:
½ Fruit, 2 Starch

Nonstick cooking spray

1/4 **cup butter or margarine**

2/3 **cup granulated sugar**

1/2 **cup cold water**

1 **teaspoon vanilla**

1 **cup all-purpose flour**

1/4 **cup unsweetened cocoa powder**

1 **teaspoon baking powder**

1/4 **cup miniature semisweet chocolate pieces**

2 **teaspoons sifted powdered sugar**

1 Lightly coat the bottom of a 9×9×2-inch baking pan with nonstick cooking spray, being careful not to coat the sides of pan.

2 In a medium saucepan melt butter; remove from heat. Stir in granulated sugar, the water, and vanilla. Stir in flour, cocoa powder, and baking powder until combined. Stir in chocolate pieces. Pour batter into prepared pan.

3 Bake in a 350° oven for 15 to 18 minutes or until a wooden toothpick inserted near the center comes out clean. Cool on a wire rack. Remove from pan. Cut into 16 bars. Sprinkle with the powdered sugar.

Double Chocolate Brownies

One small brownie square served after dinner satisfies every kid's need for sweets.

Prep: 10 minutes   **Bake:** 15 minutes
Oven: 350°F   **Makes:** 16 brownies

103 CALORIES

Nutrition Facts per brownie:
103 cal., 4 g total fat (2 g sat. fat), 8 mg chol., 56 mg sodium, 16 g carbo., 0 g fiber, 1 g pro.
Daily Values:
2% vit. A, 3% calcium, 3% iron
Exchanges:
1 Starch, 1/2 Fat

Cakey Chocolate Chip Cookies

These are the chocolate chip cookies your children will beg for. Soft and satisfying, they feature good-for-you oats and yogurt.

Prep: 20 minutes   **Bake:** 9 minutes per batch
Oven: 375°F   **Makes:** about 60 cookies

82 CALORIES

1 cup rolled oats
1/2 cup butter, softened
1 cup packed brown sugar
1 teaspoon baking soda
1/4 teaspoon salt
1 8-ounce container plain low-fat yogurt
2 eggs
1 teaspoon vanilla
2 1/2 cups all-purpose flour
2 cups semisweet chocolate pieces (12 ounces)

1 Place oats in a shallow baking pan. Bake in a 375° oven about 10 minutes or until toasted, stirring once. Place oats in a food processor bowl or blender container. Cover and process or blend until ground; set aside.

2 In a large mixing bowl beat butter with an electric mixer on medium to high speed for 30 seconds. Add brown sugar, baking soda, and salt; beat until combined. Beat in the yogurt, eggs, and vanilla until combined. Beat in as much of the flour as you can with the mixer. Using a wooden spoon, stir in the oats and any remaining flour. Stir in chocolate pieces.

3 Drop dough by rounded teaspoons 2 inches apart on an ungreased cookie sheet. Bake in the 375° oven for 9 to 11 minutes or until bottoms are light brown. Transfer to a wire rack to cool.

Nutrition Facts per cookie:
82 cal., 3 g total fat (2 g sat. fat), 12 mg chol., 54 mg sodium, 12 g carbo., 1 g fiber, 2 g pro.
Daily Values:
1% vit. A, 1% calcium, 3% iron
Exchanges:
1 Starch

2 cups assorted fresh vegetables, such as baby carrots with tops; radishes; 1-inch green sweet pepper squares, halved; and/or small pattypan squash

4 ounces firm cheese, such as peppercorn cheese or smoked Gouda, cut into 1/2-inch chunks

4 ounces cooked smoked turkey sausage or summer sausage, cut into 3/4-inch slices and quartered

2 tablespoons refrigerated basil pesto

1 tablespoon white wine vinegar

1 Place vegetables, cheese, and sausage in a plastic bag set in a bowl. For the marinade, in a small bowl stir together pesto sauce and vinegar. Pour over vegetable mixture in plastic bag. Close bag. Marinate in the refrigerator for 1 to 24 hours.

2 Remove vegetable mixture from the refrigerator. Alternately thread the vegetables, cheese, and sausage onto twelve 6-inch skewers.

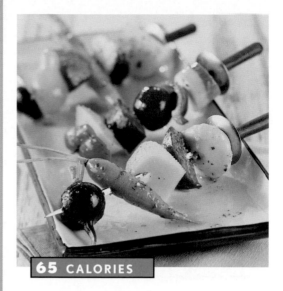

65 CALORIES

Antipasto Kabobs

Here's a no-cook kabob with lots of crunch. Follow the recipe or set a table with ingredients and let everyone make a skewer of favorites for themselves.

Prep: 30 minutes   **Marinate:** 1 to 24 hours
Makes: 12 servings

Nutrition Facts per serving:
65 cal., 4 g total fat (2 g sat. fat), 15 mg chol., 252 mg sodium, 3 g carbo., 1 g fiber, 4 g pro.
Daily Values:
102% vit. A, 2% vit. C, 8% calcium, 2% iron
Exchanges:
1 Vegetable, 1/2 Meat

28 CALORIES

Vegetable-Stuffed Tomato Bites

You won't believe this creamy appetizer fits into your diet. It's a good one for entertaining because it can be prepped ahead of time.

Start to Finish: 20 minutes

Makes: 16 servings

8 small roma tomatoes (about 1 pound)

3 tablespoons crumbled blue cheese

2 tablespoons thinly sliced green onion (1)

2 tablespoons light dairy sour cream

2 tablespoons low-fat mayonnaise dressing or light salad dressing

1 teaspoon snipped fresh oregano or basil

3/4 cup frozen whole kernel corn, thawed and drained

1/4 cup chopped, peeled jicama

Freshly ground black pepper

Shredded romaine (optional)

1 Cut tomatoes into halves lengthwise or at an angle, and remove a small slice from the bottom of each portion so tomato will stand up. Scoop out the pulp, leaving 1/4-inch shells. Discard pulp. Place the tomato shells, cut sides down, on paper towels. Let stand while preparing filling.

2 For filling, in a medium bowl combine cheese, green onion, sour cream, mayonnaise dressing, and oregano. Stir in corn and jicama.

3 To serve, spoon about 1 tablespoon of the vegetable mixture into each tomato shell. Sprinkle with pepper. If desired, place on a bed of shredded romaine.

Make-ahead directions: Prepare as above through step 2. Cover and chill tomato shells and filling separately up to 6 hours. Stuff tomatoes before serving.

Nutrition Facts per serving:
28 cal., 1 g total fat (1 g sat. fat), 2 mg chol., 37 mg sodium, 4 g carbo., 0 g fiber, 1 g pro.
Daily Values:
4% vit. A, 11% vit. C, 1% calcium, 1% iron
Exchanges:
1/2 Vegetable, 1/2 Fat

2 tablespoons raspberry vinegar

2 teaspoons honey mustard

1/4 teaspoon freshly ground black pepper
   Dash salt

3 tablespoons cooking oil

3 tablespoons olive oil

1 pound medium asparagus spears

8 ounces fresh sugar snap peas

1 For dipping sauce, in a blender container combine vinegar, mustard, pepper, and salt. Cover and blend until combined. With the blender running, slowly add oils in a thin, steady stream. Continue blending until mixture is thick. Transfer to a covered container and chill up to 4 hours.

2 Snap off and discard woody bases from asparagus. If desired, remove tips and strings from sugar snap peas. In a large deep skillet bring 1 inch of lightly salted water to boiling. Add asparagus. Reduce heat and simmer, uncovered, about 4 minutes or until crisp-tender. Using tongs, transfer asparagus to a large bowl of ice water to cool quickly. Add peas to simmering water; cook about 2 minutes or until crisp-tender. Drain and transfer vegetables to a bowl of ice water to quickly chill; drain.

3 To serve, transfer vegetables to a serving bowl. Drizzle sauce over vegetables; toss to coat.

Veggies with Mustard Sauce

A quick dip in ice water preserves the crisp-tender texture of the asparagus and the sugar snap peas.

Start to Finish: 20 minutes
Makes: 12 servings

73 CALORIES

Nutrition Facts per serving (about 1/3 cup):
73 cal., 7 g total fat (1 g sat. fat), 0 mg chol., 21 mg sodium, 3 g carbo., 1 g fiber, 1 g pro.
Daily Values:
9% vit. A, 9% vit. C, 2% calcium, 2% iron
Exchanges:
1/2 Vegetable, 11/2 Fat

Honey-Nut Spread

Although this spread tastes great on fruit, you'll want to slather some on graham crackers as well.

Start to Finish: 10 minutes

Makes: about 2/3 cup spread

99 CALORIES

1/3 cup reduced-fat cream cheese (Neufchâtel) (about 3 ounces), softened

1 tablespoon honey

1 tablespoon chopped walnuts

1/8 teaspoon ground cinnamon or cardamom

2 tablespoons snipped dried figs, dates, or dried apricots

Milk (optional)

Graham crackers; apple or pear slices

1 In a small bowl stir together the cream cheese, honey, walnuts, and cinnamon; stir in dried fruit.

2 If necessary, stir in 2 to 3 teaspoons milk until desired spreading consistency. Serve with graham crackers or fruit.

Make-ahead directions: Prepare as above through step 1. Cover and chill the spread up to 24 hours. Stir in milk, if necessary, before serving.

Nutrition Facts per 1 tablespoon spread with 2 graham cracker squares:
99 cal., 4 g total fat (2 g sat. fat), 6 mg chol., 119 mg sodium, 14 g carbo., 1 g fiber, 2 g pro.
Daily Values:
2% vit. A, 1% calcium, 4% iron
Exchanges:
1 Starch, 1/2 Fat

1   **cup sliced carrots (2 medium)**

¼   **cup chopped onion**

1   **clove garlic, minced**

½   **teaspoon curry powder**

¼   **teaspoon ground cumin**

2   **tablespoons olive oil or cooking oil**

½   **cup drained canned white beans
    (such as navy or cannellini beans)**

⅛   **teaspoon salt**

    **Thinly sliced green onions or snipped
    fresh cilantro (optional)**

    **Crackers, melba toast, or toasted
    baguette-style French bread slices**

1 In a small covered saucepan cook carrots in a small amount of boiling water about 8 minutes or until tender. Drain.

2 Meanwhile, in a small skillet cook onion, garlic, curry powder, and cumin in oil until onion is tender. Transfer carrots and onion mixture to a food processor bowl or blender container; add beans and salt. Cover and process or blend until smooth.

3 Transfer to a bowl. If desired, garnish with green onions. Serve with crackers.

Make-ahead directions: Prepare as above through step 2. Cover and chill up to 3 days. Let stand at room temperature for 30 minutes before serving.

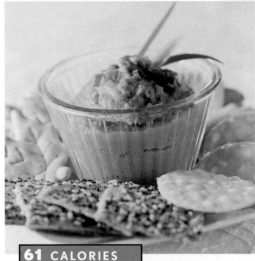

61 CALORIES

Curried Carrot Spread

Wow! This carrot spread packs a lot of flavor into each bite. Colorful as well as delicious, it looks great on your appetizer table.

Start to Finish: 25 minutes
Makes: 1 cup spread

**Nutrition Facts per 1 tablespoon spread
with 2 crackers:**
61 cal., 3 g total fat (0 g sat. fat), 0 mg chol., 93 mg sodium, 7 g carbo., 1 g fiber, 1 g pro.
Daily Values:
38% vit. A, 1% vit. C, 1% calcium, 3% iron
Exchanges:
½ Starch, ½ Fat

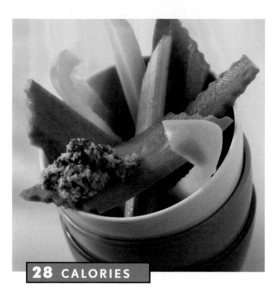

28 CALORIES

Spicy Broccoli Spread

What a way to incorporate a healthful vegetable into your diet. Who would have thought that broccoli could be blended into a flavorful spread.

Prep: 25 minutes   **Chill:** 3 to 24 hours
Makes: 1 cup spread

- 2 cups broccoli florets
- ¹/₂ cup chopped onion (1 medium)
- 1 tablespoon olive oil
- 2 tablespoons grated Parmesan cheese
- ¹/₄ to ¹/₂ teaspoon crushed red pepper
  Assorted vegetables dippers, baked tortilla wedges, or assorted crackers

1 In a medium covered saucepan cook broccoli in a small amount of boiling salted water about 10 minutes or until broccoli is tender. Drain well, reserving cooking liquid.

2 In a small skillet cook onion in hot oil about 8 to 10 minutes or until onion is soft and browned. In a food processor bowl or blender container combine broccoli, onion mixture, Parmesan cheese, and crushed red pepper. Cover and process or blend until nearly smooth. If mixture seems dry and thick, add reserved cooking liquid, 1 tablespoon at a time, until desired spreading consistency. Cover and chill for 3 to 24 hours. Serve with vegetable dippers.

Nutrition Facts per 1 tablespoon spread with 4 carrot sticks:
28 cal., 1 g total fat (0 g sat. fat), 0 mg chol., 25 mg sodium, 4 g carbo., 1 g fiber, 1 g pro.
Daily Values:
175% vit. A, 18% vit. C, 2% calcium, 1% iron
Exchanges:
1 Vegetable

1½ **cups chopped sweet onions (such as Vidalia or Walla Walla)**

2 **tablespoons butter or margarine**

1 **8-ounce carton dairy sour cream**

¼ **teaspoon salt**

¼ **teaspoon coarsely ground black pepper**

⅛ **teaspoon cayenne pepper**

4 **teaspoons snipped fresh chives**

Milk (optional)

Fresh vegetable dippers, such as broccoli florets, sweet pepper strips, carrot sticks, and/or sliced summer squash or zucchini

1 In a medium skillet cook onions in butter about 5 minutes or until tender. Cool the onions.

2 In a blender container or food processor bowl combine cooked onions, sour cream, salt, black pepper, and cayenne pepper. Cover and blend or process until nearly smooth. Transfer to a small bowl. Stir in chives. Cover and chill for 1 to 24 hours.

3 If necessary, stir in additional milk, 1 teaspoon at a time, until desired dipping consistency. If desired, sprinkle with a little additional black pepper. Serve with a variety of vegetable dippers.

Fresh Onion Dip

Break out all your favorite veggie dippers for this creamy, low-cal onion dip. Instead of a bowl, for a creative and colorful serving vessel, cut a sweet pepper (your choice of color) in half lengthwise and spoon the dip into each half.

Prep: 20 minutes   **Chill:** 1 to 24 hours
Makes: about 1½ cups dip

46 CALORIES

Nutrition Facts per 1 tablespoon dip with 4 carrot sticks:
46 cal., 3 g total fat (2 g sat. fat), 7 mg chol., 51 mg sodium, 4 g carbo., 1 g fiber, 1 g pro.
Daily Values:
174% vit. A, 6% vit. C, 2% calcium, 1% iron
Exchanges:
1 Vegetable, ½ Fat

Greek Layer Dip

Purchased hummus makes this an easy dip to prepare. Look for containers of hummus in supermarkets near the better-quality cheeses.

Start to Finish: 20 minutes

Makes: 10 servings

120 CALORIES

1   **8-ounce carton plain lowfat yogurt**

¼   **cup coarsely shredded unpeeled cucumber**

1   **tablespoon finely chopped red onion**

1   **teaspoon snipped fresh mint**

1   **8-ounce container (³/₄ cup) plain hummus**

½   **cup chopped, seeded tomato**

2   **ounces feta cheese, crumbled (½ cup)**

   Chopped cucumber (optional)

   Sliced green onion (optional)

3   **large white and/or wheat pita bread rounds**

1 In a small bowl stir together the yogurt, shredded cucumber, chopped onion, and mint. Set aside.

2 Spread hummus in the bottom of a 10-inch quiche dish or 9-inch pie plate. Spread yogurt mixture over hummus. Sprinkle with tomato and feta cheese. If desired, top with chopped cucumber and sliced green onion.

3 Split each pita bread round in half, making 2 rounds; cut each round into 8 wedges.* Serve pita bread wedges with dip.

*Note: For crisper pita bread dippers, spread wedges in a single layer on baking sheets. Lightly sprinkle with water. Sprinkle wedges with paprika and crushed dried oregano. Bake in a 350°F oven about 10 minutes or until crisp. Cool; cover and store in a cool, dry place.

Nutrition Facts per about ¼ cup dip and 5 pita wedges:
120 cal., 4 g total fat (1 g sat. fat), 6 mg chol., 231 mg sodium, 17 g carbo., 2 g fiber, 5 g pro.
Daily Values:
2% vit. A, 7% vit. C, 10% calcium, 5% iron
Exchanges:
1 Starch, ½ Fat

1 **8-ounce carton light dairy sour cream**

2 **tablespoons powdered sugar**

2 **teaspoons finely shredded lime peel**

1 **tablespoon lime juice**

1 **pint small strawberries (2 to 3 cups)**

1 For lime dipping sauce, in a small bowl stir together sour cream, powdered sugar, lime peel, and lime juice.

2 Wash strawberries; do not remove stems. Drain on several layers of paper towels. Serve berries with lime dipping sauce.

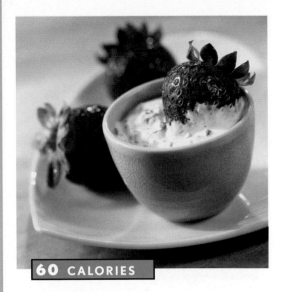

60 CALORIES

Strawberries with Lime Sauce

Don't be fooled by the simplicity of this recipe. The dipping sauce is divine.

Start to Finish: 15 minutes

Makes: 8 servings

Nutrition Facts per 2 tablespoons sauce and 3 or 4 strawberries:
60 cal., 2 g total fat (1 g sat. fat), 9 mg chol., 19 mg sodium, 7 g carbo., 1 g fiber, 2 g pro.
Daily Values:
4% vit. A, 53% vit. C, 6% calcium, 1% iron
Exchanges:
1/2 Fruit, 1/2 Fat

Marinated Zucchini and Mushrooms

Lemony and refreshing, the dressing for this appetizer requires only a little olive oil for flavor. Though high in calories, olive oil packs big flavor in every drop.

Prep: 20 minutes **Marinate:** 8 to 24 hours
Makes: about 8 servings

Nutrition Facts per serving (about 2/3 cup):
60 cal., 4 g total fat (1 g sat. fat), 0 mg chol., 76 mg sodium, 6 g carbo., 1 g fiber, 1 g pro.
Daily Values:
13% vit. A, 47% vit. C, 1% calcium, 3% iron
Exchanges:
1 Vegetable, 1/2 Fat

2 **cups small whole fresh mushrooms (about 6 ounces)**

2 **small zucchini and/or yellow summer squash, halved lengthwise and bias-sliced into 1/2-inch slices (2 cups)**

1 **small red sweet pepper, cut into bite-size pieces (1/2 cup)**

1 **cup cubed, peeled jicama (half of a medium)**

2 **tablespoons olive oil or salad oil**

1/2 **teaspoon cumin seeds**

1/4 **teaspoon chili powder**

1 **clove garlic, minced**

1/4 **cup lemon juice**

1 **tablespoon sugar**

1/4 **teaspoon salt**

1/4 **teaspoon black pepper**

1 Place mushrooms, zucchini, sweet pepper, and jicama in a plastic bag set in a deep bowl.

2 For marinade, in small skillet heat oil over medium heat for 1 minute. Add cumin seeds, chili powder, and garlic; cook and stir about 1 minute or until garlic is golden and seasonings are fragrant. Remove from heat and transfer to a small bowl. Stir in lemon juice, sugar, salt, and black pepper. Mix well. Pour marinade over vegetables in bag. Seal bag. Marinate vegetables in the refrigerator for at least 8 hours or overnight, turning bag occasionally.

3 To serve, pour vegetables and marinade into serving dish. Serve with toothpicks.

- **3** 7- to 8-inch spinach and/or jalapeño flour tortillas
- **1** 5.2-ounce carton boursin cheese or one 5-ounce container semisoft cheese with garlic and herb
- **12** large fresh basil leaves
- **½** of a 7-ounce jar roasted red sweet peppers, cut into ¼-inch strips
- **4** ounces thinly sliced cooked roast beef, ham, or turkey
- **1** tablespoon low-fat mayonnaise dressing

  Fresh basil leaves (optional)

1 Spread each tortilla with one-third of the boursin cheese. Add a layer of the large basil leaves to cover cheese. Divide sweet pepper strips among the tortillas, arranging pepper strips over the basil leaves 1 to 2 inches apart. Top with meat slices. Spread 1 teaspoon mayonnaise dressing over the meat on each tortilla. Roll tortillas tightly into a spiral, enclosing the filling. Wrap each roll in plastic wrap. Chill rolls in the refrigerator for 2 to 4 hours to blend flavors.

2 To serve, remove the plastic wrap from the tortilla rolls; cut each roll into 1-inch slices, making diagonal slices, if desired. If desired, garnish with the remaining basil leaves.

Wrap and Roll Basil Pinwheels

If you can't locate colorful spinach or jalapeño tortillas, use plain or whole wheat tortillas to wrap these cheese and meat-filled finger foods.

Prep: 20 minutes   **Chill:** 2 to 4 hours

Makes: about 24 pinwheels

45 CALORIES

Nutrition Facts per pinwheel:
45 cal., 3 g total fat (2 g sat. fat), 4 mg chol., 60 mg sodium, 2 g carbo., 0 g fiber, 2 g pro.
Daily Values:
14% vit. C, 1% calcium, 1% iron
Exchanges:
½ Meat

Picadillo Chicken Pizzettas

Sweet dried fruit, spicy salsa, and salty olives make this an out-of-the-ordinary pizza-style appetizer.

Prep: 25 minutes **Bake:** 20 minutes
Oven: 425°F **Makes:** 24 servings

87 CALORIES

- **1** 6- or 6½-ounce package pizza crust mix
- **1** cup bottled salsa
- **¼** teaspoon ground cinnamon
- **¼** teaspoon ground cumin
- **2** cups sliced or chopped cooked chicken or turkey
- **½** cup dried cranberries or raisins
- **½** cup pitted green olives coarsely chopped
- **¼** cup sliced green onions or chopped onion
- **1** tablespoon sliced almonds
- **1** cup shredded Manchego or Monterey Jack cheese (4 ounces)
- **1** tablespoon snipped fresh cilantro

1 Prepare pizza crust according to package directions. Pat dough into a greased 15×10×1-inch baking pan (crust will be thin). Bake in a 425° oven for 5 minutes.

2 In a small bowl combine salsa, cinnamon, and cumin; spread evenly over crust. Top with chicken, cranberries, olives, onions, and almonds. Sprinkle with cheese.

3 Bake for 15 minutes or until edges of crust are golden. Remove from oven; sprinkle with snipped cilantro. Cut into 12 squares; cut each piece in half diagonally.

Nutrition Facts per serving:
87 cal., 4 g total fat (1 g sat. fat), 15 mg chol., 226 mg sodium, 8 g carbo., 1 g fiber, 6 g pro.
Daily Values:
2% vit. A, 2% vit. C, 4% calcium, 3% iron
Exchanges:
½ Starch, ½ Meat

6 4-inch or four 6-inch white corn
   tortillas

   Cooking oil or nonstick cooking spray

½ cup shredded Monterey Jack cheese
   (2 ounces)

2 to 3 medium fresh serrano chile
   peppers, halved, seeded, and cut
   into thin slices (see note on page 76)

1 roma tomato, chopped

2 tablespoons snipped fresh cilantro

2 tablespoons light dairy sour cream

1 Lightly brush 1 side of each tortilla with
cooking oil or lightly coat with cooking
spray. Divide cheese evenly among
unoiled sides of 2 larger or 3 smaller
tortillas. Top with pepper slices, chopped
tomato, and cilantro. Top with remaining
tortillas, oiled sides up.

2 Heat a heavy skillet or griddle over
medium heat. Cook quesadillas, one at a
time, about 1 to 2 minutes per side or
until cheese melts and tortillas are lightly
browned. Cut each quesadilla into
4 wedges. Serve warm with sour cream.

105 CALORIES

Texas-Style Quesadillas

Generally made with flour tortillas, these
quesadillas use white corn tortillas. If you
have access to a Mexican market that
sells homemade corn tortillas, use them.
There's nothing better.

Prep: 10 minutes   **Cook:** 4 to 6 minutes
Makes: 6 servings

Nutrition Facts per serving:
105 cal., 5 g total fat (2 g sat. fat), 10 mg chol.,
57 mg sodium, 11 g carbo., 1 g fiber, 4 g pro.
Daily Values:
6% vit. A, 9% vit. C, 10% calcium, 6% iron
Exchanges:
½ Starch, ½ Meat, ½ Fat

80 CALORIES

Polynesian Glazed Wings

You'll enjoy serving these succulent and delicious wings at your next party. The recipe starts with chicken wing drummettes, a frozen product you'll find in the freezer section of the supermarket.

Prep: 10 minutes **Bake:** 1 hour
Oven: 400°F **Makes:** 30 appetizers

3 pounds (about 30) frozen plain chicken wing drummettes
1/2 cup packed brown sugar
1 tablespoon cornstarch
2 teaspoons grated fresh ginger
1/4 to 1/2 teaspoon crushed red pepper
1/2 cup pineapple juice
1/2 cup reduced-sodium chicken broth or water
1/4 cup finely chopped green sweet pepper
2 tablespoons soy sauce
Thinly sliced green onions (optional)

1 Place frozen chicken drummettes in a 15×10×1-inch baking pan. Bake in a 400° oven for 50 to 60 minutes or until skins are crispy.

2 Meanwhile, in a small saucepan combine brown sugar, cornstarch, ginger, and crushed red pepper. Stir in pineapple juice, broth, sweet pepper, and soy sauce. Cook and stir over medium heat until thickened and bubbly; cook and stir 2 minutes more. Set aside.

3 Carefully drain off any juices from baking pan. Brush drummettes with some of the glaze mixture. Bake for 10 minutes more. Brush with more of the glaze mixture. Place on serving plate. If desired, sprinkle with green onions. Pass remaining glaze mixture.

Nutrition Facts per appetizer:
80 cal., 5 g total fat (1 g sat. fat), 29 mg chol., 98 mg sodium, 5 g carbo., 0 g fiber, 5 g pro.
Daily Values:
3% vit. C, 1% iron
Exchanges:
1/2 Other Carbo, 1/2 Meat

- ¼ **cup chopped onion**
- 2 **tablespoons water**
- 2 **cloves garlic, minced**
- 1 **14½-ounce can stewed tomatoes, drained and cut up**
- 1 **4½-ounce can chopped green chile peppers, drained**
- ½ **to ¾ teaspoon chili powder**
- ¼ **teaspoon bottled hot pepper sauce**
- 1 **cup shredded reduced-fat cheddar cheese (4 ounces)**
- 1 **3-ounce package cream cheese, cubed**
- 3 **ounces fat-free cream cheese, cubed**
- **Chopped fresh tomato (optional)**
- 1 **recipe Tortilla Crisps**

1 In a medium saucepan combine onion, water, and garlic. Bring to boiling; reduce heat. Cook, uncovered, over medium heat about 2 to 3 minutes or until water has evaporated. Add stewed tomatoes, chile peppers, chili powder, and hot pepper sauce. Cook and stir until hot.

2 Add cheddar cheese and cream cheeses. Cook and stir over low heat until cheese is melted. Transfer to a serving bowl. If desired, top dip with chopped fresh tomato. Serve immediately with Tortilla Crisps.

Tortilla Crisps: Cut nine 7- or 8-inch flour tortillas into 8 wedges. Spread one-third of the wedges in a 15×10×1-inch baking pan. Bake in a 350°F oven for 5 to 10 minutes or until wedges are dry and crisp. Repeat with remaining wedges; cool. Store in an airtight container at room temperature up to 4 days or in the freezer up to 3 weeks. Makes 72 crisps.

Queso Dip

If you like, substitute a can of Mexican-style stewed tomatoes for the stewed tomatoes, green chiles, chili powder, and hot pepper sauce.

Start to Finish: 20 minutes
Makes: 2¼ cups dip

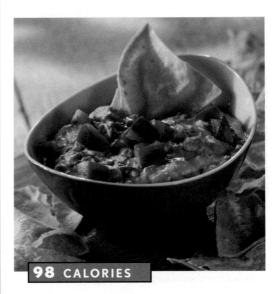

98 CALORIES

Nutrition Facts per 2 tablespoons dip with 4 tortilla crisps:
98 cal., 4 g total fat (2 g sat. fat), 10 mg chol., 189 mg sodium, 10 g carbo., 1 g fiber, 4 g pro.
Daily Values:
2% vit. A, 5% vit. C, 9% calcium, 4% iron
Exchanges:
½ Vegetable, ½ Starch, ½ Meat

Savory Bites

Have a few of these snacks leftover from your party? Top your favorite salad or soup broken pieces of these snack treats in place of ordinary croutons.

Prep: 10 minutes   **Bake:** 15 minutes
Oven: 300°F   **Makes:** 10 servings

70 CALORIES

1   5¼-ounce package plain melba toast rounds (3 cups)
4   teaspoons olive oil
2   teaspoons white wine Worcestershire sauce
2   teaspoons water
½   teaspoon dried basil, crushed
¼   teaspoon garlic powder
    Dash cayenne pepper

1 Place toast rounds in a medium bowl; set aside. In a small bowl stir together oil, Worcestershire sauce, water, basil, garlic powder, and cayenne pepper. Drizzle oil mixture over toast rounds; toss to coat. Spread toast rounds in an even layer in a shallow baking pan.

2 Bake in a 300° oven for 15 minutes. Cool in pan on a wire rack.

Make-ahead directions: Prepare as above. Store in an airtight container at room temperature up to 1 week.

Nutrition Facts per 5 toast rounds:
70 cal., 2 g total fat (0 g sat. fat), 0 mg chol., 109 mg sodium, 12 g carbo., 1 g fiber, 2 g pro.
Daily Values:
4% iron
Exchanges:
1 Starch

1   medium eggplant (1 pound)

2   tablespoons olive oil

$^1/_2$ cup chopped onion (1 medium)

1   14$^1/_2$-ounce can stewed tomatoes, cut up

$^1/_4$ cup dry red wine

2   tablespoons red wine vinegar

2   tablespoons capers, drained

$^1/_8$ teaspoon salt

$^1/_8$ teaspoon cracked black pepper

1   8-ounce loaf baguette-style French bread

2   tablespoons olive oil

1 Peel eggplant, if desired, and cut into $^1/_4$-inch cubes (you should have about 5 cups). In a large skillet heat the 2 tablespoons olive oil; add eggplant and onion. Cook, uncovered, over medium-high heat for 8 to 10 minutes or until tender, stirring occasionally. Stir in undrained tomatoes, red wine, vinegar, capers, salt, and pepper. Bring to boiling; reduce heat. Simmer, uncovered, for 10 minutes or until most of the liquid has evaporated. Cool slightly. Cover and chill at least 3 hours.

2 Before serving, cut baguette into $^1/_4$-inch slices. Brush 1 side of each slice with a little remaining olive oil. Arrange slices in a single layer on the unheated rack of a broiler pan. Broil a few inches from heat for 2 to 3 minutes, turning once. Serve with eggplant topper.

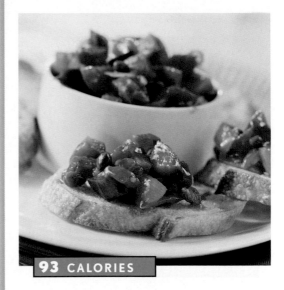

93 CALORIES

Sicilian Eggplant Topper

Serve this diverse Mediterranean topper in a bowl surrounded by baguette toasts or heap it on a bed of colorful kale.

Prep: 20 minutes   **Cook:** 20 minutes
Chill: 3 hours   **Broil:** 2 minutes
Makes: 16 servings

Nutrition Facts per serving:
93 cal., 4 g total fat (1 g sat. fat), 0 mg chol.,
184 mg sodium, 12 g carbo., 1 g fiber, 2 g pro.
Daily Values:
2% vit. C, 2% calcium, 4% iron
Exchanges:
1 Starch, $^1/_2$ Fat

50 CALORIES

Mushrooms Stuffed with Blue Cheese

Blue cheese packs so much flavor, you never need more than a little. Don't be afraid to eat "forbidden foods" like blue cheese; just be careful not to overindulge.

Prep: 30 minutes **Bake:** 12 minutes
Oven: 400°F **Makes:** 14 to 16 servings

14 to 16 medium crimini and/or button mushrooms (2-inch diameter)
 4 green onions, sliced
 1 clove garlic, minced
 1 tablespoon butter or margarine
 2 ounces blue cheese, crumbled ($^1/_2$ cup)
 $^1/_3$ cup toasted pine nuts

1 Remove mushroom stems; chop stems to make about 1 cup. Set caps aside. In a large skillet cook mushroom stems, green onions, and garlic in butter over medium heat for 5 minutes or until mushroom stems are tender. Remove from heat. Stir in cheese and pine nuts.

2 Place mushroom caps, stem sides up, in a 15×10×1-inch baking pan. Spoon about 1 tablespoon cheese mixture into each.

3 Bake in a 400° oven for 12 to 15 minutes or until mushrooms are tender.

Make-ahead directions: Prepare as above through step 2. Cover and chill up to 2 hours. Bake as directed above.

Nutrition Facts per serving:
50 cal., 4 g total fat (2 g sat. fat), 5 mg chol., 67 mg sodium, 2 g carbo., 0 g fiber, 3 g pro.
Daily Values:
2% vit. A, 1% vit. C, 3% calcium, 3% iron
Exchanges:
1 Vegetable, $^1/_2$ Fat

Nonstick cooking spray

3 cups bite-size rice square cereal

2 cups bite-size shredded wheat biscuits

³/₄ cup shelled pumpkin seeds

¹/₄ cup maple-flavored syrup

2 tablespoons Dijon-style mustard

¹/₂ teaspoon garlic powder

1 Lightly coat a 13×9×2-inch baking pan with cooking spray. Combine cereal, wheat biscuits, and pumpkin seeds in pan; set aside. In a small bowl stir together syrup, mustard, and garlic powder until combined. Drizzle over cereal mixture in roasting pan; toss to coat.

2 Bake mixture in a 300° oven for 45 minutes, gently stirring 3 times. Spread baked mixture on foil to cool.

Make-ahead directions: Prepare as above. Store in an airtight container at room temperature up to 2 weeks.

Maple-Mustard Crunch

Be ready when your craving for chips attacks! Armed with this roasted snack mix, you'll be able to conquer the craving.

Prep: 10 minutes   **Bake:** 45 minutes
Oven: 300°F   **Makes:** 15 (¹/₃-cup) servings

118 CALORIES

Nutrition Facts per serving:
118 cal., 5 g total fat (1 g sat. fat), 0 mg chol., 163 mg sodium, 15 g carbo., 1 g fiber, 5 g pro.
Daily Values:
2% vit. A, 2% vit. C, 2% calcium, 19% iron
Exchanges:
1 Starch, 1 Fat

Pretzels and Fruit Snack Mix

For a quicker snack—without the extra sweetness—combine pretzel twists and sticks, dried fruit, and almonds, and omit the brown sugar mixture and baking time.

Prep: 10 minutes
Bake: 10 minutes   **Oven:** 350°F
Makes: 12 (about ⅓-cup) servings

147 CALORIES

Nonstick cooking spray
2½ cups small pretzel twists and/or pretzel sticks (about 6 ounces)
½ cup whole almonds
2 tablespoons packed brown sugar
1 tablespoon butter or margarine
1 tablespoon honey
1 teaspoon vanilla
1 6-ounce package dried tart cherries or dried cranberries (1½ cups)

1 Line a 15×10×1-inch baking pan with foil. Lightly coat with nonstick cooking spray. Combine the pretzels and almonds in the pan; set aside.

2 In a small saucepan combine the brown sugar, butter, and honey. Cook over medium heat until butter is melted and mixture is combined. Remove from heat. Stir in vanilla.

3 Pour warm brown sugar mixture over pretzel mixture. Stir until ingredients are well coated. Bake in a 350° oven for 10 minutes or until mixture is golden brown, stirring once. Stir in cherries. Cool in pan on a wire rack.

Make-ahead directions: Prepare as above. Store in an airtight container in the refrigerator or freezer up to 1 week.

Nutrition Facts per serving:
147 cal., 4 g total fat (1 g sat. fat), 3 mg chol., 164 mg sodium, 25 g carbo., 2 g fiber, 3 g pro.
Daily Values:
1% vit. A, 2% calcium, 3% iron
Exchanges:
½ Starch, 1 Other Carbo., 1 Fat

9 cups popped popcorn*

²/₃ cup packed brown sugar

¹/₃ cup light-colored corn syrup

3 tablespoons butter

¹/₂ teaspoon vanilla

¹/₄ teaspoon baking soda

1 Remove all unpopped kernels from the popped corn. Put popcorn in a 17×11×2-inch baking pan.

2 In a 1½-quart saucepan combine brown sugar, corn syrup, and butter. Cook and stir over medium heat until butter melts and mixture boils. Reduce heat to medium-low. Cook, without stirring, for 5 minutes more. Remove from heat. Stir in vanilla and baking soda. Pour syrup mixture over popcorn in baking pan and gently stir to coat.

3 Bake in a 300° oven for 15 minutes; stir. Bake 5 minutes more. Transfer popcorn mixture to a large piece of foil; cool completely. Break into clusters.

*Note: For 9 cups of popped popcorn, start with ⅓ cup unpopped kernels.

Make-ahead directions: Prepare as above. Store in an airtight container at room temperature up to 3 days.

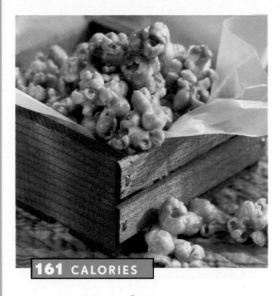

161 CALORIES

Caramel Corn

Many caramel corn recipes contain lots of butter that, of course, adds lots of calories. This version cuts down the amount of butter without sacrificing the buttery flavor caramel corn is known for.

Prep: 15 minutes **Bake:** 20 minutes
Oven: 300°F **Makes:** 9 (1-cup) servings

Nutrition Facts per serving:
161 cal., 4 g total fat (3 g sat. fat), 11 mg chol., 97 mg sodium, 31 g carbo., 1 g fiber, 1 g pro.
Daily Values:
3% vit. A, 2% calcium, 3% iron
Exchanges:
2 Other Carbo., ½ Fat

101 CALORIES

Carrot Cocktail

This type of drink tends to be pricey in the big city juice bars. Now you can make it at home.

Prep: 10 minutes
Cook: 10 minutes   **Cool:** 10 minutes
Makes: 2 (8-ounce) servings

$1/2$ cup sliced carrots

$1^1/2$ cups apple juice or apple cider, chilled

1 teaspoon snipped fresh lemon thyme or 1 teaspoon snipped fresh thyme plus $1/4$ teaspoon finely shredded lemon peel

$1/2$ cup ice cubes

1 lemon slice, halved (optional)

1 In a small covered saucepan cook carrots in a small amount of boiling water about 10 minutes or until very tender. Drain well. Cool carrots.

2 Place drained carrots in a blender container. Add apple juice and lemon thyme or thyme and peel. Cover and blend until smooth. With blender running, add ice cubes, 1 at a time, through opening in lid until blended. Pour into glasses. If desired, garnish with lemon slices.

Nutrition Facts per serving:
101 cal., 0 g total fat (0 g sat. fat), 0 mg chol., 16 mg sodium, 25 g carbo., 1 g fiber, 0 g pro.
Daily Values:
154% vit. A, 7% vit. C, 2% calcium, 5% iron
Exchanges:
$1/2$ Vegetable, $1^1/2$ Fruit

1 **lemon**
4 **cups apple juice**
2 **cups water**
4 **inches stick cinnamon**
1 **tablespoon whole cardamom pods, crushed**
1 **teaspoon whole cloves**
6 **regular-size tea bags**
¼ **cup maple syrup**
   Thin apple slices (optional)
   Cinnamon sticks (optional)

1 Use a vegetable peeler to remove strips of peel from half of the lemon; set peel aside. Squeeze juice from lemon.

2 In a large saucepan combine apple juice, water, and 1 tablespoon of the lemon juice. (Save remaining lemon juice for another use.) For the spice bag, place cinnamon, cardamom, cloves, and the lemon peel strips in the center of a 6-inch square of double-thick 100-percent-cotton cheesecloth. Bring corners together and tie with a clean string. Add bag to apple juice mixture.

3 Bring mixture to boiling; reduce heat. Cover and simmer 10 minutes. Remove from heat. Add tea bags; cover and let stand 5 minutes. Remove tea bags and spice bag and discard them. Stir in maple syrup. Serve in mugs. If desired, float apple slices on top of each serving and serve with cinnamon stick stirrers.

Spiced Apple Tea

This soothing treat satisfies any sweet craving you might experience when the afternoon doldrums roll in.

Start to Finish: 20 minutes
Makes: about 8 (6-ounce) servings

85 CALORIES

Nutrition Facts per serving:
85 cal., 0 g total fat (0 g sat. fat), 0 mg chol., 6 mg sodium, 21 g carbo., 0 g fiber, 0 g pro.
Daily Values:
3% vit. C, 2% calcium, 3% iron
Exchanges:
1½ Fruit

Mulled Raspberry Tea

Frozen raspberries (when fresh aren't in season) allow you to enjoy this fanciful tea any time of year. It's a nice change from the more common orange and spice variety.

Start to Finish: 15 minutes

Makes: 6 (about 7-ounce) servings

74 CALORIES

1 cup frozen loose-pack raspberries, slightly thawed
2 cups brewed tea
2 cups cranberry-raspberry drink
1 cup prepared lemonade
¼ cup water
3 whole allspice
1 lemon, cut into thin wedges
  Fresh raspberries (optional)

1 In a medium saucepan slightly mash the 1 cup raspberries with a potato masher. Stir in the tea, cranberry-raspberry drink, lemonade, the water, and allspice. Bring to boiling; reduce heat. Simmer, uncovered, for 10 minutes. Strain and discard the fruit pulp and spices.

2 Serve in mugs with lemon wedges and, if desired, additional fresh raspberries.

Nutrition Facts per serving:
74 cal., 0 g total fat (0 g sat. fat), 0 mg chol., 15 mg sodium, 18 g carbo., 1 g fiber, 0 g pro.
Daily Values:
1% vit. A, 55% vit. C, 1% calcium, 1% iron
Exchanges:
1 Fruit

6 **cups water**

4 **teaspoons sugar**

1 **1-inch piece fresh ginger, thinly sliced**

8 **lemon peel strips (2¹/₂×1 inch each)**

8 **green tea bags**

Lemon slices (optional)

1 In a large saucepan combine the water, sugar, ginger, and lemon peel strips. Bring to boiling; reduce heat. Simmer, uncovered, for 10 minutes. Remove ginger and lemon strips with a slotted spoon and discard.

2 Place tea bags in a teapot; immediately add simmering water mixture. Cover and let stand 3 to 5 minutes. Remove tea bags and discard. Serve immediately in mugs. If desired, garnish with lemon slices.

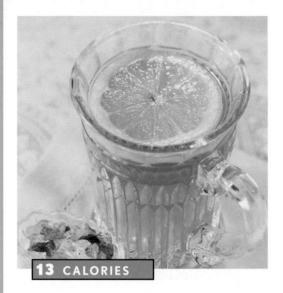

13 CALORIES

Ginger-Lemon Tea

Tea does a good job of chasing hunger come midafternoon. This version features ginger, which not only infuses its wonderful flavor but is said to calm a nervous stomach. Note, also, that it's a free exchange!

Start to Finish: 25 minutes
Makes: 6 (8-ounce) servings

Nutrition Facts per serving:
13 cal., 0 g total fat (0 g sat. fat), 0 mg chol., 7 mg sodium, 3 g carbo., 0 g fiber, 0 g pro.
Daily Values:
1% vit. C
Exchanges:
Free

91 CALORIES

Mixed-Fruit Smoothies

Why spend the money for a meal-replacement drink when you can prepare your own at home? For an impressive party drink, make two-tone smoothies with mango and strawberry flavors.

Start to Finish: 15 minutes

Makes: 6 (about 5-ounce) servings

2 **bananas, chilled and cut up**

²/₃ **cup strawberries or mango slices**

1¹/₂ **cups grape juice or mango, apricot, or other fruit nectar, chilled**

1 **8-ounce carton plain fat-free yogurt**

1 **tablespoon honey (optional)**

Fresh strawberries and mango slices (optional)

1 In a blender container combine cut-up bananas, strawberries, grape juice, yogurt, and, if desired, honey. Cover and blend until smooth. Pour into 6 chilled glasses. If desired, garnish with additional strawberries and mango slices.

Note: For two-tone smoothies, make mango smoothies and strawberry smoothies. Transfer to separate pitchers or glass measuring cups. Taking a pitcher or cup in each hand, slowly pour both smoothies at the same time into opposite sides of the glass.

Nutrition Facts per serving:
91 cal., 0 g total fat (0 g sat. fat), 1 mg chol., 31 mg sodium, 20 g carbo., 1 g fiber, 3 g pro.
Daily Values:
1% vit. A, 44% vit. C, 8% calcium, 2% iron
Exchanges:
1¹/₂ Fruit

1 **4-inch piece fresh peeled ginger, finely chopped**

3 **cups pineapple juice, chilled**

1 **cup orange juice, chilled**

¹/₂ **cup vanilla low-fat yogurt**

3 **tablespoons lime juice**

¹/₄ **cup finely chopped fresh cilantro leaves**

1 Place ginger, a little at at time, in a garlic press to extract juice; reserve juice (you should have about 1½ teaspoons).

2 In a blender container or food processor bowl combine ginger juice, pineapple juice, orange juice, yogurt, lime juice, and cilantro. Cover and blend or process until nearly smooth. Serve immediately.

Herbed Pineapple Refresher

A refreshing combo of ginger, pineapple juice, orange juice, lime juice, and cilantro makes this blended drink just the thing to shake the hungries.

Start to Finish: 15 minutes

Makes: 6 (about 6-ounce) servings

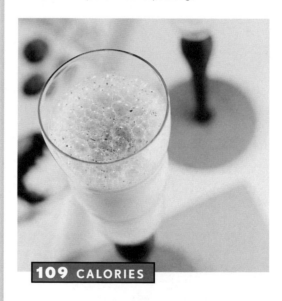

109 CALORIES

Nutrition Facts per serving:
109 cal., 0 g total fat (0 g sat. fat), 1 mg chol.,
17 mg sodium, 25 g carbo., 0 g fiber, 2 g pro.
Daily Values:
5% vit. A, 66% vit. C, 6% calcium, 3% iron
Exchanges:
1½ Fruit

Golden Sparklers

This festive drink contains orange juice, apricot nectar, and sparkling water. For an impressive party presentation, place it in a punch bowl and float very thinly sliced rounds of orange, lemon, and lime on top or make citrus ice cubes (see recipe).

Prep: 15 minutes   **Freeze:** 2 hours
Makes: about 20 (1/2-cup) servings

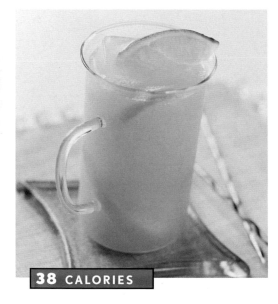

38 CALORIES

12 thin half-slices of orange, lemon, or lime
    Water
 3 cups orange juice, chilled
 3 cups apricot nectar, chilled
 2 cups ice cubes
 1 750-milliliter bottle sparkling water, chilled

1 For citrus ice cubes, place a thin half-slice of orange, lemon, or lime in each compartment of an ice cube tray, with one end of the slice extending above the tray about ¾ inch. Fill tray with water and freeze for 2 hours or until firm.

2 Pour orange juice and apricot nectar over plain ice cubes in a large (11-cup) glass pitcher or punch bowl. Add sparkling water, stirring gently. Place a citrus ice cube in each punch cup. Pour or ladle juice mixture into cup.

Nutrition Facts per serving:
38 cal., 0 g total fat (0 g sat. fat), 0 mg chol., 9 mg sodium, 9 g carbo., 0 g fiber, 0 g pro.
Daily Values:
11% vit. A, 31% vit. C, 1% calcium, 1% iron
Exchanges:
1/2 Fruit

On the divider: Blueberry-Cornmeal Pancakes (see recipe, page 207)

- **1** 12-inch Italian bread shell (Boboli)
- **6** eggs
- **1/3** cup milk
- **2** teaspoons snipped fresh tarragon or oregano
- **1/8** teaspoon salt
- **1/8** teaspoon black pepper
- **1** cup fresh asparagus bias-cut into 1-inch pieces
- **1** clove garlic, minced
- **1** tablespoon butter or margarine
- **1** large tomato, halved and sliced

1 Place bread shell on a 12-inch pizza pan. Bake in a 450° oven for 8 to 10 minutes or until heated through.

2 Meanwhile, in a medium bowl beat together eggs, milk, tarragon, salt, and pepper. In a large nonstick skillet cook asparagus and garlic in hot butter over medium heat for 3 minutes; pour egg mixture over asparagus mixture in skillet. Cook over medium heat, without stirring, until mixture begins to set on the bottom and around edge.

3 Using a spatula, lift and fold the partially cooked egg mixture so the uncooked portion flows underneath. Continue cooking over medium heat for 2 to 3 minutes or until egg mixture is cooked through but still glossy and moist. Remove from heat.

4 Arrange tomato slices evenly around the edge of the baked bread shell. Spoon scrambled egg mixture in the center. Cut into wedges; serve immediately.

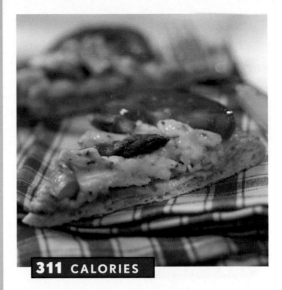

311 CALORIES

Tomato and Asparagus Pizza

Eggs scrambled with fresh herbs and garden vegetables aren't just for breakfast. They make a great topping for pizza too. Using prepared Boboli crust trims preparation time.

Start to Finish: 20 minutes
Oven: 450°F   **Makes:** 6 servings

Nutrition Facts per serving:
311 cal., 12 g total fat (3 g sat. fat), 222 mg chol., 555 mg sodium, 36 g carbo., 2 g fiber, 16 g pro.
Daily Values:
14% vit. A, 14% vit. C, 13% calcium, 14% iron
Exchanges:
1 Vegetable, 2 Starch, 1 Meat, 1 Fat

258 CALORIES

Sweet Potato Frittata with Cranberry Salsa

Chutney, the traditional Indian relish responsible for adding verve to this slightly sweet salsa, contains fruit (usually mangoes or limes), vinegar, sugar, and spices combined in proportions that play up contrasting flavors: sweet, sour, spicy, and piquant.

Prep: 20 minutes   **Bake:** 15 minutes
Oven: 350°F   **Makes:** 6 servings

1	cup fresh cranberries, coarsely chopped
1/4	cup sugar
1	tablespoon water
1/3	cup chutney
1/4	cup chopped red onion
1	tablespoon butter or margarine
1 1/2	cups sliced, halved, peeled sweet potato
2	ounces Canadian-style bacon, chopped (about 1/3 cup)
1/4	cup thinly sliced green onions (2)
	Dash salt
	Dash ground white pepper
8	beaten eggs

1 For cranberry salsa, in a small saucepan combine cranberries, sugar, and the water. Bring to boiling, stirring occasionally. Remove from heat. Snip any large pieces of chutney. Stir chutney and red onion into cranberry mixture. Set aside.

2 In a 10-inch oven-going skillet melt butter over medium heat. Add sweet potato. Cook, covered, for 5 to 7 minutes or until sweet potato is almost tender, turning once. Sprinkle with Canadian bacon, green onions, salt, and pepper.

3 Pour eggs over potato mixture in skillet. Bake, uncovered, in a 350° oven for 15 to 18 minutes or until egg mixture is set. Cut into wedges. Serve with warm cranberry salsa.

Nutrition Facts per serving:
258 cal., 10 g total fat (4 g sat. fat), 294 mg chol., 283 mg sodium, 32 g carbo., 2 g fiber, 11 g pro.
Daily Values:
156% vit. A, 30% vit. C, 5% calcium, 8% iron
Exchanges:
1 Fruit, 1 Starch, 1 1/2 Meat, 1/2 Fat

- **2** tablespoons sliced almonds
- **1** yellow sweet pepper, cut into thin bite-size strips
- **1** fresh jalapeño chile pepper, seeded and chopped (see note on page 76)
- **1** tablespoon olive oil or cooking oil
- **4** medium tomatoes (about 1¼ pounds), peeled and chopped
- **1½** to 2 teaspoons purchased or homemade Mexican seasoning*
- **¼** teaspoon salt
- **4** eggs
  Salt (optional)
  Black pepper (optional)
- **1** medium ripe avocado, seeded, peeled, and sliced (optional)

1 Spread almonds in a large skillet. Cook, stirring occasionally, over medium heat for 4 to 5 minutes or until lightly browned. Remove toasted almonds from skillet; set aside. In the same skillet cook sweet pepper and jalapeño pepper in hot oil about 2 minutes or until tender. Stir in tomatoes, Mexican seasoning, and the ¼ teaspoon salt. Bring to boiling; reduce heat. Simmer, covered, for 5 minutes.

2 Break 1 of the eggs into a measuring cup. Carefully slide the egg into simmering tomato mixture. Repeat with remaining eggs. If desired, sprinkle the eggs lightly with additional salt and pepper.

3 Cover and simmer the eggs over medium-low heat for 3 to 5 minutes or until the whites are completely set and yolks begin to thicken but are not hard. If desired, top with avocado slices. Sprinkle with the toasted almonds.

*Note: For homemade Mexican seasoning, combine 1 to 1½ teaspoons chili powder and ½ teaspoon ground cumin.

Southwest Skillet

It's home on the range with a stove-top main course built on classic Southwestern flavors. Round up everything you need in the aisles of most supermarkets.

Start to Finish: 25 minutes
Makes: 4 servings

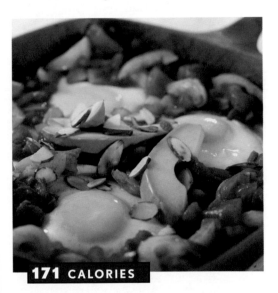

171 CALORIES

Nutrition Facts per serving:
171 cal., 11 g total fat (2 g sat. fat), 213 mg chol., 289 mg sodium, 11 g carbo., 3 g fiber, 9 g pro.
Daily Values:
24% vit. A, 163% vit. C, 5% calcium, 11% iron
Exchanges:
2 Vegetable, 1 Meat, 1 Fat

Salmon and Bagel Bake

This bagel casserole might become your favorite Sunday brunch. It goes together quickly and gives you extra time to read the paper while it bakes.

Prep: 20 minutes **Bake:** 35 minutes
Stand: 10 minutes **Oven:** 350°F
Makes: 6 to 8 servings

237 CALORIES

- 4 eggs
- 1 14-ounce can reduced-sodium chicken broth
- 1/4 cup thinly sliced green onions
- 2 cloves garlic, minced
- 1 tablespoon snipped fresh dill or 3/4 teaspoon dried dill
- 7 mini bagels or 4 medium bagels, split (8 to 10 ounces total)
   Nonstick cooking spray
- 1 3-ounce package thinly sliced smoked salmon (lox-style)
- 3 ounces Havarti cheese, shredded (3/4 cup)

1 In a medium bowl beat together eggs and broth. Stir in green onions, garlic, and dill; set aside. If using medium bagels, cut each bagel half into 2 or 3 pieces. (Do not cut mini bagels into pieces.)

2 Lightly coat a 2-quart round or square baking dish with nonstick cooking spray. Arrange bagel bottom pieces, cut sides up, in prepared dish, overlapping as necessary. Arrange salmon on bagel pieces in baking dish; sprinkle with cheese. Arrange bagel top pieces over the layers, cut sides down. Gradually pour egg mixture over all. Lightly press down with the back of a spoon.

3 Bake, uncovered, in a 350° oven for 35 to 40 minutes or until a knife inserted near the center comes out clean. Let stand for 10 minutes before serving.

Nutrition Facts per serving:
237 cal., 10 g total fat (1 g sat. fat), 162 mg chol., 779 mg sodium, 22 g carbo., 1 g fiber, 15 g pro.
Daily Values:
5% vit. A, 2% vit. C, 13% calcium, 11% iron
Exchanges:
1 1/2 Starch, 1 1/2 Meat

Nonstick cooking spray

1 **large onion, halved and thinly sliced**

1 **15-ounce can chunky chili-style tomato sauce**

1 **fresh jalapeño chile pepper, seeded and chopped (see note on page 76)**

3 **tablespoons snipped fresh cilantro**

6 **eggs**

¹/₄ **teaspoon salt**

¹/₈ **teaspoon black pepper**

³/₄ **cup shredded Monterey Jack or cheddar cheese (3 ounces)**

6 **8-inch flour tortillas, warmed, or 6 slices bread, toasted**

1 Coat a 12-inch ovenproof skillet with nonstick cooking spray. Preheat skillet over medium-high heat. Cook onion in hot skillet for 4 to 5 minutes or until tender. Remove from heat.

2 In a small bowl stir together the tomato sauce, jalapeño pepper, and cilantro. Pour sauce mixture over onions in skillet. Break 1 of the eggs into a measuring cup. Carefully slide the egg into simmering tomato sauce mixture. Repeat with remaining eggs. Sprinkle eggs with salt and black pepper.

3 Bake, uncovered, in a 400° oven for 15 to 20 minutes or until eggs are set. Sprinkle with cheese; bake for 1 minute more. Serve with warmed tortillas or toast.

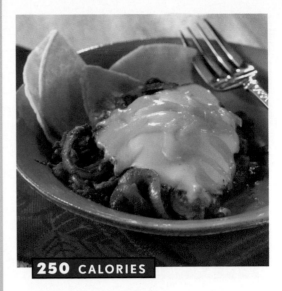

250 CALORIES

Ranch Eggs

Your taste buds get a wake-up call with this Mexican-style casserole. If hot and spicy doesn't suit you in the morning, serve this meatless main dish for supper.

Prep: 15 minutes **Bake:** 16 minutes
Oven: 400°F **Makes:** 6 servings

Nutrition Facts per serving:
250 cal., 12 g total fat (5 g sat. fat), 225 mg chol., 717 mg sodium, 22 g carbo., 2 g fiber, 12 g pro.
Daily Values:
11% vit. A, 13% vit. C, 22% calcium, 13% iron
Exchanges:
1 Vegetable, 1 Starch, 1¹/₂ Meat

214 CALORIES

Provençal Omelet

In Provence, that famous southeastern region of France, garlic, tomatoes, and olive oil are indispensable to the local cuisine. It's the melding of these three flavors that puts the Provençal in dishes such as this one.

Start to Finish: 30 minutes
Makes: 2 servings

Nutrition Facts per serving:
214 cal., 9 g total fat (2 g sat. fat), 8 mg chol., 557 mg sodium, 16 g carbo., 1 g fiber, 17 g pro.
Daily Values:
14% vit. A, 8% vit. C, 15% calcium, 19% iron
Exchanges:
3 Vegetable, 2 Meat, 1/2 Fat

1/2 of a medium onion, cut into very thin wedges
  1 teaspoon olive oil
  1 cup sliced fresh mushrooms
  2 cloves garlic, minced
1/4 teaspoon dried thyme, crushed
  1 8-ounce can (about 1 cup) stewed tomatoes, drained
  1 cup refrigerated or frozen egg product, thawed, or 2 eggs plus 2 egg whites
  2 tablespoons water
1/4 teaspoon coarsely ground black pepper
     Dash salt
     Nonstick cooking spray
  1 teaspoon olive oil
  2 tablespoons finely shredded Asiago or Parmesan cheese

1 In a small skillet cook and stir onion in 1 teaspoon hot oil over medium heat for 3 minutes. Add mushrooms, garlic, and thyme; cook and stir for 3 minutes more. Add tomatoes. Bring to boiling; reduce heat. Simmer, uncovered, for 5 minutes.

2 Meanwhile, in a medium bowl beat together egg product or eggs and egg whites, the water, pepper, and salt. Coat a 10-inch nonstick skillet with sloped sides with nonstick cooking spray. Preheat over medium heat. Add 1 teaspoon oil, swirling to coat skillet. Add egg mixture. Immediately begin stirring egg mixture gently but continuously with a wooden or plastic spatula until mixture resembles small pieces of cooked egg surrounded by liquid egg. Stop stirring. Cook 30 to 60 seconds more or until egg mixture is set but shiny.

3 Spoon half of the tomato mixture onto half of omelet; sprinkle with some of the cheese. Using a pancake turner, fold omelet in half. Cut omelet in half. Spoon remaining tomato mixture over omelet halves. Top with remaining cheese.

- 3 medium roma tomatoes, seeded and chopped
- ½ cup canned black beans, rinsed and drained
- 2 tablespoons chopped red onion
- 1 fresh jalapeño chile pepper, seeded and finely chopped (see note on page 76)
- 1 tablespoon snipped fresh cilantro
- 2 teaspoons lime juice
- 1 teaspoon olive oil
- ⅛ teaspoon black pepper
- 1 16-ounce tube refrigerated cooked polenta, cut into 12 slices
- 1 tablespoon olive oil
- 4 eggs
  Salt (optional)
  Black pepper (optional)
- 2 teaspoons snipped fresh cilantro
  Fresh cilantro sprigs (optional)
  Lime wedges

1 For salsa, in a small bowl combine the tomatoes, black beans, red onion, jalapeño pepper, the 1 tablespoon cilantro, the lime juice, the 1 teaspoon oil, and the ⅛ teaspoon black pepper. Set aside.

2 In a 12-inch nonstick skillet cook the polenta slices in the 1 tablespoon hot oil over medium heat for 14 to 16 minutes or until polenta is browned; turn once.

3 Meanwhile, fill a large skillet half full with water. Bring to boiling; reduce heat to simmering. Break 1 of the eggs into a measuring cup. Carefully slide egg into simmering water, holding the lip of the cup as close to the water as possible. Repeat with the remaining eggs. If desired, sprinkle with salt and black pepper. Simmer, uncovered, for 3 to 5 minutes or until the egg whites are completely set and yolks begin to thicken but are not hard. Using a slotted spoon, remove eggs.

4 To serve, divide the polenta slices among 4 dinner plates. Top with eggs and salsa. Sprinkle with the 2 teaspoons cilantro. If desired, garnish with cilantro sprigs. Serve with lime wedges.

Poached Eggs with Polenta and Black Beans

Discover a wonderful way to take advantage of easy-to-use tubes of prepared polenta in this Southwestern-inspired creation.

Start to Finish: 35 minutes
Makes: 4 servings

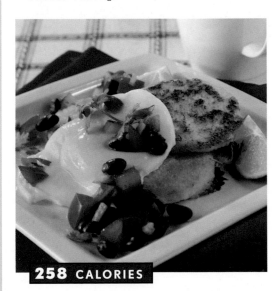

258 CALORIES

Nutrition Facts per serving:
258 cal., 10 g total fat (2 g sat. fat), 213 mg chol., 610 mg sodium, 30 g carbo., 5 g fiber, 11 g pro.
Daily Values:
16% vit. A, 30% vit. C, 4% calcium, 9% iron
Exchanges:
2 Starch, 1 Meat, ½ Fat

Ham and Potato Scramble

This all-in-one skillet breakfast needs nothing more than orange juice and some fresh fruit to round out the menu.

Start to Finish: 25 minutes

Makes: 4 servings

175 CALORIES

1   **16-ounce container refrigerated egg product or 8 slightly beaten eggs**

¼   **cup milk**

¼   **cup thinly sliced green onions (2)**

¼   **teaspoon garlic salt**

¼   **teaspoon black pepper**

1   **tablespoon butter or margarine**

1   **cup refrigerated shredded hash brown potatoes**

½   **cup diced low-fat, reduced-sodium cooked boneless ham (2 ounces)**

⅓   **cup shredded reduced-fat cheddar cheese**

1 In a medium bowl beat together egg product or eggs, milk, green onions, garlic salt, and pepper; set aside. In a large nonstick skillet heat butter over medium heat until melted. Add potatoes and ham to skillet. Cook for 6 to 8 minutes or until light brown, stirring occasionally. Add egg mixture. Cook over medium heat, without stirring, until mixture begins to set on the bottom and around edge.

2 With a spatula or large spoon, lift and fold the partially cooked egg product mixture so the uncooked portion flows underneath. Continue cooking for 2 to 3 minutes more or until egg product mixture is cooked through but is still glossy and moist. Remove from heat immediately. Sprinkle with shredded cheese. Serve warm.

Nutrition Facts per serving:
175 cal., 6 g total fat (3 g sat. fat), 23 mg chol., 593 mg sodium, 10 g carbo., 1 g fiber, 19 g pro.
Daily Values:
11% vit. A, 14% vit. C, 14% calcium, 14% iron
Exchanges:
½ Starch, 2½ Meat

2 small zucchini, cut crosswise into
    ¹/₄-inch slices (about 2 cups)

   Nonstick cooking spray

6 cups crusty sourdough bread torn into
    bite-size pieces (6 ounces)

1 4.4-ounce package Brie cheese, cut
    into ¹/₂-inch cubes

1 cup halved grape or cherry tomatoes

1 cup refrigerated or frozen egg product,
    thawed, or 4 beaten eggs

²/₃ cup evaporated fat-free milk

¹/₃ cup sliced green onions

3 tablespoons snipped fresh dill

¹/₂ teaspoon salt

¹/₈ teaspoon black pepper

1 In a covered medium saucepan cook
zucchini in a small amount of boiling
lightly salted water for 2 to 3 minutes or
just until tender. Drain zucchini. Set aside.

2 Meanwhile, coat a 2-quart rectangular
baking dish with nonstick cooking spray.
Arrange 4 cups of the bread pieces in the
prepared baking dish. If desired, remove
and discard rind from cheese. Sprinkle
cheese evenly over bread in baking dish.
Arrange zucchini and tomatoes on
top. Sprinkle with remaining 2 cups
bread pieces.

3 In a medium bowl combine egg product,
evaporated fat-free milk, green onions,
dill, salt, and pepper. Pour evenly over
mixture in baking dish. Lightly press
down layers with back of spoon. Cover
with plastic wrap; chill for at least
4 hours or up to 24 hours.

4 Remove plastic wrap from strata; cover
with foil. Bake in a 325° oven for
30 minutes. Uncover; bake for 25 to
30 minutes more or until a knife inserted
near the center comes out clean. Let
stand for 10 minutes before serving.

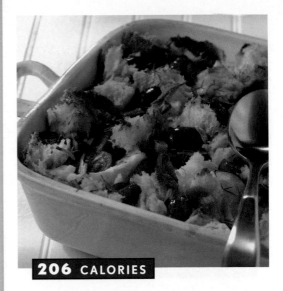

206 CALORIES

Baked Brie Strata

Make this strata the night before and pop
it in the oven the next morning. The Brie
may seem decadent to a dieter, but each
portion of this dish has only 206 calories
and 6 grams of fat.

Prep: 25 minutes   **Bake:** 55 minutes
Stand: 10 minutes   **Chill:** 4 to 24 hours
Oven: 325°F   **Makes:** 6 servings

Nutrition Facts per serving:
206 cal., 6 g total fat (4 g sat. fat), 22 mg chol.,
596 mg sodium, 24 g carbo., 1 g fiber, 14 g pro.
Daily Values:
14% vit. A, 15% vit. C, 14% calcium, 11% iron
Exchanges:
2 Vegetable, 1 Starch, 1 Meat

130 CALORIES

Vegetable Frittata

Packed with colorful vegetables, this fresh-flavored baked egg dish satisfies at breakfast, lunch, or supper.

Prep: 30 minutes   **Bake:** 35 minutes
Stand: 10 minutes   **Oven:** 350°F
Makes: 8 servings

1½ pounds fresh asparagus or two 9- or 10-ounce packages frozen cut asparagus
1 medium yellow sweet pepper, cut into ¼-inch-wide strips
⅓ cup chopped onion (1 small)
1 small zucchini, halved lengthwise and cut into ¼-inch slices (about 1 cup)
10 slightly beaten eggs
1 cup milk
2 tablespoons snipped fresh flat-leaf parsley
1¼ teaspoons salt
¼ to ½ teaspoon black pepper

1 Butter a 2-quart rectangular baking dish; set aside.

2 If using fresh asparagus, snap off and discard woody bases. If desired, scrape off scales. Cut into 1-inch pieces.

3 In a large saucepan bring about 1 inch water to boiling. Add asparagus, pepper strips, and onion. Bring just to boiling; reduce heat slightly. Cover and boil about 1 minute or until vegetables are crisp-tender. Drain well. Stir zucchini into vegetable mixture; spread vegetables evenly in prepared baking dish.

4 In a large bowl combine eggs, milk, parsley, salt, and black pepper. Pour over vegetables in baking dish. Bake, uncovered, in a 350° oven about 35 minutes or until a knife inserted near the center comes out clean. Let stand for 10 minutes before serving.

Nutrition Facts per serving:
130 cal., 7 g total fat (2 g sat. fat), 268 mg chol., 460 mg sodium, 7 g carbo., 1 g fiber, 10 g pro.
Daily Values:
17% vit. A, 74% vit. C, 9% calcium, 9% iron
Exchanges:
1 Vegetable, 1 Meat

Nonstick cooking spray

3 eggs

$1/2$ cup all-purpose flour

$1/2$ cup milk

$1/4$ teaspoon salt

$1/4$ cup orange marmalade

3 cups sliced fresh fruit (such as strawberries, peeled kiwifruit, nectarines, pears, or peeled peaches)

1 Lightly coat six 5-inch individual baking dishes, 4½-inch pie plates, or 10-ounce custard cups with nonstick cooking spray; set aside.

2 For batter, in a medium bowl use a wire whisk or rotary beater to beat eggs until combined. Add flour, milk, and salt; beat until mixture is smooth. Immediately pour batter into prepared baking dishes. Bake in a 400° oven for 20 to 25 minutes or until puffed and brown.

3 Meanwhile, in a small saucepan melt the orange marmalade over low heat. To serve, top pancakes with fruit; spoon melted marmalade over fruit. Serve warm.

Puffed Oven Pancake: Place 2 tablespoons butter or margarine in a 10-inch ovenproof skillet. Place skillet in a 400° oven for 3 to 5 minutes or until butter melts. Meanwhile, prepare batter as above. Immediately pour batter into the hot skillet. Bake in the 400° oven for 20 to 25 minutes or until puffed and brown. Serve as above.

Nutrition Facts per serving:
172 cal., 7 g total fat (4 g sat. fat), 119 mg chol., 188 mg sodium, 22 g carbo., 3 g dietary fiber, 5 g pro.
Daily Values:
8% vit. A, 70% vit. C, 5% calcium, 6% iron
Exchanges:
1½ Fruit, ½ Meat, ½ Fat

Individual Puffed Oven Pancakes

All well-made pancakes can be described as light and airy, but oven pancakes actually puff up as they bake, creating ample bowls for the fresh fruit.

Prep: 10 minutes   **Bake:** 20 minutes
Oven: 400°F   **Makes:** 6 servings

140 CALORIES

Nutrition Facts per serving:
140 cal., 3 g total fat (1 g sat. fat), 108 mg chol., 147 mg sodium, 23 g carbo., 2 g fiber, 5 g pro.
Daily Values:
5% vit. A, 69% vit. C, 5% calcium, 6% iron
Exchanges:
1½ Fruit, 1 Meat

Cranberry-Apple Pancake

The beauty of this massive pancake—large enough to serve eight—is that it bakes in the oven, so there's no tending to a griddle.

Prep: 15 minutes **Bake:** 15 minutes
Cool: 5 minutes **Oven:** 350°F
Makes: 8 servings

163 CALORIES

Nutrition Facts per serving:
163 cal., 6 g total fat (3 g sat. fat), 35 mg chol., 199 mg sodium, 25 g carbo., 1 g fiber, 3 g pro.
Daily Values:
4% vit. A, 9% vit. C, 5% calcium, 5% iron
Exchanges:
1 Fruit, 1/2 Starch, 1 Fat

2 tablespoons butter or margarine
1 small apple, peeled, cored, and chopped
1/4 cup dried cranberries
1/4 cup packed brown sugar
1 teaspoon finely shredded orange peel (set aside)
1/4 cup orange juice
3/4 cup all-purpose flour
4 teaspoons granulated sugar
1/2 teaspoon baking powder
1/2 teaspoon baking soda
1/8 teaspoon salt
1 beaten egg
1/2 cup buttermilk or sour milk*
4 teaspoons cooking oil

1 Place butter in a 9-inch pie plate. Place pie plate in a 350° oven just until butter is melted. Remove from oven; cover bottom with apple and cranberries.

2 Meanwhile, in a small saucepan combine brown sugar and orange juice. Bring to boiling; reduce heat to medium. Boil gently, uncovered, for 5 minutes. Pour over apple and cranberries in pie plate.

3 In a medium bowl stir together flour, granulated sugar, baking powder, baking soda, and salt; set aside. In another medium bowl combine egg, buttermilk, oil, and orange peel. Add egg mixture all at once to flour mixture. Stir just until mixed. Pour batter evenly over fruit mixture in pie plate.

4 Bake in the 350° oven about 15 minutes or until top springs back when lightly touched. Cool in pie plate for 5 minutes. Carefully invert pancake onto a serving platter. Cut into wedges and serve warm.

*Note: To make 1/2 cup sour milk, place 1 1/2 teaspoons lemon juice or vinegar in a glass measuring cup. Add enough milk to make 1/2 cup total liquid; stir. Let the mixture stand for 5 minutes before using it in a recipe.

1 cup all-purpose flour

2 tablespoons cornmeal

1 tablespoon granulated sugar

1 teaspoon baking powder

1/2 teaspoon baking soda

1/4 teaspoon salt

1/4 teaspoon ground cinnamon

1 beaten egg

1 cup buttermilk or sour milk*

2 tablespoons cooking oil

1 cup fresh or frozen blueberries

Sifted powdered sugar (optional)

Maple or blueberry-flavored syrup (optional)

1 In a medium bowl combine flour, cornmeal, granulated sugar, baking powder, baking soda, salt, and cinnamon. Make a well in center of flour mixture; set aside.

2 In another medium bowl stir together the egg, buttermilk, and oil. Add egg mixture all at once to flour mixture. Stir just until moistened (batter should be lumpy). Gently fold in blueberries.

3 For each pancake, pour or spread about 1/4 cup of the batter into a 4-inch circle onto a hot, lightly greased griddle or heavy skillet. Cook over medium heat about 2 minutes on each side or until pancakes are golden brown, turning to second sides when pancakes have bubbly surfaces and edges are slightly dry. Serve warm. If desired, sprinkle with powdered sugar. If desired, pass syrup.

*Note: To make 1 cup sour milk, place 1 tablespoon lemon juice or vinegar in a glass measuring cup. Add enough milk to make 1 cup total liquid; stir. Let the mixture stand for 5 minutes before using it in a recipe.

253 CALORIES

Blueberry-Cornmeal Pancakes

These soul-satisfying pancakes contain a little cornmeal, which gives them a wonderful texture and flavor. You can use frozen blueberries in place of fresh when not in season.

Prep: 10 minutes   **Cook:** 4 minutes per batch
Makes: 4 or 5 servings

Nutrition Facts per serving:
253 cal., 9 g total fat (2 g sat. fat), 56 mg chol., 484 mg sodium, 35 g carbo., 3 g fiber, 7 g pro.
Daily Values:
3% vit. A, 7% vit. C, 15% calcium, 10% iron
Exchanges:
1 Starch, 1 1/2 Other Carbo., 1 Fat

236 CALORIES

Three-Grain Flapjacks

Top these wholesome flapjacks with fruit. If your favorite isn't in season, choose unsweetened frozen or juice-pack canned, which are processed at the peak of freshness and offer the same health benefits as fresh.

Prep: 15 minutes **Cook:** 3 minutes per batch
Stand: 10 minutes **Makes:** 8 to 10 servings

Nutrition Facts per serving (about 6 silver-dollar size pancakes or 2 regular pancakes):
236 cal., 7 g total fat (2 g sat. fat), 29 mg chol., 314 mg sodium, 36 g carbo., 2 g fiber, 7 g pro.
Daily Values:
4% vit. A, 1% vit. C, 17% calcium, 10% iron
Exchanges:
2½ Starch, 1 Fat

1½ cups all-purpose flour
½ cup yellow cornmeal
2½ teaspoons baking powder
½ teaspoon salt
½ cup regular rolled oats
3 tablespoons packed brown sugar
1 beaten egg
1¾ cups light or low-fat milk
¼ cup plain low-fat yogurt
3 tablespoons cooking oil
½ cup dried blueberries or currants (optional)
Nonstick cooking spray
Canned crushed pineapple (juice pack) or maple syrup (optional)

1 In a large bowl stir together flour, cornmeal, baking powder, and salt. In a blender container or food processor bowl combine oats and brown sugar. Cover and blend or process until oats are coarsely ground. Stir oat mixture into flour mixture. Make a well in the center of flour mixture.

2 In a medium bowl combine the egg, milk, yogurt, and oil. Add the egg mixture all at once to flour mixture. Stir just until moistened (batter should be lumpy and thin). Let stand for 10 minutes to thicken slightly, stirring once or twice. If desired, gently fold in blueberries or currants.

3 Lightly coat an unheated nonstick griddle or heavy skillet with nonstick cooking spray. Preheat over medium heat. For silver-dollar-size pancakes, pour or spread about 1 tablespoon batter into a 1-inch circle onto hot griddle or skillet. For standard-size pancakes, pour or spread about ¼ cup batter into a 3-inch circle onto hot griddle or skillet. Cook over medium heat for 1½ to 2 minutes on each side or until pancakes are golden brown, turning to second sides when pancakes have bubbly surfaces and edges are slightly dry. Serve warm. If desired, serve with pineapple or syrup.

- 2 **cups all-purpose flour**
- 2 **tablespoons brown sugar**
- 1 **tablespoon baking powder**
- 1/2 **teaspoon salt**
- 1/2 **teaspoon pumpkin pie spice**
- 1 1/2 **cups fat-free milk**
- 1 **cup canned pumpkin**
- 1/2 **cup refrigerated or frozen egg product, thawed**
- 2 **tablespoons cooking oil**
- 1 **recipe Orange Syrup**
- 1 **orange, peeled and sectioned (optional)**

1 In a medium bowl stir together the flour, brown sugar, baking powder, salt, and pumpkin pie spice. Make a well in the center of the flour mixture.

2 In another medium bowl combine the milk, pumpkin, egg product, and oil. Add milk mixture all at once to flour mixture. Stir just until moistened (batter should be lumpy).

3 Pour about ¾ cup batter onto grids of a preheated, lightly greased waffle baker. Close lid quickly; do not open until golden brown. Bake according to manufacturer's directions. When done, use a fork to lift waffle off grids. Repeat with remaining batter. Serve waffles warm with Orange Syrup and, if desired, orange sections.

Orange Syrup: In a small saucepan stir together 1 cup orange juice, 2 tablespoons honey, 2½ teaspoons cornstarch, and ¼ teaspoon ground cinnamon. Cook and stir until thickened and bubbly. Cook and stir for 2 minutes more. Serve warm. Makes about 1 cup.

Pumpkin Waffles with Orange Syrup

If your family is tired of ordinary waffles, they'll sit up and take notice when you set this pumpkin-infused version and its orange syrup partner on the table.

Prep: 10 minutes   **Bake:** per waffle baker directions
Makes: 10 waffles

173 CALORIES

Nutrition Facts per waffle:
173 cal., 3 g total fat (1 g sat. fat), 1 mg chol., 279 mg sodium, 31 g carbo., 1 g fiber, 5 g pro.
Daily Values:
111% vit. A, 23% vit. C, 14% calcium, 10% iron
Exchanges:
2 Starch

Blueberry Blintzes

Showcase naturally sweet and pretty summer blueberries in this spectacular brunch entrée. Blackberries or sliced strawberries are scrumptious too.

Prep: 30 minutes **Bake:** 15 minutes
Oven: 400°F **Makes:** 8 servings

231 CALORIES

Nutrition Facts per serving (2 blintzes):
231 cal., 8 g total fat (3 g sat. fat), 70 mg chol., 182 mg sodium, 31 g carbo., 2 g fiber, 11 g pro.
Daily Values:
10% vit. A, 35% vit. C, 22% calcium, 6% iron
Exchanges:
1 Fruit, 1 Starch, 1 Medium-Fat Meat, ½ Fat

2	**eggs**
1⅓	**cups fat-free milk**
¾	**cup whole wheat flour**
1	**tablespoon cooking oil**
¼	**teaspoon salt**
1	**15-ounce carton part-skim ricotta cheese**
2	**cups fresh blueberries**
¼	**cup packed brown sugar**
1½	**teaspoons finely shredded orange peel**
1	**cup orange juice**
1	**tablespoon cornstarch**
1	**tablespoon granulated sugar**
¼	**teaspoon ground cardamom**

1 For crepes, in a medium bowl combine eggs, milk, flour, oil, and salt; beat until well mixed. Heat a lightly greased 6-inch skillet over medium heat; remove from heat. Spoon in 2 tablespoons batter; lift and tilt skillet to spread batter. Return to heat; cook on 1 side only for 1 to 2 minutes or until brown. (Or cook on a crepemaker according to manufacturer's directions.) Invert over clean, white paper towels; remove crepe. Repeat with the remaining batter, lightly greasing skillet occasionally.

2 For filling, in another medium bowl combine ricotta cheese, 1 cup of the blueberries, the brown sugar, and 1 teaspoon of the orange peel. Fill each crepe, browned side down, with a rounded tablespoon of the filling. Roll up. Place blintzes in a 3-quart rectangular baking dish. Bake, uncovered, in a 400° oven for 15 to 20 minutes or until heated through.

3 Meanwhile, for sauce, in a small saucepan stir together the remaining ½ teaspoon orange peel, the orange juice, cornstarch, granulated sugar, and cardamom. Cook and stir until thickened and bubbly. Cook and stir for 2 minutes more. Stir in the remaining 1 cup blueberries. Spoon the sauce over warm blintzes.

2 medium ripe bananas, cut into
   ¼-inch slices (about 1⅓ cups)
1 tablespoon lemon juice
12 ½-inch slices French bread
¼ cup miniature semisweet chocolate
   pieces
2 beaten eggs
¾ cup milk
2 tablespoons honey
½ teaspoon vanilla
¼ teaspoon ground cinnamon
¼ cup sliced almonds
1 teaspoon sugar
   Maple-flavored syrup (optional)

1 In a small bowl gently toss bananas with lemon juice. Grease a 2-quart square baking dish. Arrange half of the bread slices in the bottom of the prepared baking dish. Layer bananas over bread in baking dish. Top with chocolate pieces and remaining bread slices.

2 In a medium bowl combine eggs, milk, honey, vanilla, and cinnamon. Pour liquid slowly over bread to coat evenly. Cover and chill for at least 6 hours or up to 24 hours.

3 Uncover the baking dish. Sprinkle bread with almonds and sugar. Bake in a 425° oven for 5 minutes. Reduce oven temperature to 325°. Bake for 20 to 25 minutes more or until knife inserted near the center comes out clean and top of French toast is light brown. Let stand for 10 minutes before serving. If desired, serve with maple-flavored syrup.

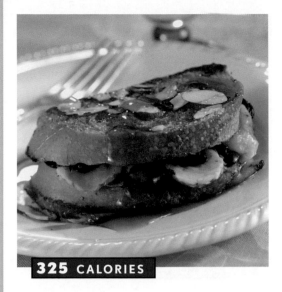

325 CALORIES

Banana French Toast

Sandwiched between French bread slices, bananas and chocolate create a French toast to behold. It seems so decadent, you might feel guilty for eating it. But don't—with 325 calories and only 9 grams of fat, this is a dieter's delight.

Prep: 25 minutes **Bake:** 25 minutes
Stand: 10 minutes **Chill:** 6 to 24 hours
Oven: 425°F/ 325°F **Makes:** 6 servings

Nutrition Facts per serving:
325 cal., 9 g total fat (3 g sat. fat), 73 mg chol.,
342 mg sodium, 51 g carbo., 3 g fiber, 10 g pro.
Daily Values:
4% vit. A, 9% vit. C, 10% calcium, 12% iron
Exchanges:
1½ Fruit, 2 Starch, ½ Meat, 1 Fat

181 CALORIES

Stuffed French Toast

For a change of taste, top fruit and cheese-filled French toast with a drizzle of maple syrup or in place of the honey or spreadable fruit.

Start to Finish: 30 minutes

Makes: 8 servings

¹/₂ cup fat-free cream cheese (about 5 ounces)

2 tablespoons apricot or strawberry spreadable fruit

8 1-inch slices French bread

2 slightly beaten egg whites

1 beaten egg

³/₄ cup fat-free milk

¹/₂ teaspoon vanilla

¹/₈ teaspoon apple pie spice

Nonstick cooking spray

¹/₂ cup honey, or apricot or strawberry spreadable fruit

Sifted powdered sugar (optional)

1 In a small bowl stir together cream cheese and the 2 tablespoons spreadable fruit. Using a serrated knife, cut a pocket in each bread slice by making a cut in the crust top of each slice from the top almost to the bottom. Fill each pocket with some of the cream cheese mixture.

2 In a shallow bowl beat together the egg whites, whole egg, milk, vanilla, and apple pie spice. Coat an unheated nonstick griddle with nonstick cooking spray. Preheat over medium heat.

3 Dip bread slices into egg white mixture, coating both sides. Cook bread slices on hot griddle about 3 minutes or until golden brown, turning once to cook second sides.

4 Meanwhile, in a small saucepan heat the ½ cup spreadable fruit (if using) until melted, stirring frequently. If desied, sift with powdered sugar. Serve honey or spreadable fruit with French toast.

Nutrition Facts per serving:
181 cal., 1 g total fat (0 g sat. fat), 30 mg chol., 187 mg sodium, 36 g carbo., 1 g fiber, 7 g pro.
Daily Values:
2% vit. A, 1% vit. C, 11% calcium, 5% iron
Exchanges:
1 Starch, 1 Other Carbo., 1 Meat

2 1-ounce envelopes instant oatmeal (plain)

1 medium banana, peeled and sliced

Desired fresh fruit (such as blueberries, sliced strawberries, and/or sliced peaches)

2 tablespoons chopped pecans, toasted

2 teaspoons caramel-flavored ice cream topping

Milk (optional)

1 In 2 microwave-safe bowls prepare oatmeal according to package directions. Top each serving with banana slices, desired fresh fruit, and pecans. Drizzle with ice cream topping. If desired, heat in microwave on 100% power (high) for 30 seconds. If desired, serve with milk.

Fruit and Caramel Oatmeal

Kids love this warm oatmeal, thanks to the banana, nuts, and drizzling of caramel. Moms love it because it's microwaveable and takes just minutes to make.

Start to Finish: 10 minutes

Makes: 2 servings

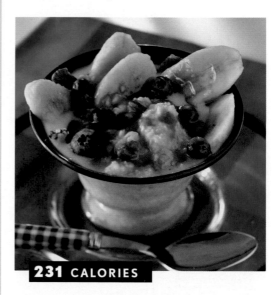

231 CALORIES

Nutrition Facts per serving:
231 cal., 7 g total fat (1 g sat. fat), 0 mg chol., 302 mg sodium, 39 g carbo., 6 g fiber, 6 g pro.
Daily Values:
31% vit. A, 11% vit. C, 17% calcium, 37% iron
Exchanges:
1½ Fruit, 1 Starch, 1 Fat

Fruit and Grain Cereal

If you're looking for a hot cereal that tastes great and is good for you too, look no further. Keep a batch of this cracked wheat, brown rice, dried fruit, and cinnamon cereal in the refrigerator so you can cook up a fuss-free hot breakfast any day of the week.

Prep: 5 minutes   **Cook:** 15 minutes
Cool: 3 minutes   **Makes:** 5 servings

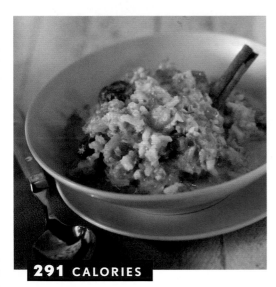

291 CALORIES

1½   **cups cracked wheat cereal**
¾   **cup quick-cooking brown rice**
½   **cup mixed dried fruit bits**
½   **teaspoon ground cinnamon**
¼   **teaspoon salt**
3⅓   **cups water**
2½   **cups milk**
   Stick cinnamon (optional)

1 In a self-sealing plastic bag combine wheat cereal, rice, dried fruit bits, cinnamon, and salt. Mix thoroughly to ensure fruit and seasonings are evenly distributed. (You may have to use your hands to separate fruit bits.) Seal bag. Store in refrigerator for up to 1 month.

2 In a large saucepan combine water and milk. Bring to boiling; reduce heat. Stir in cereal mixture. (For 1 serving, in a small saucepan bring ⅔ cup of the water and ½ cup of the milk to boiling; reduce heat. Stir in ½ cup of the cereal mixture.) Simmer, uncovered, for 15 to 20 minutes or until most of the liquid is absorbed, mixture is creamy, and wheat is just tender,* stirring occasionally. Cool for 3 to 5 minutes before serving. If desired, garnish with stick cinnamon.

*Note: If mixture is dry before wheat is tender, stir in additional water.

Nutrition Facts per serving:
291 cal., 3 g total fat (2 g sat. fat), 10 mg chol., 199 mg sodium, 58 g carbo., 9 g fiber, 11 g pro.
Daily Values:
5% vit. A, 3% vit. C, 17% calcium, 8% iron
Exchanges:
½ Milk, 2½ Starch, 1 Other Carbo.

Nonstick cooking spray

2¹/₂ cups regular rolled oats

1 cup wheat flakes

¹/₃ cup toasted wheat germ

¹/₃ cup sliced almonds or pecan pieces

¹/₃ cup unsweetened pineapple juice or apple juice

¹/₃ cup honey

¹/₄ teaspoon ground allspice

¹/₄ teaspoon ground cinnamon

6 cups desired fat-free yogurt

4 cups fresh fruit (such as blueberries, seedless green grapes, raspberries, sliced strawberries, and/or chopped peaches)

1 Coat a 15×10×1-inch baking pan with nonstick cooking spray; set aside. In a large bowl stir together the oats, wheat flakes, wheat germ, and nuts. In a small saucepan stir together juice, honey, allspice, and cinnamon. Cook and stir just until boiling. Remove from heat. Pour over oat mixture, tossing just until coated.

2 Spread the oat mixture evenly in prepared pan. Bake in a 325° oven for 30 to 35 minutes or until oats are lightly browned, stirring twice. Remove from oven. Immediately turn out onto a large piece of foil; cool completely.

3 For each serving, spoon ¹/₂ cup of the yogurt into a bowl. Top with ¹/₃ cup of the oat mixture and ¹/₃ cup desired fruit.

Make-ahead directions: Prepare as above through step 2. Cover and chill for up to 2 weeks. For longer storage, seal in freezer bags and freeze for up to 3 months.

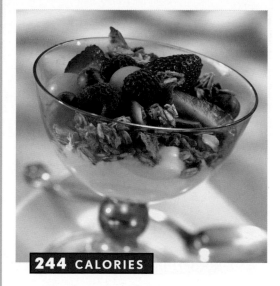

244 CALORIES

Honey Granola with Yogurt

Fruits, nuts, grains, and yogurt blend to make a nutritionally powerful breakfast. The contrast of smooth yogurt and crunchy granola will wake up everyone's taste buds.

Prep: 15 minutes **Bake:** 30 minutes
Oven: 325°F **Makes:** 12 servings

Nutrition Facts per serving:
244 cal., 4 g total fat (1 g sat. fat), 2 mg chol., 96 mg sodium, 44 g carbo., 5 g fiber, 11 g pro.
Daily Values:
4% vit. A, 45% vit. C, 24% calcium, 21% iron
Exchanges:
1 Milk, ¹/₂ Fruit, 1¹/₂ Starch, ¹/₂ Fat

156 CALORIES

Plum-Oat Drop Biscuits

Dried plums (formerly known as prunes) are nutritional powerhouses. Teamed with rolled oats, they supply these cinnamon-spiced biscuits with a heart-healthy dose of fiber.

Prep: 20 minutes   **Bake:** 10 minutes
Oven: 450°F   **Makes:** 12 biscuits

- 2 **tablespoons sugar**
- 1/2 **teaspoon ground cinnamon**
- 11/3 **cups all-purpose flour**
- 11/3 **cups regular rolled oats**
- 1 **tablespoon baking powder**
- 1/4 **teaspoon salt**
- 3 **tablespoons butter or margarine**
- 3/4 **cup snipped orange-flavored pitted dried plums (prunes)**
- 1 **cup fat-free milk**

1 In a small bowl stir together sugar and cinnamon; set aside. In a large bowl stir together flour, oats, baking powder, salt, and 1 tablespoon of the sugar mixture. Using a pastry blender, cut in butter until mixture resembles coarse crumbs. Stir in dried plums. Make a well in the center of the flour mixture. Add the milk all at once. Using a fork, stir just until moistened.

2 Grease a large baking sheet. Drop dough into 12 mounds (about ¼ cup each) onto prepared baking sheet. Sprinkle the remaining sugar mixture evenly over all. Bake in a 450° oven for 10 to 12 minutes or until golden brown. Remove biscuits from baking sheet. Serve immediately.

Nutrition Facts per biscuit:
156 cal., 4 g total fat (2 g sat. fat), 9 mg chol., 191 mg sodium, 27 g carbo., 2 g fiber, 4 g pro.
Daily Values:
7% vit. A, 1% vit. C, 10% calcium, 8% iron
Exchanges:
1 Starch, ½ Other Carbo., ½ Fat

Nonstick cooking spray

1 16-ounce loaf frozen sweet roll dough, thawed

1 tablespoon butter or margarine, melted

¼ cup granulated sugar

1 tablespoon finely shredded orange peel

⅓ cup sifted powdered sugar

1 to 2 teaspoons orange juice or milk

1 Lightly coat twelve 2½-inch muffin cups with nonstick cooking spray; set aside.

2 On a lightly floured surface, roll thawed dough to a 12×8-inch rectangle. Brush with melted butter. In a small bowl combine granulated sugar and orange peel; sprinkle evenly over dough. Roll up into a spiral, starting from a long side. Pinch seam to seal. Slice roll into 12 equal pieces. Place pieces, cut sides down, in prepared muffin cups. Cover; let rise in a warm place for 30 minutes.

3 Bake rolls in a 350° oven about 20 minutes or until golden brown. Remove from muffin cups. Place on a wire rack.

4 For icing, in a small bowl stir together the powdered sugar and enough of the orange juice or milk to make drizzling consistency. Drizzle icing over rolls. Serve warm.

Orange Sweet Rolls

Best when served warm, these little rolls melt in your mouth as they satisfy your desire for a touch of early morning sweetness.

Prep: 20 minutes   **Rise:** 30 minutes
Bake: 20 minutes   **Oven:** 350°F
Makes: 12 rolls

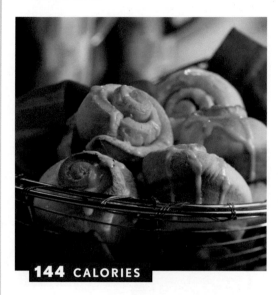

144 CALORIES

Nutrition Facts per roll:
144 cal., 4 g total fat (2 g sat. fat), 24 mg chol., 79 mg sodium, 25 g carbo., 1 g fiber, 3 g pro.
Daily Values:
1% vit. A, 2% vit. C, 2% calcium, 6% iron
Exchanges:
1 Starch, ½ Other Carbo., ½ Fat

Dried Fruit Coffee Cake

Sweet, tender coffee cake—studded with dried plums and dried apricots—is a tasty way to add interest to weekday breakfasts.

Prep: 20 minutes **Bake:** 25 minutes
Cool: 10 minutes **Oven:** 350°F
Makes: 10 servings

211 CALORIES

Nonstick cooking spray
1½ **cups all-purpose flour**
1 **teaspoon baking powder**
¼ **teaspoon salt**
1 **slightly beaten egg**
½ **cup snipped dried pitted plums (prunes)**
¼ **cup snipped dried apricots**
½ **cup packed brown sugar**
¼ **cup unsweetened applesauce**
4 **tablespoons butter, melted**
1 **teaspoon vanilla**
2 **tablespoons sliced almonds**
2 **tablespoons toasted wheat germ**
1 **tablespoon packed brown sugar**

1 Lightly coat an 8×1½-inch round baking pan with nonstick cooking spray; set aside. In a medium bowl stir together flour, baking powder, and salt.

2 In a small bowl combine egg, dried plums, and apricots. Stir in the ½ cup brown sugar, the applesauce, 3 tablespoons of the melted butter, and the vanilla. Add fruit mixture all at once to flour mixture; stir to combine. Spread batter evenly into prepared baking pan.

3 For topping, in a small bowl stir together almonds, wheat germ, the 1 tablespoon brown sugar, and the remaining 1 tablespoon melted butter. Sprinkle the topping over batter; lightly press into batter.

4 Bake in a 350° oven for 25 to 30 minutes or until a wooden toothpick inserted near the center comes out clean. Cool in pan on a wire rack for 10 minutes. Serve warm.

Nutrition Facts per serving:
211 cal., 7 g total fat (3 g sat. fat), 34 mg chol., 160 mg sodium, 35 g carbo., 2 g fiber, 4 g pro.
Daily Values:
13% vit. A, 1% vit. C, 5% calcium, 10% iron
Exchanges:
1 Fruit, 1 Other Carbo., 1 Fat

- $^1/_3$ **cup sugar**
- 1 **to 2 tablespoons instant coffee crystals**
- 1$^1/_2$ **teaspoons ground cinnamon**
- 1$^1/_2$ **cups all-purpose flour**
- $^1/_2$ **cup sugar**
- 1 **teaspoon baking powder**
- $^1/_2$ **teaspoon baking soda**
- $^1/_8$ **teaspoon salt**
- 1 **slightly beaten egg**
- 1 **8-ounce carton plain low-fat yogurt**
- 3 **tablespoons butter or margarine, melted**
- 1 **teaspoon vanilla**
- $^1/_4$ **cup chopped walnuts**

1 Grease bottom and $^1/_2$ inch up the sides of an 8×8×2-inch baking pan; set aside.

2 In a small bowl stir together the $^1/_3$ cup sugar, the coffee crystals, and cinnamon; set aside.

3 In a large bowl stir together flour, the $^1/_2$ cup sugar, the baking power, baking soda, and salt. In another bowl combine egg, yogurt, melted butter, and vanilla; add to flour mixture, stirring until moistened. Spread half of the batter in prepared baking pan. Sprinkle with half of the sugar-coffee mixture. Drop remaining batter by spoonfuls evenly over mixture in baking pan. Spread batter evenly over the mixture. Sprinkle with remaining sugar-coffee mixture. Sprinkle with nuts.

4 Bake in a 350° oven for 30 to 35 minutes or until a wooden toothpick inserted in center comes out clean. Serve warm.

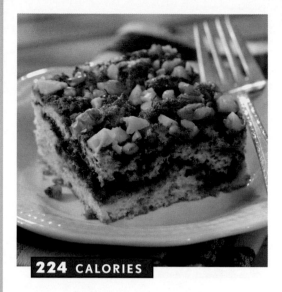

224 CALORIES

Double Coffee Cake

Double your coffee pleasure with this java-spiked quick bread. Want even more flavor? Use an extra tablespoon of instant coffee crystals.

Prep: 30 minutes **Bake:** 30 minutes
Oven: 350°F **Makes:** 9 servings

Nutrition Facts per serving:
224 cal., 7 g total fat (3 g sat. fat), 36 mg chol., 214 mg sodium, 35 g carbo., 1 g fiber, 5 g pro.
Daily Values:
4% vit. A, 1% vit. C, 9% calcium, 7% iron
Exchanges:
1 Starch, 1 Other Carbo., 1 Fat

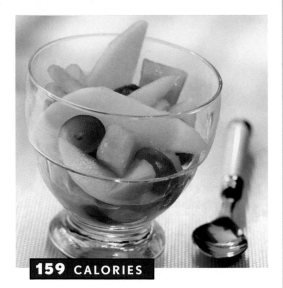

159 CALORIES

Sunrise Fruit Compote

By definition, a compote consists of fresh or dried fruit cooked in a sugary syrup and chilled before served. It's a cool, refreshing start to a summer day or, served over piping hot oatmeal, an early warmer-upper in winter.

Prep: 20 minutes   **Chill:** 1 to 4 hours
Makes: 6 servings

- 1 **lemon**
- 1 **orange or tangerine**
- 1 **lime**
- ⅓ **cup sugar**
- 2 **large pears, cored and sliced**
- 2 **medium papayas, peeled, seeded, and cubed**
- 1 **cup seedless red grapes, halved**

1 Halve lemon, orange, and lime; squeeze out all of the juices (about ¾ cup total), reserving citrus shells. In a small saucepan combine the juices, sugar, and half of the citrus shells; bring to boiling. Discard remaining shells. Cook and stir until sugar dissolves; reduce heat. Simmer, uncovered, for 5 minutes. Carefully remove shells; discard.

2 Place pears, papayas, and grapes in a large bowl. Pour hot juice mixture over fruit, gently stirring to mix. Cover and chill for at least 1 hour or up to 4 hours.

Nutrition Facts per serving:
159 cal., 1 g total fat (0 g sat. fat), 0 mg chol., 7 mg sodium, 40 g carbo., 4 g fiber, 1 g pro.
Daily Values:
7% vit. A, 147% vit. C, 4% calcium, 3% iron
Exchanges:
2½ Fruit

1　cup vanilla-flavored soy milk or 1 cup light or low-fat milk plus ¼ teaspoon vanilla

¼　cup orange juice

¼　cup refrigerated or frozen egg product, thawed

1　to 2 tablespoons honey

½　cup chopped mango

½　cup frozen strawberries, raspberries, blueberries, or boysenberries

Fresh mint sprigs (optional)

1 In a blender container combine soy milk, orange juice, egg product, and honey. Cover and blend for 10 seconds.

2 Add mango and frozen berries. Cover and blend until smooth. Immediately pour into 2 glasses. If desired, garnish with fresh mint.

Berry-Mango Soy Smoothie

Not your ordinary fruit smoothie, this one reaps the nutritional benefits of soy milk, making it low in fat and high in protein.

Start to Finish: 10 minutes
Makes: 2 (10-ounce) servings

168 CALORIES

Nutrition Facts per serving:
168 cal., 2 g total fat (0 g sat. fat), 0 mg chol., 117 mg sodium, 31 g carbo., 3 g fiber, 7 g pro.
Daily Values:
41% vit. A, 79% vit. C, 17% calcium, 10% iron
Exchanges:
½ Milk, 1½ Fruit, ½ Meat

Melon Smoothie

Breakfast doesn't get any easier than this. Even the family sleepyheads will look forward to starting the day off with a yummy smoothie.

Start to Finish: 10 minutes

Makes: 4 (8-ounce) servings

130 CALORIES

2 cups orange or orange-tangerine juice, chilled

1 cup cubed cantaloupe

1 8-ounce carton plain low-fat yogurt

2 to 4 tablespoons sugar or honey

1/2 teaspoon vanilla

   Toasted wheat germ (optional)

   Peeled cantaloupe wedges (optional)

1 In a blender container combine the orange-tangerine juice, cantaloupe, yogurt, sugar, and vanilla. Cover and blend until nearly smooth.

2 Divide among 4 glasses. If desired, sprinkle with wheat germ and garnish with cantaloupe wedges.

Nutrition Facts per serving:
130 cal., 1 g total fat (1 g sat. fat), 3 mg chol., 45 mg sodium, 26 g carbo., 1 g fiber, 4 g pro.
Daily Values:
32% vit. A, 132% vit. C, 12% calcium, 2% iron
Exchanges:
1/2 Milk, 1 1/2 Fruit

On the divider: **Peppercorn Steaks** (see recipe, page 232)

- 1   1¼-pound beef flank steak
- ½   cup beef broth
- ⅓   cup hoisin sauce
- ¼   cup reduced-sodium soy sauce
- ¼   cup sliced green onions (2)
- 3   tablespoons dry sherry or apple, orange, or pineapple juice
- 1   tablespoon sugar
- 1   teaspoon grated fresh ginger
- 4   cloves garlic, minced
      Nonstick cooking spray

1 Trim fat from steak. Place steak in a plastic bag set in a shallow dish. For marinade, in a small bowl stir together broth, hoisin sauce, soy sauce, green onions, sherry or juice, sugar, ginger, and garlic. Pour over steak; seal bag. Marinate in refrigerator for at least 4 hours or up to 24 hours, turning bag occasionally.

2 Preheat broiler. Drain steak, discarding the marinade. Lightly coat the unheated rack of a broiler pan with nonstick cooking spray. Place steak on the prepared rack. Broil 4 to 5 inches from heat for 15 to 18 minutes or until medium doneness (160°F), turning once. (Or grill steak on the rack of an uncovered grill directly over medium coals for 17 to 21 minutes or until medium doneness [160°F], turning once.) To serve, thinly slice the steak across the grain.

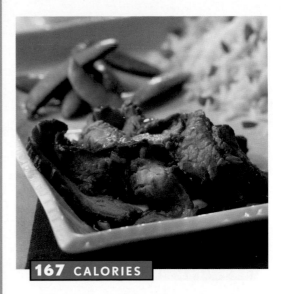

167 CALORIES

Asian Flank Steak

Anyone who has marinated a flank steak knows how tender it becomes—and how flavorful. Hoisin and soy sauces, sherry, ginger, and garlic combine for this delicious marinade.

Prep: 15 minutes   **Marinate:** 4 to 24 hours
Broil: 15 minutes   **Makes:** 6 servings

Nutrition Facts per serving:
167 cal., 7 g total fat (3 g sat. fat), 47 mg chol., 344 mg sodium, 4 g carbo., 0 g fiber, 20 g pro.
Daily Values:
1% vit. A, 2% vit. C, 2% calcium, 11% iron
Exchanges:
3 Meat

224 CALORIES

Flank Steak with Corn Salsa

Both the salsa and marinade for this Mexican-inspired dish are quick and easy to make. The prep work, which can be done ahead, takes only 15 minutes.

Prep: 15 minutes   **Marinate:** 6 to 24 hours
Broil: 15 minutes   **Makes:** 6 servings

1   8³/₄-ounce can whole kernel corn, drained
³/₄   cup bottled salsa verde
²/₃   cup chopped tomato (1 medium)
1   1¹/₄- to 1¹/₂-pound beef flank steak
³/₄   cup bottled Italian salad dressing
2   tablespoons cracked black pepper
1   tablespoon Worcestershire sauce
1   teaspoon ground cumin
   Flour tortillas (optional)

1 For corn salsa, in medium bowl combine corn, salsa verde, and tomato. Cover and chill for at least 6 hours or up to 24 hours.

2 Meanwhile, trim fat from steak. Score both sides of steak in a diamond pattern by making shallow diagonal cuts at 1-inch intervals. Place steak in a plastic bag set in a shallow dish.

3 For marinade, in a small bowl combine salad dressing, pepper, Worcestershire sauce, and cumin. Pour over steak; seal bag. Marinate in the refrigerator for at least 6 hours or up to 24 hours, turning bag occasionally. Drain steak, discarding marinade.

4 Preheat broiler. Place steak on the unheated rack of a broiler pan. Broil 3 to 4 inches from the heat for 15 to 18 minutes or until medium doneness (160°F), turning once.

5 To serve, thinly slice steak diagonally across the grain. Serve steak with corn salsa and, if desired, tortillas.

Nutrition Facts per serving:
224 cal., 12 g total fat (4 g sat. fat), 38 mg chol., 201 mg sodium, 8 g carbo., 1 g fiber, 22 g pro.
Daily Values:
4% vit. A, 11% vit. C, 1% calcium, 12% iron
Exchanges:
¹/₂ Starch, 3 Meat

1 1¹/₄-pound beef flank steak
¹/₂ cup dry red wine
¹/₃ cup finely chopped onion (1 small)
2 tablespoons lime juice
1 tablespoon reduced-sodium soy sauce
1 tablespoon cooking oil
1 teaspoon crushed red pepper
¹/₂ teaspoon coarsely ground black pepper
¹/₂ teaspoon dried whole green peppercorns, crushed
3 cloves garlic, minced
3 pita bread rounds, halved crosswise
6 lettuce leaves
1 small red onion, sliced and separated into rings

1 Trim fat from steak. Score both sides of steak in a diamond pattern by making shallow diagonal cuts at 1-inch intervals. Place steak in a plastic bag set in a shallow dish.

2 For marinade, in a small bowl stir together wine, chopped onion, lime juice, soy sauce, oil, red pepper, black pepper, green peppercorns, and garlic. Pour over steak; seal bag. Marinate in the refrigerator for at least 6 hours or up to 24 hours, turning bag occasionally.

3 Preheat broiler. Drain steak, reserving marinade. Place steak on the unheated rack of a broiler pan. Broil 3 to 4 inches from the heat for 15 to 18 minutes or until medium doneness (160°F), turning and brushing once with reserved marinade halfway through broiling time. Discard any remaining marinade.

4 To serve, thinly slice steak diagonally across the grain. Fill pita bread halves with meat, lettuce, and onion.

Pepper-Marinated Flank Steak

Have you ever stopped to think about the origins of pepper, that everyday spice you sprinkle on so many foods? Peppercorns are the tiny berries of a tropical vine and come in an array of colors, depending on when they're harvested. Green peppercorns are picked underripe, black are not quite ripe, and white have been allowed to fully ripen.

Prep: 10 minutes   **Marinate:** 6 to 24 hours
Broil: 15 minutes   **Makes:** 6 servings

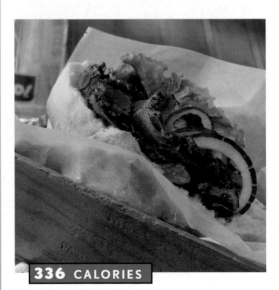

336 CALORIES

Nutrition Facts per serving:
336 cal., 10 g total fat (4 g sat. fat), 40 mg chol., 612 mg sodium, 26 g carbo., 4 g fiber, 34 g pro.
Daily Values:
10% vit. A, 18% vit. C, 14% calcium, 19% iron
Exchanges:
2 Vegetable, 1 Starch, 3¹/₂ Meat

Beef Satay with Peanut Sauce

It seems odd that you would be instructed to freeze a piece of meat before you cook it, but in this case it makes perfect sense. Doing so eases the task of slicing it into thin strips.

Prep: 25 minutes **Marinate:** 30 minutes
Broil: 4 minutes **Makes:** 5 servings

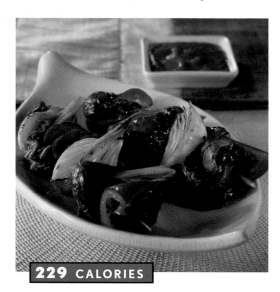

229 CALORIES

Nutrition Facts per serving:
229 cal., 10 g total fat (3 g sat. fat), 36 mg chol., 491 mg sodium, 11 g carbo., 2 g fiber, 23 g pro.
Daily Values:
4% vit. A, 40% vit. C, 2% calcium, 11% iron
Exchanges:
2 Vegetable, 2½ Meat, ½ Fat

1 1- to 1¼-pound beef flank steak
⅓ cup light teriyaki sauce
½ teaspoon bottled hot pepper sauce
1 medium onion, cut into thin wedges
4 green onions, cut into 1-inch pieces
1 red or green sweet pepper, cut into ¾-inch chunks
3 tablespoons reduced-fat or regular peanut butter
3 tablespoons water
2 tablespoons light teriyaki sauce

1 If desired, partially freeze steak for easier slicing. For satay, trim fat from steak. Cut steak crosswise into thin slices. For marinade, in a medium bowl combine the ⅓ cup teriyaki sauce and ¼ teaspoon of the hot pepper sauce. Add steak; toss to coat. Cover and marinate in the refrigerator for 30 minutes. If using bamboo skewers, soak them in water for 30 minutes to prevent scorching.

2 Preheat broiler. Drain steak, reserving marinade. On bamboo or metal skewers, alternately thread steak strips (accordion style), onion wedges, green onion pieces, and sweet pepper pieces. Brush with reserved marinade. Discard any remaining marinade.

3 Place skewers on the unheated rack of a broiler pan. Broil 4 to 5 inches from the heat about 4 minutes or until meat is slightly pink in center, turning once.

4 For peanut sauce, in a small saucepan combine peanut butter, the water, the 2 tablespoons teriyaki sauce, and the remaining ¼ teaspoon hot pepper sauce. Heat, stirring constantly, over medium heat just until smooth and hot.

5 Serve satay with warm peanut sauce.

1 slice bacon, chopped
4 4-ounce beef tenderloin steaks,
  cut 1 inch thick
  Salt
  Black pepper
3 cups very thinly sliced fresh Swiss
  chard leaves (4 ounces)
½ teaspoon dried thyme, crushed
⅛ teaspoon salt
⅛ teaspoon black pepper

1 Preheat broiler. In a large skillet cook
bacon over medium heat until crisp.
Remove from skillet, reserving drippings.
Crumble bacon; set aside. Remove skillet
from heat; set aside.

2 Season steaks with salt and pepper. Place
steaks on the unheated rack of a broiler
pan. Broil 4 to 5 inches from the heat
until desired doneness, turning once
halfway through broiling time. (Allow
12 to 14 minutes for medium-rare
doneness [145°F] or 15 to 18 minutes for
medium doneness [160°F].)

3 Meanwhile, cook and stir Swiss chard in
drippings in skillet over medium heat for
4 to 6 minutes or just until tender. Stir in
reserved bacon, thyme, the ⅛ teaspoon
salt, and the ⅛ teaspoon pepper. To
serve, spoon Swiss chard mixture on top
of the steaks.

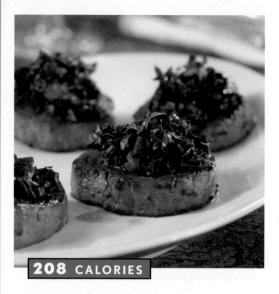

208 CALORIES

Chard-Topped Steaks

These elegant steaks make great dinner
party fare. The tender, tangy Swiss chard
greens complement the succulent beef.

Prep: 20 minutes   **Broil:** 12 minutes
Makes: 4 servings

Nutrition Facts per serving:
208 cal., 11 g total fat (4 g sat. fat), 60 mg chol.,
363 mg sodium, 1 g carbo., 1 g fiber, 25 g pro.
Daily Values:
20% vit. A, 14% vit. C, 2% calcium, 20% iron
Exchanges:
3½ Meat

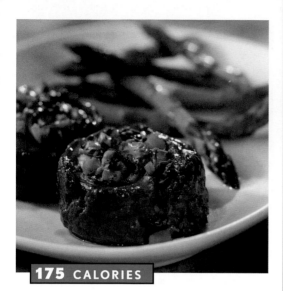

175 CALORIES

Teriyaki Beef Spirals

Chopped water chestnuts, a common ingredient in Asian cooking, give the fresh spinach filling added crunch. The toothpicks and skewers help hold the spirals together as they broil.

Prep: 20 minutes **Broil:** 12 minutes
Makes: 5 servings

Nutrition Facts per serving:
175 cal., 8 g total fat (3 g sat. fat), 56 mg chol., 139 mg sodium, 1 g carbo., 1 g fiber, 23 g pro.
Daily Values:
7% vit. A, 5% vit. C, 2% calcium, 15% iron
Exchanges:
3 Meat

---

1 **cup loosely packed fresh spinach leaves**
$^1/_2$ **cup finely chopped water chestnuts**
$^1/_4$ **cup thinly sliced green onions (2)**
$^1/_4$ **cup bottled reduced-sodium teriyaki sauce**
1 **1$^1/_4$-pound beef flank steak**
Salt
Black pepper

1 Preheat broiler. Remove stems from spinach leaves. Layer leaves on top of each other; slice crosswise into thin strips. In a medium bowl combine spinach, water chestnuts, green onions, and 2 tablespoons of the teriyaki sauce.

2 Trim fat from steak. Score both sides of steak in a diamond pattern by making shallow diagonal cuts at 1-inch intervals. Place steak between 2 sheets of plastic wrap. Working from center to edges, use the flat side of a meat mallet to pound the steak into a 12×8-inch rectangle. Remove plastic wrap. Sprinkle steak lightly with salt and pepper.

3 Spread spinach mixture over steak. Starting from a long side, roll rectangle into a spiral. Starting $^1/_2$ inch from 1 end, secure with wooden toothpicks at 1-inch intervals. Cut between toothpicks into 10 pinwheels. Thread 2 pinwheels onto each of 5 long skewers. Brush with some of the remaining teriyaki sauce.

4 Place skewers on the rack of an unheated broiler pan. Broil 3 to 4 inches from heat for 12 to 14 minutes or until medium doneness, turning once and brushing with teriyaki sauce halfway through broiling time. Discard any of the remaining teriyaki sauce. Remove toothpicks and skewers.

4 3- to 4-ounce beef tenderloin steaks,
   cut 1 inch thick

   Salt

1 tablespoon reduced-sodium soy sauce

1 tablespoon olive oil

1 tablespoon snipped fresh chives

2 cloves garlic, minced

1/2 teaspoon coriander seeds or cumin
     seeds, crushed

1/2 teaspoon celery seeds

1/2 teaspoon coarsely ground black pepper

1 Preheat broiler. Trim fat from steaks.
Sprinkle lightly with salt. In a small bowl
combine soy sauce, oil, chives, garlic,
coriander seeds or cumin seeds, celery
seeds, and pepper. Brush the mixture
onto both sides of each steak.

2 Place steaks on the unheated rack of a
broiler pan. Broil 3 to 4 inches from heat
until desired doneness, turning once
halfway through broiling time. (Allow
12 to 14 minutes for medium-rare
doneness [145°F] or 15 to 18 minutes for
medium doneness [160°F].)

Coriander-Studded Tenderloin Steak

Coriander seeds come from the plant
commonly called cilantro, but they don't
share the same flavor. The seeds taste like
a combination of lemon, caraway, and
sage. Use a mortar and pestle to crush them.
If you don't have a mortar and pestle, crush
the seeds with a rolling pin.

Prep: 10 minutes **Broil:** 12 minutes
Makes: 4 servings

164 CALORIES

Nutrition Facts per serving:
164 cal., 9 g total fat (3 g sat. fat), 42 mg chol.,
256 mg sodium, 1 g carbo., 0 g fiber, 18 g pro.
Daily Values:
1% vit. A, 2% vit. C, 2% calcium, 14% iron
Exchanges:
2 1/2 Meat, 1/2 Fat

Peppercorn Steaks

A little molasses goes a long way, so this recipe calls for only a couple of teaspoons. Be sure to use a lighter, milder-flavored molasses so it doesn't overpower the dish.

Start to Finish: 35 minutes

Makes: 4 servings

247 CALORIES

2 **6-ounce boneless beef ribeye steaks or beef top sirloin steaks, cut about 1 inch thick**

1 **tablespoon multicolor peppercorns, crushed**

¹/₂ **teaspoon salt**

2 **tablespoons butter or margarine, softened**

2 **teaspoons mild-flavored molasses**

¹/₄ **teaspoon finely shredded lemon peel**

1 **teaspoon lemon juice**

2 **cups sugar snap peas**

¹/₂ **cup carrot cut into thin bite-size strips**

   Lemon peel strips (optional)

1 Preheat broiler. Trim fat from steaks. Using your fingers, press the crushed peppercorns and salt onto both sides of each steak.

2 Place steaks on the unheated rack of a broiler pan. Broil 3 to 4 inches from the heat until desired doneness, turning once halfway through broiling time. (For ribeye steaks, allow 12 to 14 minutes for medium-rare doneness [145°F] or 15 to 18 minutes for medium doneness [160°F].) (For sirloin steaks, allow 15 to 17 minutes for medium-rare doneness [145°F] or 20 to 22 minutes for medium doneness [160°F].)

3 Meanwhile, in a small bowl combine softened butter, molasses, finely shredded lemon peel, and lemon juice (mixture will appear curdled). Set aside.

4 Remove strings and tips from sugar snap peas. In a covered medium saucepan cook peas and carrot in a small amount of boiling salted water for 2 to 4 minutes or until crisp-tender. Drain well. Stir in 1 tablespoon of the molasses mixture.

5 To serve, dot remaining molasses mixture evenly over steaks. Slice steaks and toss with vegetable mixture. If desired, garnish with lemon peel strips.

Nutrition Facts per serving:
247 cal., 12 g total fat (6 g sat. fat), 66 mg chol., 418 mg sodium, 13 g carbo., 3 g fiber, 20 g pro.
Daily Values:
81% vit. A, 35% vit. C, 7% calcium, 19% iron
Exchanges:
2 Vegetable, 2¹/₂ Meat, 1 Fat

2 beef top loin steaks, cut 1 inch thick (about 1¼ pounds total)

¼ teaspoon salt

¼ teaspoon black pepper

1 8-ounce carton plain low-fat yogurt

¼ cup low-fat mayonnaise dressing

¼ cup very thinly sliced green onions (2)

¼ cup apple juice or apple cider

1 tablespoon snipped fresh parsley

1½ teaspoons snipped fresh tarragon or ½ teaspoon dried tarragon, crushed

¼ teaspoon salt

¼ teaspoon crushed red pepper or ⅛ teaspoon cayenne pepper

1 Preheat broiler. Trim fat from steaks. Cut steaks into 4 serving-size portions. Sprinkle steaks with ¼ teaspoon salt and the black pepper.

2 Place steaks on the unheated rack of a broiler pan. Broil 3 to 4 inches from heat until desired doneness, turning once. (Allow 12 to 14 minutes for medium-rare doneness [145°F] or 15 to 18 minutes for medium doneness [160°F].)

3 Meanwhile, for sauce, in a small bowl combine yogurt, mayonnaise dressing, green onions, juice or cider, parsley, tarragon, ¼ teaspoon salt, and the crushed or cayenne pepper. Slice steaks. Serve sauce with steak slices.

277 CALORIES

Beef Loin with Tarragon Sauce

A creamy, tarragon-flavored sauce is the standout here. Use tarragon in small amounts, because it can be too potent in larger doses. If you have extra sauce, it can double as dressing for salad greens.

Prep: 20 minutes **Broil:** 12 minutes
Makes: 4 servings

Nutrition Facts per serving:
277 cal., 10 g total fat (4 g sat. fat), 89 mg chol., 543 mg sodium, 11 g carbo., 1 g fiber, 34 g pro.
Daily Values:
4% vit. A, 6% vit. C, 13% calcium, 16% iron
Exchanges:
½ Milk, 4 Meat

358 CALORIES

Steak with Onions and Carrots

Beer gives this dish character; caramelized onions and carrots provide sweetness. If you don't have a 12-inch skillet, brown the onions in two batches in a 9- or 10-inch skillet.

Start to Finish: 1 hour   **Makes:** 4 servings

Nutrition Facts per serving:
358 cal., 9 g total fat (2 g sat. fat), 86 mg chol., 349 mg sodium, 34 g carbo., 5 g fiber, 34 g pro.
Daily Values:
289% vit. A, 39% vit. C, 6% calcium, 33% iron
Exchanges:
2 Vegetable, 1½ Starch, 3½ Meat

- 4 small onions, peeled and cut into wedges
- 1 tablespoon cooking oil
- 8 baby carrots with tops
- 4 small red potatoes, cut up (1 pound total)
- ½ cup beef broth
- ¼ cup beer, dark beer, or beef broth
- 1 tablespoon brown sugar
- 1 teaspoon dried thyme, crushed
- 1 1¼-pound boneless beef top sirloin steak, cut 1½ inches thick
- ¼ teaspoon salt
- ¼ teaspoon black pepper
  Snipped fresh thyme (optional)

1 In a 12-inch skillet cook onions in hot oil about 5 minutes or until browned, turning occasionally. Remove onions; set aside. Add carrots to skillet; cook about 5 minutes or until light brown, turning occasionally. Remove skillet from heat. Carefully add potatoes, the ½ cup broth, beer or additional broth, the brown sugar, and ½ teaspoon of the dried thyme. Return onions to skillet. Return skillet to heat. Bring to boiling; reduce heat. Simmer, covered, for 30 to 35 minutes or until vegetables are tender.

2 Meanwhile, preheat broiler. Season steak with the remaining ½ teaspoon dried thyme, the salt, and pepper. Place steak on unheated rack of broiler pan. Broil 4 to 5 inches from heat until desired doneness, turning once. (Allow 25 to 27 minutes for medium-rare doneness [145°F] or 30 to 32 minutes for medium doneness [160°F].) Cut into 4 pieces.

3 Remove vegetables from skillet with a slotted spoon. Gently boil juices, uncovered, for 1 to 2 minutes or until slightly thickened. Divide steak and vegetables among 4 dinner plates. Spoon juices over. If desired, sprinkle with fresh thyme.

- **12** ounces boneless beef top sirloin steak, cut 1 inch thick
- **⅓** cup bottled reduced-sodium teriyaki sauce or soy sauce
- **¼** cup lemon juice
- **¼** cup water
- **2** teaspoons toasted sesame oil
- **⅛** teaspoon bottled hot pepper sauce
- **3** cups shredded napa cabbage
- **1** cup torn or shredded fresh sorrel or fresh spinach
- **2** cups fresh fruit (such as sliced kiwifruit, plums, or nectarines; halved strawberries or seedless grapes; raspberries; and/or blueberries)

1 Trim fat from steak. Place steak in a plastic bag set in a shallow dish. For marinade, in a small bowl combine teriyaki sauce or soy sauce, lemon juice, the water, oil, and hot pepper sauce; reserve ⅓ cup for dressing. Pour remaining marinade over steak; close bag. Marinate in refrigerator for at least 2 hours or up to 8 hours.

2 Preheat broiler. Drain steak, reserving marinade. Place steak on the unheated rack of a broiler pan. Broil 3 to 4 inches from heat to desired doneness, turning once and brushing occasionally with reserved marinade up to the last 5 minutes of broiling time. (Allow 15 to 17 minutes for medium-rare doneness [145°F] or 20 to 22 minutes for medium doneness [160°F].) Discard any remaining marinade.

3 To serve, divide cabbage and sorrel or spinach among 4 dinner plates. Thinly slice steak diagonally. Arrange steak and fruit on top of greens. Drizzle with the reserved dressing.

Beef and Fruit Salad

This salad boasts the flavors of Japanese cuisine. A mix of teriyaki, sesame oil, and pepper sauce does twice the work as both marinade and dressing. For a splashy table presentation, cut the fruit into interesting shapes with cookie cutters.

Prep: 20 minutes **Marinate:** 2 to 8 hours
Broil: 15 minutes **Makes:** 4 servings

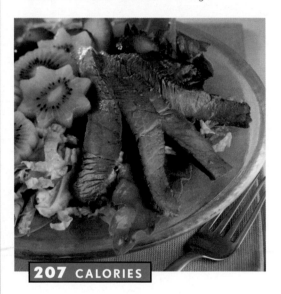

207 CALORIES

Nutrition Facts per serving:
207 cal., 7 g total fat (2 g sat. fat), 52 mg chol., 380 mg sodium, 17 g carbo., 3 g fiber, 21 g pro.
Daily Values:
18% vit. A, 63% vit. C, 6% calcium, 14% iron
Exchanges:
1 Vegetable, 1 Fruit, 2½ Meat

Sweet Onion and Spinach Burgers

Sweet onions star in this recipe. Look for Walla Wallas or Vidalias. The combination of herbed cheese and onion can't be beat.

Prep: 35 minutes   **Broil:** 10 minutes

Makes: 6 servings

281 CALORIES

Nutrition Facts per serving:
281 cal., 12 g total fat (5 g sat. fat), 113 mg chol., 557 mg sodium, 24 g carbo., 4 g fiber, 21 g pro.
Daily Values:
17% vit. A, 5% vit. C, 6% calcium, 15% iron
Exchanges:
1 Vegetable, 1 Starch, 2¹/₂ Meat, ¹/₂ Fat

1   **beaten egg**
¹/₄   **cup rolled oats**
2   **tablespoons water**
¹/₂   **teaspoon salt**
¹/₄   **teaspoon black pepper**
1   **pound lean ground veal or lean ground beef**
1   **tablespoon butter or margarine**
1   **small sweet onion, sliced (1 cup)**
2   **teaspoons brown sugar**
¹/₂   **teaspoon dry mustard**
2   **cups loosely packed fresh baby spinach leaves or spinach leaves, coarsely chopped**
6   **tablespoons light semisoft cheese with garlic and herbs**
3   **whole wheat pita bread rounds, halved**

1 Preheat broiler. In a medium bowl stir together egg, oats, the water, salt, and pepper. Add veal or beef; mix well. Shape mixture into six ¹/₂-inch oval-shape patties. Place patties on the unheated rack of a broiler pan. Broil 3 to 4 inches from heat for 10 to 12 minutes or until internal temperature registers 160°F on an instant-read thermometer, turning once.

2 Meanwhile, in a medium nonstick skillet melt butter over medium-low heat. Add onion. Cook, covered, for 13 to 15 minutes or until onion is tender. Add brown sugar and dry mustard. Cook, uncovered, over medium-high heat for 3 to 4 minutes or until onions are golden brown, stirring constantly. Stir in spinach. Toss lightly to coat; heat through.

3 Spread 1 tablespoon of the semisoft cheese on 1 side of the inside of each pita bread half. Fill each pita bread half with a patty and some of the onion-spinach mixture.

- 1½ **pounds tiny new potatoes (15 to 18 total), halved**
- 1½ **teaspoons chili powder**
- ½ **teaspoon ground cumin**
- ¼ **teaspoon garlic powder**
- ¼ **teaspoon salt**
- ¼ **teaspoon dried oregano, crushed**
- ⅛ **teaspoon cayenne pepper**
- 3 **tablespoons lemon juice**
- 1 **tablespoon cooking oil**
- 1 **1½- to 2-pound boneless tri-tip roast**

1 In a covered medium saucepan cook potatoes in a small amount of boiling salted water about 10 minutes or until nearly tender. Drain well.

2 Meanwhile, in a small bowl combine chili powder, cumin, garlic powder, salt, oregano, and cayenne pepper. Gently toss potatoes with 2 tablespoons of the lemon juice and the oil. Sprinkle with 1½ teaspoons of the chili powder mixture. Toss again to coat potatoes evenly. Arrange potatoes in a single layer in a lightly greased 15×10×1-inch baking pan; set aside.

3 Brush both sides of roast with remaining 1 tablespoon lemon juice. Sprinkle with remaining chili powder mixture. Place roast on a rack set in a shallow roasting pan. Insert an oven-going thermometer into center of roast. Roast, uncovered, in a 425° oven until desired doneness. (Allow 30 to 35 minutes for medium-rare doneness [140°F] or 40 to 45 minutes for medium doneness [155°F].) Remove roast from oven. Cover with foil and let stand for 15 minutes before carving. (The temperature of the meat will rise 5°F during standing.)

4 Meanwhile, while roast is standing, place the potatoes in the 425° oven. Bake, uncovered, about 15 minutes or until potatoes are tender and browned, carefully turning potatoes once.

5 To serve, thinly slice roast across the grain. Serve potatoes with roast.

265 CALORIES

Roast with Spicy Potatoes

Tri-tip roast is a boneless cut of beef from the bottom sirloin. Because of its triangular shape, it's also sometimes called triangular roast. This versatile cut can be roasted, grilled, or broiled, and best of all, it's low in calories. Serve it with your favorite horseradish sauce or flavored mustard.

Prep: 25 minutes   **Roast:** 30 minutes
Stand: 15 minutes   **Oven:** 425°F
Makes: 6 to 8 servings

Nutrition Facts per serving:
265 cal., 8 g total fat (2 g sat. fat), 54 mg chol., 175 mg sodium, 20 g carbo., 2 g fiber, 28 g pro.
Daily Values:
5% vit. A, 34% vit. C, 2% calcium, 22% iron
Exchanges:
1½ Starch, 3 Meat

225 CALORIES

Deviled Roast Beef

When spicy ingredients, such as mustard, pepper, and hot pepper sauce, combine to flavor foods, the foods are said to be deviled. Here mustard and black pepper are rubbed onto the beef. Mustard flavors the mushroom sauce as well.

Prep: 25 minutes   **Roast:** 1½ hours
Stand: 15 minutes   **Oven:** 325°F
Makes: 8 to 10 servings

Nutrition Facts per serving:
225 cal., 10 g total fat (4 g sat. fat), 64 mg chol., 351 mg sodium, 5 g carbo., 0 g fiber, 26 g pro.
Daily Values:
1% vit. A, 1% vit. C, 3% calcium, 11% iron
Exchanges:
1 Vegetable, 3½ Meat

1   **2- to 2½-pound beef eye round roast**
¼   **cup Dijon-style mustard**
¼   **teaspoon coarsely ground black pepper**
2   **cups sliced fresh mushrooms**
1   **cup beef broth**
1   **small onion, cut into thin wedges**
¼   **cup water**
2   **cloves garlic, minced**
1   **teaspoon Worcestershire sauce**
¼   **teaspoon dried thyme, crushed**
½   **cup fat-free milk**
3   **tablespoons all-purpose flour**

1 Trim fat from roast. In a small bowl stir together 2 tablespoons of the mustard and the pepper; rub onto the roast. Place the roast on a rack in a shallow roasting pan. Insert an oven-going thermometer into center of roast. Roast in a 325° oven, uncovered, for 1½ to 1¾ hours or until medium-rare doneness (135°F). Remove roast from oven. Cover with foil and let stand for 15 minutes before carving. (The temperature of the meat will rise 10°F during standing.)

2 Meanwhile, for sauce, in a medium saucepan combine the mushrooms, broth, onion, the water, garlic, Worcestershire sauce, and thyme. Bring to boiling; reduce heat. Simmer, covered, about 5 minutes or until vegetables are tender. In a small bowl stir together milk and the remaining 2 tablespoons mustard; gradually stir into flour. Add to mushroom mixture in saucepan. Cook and stir over medium heat until thickened and bubbly. Cook and stir for 1 minute more.

3 To serve, thinly slice beef across the grain. Serve with sauce.

1 **2-pound beef tenderloin roast**

½ **teaspoon salt**

½ **teaspoon coarsely ground black pepper**

1 **lemon**

⅔ **cup apple butter or spiced apple butter**

1½ **teaspoons grated fresh ginger**

1 Trim fat from roast. Sprinkle all sides of roast with salt and pepper. Place on a rack in a shallow roasting pan. Insert an oven-going thermometer into center of roast. Roast, uncovered, in a 425° oven until desired doneness. (Allow 35 to 40 minutes for medium-rare doneness [140°F] or 45 to 50 minutes for medium doneness [155°F].) Remove from oven. Cover with foil and let stand for 15 minutes before carving. (The temperature of the meat will rise 5°F during standing.)

2 Meanwhile, finely shred ½ teaspoon peel from the lemon; set peel aside. Cut lemon in half; squeeze 3 tablespoons lemon juice. In a small bowl combine the lemon peel, lemon juice, apple butter, and ginger. Brush mixture over meat 2 or 3 times during the last 10 minutes of roasting.

3 To serve, thinly slice meat. Serve with any remaining apple butter mixture.

Tenderloin with Apple Butter

This is the ultimate in comfort food. Beef tenderloin pairs with apple butter and a hint of ginger for a laid-back, yet sophisticated, dish.

Prep: 15 minutes   **Roast:** 35 minutes

Stand: 15 minutes   **Oven:** 425°F

Makes: 8 servings

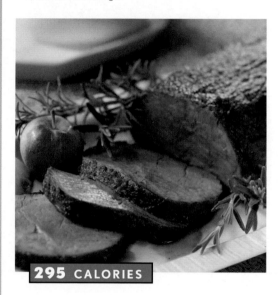

295 CALORIES

Nutrition Facts per serving:
295 cal., 7 g total fat (3 g sat. fat), 57 mg chol., 200 mg sodium, 32 g carbo., 1 g fiber, 24 g pro.
Daily Values:
2% vit. A, 6% vit. C, 2% calcium, 18% iron
Exchanges:
1 Fruit, 1 Other Carbo., 3 Meat

Chutney and Herb Rump Roast

One key ingredient here is apricot nectar. Not only does it flavor the liquid in which the roast cooks, it's also used to thin the mango chutney, which serves as a sauce.

Prep: 15 minutes **Cook:** 2 hours
Makes: 8 servings

266 CALORIES

1 2¹/₂-pound beef round rump roast
¹/₂ teaspoon dried basil, crushed
¹/₂ teaspoon dried marjoram, crushed
¹/₂ teaspoon salt
¹/₄ teaspoon black pepper
1 tablespoon cooking oil
1¹/₄ cups water
³/₄ cup apricot nectar or peach nectar
1 9-ounce jar (about ³/₄ cup) mango chutney
¹/₄ cup sliced green onions (2)
2 tablespoons apricot nectar or peach nectar
1 teaspoon chile oil or ¹/₄ teaspoon crushed red pepper

1 Trim fat from roast. In a small bowl combine basil, marjoram, salt, and black pepper. Rub the mixture onto all sides of the roast. In a 4-quart Dutch oven brown roast on all sides in hot oil. Drain off fat. Combine the water and the ¾ cup apricot or peach nectar. Pour over roast. Bring to boiling; reduce heat. Simmer, covered, for 1 hour.

2 Carefully turn over roast. Cook, covered, for 1 hour more or until meat is tender. Transfer meat to a platter; discard cooking liquid. Meanwhile, place chutney in a small bowl; snip any large pieces. Stir in sliced green onions, the 2 tablespoons apricot or peach nectar, and the chile oil or crushed red pepper. Serve chutney mixture with roast.

Nutrition Facts per serving:
266 cal., 8 g total fat (2 g sat. fat), 74 mg chol., 256 mg sodium, 15 g carbo., 1 g fiber, 33 g pro.
Daily Values:
16% vit. A, 14% vit. C, 2% calcium, 17% iron
Exchanges:
1 Fruit, 4 Meat

1 **2- to 2½-pound fresh beef brisket**

1 **14-ounce can beef broth**

½ **cup dry red wine**

¼ **cup finely chopped shallots or ½ cup chopped onion (1 medium)**

¾ **cup finely chopped fresh poblano chile pepper (see note on page 76) or finely chopped green sweet pepper**

1 **tablespoon brown sugar**

1 **teaspoon paprika**

1 **8-ounce carton light dairy sour cream**

2 **tablespoons all-purpose flour**

   Salt (optional)

   Black pepper (optional)

1 Trim fat from brisket. Place brisket in a 13×9×2-inch baking pan. In a medium bowl combine broth, red wine, shallots or onion, poblano or sweet pepper, brown sugar, and paprika. Pour over brisket. Cover with foil. Bake in a 325° oven about 3 hours or until tender, turning once. Remove meat, reserving juices. Cover meat; keep warm.

2 For sauce, skim fat from pan juices. Measure 1¼ cups pan juices; transfer to a medium saucepan. (Discard remaining pan juices.) In a small bowl combine sour cream and flour; whisk into pan juices in saucepan. Cook and stir until slightly thickened and bubbly. Cook and stir for 1 minute more. If desired, season to taste with salt and black pepper. Thinly slice meat across the grain. Serve with sauce.

237 CALORIES

Brisket with Sour Cream Sauce

Brisket requires slow cooking, but it's worth the long wait. A delicious mix of sour cream and pan juices tops off this tender meat.

Prep: 25 minutes   **Bake:** 3 hours
Oven: 325°F   **Makes:** 8 servings

Nutrition Facts per serving:
237 cal., 9 g total fat (4 g sat. fat), 64 mg chol., 281 mg sodium, 8 g carbo., 0 g fiber, 26 g pro.
Daily Values:
10% vit. A, 58% vit. C, 7% calcium, 16% iron
Exchanges:
1 Vegetable, 3½ Meat

312 CALORIES

Zesty Swiss Steak

Swiss steak typically is smothered with chopped tomatoes, broth, onions, and vegetables before being braised for several hours. With salsa, cumin, cayenne pepper, and fajita seasoning, this spicy version has a south-of-the-border attitude.

Prep: 20 minutes   **Cook:** 1¼ hours
Makes: 4 servings

1 **pound boneless beef round steak, cut ¾ inch thick**
2 **tablespoons all-purpose flour**
¾ **teaspoon fajita seasoning**
⅛ **teaspoon ground cumin**
⅛ **teaspoon cayenne pepper**
2 **teaspoons cooking oil**
1½ **cups bottled salsa**
½ **cup water**
1 **cup yellow and/or green sweet pepper cut into thin bite-size strips**
2 **cloves garlic, minced**
2 **cups hot cooked rice**
    Snipped fresh cilantro (optional)

1 Trim fat from steak. Cut steak into 4 serving-size pieces. In a large plastic bag combine flour, fajita seasoning, cumin, and cayenne pepper; set aside. Place meat between 2 pieces of plastic wrap. Using the notched edge of a meat mallet, pound meat lightly to ½-inch thickness. Remove plastic wrap. Add meat pieces, 2 at a time, to flour mixture in bag. Seal bag; shake to coat evenly.

2 In a large nonstick skillet brown meat on both sides in hot oil. Drain off fat. Add salsa, the water, sweet pepper strips, and garlic. Bring to boiling; reduce heat. Simmer, covered, about 1¼ hours or until meat is tender. Skim off fat. Serve with hot cooked rice. If desired, sprinkle with snipped fresh cilantro.

Nutrition Facts per serving:
312 cal., 8 g total fat (2 g sat. fat), 66 mg chol., 305 mg sodium, 31 g carbo., 2 g fiber, 28 g pro.
Daily Values:
40% vit. A, 106% vit. C, 3% calcium, 24% iron
Exchanges:
2 Starch, 3 Meat

1 2-pound boneless beef chuck pot roast

Salt

Black pepper

1 tablespoon cooking oil

1 teaspoon finely shredded orange peel

1½ cups orange juice

1 cup water

¼ cup maple syrup or maple-flavored syrup

½ teaspoon salt

¼ teaspoon ground ginger

⅛ teaspoon ground allspice

1½ pounds sweet potatoes (about 2 medium), peeled and cut into bite-size chunks

1 medium onion, cut into thin wedges

1 tablespoon cornstarch

1 tablespoon cold water

1 Trim fat from pot roast. Sprinkle pot roast with salt and pepper. In a 4-quart Dutch oven brown roast on all sides in hot oil. Drain off fat.

2 In a medium bowl combine orange peel, orange juice, the 1 cup water, the syrup, the ½ teaspoon salt, the ginger, and allspice. Pour over pot roast. Bring to boiling; reduce heat. Simmer, covered, for 1¼ hours. Add sweet potatoes and onion to meat. Return to boiling; reduce heat. Simmer, covered, about 30 minutes more or until meat and vegetables are tender, adding additional water if necessary.

3 Transfer meat and vegetables to a platter; reserve juices in Dutch oven. If desired, cut meat into bite-size pieces. Keep warm.

4 For sauce, measure juices; skim off fat. If necessary, add enough water to make 2 cups total liquid. Return to Dutch oven. In a small bowl stir together cornstarch and the 1 tablespoon cold water. Stir into juices in Dutch oven. Cook and stir over medium heat until thickened and bubbly. Cook and stir for 2 minutes more. If desired, season to taste with additional pepper. Serve sauce over meat and vegetables.

Maple Harvest Pot Roast

When you're looking for real comfort food that fits into your calorie budget, turn to this satisfying roast with sweet potatoes. Subtle spices, orange juice, and maple syrup create a mouthwatering sauce.

Prep: 25 minutes   **Cook:** 1³/₄ hours
Makes: 6 to 8 servings

399 CALORIES

Nutrition Facts per serving:
399 cal., 8 g total fat (2 g sat. fat), 89 mg chol., 362 mg sodium, 46 g carbo., 4 g fiber, 35 g pro.
Daily Values:
435% vit. A, 86% vit. C, 5% calcium, 26% iron
Exchanges:
1 Starch, 2 Other Carbo., 4 Meat

Quick Honey-Garlic Pot Roast

Imagine a pot roast dinner that's ready to eat in only 30 minutes. Thanks to a precooked pot roast you'll find at your supermarket, all you have to do is add a few ingredients to give it a personal touch.

Prep: 10 minutes **Cook:** 20 minutes
Makes: 4 servings

305 CALORIES

- 1 **17-ounce package refrigerated cooked beef roast au jus or beef pot roast with juices**
- 2 **tablespoons honey**
- 1 **tablespoon Worcestershire sauce**
- 1 **to 1½ teaspoons bottled roasted minced garlic**
- ¼ **teaspoon black pepper**
- 2 **cups packaged peeled baby carrots, halved lengthwise**
- 12 **ounces tiny new potatoes, halved**
- 1 **medium red onion, cut into thin wedges**

1 Remove meat from package, reserving juices. In a medium bowl combine reserved juices, honey, Worcestershire sauce, roasted garlic, and pepper. Place meat in a large nonstick skillet. Arrange carrots, potatoes, and onion around meat. Pour honey mixture over meat and vegetables.

2 Bring mixture to boiling; reduce heat. Cover and simmer for 20 to 25 minutes or until vegetables are tender and meat is heated through. Transfer meat and vegetables to a serving platter. Spoon sauce over meat and vegetables.

Nutrition Facts per serving:
305 cal., 9 g total fat (4 g sat. fat), 64 mg chol., 502 mg sodium, 35 g carbo., 4 g fiber, 26 g pro.
Daily Values:
307% vit. A, 31% vit. C, 3% calcium, 22% iron
Exchanges:
1 Vegetable, 2 Starch, 3 Meat

1 **17-ounce package refrigerated cooked beef pot roast with juices**

2 **tablespoons minced shallots**

1 **tablespoon butter or margarine**

2 **tablespoons tarragon vinegar**

2 **cups pitted fresh fruit cut into wedges (such as apples, plums, and peaches)**

Hot cooked wide noodles (optional)

1 **teaspoon snipped fresh tarragon**

Fresh tarragon sprigs (optional)

1 Remove meat from package, reserving juices. In a large skillet cook shallots in hot butter over medium heat for 1 minute. Add pot roast; reduce heat. Cover and simmer about 10 minutes or until pot roast is heated through.

2 In a small bowl stir together reserved meat juices and tarragon vinegar. Pour over meat. Spoon fruit on top. Cover; heat for 2 minutes more. If desired, serve with hot cooked noodles. Top with snipped tarragon. If desired, garnish with tarragon sprigs.

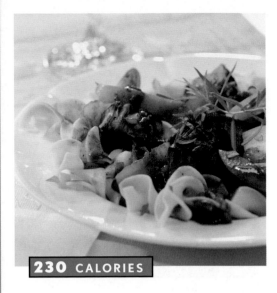

230 CALORIES

Easy Pot Roast

Tarragon and shallots boost the flavor of this ready-in-a-flash roast. Any noodle will complement this dish. Another time, try serving it with spaetzle.

Start to Finish: 25 minutes
Makes: 4 servings

Nutrition Facts per serving:
230 cal., 8 g total fat (3 g sat. fat), 72 mg chol., 386 mg sodium, 15 g carbo., 2 g fiber, 23 g pro.
Daily Values:
7% vit. A, 10% vit. C, 1% calcium, 15% iron
Exchanges:
1 Fruit, 3 Meat

170 CALORIES

Teriyaki Beef Soup

For an even quicker stove-to-table time, cut up the beef and vegetables for this soup the evening before. The next day, you'll be able to toss the whole meal together in record time.

Prep: 20 minutes   **Cook:** 18 minutes
Makes: 5 servings (about 7½ cups)

8   ounces boneless beef top sirloin steak
1   large shallot, cut into thin rings
2   teaspoons olive oil
4   cups water
1   cup apple juice or apple cider
2   medium carrots, cut into thin bite-size strips (1 cup)
⅓   cup long grain rice
1   tablespoon grated fresh ginger
1   teaspoon instant beef bouillon granules
3   cloves garlic, minced
2   cups coarsely chopped broccoli
1   to 2 tablespoons bottled reduced-sodium teriyaki sauce
1   tablespoon dry sherry (optional)

1 If desired, partially freeze steak for easier slicing. Trim fat from steak. Cut steak into bite-size strips. In a large saucepan cook and stir steak and shallot in hot oil over medium-high heat for 2 to 3 minutes or until beef is browned. Remove beef mixture with a slotted spoon; set aside.

2 In the same saucepan combine the water, juice or cider, carrots, uncooked rice, ginger, bouillon granules, and garlic. Bring to boiling; reduce heat. Simmer, covered, about 15 minutes or until the carrots are tender.

3 Stir in broccoli and the beef mixture. Simmer, covered, for 3 minutes. Stir in the teriyaki sauce. If desired, stir in sherry.

Nutrition Facts per serving:
170 cal., 4 g total fat (1 g sat. fat), 21 mg chol., 277 mg sodium, 22 g carbo., 2 g fiber, 12 g pro.
Daily Values:
135% vit. A, 52% vit. C, 5% calcium, 13% iron
Exchanges:
1 Vegetable, ½ Fruit, ½ Starch, 1 Meat

- **6** ounces boneless beef top sirloin steak
- **1** teaspoon olive oil
- **½** cup chopped onion (1 medium)
- **2** cups water
- **1** 14-ounce can beef broth
- **1** 14½-ounce can low-sodium tomatoes, undrained and cut up
- **½** cup thinly sliced carrot (1 medium)
- **1** teaspoon unsweetened cocoa powder
- **1** clove garlic, minced
- **1** cup thinly sliced cabbage
- **1** ounce dried wide noodles (about ½ cup)
- **2** teaspoons paprika
- **¼** cup light dairy sour cream
  Snipped fresh parsley (optional)
  Paprika (optional)

1 Trim fat from steak. Cut steak into ½-inch cubes. In a large saucepan cook and stir steak cubes in hot oil over medium-high heat about 6 minutes or until beef is browned. Add onion; cook and stir about 3 minutes more or until tender.

2 Stir in the water, broth, undrained tomatoes, carrot, cocoa powder, and garlic. Bring to boiling; reduce heat. Simmer, uncovered, about 15 minutes or until beef is tender.

3 Stir in the cabbage, uncooked noodles, and the 2 teaspoons paprika. Simmer, uncovered, for 5 to 7 minutes more or until noodles are tender but still firm. Remove from heat. Top each serving with some of the sour cream. If desired, sprinkle with the parsley and the additional paprika.

Beef Goulash Soup

A single teaspoon of unsweetened cocoa powder contributes a hint of New World flavor to an Old World Hungarian goulash. Don't be surprised if your family asks for this soup time and again.

Prep: 30 minutes   **Cook:** 20 minutes
Makes: 4 servings (about 6 cups)

188 CALORIES

Nutrition Facts per serving:
188 cal., 7 g total fat (3 g sat. fat), 36 mg chol., 397 mg sodium, 16 g carbo., 3 g fiber, 14 g pro.
Daily Values:
104% vit. A, 39% vit. C, 10% calcium, 14% iron
Exchanges:
2 Vegetable, ½ Starch, 1½ Meat

Beef Soup with Root Vegetables

With a hearty dose of potatoes, turnips, and sweet potatoes, this traditional beef soup will fill you up. As an added plus, root vegetables pack in healthy nutrients necessary for everyone.

Prep: 25 minutes **Cook:** 1½ hours
Makes: 6 servings (about 8 cups)

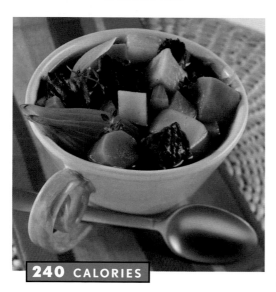

240 CALORIES

1 **pound boneless beef round steak**
2 **tablespoons olive oil**
2 **stalks celery, sliced**
1 **large onion, cut into thin wedges**
1 **medium carrot, cut into ½-inch slices**
2 **cloves garlic, minced**
2 **14-ounce cans beef broth**
1 **cup water**
2 **sprigs fresh thyme**
1 **bay leaf**
2 **medium potatoes, peeled and cut into ¾-inch cubes**
2 **medium turnips, peeled and cut into ¾-inch cubes**
1 **large sweet potato, peeled and cut into ¾-inch cubes**

1 Trim fat from steak. Cut steak into ¾-inch cubes. In a 4-quart Dutch oven cook meat, half at a time, in 1 tablespoon of the hot oil over medium heat until browned. Remove meat.

2 In the same Dutch oven heat the remaining 1 tablespoon oil over medium heat. Add celery, onion, carrot, and garlic; cook for 3 minutes, stirring frequently. Drain off fat. Return meat to Dutch oven.

3 Stir in broth, the water, thyme, and bay leaf. Bring to boiling; reduce heat. Simmer, covered, about 1¼ hours or until meat is almost tender. Discard thyme and bay leaf. Stir in potatoes, turnips, and sweet potato. Bring to boiling; reduce heat. Simmer, covered, about 15 minutes more or until meat and vegetables are tender.

Nutrition Facts per serving:
240 cal., 9 g total fat (2 g sat. fat), 44 mg chol., 545 mg sodium, 21 g carbo., 3 g fiber, 20 g pro.
Daily Values:
150% vit. A, 31% vit. C, 4% calcium, 16% iron
Exchanges:
1 Vegetable, 1 Starch, 2 Meat, ½ Fat

Nonstick cooking spray

8 ounces boneless beef top sirloin or top round steak, cut into $^3/_4$-inch cubes

$^1/_2$ cup chopped onion (1 medium)

$^1/_2$ cup sliced celery (1 stalk)

2 cloves garlic, minced

1 cup water

1 15$^1/_4$-ounce can pineapple tidbits (juice pack)

1 15- to 15$^3/_4$-ounce can chili beans with chili gravy

1 14$^1/_2$-ounce can diced tomatoes, undrained

1 8-ounce can low-sodium tomato sauce

1 tablespoon brown sugar

2 teaspoons chili powder

$^1/_4$ teaspoon salt

$^1/_8$ teaspoon cayenne pepper

Light dairy sour cream (optional)

1 Lightly coat an unheated 4-quart Dutch oven with nonstick cooking spray. Preheat over medium-high heat. Add meat, onion, celery, and garlic. Cook and stir until meat is browned and onion is tender.

2 Carefully stir in the water, undrained pineapple, undrained chili beans, undrained tomatoes, tomato sauce, brown sugar, chili powder, salt, and cayenne pepper. Bring to boiling; reduce heat. Simmer, covered, for 45 to 60 minutes or until meat is tender. If desired, serve with sour cream.

239 CALORIES

Spicy Sweet Chili

When it comes to chili recipes, you don't normally find pineapple in the ingredient list. This chili boasts a little sweetness from pineapple along with the usual chili spices. It's even better with a dollop of the optional sour cream.

Prep: 20 minutes   **Cook:** 45 minutes
Makes: 5 or 6 servings (about 6 cups)

Nutrition Facts per serving:
239 cal., 2 g total fat (0 g sat. fat), 27 mg chol., 524 mg sodium, 38 g carbo., 7 g fiber, 16 g pro.
Daily Values:
25% vit. A, 35% vit. C, 8% calcium, 27% iron
Exchanges:
2 Vegetable, 1 Fruit, 1 Starch, 1 Meat

306 CALORIES

Pinot Noir Beef Stew

Easy to find and relatively inexpensive, Pinot Noir is the red wine of choice for this stew. Why? It doesn't overpower the stew's subtle flavors.

Prep: 20 minutes **Cook:** 1 hour 10 minutes
Makes: 4 servings (about 5 cups)

12 ounces boneless beef chuck roast or 12 ounces lean beef stew meat

3 medium leeks, halved lengthwise and sliced

2 cloves garlic, minced

1 tablespoon cooking oil

2¼ cups beef broth

1 cup Pinot Noir

1 teaspoon dried thyme, crushed

¼ teaspoon salt

⅛ teaspoon black pepper

2 medium potatoes, peeled (if desired) and cut into 1-inch cubes

2 cups packaged, peeled baby carrots (10 ounces)

1 cup sliced celery (2 stalks)

1 tablespoon cold water

1½ teaspoons cornstarch

1 If using chuck roast, trim fat from roast. Cut roast into ¾-inch cubes. In a 3-quart saucepan cook the meat, leeks, and garlic in the hot oil over medium-high heat until meat is browned.

2 Stir in broth, wine, thyme, salt, and pepper. Bring to boiling; reduce heat. Simmer, covered, for 45 minutes. Add potatoes, carrots, and celery. Return to boiling; reduce heat. Simmer, covered, for 25 to 30 minutes more or until meat and vegetables are tender.

3 In a small bowl stir together the cold water and the cornstarch; stir into meat mixture. Cook and stir until mixture is thickened and bubbly. Cook and stir for 2 minutes more.

Nutrition Facts per serving:
306 cal., 7 g total fat (2 g sat. fat), 50 mg chol., 718 mg sodium, 26 g carbo., 4 g fiber, 22 g pro.
Daily Values:
310% vit. A, 32% vit. C, 6% calcium, 28% iron
Exchanges:
2 Vegetable, 1 Starch, 2 Meat

12 ounces boneless beef chuck roast

2 tablespoons all-purpose flour

12 peeled pearl onions or 1 cup chopped onion (1 large)

2 tablespoons olive oil or cooking oil

1 14-ounce can beef broth

1 cup water

1/2 cup dry red wine

1 tablespoon Worcestershire sauce

1/2 teaspoon dried thyme, crushed

1/4 teaspoon black pepper

10 cloves garlic, peeled

1 bay leaf

1 pound rutabaga, peeled and cut into 3/4-inch cubes

6 ounces green beans, trimmed and cut into 2 1/2-inch pieces, or 1 cup loose-pack frozen cut green beans

1 tablespoon tomato paste or catsup

1 Trim fat from roast. Cut roast into 3/4-inch cubes. Place flour in a plastic bag. Add meat cubes, a few at a time, shaking to coat.

2 In a large saucepan or Dutch oven cook meat and onions in hot oil over medium heat for 4 to 5 minutes or until meat is browned. Drain off fat. Stir in broth, the water, wine, Worcestershire sauce, thyme, pepper, garlic, and bay leaf. Bring to boiling; reduce heat. Simmer, covered, for 30 minutes.

3 Stir in rutabaga. Bring to boiling; reduce heat. Simmer, covered, about 1 hour more or until meat and rutabaga are tender, adding fresh green beans for the last 20 minutes or frozen green beans for the last 10 minutes of cooking. Discard bay leaf. Stir in tomato paste or catsup.

Beef and Rutabaga Stew

Ten cloves of garlic may sound like overkill, but the garlic's flavor mellows as it slowly simmers in the thyme-seasoned broth.

Prep: 25 minutes   **Cook:** 1 1/2 hours
Makes: 4 or 5 servings (about 8 cups)

285 CALORIES

Nutrition Facts per serving:
285 cal., 10 g total fat (3 g sat. fat), 45 mg chol., 487 mg sodium, 22 g carbo., 5 g fiber, 21 g pro.
Daily Values:
16% vit. A, 49% vit. C, 11% calcium, 22% iron
Exchanges:
1 Vegetable, 1 Starch, 2 Meat, 1/2 Fat

Pasta with Beef and Asparagus

Whenever asparagus and steak get together, the result is both elegant and delicious. This dish may appear complicated but comes together in almost no time.

Start to Finish: 30 minutes

Makes: 4 servings

421 CALORIES

8 ounces boneless beef top sirloin steak
1 pound fresh asparagus
8 ounces dried bow tie pasta
1 8-ounce carton light dairy sour cream
2 tablespoons all-purpose flour
²/₃ cup water
1 tablespoon honey
¹/₂ teaspoon salt
¹/₄ teaspoon black pepper
2 tablespoons finely chopped shallot
1 teaspoon cooking oil
2 teaspoons snipped fresh tarragon
   Fresh tarragon sprigs (optional)

1 If desired, partially freeze steak before slicing. Cut off and discard woody bases from fresh asparagus. If desired, scrape off scales. Bias-slice asparagus into 1-inch pieces; set aside. Cook pasta according to package directions, adding asparagus for the last 3 minutes of cooking. Drain well; keep warm.

2 Meanwhile, trim fat from steak. Thinly slice steak across the grain into bite-size strips. In a medium bowl stir together sour cream and flour. Stir in the water, honey, salt, and pepper. Set aside.

3 In a large nonstick skillet cook and stir the meat and shallot in hot oil over medium-high heat about 5 minutes or until meat is browned. Drain off fat.

4 Stir sour cream mixture into meat mixture in skillet. Cook and stir until thickened and bubbly. Cook and stir for 1 minute more. Stir in drained pasta, asparagus, and snipped tarragon. Heat through. If desired, garnish with tarragon sprigs.

Nutrition Facts per serving:
421 cal., 11 g total fat (4 g sat. fat), 107 mg chol., 373 mg sodium, 54 g carbo., 3 g fiber, 26 g pro.
Daily Values:
11% vit. A, 28% vit. C, 14% calcium, 23% iron
Exchanges:
2 Vegetable, 3 Starch, 2 Meat, ¹/₂ Fat

- **12** ounces beef top round steak
- **³/₄** cup water
- **¹/₂** cup bottled plum sauce
- **2** tablespoons reduced-sodium soy sauce
- **1** tablespoon cornstarch
- **1** teaspoon grated fresh ginger
- **1** tablespoon cooking oil
- **1** cup broccoli florets
- **1** small onion, cut into 1-inch pieces
- **2** cloves garlic, minced
- **3** cups lightly packed, coarsely chopped bok choy
- **2** medium plums, pitted and cut into thin wedges
- **2** cups hot cooked Chinese egg noodles, fine egg noodles, or rice

1 If desired, partially freeze steak for easier slicing. Trim fat from steak. Thinly slice steak across the grain into bite-size strips. Set aside. For sauce, in a small bowl stir together the water, plum sauce, soy sauce, cornstarch, and ginger. Set aside.

2 In a nonstick wok or large skillet heat oil over medium-high heat. (Add more oil as necessary during cooking.) Add broccoli, onion, and garlic; stir-fry for 3 minutes. Remove broccoli mixture from wok. Add beef to hot wok. Cook and stir for 2 to 3 minutes or until browned. Push beef from center of wok. Stir sauce. Add sauce to center of wok. Cook and stir until thickened and bubbly.

3 Return broccoli mixture to wok. Add bok choy and plums. Stir all ingredients together to coat with sauce. Cover and cook about 2 minutes more or until heated through. Serve over hot cooked noodles or rice.

413 CALORIES

Beef and Broccoli with Plum Sauce

Many supermarkets don't sell plums year-round. When you can't find them, substitute frozen peaches, thawed and thinly sliced.

Start to Finish: 30 minutes
Makes: 4 servings

Nutrition Facts per serving:
413 cal., 10 g total fat (3 g sat. fat), 74 mg chol., 533 mg sodium, 54 g carbo., 4 g fiber, 26 g pro.
Daily Values:
45% vit. A, 90% vit. C, 10% calcium, 24% iron
Exchanges:
3 Vegetable, 1 Fruit, 1¹/₂ Starch, 2 Meat, ¹/₂ Fat

237 CALORIES

Five-Spice Steak Wraps

These wraps unite Asian and Mexican cuisine into one freshly fused dish.

Start to Finish: 25 minutes
Makes: 4 servings

12 ounces boneless beef round steak

2 cups packaged shredded cabbage with carrot (coleslaw mix)

¼ cup red and/or green sweet pepper cut into thin bite-size strips

¼ cup carrot cut into thin bite-size strips

¼ cup snipped fresh chives

2 tablespoons rice vinegar

½ teaspoon toasted sesame oil

½ teaspoon five-spice powder

¼ teaspoon salt

Nonstick cooking spray

¼ cup plain low-fat yogurt or light dairy sour cream

4 8-inch flour tortillas

1 If desired, partially freeze steak for easier slicing. In a medium bowl combine coleslaw mix, sweet pepper, carrot, and chives. In a small bowl combine vinegar and sesame oil. Pour vinegar mixture over coleslaw mixture; toss to coat. Set aside.

2 Trim fat from steak. Thinly slice steak across the grain into bite-size strips. Sprinkle steak with five-spice powder and salt. Coat an unheated large nonstick skillet with nonstick cooking spray. Preheat over medium-high heat. Add steak strips; stir-fry for 3 to 4 minutes or until browned.

3 To assemble, spread 1 tablespoon of the yogurt down the center of each tortilla. Top with steak strips. Stir coleslaw mixture; spoon over steak. Fold in sides of tortillas. If desired, secure with wooden toothpicks.

Nutrition Facts per serving:
237 cal., 7 g total fat (2 g sat. fat), 51 mg chol., 329 mg sodium, 20 g carbo., 2 g fiber, 22 g pro.
Daily Values:
58% vit. A, 54% vit. C, 9% calcium, 19% iron
Exchanges:
1 Vegetable, 1 Starch, 2 Meat

- **2** medium oranges
- **12** ounces veal scaloppini or boneless veal leg round steak or sirloin steak, cut ¼ inch thick
- **¼** teaspoon salt
- **¼** teaspoon black pepper
- **2** teaspoons olive oil
- **⅓** cup sliced green onions
- **2** cloves garlic, minced
- **1** teaspoon grated fresh ginger
- **1** cup orange juice
- **1** tablespoon white wine vinegar
- **2** teaspoons cornstarch
- **¼** cup golden raisins
- **⅛** teaspoon salt
- Hot cooked pasta or rice (optional)

1 Finely shred ½ teaspoon peel from 1 of the oranges; set peel aside. Peel and section oranges, discarding seeds. Set orange sections aside.

2 Sprinkle meat with the ¼ teaspoon salt and the pepper. In a large nonstick skillet cook meat in hot oil over medium-high heat for 4 to 6 minutes or until browned, turning once. Remove meat from skillet, reserving drippings in skillet. Add green onions, garlic, and ginger to drippings in skillet. Cook and stir over medium heat for 1 minute.

3 In a small bowl stir together orange juice, vinegar, and cornstarch; add to skillet. Cook and stir until slightly thickened and bubbly. Add the orange peel, orange sections, raisins, and the ⅛ teaspoon salt to skillet. Toss gently to coat. Return meat to skillet; spoon sauce over meat. Heat through. If desired, serve meat over hot cooked pasta.

Veal with Orange Sauce

Orange juice, ginger, garlic, and green onions combine for this quick-and-easy sauce, which happens to taste great with pork too.

Start to Finish: 25 minutes

Makes: 4 servings

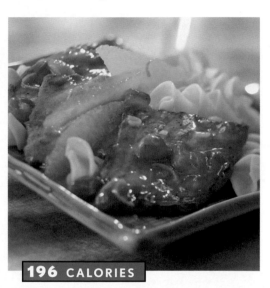

196 CALORIES

Nutrition Facts per serving:
196 cal., 4 g total fat (1 g sat. fat), 66 mg chol., 265 mg sodium, 21 g carbo., 2 g fiber, 19 g pro.
Daily Values:
4% vit. A, 83% vit. C, 4% calcium, 6% iron
Exchanges:
1½ Fruit, 2½ Meat

Steak Salad with Buttermilk Dressing

Those watching their weight needn't shy away from beef. This salad makes a perfect light lunch. You can cook the meat ahead of time or substitute deli beef.

Start to Finish: 35 minutes

Makes: 4 servings

187 CALORIES

8   ounces boneless beef top sirloin steak

8   cups torn mixed salad greens

    Nonstick cooking spray

¼   cup finely shredded fresh basil

    Salt (optional)

    Black pepper (optional)

2   medium carrots, cut into thin bite-size strips

1   medium yellow sweet pepper, cut into thin bite-size strips

1   cup yellow and/or red pear-shaped tomatoes, halved

1   recipe Buttermilk Dressing

1 If desired, partially freeze steak for easier slicing. Arrange salad greens on 4 dinner plates. Set aside. Trim fat from steak. Cut steak across the grain into thin bite-size strips.

2 Lightly coat an unheated large skillet with nonstick cooking spray. Preheat over medium-high heat. Add steak strips. Cook and stir for 2 to 3 minutes or until meat is browned. Remove from heat. Stir in basil. If desired, lightly sprinkle with salt and black pepper to taste.

3 To serve, spoon the warm meat mixture over greens. Top with carrots, sweet pepper, and tomatoes. Drizzle with Buttermilk Dressing. Serve immediately.

Buttermilk Dressing: In a small bowl combine ½ cup plain low-fat yogurt; ⅓ cup buttermilk; 3 tablespoons freshly grated Parmesan cheese; 3 tablespoons finely chopped red onion; 3 tablespoons low-fat mayonnaise dressing; 2 tablespoons snipped fresh parsley; 1 tablespoon white wine vinegar or lemon juice; 1 clove garlic, minced; ¼ teaspoon salt; and ⅛ teaspoon black pepper. Cover and refrigerate for at least 30 minutes or up to 24 hours.

Nutrition Facts per serving:
187 cal., 5 g total fat (2 g sat. fat), 35 mg chol., 419 mg sodium, 18 g carbo., 4 g fiber, 19 g pro.
Daily Values:
192% vit. A, 176% vit. C, 20% calcium, 15% iron
Exchanges:
3 Vegetable, 2 Meat

12 ounces boneless beef top sirloin steak, cut 1/2 inch thick

1/2 cup reduced-fat, reduced-calorie bottled balsamic-, raspberry-, or Italian-flavored vinaigrette

1/2 teaspoon crushed red pepper

1 clove garlic, minced

1/4 cup low-fat mayonnaise dressing

1 small red onion, thinly sliced

2 teaspoons cooking oil

4 hoagie rolls (about 2 ounces each), split and toasted

1 1/4 cups small lettuce leaves

2/3 cup fresh basil leaves, thinly sliced

1 If desired, partially freeze steak for easier slicing. Trim fat from steak. Thinly slice steak across the grain into bite-size strips. In a medium bowl combine vinaigrette, red pepper, and garlic. In a small bowl combine 1 tablespoon of the vinaigrette mixture and the mayonnaise dressing. Cover and chill.

2 Add steak strips to the remaining vinaigrette mixture; stir to coat evenly. Cover and marinate in the refrigerator for 1 hour. Drain steak strips, discarding the marinade.

3 In a large nonstick skillet cook steak strips and onion in hot oil over medium-high heat for 2 to 3 minutes or until meat is browned and onion is crisp-tender.

4 To assemble, spread mayonnaise dressing-vinaigrette mixture evenly onto cut sides of hoagie rolls. Top roll bottoms with lettuce and basil. With a slotted spoon, divide steak and onion mixture among the roll bottoms. Add roll tops.

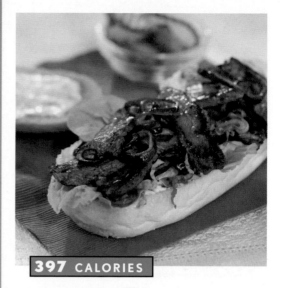

397 CALORIES

Vinaigrette-Dressed Steak Sandwich

Choose your favorite vinaigrette for this steak sandwich—any one will do. A small amount is mixed with mayonnaise dressing for the sandwich spread. Fresh basil livens up the greens.

Prep: 25 minutes   **Marinate:** 1 hour
Makes: 4 servings

Nutrition Facts per serving:
397 cal., 12 g total fat (2 g sat. fat), 55 mg chol., 500 mg sodium, 48 g carbo., 3 g fiber, 23 g pro.
Daily Values:
8% vit. A, 6% vit. C, 8% calcium, 24% iron
Exchanges:
2 Vegetable, 2 1/2 Starch, 2 Meat, 1/2 Fat

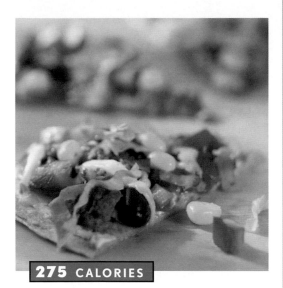

275 CALORIES

Southwestern Tortilla Wedges

The trick to buying the kind of ground beef that's easy on your waistline is to look for the leanest beef possible. What you want is a high percentage of lean meat to fat (for example, 95% lean is very lean). If you're not sure, ask the butcher which ground beef is the leanest.

Prep: 20 minutes **Bake:** 5 minutes
Oven: 400°F **Makes:** 4 servings

Nutrition Facts per serving:
275 cal., 12 g total fat (6 g sat. fat), 44 mg chol., 448 mg sodium, 26 g carbo., 3 g fiber, 17 g pro.
Daily Values:
8% vit. A, 8% vit. C, 18% calcium, 14% iron
Exchanges:
1 Vegetable, 1½ Starch, 1½ Meat, ½ Fat

Nonstick cooking spray
6 ounces lean ground beef
½ cup bottled salsa or picante sauce
¼ cup water
1 teaspoon fajita seasoning
4 8-inch spinach-flavored, tomato-basil-flavored, or plain flour tortillas
¼ cup light dairy sour cream
½ cup canned red kidney beans, rinsed and drained
¼ cup canned whole kernel corn with sweet peppers, drained
½ cup shredded Monterey Jack cheese with peppers or shredded Colby Jack cheese (2 ounces)
1 tablespoon snipped fresh cilantro
Chopped tomato (optional)
Shredded lettuce (optional)
Bottled salsa or picante sauce (optional)

1 Coat an unheated medium nonstick skillet with nonstick cooking spray. Preheat over medium heat. Add ground beef. Cook and stir until brown. Drain off fat. Stir in the ½ cup salsa, the water, and fajita seasoning. Bring to boiling; reduce heat. Simmer, covered, for 5 minutes.

2 Spread 1 side of each tortilla with some of the sour cream. Top evenly with beef mixture, beans, and corn. In a small bowl combine shredded cheese and cilantro. Sprinkle cheese mixture evenly over tortillas. Place on a very large baking sheet (or use 2 regular baking sheets).

3 Bake in a 400° oven for 5 to 7 minutes or until heated through and cheese is melted. Cut into wedges to serve. If desired, top with chopped tomato and shredded lettuce. If desired, serve with additional salsa.

1 head garlic

1 teaspoon olive oil

½ of an 8-ounce package reduced-fat cream cheese (Neufchâtel), softened

1 tablespoon fat-free milk

¾ teaspoon herb-pepper seasoning

4 small pita bread rounds

1 small zucchini, thinly sliced lengthwise

1 medium tomato, halved and thinly slices

1 small fresh jalapeño chile pepper, sliced (see note on page 76), or 2 tablespoons finely chopped green sweet pepper

6 ounces thinly sliced cooked beef

1 Peel away the dry outer layers of peel from the head of garlic, leaving skins and cloves intact. Cut off the pointed top portion (about ¼ inch), leaving the bulb intact but exposing the individual cloves. Place the garlic head, cut side up, in a muffin cup or custard cup. Drizzle with oil. Cover with foil. Bake in a 425° oven for 25 to 35 minutes or until the cloves feel soft when pressed. Set aside just until cool enough to handle. Squeeze out the garlic paste from individual cloves.

2 In a small mixing bowl combine garlic paste, cream cheese, milk, and herb-pepper seasoning. Beat with an electric mixer or stir by hand until mixture is smooth.

3 For roll-ups, spread cream cheese mixture over 1 side of each pita bread round. Top each with some of the zucchini, tomato, and jalapeño pepper. Top with cooked beef. Roll up pita bread rounds, securing with wooden picks, if necessary.

Beef and Garlic Pita Roll-Ups

A lively spread of roasted garlic and cream cheese provides a velvety base for colorful layers of zucchini, tomato, peppers, and thinly sliced beef in this tasty roll-up.

Prep: 20 minutes   **Bake:** 25 minutes
Oven: 425°F
Makes: 4 servings

346 CALORIES

Nutrition Facts per serving:
346 cal., 11 g total fat (5 g sat. fat), 51 mg chol., 469 mg sodium, 41 g carbo., 2 g fiber, 22 g pro.
Daily Values:
13% vit. A, 24% vit. C, 10% calcium, 16% iron
Exchanges:
1 Vegetable, 2½ Starch, 1½ Meat

Beef Sandwich with Horseradish Slaw

Horseradish and beef, common sandwich partners, pair up once again. Here the horseradish seasons crunchy broccoli slaw.

Start to Finish: 15 minutes

Makes: 4 servings

315 CALORIES

1/3 cup light dairy sour cream

2 tablespoons snipped fresh chives

2 tablespoons spicy brown mustard

1 teaspoon prepared horseradish

1/2 teaspoon sugar

1/4 teaspoon salt

1 cup packaged shredded broccoli (broccoli slaw mix)

8 ounces thinly sliced cooked roast beef

8 1/2-inch slices sourdough bread, toasted

1 In a medium bowl combine sour cream, chives, brown mustard, horseradish, sugar, and salt. Add shredded broccoli; toss to coat.

2 To assemble, divide roast beef among 4 of the bread slices. Top with broccoli mixture. Top with remaining bread slices. If desired, secure sandwiches with wooden toothpicks.

Nutrition Facts per serving:
315 cal., 11 g total fat (4 g sat. fat), 53 mg chol., 630 mg sodium, 30 g carbo., 2 g fiber, 23 g pro.
Daily Values:
11% vit. A, 36% vit. C, 11% calcium, 18% iron
Exchanges:
2 Starch, 2 Meat, 1/2 Fat

On the divider: Squirt-of-Orange Pork Chops (see recipe, page 276)

1½ cups chopped honeydew melon

1½ cups chopped cantaloupe

1 cup strawberries, coarsely chopped

1 tablespoon snipped fresh mint

1 tablespoon lemon juice

1 tablespoon honey

4 teaspoons Jamaican jerk seasoning

2 12-ounce pork tenderloins

Fresh mint sprigs (optional)

1 For salsa, in a medium bowl combine honeydew melon, cantaloupe, strawberries, the snipped mint, lemon juice, and honey. Cover and chill for up to 1 hour.

2 Sprinkle jerk seasoning evenly over tenderloins, pressing onto surface. Place tenderloins on a rack in a shallow roasting pan. Roast in a 425° oven for 25 to 35 minutes or until pork juices run clear (160°F).

3 To serve, slice pork and serve with salsa. If desired, garnish with mint sprigs.

187 CALORIES

Tenderloin with Melon Salsa

Two kinds of melon plus fresh strawberries combine in this simple salsa. The sweet, juicy relish is the perfect counterpoint to jerk-seasoned pork tenderloin.

Prep: 25 minutes   **Roast:** 25 minutes
Oven: 425°F   **Makes:** 6 servings

Nutrition Facts per serving:
187 cal., 3 g total fat (1 g sat. fat), 66 mg chol., 254 mg sodium, 12 g carbo., 1 g fiber, 28 g pro.
Daily Values:
26% vit. A, 73% vit. C, 2% calcium, 10% iron
Exchanges:
1 Fruit, 3½ Meat

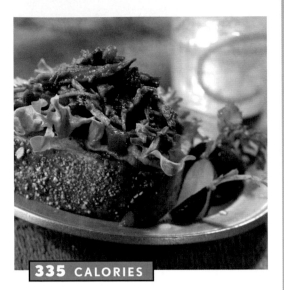

335 CALORIES

Smoky-Sweet Pork

Dates and smoky chipotle peppers take bottled barbecue sauce to new heights. If you prefer, pile the shredded meat into kaiser rolls or hoagie buns instead of on bread slices.

Prep: 25 minutes **Cook:** 1½ hours
Makes: 8 servings

1½ **pounds boneless pork top loin roast (single loin) or boneless pork blade roast**

2 **teaspoons cooking oil**

1½ **cups water**

½ **cup catsup**

½ **cup bottled barbecue sauce**

1 **cup chopped red onion**

½ **cup chopped celery**

¼ **cup packed brown sugar**

¼ **cup snipped pitted dates**

2 **tablespoons finely chopped canned chipotle peppers in adobo sauce**

1 **teaspoon dry mustard**

1 **teaspoon bottled minced garlic or 2 cloves garlic, minced**

8 **thick bread slices**

8 **lettuce leaves (optional)**

1 Trim fat from roast. In a large saucepan brown roast on all sides in hot oil. Drain off fat. Add the water, catsup, barbecue sauce, red onion, celery, brown sugar, dates, chipotle peppers, mustard, and garlic. Bring to boiling; reduce heat. Simmer, covered, for 1½ to 2 hours or until meat is very tender, stirring sauce occasionally.

2 Remove meat from sauce. Pour sauce into large glass measure or bowl; set aside. Using 2 forks, pull meat apart into shreds. Skim fat from sauce, if necessary. Return meat to saucepan; stir in enough of the sauce to make desired consistency. Heat through.

3 To serve, top bread slices with lettuce leaves (if desired); spoon meat mixture onto lettuce.

Nutrition Facts per serving:
335 cal., 8 g total fat (2 g sat. fat), 50 mg chol., 606 mg sodium, 41 g carbo., 3 g fiber, 23 g pro.
Daily Values:
7% vit. A, 9% vit. C, 10% calcium, 15% iron
Exchanges:
½ Fruit, 2 Starch, 2½ Meat

1 2- to 2½-pound boneless pork top
   loin roast (single loin)
   Salt
   Black pepper
⅓ cup pineapple preserves
2 tablespoons coarse-grain mustard
¼ teaspoon dried mint or basil, crushed
1 15¼-ounce can pineapple chunks
   (juice pack), drained

1 Trim fat from roast. Place roast in a
shallow roasting pan. Season with salt
and pepper. Insert an oven-going meat
thermometer into center of roast. Roast,
uncovered, in a 325° oven for 1 hour.

2 Meanwhile, for glaze, in a small bowl
combine preserves, mustard, and mint.

3 Spoon about half of the glaze onto the
meat; add pineapple chunks to roasting
pan. Roast for 15 to 45 minutes more or
until thermometer registers 155°F,
spooning remaining glaze over once.

4 Remove from oven. Cover with foil and
let stand for 15 minutes before carving.
(The temperature of the meat will rise
5°F during standing.) Transfer roast to
serving platter. Stir together pineapple
and pan drippings; serve with meat.

Pineapple Pork Roast

Fruit flavors and pork go together naturally.
In this fuss-free pork loin recipe, a
pineapple-accented mustard glaze and
pineapple chunks enhance the delicate
flavor of the meat.

Prep: 20 minutes   **Roast:** 1¼ hours
Oven: 325°F   **Stand:** 15 minutes
Makes: 8 to 10 servings

231 CALORIES

Nutrition Facts per serving:
231 cal., 6 g total fat (2 g sat. fat), 66 mg chol.,
146 mg sodium, 18 g carbo., 1 g fiber, 25 g pro.
Daily Values:
1% vit. A, 11% vit. C, 3% calcium, 7% iron
Exchanges:
1 Fruit, 3 Meat

Rhubarb-Sauced Pork Roast

Depending on the weather and your mood, you can choose to either roast or grill this mustard-and-rosemary-infused pork. Whichever cooking method you choose, the tender slices taste delectable drizzled with the accompanying homemade rhubarb and orange sauce.

Prep: 20 minutes **Roast:** 1¼ hours
Oven: 325°F **Stand:** 15 minutes
Makes: 8 to 10 servings

212 CALORIES

Nutrition Facts per serving:
212 cal., 5 g total fat (2 g sat. fat), 71 mg chol., 380 mg sodium, 12 g carbo., 1 g fiber, 26 g pro.
Daily Values:
2% vit. A, 17% vit. C, 7% calcium, 6% iron
Exchanges:
1 Fruit, 3½ Meat

1 2- to 2½-pound boneless pork top loin roast (single loin)
¼ cup Dijon-style mustard
1 tablespoon snipped fresh rosemary
½ teaspoon salt
¼ teaspoon black pepper
1 to 2 tablespoons bottled minced garlic
3 cups fresh or frozen sliced rhubarb (about 1 pound)
⅓ cup orange juice
⅓ to ½ cup sugar
1 tablespoon cider vinegar
   Fresh rosemary sprig (optional)

1 Score the top and bottom of roast in a diamond pattern by making shallow diagonal cuts at 1-inch intervals. In a small bowl combine mustard, the snipped rosemary, salt, pepper, and garlic. Rub the mustard mixture evenly onto all sides of roast. Insert an oven-going meat thermometer into center of roast. Place roast on a rack in a shallow roasting pan.

2 Roast, uncovered, in a 325° oven for 1¼ to 1¾ hours or until thermometer registers 155°F. Remove from oven.

3 Cover with foil; let stand for 15 minutes before carving. (The temperature of the meat will rise 5°F during standing.)

4 Meanwhile, for sauce, in a medium saucepan stir together rhubarb, orange juice, sugar, and vinegar. Bring to boiling; reduce heat. Simmer, covered, about 15 minutes or until rhubarb is very tender.

5 To serve, slice the roast and serve with warm sauce. If desired, garnish with rosemary sprig.

Grilling directions: Prepare as above through step 1. In a grill with a cover arrange medium coals around edge of grill. Test for medium-low heat in center of grill (not over coals). Place roast in roasting pan on grill rack in center of grill. Cover and grill for 1 to 1¼ hours or until meat thermometer registers 155°F, adding hot coals as necessary to maintain heat. Continue as above in steps 3 to 5.

1 15-ounce can black beans, rinsed and drained

1 14-ounce can beef broth

1³/₄ cups water

12 ounces cooked pork, cut into bite-size strips

3 plantains, peeled and sliced

1 cup chopped tomatoes

¹/₂ of a 16-ounce package (2 cups) frozen pepper stir-fry vegetables (yellow, green, and red sweet peppers and onion)

1 tablespoon grated fresh ginger

1 teaspoon ground cumin

¹/₄ teaspoon salt

¹/₄ teaspoon crushed red pepper

3 cups hot cooked rice

Dried chile peppers (optional)

1 In a Dutch oven combine the beans, broth, and the water; heat to boiling.

2 Add the pork, plantains, and tomatoes to the bean mixture. Stir in the frozen vegetables, ginger, cumin, salt, and crushed red pepper. Return mixture to boiling; reduce heat. Simmer, covered, about 10 minutes or until plantains are tender. Serve with hot cooked rice. If desired, garnish with chile peppers.

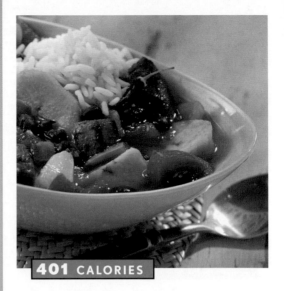

401 CALORIES

Caribbean-Style Pork Stew

The flavor of a plantain depends on its ripeness. A ripe, black-skinned plantain tastes like a banana. An almost-ripe, yellow plantain tastes similar to sweet potatoes. An unripe, green plantain tastes starchy, but it loses the starchy flavor when cooked and develops a flavor reminiscent of squash.

Start to Finish: 30 minutes
Makes: 6 servings (8½ cups)

Nutrition Facts per serving:
401 cal., 7 g total fat (2 g sat. fat), 46 mg chol., 543 mg sodium, 64 g carbo., 7 g fiber, 25 g pro.
Daily Values:
29% vit. A, 60% vit. C, 5% calcium, 18% iron
Exchanges:
1 Vegetable, 2 Fruit, 2 Starch, 2½ Meat

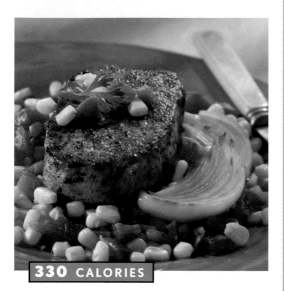

330 CALORIES

Spicy Skillet Pork Chops

Prepare these chops to suit your taste. If you prefer a milder dish, use regular chili powder; if fiery is more your style, use hot chili powder.

Start to Finish: 40 minutes

Makes: 4 servings

1½ cups loose-pack frozen whole kernel corn

1 10-ounce can chopped tomatoes and green chile peppers

½ teaspoon ground cumin

¼ teaspoon bottled hot pepper sauce

2 cloves garlic, minced

4 boneless pork loin chops, cut ¾ inch thick (about 1½ pounds total)

½ teaspoon chili powder

2 teaspoons cooking oil

1 medium onion, cut into thin wedges

1 tablespoon snipped fresh cilantro

Fresh cilantro leaves (optional)

1 In a medium bowl combine corn, undrained tomatoes, cumin, hot pepper sauce, and garlic; set aside.

2 Trim fat from chops. Sprinkle both sides of each chop with chili powder. In a 12-inch nonstick skillet heat oil over medium-high heat. Add chops; cook chops about 4 minutes or until browned, turning once. Remove chops from skillet, reserving drippings. Reduce heat to medium. Add onion to skillet. Cook and stir for 3 minutes. Stir corn mixture into onion mixture in skillet. Place chops on corn mixture. Bring to boiling; reduce heat. Simmer, covered, for 10 to 12 minutes or until pork juices run clear (160°F).

3 To serve, remove chops from skillet. Stir snipped cilantro into corn mixture in skillet; serve corn mixture with chops. If desired, garnish with cilantro leaves.

Nutrition Facts per serving:
330 cal., 11 g total fat (3 g sat. fat), 93 mg chol., 360 mg sodium, 18 g carbo., 2 g fiber, 40 g pro.
Daily Values:
7% vit. A, 19% vit. C, 5% calcium, 9% iron
Exchanges:
1 Vegetable, 1 Starch, 5 Meat

2 boneless pork loin chops, cut ³/₄ inch thick (about 12 ounces total)

¹/₄ teaspoon salt

¹/₄ teaspoon ground ginger

¹/₈ teaspoon black pepper

1 teaspoon cooking oil

1 teaspoon bottled minced garlic or 2 cloves garlic, minced

¹/₂ cup fresh sugar snap peas

¹/₃ cup sliced fresh mushrooms

²/₃ cup bottled reduced-fat raspberry vinaigrette salad dressing

¹/₂ cup fresh raspberries

8 cups torn fresh spinach and/or romaine or purchased torn mixed salad greens

1 Trim fat from chops. Sprinkle both sides of each chop with salt, ginger, and pepper. In a large nonstick skillet heat oil over medium heat. Add chops; cook for 8 to 12 minutes or until pork juices run clear (160°F), turning once. Remove chops from skillet, reserving drippings. Cover chops; keep warm.

2 In the same skillet cook and stir garlic in reserved drippings for 30 seconds. Add sugar snap peas and mushrooms to skillet. Pour raspberry vinaigrette dressing over all. Cover and cook for 2 to 3 minutes or until heated through. Remove from heat. Gently stir in the raspberries; set aside and keep warm.

3 Divide spinach evenly among 4 dinner plates. Thinly slice pork. Arrange pork on spinach. Pour warm raspberry mixture over all.

Pork with Berry-Dressed Greens

Think of this salad when raspberry season rolls around. Reduced-fat raspberry vinaigrette and lean pork loin help keep this fresh-tasting salad low in calories and fat.

Start to Finish: 20 minutes
Makes: 4 servings

248 CALORIES

Nutrition Facts per serving:
248 cal., 12 g total fat (2 g sat. fat), 46 mg chol., 617 mg sodium, 12 g carbo., 7 g fiber, 21 g pro.
Daily Values:
68% vit. A, 40% vit. C, 7% calcium, 30% iron
Exchanges:
2 Vegetable, 2¹/₂ Meat, 1 Fat

Pork Chops with Raspberries

Pan drippings mix with vinegar, brown sugar, and spices to create a thick and bubbly sauce dotted with fresh berries.

Start to Finish: 25 minutes
Makes: 4 servings

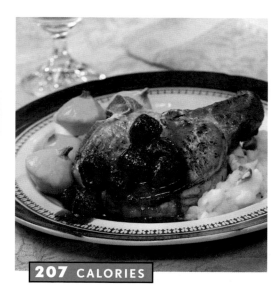

207 CALORIES

<table>
<tr><td>³/₄</td><td>cup reduced-sodium chicken broth</td></tr>
<tr><td>1</td><td>tablespoon white balsamic vinegar</td></tr>
<tr><td>1</td><td>tablespoon brown sugar</td></tr>
<tr><td>1¹/₂</td><td>teaspoons cornstarch</td></tr>
<tr><td></td><td>Dash ground allspice</td></tr>
<tr><td>4</td><td>pork rib chops, cut ³/₄ inch thick (about 1¹/₂ pounds total)</td></tr>
<tr><td>¹/₂</td><td>teaspoon salt</td></tr>
<tr><td>¹/₄</td><td>teaspoon black pepper</td></tr>
<tr><td>¹/₄</td><td>teaspoon dried basil, crushed</td></tr>
<tr><td>1</td><td>tablespoon cooking oil</td></tr>
<tr><td>1</td><td>cup fresh raspberries</td></tr>
</table>

1 In a small bowl stir together broth, balsamic vinegar, brown sugar, cornstarch, and allspice; set aside.

2 Trim fat from chops. Sprinkle both sides of each chop with salt, pepper, and basil. In a 12-inch skillet heat oil over medium heat. Add chops; cook for 8 to 12 minutes or until pork juices run clear (160°F). Transfer chops to a serving platter. Cover and keep warm. Drain fat from skillet.

3 Stir vinegar mixture. Add to skillet. Cook and stir over medium heat until slightly thickened and bubbly. Cook and stir for 2 minutes more. Gently stir in raspberries; heat through. To serve, spoon raspberry mixture over chops.

Nutrition Facts per serving:
207 cal., 9 g total fat (2 g sat. fat), 53 mg chol., 444 mg sodium, 8 g carbo., 2 g fiber, 22 g pro.
Daily Values:
1% vit. A, 11% vit. C, 3% calcium, 6% iron
Exchanges:
¹/₂ Fruit, 3 Meat

4 **boneless pork top loin chops, cut 1 inch thick (about 1¼ pounds total)**

¼ **teaspoon salt**

¼ **teaspoon black pepper**

2 **teaspoons olive oil**

⅓ **cup water**

¼ **cup plum jam**

1 **tablespoon balsamic vinegar**

2 **teaspoons Dijon-style mustard**

½ **teaspoon chicken bouillon granules**

1 **clove garlic, minced**

1 **small plum, seeded and cut into thin wedges**

½ **cup seedless red or green grapes, halved**

Snipped fresh chives (optional)

1 Trim fat from chops. Sprinkle both sides of each chop with salt and pepper. In a large nonstick skillet heat oil over medium heat. Add chops; cook for 8 to 12 minutes or until pork juices run clear (160°F), turning once. Transfer chops to a serving platter. Cover and keep warm.

2 Add the water, jam, balsamic vinegar, mustard, chicken bouillon granules, and garlic to skillet. Whisk over medium heat until bubbly. Remove from heat. Gently stir in plum wedges and grapes. To serve, spoon plum-grape mixture over chops. If desired, sprinkle with snipped chives.

305 CALORIES

Pork Chops with Plum-Grape Sauce

The plums and grapes in this recipe provide color and variety. You can choose a yellow, green, or red plum to go with the red grapes. Or select seedless green grapes and opt for a red or purple plum.

Start to Finish: 25 minutes

Makes: 4 servings

Nutrition Facts per serving:
305 cal., 10 g total fat (3 g sat. fat), 83 mg chol., 386 mg sodium, 21 g carbo., 1 g fiber, 31 g pro.
Daily Values:
2% vit. A, 11% vit. C, 3% calcium, 7% iron
Exchanges:
1½ Fruit, 4½ Meat

385 CALORIES

Fajita Pork Chops

A spunky Great Northern bean and mango salad is the ideal accompaniment for grilled or broiled fajita-seasoned pork. You also can make the salad with black beans or pinto beans.

Prep: 20 minutes   **Stand:** 30 minutes
Broil: 9 minutes   **Makes:** 4 servings

Nutrition Facts per serving:
385 cal., 9 g total fat (3 g sat. fat), 93 mg chol., 402 mg sodium, 32 g carbo., 7 g fiber, 43 g pro.
Daily Values:
57% vit. A, 48% vit. C, 13% calcium, 17% iron
Exchanges:
1/2 Fruit, 11/2 Starch, 5 Meat

1   **lime**
1   **15-ounce can Great Northern beans, rinsed and drained**
1   **large mango, pitted, peeled, and chopped, or 2 medium nectarines or peaches, peeled, pitted, and chopped**
1   **small roma tomato, seeded and chopped**
1/4   **cup sliced green onions (2)**
2   **tablespoons cider vinegar**
1   **tablespoon fresh jalapeño chile pepper, seeded and finely chopped (see note on page 76)**
1   **teaspoon sugar**
1/2   **teaspoon fajita seasoning**
2   **cloves garlic, minced**
4   **boneless pork loin chops, cut 3/4 inch thick (about 11/2 pounds total)**
1   **teaspoon fajita seasoning**
    Lime wedges (optional)

1 Finely shred 1/2 teaspoon peel from lime. Squeeze juice from lime. Reserve 2 teaspoons lime juice for pork chops.

2 For salad, in a medium bowl combine finely shredded lime peel, remaining lime juice, beans, mango, tomato, green onions, vinegar, jalapeño, sugar, the 1/2 teaspoon fajita seasoning, and the garlic. Let stand at room temperature for 30 minutes, stirring occasionally. (Or, if desired, cover and refrigerate for up to 24 hours.)

3 Trim fat from chops. Brush the reserved 2 teaspoons lime juice onto both sides of each chop. Sprinkle chops with the 1 teaspoon fajita seasoning.

4 Preheat broiler. Place chops on the unheated rack of a broiler pan. Broil 3 to 4 inches from the heat for 9 to 11 minutes or until pork juices run clear (160°F), turning once. Slice chops and serve with salad. If desired, serve with lime wedges.

Grilling directions: Prepare as above through step 3. Place chops on the rack of an uncovered grill directly over medium coals. Grill for 12 to 15 minutes or until done (160°F), turning once. Slice chops and serve with salad.

¼ cup frozen orange juice concentrate, thawed

1 tablespoon lemon juice

1 tablespoon reduced-sodium soy sauce

1 teaspoon ground coriander

¼ teaspoon black pepper

1 clove garlic, minced

4 pork rib or loin chops, cut ¾ inch thick (about 1½ pounds total)

1 For marinade, in a small bowl combine orange juice concentrate, lemon juice, soy sauce, coriander, pepper, and garlic; set aside.

2 Trim fat from chops. Place chops in a plastic bag set in a bowl. Pour marinade over chops; seal bag. Marinate in the refrigerator for at least 4 hours or up to 6 hours, turning bag occasionally. Drain chops, discarding marinade.

3 Preheat broiler. Place chops on the unheated rack of a broiler pan. Broil 3 to 4 inches from heat for 9 to 12 minutes or until pork juices run clear (160°F), turning once.

Coriander Pork Chops

With as little as 4 hours' marinating time, the juicy chops take on a delectable citrus and coriander flavor. Cap off the meal with rice pilaf and steamed whole green beans.

Prep: 10 minutes **Marinate:** 4 to 6 ho

Broil: 9 minutes **Makes:** 4 servings

263 CALORIES

Nutrition Facts per serving:
263 cal., 9 g total fat (3 g sat. fat), 92 mg chol., 141 mg sodium, 4 g carbo., 0 g fiber, 38 g pro.
Daily Values:
1% vit. A, 25% vit. C, 3% calcium, 6% iron
Exchanges:
½ Fruit, 5 Meat

Barley and Fruit-Stuffed Chops

The pork's flavorful juices moisten the fruit and barley stuffing as they broil. Team them with steamed Brussels sprouts for a top-notch meal.

Prep: 30 minutes   **Broil:** 12 minutes
Makes: 4 servings

216 CALORIES

1/3   **cup water**

1/4   **cup chopped onion**

2   **tablespoons quick-cooking barley**

2   **tablespoons mixed dried fruit bits**

1/2   **teaspoon finely shredded orange peel or lemon peel**

1/4   **teaspoon salt**

1   **tablespoon fine dry bread crumbs**

1/4   **teaspoon dried thyme, crushed**

1/4   **teaspoon black pepper**

1   **teaspoon bottled minced garlic or 2 cloves garlic, minced**

4   **4- to 5-ounce boneless pork loin chops, cut 3/4 inch thick**

2   **tablespoons orange juice**

1   **tablespoon honey**

1 For stuffing, in a small saucepan combine the water, onion, barley, fruit bits, orange peel, and salt. Bring to boiling; reduce heat. Simmer, covered, for 5 minutes. Remove from heat. Cover and let stand for 5 minutes. Stir in fine dry bread crumbs, thyme, pepper, and garlic. Set aside.

2 Meanwhile, trim fat from chops. Make a pocket in each chop by cutting horizontally from the fat side almost to the opposite side.

3 Divide stuffing among pockets in chops. If necessary, secure each opening with a wooden toothpick.

4 Preheat broiler. Place chops on the unheated rack of a broiler pan. Broil 3 to 4 inches from the heat for 12 to 15 minutes or until pork juices run clear (meat and stuffing reach 160°F), turning once.

5 Meanwhile, in a small bowl combine orange juice and honey. Brush orange juice mixture on the chops for the last 2 minutes of broiling. Before serving, discard toothpicks.

Nutrition Facts per serving:
216 cal., 6 g total fat (2 g sat. fat), 66 mg chol., 236 mg sodium, 14 g carbo., 1 g fiber, 25 g pro.
Daily Values:
1% vit. A, 10% vit. C, 3% calcium, 6% iron
Exchanges:
1/2 Fruit, 1/2 Starch, 3 1/2 Meat

2 tablespoons golden raisins

1/4 cup boiling water

1 15 1/4-ounce can unpeeled apricot halves in light syrup, drained

1 1/2 teaspoons olive oil

1/2 teaspoon snipped fresh thyme or 1/8 teaspoon dried thyme, crushed

1/4 teaspoon salt

1/4 teaspoon curry powder

4 pork loin or rib chops, cut 3/4 inch thick (about 1 1/2 pounds total)

1/4 teaspoon salt

1/4 teaspoon black pepper

1/8 teaspoon curry powder

1 Place raisins in a small bowl; add boiling water. Cover and let stand for 15 minutes or until plump. Drain; set aside.

2 Chop 1/2 cup of the apricots; set aside. In a blender container or small food processor bowl combine remaining apricots, 1/2 teaspoon of the oil, the thyme, 1/4 teaspoon salt, and the 1/4 teaspoon curry powder. Blend or process until smooth. Set aside half of the mixture for glaze. For apricot chutney, gently stir raisins and reserved chopped apricots into remaining thyme mixture; set aside.

3 Brush both sides of pork chops with remaining 1 teaspoon oil. In a small bowl combine 1/4 teaspoon salt, the pepper, and the 1/8 teaspoon curry powder. Rub on both sides of chops.

4 Preheat broiler. Place chops on unheated rack of a broiler pan. Broil 3 to 4 inches from the heat for 9 to 12 minutes or until pork juices run clear (160°F), turning once and brushing with the reserved apricot glaze for the last 2 to 3 minutes of broiling. Serve apricot chutney with chops.

Grilling directions: Prepare as above through step 3. Place chops on the rack of an uncovered grill directly over medium coals. Grill for 11 to 14 minutes or until pork juices run clear (160°F), turning once and brushing with the reserved apricot glaze during the last 3 minutes of grilling. Serve apricot chutney with chops.

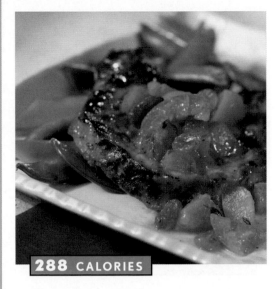

288 CALORIES

Pork Chops with Apricot Chutney

Apricot puree seasoned with thyme serves as a glaze and a chutney for these curry-rubbed chops. Juicy and sweet— how's that for diet fare?

Prep: 20 minutes **Stand:** 15 minutes
Broil: 9 minutes **Makes:** 4 servings

Nutrition Facts per serving:
288 cal., 11 g total fat (3 g sat. fat), 76 mg chol., 366 mg sodium, 21 g carbo., 2 g fiber, 26 g pro.
Daily Values:
27% vit. A, 6% vit. C, 4% calcium, 9% iron
Exchanges:
1 1/2 Fruit, 3 1/2 Meat

262 CALORIES

Squirt-of-Orange Pork Chops

A splash of juice and an orange marmalade brush-on give these garlicky chops a burst of citrus flavor. For an extra-special treat, use blood oranges in place of the regular ones.

Prep: 10 minutes **Broil:** 9 minutes
Makes: 4 servings

1 **large orange**
4 **boneless pork top loin chops, cut
1 inch thick (about 1¹/₄ pounds total)**
¹/₂ **teaspoon garlic-pepper seasoning**
¹/₄ **teaspoon salt**
¹/₄ **cup orange marmalade**
2 **teaspoons snipped fresh rosemary
Fresh rosemary sprig (optional)**

1 Cut orange in half. Cut one half of the orange into 4 wedges; set wedges aside. Squeeze juice from remaining orange half. Remove 1 tablespoon of the juice and brush on both sides of each chop. Sprinkle chops with garlic-pepper seasoning and salt. In a small bowl combine remaining orange juice, orange marmalade, and the snipped rosemary; set aside.

2 Preheat broiler. Place chops on the unheated rack of a broiler pan. Broil 3 to 4 inches from the heat for 9 to 12 minutes or until pork juices run clear (160°F), turning once and brushing with orange marmalade mixture for the last 2 to 3 minutes of broiling.

3 Serve orange wedges with chops. If desired, garnish with rosemary sprig. If desired, squeeze juice from orange wedges over chops.

Nutrition Facts per serving:
262 cal., 7 g total fat (3 g sat. fat), 83 mg chol., 343 mg sodium, 17 g carbo., 1 g fiber, 31 g pro.
Daily Values:
2% vit. A, 32% vit. C, 4% calcium, 6% iron
Exchanges:
1 Fruit, 4¹/₂ Meat

Nonstick cooking spray

12 ounces lean boneless pork, cut into ¹/₂-inch cubes

1 teaspoon cooking oil

1 cup chopped onion (1 large)

1 cup chopped carrots (2 medium)

3 cloves garlic, minced

2 15-ounce cans white kidney beans (cannellini), rinsed and drained

4 roma tomatoes, chopped

²/₃ cup reduced-sodium chicken broth

²/₃ cup water

2 ounces smoked turkey sausage, halved lengthwise and cut into ¹/₄-inch slices

1 teaspoon dried thyme, crushed

¹/₄ teaspoon dried rosemary, crushed

¹/₄ teaspoon black pepper

2 tablespoons snipped fresh thyme or flat-leaf parsley

1 Lightly coat an unheated Dutch oven with nonstick cooking spray. Preheat over medium-high heat. Add pork to Dutch oven; cook and stir until pork is browned. Remove pork from Dutch oven. Reduce heat. Carefully add oil to hot Dutch oven. Add onion, carrots, and garlic; cook until onion is tender. Stir pork, beans, tomatoes, broth, the water, turkey sausage, thyme, rosemary, and pepper into Dutch oven.

2 Bake, covered, in a 325° oven for 40 to 45 minutes or until pork and carrots are tender. To serve, spoon into individual casseroles or bowls; sprinkle each serving with thyme.

Range top directions: Prepare as above through step 1. Simmer, covered, about 15 minutes or until the pork and carrots are tender. Serve as above.

Oven-Baked Cassoulet

A French cassoulet traditionally simmers for hours. This version slashes the cooking time. For a touch of freshness, top with snipped fresh thyme or parsley just before serving.

Prep: 20 minutes   **Bake:** 40 minutes
Oven: 325°F   **Makes:** 5 servings (6²/₃ cups)

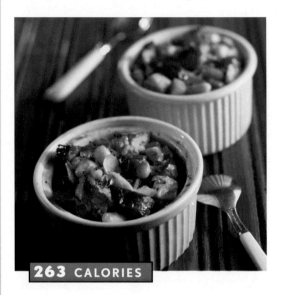

263 CALORIES

Nutrition Facts per serving:
263 cal., 6 g total fat (2 g sat. fat), 48 mg chol., 500 mg sodium, 33 g carbo., 10 g fiber, 28 g pro.
Daily Values:
134% vit. A, 32% vit. C, 8% calcium, 19% iron
Exchanges:
2¹/₂ Vegetable, 1¹/₂ Starch, 2¹/₂ Meat

Jamaican Pork Kabobs

Jamaican cooking doesn't always call for jerk seasoning. These pork and vegetable kabobs get their island flair from mango chutney and a liberal dose of Pickapeppa sauce, which can be described as a spicy Worcestershirelike sauce.

Prep: 15 minutes   **Broil:** 12 minutes
Makes: 4 servings

259 CALORIES

2	ears of corn, husked and cleaned
1	12- to 14-ounce pork tenderloin
16	baby pattypan squash (each about 1 inch in diameter) or 4 fresh tomatillos, quartered
1	small red onion, cut into ½-inch wedges
¼	cup mango chutney, finely chopped
3	tablespoons Pickapeppa sauce*
1	tablespoon cooking oil
1	tablespoon water
	Hot cooked rice (optional)

1 Cut corn crosswise into 1-inch pieces. In medium saucepan cook corn pieces in a small amount of boiling water for 3 minutes; drain and rinse with cold water. Meanwhile, cut tenderloin into 1-inch slices. For kabobs, on long metal skewers, alternately thread corn, tenderloin slices, squash or tomatillos, and onion wedges, leaving a ¼-inch space between pieces. In a small bowl combine chutney, Pickapeppa sauce, oil, and the water; set aside.

2 Preheat broiler. Place kabobs on the unheated rack of a broiler pan. Broil 3 to 4 inches from the heat for 12 to 14 minutes or until pork is cooked through and the vegetables are tender, turning once and brushing with the chutney mixture for the last 5 minutes of broiling. If desired, serve with hot cooked rice.

***Note:** If you can't find Pickapeppa sauce, substitute 3 tablespoons Worcestershire sauce mixed with a dash of bottled hot pepper sauce.

Nutrition Facts per serving:
259 cal., 6 g total fat (1 g sat. fat), 50 mg chol., 150 mg sodium, 29 g carbo., 4 g fiber, 23 g pro.
Daily Values:
20% vit. A, 42% vit. C, 3% calcium, 10% iron
Exchanges:
3 Vegetable, 1 Starch, 2 Meat

- **2** teaspoons cooking oil
- **1/3** cup chopped onion (1 small)
- **4** cloves garlic, minced
- **12** ounces pork tenderloin, cut into 3/4-inch cubes
- **2** teaspoons chili powder
- **2** teaspoons ground cumin
- **1** yellow or red sweet pepper, cut into 1/2-inch chunks
- **1** cup beer or beef broth
- **1/2** cup bottled picante sauce or salsa
- **1** to 2 tablespoons finely chopped canned chipotle peppers in adobo sauce
- **1** 15-ounce can small red beans or pinto beans, rinsed and drained

1 In a large saucepan heat oil over medium-high heat. Add onion and garlic; cook about 3 minutes or until tender. In a large bowl toss pork with chili powder and cumin; add to saucepan. Cook and stir about 3 minutes or until pork is browned.

2 Stir in sweet pepper, beer or broth, picante sauce or salsa, and chipotle peppers. Bring to boiling; reduce heat. Simmer, uncovered, about 5 minutes or just until pork is tender. Add beans; heat through.

281 CALORIES

Chunky Chipotle Pork Chili

This hearty bowl of red goes together in minutes. The secret? Lean pork tenderloin, which cooks in practically no time. As for the simmered-all-day flavor, the credit goes to smoky chipotle peppers.

Start to Finish: 30 minutes
Makes: 4 servings (4 cups)

Nutrition Facts per serving:
281 cal., 5 g total fat (1 g sat. fat), 50 mg chol., 630 mg sodium, 27 g carbo., 7 g fiber, 27 g pro.
Daily Values:
15% vit. A, 127% vit. C, 9% calcium, 17% iron
Exchanges:
1 Vegetable, 1 1/2 Starch, 3 Meat

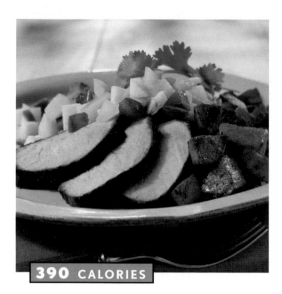

390 CALORIES

Caribbean Pork with Sweet Potatoes

This dish is pretty to look at and pretty hot-tasting too. Pickapeppa sauce and a fruit salsa give this meat-and-potatoes roast a Caribbean kick.

Prep: 30 minutes   **Roast:** 1¼ hours
Oven: 325°F   **Makes:** 4 servings

Nutrition Facts per serving:
390 cal., 6 g total fat (2 g sat. fat), 66 mg chol., 231 mg sodium, 55 g carbo., 6 g fiber, 28 g pro.
Daily Values:
479% vit. A, 100% vit. C, 7% calcium, 14% iron
Exchanges:
1 Vegetable, 1 Fruit, 2 Starch, 3 Meat

3   tablespoons Pickapeppa sauce*
1   clove garlic, minced
⅛   teaspoon dried thyme, crushed
1   1-pound boneless pork top loin roast (single loin)
2   large sweet potatoes, peeled and cut into ¾-inch pieces (1 to 1¼ pounds total)
1   recipe Mango-Jicama Salsa
    Fresh cilantro sprigs (optional)

1 In a small bowl combine 2 tablespoons of the Pickapeppa sauce, the garlic, and thyme; set aside.

2 Trim fat from roast. Brush garlic mixture on all sides of roast. Place roast on a rack in a shallow roasting pan. Roast in a 325° oven for 45 minutes.

3 Meanwhile, in a medium saucepan cook sweet potatoes in boiling, lightly salted water about 8 minutes or just until tender; drain. Toss sweet potatoes with remaining 1 tablespoon Pickapeppa sauce. Place sweet potatoes around roast in pan. Continue roasting for 30 to 45 minutes more or until pork juices run clear (160°F).

4 To serve, slice pork. Serve sliced pork with sweet potatoes and Mango-Jicama Salsa. If desired, garnish with cilantro.

Mango-Jicama Salsa: Drain one 8-ounce can pineapple tidbits (juice pack), reserving 2 tablespoons of the juice. In a medium bowl combine pineapple; reserved pineapple juice; 1 cup peeled, chopped jicama; 1 medium mango, peeled, seeded, and chopped; 1 large tomato, seeded and chopped; 1 green onion, sliced; 1 or 2 fresh jalapeño chile peppers, seeded and finely chopped (see note on page 76); 1 tablespoon lime juice; and ⅛ teaspoon salt. Cover and refrigerate until serving time or up to 24 hours.

*Note: If you can't find Pickapeppa sauce, substitute 3 tablespoons Worcestershire sauce mixed with a dash of bottled hot pepper sauce.

- 1 **12-ounce pork tenderloin**
  Nonstick cooking spray
- 1 **tablespoon olive oil**
- 2 **medium onions, sliced and separated into rings**
- 1 **tablespoon brown sugar**
- 1/3 **cup water**
- 3 **tablespoons balsamic vinegar or white wine vinegar**
- 2 **teaspoons cornstarch**
- 1/4 **teaspoon salt**
- 1/4 **teaspoon black pepper**
  Hot cooked orzo (optional)
- 2 **tablespoons snipped fresh parsley**

1 Trim fat from pork. Cut pork crosswise into ½-inch slices. Lightly coat an unheated large nonstick skillet with nonstick cooking spray. Preheat skillet over medium-high heat. Add half of the pork to the hot skillet; cook about 4 minutes or until pork is cooked through, turning once. Remove pork from skillet. Repeat with remaining pork.

2 Carefully add oil to skillet; add the onions. Cook, covered, over medium-low heat for 13 to 15 minutes or until onions are tender. Uncover; stir in the brown sugar. Cook and stir over medium-high heat for 4 to 5 minutes or until onions are golden.

3 Meanwhile, in a small bowl stir together the water, vinegar, cornstarch, salt, and pepper; carefully stir into onion mixture in skillet. Cook and stir until thickened and bubbly. Cook and stir for 2 minutes more. Return pork to skillet; heat through.

4 If desired, serve the pork and onion mixture over hot cooked orzo. Sprinkle with parsley.

Pork with Glazed Onions

A small amount of brown sugar melts during cooking to coat the onions with a light caramel glaze. For extra flavor, use a variety of sweet onion, such as Maui, Walla Walla, or Vidalia.

Start to Finish: 35 minutes
Makes: 4 servings

185 CALORIES

Nutrition Facts per serving:
185 cal., 5 g total fat (1 g sat. fat), 50 mg chol., 186 mg sodium, 12 g carbo., 1 g fiber, 21 g pro.
Daily Values:
2% vit. A, 9% vit. C, 2% calcium, 8% iron
Exchanges:
2 Vegetable, 2½ Meat

Tangy Stir-Fried Pork

When fresh kumquats are in season, use them to add flavor and interest to pork tenderloin. Other times of the year, substitute thinly sliced orange.

Start to Finish: 25 minutes

Makes: 4 servings

244 CALORIES

1 teaspoon cooking oil

12 ounces pork tenderloin, cut into 1/2-inch slices

1/4 cup dry white wine or reduced-sodium chicken broth

6 kumquats, thinly sliced, or 1/4 of an orange, thinly sliced

2 tablespoons bottled hoisin sauce

1 green onion, bias-sliced into 1/4-inch pieces

1 teaspoon sesame seeds, toasted

2 cups hot, cooked quick-cooking brown rice

1 In a wok or large nonstick skillet heat oil over medium-high heat. Add pork; cook for 6 to 8 minutes or until cooked through. Remove from wok or skillet.

2 Add wine or broth, kumquat or orange slices, and hoisin sauce to wok or skillet. Cook and stir for 1 minute.

3 Return pork to wok or skillet. Heat through. Stir in green onion and sesame seeds. Serve over hot cooked rice.

Nutrition Facts per serving:
244 cal., 4 g total fat (1 g sat. fat), 50 mg chol., 126 mg sodium, 26 g carbo., 3 g fiber, 23 g pro.
Daily Values:
3% vit. A, 20% vit. C, 3% calcium, 9% iron
Exchanges:
1/2 Fruit, 1 1/2 Starch, 2 1/2 Meat

Nonstick cooking spray

1 tablespoon finely chopped, drained canned whole cherry pepper (1 pepper) or pepperoncini salad peppers

¼ cup bottled chili sauce

¼ cup seasoned fine dry bread crumbs

2 tablespoons finely chopped onion

1 tablespoon grated Parmesan cheese or Romano cheese

1½ teaspoons fennel seeds, crushed

1 pound very lean ground pork

1 26- or 27-ounce jar chunky-style pasta sauce

¼ cup chopped, drained canned whole cherry peppers (4 peppers) or pepperoncini salad peppers

3 cups hot cooked wide noodles

1 Lightly coat a 15×10×1-inch baking pan with nonstick cooking spray; set aside. In a large bowl combine the 1 tablespoon finely chopped pepper, the chili sauce, bread crumbs, onion, cheese, and fennel seeds. Add pork. Mix well. Shape into 36 meatballs. Place in prepared pan.

2 Bake, uncovered, in a 350° oven for 20 to 25 minutes or until browned and cooked through. Remove from oven; drain off fat.

3 Meanwhile, in a medium saucepan heat the pasta sauce until bubbly. Add baked meatballs and the ¼ cup chopped peppers; heat through. Serve over hot noodles.

294 CALORIES

Feisty Italian Meatballs

Marvelous pork meatballs seasoned with chili sauce and cherry peppers—and served with hot cooked noodles—add up to a stick-to-the-ribs entrée. Complete the menu with fresh spinach salad.

Prep: 20 minutes   **Bake:** 20 minutes
Oven: 350°F   **Makes:** 6 servings

Nutrition Facts per serving:
294 cal., 9 g total fat (3 g sat. fat), 62 mg chol., 993 mg sodium, 38 g carbo., 2 g fiber, 16 g pro.
Daily Values:
2% vit. A, 12% vit. C, 7% calcium, 15% iron
Exchanges:
1 Vegetable, 2 Starch, 2 Meat

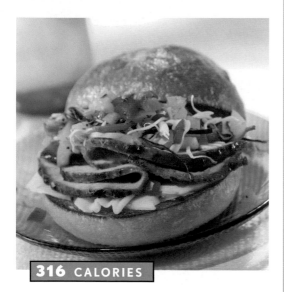

316 CALORIES

Pork Sandwiches with Mojo Sauce

These Cuban-style sandwiches feature mojo sauce, which is a combination of garlic, citrus juices, and spices. Although not a component of traditional Cuban-style sandwiches, the coleslaw mix adds a fitting crunch.

Start to Finish: 35 minutes

Makes: 4 servings

- $3/4$ cup finely chopped red and/or yellow sweet pepper
- 4 large cloves garlic, minced
- 1 teaspoon olive oil
- $1/4$ cup orange juice
- 1 tablespoon lime juice
- 1 teaspoon ground cumin
- 1 teaspoon dried oregano, crushed
- $1/4$ teaspoon salt
- $1/4$ teaspoon black pepper
- 2 ounces mozzarella cheese, thinly sliced
- 4 small rolls, toasted if desired
- 8 ounces cooked pork loin, thinly sliced
- 1 cup packaged shredded cabbage with carrot (coleslaw mix)

1 For mojo sauce, in a small saucepan cook sweet pepper and garlic in hot oil until tender. Stir in orange juice, lime juice, cumin, oregano, salt, and black pepper. Bring to boiling; reduce heat. Boil gently for 1 minute. Cool to room temperature. (If desired, store tightly covered in the refrigerator for up to 1 week.)

2 For sandwiches, divide cheese among roll bottoms. Top each with one-quarter of the pork slices and ¼ cup of the cabbage. Spoon 2 tablespoons of the mojo sauce onto each sandwich. Top with roll tops.

Nutrition Facts per serving:
316 cal., 11 g total fat (4 g sat. fat), 54 mg chol., 490 mg sodium, 28 g carbo., 3 g fiber, 24 g pro.
Daily Values:
36% vit. A, 107% vit. C, 19% calcium, 14% iron
Exchanges:
1 Vegetable, 1½ Starch, 2½ Meat

8   ounces fresh Chinese egg noodles or
    dried fine egg noodles

12 ounces ground pork

4   cloves garlic, minced

2   teaspoons peanut oil or cooking oil

1   teaspoon toasted sesame oil

2   cups chopped broccoli or packaged
    shredded broccoli (broccoli slaw)

1   medium carrot, cut into thin
    2-inch-long strips

1   tablespoon grated fresh ginger

1/4 teaspoon crushed red pepper

1/4 cup chicken broth

1/4 cup bottled hoisin sauce

1 Cook noodles according to package
directions. Drain. Meanwhile, preheat a
large skillet or a wok over medium-high
heat. Add ground pork and garlic; cook
until meat is brown. Drain off fat.
Remove meat from skillet or wok.

2 Add peanut oil and sesame oil to skillet.
Add broccoli, carrot, ginger, and crushed
red pepper; stir-fry for 2 minutes. Stir
in broth and hoisin sauce. Cook and
stir until bubbly.

3 Stir noodles into vegetable mixture. Stir
in cooked meat; heat through.

Garlic Pork

The exotic flavors of the Orient—fresh
ginger, sesame oil, and hoisin sauce—
make this hearty stir-fry as delicious as
it is easy. Using broccoli slaw saves
precious prep time.

Start to Finish: 25 minutes

Makes: 4 servings

407 CALORIES

Nutrition Facts per serving:
407 cal., 13 g total fat (4 g sat. fat), 94 mg chol.,
280 mg sodium, 52 g carbo., 3 g fiber, 21 g pro.
Daily Values:
102% vit. A, 73% vit. C, 6% calcium, 18% iron
Exchanges:
2 Vegetable, 2½ Starch, 1½ Meat, ½ Fat

Maple-Bourbon Smoked Chops

Smoked pork chops are hard to resist when they're topped with this sensational maple syrup, bourbon, and onion combo. And, with only 229 calories and 8 grams of fat, there's no need to!

Start to Finish: 30 minutes

Makes: 4 servings

229 CALORIES

2 teaspoons cooking oil

1 medium onion, halved lengthwise and sliced

1/4 cup pure maple syrup or maple-flavored syrup

1 tablespoon bourbon

1 tablespoon Dijon-style mustard

1/8 teaspoon crushed red pepper

2 cloves garlic, minced

4 cooked smoked boneless pork chops, cut 3/4 inch thick (about 1 pound total)

1 In a large skillet heat oil over medium heat. Add onion; cook for 4 to 5 minutes or until tender, stirring occasionally. Increase heat to medium-high; cook and stir for 3 to 4 minutes more or until onion is golden. Remove onion from skillet with a slotted spoon, reserving drippings. In a medium bowl stir together cooked onion, syrup, bourbon, mustard, red pepper, and garlic; set aside.

2 Trim fat from chops. In the same skillet cook chops in reserved drippings over medium heat for 5 minutes. Turn chops over. Add onion mixture to skillet. Cook, uncovered, for 4 to 5 minutes more or until chops are heated through.

3 To serve, transfer chops to a serving platter. Spoon onion mixture over chops.

Nutrition Facts per serving:
229 cal., 8 g total fat (2 g sat. fat), 60 mg chol., 1,382 mg sodium, 16 g carbo., 0 g fiber, 20 g pro.
Daily Values:
3% vit. C, 2% calcium, 4% iron
Exchanges:
1 Starch, 2 1/2 Meat

- 2 **cups sliced fresh shiitake or button mushrooms**
- 1 **small red or green sweet pepper, cut into thin strips**
- 1/2 **cup chopped onion (1 medium)**
- 1 **clove garlic, minced**
- 1 **tablespoon butter or margarine**
- 1 **12-ounce can (1 1/2 cups) evaporated fat-free milk**
- 2 **tablespoons snipped fresh basil or 1/2 teaspoon dried basil, crushed**
- 4 **teaspoons cornstarch**
- 1/4 **teaspoon black pepper**
- 4 **ounces cooked ham, cut into thin bite-size strips**
- 1 **9-ounce package refrigerated fettuccine**
   Finely shredded Parmesan cheese (optional)

1 For sauce, in a large skillet cook mushrooms, sweet pepper, onion, and garlic in hot butter until tender. In a medium bowl combine evaporated milk, basil, cornstarch, and black pepper. Stir into vegetable mixture in skillet. Cook and stir over medium heat until bubbly. Cook and stir for 2 minutes more. Stir in ham. Remove from heat.

2 Meanwhile, cook pasta according to package directions. Drain. Serve sauce over pasta. If desired, sprinkle with Parmesan cheese.

385 CALORIES

Pasta with Ham-Mushroom Sauce

This creamy, satisfying dish resembles a vegetable-studded fettuccine Alfredo. However, Alfredo sauce usually relies on heavy cream for its richness, and this flavorful sauce is made with evaporated fat-free milk, which is a lot lighter.

Start to Finish: 30 minutes
Makes: 4 servings

Nutrition Facts per serving:
385 cal., 10 g total fat (4 g sat. fat), 96 mg chol., 600 mg sodium, 52 g carbo., 3 g fiber, 22 g pro.
Daily Values:
30% vit. A, 54% vit. C, 28% calcium, 18% iron
Exchanges:
1 Milk, 2 Vegetable, 2 Starch, 1 Meat

315 CALORIES

Deli Sandwich Stacks

A creamy cheese and honey mustard spread serves as the irresistible and innovative base for sliced ham, turkey, and mild cheese. Team this hearty sandwich with your favorite soup for a super-satisfying lunch or supper.

Start to Finish: 20 minutes

Makes: 4 servings

½ of a 4-ounce container light semisoft cheese with garlic and herb

2 tablespoons honey mustard

¼ teaspoon lemon-pepper seasoning

6 slices marble rye, cracked wheat, or seven-grain bread

2 small roma tomatoes, thinly sliced

⅓ cup sliced canned banana peppers, well drained

1 cup loosely packed fresh spinach leaves or 4 lettuce leaves

4 thin slices Colby or Monterey Jack cheese

4 ounces thinly sliced cooked turkey breast

4 ounces low-fat, reduced-sodium thinly sliced cooked ham

Fresh banana peppers (optional)

1 In a small bowl combine semisoft cheese, honey mustard, and lemon-pepper seasoning. Spread the cheese mixture evenly onto 1 side of 4 of the bread slices.

2 To assemble sandwiches, divide tomatoes, sliced banana peppers, spinach or lettuce, and Colby or Monterey Jack cheese evenly among the 4 bread slices, spread sides up. Top 2 stacks with turkey and 2 stacks with ham. Arrange the stacks with ham on top of the stacks with turkey. Top with remaining bread slices. Cut stacks in half. If desired, garnish each half with a banana pepper and secure with a wooden pick.

Nutrition Facts per serving:
315 cal., 12 g total fat (6 g sat. fat), 51 mg chol., 1,245 mg sodium, 31 g carbo., 4 g fiber, 22 g pro.
Daily Values:
22% vit. A, 48% vit. C, 22% calcium, 16% iron
Exchanges:
2 Starch, 3 Meat

- 1 15-inch round Armenian cracker bread (lavash)
- ½ of an 8-ounce package reduced-fat cream cheese (Neufchâtel), softened
- 2 tablespoons peach butter or apple butter
- 1 tablespoon milk
- ¼ cup finely chopped green or yellow sweet pepper
- 2 tablespoons thinly sliced green onion
- 8 ounces thinly sliced low-fat, reduced-sodium cooked honey ham or thinly sliced deli-roasted pork
- 4 small butterhead (Boston or Bibb) lettuce leaves

1 Soften cracker bread according to package directions.

2 Meanwhile, in a medium bowl combine cream cheese, peach or apple butter, and milk; stir until smooth. Stir in sweet pepper and green onion.

3 Spread cream cheese mixture onto softened cracker bread. Top with ham or pork and lettuce leaves. Roll up tightly into a spiral. (If desired, wrap and chill up to 6 hours.) Cut crosswise into 8 pieces to serve.

Creamy Ham Sandwich Rolls

Look for Armenian cracker bread in the bakery section of large supermarkets. This Middle Eastern specialty may be labeled lavash, lavosh, or lahvosh.

Prep: 25 minutes
Stand: Per cracker bread package directions
Makes: 8 servings

166 CALORIES

Nutrition Facts per serving:
166 cal., 6 g total fat (3 g sat. fat), 26 mg chol., 429 mg sodium, 21 g carbo., 0 g fiber, 9 g pro.
Daily Values:
5% vit. A, 8% vit. C, 2% calcium, 4% iron
Exchanges:
1½ Starch, 1 Meat

Rosemary-Rubbed Lamb Chops

This succulent apricot-glazed lamb is special enough to headline the most elegant menu. Mustard and rosemary add savory flavor to its sweet brush-on.

Start to Finish: 25 minutes

Makes: 4 servings

289 CALORIES

8 lamb rib chops, cut 1 inch thick (about 1½ pounds total)

2 tablespoons olive oil

2 teaspoons snipped fresh rosemary or ½ teaspoon dried rosemary, crushed

½ teaspoon coarsely ground black pepper

2 cloves garlic, minced

½ cup apricot preserves or peach preserves

¼ cup water

1 tablespoon Dijon-style mustard

1 teaspoon chicken bouillon granules

½ teaspoon snipped fresh rosemary or ⅛ teaspoon dried rosemary, crushed

¼ teaspoon coarsely ground black pepper

Fresh rosemary sprigs (optional)

1 Trim fat from chops. In a small bowl combine 1 tablespoon of the oil, the 2 teaspoons snipped rosemary or ½ teaspoon dried rosemary, the ½ teaspoon pepper, and the garlic. Use your fingers or a pastry brush to rub or brush the garlic mixture onto all sides of chops.

2 For glaze, in a small saucepan combine apricot or peach preserves, the water, mustard, bouillon granules, the ½ teaspoon snipped rosemary or ⅛ teaspoon dried rosemary, and the ¼ teaspoon pepper; heat and stir until bubbly. Remove from heat; set aside.

3 In a large skillet heat the remaining 1 tablespoon oil over medium heat. Add chops; cook for 9 to 11 minutes or until medium doneness (160°F), turning once. Serve chops with glaze. If desired, garnish with rosemary sprigs.

Nutrition Facts per serving:
289 cal., 12 g total fat (3 g sat. fat), 48 mg chol., 361 mg sodium, 29 g carbo., 1 g fiber, 15 g pro.
Daily Values:
7% vit. C, 2% calcium, 9% iron
Exchanges:
2 Fruit, 2 Meat, 1 Fat

- 12 ounces lean boneless lamb, cut into thin bite-size strips
- ½ cup water
- ⅓ cup orange marmalade or apricot spread
- 1 tablespoon snipped fresh thyme or 1 teaspoon dried thyme, crushed
- ½ teaspoon coarsely ground black pepper
- ¼ teaspoon salt
- ⅛ teaspoon cayenne pepper
- 1 clove garlic, minced
- 1 tablespoon cooking oil
- 2 medium pears, cored and thinly sliced
- 1 small red onion, thinly sliced
- ½ of a medium red sweet pepper, cut into thin strips
- Hot cooked rice sticks (optional)

1 Place lamb in a plastic bag set in a shallow dish; set aside. For marinade, in a small bowl combine the water, orange marmalade or apricot spread, thyme, black pepper, salt, cayenne pepper, and garlic. Pour over lamb; seal bag. Marinate in refrigerator for at least 2 hours or up to 24 hours, turning bag occasionally.

2 Drain lamb, reserving marinade. In a large nonstick skillet heat oil over medium heat. Add pears, onion, and sweet pepper; cook for 2 to 4 minutes or just until pears are tender. Remove from skillet; set aside.

3 In the same skillet stir-fry the lamb over medium-high heat for 2 to 3 minutes or until desired doneness. Remove from skillet and spoon onto serving platter. Return the onion-pear mixture to the skillet. Stir in reserved marinade. Bring to boiling; reduce heat. Simmer, uncovered, about 2 minutes more or until onion is tender. If desired, serve over hot cooked rice sticks.

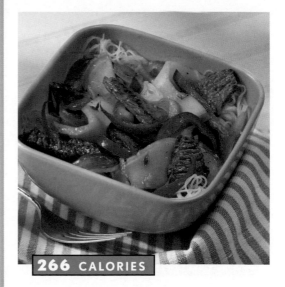

266 CALORIES

Lamb with Peppered Pears

This dish takes full advantage of pepper in several of its many forms: coarsely ground black pepper, cayenne pepper, and red sweet pepper. For a more colorful presentation, use a mixture of red and yellow sweet pepper strips.

Prep: 20 minutes **Marinate:** 2 to 24 hours
Cook: 10 minutes **Makes:** 4 servings

Nutrition Facts per serving:
266 cal., 8 g total fat (2 g sat. fat), 56 mg chol., 203 mg sodium, 33 g carbo., 3 g fiber, 18 g pro.
Daily Values:
18% vit. A, 51% vit. C, 3% calcium, 12% iron
Exchanges:
1 Vegetable, 1½ Fruit, 2½ Meat

239 CALORIES

Lamb with Orange Compote

Mint heightens the flavors of ruby cranberries and bright orange sections in the colorful compote served with this garlic-rubbed lamb spiral. Round out the meal with healthful roasted potatoes and steamed broccoli.

Prep: 25 minutes   **Roast:** 25 minutes
Oven: 400°F   **Stand:** 10 minutes
Makes: 4 servings

Nutrition Facts per serving:
239 cal., 10 g total fat (3 g sat. fat), 74 mg chol.,
288 mg sodium, 12 g carbo., 1 g fiber, 24 g pro.
Daily Values:
4% vit. A, 42% vit. C, 4% calcium, 15% iron
Exchanges:
1 Fruit, 3 Meat

2   **medium oranges**
1   **tablespoon snipped fresh mint**
1   **tablespoon rice vinegar**
1   **tablespoon mint jelly**
½   **cup chopped, seeded cucumber**
2   **tablespoons snipped dried cranberries**
1   **boneless lamb loin roast (about 1 pound)**
2   **tablespoons snipped fresh parsley**
4   **cloves garlic, minced**
¼   **teaspoon salt**
¼   **teaspoon black pepper**
    Salt
    Black pepper
1   **tablespoon olive oil**

1 For compote, peel, seed, and section the oranges over a small bowl to catch juice. Reserve 2 tablespoons of the juice in bowl. Whisk in mint, rice vinegar, and jelly. Stir in the orange sections, cucumber, and cranberries. Cover and refrigerate until serving time or for up to 2 hours.

2 Trim fat from roast. Place roast between 2 pieces of plastic wrap. Working from the center to the edges, pound with the flat side of a meat mallet to a rectangle about ½ inch thick. Remove plastic wrap. Sprinkle meat with parsley, garlic, the ¼ teaspoon salt, and the ¼ teaspoon pepper. Starting from a long side, roll up into a spiral. Tie with 100-percent-cotton string at 1½-inch intervals. Lightly sprinkle with additional salt and pepper.

3 In a large ovenproof skillet cook meat in hot oil until browned, turning to brown evenly. Insert an oven-going meat thermometer into the center of meat. Place skillet in a 400° oven. Roast for 25 to 30 minutes or until the thermometer registers 155°F. Remove meat from oven.

4 Cover meat with foil; let stand for 10 minutes. (The temperature of the meat will rise 5°F during standing.) To serve, cut meat into ½-inch slices. Serve meat with compote.

8 lamb loin chops, cut 1 inch thick
   (about 1½ pounds total)
2 teaspoons olive oil
1 small onion, thinly sliced
2 cups sliced fresh mushrooms
1 tablespoon balsamic vinegar
¼ teaspoon salt
¼ teaspoon black pepper
2 cloves garlic, minced
1 teaspoon snipped fresh tarragon or
   basil or ¼ teaspoon dried tarragon
   or basil, crushed

1 Trim fat from chops. In a large nonstick skillet heat oil over medium heat. Add chops; cook for 9 to 11 minutes or until medium doneness (160°F), turning once. Transfer chops to a serving platter; keep warm.

2 Stir onion into drippings in skillet. Cook and stir for 2 minutes. Stir in mushrooms, balsamic vinegar, salt, pepper, and garlic. Cook and stir for 3 to 4 minutes or until mushrooms are tender. Stir in tarragon or basil. Spoon mushroom mixture over chops on platter.

Lamb with Herbed Mushrooms

Featuring fresh tarragon, the low-calorie mushroom topper makes an ideal accent to the full-bodied flavor of the lamb. If you like it paired with lamb, try it with broiled or grilled pork or chicken too.

Start to Finish: 25 minutes
Makes: 4 servings

165 CALORIES

Nutrition Facts per serving:
165 cal., 9 g total fat (3 g sat. fat), 48 mg chol., 280 mg sodium, 4 g carbo., 1 g fiber, 16 g pro.
Daily Values:
2% vit. C, 2% calcium, 9% iron

Exchanges:
1 Vegetable, 2 Meat

Aloha Lamb Chops

A curry-seasoned lime and pineapple juice mixture starts out as a marinade for tender lamb chops and subsequently simmers down to a delicate sauce. Fresh papaya or mango brings to mind the sultry sun and fun of the tropics.

Prep: 20 minutes **Marinate:** 4 to 6 hours
Broil: 10 minutes **Makes:** 4 servings

275 CALORIES

Nutrition Facts per serving:
275 cal., 4 g total fat (1 g sat. fat), 40 mg chol., 190 mg sodium, 43 g carbo., 3 g fiber, 17 g pro.
Daily Values:
5% vit. A, 101% vit. C, 5% calcium, 16% iron
Exchanges:
1 Fruit, 1½ Starch, 2 Meat

4   lamb loin chops, cut 1 inch thick
    (about 1 pound total)
1   lime
1   6-ounce can (³/₄ cup) unsweetened
    pineapple juice
¼   cup sliced green onions (2)
1   tablespoon brown sugar
1   teaspoon curry powder
¼   teaspoon salt
¼   teaspoon crushed red pepper
½   cup cold water
1   tablespoon cornstarch
1   medium papaya or mango, pitted,
    peeled, and chopped
2   cups hot cooked orzo or rice
    Sliced papaya or mango (optional)

1 Trim fat from chops. Place chops in a plastic bag set in a shallow dish; set aside.

2 Finely shred ½ teaspoon peel from the lime; cover peel with plastic wrap and set aside. Squeeze juice from lime.

3 For marinade, in a small bowl combine the lime juice, pineapple juice, green onions, brown sugar, curry powder, salt, and crushed red pepper. Pour over meat; seal bag. Marinate in refrigerator for at least 4 hours or up to 6 hours, turning bag occasionally.

4 Drain chops, reserving marinade. Preheat broiler. Place chops on the unheated rack of a broiler pan. Broil 3 to 4 inches from the heat for 10 to 15 minutes or until medium doneness (160°F), turning once.

5 Meanwhile, pour reserved marinade into a small saucepan. In a small bowl stir together the water and cornstarch; stir into marinade in saucepan. Cook and stir over medium heat until bubbly. Cook and stir for 2 minutes more. Stir in the chopped papaya or mango and reserved lime peel.

6 Serve chops and sauce over hot cooked orzo. If desired, garnish with sliced papaya or mango.

1½ pounds lean boneless lamb

1 tablespoon cooking oil

1 14-ounce can reduced-sodium chicken broth

1¼ cups apple juice or apple cider

2 medium sweet potatoes, peeled and cut into bite-size pieces

1 cup loose-pack frozen small whole onions

½ teaspoon salt

½ teaspoon ground allspice

¼ teaspoon black pepper

2 cups loose-pack frozen cut green beans

1 large Jonathan, Jonagold, or Fuji apple, peeled, if desired, and cut into bite-size pieces

¼ cup apple juice or apple cider

2 tablespoons cornstarch

1 Trim fat from meat. Cut meat into 1-inch cubes. In a 4-quart Dutch oven brown meat, half at a time, in hot oil. Drain off fat. Return all meat to Dutch oven. Add broth and the 1¼ cups apple juice. Stir in sweet potatoes, onions, salt, allspice, and pepper.

2 Bake, covered, in a 350° oven for 1 hour. Stir in green beans and apple. Cover and bake for 15 to 20 minutes more or until meat is tender. Remove Dutch oven from the oven; place on the range top.

3 In a small bowl stir together the ¼ cup apple juice and the cornstarch. Stir into meat mixture. Cook and stir over medium heat until thickened and bubbly. Cook and stir for 2 minutes more.

297 CALORIES

Sweet Potato and Lamb Stew

Though this stew takes almost 2 hours to make, the cooking is mostly untended. Serve it with crisp vinaigrette-tossed greens and chunks of your favorite bread to sop up the sweet apple juices.

Prep: 30 minutes   **Bake:** 1¼ hours
Oven: 350°F   **Makes:** 6 servings (8 cups)

Nutrition Facts per serving:
297 cal., 6 g total fat (2 g sat. fat), 71 mg chol., 447 mg sodium, 34 g carbo., 4 g fiber, 26 g pro.
Daily Values:
209% vit. A, 30% vit. C, 5% calcium, 18% iron
Exchanges:
1 Vegetable, 1 Fruit, 1 Starch, 3 Meat

Lamb and Bulgur Burgers

Garlic, coriander, and thyme season these juicy burgers. For the most healthful option, ask your butcher to grind leg of lamb—it will be leaner than the meat used for ordinary ground lamb.

Prep: 20 minutes **Bake:** 20 minutes
Oven: 350°F **Makes:** 6 servings

307 CALORIES

- 1 **8-ounce carton plain low-fat yogurt**
- 2 **teaspoons snipped fresh dill or 1/2 teaspoon dried dill**
- 3/4 **cup water**
- 1/2 **cup bulgur**
- 1/2 **teaspoon salt**
- 1/4 **cup finely chopped onion**
- 3 **tablespoons snipped fresh parsley**
- 1 **teaspoon ground coriander**
- 1 **teaspoon snipped fresh thyme or 1/4 teaspoon dried thyme, crushed**
- 1/8 **teaspoon black pepper**
- 2 **cloves garlic, minced**
- 12 **ounces lean ground lamb**
- 1/2 **of a medium cucumber, cut lengthwise into thin ribbons**
- 6 **sandwich rolls or whole wheat hamburger buns, split**
  Tomato slices (optional)

1 For sauce, in a small bowl stir together yogurt and dill. Cover and refrigerate until serving time.

2 In a small saucepan bring the water to boiling. Stir in bulgur and ¼ teaspoon of the salt. Reduce heat to low. Cook, covered, for 10 minutes. Remove from heat. Let stand, covered, for 5 minutes.

3 Meanwhile, in a large bowl combine the onion, parsley, coriander, thyme, pepper, garlic, and the remaining ¼ teaspoon salt. Stir in cooked bulgur and ground lamb; mix well. Shape meat mixture into six ½-inch-thick patties. Place in a shallow baking pan. Bake in a 350° oven for 20 to 25 minutes or until internal temperature registers 160°F on an instant-read thermometer.

4 To serve, arrange the cucumber ribbons on roll bottoms. Add burgers, tomato slices (if desired), sauce, and roll tops.

Nutrition Facts per serving:
307 cal., 11 g total fat (4 g sat. fat), 40 mg chol., 498 mg sodium, 35 g carbo., 3 g fiber, 17 g pro.
Daily Values:
4% vit. A, 9% vit. C, 15% calcium, 15% iron
Exchanges:
2½ Starch, 1½ Meat

On the divider: Peppered Chicken in Marsala Sauce (see recipe, page 316)

- **2** tablespoons all-purpose flour
- **4** skinless, boneless chicken breast halves (1¼ to 1½ pounds total)
- **1** tablespoon olive oil
- **2** large green and/or yellow sweet peppers, cut into thin bite-size strips
- **1** large onion, halved lengthwise and thinly sliced
- **3** cloves garlic, minced
- **1** teaspoon paprika
- **⅛** teaspoon cayenne pepper
- **1** 14½-ounce can diced tomatoes, undrained
- **¼** cup reduced-sodium chicken broth
- **¼** cup sliced pitted ripe olives
- **1** tablespoon snipped fresh oregano
  Fresh oregano leaves (optional)

1 Place flour in a shallow dish. Dip chicken into flour to coat. In a large skillet cook chicken in hot oil over medium-high heat about 4 minutes or until chicken is browned, turning once. Remove chicken.

2 Add sweet peppers, onion, and garlic to skillet. Cook and stir for 3 to 4 minutes or until vegetables are nearly tender. Add paprika and cayenne pepper. Cook and stir for 1 minute more.

3 Stir in undrained tomatoes, broth, and olives. Bring to boiling. Return chicken to skillet, spooning tomato mixture over chicken. Reduce heat. Simmer, covered, about 10 minutes or until chicken is tender and no longer pink (170°F).

4 Transfer chicken to a serving platter. Stir snipped oregano into tomato mixture. Spoon the tomato mixture over chicken. If desired, garnish with oregano leaves.

271 CALORIES

Basque Chicken

Piquant garlic, cayenne pepper, and oregano create a saucy fusion with tomatoes, sweet peppers, and onion in a dish that's reminiscent of dishes prepared in the Basque region between France and Spain.

Start to finish: 35 minutes

Makes: 4 servings

Nutrition Facts per serving:
271 cal., 7 g total fat (1 g sat. fat), 82 mg chol., 361 mg sodium, 15 g carbo., 2 g fiber, 35 g pro.
Daily Values:
11% vit. A, 76% vit. C, 8% calcium, 13% iron
Exchanges:
3 Vegetable, 4 Meat

252 CALORIES

Chicken with Apples and Sage

The use of apple juice instead of broth adds a pleasant sweetness to this one-skillet dish. Serve it with hot cooked rice or wild rice.

Start to Finish: 30 minutes

Makes: 4 servings

4 **skinless, boneless chicken breast halves (1^1/$_4$ to 1^1/$_2$ pounds total)**

^{1}/$_8$ **teaspoon salt**

Nonstick cooking spray

1 **cup apple juice or apple cider**

1 **red or green sweet pepper, cut into 1-inch pieces**

^{1}/$_4$ **cup chopped onion**

1 **clove garlic, minced**

1^1/$_2$ **teaspoons snipped fresh sage or ^{1}/$_2$ teaspoon dried sage, crushed**

^{1}/$_4$ **teaspoon black pepper**

1 **tablespoon cornstarch**

1 **tablespoon cold water**

2 **medium green and/or red cooking apples, sliced**

1 Sprinkle chicken with salt. Coat an unheated large skillet with nonstick cooking spray. Preheat over medium-high heat. Add chicken; cook for 8 to 10 minutes or until chicken is tender and no longer pink (170°F), turning once. Remove from skillet; keep warm.

2 Add apple juice, sweet pepper, onion, garlic, dried sage (if using), and black pepper to skillet. Bring to boiling; reduce heat. Simmer, covered, for 2 minutes.

3 In a small bowl combine cornstarch and cold water; stir into mixture in skillet. Stir in apples. Cook and stir until thickened and bubbly. Cook and stir for 2 minutes more. If using, stir in the fresh sage. Return the chicken to the skillet; heat through.

Nutrition Facts per serving:
252 cal., 3 g total fat (1 g sat. fat), 82 mg chol., 153 mg sodium, 23 g carbo., 3 g fiber, 34 g pro.
Daily Values:
34% vit. A, 91% vit. C, 3% calcium, 8% iron
Exchanges:
1^1/$_2$ Fruit, 4 Meat

2 tablespoons all-purpose flour

4 skinless, boneless chicken breast halves (1¼ to 1½ pounds total)

1 cup finely chopped onion (1 large)

1 tablespoon olive oil

2 cloves garlic, minced

1 14½-ounce can diced tomatoes, undrained

1 14-ounce can artichoke hearts, drained and halved

⅓ cup reduced-sodium chicken broth

1 tablespoon snipped fresh oregano or 1 teaspoon dried oregano, crushed

Dash black pepper

2 teaspoons drained capers or 2 tablespoons chopped, pitted ripe olives

2 cups hot cooked couscous

¼ cup sliced green onions (2)

½ teaspoon shredded lemon peel

1 Place flour in a shallow dish. Dip chicken in flour to coat. Set aside.

2 In a large skillet cook chopped onion in hot oil over medium heat for 3 minutes. Stir in garlic; push onion mixture to side of skillet. Add chicken. Cook about 4 minutes or until chicken is browned, turning once. Add undrained tomatoes, artichoke hearts, broth, dried oregano (if using), and pepper; stir just to combine.

3 Bring to boiling; reduce heat. Simmer, covered, about 10 minutes or until chicken is tender and no longer pink (170°F). Remove chicken; cover and keep warm.

4 Simmer tomato mixture, uncovered, about 3 minutes or until reduced to desired consistency. Stir in capers or chopped olives and, if using, fresh oregano. To serve, toss couscous with green onions and lemon peel. Serve chicken with couscous mixture. Spoon tomato mixture over chicken.

Chicken with Vegetable Sauce

Count on this Mediterranean-inspired chicken entrée to provide nutrition and flavor every time. The chunky sauce features juicy diced tomatoes, oregano, and artichoke hearts mingled with capers and garlic.

Start to Finish: 35 minutes
Makes: 4 servings

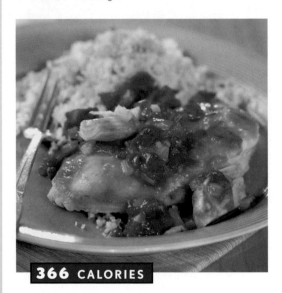

366 CALORIES

Nutrition Facts per serving:
366 cal., 6 g total fat (1 g sat. fat), 82 mg chol., 676 mg sodium, 35 g carbo., 6 g fiber, 39 g pro.
Daily Values:
4% vit. A, 34% vit. C, 11% calcium, 24% iron

Exchanges:
2 Vegetable, 1½ Starch, 4 Meat

Fusion Chicken

Simple yet delicious, these chicken breast halves are browned, quickly glazed with an Asian-style sauce, and served with an easy South American-inspired relish.

Start to Finish: 40 minutes

Makes: 4 servings

293 CALORIES

¼ cup water

3 **tablespoons bottled hoisin sauce**

2 **tablespoons peach preserves**

1 **tablespoon sugar**

2 **teaspoons soy sauce**

4 **medium tangerines or 2 large oranges**

3 **tablespoons snipped fresh cilantro**

4 **skinless, boneless chicken breast halves (1¼ to 1½ pounds total)**

1 **tablespoon cooking oil**

 Hot cooked jasmine rice or long grain rice (optional)

1 In a small bowl combine the water, hoisin sauce, preserves, sugar, and soy sauce. Finely shred 1 teaspoon peel from 1 of the tangerines or oranges. Add peel to hoisin mixture; set aside. Peel and coarsely chop tangerines or oranges; remove seeds. In a medium bowl gently toss chopped tangerines or oranges and cilantro; set aside.

2 In a large skillet cook chicken in hot oil over medium heat for 3 to 5 minutes or until chicken is browned, turning once. Drain off fat. Carefully pour hoisin mixture over chicken. Bring to boiling; reduce heat. Simmer, covered, for 8 to 10 minutes or until chicken is tender and no longer pink (170°F).

3 Remove chicken from skillet. Boil sauce gently, uncovered, about 5 minutes or until reduced to ⅓ cup. Return chicken to skillet. Heat through, turning once to coat with sauce. If desired, serve on hot cooked rice. Spoon sauce over chicken. Serve tangerine mixture with chicken.

Nutrition Facts per serving:
293 cal., 6 g total fat (1 g sat. fat), 82 mg chol., 369 mg sodium, 24 g carbo., 2 g fiber, 34 g pro.
Daily Values:
20% vit. A, 53% vit. C, 4% calcium, 8% iron
Exchanges:
1½ Fruit, 4 Meat

- 1 6-ounce jar marinated artichoke hearts
- 1 tablespoon olive oil
- 12 ounces skinless, boneless chicken breasts, cut into bite-size pieces
- 3 cloves garlic, thinly sliced
- ¼ cup chicken broth
- ¼ cup dry white wine
- 1 tablespoon small fresh oregano leaves or 1 teaspoon dried oregano, crushed
- 1 7-ounce jar roasted red sweet peppers, drained and cut into strips
- ¼ cup pitted kalamata olives
- 3 cups hot cooked campanelle or penne pasta
- ¼ cup crumbled feta cheese (optional)

1 Drain artichokes, reserving marinade. Cut up any large pieces. Set aside. In a large skillet heat oil over medium-high heat. Add chicken and garlic. Cook and stir until chicken is browned. Add the reserved artichoke marinade, broth, wine, and, if using, dried oregano.

2 Bring to boiling; reduce heat. Simmer, covered, for 10 minutes. Stir in artichokes, roasted peppers, olives, and, if using, fresh oregano. Heat through.

3 To serve, spoon the chicken mixture over pasta. If desired, sprinkle with feta cheese.

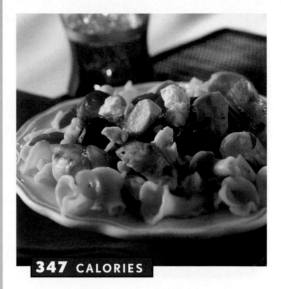

347 CALORIES

Mediterranean Chicken and Pasta

The zesty flavors of the Mediterranean dominate this dish. Artichokes, oregano, kalamata olives, and feta cheese mingle with chicken pieces, garlic, and a splash of white wine.

Prep: 15 minutes   **Cook:** 10 minutes
Makes: 4 servings

Nutrition Facts per serving:
347 cal., 9 g total fat (1 g sat. fat), 49 mg chol., 323 mg sodium, 38 g carbo., 3 g fiber, 26 g pro.
Daily Values:
1% vit. A, 189% vit. C, 3% calcium, 16% iron
Exchanges:
1 Vegetable, 2 Starch, 2½ Meat, ½ Fat

346 CALORIES

Chicken with Brandied Fruit

Cayenne pepper adds just enough heat to this scaloppini-style chicken dressed in brandied nectarine sauce. Serve a tossed spinach salad on the side.

Start to Finish: 30 minutes

Makes: 4 servings

4 **skinless, boneless chicken breast halves (1¼ to 1½ pounds total)**

¼ **cup all-purpose flour**

¼ **teaspoon salt**

⅛ **teaspoon cayenne pepper**

1 **tablespoon olive oil**

1 **tablespoon butter or margarine**

3 **medium nectarines, pitted and cut into thin wedges***

3 **tablespoons brandy**

2 **tablespoons water**

1 **tablespoon lemon juice**

2 **tablespoons sliced almonds, toasted**

Fresh oregano sprigs (optional)

1 Place each chicken piece between 2 pieces of plastic wrap. Pound lightly with the flat side of a meat mallet to ¼-inch thickness. Remove plastic wrap. In a shallow dish combine flour, salt, and cayenne pepper. Dip chicken in flour mixture to coat.

2 In a large skillet heat olive oil and butter over medium heat. Add chicken and cook for 6 to 8 minutes or until chicken is tender and no longer pink, turning once. Remove skillet from heat. Transfer chicken to a serving platter; cover and keep warm. Add nectarines, brandy, the water, and lemon juice to the skillet. Return to heat and cook for 1 minute, stirring gently.

3 Serve the fruit mixture over chicken. Sprinkle with almonds. If desired, garnish with oregano.

***Note:** You can substitute fresh plums, peaches, or pears for the nectarines.

Nutrition Facts per serving:
346 cal., 11 g total fat (3 g sat. fat), 90 mg chol., 254 mg sodium, 19 g carbo., 2 g fiber, 36 g pro.
Daily Values:
18% vit. A, 14% vit. C, 3% calcium, 9% iron
Exchanges:
1½ Fruit, 4½ Meat

2 tablespoons fish sauce (nam pla)

1 tablespoon lime juice

2 teaspoons minced fresh lemongrass
   or 1 teaspoon finely shredded
   lemon peel

4 teaspoons cooking oil

1 large red onion, halved lengthwise
   and sliced

3 cloves garlic, minced

¼ of a fresh pineapple, peeled, cored,
   and cut into ¼-inch wedges

1 small cucumber, cut into thin bite-size
   strips (about 1 cup)

1 or 2 fresh jalapeño chile peppers,
   seeded and finely chopped (see note
   on page 76)

12 ounces skinless, boneless chicken
    breasts, cut into bite-size strips

3 cups hot cooked aromatic rice (such
   as jasmine or basmati)

   Snipped fresh cilantro or parsley
   (optional)

1 For sauce, in a small bowl stir together
fish sauce, lime juice, and lemongrass or
lemon peel; set aside.

2 Pour 2 teaspoons of the oil into a wok
or large skillet. Heat wok or skillet over
medium-high heat. Stir-fry onion and
garlic in hot oil for 2 minutes. Add
pineapple, cucumber, and jalapeño
peppers. Stir-fry for 2 minutes more.
Remove from wok.

3 Add the remaining 2 teaspoons oil to
hot wok. Add chicken. Stir-fry for 2 to
3 minutes or until chicken is tender and
no longer pink. Return onion mixture
to wok. Add sauce. Cook and stir about
1 minute more or until heated through.
Serve immediately over rice. If desired,
sprinkle with snipped cilantro.

Bangkok Stir-Fry

Stir-fries are known for their diverse
mixes of flavors. This one features
lemongrass, pineapple, cucumber, and
jalapeño peppers. If you've never tried
fish sauce, don't be deterred by its
pungent odor; its flavor greatly enhances
the sauce.

Start to Finish: 30 minutes
Makes: 4 servings

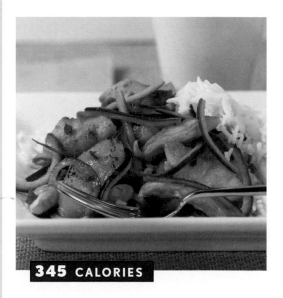

345 CALORIES

Nutrition Facts per serving:
345 cal., 6 g total fat (1 g sat. fat), 49 mg chol.,
747 mg sodium, 46 g carbo., 2 g fiber, 25 g pro.
Daily Values:
3% vit. A, 25% vit. C, 5% calcium, 14% iron
Exchanges:
½ Fruit, 2½ Starch, 2½ Meat

Shortcut Chicken Mole

Depending on the type of chile peppers available, traditional mole sauces vary in color and kick, but they always have one thing in common, and that's a pinch of chocolate. This streamlined version relies on chiles for bite, cocoa powder for richness, and cumin for an intriguing taste of Mexico.

Start to Finish: 15 minutes

Makes: 4 servings

334 CALORIES

1½ cups quick-cooking rice

12 ounces boneless chicken strips for stir-frying or 12 ounces skinless, boneless chicken breasts, cut into bite-size strips

1 tablespoon cooking oil

1 tablespoon unsweetened cocoa powder

1 teaspoon ground cumin

1 16-ounce jar thick and chunky salsa

½ of a 16-ounce package (2 cups) frozen yellow, green, and red sweet peppers with onion

Fresh herb sprigs (optional)

1 Cook rice according to package directions.

2 Meanwhile, in a large skillet cook and stir chicken strips in hot oil for 2 to 3 minutes or until light brown. Drain off fat.

3 Sprinkle chicken with cocoa powder and cumin; stir to combine. Stir in salsa and sweet peppers with onion. Bring to boiling; reduce heat. Simmer, covered, about 5 minutes or just until sweet peppers are tender.

4 Serve chicken mixture with the hot cooked rice. If desired, garnish with fresh herb sprigs.

Nutrition Facts per serving:
334 cal., 5 g total fat (1 g sat. fat), 49 mg chol., 549 mg sodium, 44 g carbo., 3 g fiber, 26 g pro.
Daily Values:
27% vit. A, 94% vit. C, 7% calcium, 21% iron
Exchanges:
1 Vegetable, 2½ Starch, 2½ Meat

- **8** ounces dried penne
- **8** ounces asparagus, trimmed and cut into 1¹/₂-inch pieces
- **1** tablespoon olive oil
- **3** cups sliced fresh shiitake or crimini mushrooms
- **1** medium leek, thinly sliced, or ¹/₂ cup chopped onion (1 medium)
- **3** cloves garlic, minced
- **¹/₃** cup mushroom broth or vegetable broth
- **¹/₄** cup half-and-half or light cream
- **¹/₄** teaspoon salt
- **¹/₈** teaspoon black pepper
- **12** ounces shredded cooked chicken (about 2¹/₂ cups)
- **1** cup chopped roma tomatoes
- **1** tablespoon finely shredded fresh basil
- **1** tablespoon finely shredded fresh oregano

  Finely shredded Parmesan cheese (optional)

1 Cook penne according to package directions, adding asparagus for the last 2 minutes of cooking; drain. Return pasta mixture to saucepan; cover and keep warm.

2 Meanwhile, in a large skillet heat oil over medium-high heat. Add mushrooms, leek or onion, and garlic; cook for 4 to 5 minutes or until most of the liquid is evaporated. Stir in broth, half-and-half, salt, and pepper. Bring to boiling. Boil gently, uncovered, for 4 to 5 minutes or until mixture is slightly thickened. Stir in chicken, tomatoes, basil, and oregano; heat through.

3 Spoon the mushroom mixture over pasta mixture; toss gently to coat. Serve immediately. If desired, serve with Parmesan cheese.

396 CALORIES

Chicken-Vegetable Pasta

The flavors of Italy fuse in this creamy combo of veggies and chicken. The small amount of half-and-half adds just the right amount of richness.

Start to Finish: 25 minutes
Makes: 5 servings

Nutrition Facts per serving:
396 cal., 8 g total fat (2 g sat. fat), 62 mg chol., 199 mg sodium, 53 g carbo., 4 g fiber, 30 g pro.
Daily Values:
9% vit. A, 22% vit. C, 6% calcium, 18% iron
Exchanges:
4 Vegetable, 2 Starch, 2 Meat

271 CALORIES

Spicy Chicken with Fruit

Caribbean cuisine is known for its jerk seasoning, which generally contains chiles, thyme, garlic, onion, and spices such as cinnamon, ginger, allspice, and/or cloves. It's also known for its luscious fruits. Here peach nectar, peaches, and plums create a complementary sauce. If plums aren't in season, substitute nectarines or more peaches.

Start to Finish: 35 minutes

Makes: 4 servings

Nutrition Facts per serving:
271 cal., 3 g total fat (1 g sat. fat), 82 mg chol., 323 mg sodium, 27 g carbo., 3 g fiber, 34 g pro.
Daily Values:
15% vit. A, 33% vit. C, 4% calcium, 9% iron
Exchanges:
1¹/₂ Fruit, 4¹/₂ Meat

2 teaspoons Jamaican jerk seasoning

2 fresh serrano chile peppers, seeded and finely chopped (see note on page 76)

4 skinless, boneless chicken breast halves (1¹/₄ to 1¹/₂ pounds total)

Nonstick cooking spray

¹/₂ cup peach nectar

3 green onions, bias-sliced into 1-inch pieces

2 cups sliced, peeled peaches

1 cup sliced, pitted plums

1 tablespoon brown sugar

¹/₈ teaspoon salt

¹/₂ cup pitted dark sweet cherries, halved

Fresh serrano pepper, cut into a flower (see note on page 76) (optional)

1 In a small bowl combine jerk seasoning and 1 of the finely chopped serrano peppers. Rub mixture onto both sides of each chicken breast. Lightly coat an unheated large skillet with nonstick cooking spray. Preheat skillet over medium heat. Add chicken. Cook for 8 to 10 minutes or until tender and no longer pink (170°F), turning once. Transfer to a serving platter; keep warm.

2 Add 2 tablespoons of the peach nectar and the green onions to skillet. Cook and stir over medium heat for 4 to 5 minutes or just until green onions are tender.

3 In a medium bowl combine remaining finely chopped serrano pepper, remaining peach nectar, half of the peaches, half of the plums, the brown sugar, and salt. Add to skillet. Cook and stir over medium heat about 2 minutes or until slightly thickened and bubbly. Remove from heat. Stir in remaining peaches and plums. Stir in cherries. Spoon over chicken. If desired, garnish with pepper flower.

$2^2/_3$ **cups dried penne pasta (8 ounces)**

12 **ounces skinless, boneless chicken breasts, cut into bite-size strips**

$^1/_4$ **teaspoon salt**

$^1/_8$ **teaspoon freshly ground black pepper**

2 **tablespoons olive oil or cooking oil**

3 **large cloves garlic, minced**

3 **cups sliced fresh mushrooms (8 ounces)**

1 **medium onion, thinly sliced**

$^1/_2$ **cup chicken broth**

$^1/_4$ **cup dry white wine**

1 **cup cut-up roma tomatoes**

$^1/_4$ **cup shredded basil leaves**

3 **tablespoons snipped fresh oregano**

$^1/_4$ **cup shredded Parmesan cheese**

$^1/_8$ **teaspoon freshly ground black pepper**

1 Cook pasta in lightly salted boiling water according to package directions. Drain and return to saucepan; keep warm.

2 Meanwhile, season chicken with salt and $^1/_8$ teaspoon pepper. In a large skillet heat 1 tablespoon of the oil over medium-high heat. Add chicken and garlic; cook and stir about 5 minutes or until chicken is tender and no longer pink. Remove from skillet; keep warm.

3 Add remaining 1 tablespoon oil to skillet. Cook mushrooms and onion in hot oil just until tender, stirring occasionally. Carefully add broth and wine. Bring to boiling; reduce heat. Boil gently, uncovered, about 2 minutes or until liquid is reduced by half. Remove skillet from heat.

4 Add cooked pasta, chicken, tomatoes, basil, and oregano to mushroom mixture; toss to coat. Transfer to a serving dish; sprinkle with Parmesan cheese and $^1/_8$ teaspoon pepper. Serve immediately.

Chicken-Mushroom Pasta

With a mellow base of broth and white wine, the tender medley of chicken, mushrooms, and herbs shines through. A glass of white wine served with dinner makes the perfect accompaniment.

Start to Finish: 30 minutes
Makes: 6 servings

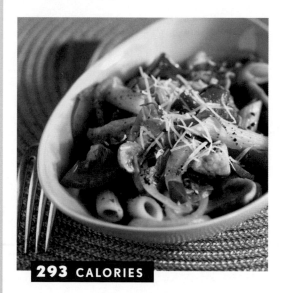

293 CALORIES

Nutrition Facts per serving:
293 cal., 8 g total fat (2 g sat. fat), 35 mg chol., 255 mg sodium, 33 g carbo., 2 g fiber, 22 g pro.
Daily Values:
5% vit. A, 11% vit. C, 7% calcium, 12% iron
Exchanges:
1 Vegetable, $1^1/_2$ Starch, $2^1/_2$ Meat

Szechwan-Fried Chicken Breasts

Szechwan Chinese cuisine is known for its hot, spicy dishes. While chile oil spikes up the heat, here the sweetness from the apricot preserves tempers it.

Start to Finish: 30 minutes

Makes: 4 servings

314 CALORIES

- 1   tablespoon reduced-sodium soy sauce
- 1   teaspoon grated fresh ginger
- 1   teaspoon chile oil
- ¹⁄₂   teaspoon sugar
- ¹⁄₂   cup all-purpose flour
- 4   skinless, boneless chicken breast halves (1¹⁄₄ to 1¹⁄₂ pounds total)
- 1   tablespoon cooking oil
- ¹⁄₄   cup apricot preserves
- ¹⁄₄   cup reduced-sodium chicken broth
    Hot cooked rice (optional)
    Shredded orange peel (optional)

1 In a small bowl stir together soy sauce, ginger, ¹⁄₂ teaspoon of the chile oil, and the sugar; set aside.

2 Place flour in a shallow bowl. Brush both sides of each chicken breast half with soy mixture; dip in flour to coat. In a large nonstick skillet cook chicken in hot cooking oil over medium-high heat for 8 to 10 minutes or until tender and no longer pink (170°F), turning once. Remove chicken from skillet; cover and keep warm.

3 For sauce, add apricot preserves, broth, and remaining ¹⁄₂ teaspoon chile oil to skillet. Cook and stir over medium heat until preserves melt and mixture is heated through. Spoon sauce over chicken. If desired, serve with hot cooked rice and sprinkle with orange peel.

Nutrition Facts per serving:
314 cal., 7 g total fat (1 g sat. fat), 82 mg chol., 267 mg sodium, 26 g carbo., 1 g fiber, 35 g pro.
Daily Values:
1% vit. A, 6% vit. C, 3% calcium, 10% iron
Exchanges:
1¹⁄₂ Other Carbo., 4 Meat, ¹⁄₂ Fat

- **12** ounces skinless, boneless chicken breasts, cut into bite-size strips
- **¹/₂** cup orange juice
- **¹/₄** cup snipped fresh cilantro
- **1** teaspoon finely shredded lime peel
- **2** tablespoons lime juice
- **1** fresh jalapeño chile pepper, seeded and finely chopped (see note on page 76)
- **¹/₈** teaspoon salt
- **¹/₈** teaspoon black pepper
- **3** cloves garlic, minced
- **1** medium red sweet pepper, cut into thin strips
- **2** teaspoons cooking oil
- **1** cup loose-pack frozen whole kernel corn
- **1¹/₂** teaspoons cornstarch
- **8** 6-inch corn tortillas
- **¹/₂** cup light dairy sour cream (optional)
- Fresh cilantro sprigs (optional)

1 Place chicken in a plastic bag set in a shallow dish. For marinade, in a small bowl combine orange juice, snipped cilantro, lime peel, lime juice, jalapeño pepper, salt, black pepper, and garlic. Pour over chicken; seal bag. Marinate in the refrigerator for at least 1 hour or up to 2 hours, turning bag occasionally.

2 Drain chicken, reserving marinade. In a large nonstick skillet cook and stir sweet pepper in hot oil over medium-high heat until crisp-tender. Remove sweet pepper.

3 Add chicken to skillet. Cook and stir for 3 to 4 minutes or until chicken is tender and no longer pink. Stir in corn; heat through. In a small bowl stir together the reserved marinade and the cornstarch; add to chicken mixture. Cook and stir until thickened and bubbly. Cook and stir for 2 minutes more. Return sweet pepper to skillet; stir to combine.

4 Wrap tortillas in microwave-safe paper towels. Microwave on 100% power (high) for 45 to 60 seconds or until warm. Divide the chicken mixture among tortillas. If desired, top with sour cream and garnish with cilantro sprigs.

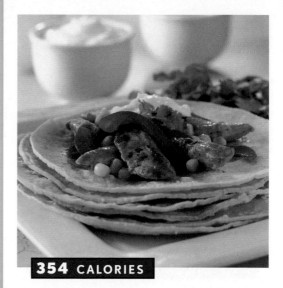

354 CALORIES

Tex-Mex Chicken Tacos

Orange, lime, jalapeño pepper, and cilantro create this chicken's big Tex-Mex marinade. Sweet peppers and corn enhance the hearty chicken mixture that's spooned onto corn tortillas.

Prep: 20 minutes **Cook:** 15 minutes
Marinate: 1 to 2 hours **Makes:** 4 servings

Nutrition Facts per serving:
354 cal., 7 g total fat (1 g sat. fat), 49 mg chol., 336 mg sodium, 49 g carbo., 4 g fiber, 26 g pro.
Daily Values:
45% vit. A, 128% vit. C, 8% calcium, 23% iron
Exchanges:
1 Vegetable, 1 Starch, 1¹/₂ Other Carbo., 2 Meat

293 CALORIES

Sesame Chicken

Dipped in teriyaki sauce and coated with sesame seeds, this no-fuss chicken brings home the flavors of the Orient.

Prep: 15 minutes **Bake:** 45 minutes
Oven: 400°F **Makes:** 4 servings

4 **chicken breast halves (about 2¹/₂ pounds total)**
Nonstick cooking spray
3 **tablespoons sesame seeds**
3 **tablespoons all-purpose flour**
¹/₄ **teaspoon salt**
¹/₄ **teaspoon cayenne pepper**
3 **tablespoons bottled reduced-sodium teriyaki sauce**
1 **tablespoon butter or margarine, melted**
Fresh pineapple wedges (optional)
Shredded spinach (optional)

1 Skin chicken; set aside. Lightly coat a large baking sheet with nonstick cooking spray; set aside. In a large plastic bag combine sesame seeds, flour, salt, and cayenne pepper. Dip chicken in teriyaki sauce. Add chicken to the mixture in the plastic bag. Seal bag. Shake bag to coat the chicken.

2 Place chicken, bone sides down, on prepared baking sheet. Drizzle melted butter over chicken.

3 Bake in a 400° oven about 45 minutes or until chicken is tender and no longer pink (170°F). If desired, garnish with pineapple wedges and spinach.

Nutrition Facts per serving:
293 cal., 9 g total fat (3 g sat. fat), 115 mg chol., 460 mg sodium, 7 g carbo., 1 g fiber, 45 g pro.
Daily Values:
4% vit. A, 3% vit. C, 3% calcium, 11% iron
Exchanges:
6 Meat

4 **skinless, boneless chicken breast halves (1¼ to 1½ pounds total)**
½ **cup finely chopped green onions (4)**
½ **cup orange juice**
1 **tablespoon brown sugar**
1 **tablespoon finely chopped fresh ginger**
1 **tablespoon olive oil**
2 **cloves garlic, minced**
1 **teaspoon ground coriander**
½ **teaspoon paprika**
¼ **teaspoon salt**
¼ **teaspoon ground cinnamon**
¼ **teaspoon black pepper**
 Nonstick cooking spray
2 **cups hot cooked rice**

1 Place chicken in a plastic bag set in a shallow dish. For marinade, in a small bowl combine green onions, orange juice, brown sugar, ginger, oil, garlic, coriander, paprika, salt, cinnamon, and pepper. Pour over chicken; seal bag. Marinate in the refrigerator for at least 2 hours or up to 6 hours, turning bag occasionally. Drain chicken, reserving the marinade.

2 Lightly coat a 2-quart rectangular baking dish with nonstick cooking spray. Arrange chicken in the prepared baking dish; pour marinade over chicken.

3 Bake, uncovered, in a 375° oven about 20 minutes or until chicken is tender and no longer pink (170°F). Spoon rice onto 4 dinner plates. Transfer chicken to dinner plates. Strain the juices remaining in baking dish; spoon juices over chicken.

Ginger-Spiced Chicken

A marinade of orange juice with coriander, cinnamon, ginger, and paprika gives these chicken breasts a hint of North African flavor.

Prep: 15 minutes **Marinate:** 2 to 6 hours
Bake: 20 minutes **Oven:** 375°F
Makes: 4 servings

332 CALORIES

Nutrition Facts per serving:
332 cal., 6 g total fat (1 g sat. fat), 82 mg chol., 228 mg sodium, 31 g carbo., 1 g fiber, 36 g pro.
Daily Values:
6% vit. A, 34% vit. C, 5% calcium, 14% iron
Exchanges:
½ Starch, 1 Other Carbo., 4 Meat

German-Style Chicken

Dusseldorf, Germany's most famous mustard, is usually dark in color and has a sweet-and-sour flavor. It's equally delicious on sausage or cold meats.

Prep: 15 minutes **Bake:** 45 minutes
Oven: 375°F **Makes:** 4 servings

243 CALORIES

4 **chicken breast halves (about 2¹/₂ pounds total)**
¹/₄ **cup Dusseldorf or horseradish mustard**
2 **tablespoons dry sherry**
¹/₂ **teaspoon sweet Hungarian paprika or ¹/₄ teaspoon hot Hungarian paprika**
¹/₂ **cup soft rye bread crumbs**

1 Skin chicken breasts. In a small bowl combine mustard, sherry, and paprika. Transfer 2 tablespoons of the mustard mixture to another small bowl; brush evenly over tops of chicken breast halves. Set aside remaining mustard mixture. Place chicken halves, mustard sides up, in a 3-quart rectangular baking dish. Sprinkle with bread crumbs. Lightly pat onto chicken.

2 Bake, uncovered, in a 375° oven for 45 to 50 minutes or until chicken is tender and no longer pink (170°F). Serve with reserved mustard mixture.

Nutrition Facts per serving:
243 cal., 4 g total fat (1 g sat. fat), 107 mg chol., 363 mg sodium, 4 g carbo., 1 g fiber, 44 g pro.
Daily Values:
4% vit. A, 3% vit. C, 5% calcium, 10% iron
Exchanges:
6 Meat

1   **large fresh poblano chile pepper
     (see note on page 76)**

1   **large clove garlic**

    Nonstick cooking spray

1/3   **cup fine dry bread crumbs**

1   **tablespoon chili powder**

1   **teaspoon ground cumin**

4   **skinless, boneless chicken breast
     halves (1 1/4 to 1 1/2 pounds total)**

1   **beaten egg**

2/3   **cup chopped tomato (1 medium)**

1/2   **cup chopped tomatillo or tomato**

1/4   **cup chopped onion**

2   **tablespoons snipped fresh cilantro**

1 To roast poblano pepper and garlic, quarter the pepper, removing seeds and membranes. Place pepper pieces and unpeeled garlic clove on a foil-lined baking sheet. Bake, uncovered, in a 450° oven for 20 to 25 minutes or until the skin on pepper pieces is charred. Remove garlic; set aside to cool. Bring up the edges of foil and seal around the pepper pieces. Let pepper stand for 20 minutes to steam. Peel pepper pieces and garlic. Chop pepper; mash garlic.

2 Meanwhile, coat a 2-quart rectangular baking dish with nonstick cooking spray; set aside. In a shallow dish combine the bread crumbs, chili powder, and cumin. Dip chicken into egg; dip into bread crumb mixture to coat. Arrange chicken in prepared baking dish. Bake, uncovered, in a 375° oven for 15 to 20 minutes or until chicken is tender and no longer pink (170°).

3 For salsa, in a medium bowl combine the poblano pepper, garlic, the 2/3 cup tomato, tomatillo or additional tomato, onion, and cilantro. To serve, slice chicken and spoon salsa over slices.

233 CALORIES

Chicken with Poblano Salsa

Here the dark green poblano, best known for its role in the Mexican classic chile rellenos, brings on a medium to hot, rich flavor. If you can't find poblanos, use Anaheim peppers instead.

Prep: 30 minutes
Bake: 20 minutes + 15 minutes
Oven: 450°/375°F
Makes: 4 servings

Nutrition Facts per serving:
233 cal., 5 g total fat (1 g sat. fat), 135 mg chol., 294 mg sodium, 11 g carbo., 2 g fiber, 36 g pro.
Daily Values:
23% vit. A, 61% vit. C, 6% calcium, 12% iron
Exchanges:
1 Vegetable, 4 1/2 Meat

255 CALORIES

Peppered Chicken in Marsala Sauce

Coated with ground pepper, this chicken, in a simple Marsala and mushroom sauce, boasts a big flavor you won't soon forget.

Prep: 20 minutes   **Bake:** 35 minutes
Oven: 425°F   **Makes:** 6 servings

6 chicken breast halves (about 3¹/₂ pounds total)
2 teaspoons olive oil or cooking oil
1 teaspoon coarsely ground black pepper
¹/₄ teaspoon salt
2 cups sliced fresh mushrooms
2 tablespoons butter
3 tablespoons all-purpose flour
¹/₄ teaspoon salt
1¹/₄ cups reduced-sodium chicken broth
¹/₄ cup dry Marsala
Coarsely ground black pepper (optional)

1 Skin chicken. Brush chicken with oil; sprinkle the 1 teaspoon pepper and ¼ teaspoon salt over chicken. Arrange chicken in a 15×10×1-inch baking pan. Bake, uncovered, in a 425° oven for 35 to 40 minutes or until chicken is tender and no longer pink (170°F).

2 Meanwhile, for sauce, in a medium saucepan cook mushrooms in hot butter until tender. Stir in flour and ¼ teaspoon salt. Add broth and Marsala. Cook and stir over medium heat until thickened and bubbly; cook and stir for 1 minute more. Pass sauce with chicken. If desired, sprinkle with additional pepper.

Nutrition Facts per serving:
255 cal., 9 g total fat (3 g sat. fat), 95 mg chol., 465 mg sodium, 5 g carbo., 0 g fiber, 36 g pro.
Daily Values:
4% vit. A, 3% vit. C, 2% calcium, 9% iron
Exchanges:
1 Vegetable, 4¹/₂ Meat, 1¹/₂ Fat

- ¼ cup all-purpose flour
- ¼ teaspoon salt
- ¼ teaspoon black pepper
- 4 skinless, boneless chicken thighs (about 12 ounces total)
- 1 tablespoon olive oil
- 1 bulb garlic, separated into cloves, peeled, and sliced (about ¼ cup)
- 1 cup reduced-sodium chicken broth
- 3 tablespoons white wine vinegar
- 2 tablespoons honey
- 1 16-ounce package shredded broccoli (broccoli slaw mix)
- 2 tablespoons coarsely chopped pecans

1 In a plastic bag combine flour, salt, and pepper. Add chicken; seal bag Shake to coat.

2 In a large skillet cook chicken in hot oil over medium heat for 10 to 12 minutes or until chicken is tender and no longer pink (180°F), turning once. Transfer chicken to plate; cover and keep warm.

3 Add garlic to skillet. Cook and stir for 1 minute. Add broth, vinegar, and honey. Bring to boiling; reduce heat. Simmer, uncovered, for 5 minutes. Stir in broccoli. Return to boiling; reduce heat. Simmer, covered, for 8 to 10 minutes more or until broccoli is crisp-tender. Stir in pecans. Serve the broccoli mixture with the chicken.

Chicken with Broccoli and Garlic

Though moist and juicy chicken thighs contain more fat than white meat does, this dish retains its low-cal status. Broccoli slaw and pecans boost the flavor.

Start to Finish: 35 minutes
Makes: 4 servings

270 CALORIES

Nutrition Facts per serving:
270 cal., 10 g total fat (2 g sat. fat), 68 mg chol., 392 mg sodium, 24 g carbo., 3 g fiber, 23 g pro.
Daily Values:
36% vit. A, 184% vit. C, 9% calcium, 14% iron
Exchanges:
2 Vegetable, 1 Other Carbo., 2½ Meat, ½ Fat

Hearty Chicken and Noodles

Chicken legs, often a good buy, turn this hearty dish of rather ordinary vegetables into a comforting home-style dinner.

Prep: 35 minutes **Cook:** 40 minutes
Makes: 6 servings

316 CALORIES

Nutrition Facts per serving:
316 cal., 6 g total fat (2 g sat. fat), 102 mg chol.,
624 mg sodium, 37 g carbo., 4 g fiber, 27 g pro.
Daily Values:
213% vit. A, 22% vit. C, 15% calcium, 16% iron
Exchanges:
1¹/₂ Vegetable, 2 Starch, 2¹/₂ Meat

  3 **whole chicken legs (drumstick and thigh) (about 2 pounds total)**
2¹/₄ **cups water**
  1 **14-ounce can reduced-sodium chicken broth**
  1 **bay leaf**
  1 **tablespoon snipped fresh thyme or 1 teaspoon dried thyme, crushed**
³/₄ **teaspoon salt**
¹/₄ **teaspoon black pepper**
  2 **cups sliced carrots (4 medium)**
1¹/₂ **cups chopped onion (3 medium)**
  3 **cups dried wide noodles (6 ounces)**
  2 **cups milk**
  1 **cup loose-pack frozen peas**
  2 **tablespoons all-purpose flour**

1 Skin chicken. In a 4¹/₂-quart Dutch oven combine chicken, the water, broth, bay leaf, dried thyme (if using), salt, and pepper. Add carrots and onions. Bring to boiling; reduce heat. Simmer, covered, about 30 minutes or until chicken is tender and no longer pink (180°F). Discard bay leaf.

2 Remove chicken from Dutch oven; cool slightly. Remove meat from bones; discard bones. Chop or shred chicken and set aside.

3 Return vegetable mixture to boiling. Add noodles; cook, uncovered, for 5 minutes. Stir in 1¹/₂ cups of the milk and the peas.

4 In a screw-top jar combine remaining ¹/₂ cup milk and the flour. Cover and shake until smooth. Stir into noodle mixture. Cook and stir over medium heat until thickened and bubbly. Stir in chicken and fresh thyme (if using). Cook for 1 to 2 minutes more or until mixture is heated through.

- 3 **tablespoons reduced-sodium soy sauce**
- 4 **teaspoons honey**
- 4 **teaspoons red wine vinegar**
- $1/2$ **teaspoon cornstarch**
- $1/2$ **teaspoon curry powder**
- $1/4$ **teaspoon bottled hot pepper sauce**
  Dash ground allspice
- 1 **tablespoon cooking oil**
- 1 **pound skinless boneless chicken breasts, cut into bite-size strips**
- 1 **small red sweet pepper, cut into thin bite-size strips**
- 2 **medium green onions, bias-sliced**
- 2 **nectarines, pitted and cut into $1/2$-inch slices**
- 2 **cups hot cooked couscous or rice**

1 For sauce, in a small bowl stir together soy sauce, honey, vinegar, cornstarch, curry powder, hot pepper sauce, and allspice; set aside.

2 Pour oil into a large wok or skillet. Heat over medium-high heat. Add chicken, sweet pepper, and green onions to wok; cook and stir for 3 to 4 minutes or until chicken is no longer pink. Push chicken mixture from center of wok. Stir sauce; add to center of wok. Cook and stir until thickened and bubbly.

3 Add nectarine slices to chicken mixture. Cook and stir for 1 to 2 minutes more or until heated through. Serve over hot cooked couscous or rice.

319 CALORIES

Fruit and Chicken Stir-Fry

Bring fresh and bold Asian flavors to your table with this easy fruit and chicken stir-fry. If you prefer, use peaches or plums in place of the nectarines.

Start to Finish: 25 minutes
Makes: 4 servings

Nutrition Facts per serving:
319 cal., 6 g total fat (1 g sat. fat), 66 mg chol., 501 mg sodium, 35 g carbo., 3 g fiber, 31 g pro.
Daily Values:
33% vit. A, 70% vit. C, 4% calcium, 9% iron
Exchanges:
1 Vegetable, $1/2$ Fruit, $1^1/2$ Starch, $3^1/2$ Meat

173 CALORIES

Mulligatawny Soup

You can never be sure what you'll find in Mulligatawny soup, a favorite from Southern India whose name means "pepper water." This one features tart apples and curry powder.

Prep: 35 minutes   **Cook:** 20 minutes
Makes: 6 servings (about 10 cups)

1   cup chopped onion (1 large)
1   cup coarsely chopped carrots
      (2 medium)
1   cup sliced celery (2 stalks)
1   tablespoon cooking oil
1⅓ cups chopped tart apples
2   to 3 teaspoons curry powder
¼   teaspoon salt
3   cups reduced-sodium chicken broth
3   cups water
1   14½-ounce can low-sodium stewed
      tomatoes, undrained
2   cups chopped cooked chicken or
      turkey (about 10 ounces)

1 In a Dutch oven cook and stir onion, carrots, and celery in hot oil over medium heat about 10 minutes or until crisp-tender. Reduce heat to medium-low; add apples, curry powder, and salt. Cook, covered, for 5 minutes.

2 Stir in broth, the water, and undrained tomatoes. Bring to boiling; reduce heat. Simmer, uncovered, for 10 minutes. Stir in the cooked chicken; simmer for 10 minutes more.

Nutrition Facts per serving:
173 cal., 6 g total fat (1 g sat. fat), 42 mg chol.,
498 mg sodium, 14 g carbo., 3 g fiber, 16 g pro.
Daily Values:
104% vit. A, 17% vit. C, 4% calcium, 7% iron
Exchanges:
1 Vegetable, ½ Fruit, 2 Meat

- 4 ounces fresh shiitake mushrooms, stems removed and caps thinly sliced
- 2 cloves garlic, minced
- 2 teaspoons peanut oil or cooking oil
- 2 14-ounce cans reduced-sodium chicken broth
- 2 tablespoons white vinegar or seasoned rice vinegar
- 2 tablespoons reduced-sodium soy sauce
- 1/2 teaspoon crushed red pepper or 1 teaspoon chile oil
- 1 cup shredded cooked chicken (about 5 ounces)
- 2 cups packaged shredded cabbage with carrot (coleslaw mix) or shredded napa cabbage
- 2 tablespoons cold water
- 1 tablespoon cornstarch
- 1 teaspoon toasted sesame oil
- Sliced green onions (optional)

1 In a large saucepan cook mushrooms and garlic in hot oil for 4 minutes, stirring occasionally. Stir in broth, vinegar, soy sauce, and red pepper or chile oil; bring to boiling. Stir in chicken and coleslaw mix or napa cabbage. Return to boiling; reduce heat. Simmer, uncovered, for 5 minutes.

2 In a small bowl stir together cold water and cornstarch. Stir into soup; simmer about 2 minutes or until slightly thickened. Remove from heat; stir in sesame oil. If desired, sprinkle with sliced green onions.

Hot and Sour Soup

It only takes minutes to make this satisfying Chinese-style soup. Often meatless, this version contains chicken, putting it on the list of dishes that qualify as meals in and of themselves.

Start to Finish: 30 minutes

Makes: 4 servings (about 5 cups)

144 CALORIES

Nutrition Facts per serving:
144 cal., 7 g total fat (1 g sat. fat), 31 mg chol., 838 mg sodium, 6 g carbo., 1 g fiber, 15 g pro.
Daily Values:
2% vit. A, 20% vit. C, 3% calcium, 5% iron
Exchanges:
1 Vegetable, 2 Meat

Chicken-Vegetable Soup

A small amount of wine deepens the flavor of this popular classic. Serving it to your kids? You might want to substitute chicken broth for the wine.

Start to Finish: 30 minutes

Makes: 4 servings (about 5 cups)

254 CALORIES

- $1/2$ **cup chopped celery (1 stalk)**
- $1/2$ **cup sliced leek or chopped onion**
- $1/2$ **cup thinly sliced carrot (1 medium)**
- 1 **tablespoon butter or margarine**
- 1 **14-ounce can reduced-sodium chicken broth**
- $1/4$ **cup all-purpose flour**
- 2 **cups milk**
- 1 **tablespoon snipped fresh thyme or basil or 1 teaspoon dried thyme or basil, crushed**
- $1/4$ **teaspoon salt**
- $1 1/2$ **cups chopped cooked chicken or turkey (about 8 ounces)**
- $1/4$ **cup dry white wine or reduced-sodium chicken broth**
  Cracked black pepper

1 In a large saucepan cook celery, leek or onion, and carrot in hot butter until tender. In a medium bowl gradually stir the 14-ounce can of chicken broth into the flour; stir into vegetables in saucepan. Add milk, dried herb (if using), and salt. Cook and stir until slightly thickened and bubbly; cook and stir for 1 minute more.

2 Stir in chicken, wine or the $1/4$ cup chicken broth, and fresh herb (if using). Cook about 2 minutes more or until heated through.

3 To serve, ladle into soup bowls. Sprinkle with pepper.

Nutrition Facts per serving:
254 cal., 10 g total fat (5 g sat. fat), 68 mg chol., 560 mg sodium, 16 g carbo., 1 g fiber, 23 g pro.
Daily Values:
86% vit. A, 8% vit. C, 18% calcium, 9% iron
Exchanges:
$1/2$ Milk, $1 1/2$ Vegetable, $2 1/2$ Meat, 1 Fat

12 ounces turkey breast tenderloin or skinless, boneless chicken breasts or thighs

1 tablespoon cooking oil

1/2 cup chopped onion (1 medium)

1/2 cup chopped red or green sweet pepper

1 clove garlic, minced

2 14-ounce cans reduced-sodium chicken broth

1 1/2 cups loose-pack frozen cut green beans

1 cup loose-pack frozen whole kernel corn or one 8-ounce can whole kernel corn, drained

1/3 cup quick-cooking barley

2 tablespoons snipped fresh basil or 1 1/2 teaspoons dried basil, crushed

1/4 teaspoon salt

1/4 teaspoon black pepper

1 Cut turkey or chicken into bite-size pieces or cubes. In a Dutch oven cook and stir turkey or chicken in hot oil for 5 minutes. With a slotted spoon remove from pan. In pan drippings cook onion, sweet pepper, and garlic for 3 minutes, stirring occasionally. Drain off fat.

2 Return turkey or chicken to Dutch oven. Add broth, beans, corn, barley, dried basil (if using), salt, and black pepper. Bring to boiling; reduce heat. Simmer, covered, for 10 to 15 minutes or until barley is cooked. Stir in fresh basil (if using).

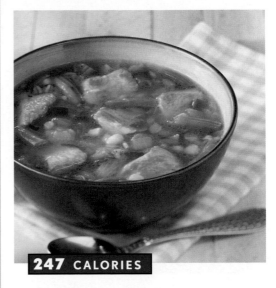

247 CALORIES

Turkey Soup with Barley

If you have some cooked turkey or chicken leftover from a prior meal, skip cooking the meat in Step 1, and add the cooked turkey or chicken to the soup in Step 2. Doing so shaves even more time off the already quick prep time.

Prep: 35 minutes   **Cook:** 10 minutes
Makes: 4 servings (about 6 cups)

Nutrition Facts per serving:
247 cal., 5 g total fat (1 g sat. fat), 51 mg chol., 703 mg sodium, 25 g carbo., 4 g fiber, 26 g pro.
Daily Values:
25% vit. A, 64% vit. C, 5% calcium, 11% iron
Exchanges:
1 Vegetable, 1 Starch, 2 Meat

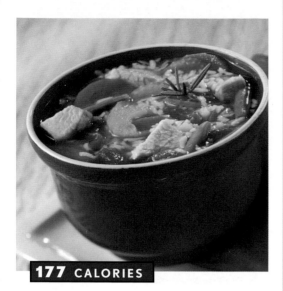

177 CALORIES

Turkey and Rice Soup

Soups make great meals when you're trying to lose weight. They're filling, satisfying, and usually nutritious. This one is all three, plus it is low in calories and fat grams.

Start to Finish: 25 minutes

Makes: 6 servings (about 8 cups)

2   **14-ounce cans reduced-sodium chicken broth**

1½   **cups water**

1   **teaspoon snipped fresh rosemary or ¼ teaspoon dried rosemary, crushed**

¼   **teaspoon black pepper**

½   **cup thinly sliced carrot (1 medium)**

½   **cup thinly sliced celery (1 stalk)**

⅓   **cup chopped onion (1 small)**

1   **cup quick-cooking rice**

½   **cup loose-pack frozen cut green beans**

2   **cups chopped cooked turkey or chicken (about 10 ounces)**

1   **14½-ounce can diced tomatoes, undrained**

    Fresh rosemary sprigs (optional)

1 In a large saucepan or Dutch oven combine broth, the water, snipped rosemary, and pepper. Add carrot, celery, and onion. Bring to boiling.

2 Stir in uncooked rice and green beans. Return to boiling; reduce heat. Simmer, covered, for 10 to 12 minutes or until vegetables are tender. Stir in turkey or chicken and undrained tomatoes; heat through. If desired, garnish with rosemary sprigs.

Nutrition Facts per serving:
177 cal., 2 g total fat (1 g sat. fat), 35 mg chol., 500 mg sodium, 20 g carbo., 1 g fiber, 17 g pro.
Daily Values:
58% vit. A, 18% vit. C, 5% calcium, 11% iron
Exchanges:
1 Vegetable, 1 Starch, 2 Meat

- 1 10-ounce package frozen red raspberries, thawed
- 2 tablespoons olive oil or salad oil
- 2 tablespoons lemon juice
- 1 clove garlic, minced
- 4 skinless, boneless chicken breast halves (about 1 pound total)
- 2 tablespoons honey-mustard
- 7 cups torn mixed salad greens
- 2 medium oranges, peeled and sectioned
- 1 avocado, halved, seeded, peeled, and sliced lengthwise
- 1 pink grapefruit, peeled and sectioned
- 2 green onions, thinly bias-sliced

1 Preheat broiler. For raspberry vinaigrette, in a blender container or food processor bowl combine raspberries, oil, lemon juice, and garlic. Cover and blend or process until smooth. Strain dressing through a sieve; discard seeds. Cover and chill dressing until serving time.

2 Place chicken on the unheated rack of a broiler pan; broil 4 to 5 inches from the heat for 12 to 15 minutes or until tender and no longer pink (170°F), turning once and brushing with honey-mustard during the last 2 minutes of broiling. Cool chicken slightly; slice into ¼-inch strips.

3 In a large bowl toss together chicken strips, greens, oranges, avocado slices, and grapefruit sections. Divide greens mixture among 4 dinner plates. Sprinkle with green onions. Drizzle each salad with 2 tablespoons of the raspberry vinaigrette. (Store remaining dressing in refrigerator for up to 1 week; use on tossed salads.)

Chicken Salad with Berry Dressing

Why buy bottled when you can have this great-tasting homemade berry vinaigrette in minutes? Frozen, unsweetened raspberries are the foundation for its delicious flavor.

Prep: 20 minutes   **Broil:** 12 minutes
Makes: 4 servings

340 CALORIES

Nutrition Facts per serving:
340 cal., 11 g total fat (2 g sat. fat), 66 mg chol., 145 mg sodium, 32 g carbo., 6 g fiber, 29 g pro.
Daily Values:
17% vit. A, 106% vit. C, 8% calcium, 13% iron
Exchanges:
2 Vegetable, 1½ Fruit, 3½ Meat, 1½ Fat

Curried Chicken Salad

Used in small doses, curry powder does a lot to perk up chicken salad. Celery and apples keep it fresh and crunchy, while the wild rice adds a satisfying chewiness.

Prep: 30 minutes   **Chill:** 1 to 4 hours
Makes: 6 servings

241 CALORIES

3 **skinless, boneless chicken breast halves (about 12 ounces total)**

1 **cup water**

¼ **teaspoon salt**

⅔ **cup low-fat mayonnaise dressing or light salad dressing**

¼ **cup fat-free milk**

2 **teaspoons curry powder**

¼ **teaspoon salt**

2 **cups chopped red apples (3 medium)**

2 **cups cooked wild rice, chilled**

1½ **cups sliced celery (3 stalks)**

½ **cup golden raisins**

Romaine or fresh spinach leaves (optional)

1 In a medium skillet combine chicken, the water, and ¼ teaspoon salt. Bring to boiling; reduce heat. Simmer, covered, for 12 to 14 minutes or until the chicken is tender and no longer pink (170°F). Drain well; cool. Cut chicken into bite-size pieces.

2 Meanwhile, for the dressing, in a small bowl stir together mayonnaise dressing, milk, curry powder, and ¼ teaspoon salt.

3 In a large bowl stir together cooked chicken, apples, chilled wild rice, celery, and raisins; stir in the dressing. Cover and chill for at least 1 hour or up to 4 hours. If desired, serve on romaine or spinach leaves.

Nutrition Facts per serving:
241 cal., 3 g total fat (1 g sat. fat), 38 mg chol., 501 mg sodium, 39 g carbo., 4 g fiber, 17 g pro.
Daily Values:
4% vit. A, 10% vit. C, 6% calcium, 9% iron
Exchanges:
1½ Fruit, 1 Starch, 2 Meat

1 recipe Thyme Vinaigrette

3 skinless, boneless chicken breast halves (about 12 ounces total)

1 cup loose-pack frozen French-cut green beans

2 cups cooked brown rice, chilled

1 14-ounce can artichoke hearts, drained and quartered

1 cup shredded red cabbage

1/2 cup shredded carrot (1 medium)

2 tablespoons sliced green onion (1)

Lettuce leaves (optional)

1 Preheat broiler. Pour 2 tablespoons of the Thyme Vinaigrette into a small bowl; brush onto chicken. Set aside the remaining vinaigrette.

2 Place chicken on the unheated rack of a broiler pan; broil 4 to 5 inches from heat for 12 to 15 minutes or until chicken is tender and no longer pink (170°F), turning once halfway through broiling time. Cut chicken into slices.

3 Meanwhile, rinse green beans with cool water for 30 seconds; drain well. In a large bowl toss together beans, chilled rice, artichoke hearts, cabbage, carrot, and green onion. Pour the remaining vinaigrette over rice mixture; toss to gently coat.

4 If desired, arrange lettuce leaves on 4 dinner plates. Top with the rice mixture and chicken slices.

Thyme Vinaigrette: In a screw-top jar combine ¼ cup white wine vinegar; 2 tablespoons olive oil; 2 tablespoons water; 1 tablespoon grated Parmesan cheese; 2 teaspoons snipped fresh thyme; 1 clove garlic, minced; ¼ teaspoon salt; and ¼ teaspoon black pepper. Cover and shake well.

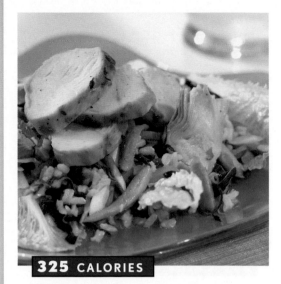

325 CALORIES

Chicken and Rice Salad

When summertime comes around, it's nice to have a variety of salad recipes at hand. You can whip up this one in minutes, leaving lots of time to enjoy the great outdoors.

Start to Finish: 30 minutes

Makes: 4 servings

Nutrition Facts per serving:
325 cal., 9 g total fat (2 g sat. fat), 50 mg chol., 545 mg sodium, 32 g carbo., 6 g fiber, 25 g pro.
Daily Values:
92% vit. A, 31% vit. C, 10% calcium, 21% iron
Exchanges:
2 Vegetable, 1½ Starch, 2½ Meat

219 CALORIES

Turkey-Peach Salad

Fresh fruit and poultry make a pleasing, naturally light pair. Here a refreshing green onion-poppy seed dressing made with yogurt is drizzled over turkey breast, peaches, and plums.

Start to Finish: 30 minutes

Makes: 4 servings

2   **turkey breast tenderloins (about 1 pound total)**
1   **teaspoon olive oil**
    Salt
    Coarsely ground black pepper
2   **peaches, pitted and sliced**
2   **plums, pitted and sliced**
2   **tablespoons lemon juice**
1/2   **cup lemon low-fat yogurt**
2   **tablespoons thinly sliced green onion (1)**
1/4   **teaspoon poppy seeds**
    Lemon juice (optional)
    Mixed salad greens

1 Cut turkey tenderloins in half horizontally to make four ½-inch portions. Rub both sides of each turkey portion with oil. Sprinkle with salt and pepper. Grill turkey on the rack of an uncovered grill directly over medium coals for 12 to 15 minutes or until turkey is tender and no longer pink (170°F), turning once. (Or preheat broiler. Place turkey on unheated rack of broiler pan; broil 4 to 5 inches from the heat for 12 to 15 minutes or until tender and no longer pink [170°F], turning once.) Cut turkey into bite-size pieces.

2 Meanwhile, in a medium bowl combine the peaches and plums. Add 2 tablespoons lemon juice; toss gently to coat. For dressing, in a small bowl combine yogurt, green onion, and poppy seeds. If necessary, stir in 1 to 2 teaspoons additional lemon juice to reach drizzling consistency.

3 Divide greens among 4 dinner plates. Arrange turkey and fruit on top of greens. Drizzle with dressing.

8 cups fresh baby spinach or torn fresh spinach

8 ounces cooked turkey, cubed

2 grapefruit, peeled and sectioned

2 oranges, peeled and sectioned

¼ cup orange juice

2 tablespoons olive oil

1 teaspoon honey

½ teaspoon poppy seeds

¼ teaspoon salt

¼ teaspoon dry mustard

2 tablespoons sliced almonds, toasted (optional)

1 Place spinach in a large bowl. Add turkey, grapefruit sections, and orange sections.

2 For dressing, in a screw-top jar combine orange juice, oil, honey, poppy seeds, salt, and dry mustard. Cover and shake well. Pour the dressing over salad; toss gently. If desired, sprinkle with almonds.

Turkey and Spinach Salad

How do you turn baby spinach into a meal? Add cubed turkey, grapefruit and orange sections, and almond slices. Toss them all together with a fresh poppy seed dressing.

Start to Finish: 25 minutes

Makes: 4 servings

228 CALORIES

Nutrition Facts per serving:
228 cal., 10 g total fat (2 g sat. fat), 43 mg chol., 261 mg sodium, 16 g carbo., 8 g fiber, 20 g pro.
Daily Values:
72% vit. A, 130% vit. C, 10% calcium, 31% iron
Exchanges:
1 Vegetable, 1 Fruit, 2 Meat, 1½ Fat

Chicken and Feta Salad-Stuffed Pitas

Where once mayonnaise reigned, a low-cal yogurt-dill sauce stands in. Ready in a snap, these chicken salad pitas surprise with an innovative mix of feta, peas, and tomato.

Start to Finish: 20 minutes

Makes: 4 servings

349 CALORIES

1 **9-ounce package frozen chopped cooked chicken, thawed**
³/₄ **cup loose-pack frozen peas, thawed**
²/₃ **cup chopped tomato (1 medium)**
¹/₄ **cup crumbled feta cheese (1 ounce)**
¹/₄ **cup sliced green onions (2)**
¹/₃ **cup plain fat-free yogurt**
1 **teaspoon dried dill**
4 **pita bread rounds, halved crosswise**
   Torn mixed salad greens

1 In a large bowl combine chicken, peas, tomato, feta cheese, and green onions. Stir in yogurt and dill; toss to combine.

2 Line pita halves with greens. Spoon chicken mixture into pita halves. If desired, cut each pita half in half.

Nutrition Facts per serving:
349 cal., 7 g total fat (3 g sat. fat), 63 mg chol., 507 mg sodium, 41 g carbo., 3 g fiber, 28 g pro.
Daily Values:
11% vit. A, 22% vit. C, 16% calcium, 18% iron
Exchanges:
1 Vegetable, 2 Starch, 3 Meat

2   tablespoons balsamic vinegar

2   tablespoons cooking oil

1   tablespoon honey

$^1/_8$ to $^1/_4$ teaspoon crushed red pepper

2   turkey breast tenderloins (about
     1 pound total)

     Salt

     Black pepper

2   medium zucchini, halved lengthwise
     and cut into $^1/_4$-inch slices

2   cups hot cooked pasta or rice

$^1/_2$ cup chopped tomato (1 small)

     Shredded fresh basil

1 For dressing, in a small bowl stir together balsamic vinegar, 1 tablespoon of the oil, the honey, and crushed red pepper; set aside. Cut turkey tenderloins in half horizontally to make four $^1/_2$-inch portions. Lightly sprinkle turkey with salt and pepper.

2 In a large nonstick skillet cook turkey in remaining 1 tablespoon hot oil over medium-high heat for 8 to 10 minutes or until tender and no longer pink (170°F), turning once. Remove from skillet; cover and keep warm.

3 Add zucchini to skillet; cook and stir about 3 minutes or until crisp-tender. Cut turkey into bite-size pieces. In a large bowl combine turkey, zucchini, and dressing. Spoon over hot cooked pasta. Sprinkle with chopped tomato and basil.

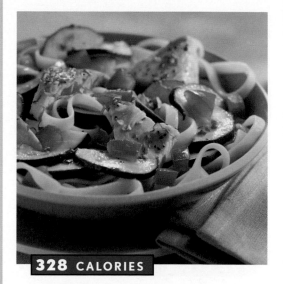

328 CALORIES

Balsamic Turkey with Zucchini

Balsamic vinegar, aged several years before it gets to store shelves, possesses a woody sweetness. For this recipe, a small amount of honey and crushed red pepper combine with the vinegar, resulting in a spicy-sweet flavor.

Start to Finish: 25 minutes
Makes: 4 servings

Nutrition Facts per serving:
328 cal., 9 g total fat (2 g sat. fat), 68 mg chol., 96 mg sodium, 30 g carbo., 2 g fiber, 31 g pro.
Daily Values:
9% vit. A, 19% vit. C, 4% calcium, 16% iron
Exchanges:
$1^1/_2$ Vegetable, $1^1/_2$ Starch, $3^1/_2$ Meat, 1 Fat

192 CALORIES

Apple-Glazed Turkey

Cooking with bold ingredients ensures flavor-packed meals. The lively tastes of garlic, sage, and apple jelly meld into an impressive brush-on glaze.

Prep: 10 minutes   **Broil:** 9 minutes
Makes: 4 servings

- **2** turkey breast tenderloins (about 1 pound total)
- **1** tablespoon lemon juice
- **1** tablespoon olive oil or cooking oil
- **1/2** teaspoon seasoned salt
- **1/2** teaspoon dried sage leaves, crushed
- **4** cloves garlic, minced
- **2** tablespoons apple jelly, melted
  Fresh sage leaves (optional)
  Apple slices (optional)

1 Preheat broiler. Cut turkey tenderloins in half horizontally to make four 1/2-inch portions. Place turkey on the unheated rack of a broiler pan. In a small bowl combine lemon juice, oil, seasoned salt, dried sage, and garlic. Brush mixture on both sides of each turkey portion.

2 Broil turkey 4 to 5 inches from the heat for 5 minutes. Turn turkey; broil for 2 minutes more. Using a clean brush, brush with apple jelly. Broil for 2 to 3 minutes more or until tender and no longer pink (170°F). Slice the turkey. If desired, garnish with sage leaves and apple slices.

Nutrition Facts per serving:
192 cal., 5 g total fat (1 g sat. fat), 68 mg chol., 247 mg sodium, 8 g carbo., 0 g fiber, 27 g pro.
Daily Values:
5% vit. C, 2% calcium, 8% iron
Exchanges:
1/2 Other Carbo., 4 Meat, 1/2 Fat

12 ounces turkey breast tenderloin steaks or boneless turkey breast, cut into 1-inch cubes

⅓ cup unsweetened pineapple juice

3 tablespoons rum or unsweetened pineapple juice

1 tablespoon brown sugar

1 tablespoon finely chopped lemongrass or 2 teaspoons finely shredded lemon peel

1 tablespoon olive oil

1 medium red onion, cut into thin wedges

2 nectarines or 3 plums, pitted and cut into thick slices

1½ cups fresh or canned pineapple chunks

Hot cooked rice (optional)

1 Place turkey in a plastic bag set in a shallow dish. For marinade, combine the ⅓ cup pineapple juice, the rum or additional pineapple juice, brown sugar, lemongrass or lemon peel, and oil. Pour over turkey. Seal bag. Marinate in refrigerator for at least 4 hours or up to 24 hours, turning bag occasionally.

2 Preheat broiler. Drain turkey, reserving marinade. In a small saucepan bring marinade to boiling. Remove from heat. On long metal skewers, alternately thread turkey and onion. Place kabobs on the unheated rack of a broiler pan; broil 3 to 4 inches from heat for 12 to 14 minutes or until turkey is tender and no longer pink, turning once and brushing occasionally with hot marinade during the first 8 minutes of broiling.

3 Meanwhile, on long metal skewers alternately thread nectarines or plums and pineapple. Brush with hot marinade. Place on broiler rack next to turkey kabobs for the last 5 minutes of broiling, turning once. Discard any remaining marinade. If desired, serve turkey and fruit kabobs with rice.

Pineapple-Rum Turkey Kabobs

The key to these turkey kabobs is the lemongrass marinade. An essential ingredient in Indonesian and Thai cooking, lemongrass imparts a woodsy, lemony flavor. If you can't find fresh lemongrass at your grocery store, look for it in Asian markets.

Prep: 15 minutes   **Marinate:** 4 to 24 hours
Broil: 12 minutes   **Makes:** 4 servings

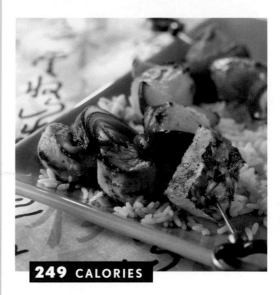

249 CALORIES

Nutrition Facts per serving:
249 cal., 4 g total fat (1 g sat. fat), 56 mg chol., 40 mg sodium, 24 g carbo., 2 g fiber, 22 g pro.
Daily Values:
10% vit. A, 31% vit. C, 3% calcium, 8% iron
Exchanges:
1½ Fruit, 3 Meat

Turkey Piccata with Fettuccine

Serve this exceptional dish with steamed broccoli, asparagus, or Brussels sprouts. The tasty juices and crusty flavor bits left in the pan after cooking the turkey jump-start a snappy pan sauce.

Start to Finish: 30 minutes

Makes: 4 servings

377 CALORIES

6 ounces dried fettuccine or linguine

¼ cup all-purpose flour

½ teaspoon lemon-pepper seasoning or black pepper

2 turkey breast tenderloins (about 1 pound total)

2 tablespoons olive oil or cooking oil

⅓ cup dry white wine

2 tablespoons lemon juice

2 tablespoons water

½ teaspoon instant chicken bouillon granules

1 tablespoon capers, rinsed and drained (optional)

2 tablespoons snipped fresh parsley

Lemon wedges (optional)

Fresh parsley sprigs (optional)

1 Cook pasta according to package directions; drain. Meanwhile, in a small bowl stir together flour and lemon-pepper seasoning; set aside.

2 Cut each turkey tenderloin in half crosswise to make ½-inch portions. Dip pieces in flour mixture to coat.

3 In a large skillet cook turkey in hot oil over medium-high heat for 6 to 10 minutes or until light golden and no longer pink (170°F), turning once. Remove turkey from pan; cover and keep warm.

4 For sauce, add wine, lemon juice, the water, and bouillon granules to skillet, scraping up crusty bits from bottom of skillet. If desired, stir in capers. Bring to boiling; reduce heat. Simmer, uncovered, for 2 minutes. Remove from heat; stir in snipped parsley.

5 To serve, divide pasta among 4 dinner plates. Divide turkey pieces among dinner plates. Spoon sauce over all. If desired, serve with lemon wedges and garnish with parsley sprigs.

Nutrition Facts per serving:
377 cal., 9 g total fat (2 g sat. fat), 68 mg chol., 301 mg sodium, 36 g carbo., 1 g fiber, 33 g pro.
Daily Values:
2% vit. A, 10% vit. C, 3% calcium, 16% iron
Exchanges:
2½ Starch, 3½ Meat, 1 Fat

- **2** turkey breast tenderloins or 4 skinless, boneless chicken breast halves (about 1 pound total)
- **½** cup sliced leeks or shallots
- **1** tablespoon olive oil or cooking oil
- **½** cup dry white wine
- **½** cup reduced-sodium chicken broth
- **1** teaspoon snipped fresh tarragon or ¼ teaspoon dried tarragon, crushed

  Dash black pepper
- **1** pound fresh asparagus spears
- **¼** cup light dairy sour cream
- **2** tablespoons Dijon-style mustard

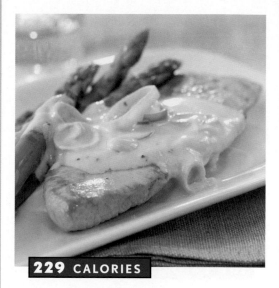

229 CALORIES

Turkey with Mustard Sauce

It's the mustard sauce that sets this dish apart from the rest. A sour cream base is dressed up with white wine, tarragon, and (what else?) Dijon-style mustard.

Start to Finish: 45 minutes
Makes: 4 servings

1 If using turkey tenderloins, cut in half horizontally to make four ½-inch portions. In a large nonstick skillet cook turkey or chicken and leeks or shallots in hot oil over medium heat about 5 minutes or until turkey is browned, turning once. Stir in wine, broth, dried tarragon (if using), and pepper. Bring to boiling; reduce heat. Simmer, covered, about 5 minutes or until turkey is tender and no longer pink (170°F).

2 Meanwhile, wash asparagus and break off woody bases where spears break easily. In a covered large saucepan cook asparagus in a small amount of boiling water for 3 to 5 minutes or until crisp-tender. Drain well.

3 Transfer turkey to a serving platter, reserving liquid in skillet; cover turkey and keep warm. Bring liquid in skillet to boiling. Continue boiling about 5 minutes more or until mixture is reduced to ½ cup.

4 In a small bowl stir together sour cream and mustard; stir in hot pan juices. Return to skillet. Heat through but do not boil. Stir in fresh tarragon (if using). Arrange cooked asparagus alongside turkey; spoon sauce over the turkey and asparagus.

Nutrition Facts per serving:
229 cal., 6 g total fat (2 g sat. fat), 73 mg chol., 319 mg sodium, 6 g carbo., 1 g fiber, 30 g pro.
Daily Values:
9% vit. A, 13% vit. C, 7% calcium, 12% iron
Exchanges:
1 Vegetable, 4 Meat, 1½ Fat

167 CALORIES

Turkey and Peppers

How can something so low in calories taste so good? The contrast of sweet and hot peppers does the trick. Serve the turkey slices over rice to soak up the flavorful juices.

Start to Finish: 25 minutes

Makes: 4 servings

4 ¹/₄- to ³/₈-inch turkey breast slices
   (about 12 ounces total)
   Salt
   Black pepper
1 **tablespoon olive oil**
2 **medium red, yellow, and/or green
   sweet peppers, cut into thin strips**
1 **medium onion, halved lengthwise and
   sliced**
1 **fresh jalapeño chile pepper, seeded and
   thinly sliced (see note on page 76)**
³/₄ **cup chicken broth**
1 **tablespoon all-purpose flour**
1 **teaspoon paprika**
   Hot cooked rice (optional)

1 Sprinkle turkey lightly with salt and black pepper. In a large nonstick skillet cook turkey in hot oil over medium-high heat for 4 to 5 minutes or until turkey is tender and no longer pink (170°F), turning once. (If necessary, reduce heat to medium to prevent overbrowning.) Transfer turkey to a serving platter; cover and keep warm.

2 Add sweet peppers, onion, and jalapeño pepper to skillet. Cook, covered, for 4 to 5 minutes or until vegetables are crisp-tender, stirring occasionally.

3 In a screw-top jar combine broth, flour, and paprika; shake well. Add to sweet pepper mixture. Cook and stir over medium heat until thickened and bubbly. Cook and stir for 1 minute more. If desired, serve turkey on hot cooked rice. Spoon the sweet pepper mixture over turkey and rice.

Nutrition Facts per serving:
167 cal., 5 g total fat (1 g sat. fat), 51 mg chol.,
260 mg sodium, 8 g carbo., 2 g fiber, 22 g pro.
Daily Values:
75% vit. A, 194% vit. C, 3% calcium, 9% iron
Exchanges:
1 Vegetable, 2¹/₂ Meat

1 beaten egg
1/4 cup fine dry bread crumbs
1 teaspoon Thai seasoning
1 pound uncooked ground turkey
4 kaiser rolls or hamburger buns,
   split and toasted
3/4 cup fresh basil leaves
2 tablespoons purchased peanut
   dipping sauce
   Green onions, bias-sliced (optional)

1 Preheat broiler. In a medium bowl
combine egg, bread crumbs, and Thai
seasoning. Add ground turkey; mix well.
Shape into four 3/4-inch patties.

2 Place patties on the unheated rack of
broiler pan. Broil 3 to 4 inches from the
heat for 14 to 18 minutes or until internal
temperature registers 165°F on an
instant-read thermometer; turn once.

3 To serve burgers, top bottom half of each
bun with some of the basil. Add patties.
Spoon peanut dipping sauce over patties.
If desired, garnish with green onions.
Add bun tops.

Thai Turkey Burgers

It's easy to give your burgers an Asian
flair. Simply add Thai seasoning and top
with peanut sauce.

Prep: 15 minutes   **Broil:** 14 minutes
Makes: 4 servings

389 CALORIES

Nutrition Facts per serving:
389 cal., 13 g total fat (3 g sat. fat), 123 mg chol.,
739 mg sodium, 36 g carbo., 2 g fiber, 31 g pro.
Daily Values:
8% vit. A, 2% vit. C, 12% calcium, 20% iron
Exchanges:
2 1/2 Starch, 3 1/2 Meat

Tall Turkey Sandwiches

The typical turkey sandwich is more than ready for a modern-day update. Here a yogurt and horseradish spread provides tang, while snow peas impart snap. For even more kick, use an extra teaspoon of horseradish.

Start to Finish: 15 minutes

Makes: 4 sandwiches

235 CALORIES

1/4 cup fat-free plain yogurt

3 tablespoons horseradish mustard

8 slices multigrain bread, toasted

12 lettuce leaves

8 to 12 ounces deli-sliced cooked turkey breast

1 tomato, sliced

1 yellow sweet pepper, sliced

1 cup fresh pea pods

1 In a small bowl stir together yogurt and horseradish mustard. Spread yogurt mixture on 4 of the toasted bread slices.

2 Top the remaining bread slices with lettuce, turkey, tomato, sweet pepper, and pea pods. Top with remaining bread slices, spread sides down.

Nutrition Facts per sandwich:
235 cal., 3 g total fat (0 g sat. fat), 23 mg chol., 1,163 mg sodium, 34 g carbo., 6 g fiber, 22 g pro.
Daily Values:
18% vit. A, 183% vit. C, 27% calcium, 27% iron
Exchanges:
1 Vegetable, 2 Starch, 2 Meat

1 **pound fresh or frozen skinless red snapper fillets, 1/2 to 3/4 inch thick**

Salt and black pepper

2 **tablespoons butter, melted**

3/4 **cup soft bread crumbs (1 slice)**

2 **tablespoons snipped fresh flat-leaf parsley**

1 **teaspoon finely shredded orange peel**

1 **tablespoon orange juice**

1 **clove garlic, minced**

1/4 **teaspoon dried oregano, crushed**

1/4 **teaspoon black pepper**

1/8 **teaspoon salt**

Orange wedges (optional)

1 Thaw fish, if frozen. Preheat broiler. Rinse fish; pat dry. Cut fish into 4 serving-size portions. Place fish on the greased unheated rack of a broiler pan. Tuck under any thin edges. Sprinkle lightly with salt and pepper. Brush 2 teaspoons of the butter over the fish. Measure thickness of the fish.

2 Broil fish 4 inches from the heat for 4 to 6 minutes per 1/2-inch thickness or until fish flakes easily when tested with a fork.

3 Meanwhile, combine remaining butter, bread crumbs, parsley, orange peel, orange juice, garlic, oregano, the 1/4 teaspoon pepper, and 1/8 teaspoon salt. Spoon mixture over broiled fish; broil 1 to 2 minutes more or until topping is light golden brown. If desired, serve with orange wedges.

187 CALORIES

Cuban Broiled Snapper with Parsley

You can almost feel Cuba's warm sun and gentle breezes when you dish up this tropical charmer. A citrus-studded parsley topping counterbalances the delicate flavor of the fish.

Start to Finish: 20 minutes
Makes: 4 servings

Nutrition Facts per serving:
187 cal., 8 g total fat (4 g sat. fat), 58 mg chol., 315 mg sodium, 4 g carbo., 0 g fiber, 24 g pro.
Daily Values:
9% vit. A, 12% vit. C, 5% calcium, 3% iron
Exchanges:
3 Meat, 1 Fat

261 CALORIES

Fish Soft Shell Tacos with Mango Salsa

Mango salsa spiked with jalapeño chile pepper and cilantro pleasantly surprises those who bite into these soft-shell tacos. The salsa is equally delicious with beef or chicken tacos.

Prep: 20 minutes   **Broil:** 8 minutes
Makes: 4 servings

1 pound fresh or frozen swordfish or halibut steaks, 1 inch thick
1/2 teaspoon Jamaican jerk seasoning
4 8- to 10-inch whole wheat or flour tortillas
2 cups small fresh spinach leaves or shredded lettuce
1 recipe Mango Salsa
   Lime wedges (optional)

1 Thaw fish, if frozen. Preheat broiler. Rinse fish; pat dry. Cut fish into 3/4-inch slices; sprinkle with jerk seasoning.

2 Place seasoned fish slices on the greased unheated rack of a broiler pan. Broil fish 4 inches from the heat for 5 minutes; turn fish. Broil for 3 to 7 minutes more or until fish flakes easily when tested with a fork. Meanwhile, wrap tortillas in foil. Heat package on lower rack of oven for 5 to 7 minutes.

3 Fill each warm tortilla with spinach, fish, and Mango Salsa. If desired, serve with lime wedges.

Mango Salsa: In a large bowl combine 1 large mango, peeled, seeded, and chopped; 1 large tomato, seeded and chopped; 1 small cucumber, seeded and chopped; 2 to 4 tablespoons snipped fresh cilantro; 1 fresh jalapeño chile pepper, seeded and chopped (see note on page 76); 1 thinly sliced green onion; and 1 tablespoon lime juice. Cover and chill until serving time. Serve with a slotted spoon. Makes about 3 cups.

Nutrition Facts per serving:
261 cal., 5 g total fat (1 g sat. fat), 43 mg chol., 346 mg sodium, 28 g carbo., 13 g fiber, 26 g pro.
Daily Values:
83% vit. A, 68% vit. C, 6% calcium, 14% iron
Exchanges:
1 Vegetable, 1/2 Fruit, 1 Starch, 3 Meat

- 4 4-ounce fresh or frozen skinless sole fillets
- 1 14½-ounce can Italian-style stewed tomatoes
- 2 cups chopped, peeled eggplant
- 1 tablespoon olive oil
- 1 small yellow, green, or red sweet pepper, coarsely chopped (³/₄ cup)
- ¼ cup bottled picante sauce
- 1 clove garlic, minced
- 1 tablespoon balsamic vinegar
- ⅛ teaspoon salt
- ⅛ teaspoon black pepper
- 2 tablespoons bottled reduced-calorie Italian salad dressing
   Lime wedges (optional)

1 Thaw fish, if frozen. Rinse fish; pat dry.

2 For caponata, cut up any large tomato pieces; set aside. In a large nonstick skillet cook the eggplant in hot oil over medium-high heat about 3 minutes or until golden brown, stirring occasionally. Stir in undrained tomatoes, sweet pepper, picante sauce, and garlic. Bring to boiling; reduce heat. Simmer, uncovered, for 4 to 5 minutes or until slightly thickened. Stir in vinegar.

3 Season fish with the salt and pepper. Brush fish with the salad dressing. Roll up, securing rolls with wooden toothpicks. Place fish in a 2-quart square baking dish. Bake, uncovered, in a 450° oven for 8 to 10 minutes or until fish flakes easily when tested with a fork. Serve caponata with fish. If desired, serve with lime wedges.

Sole with Caponata

Zesty caponata (the Italian cousin of France's ratatouille) turns ordinary fish into a fresh and lively dinner. Another time, try the caponata on your favorite sandwich or use it to top off broiled chicken.

Start to Finish: 25 minutes   **Oven:** 450°F
Makes: 4 servings

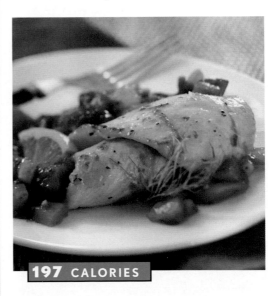

197 CALORIES

Nutrition Facts per serving:
197 cal., 6 g total fat (1 g sat. fat), 52 mg chol., 613 mg sodium, 14 g carbo., 2 g fiber, 21 g pro.
Daily Values:
4% vit. A, 94% vit. C, 6% calcium, 10% iron
Exchanges:
3 Vegetable, 3 Meat

Lemon-Herb Swordfish Steaks

Broiling is the way to go when cooking up thick dense fish, such as swordfish, tuna, and shark. Hearty fish steaks like these turn easily with tongs or a spatula without falling apart. They also taste great sprinkled with a range of seasonings.

Prep: 20 minutes **Marinate:** 30 minutes
Broil: 8 minutes **Makes:** 4 to 6 servings

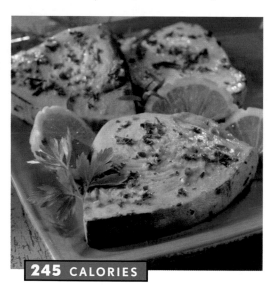

245 CALORIES

1½ pounds fresh or frozen swordfish, tuna, or shark steaks, 1 inch thick
¼ cup snipped fresh parsley
¼ cup chicken broth
1 teaspoon finely shredded lemon peel
2 tablespoons fresh lemon juice
2 tablespoons finely chopped shallot (1)
1 tablespoon snipped fresh rosemary
1 tablespoon olive oil
3 cloves garlic, minced
1½ teaspoons snipped fresh tarragon
¼ teaspoon salt
   Fresh flat-leaf parsley sprigs (optional)
   Lemon slices (optional)

1 Thaw fish, if frozen. Rinse fish; pat dry. Place fish steaks in a plastic bag set in a shallow dish. For marinade, in a bowl combine parsley, broth, lemon peel, lemon juice, shallot, rosemary, oil, garlic, tarragon, and salt. Pour marinade over fish. Seal bag. Marinate for 30 minutes in the refrigerator, turning occasionally.

2 Preheat broiler. Drain fish steaks, reserving marinade. Place fish on the greased unheated rack of a broiler pan. Broil fish 4 to 6 inches from the heat for 5 minutes, brushing once with reserved marinade. Discard any remaining marinade. Turn fish and broil for 3 to 7 minutes more or until fish flakes easily when tested with a fork. If desired, garnish with parsley sprigs and lemon slices.

Nutrition Facts per serving:
245 cal., 10 g total fat (2 g sat. fat), 64 mg chol., 350 mg sodium, 3 g carbo., 0 g fiber, 34 g pro.
Daily Values:
9% vit. A, 20% vit. C, 2% calcium, 10% iron
Exchanges:
5 Meat

- 4 5-ounce fresh or frozen halibut steaks, 1 inch thick
- 3 tablespoons hoisin sauce
- 2 tablespoons seasoned rice vinegar
- 2 tablespoons maple syrup
- 1 teaspoon grated fresh ginger
- 1 clove garlic, minced
- ¼ teaspoon crushed red pepper
- ¼ teaspoon coarsely ground black pepper
- Shredded napa cabbage (optional)

1 Thaw fish, if frozen. Rinse fish; pat dry. In a small bowl stir together hoisin sauce, vinegar, syrup, ginger, garlic, and crushed red pepper. Set aside.

2 Preheat broiler. Sprinkle fish with black pepper. Place fish on the greased unheated rack of a broiler pan. Broil fish 4 inches from the heat for 5 minutes. Brush with glaze; turn fish. Brush with remaining glaze. Broil for 3 to 7 minutes more or until fish flakes easily when tested with a fork. If desired, serve on a bed of napa cabbage.

210 CALORIES

Maple-Hoisin Glazed Halibut

Tempt your taste buds with this innovative combination of hoisin sauce, rice vinegar, and maple syrup over halibut. Side dishes of steamed carrots and boiled new potatoes are a nice touch.

Prep: 10 minutes   **Broil:** 8 minutes
Makes: 4 servings

Nutrition Facts per serving:
210 cal., 4 g total fat (1 g sat. fat), 45 mg chol., 285 mg sodium, 13 g carbo., 0 g fiber, 30 g pro.
Daily Values:
6% vit. A, 1% vit. C, 8% calcium, 8% iron
Exchanges:
1 Starch, 4 Meat

125 CALORIES

Pineapple-Glazed Orange Roughy

A glaze may seem elegant, but in some cases it's just a few tablespoons of preserves mixed with seasonings and vinegar. Be sure to try this one on chicken or pork as well.

Prep: 10 minutes
Broil: 4 to 6 minutes per ½-inch thickness
Makes: 4 servings

- 1 **pound fresh or frozen orange roughy fillets**
- 3 **tablespoons pineapple preserves**
- 2 **tablespoons rice vinegar**
- 2 **teaspoons snipped fresh thyme**
- ⅛ **teaspoon crushed red pepper**
- 1 **clove garlic, minced**
- ¼ **teaspoon black pepper**
- ⅛ **teaspoon salt**
  Fresh thyme sprigs (optional)
  Fresh pineapple wedges (optional)

1 Thaw fish, if frozen. Preheat broiler. In a small bowl stir together preserves, vinegar, snipped thyme, red pepper, and garlic; set aside.

2 Rinse fish; pat dry. Cut into 4 serving-size portions. Sprinkle fish with black pepper and salt. Place fish on the greased unheated rack of a broiler pan. Measure thickness of the fish. Broil fish 4 inches from the heat until the fish flakes easily when tested with a fork, brushing occasionally with the preserves mixture. (Allow 4 to 6 minutes per ½-inch thickness of fish; if fillets are 1 inch thick, turn once halfway through broiling.) If desired, garnish with thyme sprigs and pineapple wedges.

Nutrition Facts per serving:
125 cal., 1 g total fat (0 g sat. fat), 22 mg chol., 150 mg sodium, 11 g carbo., 0 g fiber, 17 g pro.
Daily Values:
2% vit. A, 4% vit. C, 4% calcium, 2% iron
Exchanges:
½ Fruit, 2½ Meat

4 **4-ounce fresh or frozen skinless red snapper or orange roughy fillets, 1/2 to 1 inch thick**

1/3 **cup bottled salsa**

1 **clove garlic, minced**

1 **14-ounce can vegetable broth**

1 **cup quick-cooking couscous**

1/4 **cup thinly sliced green onions (2) or coarsely chopped fresh cilantro**

Lemon wedges (optional)

1 Thaw fish, if frozen. Preheat broiler. Combine salsa and garlic; set aside. In a medium saucepan bring broth to boiling. Stir in couscous; cover and remove from heat. Let stand about 5 minutes or until liquid is absorbed. Stir in green onions.

2 Meanwhile, rinse fish; pat dry. Place fish on the greased unheated rack of a broiler pan. Measure thickness of the fish. Broil fish about 4 inches from the heat until the fish flakes easily when tested with a fork. (Allow 4 to 6 minutes per 1/2-inch thickness of fish; if fillets are 1 inch thick, turn once halfway through broiling.) Spoon the salsa mixture over fish; broil 1 minute more or until salsa is heated through.

3 To serve, arrange fish on couscous mixture. If desired, serve with lemon wedges.

Red Snapper Veracruz

Once a part of New Spain, Veracruz is located on the Gulf of Mexico and is famous for its seafood—most notably this namesake specialty. Boiled potatoes traditionally accompany the colorful snapper, but couscous is faster to prepare.

Start to Finish: 15 minutes   **Makes:** 4 servings

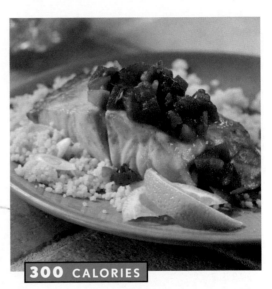

300 CALORIES

Nutrition Facts per serving:
300 cal., 2 g total fat (0 g sat. fat), 41 mg chol., 538 mg sodium, 38 g carbo., 3 g fiber, 30 g pro.
Daily Values:
5% vit. A, 7% vit. C, 6% calcium, 5% iron
Exchanges:
1 Vegetable, 2 Starch, 3 Meat

Sicilian-Style Swordfish

The licorice-flavored fennel rub and spunky olive and basil relish give meaty swordfish a one-two punch that's as delectable as it is distinctive. Look for Sicilian olives at Italian specialty stores or larger supermarkets.

Prep: 20 minutes   **Broil:** 8 minutes
Makes: 4 servings

177 CALORIES

- 2 8- to 10-ounce fresh or frozen swordfish steaks, 1 inch thick
- 1 teaspoon garlic powder
- ³/₄ teaspoon fennel seeds, crushed
- ¹/₂ teaspoon lemon-pepper seasoning
- ¹/₄ teaspoon salt
- ¹/₈ teaspoon crushed red pepper
- 1 recipe Sicilian Relish
   Fresh basil sprigs (optional)

1 Thaw fish, if frozen. Preheat broiler. Rinse fish; pat dry. Cut into 4 serving-size portions. In a small bowl stir together garlic powder, crushed fennel seeds, lemon-pepper seasoning, salt, and crushed red pepper. Rub on both sides of each fish piece.

2 Place fish on the greased unheated rack of a broiler pan. Broil 4 inches from the heat for 8 to 12 minutes or until fish flakes easily when tested with a fork, turning once halfway through broiling. Serve with Sicilian Relish. If desired, garnish with basil sprigs.

Sicilian Relish: In a small bowl toss together ¾ cup chopped roma tomatoes; 3 tablespoons chopped pitted Sicilian or kalamata olives; 3 tablespoons snipped fresh basil; 2 teaspoons lemon juice; 2 cloves garlic, minced; and 2 teaspoons olive oil.

Nutrition Facts per serving:
177 cal., 8 g total fat (2 g sat. fat), 43 mg chol., 457 mg sodium, 4 g carbo., 1 g fiber, 23 g pro.
Daily Values:
8% vit. A, 16% vit. C, 2% calcium, 7% iron
Exchanges:
3 Meat, ¹/₂ Fat

1   12-ounce fresh or frozen skinless
    salmon fillet, 1 inch thick

1½ cups apricot nectar

⅓   cup snipped dried apricots

2   tablespoons honey

2   tablespoons reduced-sodium soy
    sauce

1   tablespoon grated fresh ginger

2   cloves garlic, minced

¼   teaspoon ground cinnamon

⅛   teaspoon cayenne pepper

1 Thaw fish, if frozen. For glaze, in a medium saucepan stir together apricot nectar, apricots, honey, soy sauce, ginger, garlic, cinnamon, and cayenne pepper. Bring to boiling; reduce heat. Simmer, uncovered, about 20 minutes or until mixture is thickened and reduced by about half, stirring occasionally. Remove ¼ cup of the glaze for basting; set aside the remaining glaze until ready to serve.

2 Preheat broiler. Rinse fish; pat dry. Place fish on the greased unheated rack of a broiler pan, tucking under any thin edges.

3 Broil about 4 inches from the heat for 8 to 12 minutes or until fish flakes easily when tested with a fork, gently turning once halfway through broiling and brushing occasionally with the reserved ¼ cup glaze the last 4 minutes of broiling. Serve fish with the remaining glaze.

239 CALORIES

Sweet 'n' Heat-Glazed Salmon

The sweet for this easy broiled salmon comes from apricots and honey; the heat, from a dash of cayenne pepper. Together they're spectacular.

Prep: 30 minutes   **Broil:** 8 minutes
Makes: 4 servings

Nutrition Facts per serving:
239 cal., 6 g total fat (1 g sat. fat), 45 mg chol., 350 mg sodium, 30 g carbo., 2 g fiber, 19 g pro.
Daily Values:
42% vit. A, 3% vit. C, 5% calcium, 10% iron
Exchanges:
2 Fruit, 2½ Meat

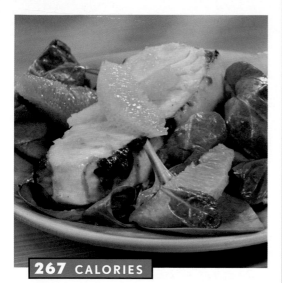

267 CALORIES

Honey-Ginger Halibut with Oranges

The spread, with the tantalizing addition of fresh ginger and wine, performs double duty, starting out as a lively marinade for the fish and winding up as a delightful dressing for the spinach.

Prep: 25 minutes   **Marinate:** 1 to 4 hours
Broil: 8 minutes   **Makes:** 4 servings

4 6-ounce fresh or frozen halibut steaks, 1 inch thick
2 medium oranges
1/2 cup dry white wine or orange juice
2 tablespoons orange-honey spread or honey
2 teaspoons grated fresh ginger
1/4 teaspoon salt
1/4 teaspoon coarsely ground black pepper
4 cups torn fresh spinach and/or baby spinach

1 Thaw fish, if frozen. Peel and section oranges over a bowl to catch juices. Reserve orange sections. Measure 1/4 cup orange juice (add additional orange juice, if necessary). For marinade, stir together the 1/4 cup orange juice, wine, honey spread, and ginger.

2 Rinse fish; pat dry. Place fish in a plastic bag set in a shallow dish. Pour marinade over fish. Seal bag. Marinate 1 to 4 hours in the refrigerator. Drain fish, reserving the marinade.

3 Preheat broiler. Pour marinade into a small saucepan. Bring to boiling. Boil, uncovered, for 2 minutes. Keep warm. Place fish on the greased unheated rack of a broiler pan. Sprinkle with the salt and pepper. Broil fish 4 inches from the heat for 8 to 12 minutes or until fish flakes easily when tested with a fork, turning once halfway through broiling.

4 Place spinach in a medium bowl. Drizzle with 1/4 cup of the hot marinade. Divide spinach among 4 dinner plates. Top with fish, reserved orange sections, and additional hot marinade.

Nutrition Facts per serving:
267 cal., 4 g total fat (1 g sat. fat), 54 mg chol., 277 mg sodium, 14 g carbo., 4 g fiber, 37 g pro.
Daily Values:
40% vit. A, 52% vit. C, 12% calcium, 21% iron
Exchanges:
1 Vegetable, 1/2 Fruit, 5 Meat

1 **pound fresh or frozen skinless whitefish fillets or other white-flesh fish fillets, about ¹/₂ inch thick**

¹/₂ **cup chopped onion (1 medium)**

¹/₂ **cup chopped carrot (1 medium)**

¹/₄ **cup reduced-sodium chicken broth**

2 **cloves garlic, minced**

¹/₄ **teaspoon salt**

¹/₄ **teaspoon smoked paprika or paprika**

¹/₄ **teaspoon black pepper**

12 **ounces fresh asparagus spears, trimmed and bias-sliced into 1-inch pieces (1¹/₂ cups)**

1 Thaw fish, if frozen. Rinse fish; pat dry. Cut fish into 4 serving-size portions; set aside. In a 2-quart rectangular baking dish stir together onion, carrot, broth, and garlic. Top with fish fillets, tucking under any thin edges. Sprinkle with salt, paprika, and pepper. Top with asparagus.

2 Bake, covered, in a 450° oven for 15 to 20 minutes or until fish flakes easily when tested with a fork. Serve fish with the vegetables.

Whitefish with Roasted Asparagus

As a member of the salmon family, whitefish has more fat than most of the other white-colored fish. The fat translates into an extra richness matched by few low-cal dishes.

Prep: 20 minutes   **Bake:** 15 minutes
Oven: 450°F   **Makes:** 4 servings

176 CALORIES

Nutrition Facts per serving:
176 cal., 6 g total fat (1 g sat. fat), 65 mg chol., 249 mg sodium, 6 g carbo., 2 g fiber, 23 g pro.
Daily Values:
86% vit. A, 13% vit. C, 5% calcium, 6% iron
Exchanges:
1 Vegetable, 3 Meat

Roasted Salmon and Tomatoes

Roasting brings out the rich, full flavor of the salmon and the tomatoes. While the main course cooks in the oven, steam some fresh asparagus or broccoli spears to complete the meal.

Prep: 15 minutes **Bake:** 12 minutes
Oven: 450°F **Makes:** 4 servings

231 CALORIES

1	1¼-pound fresh salmon fillet, about 1 inch thick
	Nonstick cooking spray
⅛	teaspoon salt
6	roma tomatoes, seeded and chopped (about 1 pound)
1	tablespoon white wine Worcestershire sauce
¼	teaspoon coarsely ground black pepper
⅛	teaspoon salt
1	tablespoon Dijon-style mustard
1	tablespoon snipped fresh marjoram or oregano
	Fresh oregano sprigs (optional)

1 Thaw fish, if frozen. Lightly coat a 13×9×2-inch baking pan with nonstick cooking spray. Rinse fish; pat dry. Cut fish into 4 serving-size portions. Sprinkle with the ⅛ teaspoon salt. Place fillet, skin side up, in pan, tucking under any thin edges. Arrange tomatoes around salmon. Sprinkle tomatoes with Worcestershire sauce, pepper, and ⅛ teaspoon salt.

2 Bake, uncovered, in a 450° oven for 12 to 16 minutes or until fish flakes easily when tested with a fork. Remove skin from fish; discard skin. Transfer fish to dinner plates. Stir mustard and marjoram into tomatoes. Serve tomato mixture with fish. If desired, garnish with oregano sprigs.

Nutrition Facts per serving:
231 cal., 10 g total fat (2 g sat. fat), 75 mg chol., 370 mg sodium, 6 g carbo., 1 g fiber, 30 g pro.
Daily Values:
16% vit. A, 37% vit. C, 5% calcium, 10% iron
Exchanges:
1 Vegetable, 4 Meat

- **1** pound fresh or frozen skinless red snapper fillets, about 1/2 inch thick
- **1** cup sliced fennel bulb
- **1/2** cup chopped onion (1 medium)
- **1/2** cup chopped carrot (1 medium)
- **2** cloves garlic, minced
- **1** tablespoon olive oil
- **1** tablespoon snipped fresh dill or 1 teaspoon dried dill
- **1/4** teaspoon salt
- **1/4** teaspoon black pepper
- **1/4** cup dry white wine or reduced-sodium chicken broth
- Fresh dill sprigs (optional)

1 Thaw fish, if frozen. Rinse fish; pat dry. In a large skillet cook fennel, onion, carrot, and garlic in hot oil over medium heat for 5 to 7 minutes or until vegetables are tender and lightly browned. Remove from heat. Stir in dill, salt, and pepper. Stir in wine.

2 Spoon about 1 cup of the vegetable mixture into a 2-quart square baking dish. Place fish on top of vegetables, tucking under any thin edges. Spoon remaining vegetable mixture on top of fish.

3 Bake, uncovered, in a 450° oven for 4 to 6 minutes or until fish flakes easily when tested with a fork. Transfer fish and vegetables to dinner plates. If desired, garnish with dill sprigs.

182 CALORIES

Red Snapper with Carrots and Fennel

It's called red snapper because of its red-tinged skin and eyes. A pretty fish, it's also a natural for low-calorie meals, not only because it's low in fat but because of how good it tastes with veggies.

Prep: 25 minutes   **Bake:** 4 minutes
Oven: 450°F   **Makes:** 4 servings

Nutrition Facts per serving:
182 cal., 6 g total fat (1 g sat. fat), 41 mg chol., 260 mg sodium, 6 g carbo., 7 g fiber, 24 g pro.
Daily Values:
79% vit. A, 9% vit. C, 5% calcium, 5% iron
Exchanges:
1 Vegetable, 3 Meat

373 CALORIES

Salmon with Feta and Pasta

Feta, the world's favorite Greek cheese, shares its tangy flavor with the salomon in this dish. Here salmon and pasta benefit. Add to the Greek flair by using kalamata olives, which have a pungent, lingering flavor.

Start to Finish: 25 minutes

Makes: 5 servings

12	ounces fresh or frozen skinless salmon fillet
8	ounces dried rotini pasta
	Nonstick cooking spray
2	cloves garlic, minced
	Salt
4	large roma tomatoes, chopped (2 cups)
1	cup sliced green onions (8)
1/3	cup sliced pitted ripe olives
3	tablespoons snipped fresh basil
1/2	teaspoon coarsely ground black pepper
2	teaspoons olive oil
1	4-ounce package crumbled feta cheese
	Fresh basil sprigs (optional)

1 Thaw fish, if frozen. Rinse fish; pat dry. Cut into 1-inch pieces. Cook pasta according to pasta directions. Drain. Keep warm.

2 Meanwhile, lightly coat a large nonstick skillet with cooking spray. Heat skillet over medium-high heat. Add garlic. Cook and stir for 15 seconds. Lightly season fish pieces with salt. Add fish to skillet. Cook fish for 4 to 6 minutes or until fish flakes easily when tested with a fork, turning fish pieces occasionally. Stir in tomatoes, green onions, olives, basil, and pepper. Heat through.

3 In a large bowl toss together hot pasta, olive oil, salmon mixture, and cheese. If desired, garnish with basil sprigs.

Nutrition Facts per serving:
373 cal., 13 g total fat (5 g sat. fat), 56 mg chol., 443 mg sodium, 41 g carbo., 3 g fiber, 24 g pro.
Daily Values:
15% vit. A, 30% vit. C, 17% calcium, 17% iron
Exchanges:
2 Vegetable, 2 Starch, 2 Meat, 1/2 Fat

1 pound fresh or frozen tilapia or other firm-flesh fish fillets, 1/2 to 1 inch thick

2 tablespoons cornmeal

2 tablespoons all-purpose flour

Nonstick cooking spray

1 teaspoon cooking oil

2 teaspoons butter or margarine

2 teaspoons all-purpose flour

1 teaspoon chili powder

1/4 teaspoon salt

1/4 teaspoon ground cumin

3/4 cup fat-free half-and-half

2 tablespoons snipped fresh parsley or cilantro (optional)

Lime slices (optional)

Tilapia with Chili Cream Sauce

Originally from the waters surrounding Africa, tilapia is raised commercially everywhere from North America to Asia. In this recipe, the sweet, mild fish—sometimes called Hawaiian sun fish—fries up crisp and tender, and soaks up all the glorious flavor of the sassy sauce. Serve fish with a side of rice and black beans.

Start to Finish: 25 minutes

Makes: 4 servings

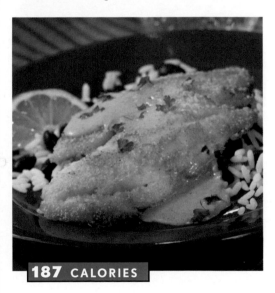

187 CALORIES

1 Thaw fish, if frozen. Rinse fish; pat dry. Cut into 4 serving-size portions. Stir together cornmeal and the 2 tablespoons flour. Sprinkle over both sides of fish. Lightly coat a 12-inch nonstick skillet with cooking spray. Add oil to skillet. Heat over medium-high heat. Add fish pieces. Cook pieces over medium to medium-high heat for 2 to 3 minutes per side or until fish flakes easily when tested with a fork. Remove fish from skillet. Keep warm.

2 Melt butter in the same skillet. Stir in the 2 teaspoons flour, chili powder, salt, and cumin. Stir in half-and-half. Cook and stir until thickened and bubbly. Cook and stir for 1 minute more. To serve, spoon sauce over fish. If desired, sprinkle with parsley, garnish with lime slices.

Nutrition Facts per serving:
187 cal., 4 g total fat (2 g sat. fat), 60 mg chol., 258 mg sodium, 12 g carbo., 1 g fiber, 23 g pro.
Daily Values:
6% vit. A, 1% vit. C, 3% calcium, 3% iron
Exchanges:
1/2 Milk, 1/2 Starch, 2 1/2 Meat

Flounder with Tomatoes and Peppers

This captivating skillet dinner showcases flounder steamed on a bed of fresh tomatoes, capers, mild chile, and olives. At the table, "catch" the delicious juices with slices of crusty bread.

Start to Finish: 25 minutes

Makes: 4 servings

188 CALORIES

1 **pound fresh or frozen flounder fillets or other thin, mild-flavor fillets**

1 **cup finely chopped onions (2 medium)**

1 **medium fresh mild green chile pepper, such as Anaheim, seeded and cut into bite-size pieces (¹⁄₂ cup) (see note on page 76)**

1 **tablespoon olive oil**

4 **medium roma tomatoes, chopped (about 2 cups)**

¹⁄₄ **cup sliced, pitted imported black olives, such as kalamata or niçoise**

2 **tablespoons capers, drained**

¹⁄₄ **teaspoon salt**

¹⁄₈ **teaspoon freshly ground black pepper**

Fresh flat-leaf parsley sprigs

1 Thaw fish, if frozen. Cut fish into 4 serving-size portions. In a large skillet cook onions and chile pepper in hot oil over medium heat about 4 minutes or until tender.

2 Stir in the tomatoes, olives, capers, and ¹⁄₈ teaspoon of the salt. Arrange the flounder fillets on top of the vegetables. Sprinkle fish with the remaining ¹⁄₈ teaspoon salt and the black pepper. Cover and simmer for 4 to 5 minutes or until fish flakes easily when tested with a fork. Transfer fish and vegetables to dinner plates. Garnish with parsley.

Nutrition Facts per serving:
188 cal., 6 g total fat (1 g sat. fat), 54 mg chol., 500 mg sodium, 10 g carbo., 2 g fiber, 23 g pro.
Daily Values:
16% vit. A, 113% vit. C, 4% calcium, 7% iron
Exchanges:
2 Vegetable, 3 Meat, 1 Fat

8 ounces fresh or frozen skinless haddock, grouper, or halibut fillets

1 small fennel bulb

3 cups reduced-sodium chicken broth or vegetable broth

1 cup finely chopped onion (1 large)

1 small yellow summer squash, cubed (about 1 cup)

1 cup dry white wine

1 teaspoon finely shredded orange or lemon peel

3 cloves garlic, minced

2 cups chopped tomatoes or one 14½-ounce can diced tomatoes

2 tablespoons snipped fresh thyme

Fresh thyme sprigs (optional)

1 Thaw fish, if frozen. Rinse fish; pat dry. Cut fish into 1-inch pieces; set aside.

2 Cut off and discard upper stalks of fennel. Remove any wilted outer layers; cut a thin slice from base. Wash fennel; cut in half lengthwise and thinly slice.

3 In a large saucepan combine fennel, broth, onion, squash, wine, orange peel, and garlic. Bring to boiling; reduce heat. Simmer, covered, for 10 minutes. Stir in fish pieces, undrained tomatoes, and the 2 tablespoons thyme. Cook about 3 minutes more or just until fish flakes easily when tested with a fork. Ladle into bowls. If desired, garnish with thyme sprigs.

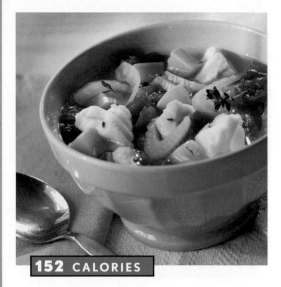

152 CALORIES

Fish Provençale

The sweet essence of fresh fennel blends nicely with the savory combination of fish, tomatoes, garlic, and onion. This Mediterranean-style soup tastes as good as it smells.

Start to Finish: 30 minutes
Makes: 4 servings (8 cups)

Nutrition Facts per serving:
152 cal., 1 g total fat (0 g sat. fat), 32 mg chol., 520 mg sodium, 13 g carbo., 8 g fiber, 15 g pro.
Daily Values:
14% vit. A, 48% vit. C, 6% calcium, 9% iron
Exchanges:
3 Vegetable, 1½ Meat

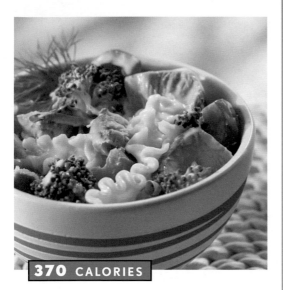

Tuna and Pasta Alfredo

It takes only minutes to cook fresh tuna for this recipe. If your schedule is really tight, a can of tuna will do. Either creates a luscious dish that is ready in minutes.

Start to Finish: 25 minutes

Makes: 6 servings

Nutrition Facts per serving:
370 cal., 10 g total fat (5 g sat. fat), 40 mg chol., 266 mg sodium, 46 g carbo., 3 g fiber, 20 g pro.
Daily Values:
51% vit. A, 99% vit. C, 13% calcium, 13% iron
Exchanges:
1 Vegetable, 2½ Starch, 1½ Meat, ½ Fat

3   cups dried mini lasagna pasta, broken mafalda, or medium noodles

2   cups chopped broccoli rabe or broccoli (6 ounces)

1   medium red sweet pepper, chopped

1   tablespoon butter or margarine

1   10-ounce container refrigerated light Alfredo sauce

2   teaspoons snipped fresh dill

1   to 2 tablespoons milk (optional)

8   ounces flaked, cooked tuna* or one 9½-ounce can tuna (water pack), drained and broken into chunks

½   cup sliced almonds, toasted (optional)

Fresh dill sprigs (optional)

1 Cook pasta according to package directions; drain. Meanwhile, in a large saucepan cook the broccoli rabe or broccoli and sweet pepper in hot butter until tender. Stir in Alfredo sauce and snipped dill. If necessary, add milk until desired consistency.

2 Gently stir in cooked pasta and tuna. Heat through. To serve, transfer pasta to a warm serving dish. If desired, sprinkle with almonds and garnish with dill sprigs.

*Note: To broil fresh tuna, place on the greased unheated rack of a broiler pan. Broil 4 inches from the heat for 4 to 6 minutes per ½-inch thickness or until fish flakes easily when tested with a fork. If fish is more than 1 inch thick, turn it over halfway through cooking. To poach tuna, add 1½ cups water to a large skillet. Bring to boiling; add fish. Simmer, uncovered, for 4 to 6 minutes per ½-inch thickness or until fish flakes easily when tested with a fork.

1 **pound fresh or frozen tuna steaks,**
  1 inch thick
3 **tablespoons sherry vinegar**
2 **tablespoons finely chopped shallots**
1 **tablespoon Dijon-style mustard**
2 **tablespoons olive oil**
1 **anchovy fillet, rinsed and mashed**
  Salt and black pepper
8 **ounces tiny new potatoes, quartered**
6 **ounces green beans**
6 **cups Bibb or Boston lettuce leaves**
³/₄ **cup thinly sliced radishes**
½ **cup pitted niçoise olives or ripe olives,**
  pitted

1 Thaw fish, if frozen. Rinse fish; pat dry. For dressing, in a small mixing bowl combine vinegar and shallots. Whisk in mustard. Add oil in a thin, steady stream, whisking constantly. Stir in the anchovy. Season to taste with salt and pepper. Remove 1 tablespoon of the dressing for brushing fish; set aside remaining dressing until ready to serve.

2 Preheat broiler. Brush the 1 tablespoon dressing over both sides of fish. Place fish on the greased unheated rack of a broiler pan. Broil about 4 inches from the heat for 8 to 12 minutes or until fish flakes easily when tested with a fork, gently turning once halfway through broiling. (Or grill the fish on the rack of an uncovered grill directly over medium coals for 8 to 12 minutes or until fish flakes easily when tested with a fork, gently turning once halfway through grilling.) Cut fish into slices.

3 Meanwhile, in a medium saucepan cook potatoes in boiling water for 7 minutes. Add green beans; cook for 2 minutes more or until potatoes are tender. Drain and cool slightly.

4 To serve, arrange fish, potatoes, green beans, lettuce leaves, radishes, and olives on 4 dinner plates. Serve with the remaining dressing.

Tuna Salad Niçoise

The term "niçoise" refers to dishes that are typically found around Nice, France. This salad is a lighter, more healthful adaptation of one of the region's classic favorites.

Prep: 30 minutes **Broil:** 8 minutes
Makes: 4 servings

280 CALORIES

Nutrition Facts per serving:
280 cal., 10 g total fat (1 g sat. fat), 51 mg chol., 400 mg sodium, 17 g carbo., 4 g fiber, 30 g pro.
Daily Values:
24% vit. A, 43% vit. C, 9% calcium, 17% iron
Exchanges:
2 Vegetable, ½ Starch, 3½ Meat, 1 Fat

Strawberries, Salmon, and Penne

Strawberries aren't strictly for dessert anymore. (Not after you've sampled this dish, anyway.) Partner their delicate sweetness with juicy broiled salmon and reap the rewards.

Prep: 30 minutes
Broil: 4 to 6 minutes per 1/2-inch thickness
Chill: 2 to 4 hours   **Makes:** 4 servings

332 CALORIES

Nutrition Facts per serving:
332 cal., 11 g total fat (2 g sat. fat), 30 mg chol., 72 mg sodium, 40 g carbo., 3 g fiber, 18 g pro.
Daily Values:
5% vit. A, 43% vit. C, 4% calcium, 13% iron
Exchanges:
1 Vegetable, 1 Fruit, 1 1/2 Starch, 1 1/2 Meat, 1 Fat

1/4   cup raspberry vinegar
2   tablespoons olive oil
1   tablespoon honey mustard
2   teaspoons sugar
1/4   teaspoon coarsely ground black pepper
1   clove garlic, minced
1   8- to 10-ounce fresh skinless, boneless salmon fillet or other fish fillet
6   ounces dried penne pasta (about 2 cups)
1   cup bias-sliced, trimmed fresh asparagus spears
1   cup sliced fresh strawberries
    Bibb lettuce leaves (optional)
1/4   cup sliced green onions (2)

1 In a small bowl whisk together raspberry vinegar, olive oil, honey mustard, sugar, pepper, and garlic. Reserve 2 teaspoons of the oil mixture; set aside.

2 Preheat broiler. Rinse fish; pat dry. Place fish on the greased unheated rack of a broiler pan; tuck under any thin edges. Measure thickness of the fish. Brush fish with reserved oil mixture. Broil fish 4 inches from the heat until the fish flakes easily when tested with a fork. (Allow 4 to 6 minutes per 1/2-inch thickness of fish; if fillet is 1 inch thick, turn once halfway through broiling.)

3 Meanwhile, cook pasta in boiling salted water according to package directions, adding the asparagus the last 2 minutes of cooking. Drain well; rinse with cold water and drain again. Return pasta mixture to saucepan. Pour remaining oil mixture over pasta; toss to coat.

4 Flake cooked salmon. Add salmon to pasta; toss gently. Cover and chill for 2 to 4 hours. To serve, add berries to pasta mixture; toss gently to mix. If desired, serve on lettuce-lined plates. Sprinkle with green onions.

1 10-ounce package light Caesar salad kit (includes lettuce, dressing, and croutons)

1 small yellow sweet pepper, cut into thin strips

1 small cucumber, quartered lengthwise and sliced

6 ounces smoked, poached, or canned salmon, skinned, boned, and broken into chunks (1 cup)

1/2 of a lemon

1 In a large bowl, combine the lettuce and dressing from the packaged salad, pepper strips, and cucumber; toss gently to coat. Add salmon and the croutons from packaged salad; toss gently to mix.

2 Divide among 3 dinner plates. Cut lemon half into 3 wedges. Before serving, squeeze juice from a lemon wedge over each salad.

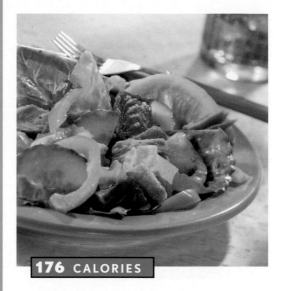

176 CALORIES

Salmon Caesar Salad

Caesar salad gets a quick makeover with the help of a salad kit and smoked salmon from your supermarket's fish counter. Keep the fixings for this five-ingredient entrée on hand for a spur-of-the-moment supper.

Start to Finish: 15 minutes
Makes: 3 servings

Nutrition Facts per serving:
176 cal., 9 g total fat (2 g sat. fat), 13 mg chol., 796 mg sodium, 12 g carbo., 3 g fiber, 14 g pro.
Daily Values:
39% vit. A, 91% vit. C, 8% calcium, 10% iron
Exchanges:
2 Vegetable, 1 1/2 Meat, 1/2 Fat

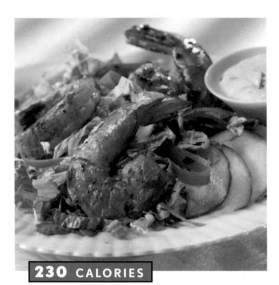

230 CALORIES

Spice-Crusted Shrimp Salad

Visit a local ethnic food market to find smoked paprika. This wonderfully earthy spice brings out the best shrimp has to offer. The versatile cilantro dressing tastes great drizzled over tossed salads as well.

Prep: 20 minutes **Cook:** 5 minutes
Makes: 4 servings

Nutrition Facts per serving:
230 cal., 7 g total fat (1 g sat. fat), 178 mg chol., 528 mg sodium, 15 g carbo., 4 g fiber, 26 g pro.
Daily Values:
120% vit. A, 57% vit. C, 19% calcium, 19% iron
Exchanges:
3 Vegetable, 3 Meat, 1 Fat

1 pound fresh or frozen peeled, deveined medium shrimp
2 cloves garlic, minced
1 teaspoon smoked paprika or paprika
1 teaspoon ground coriander
$1/4$ teaspoon salt
$1/8$ teaspoon black pepper
  Nonstick cooking spray
1 tablespoon olive oil or cooking oil
1 tablespoon lime juice
4 cups shredded napa cabbage or torn mixed salad greens
1 medium carrot, coarsely shredded
$1/2$ of a medium cucumber, halved and thinly sliced
1 recipe Cilantro-Lime Dressing
2 tablespoons snipped fresh cilantro

1 Thaw shrimp, if frozen. Rinse shrimp; pat dry. In a large bowl stir together garlic, paprika, coriander, salt, and pepper. Add shrimp. Toss to coat with spices.

2 Lightly coat a large nonstick skillet with cooking spray. Preheat skillet over medium heat. Add half of the shrimp. Cook and stir for 2 to 3 minutes or until shrimp are opaque. Remove from skillet. Add oil to skillet. Cook remaining shrimp in skillet for 2 to 3 minutes or until shrimp are opaque. Return all shrimp to skillet. Add lime juice; heat through.

3 Meanwhile, in a large bowl combine cabbage, carrot, and cucumber. Add half of the Cilantro-Lime Dressing; toss to coat. Divide cabbage mixture among 4 dinner plates. Top with shrimp. Sprinkle with snipped cilantro. Pass remaining dressing.

Cilantro-Lime Dressing: In a small bowl combine $1/3$ cup low-fat mayonnaise dressing, $1/3$ cup plain low-fat yogurt, 1 teaspoon finely shredded lime peel, 1 tablespoon lime juice, and 1 tablespoon snipped fresh cilantro. Add 1 to 2 tablespoons milk to thin dressing to desired consistency.

- **12** ounces fresh or frozen peeled, deveined medium shrimp or sea scallops
- **8** ounces dried gemelli pasta (about 2½ cups)
- **1** 6-ounce package frozen snow peas
- **1** small red sweet pepper, chopped (½ cup)
- **4** green onions, cut into 1-inch pieces
- **¼** cup rice vinegar or white wine vinegar
- **6** teaspoons salad oil
- **2** tablespoons reduced-sodium soy sauce
- **1** tablespoon honey
- **¼** teaspoon crushed red pepper
  Black sesame seeds or toasted sesame seeds (optional)

1 Thaw shrimp, if frozen. Cook pasta according to package directions, adding the peas to the pasta water the last 1 minute of cooking; drain and return to pan. Add sweet pepper and green onions to pasta mixture; toss to combine. Cover and set aside.

2 Meanwhile, for dressing, in a screw-top jar combine the vinegar, 4 teaspoons of the oil, the soy sauce, honey, and crushed red pepper. Cover and shake well to combine. Set aside.

3 Rinse shrimp; pat dry. Add remaining 2 teaspoons oil to a large nonstick skillet; add shrimp to hot oil. Cook and stir about 2 minutes or until opaque. Add the shrimp to the pasta mixture. Drizzle mixture with dressing and toss gently to coat. If desired, sprinkle with sesame seeds before serving.

Warm Shrimp and Pasta Salad

For a unique touch, go ahead and add the black sesame seeds. If they're not available, use ordinary toasted sesame seeds instead. The salad will still benefit from their crunchy texture and nutty flavor.

Start to Finish: 30 minutes

Makes: 4 servings

415 CALORIES

Nutrition Facts per serving:
415 cal., 9 g total fat (1 g sat. fat), 129 mg chol., 421 mg sodium, 54 g carbo., 4 g fiber, 27 g pro.
Daily Values:
27% vit. A, 82% vit. C, 9% calcium, 28% iron
Exchanges:
2 Vegetable, 3 Starch, 2 Meat, 1 Fat

Thai Shrimp and Snow Peas

Unsweetened coconut milk, the key ingredient in this intriguing entrée, renders this stir-fry of shrimp and snow peas irresistibly creamy and satisfying. Save time by picking up peeled and deveined shrimp at your supermarket's fish counter. Medium shrimp generally yield 36 to 40 per pound.

Start to Finish: 20 minutes

Makes: 4 servings

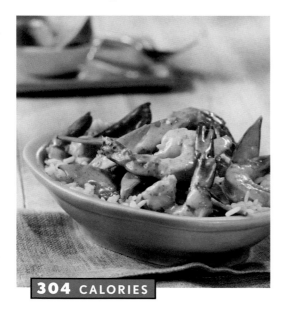

304 CALORIES

12 ounces fresh or frozen peeled, deveined medium shrimp

8 ounces snow peas, trimmed (about 2 cups)

2 teaspoons bottled minced garlic

1 teaspoon grated fresh ginger

1/8 to 1/4 teaspoon cayenne pepper

1 tablespoon cooking oil

1/2 cup purchased unsweetened coconut milk*

1/4 teaspoon salt

1/4 teaspoon finely shredded lime peel

2 cups hot cooked rice

1 Thaw shrimp, if frozen. Rinse shrimp; pat dry. Cook snow peas in a covered saucepan in a small amount of boiling salted water for 2 to 4 minutes or until crisp-tender. Drain; set aside.

2 In a large skillet cook and stir garlic, ginger, and cayenne pepper in hot oil over medium-high heat for 15 seconds. Add shrimp; cook and stir about 2 minutes or until shrimp turn opaque. Stir in coconut milk, salt, and lime peel; cook and stir until heated through. Stir in snow peas. Serve over rice.

*Note: Coconut milk can be found in the ethnic foods section of the supermarket or in Asian markets.

Nutrition Facts per serving:
304 cal., 11 g total fat (6 g sat. fat), 129 mg chol., 281 mg sodium, 30 g carbo., 2 g fiber, 21 g pro.
Daily Values:
5% vit. A, 48% vit. C, 9% calcium, 23% iron
Exchanges:
1 Vegetable, 1 1/2 Starch, 2 Meat, 1 Fat

1 pound fresh or frozen medium to large shrimp in shells

1 small red or green sweet pepper, cut into 16 pieces

¼ of a medium fresh pineapple, cut into chunks

4 green onions, cut into 1-inch pieces

¼ cup bottled barbecue sauce

1 Thaw shrimp, if frozen. Preheat broiler. Peel and devein shrimp, leaving tails intact, if desired. Rinse shrimp; pat dry. Alternately thread shrimp, sweet pepper, pineapple chunks, and green onions onto 8 metal skewers. Place skewers on the greased unheated rack of a broiler pan.

2 Broil about 4 inches from the heat for 8 to 10 minutes or until shrimp are opaque, turning skewers once and brushing with barbecue sauce halfway through broiling. (Or grill the kabobs on the rack of an uncovered grill directly over medium coals for 6 to 8 minutes or until shrimp are opaque, turning once and brushing with barbecue sauce halfway through grilling.)

134 CALORIES

Shrimp Kabobs

With broiling as well as grilling options, you can enjoy this no-fuss meal-on-a-stick no matter what the weather. For fiery palates, slather the kabobs with a spicy barbecue sauce.

Prep: 20 minutes   **Broil:** 8 minutes
Makes: 4 servings

Nutrition Facts per serving:
134 cal., 2 g total fat (0 g sat. fat), 129 mg chol., 258 mg sodium, 10 g carbo., 1 g fiber, 18 g pro.
Daily Values:
28% vit. A, 77% vit. C, 6% calcium, 13% iron
Exchanges:
½ Fruit, 2½ Meat

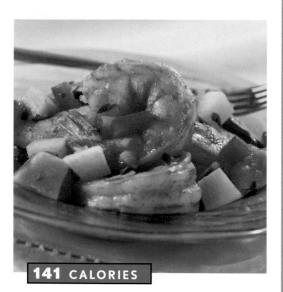

141 CALORIES

Shrimp with Papaya Salsa

Threading the shrimp onto skewers makes it easier to turn them halfway through broiling. Be sure to scoop up some of the refreshing salsa with each bite of shrimp—it's an unbeatable combo.

Prep: 40 minutes   **Broil:** 10 minutes
Makes: 6 servings

Nutrition Facts per serving:
141 cal., 4 g total fat (2 g sat. fat), 149 mg chol., 260 mg sodium, 6 g carbo., 1 g fiber, 20 g pro.
Daily Values:
16% vit. A, 60% vit. C, 6% calcium, 14% iron
Exchanges:
1/2 Fruit, 3 Meat

1 1/2   pounds fresh or frozen large shrimp in shells
1   tablespoon butter or margarine, melted
1/4   teaspoon salt
1/4   teaspoon ground cumin
1/4   teaspoon ground white pepper
1/8   teaspoon cayenne pepper
1   small papaya and/or mango, peeled, seeded, and coarsely chopped (about 1 cup)
1/3   cup chopped red sweet pepper
1/3   cup chopped, peeled jicama
2   tablespoons pineapple juice or orange juice
1   tablespoon snipped fresh cilantro or parsley
1   fresh serrano chile pepper, seeded, veins removed, and finely chopped (see note on page 76)

1 Thaw shrimp, if frozen. Peel and devein shrimp, leaving tails intact, if desired. In a small bowl stir together the melted butter, salt, cumin, white pepper, and cayenne pepper. Drizzle over shrimp, tossing to coat.

2 For salsa, in a bowl toss together papaya, sweet pepper, jicama, pineapple juice, cilantro, and chile pepper; set aside.

3 Preheat broiler. Thread shrimp onto 8 metal skewers, leaving 1/4 inch between pieces. Place skewers on the greased unheated rack of a broiler pan. Broil about 4 inches from the heat for 10 to 12 minutes or until shrimp are opaque, turning skewers once halfway through broiling. (Or arrange medium-hot coals around a drip pan in a covered grill. Test for medium heat above the pan. Place skewers on grill rack over drip pan. Cover and grill for 8 to 10 minutes or until shrimp are opaque, turning once halfway through grilling.) Serve shrimp with salsa.

- **2** cups cut-up assorted fresh vegetables from salad bar or produce department*
- **⅓** cup pitted kalamata olives or ripe olives
- **⅓** cup bottled reduced-calorie Italian salad dressing
- **12** ounces fresh or frozen peeled, deveined shrimp
- **1** 9-ounce package refrigerated fettuccine
  Nonstick cooking spray
- **½** cup crumbled goat cheese (chèvre) or feta cheese (2 ounces)
- **2** tablespoons snipped fresh basil (optional)

1 In a large bowl combine cut-up vegetables, olives, and salad dressing; toss gently to coat. Cover and store in the refrigerator 4 to 24 hours.

2 Thaw shrimp, if frozen. Rinse shrimp; pat dry. Cook fettuccine according to package directions. Drain; keep warm.

3 Meanwhile, lightly coat a large nonstick skillet with cooking spray. Cook and stir the marinated vegetables in the hot skillet over medium-high heat for 3 to 4 minutes or until crisp-tender. Remove vegetables. Add shrimp to skillet; cook and stir for 2 to 3 minutes or until shrimp turn opaque. Return vegetables to skillet; cook and stir until heated through. Serve over pasta and sprinkle with crumbled cheese. If desired, sprinkle with snipped basil.

*Note: Choose traditional vegetables such as broccoli florets, carrots, cauliflower, peas, and zucchini. Or try sugar snap peas, bite-size sticks of jicama, chopped fennel, quartered baby pattypan squash, mushrooms, or cubed sweet peppers.

Stir-Fry Shrimp and Pasta

Don't let international borders become a barrier to your good cooking. Here Chinese and Italian cuisines are tossed together with vegetables, shrimp, cheese, and, of course, pasta.

Prep: 25 minutes   **Chill:** 4 to 24 hours
Makes: 4 servings

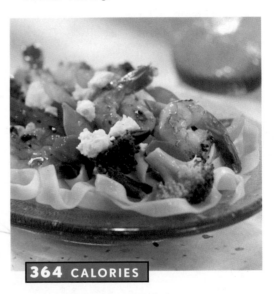

364 CALORIES

Nutrition Facts per serving:
364 cal., 10 g total fat (3 g sat. fat), 205 mg chol., 485 mg sodium, 41 g carbo., 4 g fiber, 28 g pro.
Daily Values:
114% vit. A, 91% vit. C, 10% calcium, 21% iron
Exchanges:
1 Vegetable, 2½ Starch, 2½ Meat

Zucchini with Shrimp

The Mexican flavors of jalapeño chile pepper and cilantro harmonize with the Asian accents of ginger and sesame seeds. If you like, prepare rice to serve on the side. Or give the dish a south-of-the-border twist and serve it with warmed flour tortillas.

Start to Finish: 30 minutes

Makes: 4 servings

188 CALORIES

8 ounces fresh or frozen peeled, deveined medium shrimp

5 small zucchini (about 1¼ pounds)

8 ounces fresh asparagus spears

1 fresh jalapeño chile pepper, seeded and finely chopped (see note on page 76)

1 tablespoon grated fresh ginger

2 cloves garlic, minced

2 tablespoons cooking oil

2 tablespoons snipped fresh cilantro

1 tablespoon sesame seeds, toasted

2 teaspoons toasted sesame oil

¼ teaspoon salt

¼ teaspoon black pepper

1 Thaw shrimp, if frozen. Rinse shrimp; pat dry. Halve each zucchini lengthwise. Place each half, cut side down, on a board and cut into long, thin strips. Set aside. Snap off and discard woody bases from asparagus. Cut asparagus diagonally into 1-inch pieces.

2 Place asparagus in a steamer basket over gently boiling water. Cover and steam for 2 minutes; add zucchini and steam for 2 to 3 minutes more or until vegetables are just crisp-tender (don't overcook). Drain well; keep warm.

3 Meanwhile, in a large skillet cook jalapeño, ginger, and garlic in cooking oil over medium-high heat for 30 seconds. Add shrimp. Cook over medium-high heat for 2 to 3 minutes or until shrimp are opaque, stirring often. Stir in cilantro, sesame seeds, sesame oil, salt, and black pepper. Add zucchini and asparagus to skillet; toss gently to coat. Transfer to a serving platter. If desired, sprinkle with additional cilantro and/or sesame seeds.

Nutrition Facts per serving:
188 cal., 12 g total fat (2 g sat. fat), 86 mg chol., 241 mg sodium, 7 g carbo., 3 g fiber, 15 g pro.
Daily Values:
15% vit. A, 44% vit. C, 6% calcium, 14% iron
Exchanges:
2 Vegetable, 1½ Meat, 1½ Fat

- **1** cup fresh or frozen peeled, cooked crawfish tail meat or peeled, cooked small shrimp
- **1** 15-ounce can black beans, rinsed and drained
- **³/₄** cup chopped purchased roasted red sweet peppers
- **³/₄** cup shredded Monterey Jack cheese with jalapeño peppers (3 ounces)
- **2** tablespoons snipped fresh cilantro
- **1¹/₂** teaspoons chili powder
- **¹/₄** teaspoon ground cumin
- Dash cayenne pepper
- **4** 10-inch plain or flavored flour tortillas
- Mixed salad greens (optional)
- Bottled salsa (optional)

1 Thaw crawfish, if frozen. Rinse; pat dry. For filling, in a large bowl stir together the crawfish, black beans, sweet peppers, cheese, cilantro, chili powder, cumin, and cayenne pepper.

2 Divide filling among the tortillas, spooning the mixture down the center of each tortilla. Fold in sides. Roll up tightly from bottom. Place on a foil-lined baking sheet.

3 Bake, uncovered, in a 350° oven about 20 minutes or until golden and heated through. If desired, serve on salad greens and accompany with salsa.

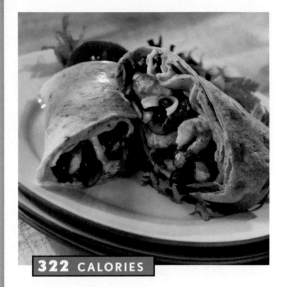

322 CALORIES

Cajun-Style Burritos

Here's a terrific example of fusion cooking: Tex-Mex burritos with a Louisiana slant. To make it a one-plate meal, serve these spicy bundles on salad greens tossed with fresh tomatoes and accompany them with a side of hot cooked rice.

Prep: 15 minutes   **Bake:** 20 minutes
Oven: 350°F   **Makes:** 4 servings

Nutrition Facts per serving:
322 cal., 11 g total fat (5 g sat. fat), 48 mg chol., 655 mg sodium, 42 g carbo., 7 g fiber, 19 g pro.
Daily Values:
13% vit. A, 136% vit. C, 26% calcium, 20% iron
Exchanges:
1 Vegetable, 2¹/₂ Starch, 1¹/₂ Meat

145 CALORIES

Lemon and Scallop Soup

The splash of lemon added just before serving ties together all the luscious flavors.

Start to Finish: 25 minutes

Makes: 4 servings (7 cups)

12 ounces fresh or frozen bay scallops

5 cups reduced-sodium chicken broth

1/2 cup dry white wine or reduced-sodium chicken broth

3 tablespoons snipped fresh cilantro

2 teaspoons finely shredded lemon peel

1/4 teaspoon black pepper

1 pound fresh asparagus spears, trimmed and cut into bite-size pieces

1 cup sliced fresh mushrooms

1/2 cup sliced green onions (4)

1 tablespoon lemon juice

1 Thaw scallops, if frozen. Rinse well and drain.

2 In a large saucepan combine the broth, wine, cilantro, lemon peel, and pepper. Bring to boiling. Add scallops, asparagus, mushrooms, and green onions. Return just to boiling; reduce heat.

3 Simmer, uncovered, for 3 to 5 minutes or until asparagus is tender and scallops are opaque. Remove from heat. Stir in the lemon juice. Serve immediately.

Nutrition Facts per serving:
145 cal., 2 g total fat (0 g sat. fat), 28 mg chol., 928 mg sodium, 7 g carbo., 2 g fiber, 21 g pro.
Daily Values:
7% vit. A, 46% vit. C, 5% calcium, 7% iron
Exchanges:
1 Vegetable, 2 1/2 Meat

8 ounces sea scallops

8 cups torn fresh spinach

2 cups sliced fresh mushrooms

1 cup shredded carrots

4 slices bacon, cut into 1/2-inch pieces

1/2 teaspoon chili powder

1/8 to 1/4 teaspoon cayenne pepper

1/4 to 1/3 cup chutney

1/4 cup water

1 to 2 teaspoons Dijon-style mustard

1 Rinse scallops; pat dry. Set scallops aside. In a large bowl toss together spinach, mushrooms, and carrots; set aside.

2 In a large nonstick skillet cook bacon over medium heat until crisp. Drain bacon, reserving 1 tablespoon drippings in skillet.

3 In a medium bowl combine chili powder and cayenne pepper; add scallops, tossing lightly to coat.

4 Cook scallops in reserved bacon drippings over medium heat for 1 to 3 minutes or until scallops turn opaque. Remove scallops from skillet; set aside. Cut up any large pieces of chutney. Add chutney, water, and mustard to skillet. Cook over medium-high heat until hot and bubbly; spoon over spinach mixture, tossing lightly to coat.

5 Divide spinach mixture among 4 plates. Top with scallops. Sprinkle with bacon.

Scallop and Spinach Salad

Give ordinary spinach salad a new lease on life by adding sea scallops and chutney to the usual lineup of ingredients. The scallops are dusted with chili powder and cayenne pepper before searing—a guaranteed wake-up call for diners.

Start to Finish: 30 minutes

Makes: 4 servings

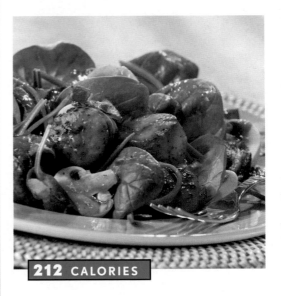

212 CALORIES

Nutrition Facts per serving:
212 cal., 9 g total fat (3 g sat. fat), 29 mg chol., 357 mg sodium, 20 g carbo., 7 g fiber, 16 g pro.
Daily Values:
255% vit. A, 46% vit. C, 8% calcium, 28% iron
Exchanges:
3 Vegetable, 1/2 Fruit, 1 1/2 Meat, 1/2 Fat

Scallops with Tropical Salsa

Mild, sweet scallops get a tropical treatment with colorful, zesty fruit salsa. The nearly fat-free scallops (3 ounces contain less than 1 gram of fat) are an obvious choice for light eating.

Start to Finish: 25 minutes

Makes: 4 servings

123 CALORIES

- 1 cup finely chopped strawberry papaya or papaya
- ½ cup seeded and finely chopped cucumber
- 1 small tomato, seeded and chopped
- 2 tablespoons snipped fresh cilantro
- 1 fresh jalapeño chile pepper, seeded and finely chopped (see note on page 76)
- 4 teaspoons lime juice
- 1 teaspoon olive oil
- 12 ounces fresh or frozen scallops
- Salt and black pepper
- 1 clove garlic, minced
- 1 teaspoon butter or margarine
- Lime wedges (optional)

1 For salsa, in a small bowl stir together the papaya, cucumber, tomato, cilantro, jalapeño pepper, lime juice, and oil. Let stand at room temperature for at least 15 minutes to allow flavors to blend.

2 Meanwhile, thaw scallops, if frozen. Rinse scallops; pat dry. Halve any large scallops. Lightly sprinkle with salt and black pepper.

3 In a large nonstick skillet cook garlic in hot butter over medium heat for 30 seconds. Add scallops. Cook and stir for 2 to 3 minutes or until scallops are opaque. Use a slotted spoon to remove scallops; drain on paper towels. Serve the scallops with salsa. If desired, serve with lime wedges.

Nutrition Facts per serving:
123 cal., 3 g total fat (1 g sat. fat), 31 mg chol., 226 mg sodium, 9 g carbo., 1 g fiber, 15 g pro.
Daily Values:
9% vit. A, 59% vit. C, 4% calcium, 3% iron
Exchanges:
½ Fruit, 2 Meat

- **1** cup chopped onion (1 large)
- **½** cup chopped red sweet pepper
- **1** clove garlic, minced
- **2** teaspoons olive oil
- **1** 14-ounce can reduced-sodium chicken broth
- **1½** cups coarsely chopped potato
- **1** fresh jalapeño chile pepper, seeded and finely chopped (see note on page 76)
- **¼** teaspoon salt
   Dash black pepper
- **8** ounces shucked oysters with their liquid
- **1** cup fresh or frozen whole kernel corn
- **1** tablespoon snipped fresh oregano
- **½** cup half-and-half or light cream
   Fresh oregano sprigs (optional)

1 In a medium saucepan cook onion, sweet pepper, and garlic in hot oil over medium heat until vegetables are tender.

2 Carefully stir chicken broth, potato, jalapeño pepper, salt, and black pepper into vegetable mixture in saucepan. Bring to boiling; reduce heat. Simmer, covered, about 10 minutes or until potato is nearly tender. Stir in undrained oysters, corn, and oregano. Return to boiling; reduce heat.

3 Cover and simmer about 5 minutes or until oysters are plump and opaque. Stir in half-and-half; heat through. If desired, garnish with oregano sprigs.

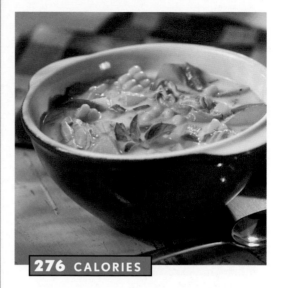

276 CALORIES

Oyster and Corn Chowder

If you think fresh oyster chowder takes a long time to make, you're in for a surprise. When you buy shucked oysters from the seafood section of the supermarket, you can cook them in just 5 minutes. This creamy jalapeño-spiced meal-in-a-bowl takes just 40 minutes more to prepare.

Start to Finish: 45 minutes
Makes: 3 servings (5 cups)

Nutrition Facts per serving:
276 cal., 10 g total fat (4 g sat. fat), 55 mg chol., 728 mg sodium, 36 g carbo., 4 g fiber, 13 g pro.
Daily Values:
36% vit. A, 107% vit. C, 10% calcium, 37% iron
Exchanges:
1 Vegetable, 2 Starch, 1 Meat, 1 Fat

122 CALORIES

Caribbean Clam Chowder

Clams team with sweet potatoes, tomatoes, chile peppers, and a hint of lime to fill this soup with exuberant island flavor. If you're purchasing fresh live clams, you can keep them in your refrigerator in an open container covered with a moist cloth up to 5 days.

Start to Finish: 35 minutes
Makes: 4 servings (6 cups)

½ pint shucked clams or one 6½-ounce can minced clams
2 cups cubed, peeled sweet potatoes (1 to 2 medium)
½ cup chopped onion (1 medium)
½ cup chopped celery (1 stalk)
¼ cup chopped red sweet pepper
2 cloves garlic, minced
1½ teaspoons snipped fresh thyme or ½ teaspoon dried thyme, crushed
1 10-ounce can chopped tomatoes and green chile peppers
1 tablespoon lime juice
1 tablespoon dark rum (optional)

1 Drain clams, reserving juice. Add enough water to clam juice to make 2½ cups liquid. If using fresh clams, chop clams; set aside.

2 In a large saucepan bring clam liquid to boiling. Stir in the sweet potatoes, onion, celery, sweet pepper, garlic, and, if using, dried thyme. Return to boiling; reduce heat. Simmer, covered, about 10 minutes or until sweet potatoes are tender.

3 Mash sweet potato mixture slightly with a potato masher. Stir in clams, undrained tomatoes, lime juice, rum (if desired), and, if using, fresh thyme. Return to boiling; reduce heat. Cook for 1 to 2 minutes more. Ladle into bowls.

Nutrition Facts per serving:
122 cal., 1 g total fat (0 g sat. fat), 12 mg chol., 322 mg sodium, 23 g carbo., 3 g fiber, 7 g pro.
Daily Values:
258% vit. A, 63% vit. C, 6% calcium, 32% iron
Exchanges:
1 Vegetable, 1 Starch, ½ Meat

1 cup dried small shell macaroni or small bow ties (4 ounces)

4 cups hot-style vegetable juice, chilled

1 tablespoon lime juice or lemon juice

6 ounces cooked crabmeat, flaked, or chopped cooked chicken (about 1¼ cups)

2 medium nectarines, chopped (1⅓ cups)

2 roma tomatoes, chopped (about 1 cup)

¼ cup chopped, seeded cucumber

2 tablespoons snipped fresh basil

Lime slices (optional)

Cucumber sticks (optional)

1 Cook pasta according to package directions; drain. Rinse with cold water; drain again.

2 Meanwhile, in a large bowl stir together vegetable juice and lime juice. Stir in pasta, crabmeat, nectarines, tomatoes, cucumber, and basil. Ladle soup into glasses or bowls. If desired, garnish with lime slices and cucumber sticks.

Crab and Pasta Gazpacho

Gazpacho—the chilled tomato and vegetable soup—was born in Spain and reinvented in California where it's a favorite on summer menus. This fast, fresh version with sweet crab, juicy nectarines, and fragrant basil couldn't come from anywhere else.

Start to Finish: 25 minutes

Makes: 6 servings (8 cups)

157 CALORIES

Nutrition Facts per serving:
157 cal., 1 g total fat (0 g sat. fat), 28 mg chol., 603 mg sodium, 27 g carbo., 2 g fiber, 10 g pro.
Daily Values:
38% vit. A, 57% vit. C, 5% calcium, 8% iron
Exchanges:
2 Vegetable, ½ Fruit, ½ Starch, 1 Meat

Chipotle-Topped Crab Cakes

The smoky flavor of chipotle chile peppers provides the gusto to make these subtly seasoned crab cakes sing. To tame a too-spicy sauce, remove the seeds from the pepper before adding to mixture.

Start to Finish: 30 minutes

Makes: 4 servings

255 CALORIES

1 egg, slightly beaten
$3/4$ cup soft bread crumbs (1 slice)
2 tablespoons sliced green onion (1)
2 tablespoons low-fat mayonnaise dressing
1 tablespoon milk
$1/2$ teaspoon lemon-pepper seasoning
2 $6^1/2$-ounce cans crabmeat, drained, flaked, and cartilage removed
Nonstick cooking spray
4 cups torn mixed salad greens
1 recipe Chipotle Sauce
Lime wedges

1 In a large bowl stir together egg, bread crumbs, green onion, mayonnaise dressing, milk, and lemon-pepper seasoning. Add crabmeat; mix well. Shape into eight $2^1/2$-inch patties.

2 Lightly coat a large nonstick skillet with cooking spray. Heat over medium heat. Add patties. Cook for 3 to 4 minutes on each side or until browned. Serve over greens with Chipotle Sauce. Garnish with lime wedges.

Chipotle Sauce: In a bowl combine $1/3$ cup low-fat mayonnaise dressing; $1/4$ cup light dairy sour cream; 2 tablespoons milk; 2 teaspoons snipped fresh cilantro; 1 canned chipotle pepper in adobo sauce, drained and finely chopped (see note on page 76); and dash salt.

Nutrition Facts per serving:
255 cal., 13 g total fat (3 g sat. fat), 144 mg chol., 739 mg sodium, 12 g carbo., 1 g fiber, 22 g pro.
Daily Values:
9% vit. A, 10% vit. C, 16% calcium, 9% iron
Exchanges:
2 Vegetable, 3 Meat, 1 Fat

On the divider: **Blackened Catfish** (see recipe, page 400)

4 **beef tenderloin steaks, cut 1 inch thick (about 1 pound total)**

3 **tablespoons cognac or brandy**

1/2 **teaspoon coarsely ground black pepper**

1 **cup sliced fresh mushrooms**

1 **tablespoon finely chopped shallot**

1 **tablespoon butter or margarine**

1/2 **cup beef broth**

1/4 **cup fat-free half-and-half**

2 **tablespoons Dijon-style mustard**

1 **tablespoon all-purpose flour**

1 Trim fat from steaks. Place in a shallow dish. Pour 2 tablespoons of the cognac over the steaks. Cover and let stand at room temperature for 15 minutes, turning once. Drain steaks, discarding cognac in dish. Sprinkle pepper over both sides of each steak.

2 Place steaks on the rack of an uncovered grill directly over medium coals. Grill to desired doneness, turning once. (Allow 11 to 15 minutes for medium-rare doneness [145°F] or 14 to 18 minutes for medium doneness [160°F].)

3 Meanwhile, in a small saucepan cook mushrooms and shallot in butter for 3 to 4 minutes or until tender. Stir in beef broth and remaining 1 tablespoon cognac. Bring to boiling; reduce heat. Boil gently, uncovered, for 5 minutes.

4 In a small bowl stir together the half-and-half, mustard, and flour until smooth. Stir into broth mixture. Cook and stir until thickened and bubbly. Cook and stir for 1 minute more. Serve sauce over steaks.

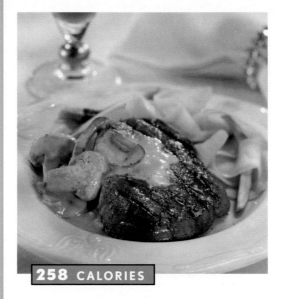

258 CALORIES

Filet Mignon with Cognac Sauce

Brandy cream sauce usually is taboo if you're dieting, unless it's this one. Based on fat-free half-and-half, this recipe lets you enjoy traditional flavor and richness without giving fat a second thought. Don't stop at steak—this versatile sauce is equally tasty over grilled pork or chicken.

Prep: 10 minutes   **Stand:** 15 minutes
Grill: 11 minutes   **Makes:** 4 servings

Nutrition Facts per serving:
258 cal., 11 g total fat (5 g sat. fat), 65 mg chol., 375 mg sodium, 4 g carbo., 0 g fiber, 25 g pro.
Daily Values:
3% vit. A, 2% calcium, 19% iron
Exchanges:
1 Vegetable, 3 1/2 Meat

Coffee-Crusted Sirloin

Thanks to innovative thinking, this sirloin steak wears a coat of ground coffee and brown sugar. It's the perfect complement to the balsamic vinegar-spiced sauce. If you feel like trying something new, use the coffee crust on pork chops.

Prep: 15 minutes   **Stand:** 15 minutes

Grill: 14 minutes   **Makes:** 4 servings

1 **pound boneless beef top sirloin steak, cut 1 inch thick**

¼ **cup balsamic vinegar**

2 **teaspoons finely ground coffee beans**

1 **tablespoon brown sugar**

¼ **teaspoon salt**

1 **small shallot, finely chopped (2 teaspoons)**

1 **tablespoon butter or margarine**

2 **teaspoons all-purpose flour**

½ **cup reduced-sodium chicken broth**

¼ **cup half-and-half or light cream**

⅛ **teaspoon black pepper**

1 Trim fat from steak. Place steak in a shallow dish. Pour 2 tablespoons of the balsamic vinegar over steak. Cover and let stand at room temperature for 15 minutes, turning once. In a small bowl combine the ground coffee beans, brown sugar, and salt. Drain steak, discarding vinegar in dish. Press coffee mixture into both sides of the steak.

2 Place steak on the rack of an uncovered grill directly over medium coals. Grill to desired doneness, turning once. (Allow 14 to 18 minutes for medium-rare doneness [145°F] or 18 to 22 minutes for medium doneness [160°F].)

3 Meanwhile, in a small saucepan cook shallot in hot butter for 2 to 3 minutes or until tender. Stir in flour. Add chicken broth. Cook and stir until thickened and bubbly. Cook and stir for 1 minute more. Remove from heat. Stir in half-and-half and pepper. Stir in the remaining 2 tablespoons balsamic vinegar.

4 To serve, slice steak. Serve sauce with steak.

Nutrition Facts per serving:
213 cal., 9 g total fat (4 g sat. fat), 83 mg chol., 319 mg sodium, 7 g carbo., 0 g fiber, 25 g pro.
Daily Values:
4% vit. A, 1% vit. C, 3% calcium, 17% iron
Exchanges:
½ Milk, 3 Meat

12 ounces boneless beef sirloin,
   cut 1 inch thick

2 tablespoons red wine vinegar

1 tablespoon cooking oil

1 tablespoon Jamaican jerk seasoning

2 ripe plantains, peeled and cut into
   1-inch chunks

1 medium red onion, cut into wedges

   Lime wedges

   Lemon leaves (optional)

1 Trim fat from meat. Cut into 1-inch
pieces. In a small bowl stir together red
wine vinegar, oil, and jerk seasoning.
Toss meat cubes with half of the vinegar
mixture. On long metal skewers,
alternately thread beef, plantain chunks,
and onion wedges, leaving a ¼-inch
space between pieces. Brush plantains
and onion wedges with remaining
vinegar mixture.

2 Place skewers on the rack of an uncovered
grill directly over medium coals. Grill
for 12 to 15 minutes or until desired
doneness, turning occasionally. Serve
with lime wedges. If desired, garnish
lemon leaves.

Jerk Beef and Plantain Kabobs

Jerk seasoning—that island combination
of garlic, thyme, spices, and chile peppers—
lends this dish a tantalizing bite. To keep
the pieces of beef, onion, and plantain
from swiveling as you turn the kabobs
on the grill, thread the pieces onto two
side-by-side skewers instead of one.

Prep: 25 minutes   **Grill:** 12 minutes
Makes: 4 servings

235 CALORIES

Nutrition Facts per serving:
235 cal., 7 g total fat (2 g sat. fat), 52 mg chol.,
271 mg sodium, 26 g carbo., 2 g fiber, 19 g pro.
Daily Values:
17% vit. A, 26% vit. C, 1% calcium, 15% iron
Exchanges:
1½ Fruit, 2½ Meat

Steak with Onion Relish

The secret to the most tender steak slices is to score the flank steak before grilling and slice it across the grain afterward.

Prep: 30 minutes   **Marinate:** 2 to 24 hours
Grill: 17 minutes   **Makes:** 8 servings

276 CALORIES

Nutrition Facts per serving:
276 cal, 11 g total fat (3 g sat. fat), 35 mg chol.,
384 mg sodium, 27 g carbo., 1 g fiber, 17 g pro.
Daily Values:
16% vit. A, 42% vit. C, 5% calcium, 15% iron
Exchanges:
1 Vegetable, 1½ Starch, 1½ Meat, ½ Fat

1 1¼- to 1½-pound beef flank steak
½ cup balsamic vinegar
2 tablespoons olive oil
2 tablespoons honey
1 tablespoon snipped fresh oregano
1 tablespoon snipped fresh sage
2 teaspoons beef bouillon granules
1 teaspoon freshly ground black pepper
2 sweet onions (such as Vidalia, Maui, Texas Sweet, or Walla Walla), halved lengthwise and thinly sliced
1 medium red or yellow sweet pepper, cut into thin bite-size strips
8 7- to 8-inch flour tortillas, warmed*

1 Trim fat from steak. Score both sides of steak in a diamond pattern by making shallow diagonal cuts at 1-inch intervals. Place steak in a plastic bag set in a shallow dish. For marinade, in a small bowl combine balsamic vinegar, olive oil, honey, oregano, sage, bouillon granules, and black pepper. Pour half of the marinade over the steak; seal bag. Set remaining marinade aside. Marinate in refrigerator for at least 2 hours or up to 24 hours, turning bag occasionally.

2 In a large nonstick skillet combine onions and reserved marinade. Bring to boiling; reduce heat to medium-low. Simmer, covered, for 13 to 15 minutes or until onions are tender, stirring occasionally. Add sweet pepper strips; cook, uncovered, over medium-high heat for 4 to 5 minutes or until pepper strips are crisp-tender, stirring constantly.

3 Drain steak, reserving marinade. Place steak on the rack of an uncovered grill directly over medium coals. Grill for 17 to 21 minutes or until medium doneness (160°F), turning and brushing once with reserved marinade halfway through grilling. Discard remaining marinade. Slice steak diagonally across the grain. Serve with onions mixture in warm tortillas.

*Note: To warm tortillas, wrap in foil and place alongside steak on grill; heat about 10 minutes, turning occasionally.

1 1½-pound beef flank steak
⅔ cup pineapple juice
⅓ cup mango chutney
1 tablespoon rum
1 tablespoon rice vinegar
1 clove garlic, minced
¼ teaspoon salt
¼ cup golden raisins
1 teaspoon cornstarch
Mango slices (optional)
Fresh parsley sprigs (optional)

1 Trim fat from steak. Score both sides of steak in a diamond pattern by making shallow diagonal cuts at 1-inch intervals. Place steak in a plastic bag set in a shallow dish. For marinade, in a small bowl stir together pineapple juice, chutney, rum, rice vinegar, garlic, and salt. Pour over steak; seal bag. Marinate in the refrigerator for at least 2 hours or up to 24 hours, turning bag occasionally.

2 Drain steak, reserving marinade. Place steak on the rack of an uncovered grill directly over medium coals. Grill for 17 to 21 minutes or until medium doneness (160°F), turning once.

3 Meanwhile, for sauce, pour reserved marinade into a small saucepan; stir in raisins and cornstarch. Cook and stir until thickened and bubbly; cook for 2 minutes more. To serve, thinly slice steak diagonally across the grain. Serve sauce with steak. If desired, garnish with mango slices and parsley.

269 CALORIES

Steak with Rum-Chutney Sauce

Marinating the flank steak a full 24 hours ensures a flavorful, tender dining experience. While the steak grills, there's enough time to whip up a side of rice or pasta, and to steam your favorite veggies.

Prep: 20 minutes   **Marinate:** 2 to 24 hours
Grill: 17 minutes   **Makes:** 6 servings

Nutrition Facts per serving:
269 cal., 8 g total fat (3 g sat. fat), 46 mg chol., 173 mg sodium, 22 g carbo., 1 g fiber, 25 g pro.
Daily Values:
12% vit. A, 17% vit. C, 2% calcium, 12% iron
Exchanges:
1½ Fruit, 3½ Meat

225 CALORIES

Rosemary Pork with Onion Jam

Pork and rosemary are a combination that goes way back. Team them with this fig and bourbon-laced onion jam, and they take on extraordinary dimensions.

Prep: 15 minutes   **Grill:** 40 minutes

Makes: 4 servings

1 12- to 16-ounce pork tenderloin
1 teaspoon olive oil
1 tablespoon snipped fresh rosemary
1/2 teaspoon coarsely ground black pepper
1/4 teaspoon salt
1 tablespoon olive oil
4 cups thinly sliced sweet onions (such as Vidalia, Maui, Texas Sweet, or Walla Walla), separated into rings
1/4 cup water
1 tablespoon brown sugar
1 tablespoon bourbon
1/4 cup snipped dried golden figs (Calimyrna)
   Fresh rosemary sprigs (optional)

1 Trim fat from pork; brush pork on all sides with the 1 teaspoon olive oil. In a small bowl stir together the snipped rosemary, the pepper, and salt. Sprinkle evenly over all sides of pork; rub in with your fingers.

2 In a grill with a cover arrange hot coals around a drip pan. Test for medium-hot heat above the pan. Place pork on the grill rack directly over the drip pan. Cover and grill for 40 to 50 minutes or until pork juices run clear (160°F).

3 Meanwhile, in a large skillet heat the 1 tablespoon oil. Add onions. Cook, covered, over medium-low heat for 13 to 15 minutes or until onions are very tender. Stir in the water, brown sugar, and bourbon. Stir in figs. Cook and stir over medium-high heat for 8 to 10 minutes or until water evaporates and onions are golden.

4 To serve, thinly slice pork. Spoon onions over pork. If desired, garnish with rosemary sprigs.

Nutrition Facts per serving:
225 cal., 7 g total fat (2 g sat. fat), 55 mg chol., 185 mg sodium, 19 g carbo., 3 g fiber, 19 g pro.
Daily Values:
1% vit. A, 9% vit. C, 4% calcium, 9% iron
Exchanges:
2 Vegetable, 1/2 Fruit, 2 Meat, 1/2 Fat

1 **12-ounce pork tenderloin**

⅓ **cup peach nectar**

3 **tablespoons bottled light teriyaki sauce**

2 **tablespoons snipped fresh rosemary or 2 teaspoons dried rosemary, crushed**

1 **tablespoon olive oil**

   Fresh peach slices (optional)

   Fresh rosemary sprigs (optional)

1 Trim fat from pork. Place pork in a plastic bag set in a shallow dish. For marinade, in a small bowl combine peach nectar, teriyaki sauce, the snipped or dried rosemary, and the olive oil. Pour over pork; seal bag. Marinate in refrigerator for at least 4 hours or up to 24 hours, turning bag occasionally.

2 Drain pork, discarding marinade. In a grill with a cover arrange hot coals around a drip pan. Test for medium-hot heat above the pan. Place pork on the grill rack directly over the drip pan. Cover and grill for 40 to 50 minutes or until pork juices run clear (160°F). Slice pork. If desired, garnish with peach slices and rosemary sprigs.

Peachy Pork Tenderloin

Fruit and pork have been a dynamic twosome for centuries because of the way fruit naturally enhances the taste of the meat. This simple five-ingredient recipe showcases the fusing of these two flavors.

Prep: 10 minutes   **Marinate:** 4 to 24 hours
Grill: 40 minutes   **Makes:** 4 servings

132 CALORIES

Nutrition Facts per serving:
132 cal., 3 g total fat (1 g sat. fat), 50 mg chol., 154 mg sodium, 3 g carbo., 0 g fiber, 21 g pro.
Daily Values:
4% vit. C, 1% calcium, 6% iron
Exchanges:
3 Meat

Pork with Pesto Cream Sauce

The traditional fines herbes is a mix of chervil, chives, parsley, and tarragon, but today it may include any number of herb favorites, depending on the brand you buy. Here the fines herbes adds a note of sophistication to the mild flavor of the pork tenderloin, while pesto gives the cream sauce zing.

Prep: 20 minutes **Grill:** 40 minutes
Makes: 4 servings

231 CALORIES

1 12-ounce pork tenderloin
1 teaspoon olive oil
1½ teaspoons fines herbes or dried basil, crushed
¼ teaspoon salt
1 tablespoon butter or margarine
4 teaspoons all-purpose flour
¼ teaspoon ground white pepper
1 cup reduced-fat milk
2 tablespoons purchased pesto
Hot cooked pasta (optional)

1 Trim fat from pork. Brush pork with olive oil. Sprinkle pork with fines herbes or basil and salt; rub in with your fingers.

2 In a grill with a cover arrange hot coals around a drip pan. Test for medium-hot heat above pan. Place pork on grill rack over the drip pan. Cover and grill for 40 to 50 minutes or until pork juices run clear (160°F).

3 Meanwhile, in a small saucepan melt butter over medium heat. Stir in flour and white pepper. Add milk all at once. Cook and stir until slightly thickened and bubbly. Cook and stir for 1 minute more. Remove from heat. Stir in pesto.

4 To serve, slice pork. If desired, serve over hot cooked pasta. Spoon sauce over pork.

Nutrition Facts per serving:
231 cal., 13 g total fat (4 g sat. fat), 69 mg chol., 299 mg sodium, 6 g carbo., 0 g fiber, 21 g pro.
Daily Values:
6% vit. A, 2% vit. C, 9% calcium, 8% iron
Exchanges:
½ Starch, 3 Meat, ½ Fat

1　**12-ounce pork tenderloin**

$1/2$　**cup unsweetened pineapple juice**

3　**tablespoons reduced-sodium soy sauce**

3　**tablespoons vinegar**

2　**cloves garlic, minced**

$1/2$　**teaspoon cayenne pepper**

1　**tablespoon olive oil**

2　**medium red and/or yellow sweet peppers, cut into 1-inch strips**

8　$1/2$**-inch slices fresh or canned pineapple**

8　**to 16 romaine leaves**

1 Trim fat from pork. Place pork in a plastic bag set in a shallow dish. For marinade, in a screw-top jar combine pineapple juice, soy sauce, vinegar, garlic, and cayenne pepper. Cover and shake well. Pour $1/2$ cup of the marinade over pork; seal bag. Marinate in refrigerator for at least 4 hours or up to 24 hours, turning bag occasionally.

2 Meanwhile, for dressing, combine the remaining marinade with the olive oil. Cover and chill until serving time.

3 Drain pork, discarding marinade. In a grill with a cover arrange hot coals around a drip pan. Test for medium-hot heat above pan. Place pork on grill rack directly over drip pan. Cover and grill for 40 to 50 minutes or until pork juices run clear (160°F). For the last 10 minutes of grilling, place sweet peppers and pineapple on the grill rack over the coals. Grill until sweet peppers are tender and pineapple is heated through, turning occasionally.

4 To serve, slice pork. Line 4 salad plates with romaine. Arrange pork, sweet peppers, and pineapple on the romaine. Shake dressing; drizzle each serving with about 2 tablespoons of the dressing.

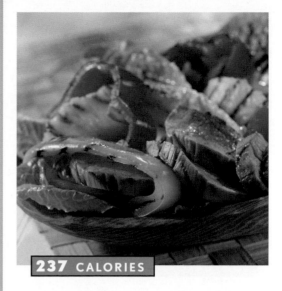

237 CALORIES

Caribbean Pork Salad

It's easy to pretend you're on a tropical island when you taste this pineapple-kissed grilled salad. Serve it with a fruity rum drink or iced tea to complete the illusion.

Prep: 15 minutes　**Marinate:** 4 to 24 hours
Grill: 40 minutes　**Makes:** 4 servings

Nutrition Facts per serving:
237 cal., 5 g total fat (1 g sat. fat), 50 mg chol., 338 mg sodium, 25 g carbo., 3 g fiber, 22 g pro.
Daily Values:
95% vit. A, 208% vit. C, 4% calcium, 14% iron
Exchanges:
1 Vegetable, $1/2$ Fruit, $2/2$ Meat

163 CALORIES

Apple-Smoked Pork Loin

This recipe relies on apple wood chips or chunks to infuse this herb-rubbed pork roast with a sweet, smoky flavor. Look for a variety of wood chips or chunks—including orange, cherry, hickory, maple, mesquite, and pecan—where grilling supplies are sold.

Prep: 10 minutes   **Soak:** 1 hour
Grill: 1 hour   **Stand:** 15 minutes
Makes: 8 servings

Nutrition Facts per serving:
163 cal., 6 g total fat (2 g sat. fat), 66 mg chol., 193 mg sodium, 1 g carbo., 0 g fiber, 24 g pro.
Daily Values:
1% vit. A, 2% vit. C, 3% calcium, 7% iron
Exchanges:
3½ Meat

3   cups apple wood or orange wood chips or 6 to 8 apple wood or orange wood chunks
1   2- to 2½-pound boneless pork top loin pork roast (single loin)
2   teaspoons dried oregano, crushed
½   teaspoon salt
½   teaspoon coarsely ground black pepper
4   cloves garlic, minced
    Fresh apple slices (optional)
    Fresh oregano sprigs (optional)

1   At least 1 hour before cooking, soak wood chips or chunks in enough water to cover.

2   Meanwhile, trim fat from roast. Place roast in a shallow dish. In a small bowl stir together the dried oregano, salt, pepper, and garlic. Sprinkle evenly over all sides of roast; rub in with your fingers.

3   Drain wood chips. In a grill with a cover arrange medium coals around a drip pan. Test for medium-low heat above pan. Sprinkle half of the drained wood chips over the coals.

4   Place roast on grill rack directly over drip pan. Cover and grill for 1 to 1¼ hours or until internal temperature registers 155°F on an instant-read thermometer. Add more coals and wood chips as needed during grilling.

5   Remove roast from grill. Cover with foil; let stand for 15 minutes. The temperature of the meat will rise 5°F during standing.

6   To serve, slice pork. If desired, garnish with apple slices and oregano sprigs.

½ cup bottled chili sauce

2 tablespoons molasses

2 tablespoons cider vinegar

1 teaspoon chili powder

4 boneless pork loin chops, cut ³/₄ to 1 inch thick (about 1¹/₄ pounds total)

1 teaspoon dried basil, crushed

½ teaspoon paprika

¼ teaspoon salt

¼ teaspoon onion powder

¼ teaspoon cayenne pepper

Purchased coleslaw (optional)

1 In a small saucepan stir together chili sauce, molasses, vinegar, and chili powder. Bring to boiling; reduce heat. Simmer, uncovered, for 3 minutes. Remove from heat.

2 Trim fat from chops. In a small bowl stir together basil, paprika, salt, onion powder, and cayenne pepper. Sprinkle evenly over both sides of each chop; rub in with your fingers.

3 Place chops on the rack of an uncovered grill directly over medium coals. Grill for 12 to 15 minutes or until pork juices run clear (160°F), turning once and brushing with chili sauce mixture during the last 5 minutes of grilling. If desired, serve with coleslaw.

Memphis-Style Pork Chops

What's considered "good" barbecue varies with the part of the country you're in. This Southern-style recipe opts out of catsup in favor of chili sauce and includes molasses and cider vinegar.

Prep: 15 minutes **Grill:** 12 minutes

Makes: 4 servings

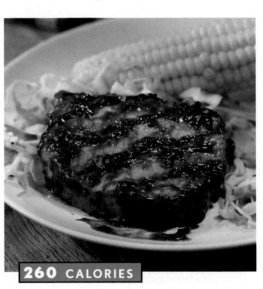

260 CALORIES

Nutrition Facts per serving:
260 cal., 7 g total fat (3 g sat. fat), 83 mg chol., 623 mg sodium, 16 g carbo., 2 g fiber, 31 g pro.
Daily Values:
13% vit. A, 10% vit. C, 5% calcium, 11% iron
Exchanges:
1 Starch, 4 Meat

Lamb with Spicy Apricot Sauce

Ginger-rubbed lamb and a sweet-hot apricot brush-on add up to a first-rate entrée that's not for timid taste buds. Present these can't-miss chops with a mixture of couscous and peas.

Prep: 15 minutes   **Grill:** 12 minutes
Makes: 4 servings

188 CALORIES

4	**lamb loin chops, cut 1 inch thick**
¼	**cup apricot spreadable fruit**
2	**tablespoons white wine vinegar**
2	**teaspoons Dijon-style mustard**
½	**teaspoon ground turmeric**
⅛	**teaspoon cayenne pepper**
1	**clove garlic, minced**
1	**tablespoon grated fresh ginger**
1	**teaspoon olive oil**
¼	**teaspoon salt**
	Hot cooked couscous (optional)
	Hot cooked peas (optional)

1 Trim fat from chops; set chops aside. In a small bowl stir together apricot spreadable fruit, white wine vinegar, mustard, turmeric, cayenne pepper, and garlic. Set aside.

2 In another small bowl stir together ginger, olive oil, and salt; rub on both sides of each chop.

3 Place chops on the rack of an uncovered grill directly over medium coals. Grill to desired doneness, turning once and brushing with apricot mixture during the last 5 minutes of grilling. (Allow 12 to 14 minutes for medium-rare doneness [145°F] or 15 to 17 minutes for medium doneness [160°F].) Discard any remaining apricot mixture.

4 If desired, toss together couscous and peas; serve with chops.

Nutrition Facts per serving:
188 cal., 6 g total fat (2 g sat. fat), 60 mg chol., 257 mg sodium, 13 g carbo., 0 g fiber, 19 g pro.
Daily Values:
1% vit. C, 1% calcium, 10% iron
Exchanges:
1 Fruit, 2½ Meat

8 **lamb rib chops, cut 1 inch thick**
¼ **teaspoon salt**
¼ **teaspoon black pepper**
½ **cup balsamic vinegar**
¼ **cup honey**
 4 **teaspoons reduced-sodium soy sauce**
    Fresh rosemary sprigs (optional)

1 Trim fat from chops. Season chops with salt and pepper. Place chops in a plastic bag set in a shallow dish. In a small bowl stir together balsamic vinegar, honey, and soy sauce. Pour over chops; seal the bag. Marinate in the refrigerator for at least 4 hours or up to 24 hours, turning the bag occasionally.

2 Drain lamb, reserving marinade. Pour marinade into a heavy small saucepan. Bring to boiling; reduce heat. Boil gently, uncovered, about 12 minutes or until reduced to about ⅓ cup; set aside. (Glaze will thicken as it cools. If it gets too thick to brush, reheat over low heat.)

3 Place chops on the rack of an uncovered grill directly over medium coals. Grill to desired doneness, turning and brushing once with glaze halfway through grilling. (Allow 12 to 14 minutes for medium-rare doneness [145°F] or 15 to 17 minutes for medium doneness [160°F].) Discard any remaining glaze. If desired, garnish with rosemary sprigs.

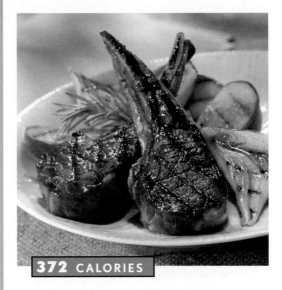

372 CALORIES

Balsamic-Glazed Lamb Chops

Tender lamb chops take on an elegant shine when marinated with a tart-sweet glaze. Once again, a few simple ingredients do a job that's dressed to impress.

Prep: 10 minutes   **Marinate:** 4 to 24 hours
Cook: 12 minutes   **Grill:** 12 minutes
Makes: 4 servings

Nutrition Facts per serving:
372 cal., 13 g total fat (5 g sat. fat), 111 mg chol., 461 mg sodium, 27 g carbo., 0 g fiber, 35 g pro.
Daily Values:
1% vit. C, 3% calcium, 16% iron
Exchanges:
1½ Fruit, 5 Meat

239 CALORIES

Minted Lamb Chops

Celebrate the arrival of the grilling season with the traditional springtime treat of lamb. An aromatic mint-infused marinade is just what the chef ordered.

Prep: 15 minutes   **Marinate:** 4 to 24 hours
Grill: 12 minutes   **Makes:** 4 servings

Nutrition Facts per serving:
239 cal., 14 g total fat (4 g sat. fat), 80 mg chol., 368 mg sodium, 2 g carbo., 0 g fiber, 25 g pro.
Daily Values:
11% vit. A, 16% vit. C, 3% calcium, 20% iron
Exchanges:
3¹/₂ Meat, ¹/₂ Fat

8	lamb rib chops, cut 1 inch thick
¹/₄	cup snipped fresh mint
¹/₄	cup lemon juice
2	tablespoons cooking oil
2	tablespoons water
1	tablespoon grated fresh ginger
1¹/₂	teaspoons paprika
1	teaspoon ground cumin
¹/₂	teaspoon salt
¹/₈	teaspoon cayenne pepper
1	large clove garlic, minced
2	tablespoons small fresh mint leaves
	Hot cooked rice pilaf (optional)
	Fresh mint sprigs (optional)

1 Trim fat from chops. Place chops in a plastic bag set in a shallow dish. For marinade, in a small bowl combine the snipped mint, lemon juice, oil, water, ginger, paprika, cumin, salt, cayenne pepper, and garlic. Pour over chops; seal bag. Marinate in the refrigerator for at least 4 hours or up to 24 hours, turning bag occasionally.

2 Drain chops, discarding marinade. Place chops on the rack of an uncovered grill directly over medium coals. Grill to desired doneness, turning once. (Allow 12 to 14 minutes for medium-rare doneness [145°F] or 15 to 17 minutes for medium doneness [160°F].)

3 Transfer chops to a serving platter; sprinkle with the mint leaves. If desired, serve with rice pilaf and garnish with mint sprigs.

- **4** skinless, boneless chicken breast halves (1¼ to 1½ pounds total)
- **1** tablespoon lemon juice
- **1** tablespoon olive oil
- **1** tablespoon snipped fresh oregano or 1 teaspoon dried oregano, crushed
- **¼** teaspoon black pepper
- **2** cloves garlic, minced
- **3** medium cucumbers, seeded and cut into ½-inch pieces
- **2** medium tomatoes, cut into ½-inch pieces
- **½** cup chopped red onion (1 medium)

  Mixed salad greens (optional)
- **⅓** cup bottled reduced-calorie creamy cucumber salad dressing
- **½** cup crumbled feta cheese
- **¼** cup chopped pitted kalamata olives or ripe olives

1 Place chicken in a plastic bag set in a shallow dish. For marinade, in a small bowl combine lemon juice, oil, oregano, pepper, and garlic. Pour over chicken; seal bag. Marinate in the refrigerator for at least 4 hours or up to 24 hours, turning bag occasionally.

2 Meanwhile, in a medium bowl toss together cucumbers, tomatoes, and red onion.

3 Drain chicken, discarding marinade. Place chicken on the rack of an uncovered grill directly over medium coals. Grill for 12 to 15 minutes or until tender and no longer pink (170°F), turning once.

4 Transfer chicken to a cutting board; cut into bite-size pieces. Toss with cucumber mixture. If desired, serve on greens. Drizzle salad dressing over. Sprinkle with feta cheese and olives.

Grilled Greek Chicken Salad

This Greek-inspired dish features lemon- and oregano-marinated grilled chicken tossed with cucumbers, feta cheese, tomatoes, kalamata olives, and onion.

Prep: 30 minutes **Marinate:** 4 to 24 hours
Grill: 12 minutes **Makes:** 4 servings

328 CALORIES

Nutrition Facts per serving:
328 cal., 13 g total fat (3 g sat. fat), 95 mg chol., 629 mg sodium, 14 g carbo., 3 g fiber, 37 g pro.
Daily Values:
19% vit. A, 48% vit. C, 13% calcium, 11% iron
Exchanges:
3 Vegetable, 4½ Meat

Chicken with Fruit Salsa

Juicy chicken breasts take on a Southwestern flair with a salsa that bursts with flavor. The chipotle peppers—actually smoked jalapeño chile peppers—are not for the faint of heart. Use the lower range for a milder salsa.

Prep: 20 minutes   **Stand:** 30 minutes
Grill: 12 minutes   **Makes:** 4 servings

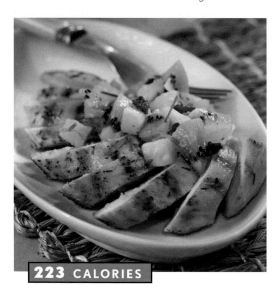

223 CALORIES

3/4 cup finely chopped pineapple
3/4 cup chopped peeled kiwifruit
1 to 2 canned chipotle peppers in adobo sauce, drained, seeded, and finely chopped
2 tablespoons snipped fresh chives
1 tablespoon honey
1 teaspoon finely shredded lime peel or lemon peel
2 teaspoons lime juice or lemon juice
4 skinless, boneless chicken breast halves (1¼ to 1½ pounds total)
1 teaspoon cooking oil
1 teaspoon dried thyme, crushed
¼ teaspoon salt
¼ teaspoon black pepper

1 For salsa, in a medium bowl stir together pineapple, kiwifruit, chipotle peppers, chives, honey, lime peel, and lime juice. Let stand at room temperature for 30 minutes.

2 Meanwhile, lightly brush chicken with cooking oil. In a small bowl stir together thyme, salt, and black pepper. Sprinkle evenly over both sides of each chicken breast half; rub in with your fingers.

3 Place chicken on the lightly greased rack of an uncovered grill directly over medium coals. Grill for 12 to 15 minutes or until chicken is tender and no longer pink (170°F), turning once. (Or preheat broiler. Place chicken on the unheated rack of broiler pan. Broil 4 to 5 inches from heat for 12 to 15 minutes or until chicken is tender and no longer pink, turning once.) Serve chicken with salsa.

Nutrition Facts per serving:
223 cal., 3 g total fat (1 g sat. fat), 82 mg chol., 239 mg sodium, 14 g carbo., 2 g fiber, 33 g pro.
Daily Values:
5% vit. A, 68% vit. C, 3% calcium, 8% iron
Exchanges:
1 Fruit, 4½ Meat

- ¹/₂ **cup fresh mint leaves**
- 1 **tablespoon lemon juice**
- 1 **tablespoon olive oil**
- 1 **tablespoon reduced-sodium soy sauce**
- 1 **teaspoon chili powder**
- ¹/₄ **teaspoon black pepper**
- 4 **cloves garlic**
- 4 **skinless, boneless chicken breast halves (1¹/₄ to 1¹/₂ pounds total)**
- **Hot cooked couscous (optional)**
- **Grilled whole green onions (optional)**
- **Fresh mint sprigs (optional)**

1 In a blender container combine the mint leaves, the lemon juice, oil, soy sauce, chili powder, pepper, and garlic. Cover and blend until smooth.

2 Place chicken in a plastic bag set in a shallow dish. Pour mint mixture over chicken; seal bag. Marinate chicken in refrigerator for at least 4 hours or up to 24 hours.

3 Place chicken on the rack of an uncovered grill directly over medium coals. Grill for 12 to 15 minutes or until tender and no longer pink (170°F), turning once. If desired, serve over hot cooked couscous. If desired, serve with grilled green onions and garnish with mint sprigs.

202 CALORIES

Garlic and Mint Chicken Breasts

Typically mild chicken shows a more aggressive side when it's bathed in a whirled-together mint marinade. Soy sauce, chili powder, and garlic add extra zing.

Prep: 15 minutes **Marinate:** 4 to 24 hours
Grill: 12 minutes **Makes:** 4 servings

Nutrition Facts per serving:
202 cal., 6 g total fat (1 g sat. fat), 82 mg chol., 228 mg sodium, 2 g carbo., 0 g fiber, 34 g pro.
Daily Values:
5% vit. A, 19% vit. C, 4% calcium, 17% iron
Exchanges:
4¹/₂ Meat

238 CALORIES

Chipotle Chicken with Pineapple Salsa

Chipotle chili powder, made with dried smoked jalapeño chile peppers and other spices, gives this chicken a rich, smoky flavor that blends deliciously with the pineapple salsa.

Prep: 20 minutes   **Grill:** 12 minutes
Makes: 4 servings

Nutrition Facts per serving:
238 cal., 2 g total fat (1 g sat. fat), 82 mg chol., 157 mg sodium, 20 g carbo., 2 g fiber, 34 g pro.
Daily Values:
16% vit. A, 55% vit. C, 4% calcium, 9% iron
Exchanges:
1½ Fruit, 4½ Meat

1   15¼-ounce can pineapple tidbits (juice pack), drained
¼   cup finely chopped red sweet pepper
½   of a fresh jalapeño chile pepper, seeded and finely chopped (see note on page 76)
2   green onions, bias-sliced
1   tablespoon coarsely chopped fresh cilantro
1   teaspoon brown sugar
½   to 1 teaspoon chipotle chili powder
½   teaspoon dried sage, crushed
¼   teaspoon garlic powder
¼   teaspoon onion powder
⅛   teaspoon salt
4   boneless, skinless chicken breast halves (1¼ to 1½ pounds total)
     Nonstick cooking spray
     Fresh cilantro sprigs (optional)

1 For pineapple salsa, in a medium bowl stir together drained pineapple, sweet pepper, jalapeño pepper, green onions, and the chopped cilantro. Set aside.

2 In a small bowl stir together brown sugar, chipotle chili powder, sage, garlic powder, onion powder, and salt. Lightly coat chicken with nonstick cooking spray. Sprinkle spice mixture evenly over chicken; rub in with your fingers.

3 Place chicken on the grill rack of an uncovered grill directly over medium coals. Grill for 12 to 15 minutes or until tender and no longer pink (170°F), turning once. Serve with pineapple salsa. If desired, garnish with cilantro sprigs.

½ teaspoon finely shredded orange peel

¼ teaspoon black pepper

8 chicken drumsticks or thighs, skinned

½ of a 10-ounce container frozen cranberry-orange sauce, thawed (½ cup)

¼ cup bottled barbecue sauce

2 teaspoons Dijon-style mustard

Lettuce leaves (optional)

1 medium orange, sectioned (optional)

1 In a small bowl stir together orange peel and pepper. Sprinkle evenly over chicken; rub in with your fingers. Place chicken on the grill rack of an uncovered grill directly over medium coals. Grill for 25 minutes, turning occasionally.

2 In a small saucepan stir together cranberry-orange sauce, barbecue sauce, and mustard. Cook and stir until heated through. Remove from heat. (Mixture will be thick.)

3 Brush cranberry mixture onto chicken. Grill for 10 to 20 minutes more or until tender and no longer pink (180°F), turning and brushing occasionally with the cranberry mixture. Discard any remaining cranberry mixture. If desired, serve with lettuce leaves and orange.

Cranberry Grilled Chicken

Time to rethink cranberries—they aren't just for the holidays. Here cranberry-orange sauce joins forces with barbecue sauce and Dijon-style mustard to glaze summery grilled drumsticks.

Prep: 20 minutes **Grill:** 35 minutes

Makes: 4 servings

318 CALORIES

Nutrition Facts per serving:
318 cal., 7 g total fat (2 g sat. fat), 157 mg chol., 335 mg sodium, 17 g carbo., 0 g fiber, 42 g pro.
Daily Values:
4% vit. A, 11% vit. C, 3% calcium, 12% iron
Exchanges:
1 Fruit, 6 Meat

Curried Turkey with Mango Salsa

Jump-start this spicy dish by soaking turkey tenderloins in the lime-curry marinade. Once they're off the grill, finish off each serving with the zesty mint-flavored fruit salsa.

Prep: 20 minutes **Marinate:** 2 to 6 hours
Grill: 25 minutes **Makes:** 4 servings

275 CALORIES

2 turkey breast tenderloins (about 1 pound total)
2 tablespoons lime juice
2 tablespoons water
1 tablespoon grated fresh ginger
1 tablespoon hot chile garlic sauce
1 tablespoon curry powder
1 tablespoon olive oil
1 tablespoon reduced-sodium soy sauce
1 recipe Mango-Mint Salsa
   Fresh mint sprigs (optional)

1 Place turkey tenderloins in a plastic bag set in a shallow dish. In a small bowl combine lime juice, the water, ginger, chile garlic sauce, curry powder, oil, and soy sauce. Pour over turkey; seal bag. Marinate in the refrigerator for at least 2 hours or up to 6 hours, turning bag occasionally.

2 Drain turkey, discarding marinade. In a grill with a cover arrange medium-hot coals around a drip pan. Test for medium heat above the pan. Place turkey tenderloins on the grill rack directly over drip pan. Cover and grill for 25 to 30 minutes or until turkey is tender and no longer pink (170°F).

3 To serve, slice turkey. Serve with Mango-Mint Salsa. If desired, garnish with mint sprigs.

Mango-Mint Salsa: Peel, seed, and chop 2 mangoes. In a medium bowl stir together chopped mango, ¼ cup finely chopped red onion, 2 tablespoons finely chopped fresh jalapeño chile pepper (see note on page 76), 2 tablespoons lime juice, 1 tablespoon snipped fresh mint, and ¼ teaspoon salt. Cover and chill until serving time.

Nutrition Facts per serving:
275 cal., 10 g total fat (2 g sat. fat), 74 mg chol., 320 mg sodium, 21 g carbo., 3 g fiber, 26 g pro.
Daily Values:
81% vit. A, 61% vit. C, 4% calcium, 12% iron
Exchanges:
1½ Fruit, 3½ Meat

2 tablespoons olive oil or cooking oil

1½ cups chopped red or yellow sweet
    pepper (2 medium)

½ cup finely chopped onion (1 medium)

¾ cup chicken broth

¼ teaspoon salt

¼ teaspoon black pepper

2 cloves garlic, minced

2 turkey breast tenderloins (about
    1 pound total)

3 cups hot cooked mafalda or fettuccine

    Fresh parsley sprigs (optional)

1 For sauce, in a large skillet heat
1 tablespoon of the oil over medium
heat. Add sweet peppers and onion; cook
about 10 minutes or until vegetables are
very tender, stirring occasionally.
Transfer vegetables to a food processor
bowl or blender container; add broth,
salt, and black pepper. Cover and process
or blend until mixture is smooth. Return
to skillet; set aside.

2 In a small bowl combine the remaining
1 tablespoon oil and the garlic. Brush
garlic mixture over turkey tenderloins.
Discard any remaining garlic mixture.

3 In a grill with a cover arrange
medium-hot coals around a drip pan.
Test for medium heat above the pan.
Place turkey on the grill rack directly
over the drip pan. Cover and grill for
25 to 30 minutes or until turkey is tender
and no longer pink (170°F).

4 To serve, slice the turkey tenderloins.
Reheat the sauce until bubbly. Spoon
sauce over pasta. Top with turkey slices.
If desired, garnish with parsley sprigs.

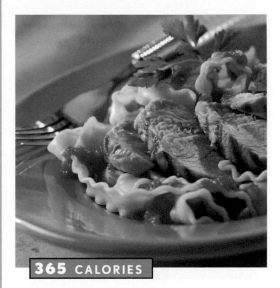

365 CALORIES

Turkey with Pepper Sauce

Grilled turkey basks in a bath of savory
sweet pepper and garlic sauce. Soak up
every little bit with squares of focaccia.

Prep: 25 minutes   **Grill:** 25 minutes
Makes: 4 servings

Nutrition Facts per serving:
365 cal., 10 g total fat (2 g sat. fat), 68 mg chol.,
347 mg sodium, 36 g carbo., 3 g fiber, 34 g pro.
Daily Values:
64% vit. A, 163% vit. C, 4% calcium, 18% iron
Exchanges:
2 Vegetable, 1½ Starch, 3½ Meat

351 CALORIES

Blackened Catfish

Catch a Cajun classic and cook it on your grill. This version of a Southern favorite is served alongside tiny new potatoes, carrots, and onions roasted on the grill in olive oil and zippy hot pepper sauce.

Prep: 25 minutes   **Grill:** 35 minutes
Makes: 4 servings

Nutrition Facts per serving:
351 cal., 12 g total fat (3 g sat. fat), 53 mg chol., 263 mg sodium, 38 g carbo., 6 g fiber, 23 g pro.
Daily Values:
312% vit. A, 92% vit. C, 6% calcium, 20% iron
Exchanges:
1 Vegetable, 2 Starch, 2 Meat

1 **tablespoon olive oil**
¼ **teaspoon salt**
  Several dashes bottled hot pepper sauce
1½ **pounds tiny new potatoes, thinly sliced**
4 **medium carrots, thinly sliced**
1 **medium green sweet pepper, cut into thin bite-size strips**
1 **medium onion, sliced**
4 **4- to 5-ounce fresh or frozen catfish or red snapper fillets, ½ to 1 inch thick**
½ **teaspoon Cajun seasoning**
  Nonstick cooking spray
  Snipped fresh sage, chervil, or fresh parsley (optional)

1 Fold a 48×18-inch piece of heavy foil in half to make a 24×18-inch rectangle. In a large bowl combine the oil, salt, and hot pepper sauce. Add the potatoes, carrots, sweet pepper, and onion; toss to coat. Place in the center of the foil rectangle. Bring up 2 opposite edges of foil; seal with a double fold. Fold remaining ends to completely enclose vegetables, leaving space for steam to build.

2 Place vegetable pack on the rack of an uncovered grill directly over medium coals. Grill for 35 to 40 minutes or until potatoes and carrots are tender.

3 Meanwhile, thaw fish, if frozen. Well grease a wire grill basket; set aside. Rinse fish; pat dry. Measure thickness of fish. Sprinkle Cajun seasoning evenly over fish fillets; lightly coat fish with nonstick cooking spray.

4 Place fish in prepared grill basket. Place the fish on the grill rack alongside the vegetable packet; grill until fish flakes easily when tested with a fork, turning the basket once. (Allow 4 to 6 minutes per ½-inch thickness of fish.) To serve, if desired, garnish fish and vegetables with sage, chervil, or parsley.

1. 1½-pound fresh or frozen salmon fillet (with skin)
¼ teaspoon salt
¼ teaspoon coarsely ground black pepper
2 tablespoons bottled barbecue sauce
1 teaspoon sugar
1 teaspoon fennel seeds, toasted* and crushed

1 Thaw fish, if frozen. Rinse fish; pat dry. Sprinkle fish with salt and pepper. Set aside.

2 In a small bowl stir together the barbecue sauce, sugar, and toasted fennel seeds.

3 In a grill with a cover arrange medium-hot coals around a drip pan. Test for medium heat above the pan. Place fish, skin side down, on a greased grill rack directly over the drip pan. Cover and grill for 18 to 20 minutes or until the thickest portion of the fish flakes easily when tested with a fork, brushing with the barbecue sauce mixture during the last 8 minutes of grilling. Discard any remaining barbecue sauce mixture.

*Note: To toast fennel seeds, place in a small skillet. Cook over medium heat for 3 to 4 minutes or until toasted and fragrant, shaking skillet occasionally.

Salmon with Fennel

In this satisfying salmon dish, fennel seeds perk up ordinary bottled barbecue sauce. Toasting the seeds brings out their rich licoricelike flavor.

Prep: 20 minutes   **Grill:** 18 minutes
Makes: 5 servings

237 CALORIES

Nutrition Facts per serving:
237 cal., 12 g total fat (2 g sat. fat), 84 mg chol., 232 mg sodium, 2 g carbo., 0 g fiber, 29 g pro.
Daily Values:
6% vit. A, 1% vit. C, 1% calcium, 5% iron
Exchanges:
4 Meat

Rosemary Trout with Lemon Butter

Here's a delicious reason why lemon and butter are timeless, classic accompaniments to fish. Grilling tomatoes alongside the trout takes maximum advantage of the grill's heat and infuses them with smoky flavor.

Prep: 20 minutes   **Grill:** 6 minutes
Makes: 4 servings

229 CALORIES

2   fresh or frozen rainbow trout, pan dressed and boned (8 to 10 ounces each)*
4   teaspoons butter, softened
1   tablespoon finely chopped shallots or onion
1   teaspoon finely shredded lemon peel
    Dash salt
    Dash black pepper
1   tablespoon snipped fresh rosemary
    Salt
    Black pepper
1   tablespoon lemon juice
2   teaspoons olive oil
2   medium tomatoes, halved crosswise
1   tablespoon snipped fresh parsley
    Lemon slices, halved (optional)

1 Thaw fish, if frozen. Rinse fish; pat dry. Set aside.

2 In a small bowl stir together the butter, half of the shallots, and the lemon peel; season with the dash salt and dash pepper. Set aside.

3 Spread open each fish. Place fish cut sides up. Rub remaining shallots and the rosemary onto cut sides of fish. Sprinkle with additional salt and pepper; drizzle with lemon juice and oil.

4 Place fish, skin sides down, on the lightly greased rack of an uncovered grill directly over medium coals. Grill for 6 to 8 minutes or until fish flakes easily with a fork.

5 Meanwhile, place tomatoes, cut sides up, on grill rack; dot each with ¼ teaspoon of the butter mixture. Grill about 5 minutes or until tomatoes are heated through. Remove fish and tomatoes from the grill. Cut each fish in half lengthwise. In a small saucepan melt remaining butter mixture; spoon over fish and tomatoes. Sprinkle fish with parsley. If desired, serve with lemon slices.

*Note: A pan-dressed fish has had the scales and internal organs removed; often the head, fins, and tail also have been removed.

Nutrition Facts per serving:
229 cal., 13 g total fat (5 g sat. fat), 78 mg chol., 233 mg sodium, 4 g carbo., 1 g fiber, 24 g pro.
Daily Values:
18% vit. A, 31% vit. C, 9% calcium, 4% iron
Exchanges:
1 Vegetable, 3 Meat, ½ Fat

- **4** 4- to 6-ounce fresh or frozen halibut steaks, cut 1 inch thick
- **2** tablespoons white balsamic vinegar
- **2** tablespoons coarse-grain mustard
- **1** tablespoon water
- **4** teaspoons olive oil
- **1** clove garlic, minced
- **4** small leeks
- **¼** teaspoon salt
- **¼** teaspoon black pepper
- **3** cloves garlic, minced

1 Thaw fish, if frozen. Rinse fish; pat dry. Refrigerate fish until needed. In a small bowl whisk together white balsamic vinegar, mustard, the water, 2 teaspoons of the olive oil, and the 1 clove garlic. Set aside.

2 Trim roots and cut off green tops of leeks. Remove 1 or 2 outer white layers. Wash well (if necessary, cut a 1-inch slit from bottom end to help separate layers for easier washing). Drain. In a medium saucepan combine leeks and a small amount of water. Bring to boiling; reduce heat. Simmer, covered, for 3 minutes. Drain. Pat dry. Brush with 1 teaspoon of the remaining olive oil.

3 Stir together the remaining 1 teaspoon olive oil, the salt, pepper, and the 3 cloves garlic. Rub on halibut steaks.

4 Place fish and leeks on the greased rack of an uncovered grill directly over medium coals. Grill for 8 to 12 minutes or until fish flakes easily when tested with a fork, gently turning fish and leeks once. Slice leeks into ½-inch pieces. Place fish and leeks on a serving platter. Drizzle with vinegar mixture.

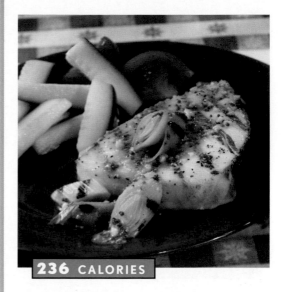

236 CALORIES

Halibut with Leeks

A new food adventure awaits you with this catch of the day. Embellished with a balsamic vinegar and mustard dressing, grilled halibut and leeks are sure to hook you and your guests.

Prep: 20 minutes **Grill:** 8 minutes
Makes: 4 servings

Nutrition Facts per serving:
236 cal., 8 g total fat (1 g sat. fat), 36 mg chol., 341 mg sodium, 15 g carbo., 2 g fiber, 26 g pro.
Daily Values:
5% vit. A, 17% vit. C, 12% calcium, 17% iron
Exchanges:
3 Vegetable, 3 Meat

162 CALORIES

Bourbon-Glazed Shrimp and Apples

The prosciutto-wrapped shrimp and crisp apple wedges absorb the spirited maple and mustard glaze as they grill. Large shrimp are easier to wrap and thread on skewers than smaller ones; purchase the kind that gives you 15 to 20 per pound.

Prep: 25 minutes   **Grill:** 8 minutes

Makes: 6 servings

1¹/₄ **pounds fresh or frozen large shrimp in shells**

   4 **thin slices prosciutto, cut into strips**

   2 **tart cooking apples**

   2 **tablespoons pure maple syrup or maple-flavored syrup**

   2 **tablespoons bourbon or orange juice**

   2 **tablespoons Dijon-style mustard**

   1 **tablespoon bottled reduced-sodium teriyaki sauce**

¹/₂ **teaspoon coarsely ground black pepper**

1 Thaw shrimp, if frozen. Peel and devein shrimp, leaving tails intact. Rinse shrimp; pat dry. Wrap a strip of prosciutto around each shrimp. Core apples. Cut each apple into wedges. On long metal skewers, alternately thread shrimp and apple wedges, leaving a ¹/₄-inch space between pieces.

2 In a small bowl stir together syrup, bourbon or orange juice, mustard, teriyaki sauce, and pepper.

3 Place kabobs on the greased rack of an uncovered grill directly over medium coals. Grill for 8 to 10 minutes or until shrimp are opaque, turning once and brushing occasionally with the syrup mixture during the last 2 minutes of grilling. Discard any remaining syrup mixture.

Nutrition Facts per serving:
162 cal., 3 g total fat (1 g sat. fat), 110 mg chol., 637 mg sodium, 13 g carbo., 1 g fiber, 18 g pro.
Daily Values:
3% vit. A, 6% vit. C, 4% calcium, 10% iron
Exchanges:
1 Fruit, 2¹/₂ Meat

1 medium cucumber, seeded and
chopped

1 cup cooked or canned black beans,
rinsed and drained

¼ cup snipped fresh cilantro

2 tablespoons cider vinegar

1 tablespoon olive oil

1 pickled jalapeño chile pepper, finely
chopped (see note on page 76)

½ to 1 teaspoon chili powder

1 clove garlic, minced

Salt

Black pepper

3 large tomatoes, halved

1 large sweet onion (such as Vidalia,
Maui, Texas Sweet, or Walla Walla),
sliced ½ inch thick

1 loaf French bread

1 In a medium bowl combine the
cucumber, beans, cilantro, vinegar, oil,
jalapeño pepper, chili powder, and garlic.
Season to taste with salt and black
pepper. Set aside.

2 Place the tomatoes and onion slices on
the lightly greased rack of an grill
directly over medium coals. Grill for
12 to 15 minutes or until lightly charred,
turning onion slices once. Transfer
vegetables to a cutting board; cool
slightly and coarsely chop. Add chopped
vegetables to the cucumber mixture; toss
to combine.

3 Meanwhile, halve the French bread
lengthwise. Cut each bread half crosswise
into 3 pieces. Using a fork, hollow out
the bread pieces slightly. Place the bread
pieces, cut sides down, on the rack of the
grill directly over medium coals. Grill
about 1 minute or until toasted. Spoon the
bean mixture into the grilled bread pieces.

Gazpacho Sandwiches

This hearty open-faced sandwich features
the flavors of the chilled Spanish soup
called gazpacho. For the filling, grilled
tomatoes and onions are stirred together
with cucumbers, jalapeño chile peppers,
and black beans. The mixture is scooped
into grilled bread "bowls."

Prep: 20 minutes **Grill:** 13 minutes
Makes: 6 servings

295 CALORIES

Nutrition Facts per serving:
295 cal., 5 g total fat (1 g sat. fat), 0 mg chol.,
671 mg sodium, 54 g carbo., 6 g fiber, 11 g pro.
Daily Values:
16% vit. A, 39% vit. C, 9% calcium, 18% iron
Exchanges:
2 Vegetable, 3 Starch, ½ Fat

Eggplant-Pepper Sandwiches

When hot summer days make kitchens unbearable, head outdoors, fire up the coals, and grill a simple feast. Here a stack of smoky eggplant slices and sweet pepper quarters anchored on French bread and sprinkled with tangy goat cheese comes together in less than 25 minutes.

Prep: 15 minutes   **Grill:** 7 minutes
Makes: 4 servings

284 CALORIES

- 2 medium red, yellow, and/or green sweet peppers
- 1 small eggplant (about 12 ounces), cut into 12 slices
- 1 tablespoon olive oil
- 8 ½-inch slices French bread, toasted
- 2 tablespoons Dijon-style mustard
- 4 ounces soft goat cheese (chèvre) crumbled

1 Quarter the sweet peppers lengthwise; remove and discard the stems, seeds, and membranes.

2 Brush eggplant slices with oil. Place eggplant slices and sweet pepper quarters on the rack of an uncovered grill directly over medium-hot coals. Grill for 4 minutes. Turn and grill for 3 to 5 minutes more or until eggplant is tender and sweet peppers are slightly charred. Remove vegetables from grill. Cool slightly. When the vegetables are cool enough to handle, cut into bite-size strips.

3 Spread 1 side of each French bread slice with mustard. Top with vegetables and goat cheese. Serve warm.

Nutrition Facts per serving:
284 cal., 11 g total fat (5 g sat. fat), 13 mg chol., 584 mg sodium, 34 g carbo., 4 g fiber, 11 g pro.
Daily Values:
8% vit. A, 73% vit. C, 9% calcium, 13% iron
Exchanges:
2 Vegetable, 1½ Starch, 1 Meat, 1 Fat

Oven Dishes

Salads and Sandwiches

Skillet and Saucepan Dishes

Skillet and Saucepan Dishes (continued)

Soups and Stews

1½ cups quick-cooking brown rice
½ cup vegetable broth or chicken broth
¼ cup dry sherry
1 tablespoon cornstarch
1 tablespoon reduced-sodium soy sauce
1 teaspoon sugar
1 teaspoon grated fresh ginger
½ teaspoon crushed red pepper (optional)
  Nonstick cooking spray
1 cup thinly bias-sliced carrots
3 cloves garlic, minced
3 cups broccoli florets
6 ounces firm tofu (fresh bean curd),
  cut into ½-inch cubes

1 Prepare rice according to package directions; keep warm.

2 For sauce, in a small bowl stir together the broth, dry sherry, cornstarch, soy sauce, sugar, ginger, and, if desired, crushed red pepper. Set sauce aside.

3 Coat an unheated wok or large skillet with nonstick cooking spray. Preheat over medium-high heat. Add carrots and garlic to hot wok or skillet; stir-fry for 2 minutes. Add broccoli; stir-fry for 3 to 4 minutes more or until vegetables are crisp-tender. Push vegetables from the center of wok.

4 Stir sauce; add to center of wok. Cook and stir until thickened and bubbly. Add tofu; stir together all ingredients to coat. Cook and stir for 1 minute more.

5 To serve, spoon vegetable mixture over hot cooked rice.

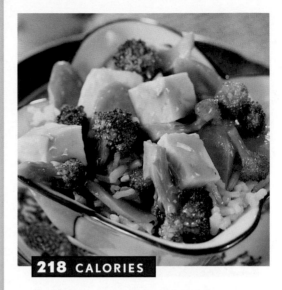

218 CALORIES

Vegetable and Tofu Stir-Fry

Use firm tofu for stir-fries because it won't fall apart when tossed about the wok. For extra flavor, sprinkle the tofu cubes with a little soy sauce before cooking.

Start to Finish: 30 minutes
Makes: 4 servings

Nutrition Facts per serving:
218 cal., 3 g total fat (0 g sat. fat), 0 mg chol., 315 mg sodium, 39 g carbo., 5 g fiber, 9 g pro.
Daily Values:
174% vit. A, 92% vit. C, 6% calcium, 9% iron
Exchanges:
1 Vegetable, 2 Starch, ½ Meat

388 CALORIES

Risotto with Beans and Vegetables

Arborio rice cooks to a creamy consistency in this easy rice dish that's brimming with vegetables and beans. If you can't find the white kidney beans, use pinto beans instead.

Start to Finish: 40 minutes

Makes: 4 servings

3   cups mushroom broth, vegetable broth, or chicken broth

2   cups sliced fresh mushrooms (such as shiitake or button mushrooms)

1/2 cup chopped onion (1 medium)

2   cloves garlic, minced

2   tablespoons olive oil

1   cup arborio rice

1   cup finely chopped zucchini

1   cup finely chopped carrots

1   15-ounce can white kidney (cannellini) beans or pinto beans, rinsed and drained

1/2 cup grated Parmesan cheese (2 ounces)

1 In a medium saucepan bring broth to boiling; reduce heat and simmer until needed. Meanwhile, in a large saucepan cook mushrooms, onion, and garlic in hot oil over medium heat about 5 minutes or until onion is tender. Add uncooked rice. Cook and stir about 5 minutes more or until rice is golden brown.

2 Slowly add 1 cup of the broth to the rice mixture, stirring constantly. Continue to cook and stir until liquid is absorbed. Add another ½ cup of the broth, the zucchini, and carrots to rice mixture, stirring constantly. Continue to cook and stir until liquid is absorbed. Add another 1 cup of the broth, ½ cup at a time, stirring constantly until the broth is absorbed. (This should take about 20 minutes.)

3 Stir the remaining ½ cup broth into rice mixture. Cook and stir until rice is slightly creamy and just tender. Stir in white kidney beans and Parmesan cheese; heat through.

Nutrition Facts per serving:
388 cal., 11 g total fat (3 g sat. fat), 8 mg chol., 539 mg sodium, 61 g carbo., 8 g fiber, 17 g pro.
Daily Values:
174% vit. A, 15% vit. C, 19% calcium, 23% iron
Exchanges:
3 Vegetable, 3 Starch, 1¹/2 Fat

- **1** large red onion, halved and cut into thin wedges
- **1** tablespoon olive oil
- **2** teaspoons curry powder
- **1** teaspoon ground cumin
- **1/4** teaspoon garam masala
- **1/8** teaspoon cayenne pepper
- **3** cups cauliflower florets
- **1** 14½-ounce can diced tomatoes, undrained
- **2** medium potatoes, peeled and cut into 1-inch cubes (about 1½ cups)
- **2** medium sweet potatoes, peeled and cut into 1-inch cubes (about 1½ cups)
- **1½** cups vegetable broth or water
- **1/4** teaspoon salt
- **1/4** teaspoon freshly ground black pepper
- **1** cup loose-pack frozen peas
- **4½** cups hot cooked couscous or brown rice

1 In a large saucepan cook onion in hot oil over medium heat about 5 minutes or until tender. Add curry powder, cumin, garam masala, and cayenne pepper. Cook and stir for 1 minute.

2 Stir in cauliflower, tomatoes, potatoes, sweet potatoes, broth, salt, and black pepper. Bring to boiling; reduce heat. Simmer, covered, for 10 to 12 minutes or until potatoes are tender. Stir in peas; heat through. Serve over couscous or brown rice.

Vegetable Curry

Who says vegetable dishes are ho-hum? Indian-style curry is well-known for its lively flavors. Curry, cumin, garam masala, and cayenne pepper all contribute to this flavorful meatless dish. Hint: You'll find garam masala in Indian markets and the gourmet sections of some supermarkets.

Start to Finish: 35 minutes
Makes: 6 servings

284 CALORIES

Nutrition Facts per serving:
284 cal., 3 g total fat (0 g sat. fat), 0 mg chol., 516 mg sodium, 55 g carbo., 7 g fiber, 9 g pro.
Daily Values:
139% vit. A, 78% vit. C, 8% calcium, 12% iron
Exchanges:
2 Vegetable, 3 Starch

Indian-Spiced Squash

When it comes to curry, it's all about making it your own. An array of traditional condiments lets diners season to taste at the table. For an interesting presentation, serve it in halved delicata squash.

Start to Finish: 35 minutes

Makes: 4 servings

369 CALORIES

1/4 cup shelled raw pumpkin seeds (pepitas)

1 tablespoon grated fresh ginger

1 tablespoon olive oil

2 pounds winter squash, peeled, seeded, and cut into 1/2-inch pieces (about 4 cups)

1/2 cup dried cranberries and/or golden raisins

1 teaspoon ground cinnamon

1 teaspoon ground coriander

1/2 teaspoon ground cumin

1/2 teaspoon curry powder

1 14-ounce can vegetable broth or chicken broth

3 cups hot cooked brown rice

Desired condiments (such as sliced bananas, pineapple chunks, sliced green onions, and/or chutney) (optional)

1 In a large skillet toast pumpkin seeds over medium heat for 4 to 5 minutes or until puffed and lightly browned, stirring occasionally. (Watch carefully because pumpkin seeds may pop in skillet.) Remove from skillet; set aside.

2 In the same skillet cook and stir ginger in hot oil over medium heat for 1 minute. Increase heat to medium-high; add squash and cook for 3 to 5 minutes or until squash starts to brown. Add cranberries or raisins, cinnamon, coriander, cumin, and curry powder; cook for 1 minute more.

3 Carefully add broth to squash mixture. Bring to boiling; reduce heat. Simmer, covered, for 10 to 15 minutes or until squash is tender but not mushy. To serve, spoon squash mixture over rice and sprinkle with pumpkin seeds.* If desired, serve with condiments.

*Note: To serve as shown in the photo, halve and seed 2 delicata squash. (If desired, place squash halves, cut sides down, in a baking dish. Bake in a 350° oven for 45 minutes. Turn cut sides up. Bake 20 to 25 minutes more or until tender.) Spoon rice into squash halves; spoon squash mixture over rice.

Nutrition Facts per serving:
369 cal., 12 g total fat (2 g sat. fat), 0 mg chol., 431 mg sodium, 60 g carbo., 6 g fiber, 11 g pro.
Daily Values:
92% vit. A, 21% vit. C, 7% calcium, 21% iron
Exchanges:
1 Fruit, 3 Starch, 1 1/2 Fat

1   **14-ounce can vegetable broth or chicken broth**

1   **teaspoon Greek seasoning or garam masala**

1   **cup loose-pack frozen green soybeans (shelled edamame)**

³/₄   **cup quick-cooking barley**

¹/₂   **cup shredded carrot**

4   **cups fresh spinach leaves**

4   **small to medium tomatoes, sliced**

1 In a medium saucepan bring broth and seasoning to boiling. Add soybeans and barley. Return to boiling; reduce heat. Simmer, covered, for 12 minutes. Stir carrot into barley mixture.

2 Meanwhile, divide spinach among 4 dinner plates. Arrange tomato slices on spinach. Using a slotted spoon, spoon barley mixture over tomatoes (or drain barley mixture; spoon over tomatoes).

Make-ahead directions: Prepare as above through step 1. Cover and chill barley mixture up to 24 hours. Arrange spinach and tomatoes as above. Spoon chilled barley mixture over tomatoes.

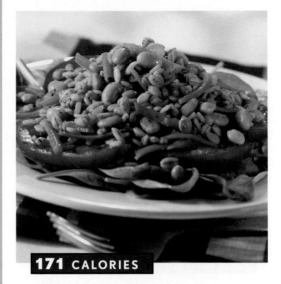

171 CALORIES

Beans, Barley, and Tomatoes

If you haven't yet tried edamame, the Japanese name for fresh green soybeans, here's a tasty way to sample them. The barley and edamame mixture spooned over spinach and tomato makes a filling summer meal.

Start to Finish: 30 minutes
Makes: 4 servings

Nutrition Facts per serving:
171 cal., 3 g total fat (0 g sat. fat), 0 mg chol., 484 mg sodium, 33 g carbo., 10 g fiber, 9 g pro.
Daily Values:
135% vit. A, 61% vit. C, 7% calcium, 24% iron
Exchanges:
2 Vegetable, 1¹/₂ Starch

273 CALORIES

Polenta with Mushrooms and Asparagus

Something bright and green always beats the winter blues. This rustic polenta, starring the first asparagus of the season, may provide the lift you need.

Prep: 30 minutes **Chill:** 2 hours
Bake: 20 minutes **Oven:** 350°F
Makes: 4 servings

Nutrition Facts per serving:
273 cal., 11 g total fat (3 g sat. fat), 8 mg chol.,
536 mg sodium, 33 g carbo., 4 g fiber, 11 g pro.
Daily Values:
5% vit. A, 26% vit. C, 9% calcium, 16% iron
Exchanges:
2 Vegetable, 1½ Starch, ½ Meat, 1 Fat

3 **cups water**
1 **cup cornmeal**
1 **cup cold water**
½ **teaspoon salt**
   Nonstick cooking spray
1 **small red onion, cut into thin wedges**
1 **tablespoon olive oil**
3 **cups sliced fresh mushrooms (such as crimini, shiitake, or oyster)**
1 **pound fresh asparagus spears, trimmed**
3 **cloves garlic, thinly sliced**
⅓ **cup dry white wine, Marsala, vegetable broth, or chicken broth**
¼ **teaspoon salt**
¼ **cup finely shredded Asiago or Parmesan cheese (1 ounce)**
2 **tablespoons pine nuts, toasted**

1 For polenta, in a medium saucepan bring the 3 cups water to boiling. In a small bowl combine the cornmeal, the 1 cup water, and the salt. Slowly add cornmeal mixture to the boiling water, stirring constantly. Cook and stir until mixture returns to boiling; reduce heat to low. Cook, uncovered, for 10 to 15 minutes or until thick, stirring frequently.

2 Coat an 8×8×2-inch baking pan with nonstick cooking spray. Spread hot polenta evenly into the pan; cool slightly. Cover and chill about 2 hours or until firm.

3 Bake the polenta in a 350° oven about 20 minutes or until heated through. Meanwhile, in a large skillet cook onion in hot oil over medium heat until tender. Add mushrooms, asparagus, and garlic; cook, uncovered, about 4 minutes or until almost tender. Stir in wine and salt. Cook, uncovered, over medium-high heat for 1 minute.

4 To serve, cut polenta into 8 pieces. Divide polenta among 4 dinner plates. Spoon the mushroom mixture over polenta. Sprinkle with cheese and pine nuts.

Make-ahead directions: Prepare as above through step 2. Cover; chill up to 24 hours. Proceed as above in steps 3 and 4.

2½ cups water

1½ cups cornmeal

1½ cups cold water

1 teaspoon salt

1 small onion, thinly sliced

1 tablespoon olive oil

4 cups fresh mushrooms, halved

¼ teaspoon salt

¼ teaspoon freshly ground black pepper

6 medium red and/or yellow sweet peppers, roasted and cut into thin bite-size strips*

1¼ cups purchased marinara sauce

1 cup shredded mozzarella cheese

Fresh basil sprigs (optional)

1 For polenta, in a medium saucepan bring the 2½ cups water to boiling. In a medium bowl combine the cornmeal, the 1½ cups water, and the 1 teaspoon salt. Slowly add cornmeal mixture to boiling water, stirring constantly. Cook and stir until mixture returns to boiling; reduce heat to low. Cook about 10 minutes or until mixture is very thick, stirring occasionally. Pour the hot mixture into a 3-quart rectangular baking dish. Cool slightly. Cover and chill about 1 hour or until firm.

2 In large nonstick skillet cook onion in hot oil over medium heat for 3 to 4 minutes or until tender. Add mushrooms, the ¼ teaspoon salt, and the black pepper. Cook and stir about 5 minutes or until mushrooms are tender. Remove from heat; stir in the roasted sweet peppers.

3 Spread the marinara sauce over chilled polenta. Top with the vegetable mixture; sprinkle with cheese. Bake, covered, in a 350° oven for 30 minutes. Uncover; bake for 10 to 15 minutes more or until edges are bubbly. If desired, garnish with basil.

*Note: To roast peppers, quarter the peppers lengthwise; remove stems, seeds, and membranes. Place peppers, cut sides down, on a foil-lined baking sheet. Roast in a 450° oven for 15 to 20 minutes or until skins are blistered and bubbly. Seal foil around peppers to form a packet. Let stand for 20 minutes. Peel peppers.

Vegetable Polenta Lasagna

With only 210 calories and 7 grams of fat, this isn't your grandmother's lasagna. Here polenta makes an unexpected alternative to the usual noodles.

Prep: 25 minutes **Chill:** 1 hour
Bake: 40 minutes **Oven:** 350°F
Makes: 8 servings

210 CALORIES

Nutrition Facts per serving:
210 cal., 7 g total fat (2 g sat. fat), 8 mg chol., 581 mg sodium, 31 g carbo., 5 g fiber, 9 g pro.
Daily Values:
62% vit. A, 177% vit. C, 12% calcium, 13% iron
Exchanges:
3 Vegetable, 1 Starch, ½ Meat, ½ Fat

Pesto Christmas Limas and Bulgur

Dappled red over pale green, Christmas limas are aptly named and easy to spot, but it's their nutty flavor that your family will rave about when you serve this Italian-inspired meal. Cook the beans ahead of time or use canned beans when dinner is really last minute.

Start to Finish: 25 minutes

Makes: 6 servings

195 CALORIES

1⅓ cups vegetable broth or chicken broth

⅔ cup bulgur

1 medium red sweet pepper, cut into thin bite-size strips

⅓ cup refrigerated basil pesto

¼ cup thinly sliced green onions

2 cups cooked Christmas lima beans, pinto beans, or cranberry beans* or one 15-ounce can pinto beans, rinsed and drained

Freshly ground black pepper

Boston or Bibb lettuce cups

Lemon wedges (optional)

1 In a medium saucepan bring broth to boiling; add bulgur. Return to boiling; reduce heat. Simmer, covered, for 10 minutes. Remove from heat. Stir in sweet pepper, pesto, and green onions. Stir in beans. Season with black pepper. To serve, spoon into lettuce cups. If desired, secure lettuce cups with wooden skewers. If desired, serve with lemon.

*Note: To cook beans, rinse ¾ cup dry beans. In a large Dutch oven combine beans and 5 cups cold water. Bring to boiling; reduce heat. Simmer, uncovered, for 2 minutes. Remove from heat. Cover and let stand for 1 hour. (Or place beans and 5 cups cold water in a Dutch oven. Cover and let soak in a cool place overnight.) Drain and rinse beans. Return beans to Dutch oven. Add 5 cups fresh water. Bring to boiling; reduce heat. Simmer, covered, for 1¼ to 1½ hours or until tender; drain.

Nutrition Facts per serving:
195 cal., 9 g total fat (0 g sat. fat), 2 mg chol., 329 mg sodium, 23 g carbo., 5 g fiber, 7 g pro.
Daily Values:
26% vit. A, 63% vit. C, 2% calcium, 4% iron
Exchanges:
1½ Starch, ½ Meat, 1 Fat

Nonstick cooking spray

3/4 **cup chopped onion**

3 **cloves garlic, minced**

1 **teaspoon olive oil or cooking oil**

2 **10-ounce packages frozen chopped spinach, thawed and well drained**

1 **cup low-fat cottage cheese, drained**

1 **cup crumbled feta cheese (4 ounces)**

1/2 **cup refrigerated or frozen egg product, thawed**

1 **tablespoon snipped fresh oregano or 1 teaspoon dried oregano, crushed**

1/4 **teaspoon coarsely ground black pepper**

1/4 **cup finely shredded Parmesan cheese (1 ounce)**

2 **tablespoons fine dry bread crumbs**

1 Lightly coat a 9-inch pie plate with nonstick cooking spray; set aside. In a medium saucepan cook onion and garlic in hot oil until onion is tender.

2 Stir spinach, cottage cheese, feta cheese, egg product, oregano, and black pepper into onion mixture. Spoon the mixture into the prepared pie plate.

3 In a small bowl combine Parmesan cheese and bread crumbs; sprinkle over spinach mixture. Bake, uncovered, in a 350° oven for 30 to 35 minutes or until a knife inserted near center comes out clean. To serve, cut into wedges.

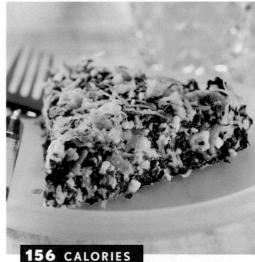

156 CALORIES

Spinach-Feta Bake

Three types of cheese not only make this spinach-and-egg ensemble good but extra rich in calcium too.

Prep: 20 minutes **Bake:** 30 minutes
Oven: 350°F **Makes:** 6 servings

Nutrition Facts per serving:
156 cal., 7 g total fat (4 g sat. fat), 22 mg chol., 666 mg sodium, 8 g carbo., 3 g fiber, 14 g pro.
Daily Values:
278% vit. A, 14% vit. C, 27% calcium, 7% iron
Exchanges:
2 Vegetable, 1¹/₂ Meat

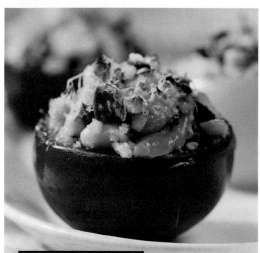

220 CALORIES

Herb-and-Bean-Stuffed Tomatoes

Basil and thyme work with a little Parmesan cheese and garlic to confer the flavors of Italy on these bean-stuffed tomatoes.

Prep: 25 minutes   **Bake:** 20 minutes
Oven: 350°F   **Makes:** 4 servings

- **4** large red and/or yellow tomatoes
- **1½** cups soft bread crumbs (2 slices)
- **½** of a 15-ounce can white kidney (cannellini) beans, rinsed and drained
- **¼** cup pine nuts, toasted
- **2** tablespoons grated Parmesan cheese
- **1** tablespoon finely shredded fresh basil or ½ teaspoon dried basil, crushed
- **1** tablespoon olive oil
- **2** cloves garlic, minced
- **⅛** teaspoon salt
- **⅛** teaspoon black pepper
- **2** teaspoons snipped fresh thyme or ½ teaspoon dried thyme, crushed
- **2** teaspoons butter or margarine, melted

1 Cut off ½ inch from the top of each tomato. Finely chop enough of the tops to equal 1 cup; set aside. Remove and discard the seeds from tomatoes.

2 In a large bowl stir together the chopped tomato, ¾ cup of the bread crumbs, the beans, pine nuts, Parmesan cheese, basil, oil, garlic, salt, and black pepper. Spoon the bean mixture into the tomatoes. Place the stuffed tomatoes in a 2-quart square baking dish.

3 In a small bowl stir together the remaining ¾ cup bread crumbs and the thyme. Sprinkle over tomatoes. Drizzle with melted butter.

4 Bake, uncovered, in a 350° oven about 20 minutes or until crumbs are golden brown and tomatoes are heated through.

Nutrition Facts per serving:
220 cal., 12 g total fat (3 g sat. fat), 8 mg chol., 327 mg sodium, 25 g carbo., 5 g fiber, 9 g pro.
Daily Values:
22% vit. A, 50% vit. C, 8% calcium, 16% iron
Exchanges:
2 Vegetable, 1 Starch, ½ Meat, 1½ Fat

1³/₄ cups water

½ cup shredded carrot

¼ cup thinly sliced green onions

1 teaspoon instant vegetable bouillon granules, 1 teaspoon instant chicken bouillon granules, or ½ of a vegetable bouillon cube, crushed

3 inches stick cinnamon or dash ground cinnamon

⅛ teaspoon salt

¾ cup bulgur

⅓ cup dried cranberries or raisins

4 small or 2 large yellow or red sweet peppers*

¾ cup shredded Muenster, brick, or mozzarella cheese (3 ounces)

½ cup water

1 In a large skillet combine the 1¾ cups water, the carrot, green onions, bouillon, cinnamon, and salt. Bring to boiling; reduce heat. Simmer, covered, for 5 minutes. Stir in the bulgur and cranberries or raisins. Remove from heat. Cover and let stand for 5 minutes. If using stick cinnamon, remove from the bulgur mixture. Drain off excess liquid.

2 Meanwhile, halve the sweet peppers lengthwise; remove and discard the seeds and membranes.

3 Stir shredded cheese into bulgur mixture; spoon into sweet pepper halves. Place the sweet pepper halves in a large skillet. Add the ½ cup water. Bring to boiling; reduce heat. Simmer, covered, for 5 to 10 minutes or until sweet peppers are crisp-tender and bulgur mixture is heated through.

*Note: You may substitute 4 large poblano peppers for the sweet peppers. Prepare as above.

Bulgur-Stuffed Peppers

Unlike most stuffed-pepper entrées, this Middle Eastern version takes only half an hour to make. It's a savory choice even on the busiest of days.

Start to Finish: 30 minutes

Makes: 4 servings

246 CALORIES

Nutrition Facts per serving:
246 cal., 7 g total fat (4 g sat. fat), 20 mg chol., 348 mg sodium, 39 g carbo., 7 g fiber, 10 g pro.
Daily Values:
97% vit. A, 431% vit. C, 19% calcium, 9% iron
Exchanges:
1 Vegetable, ½ Fruit, 1½ Starch, 1 Meat

Stuffed Shells with Fennel

Only in recent years has fennel garnered enough demand to appear regularly in produce aisles. Make up for lost time by enjoying the vegetable in this satisfying recipe.

Prep: 40 minutes **Bake:** 35 minutes
Oven: 375°F **Makes:** 5 servings

312 CALORIES

Nutrition Facts per serving:
312 cal., 12 g total fat (4 g sat. fat), 19 mg chol., 769 mg sodium, 38 g carbo., 9 g fiber, 14 g pro.
Daily Values:
23% vit. A, 62% vit. C, 26% calcium, 13% iron
Exchanges:
3 Vegetable, 1½ Starch, 1 Meat, 1 Fat

15 dried jumbo pasta shells
 1 cup chopped onion (1 large)
 1 small bulb fennel, trimmed and chopped (1 cup)
 2 cloves garlic, minced
 1 tablespoon olive oil
1½ cups chopped broccoli
¼ cup water
 1 cup part-skim or smoked ricotta cheese
⅓ cup finely shredded Pecorino Romano cheese or Parmesan cheese
 1 tablespoon snipped fresh basil
 Nonstick cooking spray
 1 26-ounce jar marinara sauce
¼ cup dry red wine (optional)
1½ teaspoons fennel seeds, crushed

1 Cook pasta shells according to package directions; drain. Rinse with cold water; drain again. Set aside.

2 Meanwhile, in a large nonstick skillet cook onion, fennel, and garlic in hot oil until onion is tender. Add broccoli and the water. Cook, covered, over medium-low heat for 4 to 5 minutes or just until vegetables are tender. Remove from heat. Drain. Stir in ricotta cheese, Romano cheese, and basil.

3 Spoon cheese mixture into cooked pasta shells. Lightly coat a 2-quart rectangular baking dish with nonstick cooking spray. Spread ½ cup of the marinara sauce in the prepared baking dish. Arrange stuffed pasta shells in baking dish.

4 In a medium bowl combine remaining marinara sauce, the wine (if desired), and fennel seeds; spoon over stuffed pasta shells. Cover dish loosely with foil. Bake in a 375° oven about 35 minutes or until heated through.

2 cups dried penne pasta (6 ounces)

2 medium bulbs fennel (about 2 pounds)

1 tablespoon olive oil or cooking oil

1 tablespoon butter or margarine

3 cloves garlic, minced

¼ teaspoon crushed red pepper

2 small yellow, green, and/or red sweet peppers, cut into thin bite-size strips (about 1 cup)

1 15-ounce can Great Northern beans, rinsed and drained

1 teaspoon snipped fresh thyme or ¼ teaspoon dried thyme, crushed

Freshly ground black pepper (optional)

1 In a large saucepan cook pasta according to package directions. Drain; return pasta to saucepan and keep warm.

2 Meanwhile, cut off feathery leaves and upper stalks of fennel bulbs. If desired, reserve some of the feathery leaves for garnish; discard upper stalks. Remove any wilted outer layers of stalks. Wash fennel and cut lengthwise into quarters. Remove core and discard; cut fennel into thin strips.

3 In a large skillet heat oil and butter over medium-high heat until butter is melted; add garlic and crushed red pepper. Cook for 30 seconds. Add fennel to skillet; cook and stir for 5 minutes. Add sweet pepper strips; cook for 3 minutes more. Add the beans and thyme; cook about 2 minutes or until heated through.

4 To serve, add fennel mixture to pasta; toss gently to combine. If desired, season to taste with freshly ground black pepper. If desired, garnish with reserved fennel leaves.

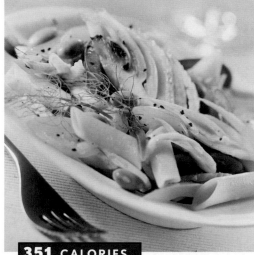

351 CALORIES

Penne with Fennel

Fennel's licoricelike tones impart an intriguing flavor. You'll find fennel at its peak in winter, so cozy up to this hearty recipe the next time the cold wind blows.

Start to Finish: 30 minutes
Makes: 4 servings

Nutrition Facts per serving:
351 cal., 8 g total fat (2 g sat. fat), 8 mg chol., 348 mg sodium, 59 g carbo., 11 g fiber, 13 g pro.
Daily Values:
46% vit. A, 125% vit. C, 16% calcium, 22% iron
Exchanges:
2 Vegetable, 3 Starch, 1 Fat

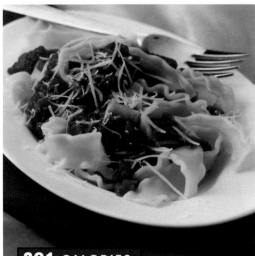

291 CALORIES

Pasta with Red Pepper Sauce

Sometimes you need a break from ordinary pasta sauce. Sweet red pepper sauce replaces chunky meat sauce and cooks in less time.

Prep: 20 minutes **Bake:** 20 minutes
Cool: 20 minutes **Oven:** 400°F
Makes: 5 servings

6 **medium red sweet peppers (8 to 10 ounces each)**

4 **cloves garlic, peeled**

10 **ounces dried pasta (such as mafalda or penne)**

1 **cup water**

1 **6-ounce can tomato paste**

1/2 **cup loosely packed fresh basil or 2 teaspoons dried basil, crushed**

2 **tablespoons balsamic vinegar**

1/4 **teaspoon salt**

Finely shredded Parmesan cheese (optional)

1 Cut peppers lengthwise into quarters; remove stems, seeds, and membranes. Place, cut sides down, on a large foil-lined baking sheet. Add garlic cloves to baking sheet. Bake in a 400° oven about 20 minutes or until peppers are tender and lightly browned. Cool about 20 minutes or until cool enough to handle.

2 Meanwhile, cook pasta according to package directions; drain and keep warm.

3 Place half each of the sweet peppers, garlic, the water, tomato paste, basil, and vinegar in a blender container or food processor bowl. Cover and blend or process until mixture is nearly smooth. Transfer to a medium saucepan. Repeat with remaining sweet peppers, garlic, water, tomato paste, basil, and vinegar. Stir in salt. Cook and stir sauce over medium-low heat until heated through.

4 To serve, spoon sauce over hot pasta. If desired, sprinkle with Parmesan cheese.

Nutrition Facts per serving:
291 cal., 1 g total fat (0 g sat. fat), 0 mg chol., 145 mg sodium, 60 g carbo., 5 g fiber, 11 g pro.
Daily Values:
156% vit. A, 438% vit. C, 3% calcium, 17% iron
Exchanges:
3 Vegetable, 3 Starch

- **2** cups dried rigatoni or penne pasta (about 6 ounces)
- **4** ounces fresh green beans and/or wax beans, bias-cut into 1-inch pieces
- **1/3** cup coarsely chopped red onion (1 small)
- **1** clove garlic, minced
- **2** teaspoons olive oil
- **6** small yellow or red roma tomatoes, halved
- **1/4** cup dry white wine, vegetable broth, or chicken broth
- **2** tablespoons finely shredded Parmesan cheese
- **1** tablespoon snipped fresh flat-leaf parsley
  Freshly ground black pepper (optional)

1 In a large saucepan cook pasta and beans in a large amount of lightly salted boiling water about 14 minutes or until pasta and beans are tender. Drain; return to pan.

2 Meanwhile, in a medium saucepan cook onion and garlic in hot oil over medium heat for 2 to 3 minutes or until onion is tender. Reduce heat to low. Add tomatoes and wine or broth; cook and stir for 2 minutes more.

3 Add tomato mixture to pasta mixture; toss lightly to combine. Transfer to a serving dish. Sprinkle with Parmesan cheese and parsley. If desired, season to taste with freshly ground black pepper.

Pasta with Beans and Tomatoes

Most string beans are stringless these days, saving you prep time. A little white wine rounds out the sauce. You can substitute vegetable or chicken broth without risking any flavor.

Start to Finish: 30 minutes
Makes: 3 servings

295 CALORIES

Nutrition Facts per serving:
295 cal., 5 g total fat (1 g sat. fat), 2 mg chol., 68 mg sodium, 50 g carbo., 4 g fiber, 10 g pro.
Daily Values:
13% vit. A, 31% vit. C, 7% calcium, 14% iron
Exchanges:
2 Vegetable, 2 1/2 Starch, 1/2 Fat

Pasta Rosa-Verde

This red, white, and green dish is enough to make any flag-waving Italian feel patriotic (not to mention eager to eat)! Fresh tomatoes are quick-cooked with peppery arugula and topped with tangy Gorgonzola cheese.

Start to Finish: 30 minutes

Makes: 4 servings

346 CALORIES

2²/₃ cups dried radiatore, cut ziti, or mostaccioli pasta (8 ounces)

1 medium onion, thinly sliced

2 cloves garlic, minced

1 tablespoon olive oil

4 to 6 medium tomatoes, seeded and coarsely chopped (3 cups)

1 teaspoon salt

¹/₂ teaspoon freshly ground black pepper

¹/₄ teaspoon crushed red pepper (optional)

3 cups arugula, watercress, and/or fresh spinach, coarsely chopped

¹/₄ cup broken walnuts or pine nuts, toasted

2 tablespoons crumbled Gorgonzola or other blue cheese

1 Cook pasta according to package directions. Drain. Cover and keep warm.

2 Meanwhile, in a large skillet cook onion and garlic in hot oil over medium heat until onion is tender. Add tomatoes, salt, black pepper, and, if desired, red pepper. Cook and stir over medium-high heat about 2 minutes or until the tomatoes are warm and release some of their juices. Stir in arugula, watercress, or spinach; heat just until wilted.

3 To serve, divide pasta among 4 dinner plates. Top with tomato mixture. Sprinkle with nuts and cheese.

Nutrition Facts per serving:
346 cal., 11 g total fat (2 g sat. fat), 3 mg chol., 660 mg sodium, 52 g carbo., 4 g fiber, 11 g pro.
Daily Values:
25% vit. A, 50% vit. C, 8% calcium, 16% iron
Exchanges:
3 Vegetable, 2¹/₂ Starch, 1¹/₂ Fat

9   medium roma tomatoes, seeded and
    cut into thin wedges

2   medium zucchini, halved lengthwise
    and cut into 1/2-inch slices

2   tablespoons olive oil

4   cloves garlic, minced

1/2   teaspoon salt

1/4   teaspoon black pepper

2   cups dried penne or rotini pasta
    (about 6 ounces)

3   tablespoons Italian-style tomato paste

1/2   cup finely shredded Parmesan cheese
    (2 ounces)

1/4   cup slivered fresh basil

1 Place tomatoes and zucchini in a 3-quart
rectangular baking dish. In a small bowl
combine oil, garlic, salt, and pepper;
drizzle over tomato mixture. Roast
vegetables, uncovered, in a 400° oven for
20 minutes, stirring once.

2 Meanwhile, cook pasta according to
package directions; drain. Stir pasta into
the roasted vegetable mixture along with
the tomato paste. Bake, uncovered, in the
400° oven for 10 minutes more.

3 To serve, stir pasta and vegetable mixture.
Divide mixture evenly among 4 dinner
plates. Sprinkle with Parmesan cheese
and basil.

327 CALORIES

Oven-Roasted Vegetable Penne

Who says pasta is fattening? This terrific
vegetarian main dish totals 11 grams of fat
and less than 350 calories per serving.
You really can eat well on a diet.

Prep: 15 minutes   **Roast:** 30 minutes
Oven: 400°F   **Makes:** 4 servings

Nutrition Facts per serving:
327 cal., 11 g total fat (3 g sat. fat), 7 mg chol.,
591 mg sodium, 47 g carbo., 5 g fiber, 12 g pro.
Daily Values:
32% vit. A, 78% vit. C, 16% calcium, 16% iron
Exchanges:
3 Vegetable, 2 Starch, 1/2 Meat, 1 Fat

250 CALORIES

Orzo with Root Vegetables

This one is just right for the summer months when quick-to-fix light suppers are the order of the day. Strips of mellow-tasting carrot and turnip keep the dish bright and colorful.

Start to Finish: 30 minutes

Makes: 4 servings

1 large onion, halved and thinly sliced
2 cloves garlic, minced
1 tablespoon olive oil
1 14-ounce can chicken broth or vegetable broth
1/4 cup water
1/2 teaspoon dried thyme, crushed
1/8 teaspoon cayenne pepper
3/4 cup dried orzo (rosamarina)
2 medium carrots, cut into thin bite-size strips
1 15-ounce can red beans, rinsed and drained
1 medium turnip, cut into thin bite-size strips
1 medium red sweet pepper, cut into thin bite-size strips

1 In a large saucepan cook onion and garlic in hot oil just until tender. Stir in broth, the water, thyme, and cayenne pepper. Bring to boiling. Add orzo and carrots. Simmer, covered, for 10 minutes.

2 Stir in red beans, turnip, and sweet pepper. Return to boiling; reduce heat. Simmer, covered, for 2 to 3 minutes more or until orzo is tender.

Nutrition Facts per serving:
250 cal., 5 g total fat (1 g sat. fat), 0 mg chol., 524 mg sodium, 43 g carbo., 9 g fiber, 13 g pro.
Daily Values:
187% vit. A, 96% vit. C, 7% calcium, 16% iron
Exchanges:
2 Vegetable, 2 1/2 Starch, 1/2 Fat

3 cups dried cavatelli or rotini pasta
   (8 ounces)
1/2 cup vegetable broth or chicken broth
2 cloves garlic, minced
2 teaspoons olive oil
6 cups torn arugula and/or fresh
   spinach
1/2 cup dried cranberries or raisins
1/3 cup sliced almonds or coarsely
   chopped pistachio nuts, toasted
1 ounce Parmesan cheese, shaved
   (optional)

1 Cook pasta according to package directions; drain. Toss with broth and keep warm.

2 Meanwhile, in a large skillet cook garlic in hot oil over medium heat for 1 minute. Add arugula and/or spinach; cook and stir for 1 to 2 minutes or just until wilted.

3 To serve, in a large bowl combine warm pasta mixture, arugula mixture, cranberries or raisins, and nuts. Toss gently to combine. If desired, top with Parmesan cheese.

Cavatelli with Arugula and Dried Cranberries

This elegant pasta supper will leave you satisfied but not stuffed. Peppery Italian arugula and pungent garlic punch up the sweetness of the dried cranberries.

Start to Finish: 20 minutes
Makes: 6 servings

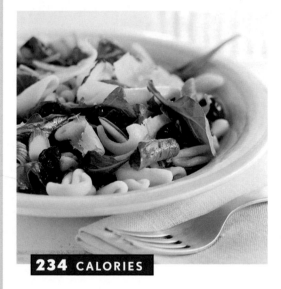

234 CALORIES

Nutrition Facts per serving:
234 cal., 6 g total fat (1 g sat. fat), 0 mg chol.,
92 mg sodium, 39 g carbo., 3 g fiber, 7 g pro.
Daily Values:
10% vit. A, 6% vit. C, 6% calcium, 10% iron
Exchanges:
1/2 Fruit, 2 Starch, 1 Fat

Zucchini, Corn, and Potato Tacos

Packed with so many flavors and so much nutrition, these tacos will tempt even picky eaters who haven't yet discovered the goodness of tofu.

Start to Finish: 40 minutes **Oven:** 350°F

Makes: 6 servings

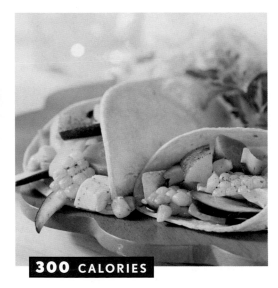

300 CALORIES

Nutrition Facts per serving:
300 cal., 12 g total fat (5 g sat. fat), 20 mg chol., 435 mg sodium, 40 g carbo., 5 g fiber, 13 g pro.
Daily Values:
118% vit. A, 18% vit. C, 26% calcium, 12% iron
Exchanges:
1 Vegetable, 2 Starch, 1 Meat, 1 Fat

- 1 medium potato, cut into ½-inch cubes (1 cup)
- 1 cup coarsely chopped carrot (2 medium)
- 12 corn tortillas
- ½ cup chopped onion (1 medium)
- 1 clove garlic, minced
- 1 tablespoon olive oil or cooking oil
- 1 small zucchini (about 6 ounces), cut into thin bite-size strips (about 1¼ cups)
- 1 cup fresh or frozen whole kernel corn
- 1 tablespoon chili powder
- ½ teaspoon salt
- ⅛ teaspoon black pepper
- 8 ounces firm tofu (fresh bean curd), cut into ½-inch cubes (1½ cups)
  Fresh cilantro sprigs (optional)
- 1 cup shredded cheddar and/or Monterey Jack cheese (4 ounces)
  Bottled salsa (optional)
  Sliced green onions (optional)
  Dairy sour cream and/or peeled avocado slices (optional)

1 In a covered medium saucepan cook the potato and carrot in a small amount of boiling water for 7 to 8 minutes or just until tender; drain and set aside.

2 Wrap tortillas tightly in foil. Heat in a 350° oven for 10 to 15 minutes or until heated through. Meanwhile, in a large skillet cook and stir onion and garlic in hot oil over medium-high heat for 2 minutes.

3 Add zucchini and corn; cook and stir for 3 minutes more. Add chili powder, salt, and pepper. Cook and stir for 1 minute more. Gently stir in potato-carrot mixture and tofu. Heat through.

4 Fill tortillas with vegetable mixture. If desired, garnish with cilantro sprigs. Pass cheese with tacos. If desired, serve with salsa, green onions, and sour cream and/or avocado.

1 15-ounce can black-eyed peas, rinsed
   and drained

1 13³/₄- to 14-ounce can artichoke
   hearts, drained and cut up

¹/₂ cup torn mixed salad greens

¹/₄ cup bottled creamy garlic salad dressing

¹/₄ teaspoon cracked black pepper

3 pita bread rounds, halved crosswise

1 small tomato, sliced

1 In a medium bowl combine black-eyed peas, artichoke hearts, mixed greens, salad dressing, and pepper. Line pita bread halves with tomato slices. Spoon artichoke mixture into pita bread halves.

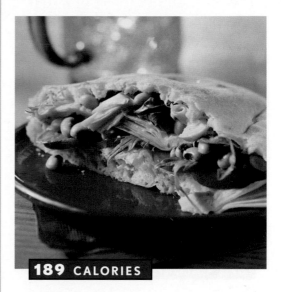

189 CALORIES

Peppery Artichoke Pitas

These pitas, filled with ingredients you can keep on hand—canned artichokes, canned beans, and bottled garlic dressing—take advantage of convenience foods to put a great dinner on the table.

Start to Finish: 20 minutes
Makes: 6 servings

Nutrition Facts per serving:
189 cal., 4 g total fat (1 g sat. fat), 0 mg chol., 632 mg sodium, 31 g carbo., 5 g fiber, 7 g pro.
Daily Values:
4% vit. A, 7% vit. C, 7% calcium, 17% iron
Exchanges:
1 Vegetable, 1¹/₂ Starch, ¹/₂ Fat

271 CALORIES

Eggplant Panini

Why say sandwich when you can say panini? The Italian word sounds so much more enticing, with a promise of unexpected delights.

Start to Finish: 25 minutes
Makes: 6 servings

- 1 cup torn arugula
- 2 teaspoons red wine vinegar
- 1 teaspoon olive oil
- 1/3 cup seasoned fine dry bread crumbs
- 2 tablespoons grated Pecorino Romano cheese or Parmesan cheese
- 1 egg
- 1 tablespoon milk
- 2 tablespoons all-purpose flour
- 1/2 teaspoon salt
- 1 medium eggplant, cut crosswise into 1/2-inch slices
- 1 tablespoon olive oil
- 3 ounces fresh mozzarella cheese, thinly sliced
- 6 individual focaccia rolls or one 12-inch plain or seasoned Italian flat bread (focaccia),* halved horizontally
- 1 large tomato, thinly sliced

1 In a small bowl toss together the arugula, red wine vinegar, and the 1 teaspoon oil; set aside. In a shallow dish stir together the bread crumbs and Romano cheese. In another shallow dish beat together the egg and milk. In a third shallow dish stir together the flour and salt. Dip the eggplant slices into flour mixture to coat. Dip the slices into egg mixture; coat both sides with bread crumb mixture.

2 In a 12-inch nonstick skillet heat the 1 tablespoon oil over medium heat. Add eggplant slices; cook for 6 to 8 minutes or until lightly browned, turning once. (Add more oil as necessary during cooking.) Top the eggplant with mozzarella cheese; reduce heat to low. Cook, covered, just until cheese begins to melt.

3 To serve, place the tomato slices on bottom halves of rolls. Top with eggplant slices, cheese sides up; the arugula mixture; and top halves of rolls. (Or place tomato slices on bottom half of bread. Top with eggplant slices, arugula mixture, and top half of bread. Cut into wedges.)

*Note: For easier slicing, purchase focaccia that is at least 2½ inches thick.

Nutrition Facts per serving:
271 cal., 10 g total fat (3 g sat. fat), 53 mg chol., 687 mg sodium, 37 g carbo., 3 g fiber, 12 g pro.
Daily Values:
9% vit. A, 11% vit. C, 22% calcium, 6% iron
Exchanges:
1 Vegetable, 2 Starch, 1 Meat, 1/2 Fat

1 **49-ounce can reduced-sodium chicken broth (about 6 cups) or 6 cups vegetable broth**

1 **10- to 12-ounce package extra-firm tofu (fresh bean curd), drained and cut into 1/2-inch cubes**

1 **tablespoon soy sauce**

1 **tablespoon toasted sesame oil**

6 **ounces fresh mushrooms (such as shiitake or button), sliced (about 2 1/4 cups)**

1 **tablespoon grated fresh ginger**

1 **clove garlic, minced**

1 **tablespoon cooking oil**

1 **16-ounce package frozen stir-fry vegetables**

2 **ounces dried udon noodles or spaghetti, broken**

1 **tablespoon snipped fresh cilantro**

1 In a large saucepan bring the broth to boiling. Meanwhile, in a medium bowl gently stir together tofu cubes, soy sauce, and sesame oil; set aside.

2 In a medium saucepan cook the sliced mushrooms, ginger, and garlic in hot oil for 4 minutes. Add to the hot broth. Stir in the frozen vegetables and udon noodles or spaghetti. Bring to boiling; reduce heat. Simmer, covered, for 10 to 12 minutes or until vegetables and noodles are tender, stirring once or twice. Gently stir in tofu mixture and cilantro; heat through.

Mushroom, Tofu, and Noodle Soup

Japanese udon (oo-DOHN) noodles are similar to spaghetti. Look for them in Asian markets or in the Asian section of your supermarket.

Start to Finish: 35 minutes
Makes: 6 servings (about 9 cups)

173 CALORIES

Nutrition Facts per serving:
173 cal., 8 g total fat (1 g sat. fat), 0 mg chol., 774 mg sodium, 15 g carbo., 1 g fiber, 12 g pro.
Daily Values:
7% vit. A, 34% vit. C, 5% calcium, 7% iron
Exchanges:
1 Vegetable, 1/2 Starch, 1 Meat, 1/2 Fat

Vegetable Soup

This ultimate vegetable soup makes the most of an array of produce—everything from green beans to sweet potatoes. Enjoy it alone for a light lunch or, for a heartier meal, serve it with a toasted cheese sandwich made with reduced-fat cheese.

Prep: 30 minutes   **Cook:** 35 minutes
Makes: 5 servings (about 7½ cups)

187 CALORIES

1/2 cup chopped onion (1 medium)
  3 cloves garlic, minced
  1 tablespoon olive oil
  3 14-ounce cans vegetable broth or reduced-sodium chicken broth
  1 cup apple juice
  1 14½-ounce can stewed tomatoes, undrained
1½ cups sliced celery (3 stalks)
  1 cup thinly sliced carrots (2 medium)
2/3 cup coarsely chopped peeled apple (1 medium)
  1 medium sweet potato, peeled and cut into ½-inch cubes (1¼ cups)
1½ cups shredded cabbage
  4 ounces fresh green beans, cut into 1½-inch pieces (1 cup), or 1 cup loose-pack frozen cut green beans
1/2 teaspoon ground coriander
1/4 teaspoon black pepper

1 In a 4-quart Dutch oven cook onion and garlic in hot oil about 3 minutes or until nearly tender.

2 Carefully add the broth, apple juice, tomatoes, celery, carrots, apple, and sweet potato. Bring to boiling; reduce heat. Simmer, covered, for 20 minutes.

3 Add cabbage, beans, coriander, and pepper. Return to boiling; reduce heat. Simmer, covered, about 15 minutes more or until vegetables are tender.

Nutrition Facts per serving:
187 cal., 5 g total fat (0 g sat. fat), 0 mg chol., 1,181 mg sodium, 35 g carbo., 5 g fiber, 5 g pro.
Daily Values:
251% vit. A, 35% vit. C, 8% calcium, 8% iron
Exchanges:
4 Vegetable, ½ Fruit, 1 Starch, ½ Fat

- 1 teaspoon cumin seeds
- ¼ teaspoon chili powder
- 2 14-ounce cans vegetable broth or chicken broth
- 1 15-ounce can chickpeas (garbanzo beans), rinsed and drained
- 1 cup peeled jicama cut into bite-size pieces
- ⅓ cup sliced green onions
- 3 cups torn fresh spinach
- ¼ cup crushed baked tortilla chips

1 In a 2-quart saucepan heat and stir cumin seeds and chili powder over medium heat for 1 to 2 minutes or until slightly fragrant. Remove from heat; carefully add broth and chickpeas.

2 Bring to boiling; stir in jicama and green onions. Return to boiling. Stir in spinach. Immediately divide among 4 soup bowls. Sprinkle each serving with some of the crushed tortilla chips.

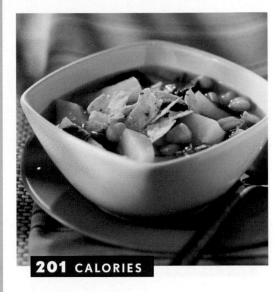

201 CALORIES

Mexican Vegetable Soup

Shredded spinach adds freshness to this no-meat chili, and chickpeas and jicama offer an unexpected twist to the traditional chili ingredients.

Start to Finish: 25 minutes
Makes: 4 servings (about 5 cups)

Nutrition Facts per serving:
201 cal., 3 g total fat (0 g sat. fat), 0 mg chol., 1,599 mg sodium, 33 g carbo., 9 g fiber, 11 g pro.
Daily Values:
40% vit. A, 34% vit. C, 9% calcium, 24% iron
Exchanges:
2 Vegetable, 1½ Starch, ½ Meat

213 CALORIES

Hearty Bean and Rice Soup

Arborio rice is an Italian-grown grain that is shorter and plumper than any other short-grain rice. Traditionally used to make creamy risotto, it lends its texture to this bean and vegetable soup.

Start to Finish: 30 minutes

Makes: 6 servings (about 10½ cups)

1 cup chopped celery (2 stalks)
1 cup chopped onion (1 large)
2 cloves garlic
1 tablespoon olive oil
5 cups vegetable broth or chicken broth
1 cup water
½ cup arborio rice
3 medium tomatoes
1 medium zucchini
6 cups torn fresh spinach
1 15-ounce can Great Northern beans, rinsed and drained
¼ cup snipped fresh thyme
¼ teaspoon cracked black pepper
½ cup crumbled feta cheese (2 ounces)

1 In a Dutch oven cook celery, onion, and garlic in hot oil until tender. Add broth, the water, and uncooked rice. Bring to boiling; reduce heat. Simmer, covered, for 15 minutes.

2 Meanwhile, chop the tomatoes; coarsely chop the zucchini. Stir tomatoes, zucchini, torn spinach, beans, thyme, and pepper into mixture in Dutch oven. Cook and stir until heated through. Top each serving with feta cheese.

Nutrition Facts per serving:
213 cal., 6 g total fat (2 g sat. fat), 8 mg chol., 1,165 mg sodium, 33 g carbo., 8 g fiber, 10 g pro.
Daily Values:
49% vit. A, 44% vit. C, 16% calcium, 27% iron
Exchanges:
2 Vegetable, 1½ Starch, ½ Meat, ½ Fat

- 3 cups loose-pack frozen whole kernel corn*
- 1 14-ounce can chicken broth or vegetable broth
- 1¼ cups cooked small pasta (such as ditalini or tiny shell macaroni)
- 1 cup milk, half-and-half, or light cream
- ¼ of a 7-ounce jar (¼ cup) roasted red sweet peppers, drained and chopped
- 1 or 2 fresh jalapeño chile peppers, seeded and finely chopped (see note on page 76)
- ½ cup crumbled feta cheese (2 ounces) (optional)

1 In a blender container or food processor bowl combine half of the corn and the broth. Cover and blend or process until nearly smooth.

2 In a large saucepan combine the broth mixture and the remaining corn.

3 Stir in cooked pasta, milk, roasted sweet peppers, and jalapeño peppers; heat through. If desired, top each serving with feta cheese.

*Note: If desired, for a roasted corn flavor, spread the corn on a baking sheet. Preheat broiler and broil corn 4 to 6 inches from the heat about 15 minutes or until tender, stirring once halfway through broiling time. Continue as directed in step 1.

Jalapeño Corn Chowder

This rich chowder features the popular Southwestern flavors of corn, jalapeño peppers, and red sweet peppers. Although not a must, crumbled feta cheese sprinkled over each serving is a salty, tangy touch you should try at least once.

Start to Finish: 20 minutes
Makes: 4 servings (about 5 cups)

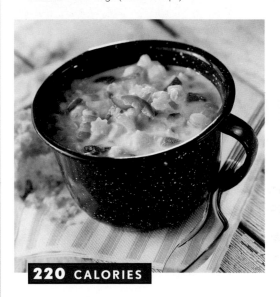

220 CALORIES

Nutrition Facts per serving:
220 cal., 3 g total fat (1 g sat. fat), 5 mg chol., 350 mg sodium, 42 g carbo., 3 g fiber, 10 g pro.
Daily Values:
3% vit. A, 59% vit. C, 9% calcium, 8% iron
Exchanges:
1 Vegetable, 2½ Starch

Chickpea Stew

Most stews are so hearty it makes sense to save them for the winter months, but this one, chock-full of veggies and the protein of chickpeas, works all year long.

Start to Finish: 25 minutes
Makes: 4 servings (about 6 cups)

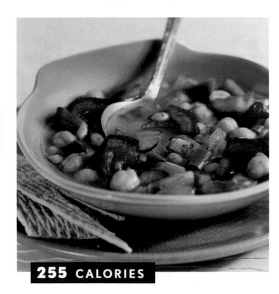

255 CALORIES

1   cup chopped onion (1 large)
³/₄ cup chopped green sweet pepper
    (1 medium)
3   cloves garlic, minced
2   teaspoons cooking oil
1¹/₂ teaspoons ground cumin
¹/₂ teaspoon paprika
¹/₈ to ¹/₄ teaspoon cayenne pepper
2   cups reduced-sodium chicken broth
    or vegetable broth
1¹/₂ cups water
1   10-ounce package (2 cups) frozen
    whole kernel corn
2   tablespoons snipped fresh oregano
1   15-ounce can chickpeas (garbanzo
    beans), rinsed and drained
²/₃ cup coarsely chopped tomato
    (1 medium)
2   tablespoons lemon juice
2   tablespoons sliced green onion

1 In a covered large saucepan cook onion, sweet pepper, and garlic in hot oil until onion is tender, stirring occasionally. Stir in cumin, paprika, and cayenne pepper; cook for 1 minute.

2 Carefully add broth, the water, corn, and oregano. Bring to boiling; reduce heat. Simmer, covered, for 5 to 10 minutes or until corn is tender. Stir in chickpeas, tomato, and lemon juice. Heat through. Ladle into serving bowls. Sprinkle with green onion.

Nutrition Facts per serving:
255 cal., 5 g total fat (1 g sat. fat), 0 mg chol.,
642 mg sodium, 48 g carbo., 8 g fiber, 10 g pro.
Daily Values:
13% vit. A, 70% vit. C, 7% calcium, 11% iron
Exchanges:
1 Vegetable, 2¹/₂ Starch, ¹/₂ Fat

3 cups cooked brown rice*

¼ cup chopped papaya or mango

3 tablespoons pitted ripe olives, coarsely chopped

2 tablespoons snipped fresh chives

2 tablespoons balsamic vinegar

1 tablespoon olive oil

3 tablespoons slivered almonds, toasted

1 papaya, seeded and cut into wedges

Lettuce or kale leaves

1 In a large bowl combine cooked rice, chopped papaya, olives, chives, balsamic vinegar, and oil; toss to combine.

2 Stir in almonds. Serve with papaya wedges. Garnish with lettuce or kale.

*Note: To cook brown rice, in a medium saucepan bring 2 cups water and ¼ teaspoon salt to boiling. Add 1 cup brown rice. Return to boiling; reduce heat. Simmer, covered, for 45 minutes. Let stand for 5 minutes. If desired, cover and chill up to 3 days.

Make-ahead directions: Prepare as above through step 1. Cover and chill up to 6 hours. Stir in almonds. Serve with papaya wedges. Garnish with lettuce or kale.

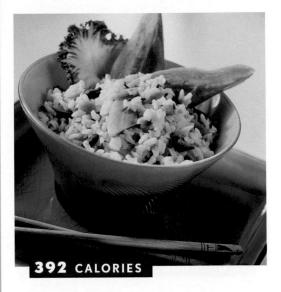

392 CALORIES

Papaya and Olives with Brown Rice

Compared to white rice, brown takes longer to cook, but it's loaded with whole grain goodness. You get the nutritious bran that white rice loses when it's polished and plenty of nutty flavor.

Cook (Rice): 45 minutes

Prep: 15 minutes

Makes: 3 servings

Nutrition Facts per serving:
392 cal., 12 g total fat (1 g sat. fat), 0 mg chol., 94 mg sodium, 65 g carbo., 6 g fiber, 8 g pro.
Daily Values:
10% vit. A, 131% vit. C, 8% calcium, 11% iron
Exchanges:
1 Fruit, 3 Starch, 2 Fat

236 CALORIES

Herb and Pepper Lentil Soup

This soup is extra heavenly served with pappadams, wafer-thin East Indian breads made with lentil flour. Look for them in specialty markets or in large supermarkets. To toast, preheat oven to 375°F. Place pappadams directly on oven rack. Bake about 1 minute or until lightly browned. Set aside to crisp.

Start to Finish: 35 minutes
Makes: 4 servings (about 6 cups)

Nutrition Facts per serving:
236 cal., 3 g total fat (1 g sat. fat), 0 mg chol., 519 mg sodium, 38 g carbo., 10 g fiber, 14 g pro.
Daily Values:
4% vit. A, 45% vit. C, 5% calcium, 17% iron
Exchanges:
1 Vegetable, 2 Starch, 1 Meat, 1/2 Fat

1   medium onion, cut into wedges
1   tablespoon cooking oil
3/4   cup chopped green sweet pepper (1 medium)
5   cups water
1¼   cups dry red lentils,* rinsed and drained
4   teaspoons instant vegetable bouillon granules, 4 teaspoons instant chicken bouillon granules, or 2 vegetable bouillon cubes, crushed
1   tablespoon snipped fresh thyme or 1 teaspoon dried thyme, crushed
1/8   to 1/4 teaspoon crushed red pepper
    Fresh thyme sprigs (optional)
    Pappadams (optional)

1 In a large saucepan cook onion in hot oil over medium heat about 8 minutes or until browned, stirring occasionally. Add sweet pepper; cook and stir for 2 minutes. Add the water, lentils, bouillon, dried thyme (if using), and crushed red pepper. Bring just to boiling; reduce heat. Simmer, uncovered, about 15 minutes or until lentils are tender. Stir in snipped fresh thyme (if using).

2 To serve, ladle soup into bowls. If desired, top with fresh thyme sprigs and serve with pappadams.

***Note:** Dry brown or green lentils may be substituted for the red lentils. Prepare as above, except simmer, covered, for 25 minutes. Uncover. Simmer about 5 minutes more or until the lentils are tender.

2²/₃ cups cooked wheat berries*
 ³/₄ cup chopped tomato
 ³/₄ cup chopped cucumber
 ¹/₂ cup snipped fresh parsley
 ¹/₄ cup thinly sliced green onions (2)
  1 tablespoon snipped fresh mint
  3 tablespoons cooking oil
  3 tablespoons lemon juice
 ¹/₄ teaspoon salt
    Sliced cucumber (optional)
    Sliced lemon (optional)

1 In a large bowl combine cooked wheat berries, tomato, chopped cucumber, parsley, green onions, and mint.

2 For dressing, in a screw-top jar combine oil, lemon juice, and salt. Cover and shake well. Drizzle dressing over wheat berry mixture; toss to coat.

3 To serve, if desired, arrange sliced cucumber and lemon around edge of bowl.

*Note: To cook wheat berries, in a medium saucepan bring one 14-ounce can vegetable broth or chicken broth and ¹/₄ cup water to boiling. Add 1 cup wheat berries. Return to boiling; reduce heat. Simmer, covered, about 1 hour or until tender; drain. Cover and refrigerate up to 3 days.

Make-ahead directions: Prepare as above through step 2. Cover and chill up to 24 hours. To serve, if desired, arrange sliced cucumber and lemon around edge of bowl.

Wheat Berry Tabouleh

Usually this Middle Eastern dish features light and fluffy cracked wheat. However, to make a more substantial salad, this version uses beanlike wheat berries. Look for them where natural foods are sold.

Start to Finish: 25 minutes
Makes: 4 servings

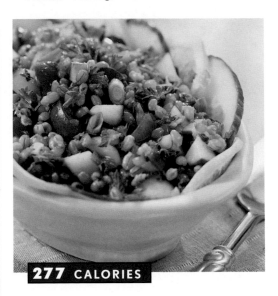

277 CALORIES

Nutrition Facts per serving:
277 cal., 12 g total fat (2 g sat. fat), 0 mg chol., 594 mg sodium, 38 g carbo., 7 g fiber, 9 g pro.
Daily Values:
17% vit. A, 43% vit. C, 5% calcium, 16% iron
Exchanges:
2 Starch, 1 Vegetable, 2 Fat

Confetti Barley Salad

No longer lost in the mix that makes up soups or stews, barley goes center stage in this refreshing color-studded recipe.

Prep: 15 minutes   **Cook:** 45 minutes
Makes: 6 servings

243 CALORIES

- 5   cups water
- 1   cup regular barley
- 2   cups loose-pack frozen soybean and sweet corn blend*
- ¼   cup white wine vinegar
- 3   tablespoons olive oil
- 1   tablespoon Dijon-style mustard
- 2   teaspoons snipped fresh oregano or ½ teaspoon dried oregano, crushed
- 2   cloves garlic, minced
- ½   teaspoon salt
- ¼   teaspoon black pepper
- 1   cup chopped red sweet pepper (1 large)
- ½   cup sliced pitted ripe olives
-    Fresh herb sprigs (optional)

1 In large saucepan bring water to boiling. Stir in barley; reduce heat. Simmer, covered, for 45 to 50 minutes or just until barley is tender, adding soybean and sweet corn blend for the last 10 minutes of cooking time. Drain. Rinse with cold water; drain again.

2 Meanwhile, for dressing, in a screw-top jar combine the vinegar, oil, mustard, oregano, garlic, salt, and black pepper. Cover and shake well. Set aside.

3 In a large bowl stir together the barley mixture, sweet pepper, and olives. Shake dressing. Pour the dressing over barley mixture; toss gently to coat. If desired, garnish with herb sprigs.

*Note: If you can't find the frozen soybean and sweet corn blend, substitute 1 cup frozen whole kernel corn, thawed, and 1 cup frozen soybeans or lima beans, thawed.

Make-ahead directions: Prepare as directed through step 3. Cover and chill up to 24 hours.

Nutrition Facts per serving:
243 cal., 10 g total fat (1 g sat. fat), 0 mg chol., 364 mg sodium, 32 g carbo., 8 g fiber, 7 g pro.
Daily Values:
30% vit. A, 86% vit. C, 5% calcium, 13% iron
Exchanges:
2 Starch, 1½ Fat

- ½ of a 16-ounce package frozen cheese-filled tortellini or one 9-ounce package refrigerated cheese-filled tortellini (about 2 cups)
- 1½ cups broccoli florets
- ¾ cup thinly sliced carrot (1 large)
- ¾ cup chopped yellow and/or red sweet pepper (1 medium)
- ¼ cup white wine vinegar
- 2 tablespoons olive oil
- 1 teaspoon dried Italian seasoning, crushed
- 1 teaspoon Dijon-style mustard
- ¼ teaspoon black pepper
- ⅛ teaspoon garlic powder
- Kale leaves (optional)

1 Cook pasta in a large saucepan according to package directions, except omit any oil and salt and add the broccoli, carrot, and sweet pepper for the last 3 minutes of cooking time. Return to boiling; reduce heat. Simmer, uncovered, about 3 minutes or until pasta is just tender and vegetables are crisp-tender. Drain. Rinse with cold water; drain again.

2 For dressing, in a screw-top jar combine the vinegar, oil, Italian seasoning, mustard, pepper, and garlic powder. Cover and shake well. Pour over pasta mixture; toss to coat. If desired, serve in kale-lined salad bowls.

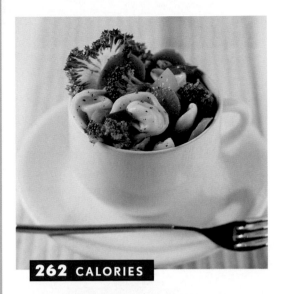

262 CALORIES

Deli-Style Pasta Salad

Want to speed things along? Substitute bottled fat-free Italian salad dressing for the homemade vinegar and oil dressing.

Start to Finish: 30 minutes
Makes: 4 servings

Nutrition Facts per serving:
262 cal., 10 g total fat (1 g sat. fat), 31 mg chol., 300 mg sodium, 33 g carbo., 2 g fiber, 11 g pro.
Daily Values:
155% vit. A, 122% vit. C, 3% calcium, 5% iron
Exchanges:
2 Vegetable, 1½ Starch, ½ Meat, 1 Fat

Egg and Vegetable Salad Cups

Old-fashioned egg salad gets a flavor boost from an assortment of vegetables, Dijon-style mustard, and fresh tarragon or basil. Serve it with crackers or breadsticks for lunch or a light supper.

Start to Finish: 30 minutes
Makes: 4 servings

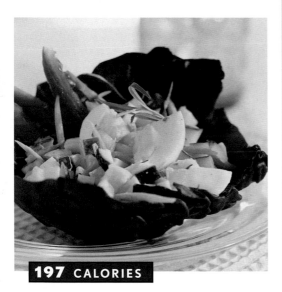

197 CALORIES

6 hard-cooked eggs, coarsely chopped
1 cup chopped cucumber
1 cup chopped zucchini or yellow summer squash
1/2 cup chopped red onion (1 medium)
1/2 cup shredded carrot (1 medium)
1/3 cup low-fat mayonnaise dressing
2 tablespoons Dijon-style mustard
1 tablespoon milk
1 teaspoon snipped fresh tarragon or basil
1/8 teaspoon paprika
   Milk (optional)
4 red cabbage cups
2 roma tomatoes, cut into thin wedges

1 In a large bowl combine eggs, cucumber, zucchini, red onion, and carrot. For dressing, in a small bowl stir together mayonnaise dressing, mustard, the 1 tablespoon milk, the tarragon or basil, and paprika. Pour the dressing over egg mixture; toss gently to coat. If desired, gently stir in enough additional milk to make desired consistency.

2 Place cabbage cups on 4 salad plates; spoon salad into cabbage cups. Arrange tomatoes in cabbage cups.

Nutrition Facts per serving:
197 cal., 10 g total fat (3 g sat. fat), 322 mg chol., 468 mg sodium, 15 g carbo., 3 g fiber, 11 g pro.
Daily Values:
105% vit. A, 45% vit. C, 9% calcium, 10% iron
Exchanges:
2 Vegetable, 1 Meat, 1/2 Fat

On the divider: Tomatoes with Fresh Mozzarella (see recipe, page 467)

12 cups mesclun or other torn mild
    salad greens

3 tablespoons olive oil

2 tablespoons regular orange juice or
   blood orange juice

2 tablespoons balsamic vinegar

8 thin slices red onion, separated into
   rings

2 cups regular orange sections and/or
   blood orange sections (6 regular
   oranges or 8 blood oranges)

2/3 cup mixed country olives or
    kalamata olives

1/8 teaspoon salt

1/8 teaspoon black pepper

3 fresh or dried figs, quartered
   (optional)

1 Place greens in a large salad bowl. For
  dressing, in a small bowl whisk together
  olive oil, orange juice, and vinegar. Pour
  dressing over greens; gently toss to mix.

2 Divide mixture among 8 salad plates. Top
  with onion rings, orange sections, and
  olives. Lightly sprinkle with salt and
  pepper. If desired, garnish salads with figs.

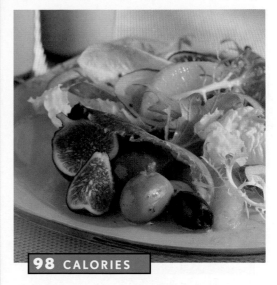

98 CALORIES

Greens with Oranges and Olives

For an exotic salad, use blood oranges or figs and arrange them on the greens along with the onions and olives.

Start to Finish: 15 minutes
Makes: 8 servings

Nutrition Facts per serving:
98 cal., 6 g total fat (1 g sat. fat), 0 mg chol.,
143 mg sodium, 10 g carbo., 3 g fiber, 1 g pro.
Daily Values:
8% vit. A, 49% vit. C, 5% calcium, 5% iron
Exchanges:
2 Vegetable, 1 Fat

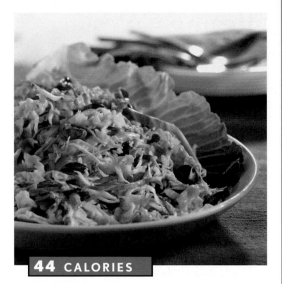

44 CALORIES

Cranberry Coleslaw

Choose fresh cranberries or more readily-available dried cranberries when putting together this simple coleslaw made with honey dressing.

Prep: 15 minutes **Chill:** Up to 45 minutes
Makes: 6 servings

¼ cup low-fat mayonnaise dressing
    or mayonnaise

1 to 2 tablespoons honey

1 tablespoon vinegar

¼ cup chopped fresh cranberries
    or snipped dried cranberries

5 cups shredded cabbage or packaged
    shredded cabbage with carrot
    (coleslaw mix)

    Cabbage leaves (optional)

1 For dressing, in a small bowl stir together mayonnaise, honey, and vinegar. Stir in the cranberries.

2 In a large bowl pour dressing over cabbage; toss to combine. Cover and chill up to 45 minutes. If desired, line a serving bowl with a few cabbage leaves and spoon in coleslaw mixture.

Nutrition Facts per serving:
44 cal., 1 g total fat (0 g sat. fat), 2 mg chol., 103 mg sodium, 10 g carbo., 2 g fiber, 1 g pro.
Daily Values:
2% vit. A, 33% vit. C, 3% calcium, 3% iron
Exchanges:
2 Vegetable

2 cups shredded cabbage

1 cup peeled jicama cut into thin bite-size strips

1 medium peach or nectarine, peeled, pitted, and chopped, or 1 medium apple, cored and chopped

¼ cup thinly sliced green onions (2)

3 tablespoons low-fat mayonnaise dressing

2 tablespoons snipped fresh cilantro

1 tablespoon cider vinegar

1½ teaspoons sugar

⅛ teaspoon cayenne pepper (optional)

1 In a large bowl combine cabbage, jicama, peach, and green onions.

2 For dressing, in a small bowl stir together mayonnaise dressing, cilantro, vinegar, sugar, and cayenne pepper, if using. Pour dressing over cabbage mixture; toss to combine. Cover and chill for 2 to 4 hours. If desired, serve in small bowls.

Jicama Coleslaw

Store whole jicama in the refrigerator up to 3 weeks. After cutting the jicama, wrap it in plastic wrap; refrigerate up to 1 week.

Prep: 25 minutes   **Chill:** 2 to 4 hours
Makes: 4 servings

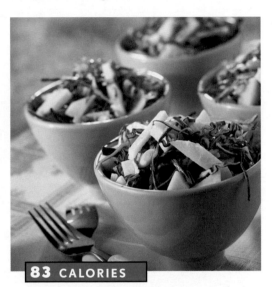

83 CALORIES

Nutrition Facts per serving:
83 cal., 4 g total fat (1 g sat. fat), 4 mg chol., 76 mg sodium, 12 g carbo., 2 g fiber, 1 g pro.
Daily Values:
6% vit. A, 41% vit. C, 3% calcium, 4% iron
Exchanges:
2½ Vegetable, ½ Fat

Honeydew and Apple Salad

When summer fruits aren't in season, try this refreshing three-ingredient, yogurt-based dressing on a combination of orange sections and banana slices.

Start to Finish: 15 minutes

Makes: 6 servings

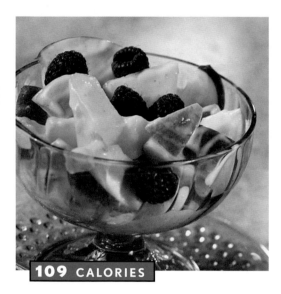

109 CALORIES

1/2	medium honeydew melon, peeled, seeded, and cut into bite-size pieces (2 cups)
2	medium tart apples, cored, halved lengthwise, and cut into bite-size pieces
2	medium nectarines or peaches, pitted and thinly sliced
1/4	cup vanilla low-fat yogurt
3	tablespoons apricot jam
1/4	teaspoon ground ginger or nutmeg
1	cup red raspberries

1 In a large bowl combine melon, apples, and nectarines. For dressing, in a small bowl stir together yogurt, jam, and spice.

2 Add dressing to fruit mixture; toss to coat. Spoon into dishes or glasses. Top with raspberries. Serve immediately.

Nutrition Facts per serving:
109 cal., 1 g total fat (0 g sat. fat), 1 mg chol., 16 mg sodium, 27 g carbo., 3 g fiber, 1 g pro.
Daily Values:
5% vit. A, 42% vit. C, 3% calcium, 2% iron
Exchanges:
2 Fruit

2 **pink or red grapefruit**

2 **navel oranges**

4 **cups Belgian endive leaves**

4 **cups torn curly endive or escarole**

1 **small jicama, peeled and cut into thin bite-size strips (about 2 cups)**

1 **recipe Citrus-Dijon Dressing**

1 Peel and section grapefruit and oranges over a bowl, reserving any juices for the dressing.

2 Place greens on individual salad plates. Arrange fruit and jicama on top of greens. Drizzle Citrus-Dijon Dressing over salads. Serve immediately.

Citrus-Dijon Dressing: In a screw-top jar combine reserved grapefruit and orange juices, ⅓ cup salad oil, 1 teaspoon finely shredded lemon peel, ¼ cup lemon juice, 1 tablespoon Dijon-style mustard, 2 teaspoons sugar, and ¼ teaspoon black pepper. Cover and shake well.

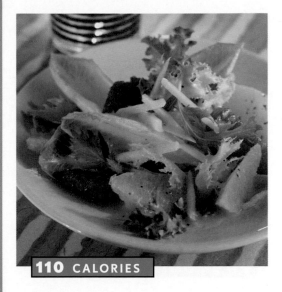

110 CALORIES

Mixed Citrus Salad

The sweet citrus fruit and tangy mustard dressing bring out the best curly endive and Belgian endive have to offer.

Start to Finish: 20 minutes
Makes: 10 servings

Nutrition Facts per serving:
110 cal., 8 g total fat (1 g sat. fat), 0 mg chol., 42 mg sodium, 11 g carbo., 2 g fiber, 1 g pro.
Daily Values:
11% vit. A, 63% vit. C, 3% calcium, 4% iron
Exchanges:
1 Vegetable, ½ Fruit, 1½ Fat

97 CALORIES

Snap Pea and Potato Salad

This is no ordinary potato salad. Colorful vegetables, fresh basil, and a creamy mayonnaise-yogurt dressing give this salad favorite a new twist.

Prep: 25 minutes   **Chill:** 2 to 8 hours
Makes: 6 servings

8 to 12 ounces Yukon gold or red potatoes, cubed (about 3 cups)

12 ounces fresh sugar snap peas, halved lengthwise, or snow peas, halved crosswise

8 ounces yellow summer squash, halved lengthwise and cut crosswise into slices (2 cups)

3 large green onions, sliced (1/2 cup)

3 tablespoons snipped fresh basil

1 recipe Creamy Dressing
   Green onion tops (optional)

1 In a covered saucepan cook potatoes covered with boiling salted water for 6 to 8 minutes. Add peas and squash for the last 2 to 3 minutes of cooking. Cook just until tender. Drain, rinse with cold water, and drain again. Transfer to a bowl.

2 Add green onions, basil, and Creamy Dressing; toss to coat. Cover and chill for 2 to 8 hours. If desired, garnish with a few green onion tops.

Creamy Dressing: In a small bowl combine 2 tablespoons low-fat mayonnaise dressing, 2 tablespoons plain low-fat yogurt, 2 tablespoons red wine vinegar, 2 teaspoons olive oil, 1/2 teaspoon salt, 1/4 teaspoon garlic powder, 1/4 teaspoon onion powder, 1/4 teaspoon paprika, and 1/4 teaspoon black pepper. Cover and refrigerate dressing up to 3 days.

Nutrition Facts per serving:
97 cal., 2 g total fat (0 g sat. fat), 1 mg chol., 257 mg sodium, 16 g carbo., 3 g fiber, 3 g pro.
Daily Values:
4% vit. A, 40% vit. C, 6% calcium, 9% iron
Exchanges:
2 Vegetable, 1/2 Starch

1　10-ounce package frozen lima beans

1　8-ounce package frozen sugar snap peas or one 9-ounce package frozen Italian green beans

1　6-ounce jar marinated artichoke hearts, undrained

1　tablespoon snipped fresh dill

1/8　teaspoon crushed red pepper

　　Romaine lettuce leaves

1　green onion, thinly sliced (optional)

　　Fresh dill (optional)

1 In a medium saucepan cook lima beans and snap peas or Italian green beans in a small amount of boiling water for 5 to 8 minutes or until crisp-tender; drain. Rinse with cold water; drain again.

2 In a medium bowl combine the lima bean mixture, undrained artichoke hearts, dill, and crushed red pepper. Cover and chill for 4 to 24 hours.

3 To serve, place the romaine leaves on salad plates. Spoon the lima bean mixture over romaine leaves. If desired, sprinkle with sliced green onion and garnish with fresh dill.

Italian-Style Vegetables

Marinated artichoke hearts provide both a vegetable and dressing for this pretty, green-hued salad combination, a welcome side to grilled or broiled meats.

Prep: 10 minutes　　**Cook:** 5 minutes
Chill: 4 to 24 hours　　**Makes:** 5 or 6 servings

131 CALORIES

Nutrition Facts per serving:
131 cal., 2 g total fat (0 g sat. fat), 0 mg chol., 141 mg sodium, 22 g carbo., 5 g fiber, 6 g pro.
Daily Values:
3% vit. A, 36% vit. C, 5% calcium, 11% iron
Exchanges:
1 Vegetable, 1 Starch

Rice Pilaf with Toasted Pecans

When you need a special side dish that goes beyond steamed rice, turn to this pilaf. With a mild lemon flavor, mushrooms, garlic, and toasted pecans, it seems a lot fancier than it really is.

Start to Finish: 30 minutes

Makes: 6 servings

161 CALORIES

2	cloves garlic, minced
2	teaspoons olive oil
1	cup uncooked long grain white rice
2½	cups reduced-sodium chicken broth
2	teaspoons finely shredded lemon peel
1½	cups sliced fresh mushrooms
½	cup thinly sliced green onions (4)
¼	cup chopped red sweet pepper
⅛	teaspoon black pepper
2	tablespoons chopped pecans, toasted
	Lemon slices (optional)

1 In a medium saucepan cook garlic in hot oil for 30 seconds. Add the rice and broth. Bring to boiling; reduce heat. Cover and simmer for 10 minutes.

2 Add the lemon peel, mushrooms, green onions, sweet pepper, and black pepper. Cover and cook 10 to 15 minutes more or until liquid is absorbed and rice is tender. Stir in toasted pecans. If desired, garnish with lemon slices.

Nutrition Facts per serving:
161 cal., 4 g total fat (0 g sat. fat), 0 mg chol., 263 mg sodium, 28 g carbo., 1 g fiber, 5 g pro.
Daily Values:
8% vit. A, 25% vit. C, 2% calcium, 10% iron
Exchanges:
1 Vegetable, 1½ Starch, ½ Fat

- **2** teaspoons olive oil
- **1** cup sliced fresh mushrooms
- **1/2** cup chopped onion
- **2/3** cup dried orzo pasta (rosamarina)
- **1** 14-ounce can reduced-sodium chicken broth
- **1/2** cup shredded carrot
- **1** teaspoon dried marjoram, crushed
- **1/8** teaspoon black pepper
- **2** cups small broccoli florets

1 In a large saucepan heat olive oil over medium-high heat. Cook and stir the mushrooms and onion in hot oil until onion is tender. Stir in orzo. Cook and stir about 2 minutes more or until orzo is lightly browned. Remove from heat.

2 Carefully stir in the chicken broth, carrot, marjoram, and pepper. Bring to boiling; reduce heat. Simmer, covered, about 15 minutes or until orzo is tender but still firm. Remove saucepan from heat; stir in broccoli. Let stand, covered, for 5 minutes.

83 CALORIES

Orzo-Broccoli Pilaf

Orzo is a tiny, rice-shape pasta, larger than a grain of rice and slightly smaller than a pine nut. For a change of pace, it makes a great substitute for the rice typically used in vegetable pilaf.

Prep: 20 minutes　**Cook:** 15 minutes
Stand: 5 minutes　**Makes:** 6 servings

Nutrition Facts per serving:
83 cal., 2 g total fat (0 g sat. fat), 0 mg chol., 184 mg sodium, 13 g carbo., 2 g fiber, 4 g pro.
Daily Values:
60% vit. A, 41% vit. C, 2% calcium, 5% iron
Exchanges:
1 Vegetable, 1/2 Starch

Vegetable Kabobs

These crisp-tender vegetable kabobs are the essence of simplicity—a coat of rosemary-scented dressing is their only embellishment.

Prep: 20 minutes   **Cook:** 8 minutes

Grill: 10 minutes   **Makes:** 8 servings

- 2 medium potatoes, quartered
- 8 red boiling onions or 2 small red onions, each cut into 8 wedges
- 8 baby squash, such as zucchini and/or yellow summer squash
- 8 medium fresh mushrooms
- 4 miniature sweet peppers, halved and seeded, and/or 1 or 2 small red and/or orange sweet peppers, cut into 1-inch pieces
- ¼ cup bottled oil-and-vinegar salad dressing
- 2 teaspoons snipped fresh rosemary or ½ teaspoon dried rosemary, crushed
- ⅛ teaspoon salt
- ⅛ teaspoon black pepper

1 In a medium covered saucepan cook potatoes and onions in a small amount of lightly salted boiling water over medium heat for 8 to 10 minutes or until nearly tender, adding the squash and mushrooms for the last 1 minute. Drain well. Cool slightly.

2 On eight 10-inch skewers alternately thread the potatoes, onions, squash, mushrooms, and sweet peppers. In a small bowl combine salad dressing, rosemary, salt, and black pepper; brush over vegetables.

3 Grill kabobs on the rack of an uncovered grill directly over medium heat for 10 to 12 minutes or until vegetables are tender and lightly browned, turning and brushing occasionally with dressing mixture. (To broil kabobs, preheat broiler. Place kabobs on the greased unheated rack of a broiler pan and broil 10 to 12 minutes, brushing occasionally with dressing mixture.)

Nutrition Facts per serving:
87 cal., 4 g total fat (1 g sat. fat), 0 mg chol., 147 mg sodium, 12 g carbo., 2 g fiber, 2 g pro.
Daily Values:
9% vit. A, 39% vit. C, 2% calcium, 5% iron
Exchanges:
1 Vegetable, ½ Starch, ½ Fat

Nonstick cooking spray

3½ cups cubed eggplant (1 small)

1 cup cubed yellow summer squash
   or zucchini (1 small)

8 pearl onions, halved

1 medium yellow sweet pepper, cut into
   1-inch strips

2 tablespoons snipped fresh flat-leaf
   parsley or regular parsley

1 tablespoon olive oil

2 cloves garlic, minced

⅛ teaspoon salt

⅛ teaspoon black pepper

2 large tomatoes, chopped

1½ teaspoons lemon juice

1 Coat a 15×10×1-inch baking pan with
cooking spray. Place eggplant, squash,
onions, sweet pepper, and parsley in the
prepared pan.

2 In a small bowl stir together oil, garlic,
salt, and black pepper. Drizzle over
vegetables; toss to coat.

3 Roast, uncovered, in a 450° oven about
20 minutes or until vegetables are tender
and lightly browned, stirring once. Stir in
the tomatoes and lemon juice. Roast,
uncovered, for 8 to 10 minutes more or
until tomatoes are very soft and starting
to juice out.

Roasted Ratatouille

Eggplant—that glossy, smooth-skinned fruit (yes, it's a fruit, although it's listed in the vegetable exchange list)—is a mainstay in ratatouille, a popular dish of France. You can serve this dish warm, cold, or at room temperature, as a side or as an appetizer with bread or crackers.

Prep: 15 minutes   **Roast:** 28 minutes
Oven: 450°F   **Makes:** 4 servings

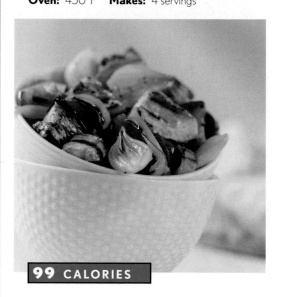

99 CALORIES

Nutrition Facts per serving:
99 cal., 4 g total fat (1 g sat. fat), 0 mg chol.,
87 mg sodium, 16 g carbo., 4 g fiber, 3 g pro.
Daily Values:
19% vit. A, 186% vit. C, 3% calcium, 7% iron
Exchanges:
3 Vegetable, ½ Fat

Four-Veggie Roast

Roasting brings out the sugars in the vegetables and caramelizes them for a mouthwatering result. Serve this side dish with a pork roast, or any simple meat-based entrée, for the ultimate weekend dinner.

Prep: 20 minutes   **Roast:** 20 minutes
Oven: 425°F   **Makes:** 4 servings

111 CALORIES

1 **tablespoon olive oil**
2 **teaspoons soy sauce**
2 **cloves garlic, minced**
1 **teaspoon grated fresh ginger**
2 **large carrots, peeled and bias-sliced into** $^1/_2$**-inch pieces**
1$^1/_2$ **cups fresh green beans (6 ounces), cut into 2-inch pieces**
5 **or 6 small new potatoes (8 ounces), halved**
1 **small onion, cut into wedges**
   Freshly ground black pepper

1 In large bowl combine olive oil, soy sauce, garlic, and ginger. Add carrots, green beans, potatoes, and onion. Stir gently to coat vegetables with seasonings.

2 Spread vegetables evenly in a 9×9×2- or 8×8×2-inch baking pan. Sprinkle with pepper. Roast the vegetables, uncovered, in a 425° oven for 20 to 25 minutes or just until tender, stirring once or twice.

Nutrition Facts per serving:
111 cal., 4 g total fat (1 g sat. fat), 0 mg chol., 175 mg sodium, 18 g carbo., 4 g fiber, 3 g pro.
Daily Values:
210% vit. A, 31% vit. C, 4% calcium, 8% iron
Exchanges:
2 Vegetable, $^1/_2$ Starch, $^1/_2$ Fat

- **2** pounds fresh asparagus spears
- **1** small onion, cut into thin wedges
- **1** small red or yellow sweet pepper, cut into thin strips
- **1** tablespoon olive oil
- **¼** teaspoon salt
- **¼** teaspoon black pepper
- **¼** cup shredded Gruyère or Swiss cheese (1 ounce)

1 Snap off and discard woody bases from asparagus spears. If desired, scrape off scales. Place asparagus, onion, and sweet pepper in a 15×10×1-inch baking pan. Drizzle with olive oil; toss gently to coat. Spread in a single layer. Sprinkle with the salt and pepper.

2 Roast, uncovered, in a 400° oven about 20 minutes or until asparagus is crisp-tender. Transfer to a serving platter; sprinkle with cheese. Let stand 2 minutes until cheese melts.

73 CALORIES

Roasted Asparagus with Gruyère

Slender stalks of asparagus and slivers of colorful sweet pepper lie under a sprinkling of Gruyère cheese. This recipe is proof that you don't have to deprive yourself to lose weight.

Prep: 15 minutes   **Roast:** 20 minutes
Oven: 400°F   **Stand:** 2 minutes
Makes: 6 servings

Nutrition Facts per serving:
73 cal., 4 g total fat (1 g sat. fat), 5 mg chol., 127 mg sodium, 4 g carbo., 2 g fiber, 4 g pro.
Daily Values:
5% vit. A, 94% vit. C, 6% calcium, 4% iron
Exchanges:
1 Vegetable, 1 Fat

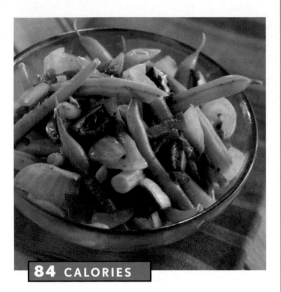

84 CALORIES

Beans and Caramelized Onions

No more boring beans! In this recipe, the familiar green bean takes on an exciting new flavor. Onions, sugar, and balsamic vinegar provide a sweet and tangy coating.

Start to Finish: 20 minutes
Makes: 5 servings

1 tablespoon butter or margarine
1¹/₂ cups chopped onion (3 medium)
1 teaspoon sugar
1 tablespoon balsamic vinegar or red wine vinegar
¹/₂ of a 7¹/₂-ounce jar roasted red sweet peppers, drained and finely chopped (¹/₂ cup)
¹/₄ cup quartered pitted ripe olives
2 tablespoons snipped fresh basil
¹/₄ teaspoon salt
¹/₄ teaspoon black pepper
1 pound fresh green beans, trimmed and cut into 2-inch pieces (about 4 cups)

1 In a large heavy skillet heat butter over medium heat until melted. Cook and stir onion and sugar in butter about 10 minutes or until the onion is very tender and golden brown. Stir in vinegar. Cook and stir for 1 to 2 minutes more or until liquid evaporates. Stir in the roasted sweet peppers, olives, basil, salt, and black pepper. Remove skillet from heat; keep warm.

2 Meanwhile, in a medium covered saucepan cook the green beans in a small amount of boiling water for 10 to 15 minutes or until crisp-tender; drain. To serve, stir onion mixture into the green beans.

Nutrition Facts per serving:
84 cal., 3 g total fat (2 g sat. fat), 7 mg chol., 207 mg sodium, 13 g carbo., 4 g fiber, 2 g pro.
Daily Values:
13% vit. A, 90% vit. C, 5% calcium, 8% iron
Exchanges:
2 Vegetable, ¹/₂ Fat

1 **pound fresh green beans, trimmed,
   or one 16-ounce package frozen
   whole or cut green beans**

2 **slices bacon**

1/2 **cup thinly sliced onion (1 small)**

2 **cloves garlic, minced**

2 **teaspoons brown mustard**

1/2 **teaspoon lemon-pepper seasoning
   or 1/4 teaspoon freshly ground
   black pepper**

1/8 **teaspoon salt**

1 In a large covered saucepan cook green beans in a small amount of boiling water for 10 to 15 minutes or until crisp-tender. (Cook frozen beans according to package directions.) Drain beans; rinse with cold water and set aside.

2 Meanwhile, in a skillet cook bacon until crisp. Remove bacon from pan, reserving 1 tablespoon drippings in skillet. Drain bacon on paper towels, crumble, and set aside. Cook onion and garlic in drippings in skillet over medium heat for 3 minutes or until tender. Stir in mustard, seasoning, and salt. Cook about 30 seconds more. Toss beans with onion mixture; heat through. Sprinkle with crumbled bacon.

Garlic-Mustard Green Beans

If green bean casserole is your idea of how to serve green beans, it's time to expand your horizons. The new way to serve these nutritious vegetables includes a mix of garlic, mustard, and bacon.

Start to Finish: 30 minutes
Makes: 6 servings

65 CALORIES

Nutrition Facts per serving:
65 cal., 4 g total fat (1 g sat. fat), 4 mg chol., 212 mg sodium, 7 g carbo., 3 g fiber, 2 g pro.
Daily Values:
9% vit. A, 17% vit. C, 3% calcium, 5% iron
Exchanges:
1 Vegetable, 1 Fat

Smoky Gouda-Sauced Broccoli

The kids will want to eat their broccoli when they taste this side dish, made irresistible with Gouda cheese. Serve it with something simple in flavor, such as a pork roast or grilled pork chops.

Prep: 20 minutes   **Bake:** 15 minutes
Oven: 425°F   **Makes:** 6 servings

145 CALORIES

1¼ **pounds broccoli, cut into spears**
½ **cup chopped onion (1 medium)**
2 **cloves garlic, minced**
1 **tablespoon butter**
2 **tablespoons all-purpose flour**
¼ **teaspoon salt**
⅛ **teaspoon black pepper**
1½ **cups light milk**
¾ **cup shredded smoked Gouda cheese (3 ounces)**
¾ **cup soft bread crumbs (1 slice bread)**
2 **teaspoons butter, melted**

1 Place a steamer basket in a large saucepan. Add water to just below the bottom of the steamer basket. Bring water to boiling. Add broccoli to steamer basket. Cover and reduce heat. Steam for 6 to 8 minutes or just until broccoli is tender.

2 Meanwhile, for sauce, in a medium saucepan cook and stir the onion and garlic in the 1 tablespoon hot butter until onion is tender. Stir in flour, salt, and pepper. Stir in the milk. Cook and stir until thickened and bubbly. Gradually add cheese, stirring until melted.

3 Transfer broccoli to a 1½-quart au gratin dish or 2-quart square baking dish. Pour sauce over broccoli. Combine bread crumbs and the 2 teaspoons melted butter; sprinkle over sauce. Bake, uncovered, in 425° oven for 15 minutes or until crumbs are lightly browned.

Nutrition Facts per serving:
145 cal., 8 g total fat (5 g sat. fat), 23 mg chol., 429 mg sodium, 13 g carbo., 2 g fiber, 7 g pro.
Daily Values:
22% vit. A, 79% vit. C, 20% calcium, 5% iron
Exchanges:
½ Milk, 1 Vegetable, ½ Meat, ½ Fat

½ cup chopped onion (1 medium)
 or leek (white part only) (1 large)

1 clove garlic, minced

1 tablespoon olive oil

½ cup reduced-sodium chicken broth

1½ pounds broccoli, cut into spears

1 tablespoon lemon juice

1 teaspoon all-purpose flour

2 tablespoons snipped fresh dill
 or 1 teaspoon dried dill

 Salt and black pepper

 Lemon slices (optional)

1 In a large saucepan cook and stir onion and garlic in hot oil about 3 minutes or until tender. Add broth; bring to boiling. Add broccoli and return to boiling. Reduce heat and cook, covered, for 8 to 10 minutes or until broccoli is tender. Transfer vegetables to a serving bowl, reserving broth in pan (add additional broth, if necessary, to measure ½ cup).

2 Combine lemon juice and flour; add to broth in saucepan. Cook and stir until thickened and bubbly; cook and stir 1 minute more. Add dill and season to taste with salt and pepper. Spoon sauce over vegetables and toss to coat. If desired, garnish with lemon slices.

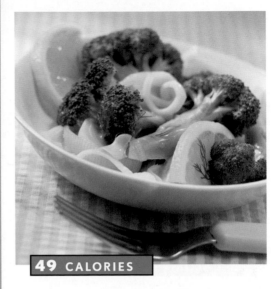

49 CALORIES

Broccoli with Lemon and Dill

A simmering in chicken broth and a splash of lemon create pleasant undertones in this broccoli side dish. Dill, along with garlic and onion, makes the perfect accent.

Start to Finish: 25 minutes
Makes: 6 to 8 servings

Nutrition Facts per serving:
49 cal., 3 g total fat (0 g sat. fat), 0 mg chol., 119 mg sodium, 6 g carbo., 2 g fiber, 3 g pro.
Daily Values:
20% vit. A, 95% vit. C, 4% calcium, 4% iron
Exchanges:
1 Vegetable, ½ Fat

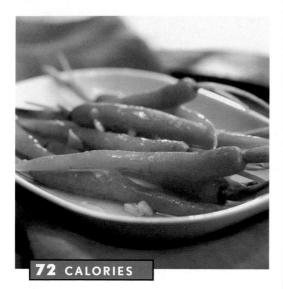

72 CALORIES

Ginger and Honey-Glazed Carrots

You'll forget that you're eating your vegetables when you taste these fresh, sweet carrots lightly coated with a buttery glaze accented with fresh ginger.

Prep: 30 minutes   **Cook:** 15 minutes
Makes: 6 servings

3   cups water
$1/2$ teaspoon salt
$1^1/2$ pounds young, small carrots with tops trimmed to 2 inches, peeled or scrubbed, or $1^1/2$ pounds packaged peeled baby carrots
1   tablespoon butter
1   tablespoon honey
2   teaspoons minced fresh ginger

1 Line a baking sheet with paper towels. In a large heavy skillet combine water and salt. Bring to boiling. Add carrots. Return to boiling; reduce heat. Cover and simmer about 10 to 12 minutes or until carrots are just tender. Drain carrots. Carefully turn out onto prepared baking sheet. (When green tops are left on carrots during cooking, the tops become very fragile; as the carrots cook, some of the tops may come off.) Pat dry with additional paper towels.

2 To glaze carrots, in the same heavy skillet combine butter, honey, and ginger. Stir constantly over medium heat until butter is melted. Carefully add carrots. Toss gently for 2 to 3 minutes or until carrots are thoroughly coated with glaze and heated through. To serve, arrange carrots in a shallow bowl; drizzle with remaining glaze from pan.

Nutrition Facts per serving:
72 cal., 2 g total fat (1 g sat. fat), 5 mg chol., 250 mg sodium, 13 g carbo., 3 g fiber, 1 g pro.
Daily Values:
513% vit. A, 12% vit. C, 3% calcium, 3% iron
Exchanges:
2 Vegetable, $1/2$ Fat

4 cups fresh boiling onions or
   2 cups frozen small whole onions

2 tablespoons honey

2 tablespoons white wine vinegar

1 tablespoon snipped fresh basil
   or 1 teaspoon dried basil, crushed

¼ teaspoon ground sage

1 If using fresh onions, in a medium covered saucepan cook onions in a small amount of boiling water for 8 to 10 minutes or just until tender; drain in a colander. Cool slightly; peel. (Or cook frozen onions according to package directions; drain in a colander.)

2 In the same saucepan combine honey, vinegar, basil, and sage. Add onions. Cook and stir until onions are glazed and heated through.

Honey-Glazed Onions

Honey, vinegar, and herbs turn ordinary onions into a sweet and savory side dish. To save time, use frozen onions—no peeling is needed.

Start to Finish: 25 minutes

Makes: 4 servings

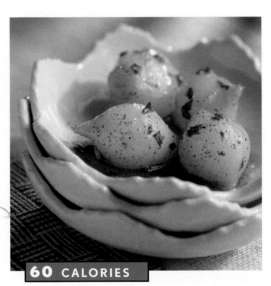

60 CALORIES

Nutrition Facts per serving:
60 cal., 0 g total fat (0 g sat. fat), 0 mg chol., 8 mg sodium, 15 g carbo., 1 g fiber, 1 g pro.
Daily Values:
1% vit. A, 7% vit. C, 3% calcium, 2% iron
Exchanges:
2 Vegetable

Cider Peas and Apples

If you always sidestep peas when thinking of a vegetable to serve, try this simple dish that pairs them up with apples. It's easy—only four ingredients—and delicious.

Start to Finish: 15 minutes

Makes: 4 servings

116 CALORIES

3   cups frozen peas

1   medium apple, cored and thinly sliced

⅓   cup apple cider or apple juice

1   teaspoon cornstarch

1 Place a steamer basket in a large saucepan. Add water to just below the bottom of the steamer basket. Bring water to boiling. Add peas to steamer basket. Cover and steam for 5 minutes. Add the apple slices; steam for 2 to 4 minutes more or until apples are just tender.

2 Meanwhile, in a medium saucepan stir cider into cornstarch. Cook and stir until mixture is thickened and bubbly. Cook about 2 minutes more, stirring often. Add the peas and apples; toss gently to coat with sauce.

Nutrition Facts per serving:
116 cal., 1 g total fat (0 g sat. fat), 0 mg chol., 122 mg sodium, 23 g carbo., 6 g fiber, 6 g pro.
Daily Values:
16% vit. A, 36% vit. C, 3% calcium, 10% iron
Exchanges:
1½ Starch

4 **large baking potatoes**
   (about 8 ounces each)

2 **tablespoons butter or margarine,**
   melted

1/3 **cup light dairy sour cream**

1 **tablespoon snipped fresh dill**
   or 3/4 teaspoon dried dill

4 **teaspoons lemon juice**

1/2 **teaspoon salt**

1/8 **teaspoon black pepper**

   Milk (optional)

   Lemon wedges (optional)

1 Scrub potatoes thoroughly with a brush. Pat dry. Prick potatoes with a fork. Bake in a 425° oven for 40 to 60 minutes or until tender. (Or microwave the potatoes, uncovered, on 100% power [high] for 13 to 17 minutes or until almost tender, rearranging once. Let stand for 5 minutes.)

2 Cut potatoes in half lengthwise. Gently scoop out each potato half, leaving a thin shell (because potatoes are hot, you may want to hold the potato halves with a pot holder while scooping). Place potato pulp in a large mixing bowl. Add 1 tablespoon of the butter, the sour cream, dill, lemon juice, salt, and pepper. With an electric mixer on low speed, beat until smooth. (If necessary, stir in 1 to 2 tablespoons milk to make desired consistency.) Spoon the mixture into the potato shells, dividing evenly among the 8 shells. Place in a 3-quart rectangular baking dish. Drizzle potatoes with remaining 1 tablespoon melted butter.

3 Bake in a 425° oven for 20 to 25 minutes or until lightly browned. If desired, serve with lemon wedges.

Make-ahead directions: Prepare as above through step 2. Cover and chill up to 24 hours. Bake, covered, for 20 minutes. Uncover and bake 10 to 15 minutes more or until heated through. Serve as above.

125 CALORIES

Lemon Dill Potatoes

Sometimes it's a small twist that turns a good recipe into a great one. With these twice-baked potatoes, the lemon and dill make all the difference.

Prep: 20 minutes   **Bake:** 1 hour
Oven: 425°F   **Makes:** 8 servings

Nutrition Facts per serving:
125 cal., 4 g total fat (2 g sat. fat), 12 mg chol., 191 mg sodium, 20 g carbo., 2 g fiber, 3 g pro.
Daily Values:
4% vit. A, 32% vit. C, 4% calcium, 9% iron
Exchanges:
1 Starch, 1 Fat

113 CALORIES

Baked Sweet Potato Fries

Here's something you won't find at fast-food restaurants! Sweet potato french fries are colorful and flavorful. Serve them alongside a turkey burger for a nutritious meal.

Prep: 15 minutes **Bake:** 20 minutes
Oven: 425°F **Makes:** 4 servings

Nonstick cooking spray
1 pound medium sweet potatoes
1 tablespoon butter or margarine, melted
¼ teaspoon seasoned salt
Dash ground nutmeg

1 Lightly coat a 15×10×1-inch baking pan with cooking spray. Scrub potatoes; cut lengthwise into quarters. Cut each quarter into 2 wedges. Arrange potatoes in a single layer in the pan. Combine butter, seasoned salt, and nutmeg. Brush mixture onto potatoes.

2 Bake in a 425° oven for 20 to 30 minutes or until brown and tender, turning once.

Nutrition Facts per serving:
113 cal., 3 g total fat (2 g sat. fat), 8 mg chol., 142 mg sodium, 20 g carbo., 2 g fiber, 1 g pro.
Daily Values:
314% vit. A, 23% vit. C, 2% calcium, 3% iron
Exchanges:
1 Starch, ½ Fat

2½ cups whole red grape tomatoes,
    small yellow pear-shape tomatoes,
    and/or cherry tomatoes
    Nonstick olive oil cooking spray
¼ cup finely chopped shallots
1 clove garlic, minced
1 teaspoon snipped fresh lemon thyme
    or thyme
¼ teaspoon salt
¼ teaspoon black pepper
4 ounces fresh mozzarella cheese,
    cut into ½-inch cubes (1 cup)

1 Halve about 1½ cups of the tomatoes; set aside. Lightly coat a large nonstick skillet with cooking spray. Add shallots, garlic, and thyme. Cook and stir over medium heat for 2 to 3 minutes or until shallots are tender.

2 Add all of the tomatoes, salt, and pepper. Cook and stir for 1 to 2 minutes more or until tomatoes are just warm. Remove from heat. Stir in mozzarella cubes.

Tomatoes with Fresh Mozzarella

This quick-to-fix tomato combination with shallots, thyme, and fresh mozzarella cheese is terrific over cooked pasta or wilted greens.

Prep: 12 minutes **Cook:** 3 minutes
Makes: 4 servings

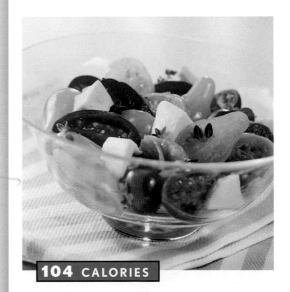

104 CALORIES

Nutrition Facts per serving:
104 cal., 5 g total fat (3 g sat. fat), 16 mg chol.,
287 mg sodium, 8 g carbo., 1 g fiber, 8 g pro.
Daily Values:
20% vit. A, 38% vit. C, 19% calcium, 4% iron
Exchanges:
1 Vegetable, 1 Meat

Mexicali Stuffed Zucchini

Make these savory stuffed zucchini wheels a day ahead, if you like. Prepare them to the baking step, cover the dish with plastic wrap, and chill. About 25 minutes before serving, remove wrap and bake.

Prep: 25 minutes   **Bake:** 21 minutes
Oven: 350°F   **Makes:** 5 or 6 servings

108 CALORIES

- 3 medium zucchini and/or yellow summer squash, ends trimmed (about 1 3/4 pounds)
- 2 cloves garlic, minced
- 2 teaspoons cooking oil
- 1 medium red sweet pepper, chopped
- 1/3 cup thinly sliced green onions (3)
- 2 tablespoons snipped fresh cilantro
- 1 fresh or canned jalapeño chile pepper, seeded and finely chopped (see note on page 76)
- 1/2 cup shredded Monterey Jack cheese (2 ounces)
- 1 recipe Cucumber Raita

1 Cut zucchini into 1½-inch rounds. Scoop out the pulp, leaving ¼- to ½-inch shells. Chop enough of the pulp to make ⅓ cup. In a medium skillet cook garlic in hot oil over medium-high heat for 1 minute. Add the reserved zucchini pulp, the sweet pepper, green onions, 1 tablespoon of the cilantro, and the jalapeño pepper. Cook and stir about 2 minutes or until the vegetables are crisp-tender.

2 Place zucchini shells in a lightly greased 2-quart rectangular baking dish. Fill each shell with pepper mixture. Bake, uncovered, in a 350° oven for 20 to 25 minutes or until zucchini is tender. Sprinkle with cheese and bake for 1 to 2 minutes more or until cheese melts.

3 Sprinkle with the remaining 1 tablespoon cilantro. Serve with the Cucumber Raita.

Cucumber Raita: In a small bowl combine ½ cup plain low-fat yogurt, ¼ cup peeled and finely chopped cucumber, 1 tablespoon snipped fresh cilantro, and ⅛ teaspoon salt.

Nutrition Facts per serving:
108 cal., 6 g total fat (3 g sat. fat), 11 mg chol., 143 mg sodium, 9 g carbo., 3 g fiber, 6 g pro.
Daily Values:
41% vit. A, 95% vit. C, 17% calcium, 7% iron
Exchanges:
2 Vegetable, 1 Fat

On the divider: Cranberry Muffins (see recipe, page 472)

Nonstick cooking spray

1½ cups all-purpose flour

⅓ cup sugar

1 teaspoon baking powder

1 teaspoon ground cinnamon

¼ teaspoon baking soda

⅛ teaspoon salt

⅔ cup buttermilk or sour milk*

1 egg or ¼ cup refrigerated or frozen
egg product, thawed

3 tablespoons cooking oil

¼ cup apricot, peach, or raspberry spread

1 Coat twelve 2½-inch muffin cups with nonstick cooking spray or line with paper bake cups; set aside. In a medium bowl stir together flour, sugar, baking powder, cinnamon, baking soda, and salt. Make a well in the center of the flour mixture; set aside.

2 In a small bowl stir together buttermilk, egg or egg product, and oil. Add buttermilk mixture all at once to flour mixture. Stir just until moistened (batter should be lumpy).

3 Spoon batter into prepared muffin cups, filling each about one-fourth full. Place 1 teaspoon of the spreadable fruit in center of each. Add remaining batter.

4 Bake in a 400° oven for 18 to 20 minutes or until golden. Cool in muffin cups on a wire rack for 5 minutes. Remove from muffin cups. Serve warm.

*Note: To make ⅔ cup sour milk, place 2 teaspoons lemon juice or vinegar in a glass measuring cup. Add enough milk to make ⅔ cup total liquid; stir. Let mixture stand for 5 minutes before using.

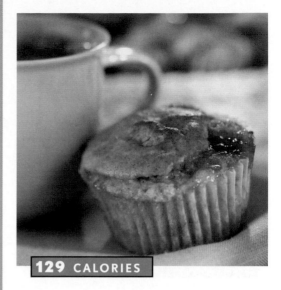

129 CALORIES

Fruit-Filled Muffins

Tucked inside each muffin is a sweet pocket of tantalizing fruit spread.

Prep: 20 minutes **Bake:** 18 minutes
Oven: 400°F **Makes:** 12 muffins

Nutrition Facts per muffin:
129 cal., 4 g total fat (1 g sat. fat), 18 mg chol., 104 mg sodium, 21 g carbo., 0 g fiber, 2 g pro.
Daily Values:
1% vit. A, 4% calcium, 5% iron
Exchanges:
½ Fruit, 1 Starch, ½ Fat

147 CALORIES

Cranberry Muffins

Bake a batch of these fruit-studded muffins for brunch or as an afternoon pick-me-up. For a breadlike muffin, use ¼ cup sugar; if you prefer a sweeter muffin, use ½ cup sugar.

Prep: 20 minutes **Bake:** 15 minutes
Oven: 400°F **Makes:** 12 to 14 muffins

1 cup fresh cranberries
2 tablespoons sugar
2 cups all-purpose flour
¼ to ½ cup sugar
4 teaspoons baking powder
1 teaspoon finely shredded orange peel
½ teaspoon salt
1 beaten egg
¾ cup milk
¼ cup butter, melted

1 Grease twelve to fourteen 2½-inch muffin cups or line with paper bake cups. Set aside. In a medium bowl toss cranberries with the 2 tablespoons sugar. Set aside.

2 In a large bowl combine flour, the ¼ to ½ cup sugar, the baking powder, orange peel, and salt. Stir well. In a small bowl combine egg, milk, and butter. Make a well in the center of the flour mixture; add egg mixture and cranberries. Stir just until moistened (batter should be lumpy). Spoon into prepared muffin cups, filling each about two-thirds full.

3 Bake in a 400° oven about 15 minutes or until golden. Cool in muffin cups on a wire rack for 5 minutes. Remove from muffin cups. Serve warm.

Nutrition Facts per muffin:
147 cal., 5 g total fat (3 g sat. fat), 30 mg chol., 285 mg sodium, 22 g carbo., 1 g fiber, 3 g pro.
Daily Values:
4% vit. A, 3% vit. C, 11% calcium, 5% iron
Exchanges:
1½ Starch, ½ Fat

- 1 **cup seven-grain cereal**
- 1 **cup dried tart cherries**
- 1/2 **cup packed brown sugar**
- 1/4 **cup cooking oil**
- 1 1/4 **cups buttermilk or sour milk***
- 1 **cup whole wheat flour**
- 1 **teaspoon baking powder**
- 1 **tablespoon crystallized ginger, finely chopped, or 1 teaspoon ground ginger**
- 1/2 **teaspoon baking soda**
- 1/2 **teaspoon salt**
- 1/2 **teaspoon ground nutmeg**
- 1 **slightly beaten egg**

1 Grease 12 muffin-top cups or sixteen 2½-inch muffin cups; set aside. In a medium bowl combine seven-grain cereal, dried cherries, brown sugar, and oil. Pour buttermilk over cereal mixture; let stand for 30 minutes.

2 Meanwhile, in a large bowl combine whole wheat flour, baking powder, ginger, baking soda, salt, and nutmeg. Make a well in the center of the flour mixture; set aside.

3 Stir beaten egg into buttermilk mixture. Add buttermilk mixture all at once to flour mixture. Stir just until moistened (batter should be lumpy). Spoon batter into prepared muffin-top cups or muffin cups, filling each muffin-top cup almost full or each muffin cup three-quarters full.

4 Bake in a 400° oven until golden. (Allow about 12 minutes for muffin-top cups or 15 to 18 minutes for 2½-inch muffins.) Cool in cups on a wire rack for 5 minutes. Remove from cups; serve warm.

*****Note:** To make 1¼ cups sour milk, place 3¾ teaspoons lemon juice or vinegar in a glass measuring cup. Add enough milk to make 1¼ cups total liquid; stir. Let mixture stand 5 minutes before using.

Multigrain and Cherry Muffins

Seasoned with ginger and nutmeg and loaded with cherries, these hearty grab-and-go treats will healthfully tide you through the morning rush hour.

Prep: 15 minutes   **Stand:** 30 minutes
Bake: 12 minutes   **Oven:** 400°F
Makes: 12 muffin tops or sixteen 2½-inch muffins

200 CALORIES

Nutrition Facts per muffin top:
200 cal., 6 g total fat (1 g sat. fat), 19 mg chol., 221 mg sodium, 34 g carbo., 2 g fiber, 4 g pro.
Daily Values:
1% vit. A, 6% calcium, 5% iron
Exchanges:
½ Fruit, 1 Starch, ½ Fat

Goat Cheese and Onion Scones

Sweet scones may be queen of the tea table, but this savory version rules at dinnertime. Substitute feta cheese, if you like, and add a favorite herb.

Prep: 20 minutes   **Bake:** 15 minutes
Oven: 400°F   **Makes:** 12 scones

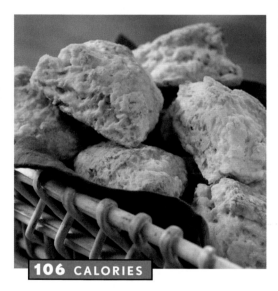

106 CALORIES

- 2 **cups all-purpose flour**
- 2 **tablespoons finely chopped green onion (1)**
- 2 **teaspoons baking powder**
- 1/4 **teaspoon baking soda**
- 1/4 **teaspoon salt**
- 1/4 **teaspoon freshly ground black pepper**
- 1 **beaten egg**
- 4 **ounces semisoft goat cheese (chèvre), crumbled or cut into small cubes**
- 1/2 **cup buttermilk or sour milk***

1 In a medium bowl combine flour, green onion, baking powder, baking soda, salt, and pepper. Make a well in center of the flour mixture; set aside.

2 In a small bowl stir together the egg, goat cheese, and buttermilk. Add egg mixture all at once to flour mixture. Using a fork, stir just until moistened.

3 Turn out dough onto a lightly floured surface. Knead dough by folding and gently pressing dough for 10 to 12 strokes or until dough is nearly smooth. Divide dough in half. Pat or lightly roll half of the dough into a 5-inch circle. Cut into 6 wedges. Repeat with remaining dough.

4 Place wedges 1 inch apart on an ungreased baking sheet. Bake in a 400° oven for 15 to 18 minutes or until golden. Remove scones from baking sheet; serve warm.

*Note: To make 1/2 cup sour milk, place 1 1/2 teaspoons lemon juice or vinegar in a glass measuring cup. Add enough milk to make 1/2 cup total liquid; stir. Let mixture stand for 5 minutes before using.

Nutrition Facts per scone:
106 cal., 3 g total fat (2 g sat. fat), 22 mg chol., 193 mg sodium, 15 g carbo., 1 g fiber, 5 g pro.
Daily Values:
1% vit. A, 1% vit. C, 7% calcium, 6% iron
Exchanges:
1 Starch, 1/2 Meat

- ³/₄ **cup all-purpose flour**
- ³/₄ **cup rye flour**
- 1 **tablespoon caraway seeds**
- ¹/₂ **teaspoon baking powder**
- ¹/₂ **teaspoon salt**
- ¹/₂ **teaspoon ground cumin**
- ¹/₄ **teaspoon ground coriander**
- ¹/₄ **cup butter, cut into 4 pieces**
- ¹/₃ **cup milk**
- 1 **beaten egg white**

1 In a food processor bowl combine all-purpose flour, rye flour, caraway seeds, baking powder, salt, cumin, and coriander. Add butter; cover and process until blended. Add milk; process just until mixture forms a dough (if necessary, add an additional 1 tablespoon milk).

2 Transfer dough to a floured surface; let stand for 5 minutes. Roll to ¹/₈-inch thickness; cut with a 2-inch round or other shape cutter or use a knife to cut into desired shapes. Transfer cutouts to an ungreased baking sheet. Brush lightly with egg white. Using a fork, prick crackers all over.

3 Bake in a 350° oven for 15 to 17 minutes or until crisp. Cool completely on wire racks; store in an airtight container.

27 CALORIES

Cumin-Caraway Crackers

These crispy crackers with caraway seeds taste as wonderful as fresh rye bread. Pair them with a chef's salad dressed with your favorite reduced-calorie salad dressing or with your favorite soup for a tasty dieter's meal.

Prep: 20 minutes   **Stand:** 5 minutes
Bake: 15 minutes   **Oven:** 350°F
Makes: 40 crackers

Nutrition Facts per cracker:
27 cal., 1 g total fat (1 g sat. fat), 3 mg chol., 49 mg sodium, 3 g carbo., 0 g fiber, 1 g pro.
Daily Values:
1% vit. A, 1% calcium, 1% iron
Exchanges:
¹/₂ Starch

144 CALORIES

Cottage Cheese-Chive Biscuits

Drop biscuits, such as these chive-stuffed morsels, are a breeze to make, so you can enjoy them warm from the oven any night of the week. Serve them with honey or just a dab of butter.

Prep: 20 minutes   **Bake:** 15 minutes
Oven: 425°F   **Makes:** 12 biscuits

2   **cups all-purpose flour**
2¹/₂   **teaspoons baking powder**
¹/₄   **teaspoon salt**
6   **tablespoons butter**
³/₄   **cup small-curd cream-style cottage cheese**
²/₃   **cup milk**
2   **tablespoons snipped fresh chives or thinly sliced green onion tops**

1 Line a baking sheet with parchment paper; set aside.

2 In a medium bowl stir together flour, baking powder, and salt. Using a pastry blender, cut in butter until mixture resembles coarse crumbs. Make a well in the center of flour mixture; set aside.

3 In a small bowl combine cottage cheese, milk, and chives or green onion tops. Add mixture all at once to flour mixture. Using a fork, stir just until moistened.

4 Drop dough by generous tablespoonfuls onto prepared baking sheet. Bake in a 425° oven for 15 to 18 minutes or until golden. Remove from parchment to wire rack; serve warm.

Nutrition Facts per biscuit:
144 cal., 7 g total fat (4 g sat. fat), 19 mg chol., 254 mg sodium, 16 g carbo., 1 g fiber, 4 g pro.
Daily Values:
6% vit. A, 1% vit. C, 8% calcium, 5% iron
Exchanges:
1 Starch, 1¹/₂ Fat

1¼ cups all-purpose flour

2 teaspoons sugar

1½ teaspoons baking powder

½ teaspoon salt

½ cup milk

2 tablespoons butter, melted

2 teaspoons sesame seeds

1 In a medium bowl stir together the flour, sugar, baking powder, and salt. Add milk, stirring just until moistened. Turn dough out onto a well floured surface; knead gently 3 to 5 times. Pat or roll dough into a 10×5-inch rectangle. Cut crosswise into 12 sticks, flouring knife between cuts.

2 Add melted butter to a 13×9×2-inch baking pan; tilt pan to coat bottom. Place breadsticks in pan, turning once to coat with butter; arrange evenly in pan. Sprinkle with sesame seeds. Bake in a 450° oven for 14 to 16 minutes or until golden. Serve warm.

Soft Breadsticks

The ideal partner for soups, pasta, or salads, these delectably moist breadsticks go together in minutes. For a change of pace, swap poppy seeds or caraway seeds for the sesame seeds.

Prep: 15 minutes **Bake:** 14 minutes
Oven: 450°F **Makes:** 12 breadsticks

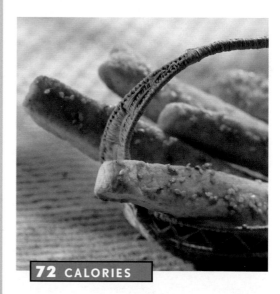

72 CALORIES

Nutrition Facts per breadstick:
72 cal., 3 g total fat (1 g sat. fat), 6 mg chol.,
173 mg sodium, 10 g carbo., 0 g fiber, 2 g pro.
Daily Values:
2% vit. A, 5% calcium, 3% iron
Exchanges:
½ Starch, ½ Fat

Old-Fashioned Corn Bread

The next time you serve stew or chili, bake a pan of this golden down-home delight to use as scoopers and dippers. For those who don't scoop or dip, pass some honey to drizzle on top.

Prep: 10 minutes   **Bake:** 20 minutes
Oven: 425°F   **Makes:** 10 servings

129 CALORIES

Nonstick cooking spray
1   cup yellow cornmeal
³/₄ cup all-purpose flour
2   tablespoons sugar
1¹/₂ teaspoons baking powder
¹/₄ teaspoon baking soda
¹/₄ teaspoon salt
³/₄ cup buttermilk or sour milk*
¹/₂ cup refrigerated or frozen egg product, thawed, or 2 beaten eggs
2   tablespoons cooking oil
    Yellow cornmeal (optional)

1 Coat a 9×1¹/₂-inch round baking pan or oven-going skillet with nonstick cooking spray. Set aside.

2 In a large bowl stir together the 1 cup cornmeal, the flour, sugar, baking powder, baking soda, and salt. In a medium bowl stir together buttermilk, egg product or eggs, and oil.

3 Add buttermilk mixture all at once to flour mixture. Stir just until moistened. Spread into prepared pan or skillet. If desired, sprinkle with additional cornmeal.

4 Bake in a 425° oven about 20 minutes or until golden. Serve warm.

*Note: To make ¾ cup sour milk, place 2¼ teaspoons lemon juice or vinegar in a glass measuring cup. Add enough milk to make ¾ cup total liquid; stir. Let mixture stand for 5 minutes before using.

Nutrition Facts per serving:
129 cal., 3 g total fat (1 g sat. fat), 1 mg chol., 190 mg sodium, 21 g carbo., 1 g fiber, 4 g pro.
Daily Values:
2% vit. A, 6% calcium, 7% iron
Exchanges:
1 Starch, ¹/₂ Fat

1 cup whole wheat flour

1 cup all-purpose flour

1 teaspoon baking powder

½ teaspoon baking soda

¼ teaspoon salt

3 tablespoons butter

2 beaten eggs

¾ cup buttermilk or sour milk*

2 tablespoons brown sugar

⅓ cup dried tart cherries or raisins

1 Grease a baking sheet; set aside. In a medium bowl combine whole wheat flour, all-purpose flour, baking powder, baking soda, and salt. Using a pastry blender, cut in butter until mixture resembles coarse crumbs. Make a well in center of flour mixture; set aside.

2 In a small bowl stir together 1 of the eggs, the buttermilk, brown sugar, and dried cherries. Add egg mixture all at once to flour mixture. Stir just until moistened.

3 Turn out dough onto a lightly floured surface. Knead dough by folding and gently pressing dough for 10 to 12 strokes or until dough is nearly smooth. Shape into a 6-inch round loaf. Cut a 4-inch cross, ½ inch deep, on the top. Place on prepared baking sheet. Brush with the remaining egg.

4 Bake in a 375° oven about 35 minutes or until golden. Serve warm.

*Note: To make ¾ cup sour milk, place 2¼ teaspoons lemon juice or vinegar in a glass measuring cup. Add enough milk to make ¾ cup total liquid; stir. Let mixture stand for 5 minutes before using.

161 CALORIES

Irish Soda Bread

Soda bread, an Irish favorite, was originally made with currants, but this version offers the choice of dried cherries or raisins. If you're feeding a crowd, double all of the ingredients, except for the eggs, and make two loaves. You'll need only one egg to brush on the loaves before baking.

Prep: 20 minutes   **Bake:** 35 minutes
Oven: 375°F   **Makes:** 1 loaf (10 servings)

Nutrition Facts per serving:
161 cal., 5 g total fat (3 g sat. fat), 53 mg chol., 232 mg sodium, 25 g carbo., 2 g fiber, 5 g pro.
Daily Values:
4% vit. A, 6% calcium, 7% iron
Exchanges:
1½ Starch, ½ Fat

146 CALORIES

Zucchini Bread

Remember this easy loaf in late summer when the markets are brimming with just-picked zucchini. Look for the small ones; they're young and their skins are extra-tender.

Prep: 20 minutes   **Bake:** 50 minutes
Oven: 350°F   **Stand:** Overnight
Makes: 1 loaf (16 servings)

1½ **cups all-purpose flour**
1 **teaspoon ground cinnamon**
½ **teaspoon baking soda**
½ **teaspoon salt**
¼ **teaspoon baking powder**
¼ **teaspoon ground nutmeg**
1 **beaten egg**
1 **cup sugar**
1 **cup finely shredded, unpeeled zucchini**
¼ **cup cooking oil**
½ **cup chopped walnuts or pecans, toasted**

1 Grease the bottom and ½ inch up sides of an 8×4×2-inch loaf pan; set aside. In a medium bowl stir together flour, cinnamon, baking soda, salt, baking powder, and nutmeg. Make a well in center of flour mixture; set aside.

2 In another medium bowl stir together egg, sugar, shredded zucchini, and oil. Add zucchini mixture all at once to flour mixture. Stir just until moistened (batter should be lumpy). Fold in nuts. Spoon batter into prepared pan.

3 Bake in a 350° oven for 50 to 55 minutes or until a wooden toothpick inserted near center comes out clean. Cool in pan on a wire rack for 10 minutes. Remove from pan. Cool completely on a wire rack. Wrap and store overnight before slicing.

Nutrition Facts per serving:
146 cal., 6 g total fat (1 g sat. fat), 13 mg chol., 123 mg sodium, 21 g carbo., 1 g fiber, 2 g pro.
Daily Values:
1% vit. A, 1% vit. C, 1% calcium, 4% iron
Exchanges:
1½ Starch, ½ Fat

1³/₄ **cups all-purpose flour**

³/₄ **cup sugar**

2 **teaspoons baking powder**

¹/₄ **teaspoon salt**

1 **beaten egg**

1 **cup milk**

¹/₄ **cup cooking oil or melted butter**

2 **teaspoons finely shredded lemon peel**

1 **tablespoon lemon juice**

¹/₃ **cup chopped almonds or walnuts**

2 **tablespoons lemon juice (optional)**

1 **tablespoon sugar (optional)**

1 Grease the bottom and ½ inch up sides of an 8×4×2-inch loaf pan; set aside. In a medium bowl stir together flour, the ³/₄ cup sugar, the baking powder, and salt. Make a well in center of flour mixture; set aside.

2 In another medium bowl stir together the egg, milk, oil or melted butter, lemon peel, and the 1 tablespoon lemon juice. Add egg mixture all at once to flour mixture. Stir just until moistened (batter should be lumpy). Fold in nuts. Spoon batter into prepared pan.

3 Bake in a 350° oven for 50 to 55 minutes or until a wooden toothpick inserted near center comes out clean. If desired, stir together the 2 tablespoons lemon juice and the 1 tablespoon sugar. While bread is still in the pan, brush lemon-sugar mixture over the top of the loaf. Cool in pan on a wire rack for 10 minutes. Remove from pan. Cool completely on a wire rack. Wrap and store overnight before slicing.

Lemon Bread

This versatile citrus loaf is equally delicious whether you make it with almonds or walnuts. When shredding the peel for this bread, be sure to get only the yellow part—the white part is bitter.

Prep: 20 minutes   **Bake:** 50 minutes
Oven: 350°F   **Stand:** Overnight
Makes: 1 loaf (16 servings)

139 CALORIES

Nutrition Facts per serving:
139 cal., 5 g total fat (1 g sat. fat), 15 mg chol., 98 mg sodium, 20 g carbo., 1 g fiber, 3 g pro.
Daily Values:
1% vit. A, 1% vit. C, 6% calcium, 4% iron
Exchanges:
1½ Starch, ½ Fat

Ginger-Date Pumpkin Loaves

Dates, crystallized ginger, and a simple glaze take this traditional pumpkin bread to a new level of sophistication.

Prep: 25 minutes   **Bake:** 35 minutes
Oven: 350°F   **Stand:** Overnight
Makes: 5 small loaves (25 servings) or 2 large loaves (24 servings)

127 CALORIES

- 2 **cups all-purpose flour**
- 1 **cup granulated sugar**
- 1 **tablespoon finely chopped crystallized ginger**
- 2 1/2 **teaspoons baking powder**
- 1/2 **teaspoon baking soda**
- 1/2 **teaspoon ground nutmeg**
- 1/4 **teaspoon salt**
- 1 **cup canned pumpkin**
- 1/2 **cup milk**
- 2 **eggs**
- 1/3 **cup shortening**
- 1 **cup coarsely chopped pitted dates**
- 1 **recipe Spiced Glaze**
  Crystallized ginger, chopped (optional)

1 Grease five 4½×2½×1½-inch loaf pans or two 8×4×2-inch loaf pans; set aside. In a large mixing bowl combine 1 cup of the flour, the granulated sugar, the 1 tablespoon ginger, the baking powder, baking soda, nutmeg, and salt. Add pumpkin, milk, eggs, and shortening. Beat with an electric mixer on low to medium speed for 30 seconds. Beat on high speed for 2 minutes, scraping side of bowl occasionally. Add the remaining flour; beat until well mixed. Stir in dates.

2 Spoon the batter into prepared pans. Bake in a 350° oven until wooden toothpicks inserted near centers comes out clean. (Allow 35 to 40 minutes for 4½×2½×1½-inch loaves or about 45 minutes for 8×4×2-inch loaves.) Cool in pans on wire racks for 10 minutes. Remove from pans. Cool completely on wire racks. Wrap bread and store overnight before slicing. Drizzle with Spiced Glaze before serving. If desired, sprinkle top with additional chopped crystallized ginger.

Spiced Glaze: In a small bowl stir together ½ cup sifted powdered sugar and ⅛ teaspoon ground ginger. Stir in enough water (2 to 3 teaspoons) to make drizzling consistency.

1 **8-ounce package pitted whole dates, snipped**

1¹⁄₂ cups boiling water

1 cup all-purpose flour

1 cup whole wheat flour

1 teaspoon baking soda

1 teaspoon baking powder

¹⁄₂ teaspoon salt

1 slightly beaten egg

1 teaspoon vanilla

¹⁄₂ cup sliced almonds, toasted and coarsely chopped

1 Place dates in a medium bowl. Pour the boiling water over dates. Let stand about 20 minutes or until dates are softened and mixture has cooled slightly.

2 Lightly grease bottom and ½ inch up sides of an 8×4×2-inch loaf pan; set aside. In a large bowl stir together all-purpose flour, whole wheat flour, baking soda, baking powder, and salt. Stir the egg and vanilla into the cooled date mixture. Add the date mixture and the almonds to the flour mixture; stir until well mixed (mixture will be thick).

3 Spoon batter evenly into prepared pan. Bake in a 350° oven for 50 to 55 minutes or until a wooden toothpick inserted near the center comes out clean. Cool in pan on wire rack for 10 minutes. Remove from pan. Cool completely on a wire rack. Wrap and store overnight before slicing.

119 CALORIES

Date-Nut Bread

Give ordinary sandwiches a boost by starting with thin slices of this fruit-and-nut loaf. Spread the bread with fat-free cream cheese and layer it with thinly sliced turkey or ham and lettuce or sliced cucumber.

Prep: 15 minutes
Stand: 20 minutes + overnight
Bake: 50 minutes   **Oven:** 350°F
Makes: 1 loaf (16 servings)

Nutrition Facts per serving:
119 cal., 3 g total fat (0 g sat. fat), 13 mg chol., 182 mg sodium, 22 g carbo., 3 g fiber, 3 g pro.
Daily Values:
1% vit. A, 4% calcium, 6% iron
Exchanges:
¹⁄₂ Fruit, 1 Starch

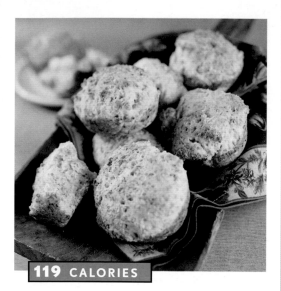

119 CALORIES

Fennel Batter Rolls

Savory onion, aromatic fennel, and pungent pepper make these no-knead rolls the perfect accompaniment for winter soups and stews. Wheat germ lends a nutty flavor and lots of nutrients.

Prep: 20 minutes   **Rise:** 50 minutes
Bake: 15 minutes   **Oven:** 375°F
Makes: 12 rolls

Nutrition Facts per roll:
119 cal., 3 g total fat (1 g sat. fat), 22 mg chol.,
149 mg sodium, 19 g carbo., 1 g fiber, 5 g pro.
Daily Values:
2% vit. A, 1% vit. C, 2% calcium, 9% iron
Exchanges:
1½ Starch

Nonstick cooking spray
2 cups all-purpose flour
1 package active dry yeast
½ cup cream-style cottage cheese
½ cup water
1 tablespoon sugar
1 tablespoon butter
2 teaspoons fennel seeds, crushed
1 teaspoon dried minced onion
½ teaspoon salt
¼ teaspoon coarsely ground black pepper
1 egg
½ cup toasted wheat germ

1 Lightly coat twelve 2½-inch muffin cups with nonstick cooking spray; set aside. In a medium mixing bowl stir together 1 cup of the flour and the yeast.

2 In a small saucepan heat and stir cottage cheese, the water, sugar, butter, fennel seeds, dried onion, salt, and pepper just until warm (120°F to 130°F) and butter almost melts. Add cottage cheese mixture to flour mixture; add egg. Beat with an electric mixer on low to medium speed for 30 seconds, scraping bowl constantly. Beat on high speed for 3 minutes. Using a wooden spoon, stir in the remaining 1 cup flour and the wheat germ (batter will be stiff).

3 Spoon the batter into the prepared muffin cups. Cover and let rise in a warm place until nearly double in size (50 to 60 minutes).

4 Bake in a 375° oven for 15 to 20 minutes or until golden. Immediately remove from muffin cups. Serve warm or cool.

2³/₄ to 3¹/₄ cups all-purpose flour

1   package active dry yeast

¹/₄   cup grated Parmesan cheese

1   teaspoon dried Italian seasoning,
     crushed

³/₄   teaspoon salt

¹/₂   teaspoon cracked black pepper

1   cup warm water (120°F to 130°F)

¹/₂   cup shredded Monterey Jack cheese
     with jalapeño peppers or shredded
     Monterey Jack cheese (2 ounces)

2   tablespoons cooking oil

1 In a large mixing bowl combine 1¼ cups of the flour, the yeast, Parmesan cheese, Italian seasoning, salt, and black pepper. Add the warm water, Monterey Jack cheese, and oil. Beat with an electric mixer on low to medium speed for 30 seconds, scraping bowl constantly. Beat on high speed for 3 minutes. Using a wooden spoon, stir in as much of the remaining flour as you can.

2 Turn out dough onto a lightly floured surface. Knead in enough of the remaining flour to make a moderately stiff dough that is smooth and elastic (6 to 8 minutes total). Shape dough into a ball. Place in a lightly greased bowl; turn once. Cover; let rise in a warm place until double (about 1 hour). Punch dough down.

3 Turn out dough onto lightly floured surface; cover and let rest for 10 minutes. Grease baking sheets; set aside. Divide the dough into thirds. On a lightly floured surface, roll each portion into a 14×10-inch rectangle. Using a pizza cutter or sharp knife, cut the dough lengthwise into ¹/₂-inch strips.

4 For each breadstick, pick up 2 dough strips together and twist several times; press ends together. Place breadsticks ¹/₂ inch apart on prepared baking sheets.

5 Bake in a 400° oven for 10 to 12 minutes or until golden. Remove from baking sheets; cool on wire racks.

Pepper Cheese Breadsticks

These breadsticks have a delightful kick. Serve them with steaming bowls of chili for a dynamite dinnertime duo.

Prep: 40 minutes   **Rise:** 1 hour
Bake: 10 minutes   **Oven:** 400°F
Makes: 30 breadsticks

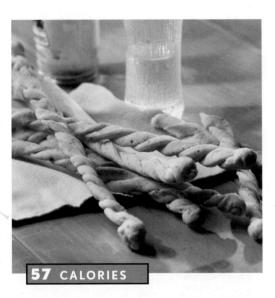

57 CALORIES

Nutrition Facts per breadstick:
57 cal., 2 g total fat (1 g sat. fat), 2 mg chol., 81 mg sodium, 8 g carbo., 0 g fiber, 2 g pro.
Daily Values:
3% calcium, 3% iron
Exchanges:
¹/₂ Starch

English Muffin Bread

For a can't-miss breakfast treat, toast slices of this delightfully sturdy bread—known for its crunchy, coarse texture—and slather them with honey butter, jam, or spreadable fruit.

Prep: 20 minutes   **Rise:** 45 minutes

Bake: 25 minutes   **Oven:** 400°F

Makes: 2 loaves (32 servings)

90 CALORIES

Cornmeal

6 cups all-purpose flour

2 packages active dry yeast

¼ teaspoon baking soda

2 cups milk

½ cup water

1 tablespoon sugar

1 teaspoon salt

1 Grease two 8×4×2-inch loaf pans. Lightly sprinkle pans with cornmeal to coat bottoms and sides; set pans aside.

2 In a large bowl combine 3 cups of the flour, the yeast, and baking soda; set aside. In a medium saucepan heat and stir milk, the water, sugar, and salt just until warm (120°F to 130°F). Using a wooden spoon, stir milk mixture into flour mixture. Stir in remaining flour.

3 Divide dough in half. Place dough in prepared pans. Sprinkle tops with additional cornmeal. Cover; let rise in a warm place until double (about 45 minutes).

4 Bake in a 400° oven about 25 minutes or until golden. Immediately remove bread from pans. Cool on wire racks.

Nutrition Facts per serving:
90 cal., 1 g total fat (0 g sat. fat), 1 mg chol., 91 mg sodium, 18 g carbo., 1 g fiber, 3 g pro.
Daily Values:
1% vit. A, 2% calcium, 6% iron
Exchanges:
1 Starch

- ³/₄ to 1¹/₄ cups all-purpose flour
- ¹/₂ cup seven-grain cereal
- 1 package active dry yeast
- ²/₃ cup water
- ¹/₃ cup applesauce
- 2 tablespoons honey
- 1 teaspoon salt
- 1 egg
- ¹/₃ cup shelled sunflower seeds
- 1³/₄ cups whole wheat flour

1 In a large mixing bowl stir together ³/₄ cup of the all-purpose flour, the ¹/₂ cup cereal, and yeast; set aside.

2 In a medium saucepan combine the water, applesauce, honey, and salt; heat and stir just until warm (120°F to 130°F). Add applesauce mixture and egg to flour mixture. Beat with an electric mixer on low to medium speed for 30 seconds, scraping bowl constantly. Beat on high speed for 3 minutes. Using a wooden spoon, stir in the ¹/₃ cup sunflower seeds, the whole wheat flour, and as much of the remaining all-purpose flour as you can.

3 Turn out dough onto a lightly floured surface. Knead in enough of the remaining all-purpose flour to make a moderately stiff dough that is smooth and elastic (6 to 8 minutes total). Shape dough into a ball. Place in a lightly greased bowl; turn once. Cover; let rise in a warm place until double (1 to 1¹/₂ hours).

4 Punch down dough. Turn out onto a lightly floured surface; cover and let rest for 10 minutes. Lightly grease an 8×4×2-inch loaf pan.

5 Shape dough into loaf. Place in prepared pan. Cover and let rise in a warm place until nearly double (30 to 45 minutes).

6 Bake in a 375° oven for 40 to 45 minutes or until bread sounds hollow when lightly tapped. (If necessary to prevent overbrowning, cover loosely with foil for the last 10 minutes of baking.) Immediately remove bread from pan. Cool on a wire rack.

111 CALORIES

Seven-Grain Bread

This loaf is full of robust wheat flavor—with a touch of honey for sweetness—and plenty of good-for-you grains too. For a special presentation, just before baking, brush the loaf with milk and sprinkle it with crushed seven-grain cereal and shelled sunflower seeds.

Prep: 30 minutes   **Rise:** 1 hour + 30 minutes
Bake: 40 minutes   **Oven:** 375°F
Makes: 1 loaf (16 servings)

Nutrition Facts per serving:
111 cal., 2 g total fat (0 g sat. fat), 13 mg chol.,
151 mg sodium, 20 g carbo., 2 g fiber, 4 g pro.
Daily Values:
1% calcium, 7% iron
Exchanges:
1¹/₂ Starch

130 CALORIES

Italian Peasant Loaf

Having pasta tonight? Use hunks of this homey bread to sop up every last trace of the sauce. Hint: If you can't find cracked wheat at the supermarket, look for it at health food stores.

Prep: 25 minutes
Rise: 45 minutes + 30 minutes
Bake: 25 minutes   **Oven:** 375°F
Makes: 1 loaf (16 servings)

Nutrition Facts per serving:
130 cal., 2 g total fat (1 g sat. fat), 16 mg chol.,
140 mg sodium, 23 g carbo., 1 g fiber, 5 g pro.
Daily Values:
1% vit. A, 4% calcium, 8% iron
Exchanges:
1½ Starch

1	**cup water**
¼	**cup cracked wheat**
¾	**cup milk**
1	**tablespoon olive oil**
¾	**teaspoon salt**
3½	**to 4 cups all-purpose flour**
¼	**cup finely shredded Parmesan cheese (1 ounce)**
1	**package active dry yeast**
1	**egg**
	Cracked wheat
	All-purpose flour

1 In a small saucepan bring the water to boiling; remove from heat. Stir in the ¼ cup cracked wheat. Let stand for 3 minutes; drain well. Add milk, oil, and salt to drained cracked wheat; let stand until cooled to lukewarm (120°F to 130°F).

2 In a large mixing bowl stir together 1½ cups of the flour, the cheese, and yeast. Add warm milk mixture and egg. Beat with an electric mixer on low to medium speed for 30 seconds, scraping bowl constantly. Beat on high speed for 3 minutes. Using a wooden spoon, stir in as much of the remaining flour as you can.

3 Turn out dough onto a lightly floured surface. Knead in enough of the remaining flour to make a moderately stiff dough that is smooth and elastic (6 to 8 minutes total). Shape dough into a ball. Place in a lightly greased bowl; turn once. Cover; let rise in a warm place until double (45 to 60 minutes).

4 Punch down dough. Turn out dough onto a lightly floured surface. Cover and let rest for 10 minutes. Grease a baking sheet.

5 Shape dough into a 6-inch round. Place on prepared baking sheet. Cover and let rise in a warm place until nearly double (30 to 40 minutes). Using a sharp knife, cut 2 or 3 slashes on top of loaf in each direction to make a diamond pattern. Brush with water; sprinkle with additional cracked wheat and flour.

6 Bake in a 375° oven for 25 to 30 minutes or until loaf sounds hollow when tapped.

4 to 4¼ cups all-purpose flour

½ cup warm water (105°F to 115°F)

1 teaspoon active dry yeast

1 cup warm water (105°F to 115°F)

2 teaspoons salt

Cornmeal (optional)

1 tablespoon olive oil

Snipped fresh rosemary

Coarse salt

Shredded Parmesan cheese (optional)

1 In a large bowl combine ½ cup of the flour, the ½ cup warm water, and the yeast. Beat with a wooden spoon until smooth. Cover loosely with plastic wrap. Let stand overnight at room temperature to ferment.

2 Gradually stir in the 1 cup warm water, the 2 teaspoons salt, and just enough of the remaining flour to make a dough that pulls away from the side of the bowl. Turn out onto a lightly floured surface. Knead in enough of the remaining flour to make a stiff dough that is smooth and elastic (8 to 10 minutes total). Place in a lightly greased bowl; turn once. Cover; let rise in a warm place until double (about 1 hour).

3 Divide dough into fourths; place dough portions onto a well floured surface. Cover; let stand for 30 minutes. Grease 2 large baking sheets. If desired, sprinkle with cornmeal; set aside.

4 Place 2 dough portions on each prepared baking sheet; shape each portion into a 6-inch circle by pulling and pressing with your fingertips. (Don't stretch dough too roughly or the dough will deflate; you want to keep air bubbles intact.)

5 Dust your fingers with flour and press into dough to make ½-inch indentations about 2 inches apart. Brush dough with olive oil; sprinkle with rosemary, coarse salt, and, if desired, Parmesan cheese.

6 Bake in a 475° oven about 20 minutes or until golden, checking after 8 minutes and popping any large air bubbles with a sharp knife. Remove from baking sheets. Cool focaccia on wire racks for 15 minutes. Serve warm.

Focaccia

A classic Italian bread, focaccia has a light, airy texture that makes it a natural for building sandwiches to serve with soups and salads, or as a snack in its own right.

Prep: 30 minutes

Stand: Overnight + 30 minutes

Rise: 1 hour **Bake:** 20 minutes

Oven: 475°F **Cool:** 15 minutes

Makes: 16 servings

113 CALORIES

Nutrition Facts per serving:
113 cal., 1 g total fat (0 g sat. fat), 0 mg chol., 413 mg sodium, 22 g carbo., 1 g fiber, 3 g pro.
Daily Values:
1% calcium, 8% iron
Exchanges:
1½ Starch

Double Chocolate Swirl

Cure your craving for chocolate with this luscious loaf that boasts both cocoa powder and semisweet chocolate but has only 139 calories and 3 grams of fat per serving. Now that's a dieter's bargain!

Prep: 30 minutes **Rise:** 1 hour + 30 minutes
Bake: 25 minutes **Oven:** 375°F
Makes: 1 loaf (16 servings)

139 CALORIES

Nutrition Facts per serving:
139 cal., 3 g total fat (2 g sat. fat), 17 mg chol., 131 mg sodium, 25 g carbo., 1 g fiber, 4 g pro.
Daily Values:
2% vit. A, 3% calcium, 8% iron
Exchanges:
1½ Starch, ½ Fat

3 to 3½ cups all-purpose flour
4 teaspoons unsweetened cocoa powder
1 package active dry yeast
1 cup milk
3 tablespoons brown sugar
1 tablespoon butter
¾ teaspoon salt
1 egg
1½ teaspoons vanilla
1 tablespoon light-colored corn syrup
½ cup miniature semisweet chocolate pieces
   Sifted powdered sugar (optional)

1 In a large mixing bowl stir together 1¼ cups of the flour, the cocoa powder, and yeast; set aside. In a saucepan heat and stir the milk, brown sugar, butter, and salt until warm (120°F to 130°F). Add to flour mixture; add egg and vanilla. Beat with an electric mixer on low to medium speed for 30 seconds, scraping bowl constantly. Beat on high speed for 3 minutes. Stir in as much of the remaining flour as you can.

2 Turn out dough onto a lightly floured surface. Knead in enough of the remaining flour to make a moderately soft dough that is smooth and elastic (3 to 5 minutes total). Shape dough into a ball. Place in a greased bowl; turn once. Cover; let rise in a warm place until double (about 1 hour).

3 Punch down dough. Turn out onto a lightly floured surface. Cover; let rest for 10 minutes. Lightly grease an 8×4×2-inch loaf pan. Roll dough into a 12×8-inch rectangle. Brush with corn syrup. Sprinkle with chocolate pieces; press lightly into dough. Starting from a short side, roll up into a spiral. Seal seam and ends. Place in prepared pan, seam side down. Cover; let rise in a warm place until nearly double (about 30 minutes).

4 Bake in a 375° oven for 25 to 30 minutes or until bread sounds hollow when tapped. If necessary, to prevent overbrowning, cover with foil after 20 minutes. Remove from pan; cool on a rack. If desired, sprinkle with powdered sugar.

2²/₃ **to 3 cups all-purpose flour**

1 **package active dry yeast**

1 **cup milk**

4 **teaspoons water**

4 **teaspoons olive oil**

1 **tablespoon sugar**

³/₄ **teaspoon salt**

2 **tablespoons milk**

1 **tablespoon sesame seeds**

1 In a large mixing bowl combine 1¼ cups of the flour and the yeast. In a small saucepan heat and stir the 1 cup milk, the water, oil, sugar, and salt just until warm (120°F to 130°F). Add milk mixture to flour mixture. Beat with an electric mixer on low to medium speed for 30 seconds, scraping bowl constantly. Beat on high speed for 3 minutes. Using a wooden spoon, stir in as much of the remaining flour as you can.

2 Turn out dough onto a lightly floured surface. Knead in enough of the remaining flour to make a stiff dough that is smooth and elastic (8 to 10 minutes total). Shape dough into a ball. Place in a lightly greased bowl; turn once. Cover; let rise in a warm place until double (45 to 60 minutes).

3 Punch down dough; turn out onto lightly floured surface. Cover; let rest for 10 minutes. Grease a large baking sheet; set aside. Divide the dough into thirds. Cover and refrigerate 2 of the portions. On a lightly floured surface, roll remaining portion into a 12-inch circle. Transfer circle to prepared baking sheet. Brush the circle with some of the 2 tablespoons milk. Using a fork, generously prick the entire surface of circle. Sprinkle with sesame seeds. Do not let rise.

4 Bake in a 350° oven for 16 to 18 minutes or until lightly browned. Remove from baking sheet; cool on a wire rack. Repeat rolling and baking with remaining dough, 1 portion at a time. Break into pieces to serve.

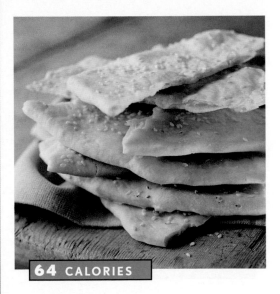

64 CALORIES

Armenian Flatbread

Although this recipe is a close cousin to crispy crackerlike Middle Eastern lavash, it bakes up chewy like a flatbread. The sesame seeds on top give it an irresistible nutty flavor.

Prep: 30 minutes   **Rise:** 45 minutes
Bake: 16 minutes per flatbread   **Oven:** 350°F
Makes: 3 flatbreads (24 servings)

Nutrition Facts per serving:
64 cal., 1 g total fat (0 g sat. fat), 1 mg chol., 79 mg sodium, 11 g carbo., 0 g fiber, 2 g pro.
Daily Values:
2% calcium, 4% iron
Exchanges:
1 Starch

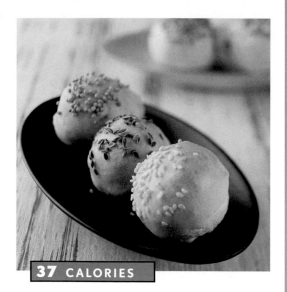

37 CALORIES

Have-a-Ball Rolls

Add a touch of pizzazz to store-bought bread dough by shaping it into tiny balls and topping it with flavorful, crunchy seeds. Take your choice of sesame, mustard, or dill seeds.

Prep: 20 minutes   **Rise:** 30 minutes
Bake: 13 minutes   **Oven:** 350°F
Makes: 30 to 36 mini rolls

1   **16-ounce loaf frozen white or whole wheat bread dough, thawed**
1   **egg white**
1   **tablespoon water**
    Sesame seeds, mustard seeds, and/or dill seeds

1 Lightly grease a large baking sheet or thirty to thirty-six 1¾-inch muffin cups; set aside.

2 Divide dough into 30 to 36 pieces. Shape into small balls. Place rolls on prepared baking sheet or in prepared muffin cups.

3 Cover; let rise until nearly double (about 30 minutes). Beat together the egg white and water. Brush over the rolls. Sprinkle generously with desired seeds.

4 Bake in a 350° oven for 13 to 15 minutes or until golden. Transfer rolls to wire racks. Serve warm.

Nutrition Facts per mini roll:
37 cal., 0 g total fat (0 g sat. fat), 0 mg chol., 2 mg sodium, 6 g carbo., 0 g fiber, 1 g pro.
Daily Values:
1% calcium,
Exchanges:
½ Starch

1 **16-ounce loaf frozen white bread dough, thawed**

2 **tablespoons salt**

3 **quarts (12 cups) boiling water**

1 **slightly beaten egg white**

1 **tablespoon water**

Coarse salt

Sesame seeds, poppy seeds, dried dill, and/or coarsely ground black pepper

1 Lightly grease 2 large baking sheets; set aside.

2 On a lightly floured surface, roll thawed dough into a 12×8-inch rectangle, occasionally stopping and letting dough rest, if necessary. Cut into twenty-four 8×½-inch strips.

3 Twist each strip. Carefully place strips on prepared baking sheets. Bake in a 475° oven for 4 minutes. Remove from oven. Reduce oven temperature to 350°.

4 Remove strips from baking sheets. Well grease the 2 large baking sheets; set aside. In a Dutch oven or kettle dissolve the 2 tablespoons salt in the boiling water. Lower a few dough strips into boiling water. Boil for 2 minutes, turning once. Using a slotted spoon, remove from water and drain on paper towels. Place about ½ inch apart on prepared baking sheets. Repeat with remaining strips.

5 In a small bowl stir together egg white and the 1 tablespoon water. Brush strips with egg white mixture. Sprinkle strips lightly with coarse salt. Sprinkle strips with seeds, dill, and/or pepper.

6 Bake in a 350° oven about 15 minutes or until golden. Immediately remove from baking sheets; cool on wire racks.

Make-ahead directions: Prepare as above through step 6. Place pretzel sticks in a freezer container. Seal, label, and freeze up to 3 months. To serve, thaw at room temperature for 2 hours. (Or wrap frozen pretzel sticks in foil; heat in a 350°F oven for 5 to 10 minutes or until warm.)

Soft 'n' Chewy Pretzel Sticks

Not all pretzels go crunch! These soft, chewy numbers are more like breadsticks than crackers, and they make great dippers for a jar of flavored mustard.

Prep: 25 minutes   **Bake:** 4 minutes + 15 minutes
Oven: 475°F/350°F
Makes: 24 pretzel sticks

47 CALORIES

Nutrition Facts per pretzel stick:
47 cal., 0 g total fat (0 g sat. fat), 0 mg chol., 357 mg sodium, 8 g carbo., 0 g fiber, 2 g pro.
Daily Values:
2% calcium
Exchanges:
½ Starch

Apple-Cherry-Filled Rolls

Fresh-from-the-oven breakfast rolls don't have to be a special-occasion luxury. With this easy recipe that starts with hot roll mix, you can enjoy them on a whim.

Prep: 30 minutes   **Rise:** 30 minutes

Bake: 13 minutes   **Oven:** 375°F

Makes: 16 rolls

165 CALORIES

Nonstick cooking spray

1 **16-ounce package hot roll mix**

1 **cup chopped, peeled apple**

¼ **cup dried tart cherries**

2 **tablespoons brown sugar**

½ **teaspoon ground cinnamon**

1 **recipe Orange Icing**

1 Lightly coat 2 baking sheets with nonstick cooking spray; set aside.

2 Prepare hot roll mix according to package directions through the resting step. Meanwhile, for filling, in a small bowl stir together apple, dried cherries, brown sugar, and cinnamon.

3 Divide dough into 16 portions. Flatten 1 portion of dough to a 4-inch circle; spoon 1 rounded teaspoon of filling onto the dough. Shape the dough around the filling to enclose, pulling dough until smooth and rounded. Place, rounded side up, on prepared baking sheet. Repeat with remaining dough and filling. Cover; let rise until double (about 30 minutes).

4 Bake in a 375° oven for 13 to 15 minutes or until golden. Cool slightly on a wire rack. Drizzle with Orange Icing. Serve warm.

Orange Icing: In a small bowl stir together 1 cup sifted powdered sugar and enough orange juice (1 to 2 tablespoons) to make of drizzling consistency.

Nutrition Facts per roll:
165 cal., 2 g total fat (0 g sat. fat), 13 mg chol., 186 mg sodium, 33 g carbo., 0 g fiber, 4 g pro.
Daily Values:
1% vit. C, 5% iron
Exchanges:
½ Fruit, 1½ Starch

- ⅓ cup sifted powdered sugar
- 2 tablespoons unsweetened cocoa powder
- 1 tablespoon cornstarch
- 1 teaspoon instant espresso coffee powder or 2 teaspoons instant coffee powder
- 3 egg whites
- ½ teaspoon vanilla
- ¼ cup granulated sugar
- ⅓ cup semisweet chocolate pieces
- 1 teaspoon shortening

1 Line a large cookie sheet with parchment paper or foil; set aside. In a small bowl stir together powdered sugar, cocoa powder, cornstarch, and espresso powder; set aside.

2 In a medium mixing bowl beat egg whites and vanilla with an electric mixer on high speed until foamy. Gradually add the granulated sugar, 1 tablespoon at a time, beating until stiff peaks form (tips stand straight). Gradually fold in the cocoa mixture.

3 Transfer the mixture to a pastry bag fitted with a large star tip. Pipe twenty-four 2-inch stars onto the prepared cookie sheet. (Or drop mixture by rounded teaspoons onto the prepared cookie sheet.) Bake in a 250° oven for 1 hour. Cool on the cookie sheet. Remove from parchment paper or foil.

4 In a small saucepan combine chocolate pieces and shortening. Cook and stir over low heat until chocolate is melted. Drizzle the melted chocolate over cookies.

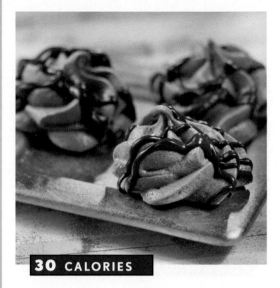

30 CALORIES

Mocha Meringue Stars

At only 30 calories each, these light-as-air morsels are practically guilt-free. The cocoa and espresso powders provide lots of flavor and no fat.

Prep: 25 minutes   **Bake:** 1 hour
Oven: 250°F   **Makes:** 24 cookies

Nutrition Facts per cookie:
30 cal., 1 g total fat (0 g sat. fat), 0 mg chol., 7 mg sodium, 5 g carbo., 0 g fiber, 1 g pro.
Daily Values:
1% calcium, 1% iron
Exchanges:
½ Other Carbo.

Brownie Cookies

Cocoa powder and brown sugar blend to make these easy drop cookies taste like rich brownies. Revisit your childhood: Enjoy them with a glass of fat-free milk.

Prep: 20 minutes   **Chill:** 1 hour

Bake: 8 minutes per batch   **Oven:** 350°F

Cool: 1 minute   **Makes:** 24 cookies

1 cup all-purpose flour
¼ teaspoon baking soda
¼ cup butter
⅔ cup granulated sugar
⅓ cup unsweetened cocoa powder
¼ cup packed brown sugar
¼ cup buttermilk or sour milk*
1 teaspoon vanilla
  Nonstick cooking spray
1 tablespoon sifted powdered sugar

1 In a small bowl stir together flour and baking soda; set aside. In a medium saucepan melt butter; remove from heat. Stir in granulated sugar, cocoa powder, and brown sugar. Stir in buttermilk and vanilla. Stir in flour mixture just until combined. Cover and chill dough for 1 hour. (Dough will be stiff.)

2 Lightly coat cookie sheets with nonstick cooking spray. Drop chilled dough by rounded teaspoons onto prepared cookie sheets.

3 Bake in a 350° oven for 8 to 10 minutes or until edges are set. Cool on cookie sheet for 1 minute. Transfer to a wire rack and let cool. Sprinkle with powdered sugar.

*Note: To make ¼ cup sour milk, place ¾ teaspoon lemon juice or vinegar in a glass measuring cup. Add enough milk to make ¼ cup total liquid; stir. Let mixture stand for 5 minutes before using.

Nutrition Facts per cookie:
73 cal., 2 g total fat (1 g sat. fat), 6 mg chol., 38 mg sodium, 12 g carbo., 0 g fiber, 1 g pro.
Daily Values:
2% vit. A, 2% calcium, 2% iron
Exchanges:
1 Other Carbo.

Nonstick cooking spray
- ¼ cup butter
- ½ cup sugar
- 1 teaspoon baking powder
- ¼ teaspoon baking soda
- 2 eggs
- ½ teaspoon vanilla
- ¼ cup unsweetened cocoa powder
- 1²/₃ cups all-purpose flour
- ⅓ cup finely chopped dried tart cherries

1 Lightly coat a large cookie sheet with nonstick cooking spray; set aside. In a large mixing bowl beat butter with an electric mixer on medium speed for 30 seconds. Add sugar, baking powder, and baking soda; beat until combined. Beat in eggs and vanilla. Beat in cocoa powder and as much of the flour as you can with the mixer. Stir in the remaining flour and the cherries.

2 Divide dough in half. Shape each half into an 8-inch-long roll. Place rolls 3 inches apart on prepared cookie sheet; flatten the rolls slightly to 2-inch width. Bake in a 375° oven for 18 to 20 minutes or until firm and a wooden toothpick inserted near center of each roll comes out clean. Remove from oven; cool on cookie sheet for 1 hour. Turn off oven.

3 Preheat oven to 325°. Using a serrated knife, cut each roll diagonally into slices about ½ inch thick. Arrange slices, cut sides down, on cookie sheet. Bake in the 325° oven for 10 minutes; turn and bake for 8 to 10 minutes more or until crisp. Transfer to a wire rack and let cool.

Chocolate-Cherry Biscotti

These Italian favorites are made by first baking the dough in a loaf, then slicing the loaf and rebaking the slices. The result is an ultra-crunchy cookie that is perfect for dipping into coffee.

Prep: 25 minutes
Bake: 18 minutes + 18 minutes
Oven: 375°F/325°F   **Cool:** 1 hour
Makes: about 24 cookies

78 CALORIES

Nutrition Facts per cookie:
78 cal., 3 g total fat (1 g sat. fat), 23 mg chol., 56 mg sodium, 12 g carbo., 0 g fiber, 2 g pro.
Daily Values:
2% vit. A, 2% calcium, 3% iron
Exchanges:
1 Other Carbo.

Orange-Blueberry Angel Food Cake

Flecked with blueberries and orange peel, this feather-light cake is capped off with a drizzle of orange glaze. Now that's a little bit of heaven!

Prep: 20 minutes **Stand:** 30 minutes
Bake: 40 minutes **Oven:** 350°F
Makes: 12 servings

208 CALORIES

Nutrition Facts per serving:
208 cal., 0 g total fat (0 g sat. fat), 0 mg chol., 48 mg sodium, 48 g carbo., 0 g fiber, 4 g pro.
Daily Values:
6% vit: C, 4% iron
Exchanges:
3 Other Carbo.

1½ cups egg whites (10 to 12 large)
1½ cups sifted powdered sugar
1   cup sifted cake flour or sifted
    all-purpose flour
1½ teaspoons cream of tartar
1   teaspoon vanilla
1   cup granulated sugar
1½ cups freeze-dried blueberries*
1   tablespoon finely shredded orange peel
1   cup sifted powdered sugar
3   to 5 teaspoons frozen orange juice
    concentrate, thawed

1 In a very large mixing bowl allow egg whites to stand at room temperature for 30 minutes. Meanwhile, sift the 1½ cups powdered sugar and the flour together 3 times. Set aside.

2 Add cream of tartar and vanilla to egg whites. Beat with an electric mixer on medium speed until soft peaks form (tips curl). Gradually add granulated sugar, about 2 tablespoons at a time, beating until stiff peaks form (tips stand straight).

3 Sift one-fourth of the powdered sugar mixture over beaten egg whites; fold in gently. Repeat, folding in the remaining powdered sugar mixture by fourths. Gently fold in freeze-dried blueberries and orange peel. Pour into an ungreased 10-inch tube pan. Gently cut through batter to remove air pockets.

4 Bake cake on the lowest rack in a 350° oven for 40 to 45 minutes or until top springs back when lightly touched. Immediately invert cake in pan; cool completely in pan. Loosen cake from pan; remove cake.

5 In a small bowl combine the 1 cup powdered sugar and 3 teaspoons of the orange juice concentrate. Stir in enough of the remaining orange juice concentrate, 1 teaspoon at a time, to reach a drizzling consistency. Drizzle over cooled cake.

*Note: Look for freeze-dried blueberries in the produce section of the supermarket. Do not substitute dried blueberries.

Nonstick cooking spray

- ³/₄ **cup sugar**
- ¹/₂ **cup water**
- 1 **tablespoon instant espresso coffee powder or 2 tablespoons instant coffee powder**
- 3 **ounces bittersweet or semisweet chocolate, chopped**
- 2 **egg yolks**
- 1 **teaspoon vanilla**
- ¹/₂ **cup unsweetened cocoa powder**
- ¹/₃ **cup all-purpose flour**
- 5 **egg whites**
- ¹/₂ **of an 8-ounce container frozen light whipped dessert topping, thawed**
- 1¹/₂ **cups fresh raspberries or sliced strawberries**

1 Lightly coat a 9-inch springform pan with nonstick cooking spray; set aside. In a medium saucepan stir together sugar, the water, and espresso powder. Cook and stir over medium-low heat until the sugar dissolves. Stir in the chocolate until melted. Remove from heat. Place egg yolks in a small bowl. Gradually stir the chocolate mixture into egg yolks; stir in vanilla (mixture may appear slightly grainy). Set aside.

2 In a medium bowl stir together the cocoa powder and flour. Stir in the melted chocolate mixture until smooth. In a large mixing bowl beat egg whites with an electric mixer on medium speed until stiff peaks form (tips stand straight). Stir a small amount of the stiffly beaten egg whites into the chocolate mixture to lighten. Fold chocolate mixture into remaining egg whites. Pour into the prepared pan.

3 Bake in a 350° oven about 30 minutes or until the top springs back when lightly touched. Cool in pan on a wire rack for 10 minutes. Loosen and remove side of pan. Cool cake completely.

4 To serve, cut cake into wedges. Top with whipped topping and berries.

156 CALORIES

Mocha Cake

Five beaten egg whites assure the lightness of this dessert. Made with espresso and bittersweet chocolate, this cake becomes a masterpiece when it's dressed in fresh red berries.

Prep: 25 minutes   **Bake:** 30 minutes
Oven: 350°F   **Makes:** 12 servings

Nutrition Facts per serving:
156 cal., 5 g total fat (3 g sat. fat), 35 mg chol., 25 mg sodium, 25 g carbo., 2 g fiber, 4 g pro.
Daily Values:
2% vit. A, 6% vit. C, 5% calcium, 6% iron
Exchanges:
1¹/₂ Other Carbo., ¹/₂ Fat

197 CALORIES

Lemon-Rosemary Cake

Lemon brings out the best in luscious berries, which is one reason this cake is so delicious. A dash of rosemary also adds a unique flavor. Use the strawberries suggested or make it a trio by adding blackberries and raspberries to the mix.

Prep: 30 minutes   **Bake:** 25 minutes
Oven: 350°F   **Makes:** 8 servings

Nutrition Facts per serving:
197 cal., 7 g total fat (1 g sat. fat), 54 mg chol., 149 mg sodium, 31 g carbo., 0 g fiber, 4 g pro.
Daily Values:
2% vit. A, 5% vit. C, 6% calcium, 5% iron
Exchanges:
2 Other Carbo., 1 Fat

Nonstick cooking spray
1 cup all-purpose flour
1 teaspoon snipped fresh rosemary
1 teaspoon baking powder
1/4 teaspoon baking soda
1/8 teaspoon salt
2/3 cup granulated sugar
2 egg yolks
3 tablespoons cooking oil
1/3 cup lemon low-fat yogurt
2 teaspoons finely shredded lemon peel
2 egg whites
1 recipe Lemon Glaze
Fresh strawberries, quartered (optional)
Lemon slices, cut into sixths (optional)
Sifted powdered sugar

1 Lightly coat an 8×1½-inch round cake pan with nonstick cooking spray; set aside. In a small bowl stir together flour, rosemary, baking powder, baking soda, and salt.

2 In a large mixing bowl beat granulated sugar, egg yolks, and oil with an electric mixer on high speed for 2 minutes. Add yogurt and lemon peel. Beat until combined. Add flour mixture. Beat just until combined. Thoroughly wash beaters. In another mixing bowl beat egg whites until stiff peaks form (tips stand straight). Stir one-third of the stiffly beaten egg whites into batter to lighten. Fold in remaining egg whites. Spread in prepared pan.

3 Bake in a 350° oven for 25 to 28 minutes or until the top springs back when lightly touched.

4 Cool in pan on a wire rack for 10 minutes. Use tines of a fork to pierce cake. Slowly drizzle Lemon Glaze over cake. Cool completely. Invert to remove from pan; turn cake top side up.

5 To serve, if desired, top each piece with strawberries and garnish with a lemon piece. Sprinkle with powdered sugar.

Lemon Glaze: In a small bowl stir together 3 tablespoons lemon juice and 2 tablespoons sifted powdered sugar.

1 cup canned pumpkin

2 slightly beaten eggs or 1/2 cup refrigerated or frozen egg product, thawed

1/3 cup packed brown sugar

3/4 teaspoon ground cinnamon

1/8 teaspoon ground allspice

1 12-ounce can (1 1/2 cups) evaporated milk

1/4 cup granulated sugar

1 In a medium bowl combine pumpkin, eggs or egg product, brown sugar, cinnamon, and allspice. Stir in evaporated milk. Pour into a 9-inch quiche dish.

2 Bake in a 300° oven for 40 to 45 minutes or until a knife inserted near the center comes out clean. Cool on a wire rack. Cover and chill for at least 2 hours or up to 24 hours.

3 Before serving, let custard stand at room temperature for 20 minutes. Meanwhile, for caramelized sugar, in a heavy 8-inch skillet heat the granulated sugar over medium-high heat until sugar begins to melt, shaking skillet occasionally to heat sugar evenly. Do not stir. Once sugar starts to melt, reduce heat to low; cook about 5 minutes more or until all of the sugar is melted and golden, stirring as needed with a wooden spoon. Quickly drizzle caramelized sugar over the custard. Serve immediately.

Cinnamon-Pumpkin Custard

When a craving for pumpkin pie hits, there's no need to ditch your diet. Treat yourself to this marvelous 195-calorie pumpkin custard.

Prep: 25 minutes **Bake:** 40 minutes
Oven: 300°F **Chill:** 2 to 24 hours
Stand: 20 minutes **Makes:** 6 servings

195 CALORIES

Nutrition Facts per serving:
195 cal., 6 g total fat (3 g sat. fat), 87 mg chol., 88 mg sodium, 30 g carbo., 1 g fiber, 6 g pro.
Daily Values:
185% vit. A, 5% vit. C, 18% calcium, 7% iron
Exchanges:
2 1/2 Other Carbo.

Coffee Custards

If you look forward to a good cup of coffee at the end of a meal, you'll flip over these captivating custards. Topped with a few berries, these custards are irresistible.

Prep: 15 minutes   **Bake:** 30 minutes
Oven: 325°F   **Cool:** 45 minutes
Makes: 6 servings

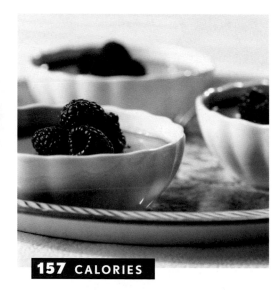

157 CALORIES

½ cup sugar
2 to 3 teaspoons instant coffee crystals
2½ cups light or low-fat milk
4 beaten eggs
1 teaspoon vanilla
   Fresh red raspberries (optional)

1 In a medium saucepan combine the sugar and coffee crystals; add milk. Cook and stir until hot and the coffee crystals are dissolved.

2 In a medium bowl gradually whisk hot milk mixture into eggs. Stir in vanilla. Place six 6-ounce custard cups or a 2-quart square baking dish in a 13×9×2-inch baking pan. Pour egg mixture into the custard cups or square baking dish. Place on the oven rack. Carefully pour boiling water into the baking pan around custard cups or square baking dish to a depth of 1 inch.

3 Bake in a 325° oven for 30 to 40 minutes or until a knife inserted near the center comes out clean. Remove the custard cups or the square baking dish from the baking pan. Cool on a wire rack for 45 minutes.

4 If desired, garnish with fresh raspberries.

Make-ahead directions: Prepare as above through step 3. Cool completely. Cover and chill up to 24 hours. Serve as above.

Nutrition Facts per serving:
157 cal., 4 g total fat (2 g sat. fat), 146 mg chol., 94 mg sodium, 21 g carbo., 0 g fiber, 8 g pro.
Daily Values:
8% vit. A, 2% vit. C, 14% calcium, 3% iron
Exchanges:
½ Milk, 1 Other Carbo., ½ Fat

6 cups fresh fruit (such as blueberries; raspberries; sliced strawberries, nectarines, peaches, pears, apricots, or bananas; and/or mango, papaya, or pineapple chunks)

1 8-ounce carton vanilla low-fat yogurt

½ cup part-skim ricotta cheese

¼ cup packed brown sugar

1 Divide fruit among four 10- to 12-ounce au gratin dishes. Place dishes in a 15×10×1-inch baking pan. In a small bowl stir together yogurt and ricotta cheese. Spoon the yogurt mixture over fruit. Sprinkle with brown sugar.

2 Bake, uncovered, in a 450° oven for 7 to 8 minutes or until brown sugar is melted. Serve immediately.

211 CALORIES

Fruited Yogurt Brûlée

When baked, this low-fat, fruit-filled dessert forms a crisp brown sugar crust. Serve it all year long with whatever fruits are in season.

Prep: 20 minutes **Bake:** 7 minutes
Oven: 450°F **Makes:** 4 servings

Nutrition Facts per serving:
211 cal., 4 g total fat (2 g sat. fat), 13 mg chol., 86 mg sodium, 39 g carbo., 5 g fiber, 7 g pro.
Daily Values:
5% vit. A, 205% vit. C, 23% calcium, 7% iron
Exchanges:
½ Milk, 1 Fruit, 1 Other Carbo.

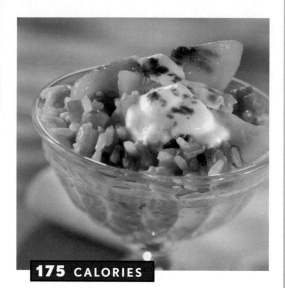

175 CALORIES

Peachy Rice Pudding

If you love rice pudding but diet variations often fall short, this peachy version will delight you. Yogurt makes it extra creamy; fresh peaches make it extra fruity.

Start to Finish: 30 minutes
Makes: 5 servings

1¹/₃ cups water

²/₃ cup long grain rice

¹/₂ of a 12-ounce can (³/₄ cup) evaporated fat-free milk

¹/₃ cup mixed dried fruit bits

2 teaspoons honey

¹/₄ teaspoon pumpkin pie spice or ground cinnamon

¹/₈ teaspoon salt

1 cup sliced, peeled peaches or frozen sliced peaches, thawed

¹/₄ cup vanilla fat-free yogurt

Pumpkin pie spice or ground cinnamon (optional)

1 In a medium saucepan stir together the water and uncooked rice. Bring to boiling; reduce heat. Simmer, covered, for 15 to 20 minutes or until rice is tender.

2 Stir evaporated milk, fruit bits, honey, the ¹/₄ teaspoon pumpkin pie spice or cinnamon, and the salt into cooked rice. Bring just to boiling; reduce heat to medium-low. Cook, uncovered, about 5 minutes or until mixture is thick and creamy, stirring frequently. Serve pudding warm topped with peaches and yogurt. If desired, sprinkle with additional pumpkin pie spice or cinnamon.

Nutrition Facts per serving:
175 cal., 0 g total fat (0 g sat. fat), 2 mg chol., 120 mg sodium, 47 g carbo., 1 g fiber, 6 g pro.
Daily Values:
7% vit. A, 5% vit. C, 14% calcium, 7% iron
Exchanges:
1¹/₂ Fruit, 1¹/₂ Starch

2 tablespoons bourbon or 2 tablespoons orange juice plus 1 teaspoon vanilla

¼ cup golden raisins or dark raisins

Nonstick cooking spray

1 slightly beaten egg white

1 slightly beaten egg

1 15-ounce can pumpkin

1 5-ounce can (²/₃ cup) evaporated milk

½ cup packed brown sugar

1 teaspoon pumpkin pie spice

⅓ cup quick-cooking rolled oats

2 tablespoons brown sugar

2 teaspoons butter or margarine, melted

1 In a small saucepan heat bourbon or orange juice and vanilla just until hot (do not boil). Add raisins; set aside to cool.

2 Lightly coat eight 6-ounce soufflé dishes or custard cups or one 1-quart casserole with nonstick cooking spray. Place soufflé dishes or custard cups in a shallow baking pan for ease of handling; set aside.

3 In a large bowl combine egg white, egg, pumpkin, evaporated milk, the ½ cup brown sugar, and the pumpkin pie spice. Stir in raisins and any liquid that is left in the saucepan. Spoon pumpkin mixture into prepared dish(es). In a small bowl stir together rolled oats and the 2 tablespoons brown sugar. Stir in melted butter. Sprinkle over pumpkin mixture.

4 Bake in a 375° oven about 30 minutes for soufflé dishes or custard cups, 40 to 45 minutes for large dish, or until a knife inserted near the center(s) comes out clean. Transfer to wire rack; cool for 1 hour before serving.

Pumpkin-Bourbon Pudding

This fancy baked pudding features pumpkin, raisins, and bourbon, making it special enough for company. Serve it in individual dishes or in one family-size casserole.

Prep: 25 minutes **Bake:** 30 minutes
Oven: 375°F **Cool:** 1 hour
Makes: 8 servings

169 CALORIES

Nutrition Facts per serving:
169 cal., 4 g total fat (2 g sat. fat), 35 mg chol., 58 mg sodium, 30 g carbo., 2 g fiber, 4 g pro.
Daily Values:
237% vit. A, 5% vit. C, 9% calcium, 8% iron
Exchanges:
2 Other Carbo., ½ Fat

Dark Chocolate Soufflés

A devil's food soufflé seems altogether too sinful to appear on any dieter's menu, but things aren't always as they seem. If you don't have espresso powder on hand, substitute instant coffee powder.

Prep: 25 minutes   **Bake:** 25 minutes
Oven: 350°F   **Makes:** 8 servings

140 CALORIES

Nutrition Facts per serving:
140 cal., 2 g total fat (1 g sat. fat), 54 mg chol., 74 mg sodium, 25 g carbo., 0 g fiber, 4 g pro.
Daily Values:
2% vit. A, 9% calcium, 5% iron
Exchanges:
2 Other Carbo.

Nonstick cooking spray
2 tablespoons granulated sugar
1 teaspoon instant espresso coffee powder or 1 teaspoon instant coffee powder
¾ cup granulated sugar
½ cup unsweetened cocoa powder
1 tablespoon all-purpose flour
⅛ teaspoon salt
½ cup milk
2 egg yolks
4 egg whites
1 teaspoon vanilla
⅛ teaspoon cream of tartar
Sifted powdered sugar (optional)

1 Lightly coat eight 4- to 6-ounce ramekins with nonstick cooking spray. In a small bowl stir together the 2 tablespoons granulated sugar and the espresso powder. Sprinkle on the side and bottom of each dish. Place in a shallow baking pan; set aside.

2 In a medium saucepan stir together ½ cup of the granulated sugar, the cocoa powder, flour, and salt. Gradually stir in milk. Cook and stir over medium-high heat until thickened and bubbly. Reduce heat; cook and stir for 1 minute more. Remove from heat. Slightly beat egg yolks. Slowly add chocolate mixture to egg yolks, stirring constantly.

3 In a large mixing bowl combine egg whites, vanilla, and cream of tartar. Beat with an electric mixer on high speed until soft peaks form (tips curl). Gradually add remaining ¼ cup granulated sugar, beating on high speed until stiff peaks form (tips stand straight). Gently fold chocolate mixture into egg whites. Spoon into prepared dishes.

4 Bake in a 350° oven about 25 minutes or until a knife inserted near centers comes out clean. If desired, sprinkle with powdered sugar. Serve immediately.

2 tablespoons sugar

1½ teaspoons unflavored gelatin

¼ cup cold water

1 16-ounce package frozen unsweetened peach slices, completely thawed and drained

½ teaspoon vanilla

½ of an 8-ounce container frozen fat-free whipped dessert topping, thawed

2 tablespoons coconut, toasted

Fresh mint sprigs (optional)

1 In a small saucepan stir together sugar and gelatin. Stir in the cold water. Cook and stir over low heat until gelatin and sugar dissolve. Remove from heat.

2 Place peaches in a blender container; add gelatin mixture and vanilla. Cover and blend until smooth. Pour peach mixture into a large bowl. Cover and chill for 1 hour. Fold whipped topping into fruit mixture. Spoon into 6 dessert dishes.

3 Cover and chill about 3 hours or until set. To serve, sprinkle with coconut. If desired, garnish with fresh mint.

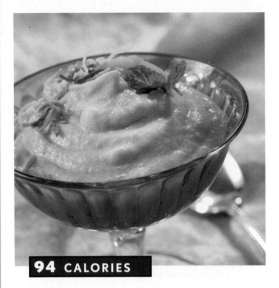

94 CALORIES

Peach-Coconut Mousse

This fruity delight is so low in calories, you can splurge and serve a cookie alongside. As an alternative to the coconut, sprinkle finely chopped crystallized ginger on top.

Prep: 25 minutes   **Chill:** 1 hour + 3 hours
Makes: 6 servings

Nutrition Facts per serving:
94 cal., 1 g total fat (1 g sat. fat), 0 mg chol., 20 mg sodium, 20 g carbo., 2 g fiber, 1 g pro.
Daily Values:
8% vit. A, 8% vit. C, 1% iron
Exchanges:
1½ Other Carbo.

3/4 cup seeded watermelon balls, chilled

3/4 cup seeded cantaloupe balls, chilled

3/4 cup seeded honeydew melon balls, chilled

1 cup lemon sorbet or mango sorbet

1/2 cup sweet sparkling wine, chilled

Fresh mint sprigs (optional)

1 Divide melon balls among 4 wine glasses or goblets. Scoop about ¼ cup sorbet on top of melon in each glass or goblet. Pour about 2 tablespoons sparkling wine over sorbet and melon in each glass or goblet. If desired, garnish with mint. Serve immediately.

Sorbet Melon Parfaits

Bring on the bubbly! Sweet sparkling wine, such as Asti Spumante, shares its effervescence in this colorful dessert.

Start to Finish: 15 minutes

Makes: 4 servings

Nutrition Facts per serving:
112 cal., 0 g total fat (0 g sat. fat), 0 mg chol.,
7 mg sodium, 24 g carbo., 1 g fiber, 1 g pro.
Daily Values:
22% vit. A, 42% vit. C, 1% calcium, 1% iron
Exchanges:
1 Fruit, ½ Other Carbo.

- ½ cup port wine
- 1 tablespoon sugar
- 2 inches stick cinnamon
- 1 teaspoon lemon juice
- 2 medium pears, peeled, cored, and cut into 6 lengthwise wedges
- 2 cups vanilla low-fat frozen yogurt

1 In a medium skillet combine wine, sugar, cinnamon, and lemon juice. Bring to boiling, stirring to dissolve sugar. Reduce heat. Simmer, uncovered, about 7 minutes or until reduced by half. Using a slotted spoon, remove and discard cinnamon.

2 Add pears to wine mixture in skillet. Cook for 6 to 8 minutes more or until pears are tender, turning occasionally. Remove from heat and let stand about 30 minutes or until cooled to room temperature. Serve fruit with frozen yogurt, drizzling sauce over yogurt.

Port-Sauced Pears

Just as port wine is a relaxing way to end an evening, these spicy red pears are a festive way to end a Yuletide meal.

Prep: 25 minutes   **Cool:** 30 minutes
Makes: 4 servings

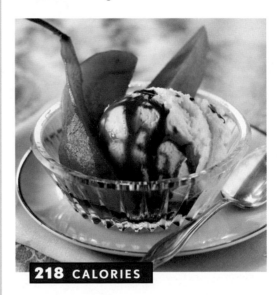

218 CALORIES

Nutrition Facts per serving:
218 cal., 3 g total fat (2 g sat. fat), 15 mg chol., 86 mg sodium, 39 g carbo., 2 g fiber, 4 g pro.
Daily Values:
7% vit. C, 9% calcium, 4% iron
Exchanges:
½ Fruit, 2 Other Carbo.

Poached Tangerines and Oranges

This dessert is as boldly flavored as it is brightly colored. Crystallized ginger, cloves, and orange liqueur create an exotic kick. Tangerines, which are actually a type of Mandarin orange, are in season from November to June.

Prep: 20 minutes   **Cool:** 30 minutes
Makes: 4 servings

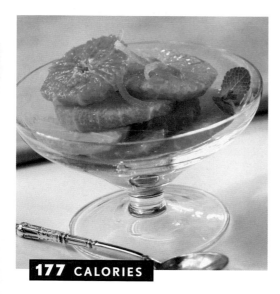

177 CALORIES

- 3 medium navel oranges
- 3 tangerines
- 1/3 cup packed brown sugar
- 1/3 cup water
- 4 whole cloves
- 2 tablespoons orange liqueur (such as Grand Marnier)
- 1 tablespoon slivered crystallized ginger
   Fresh mint sprigs

1 Remove the peel and outer membrane from the oranges and tangerines. Cut the fruit crosswise into 1/4-inch slices. Remove and discard seeds.

2 Place citrus slices in a large nonstick skillet. Add brown sugar, the water, and cloves. Bring to boiling over medium heat; reduce heat. Simmer, covered, for 2 minutes. Using a slotted spoon, remove the citrus slices from the liquid and place them in a large bowl.

3 Add orange liqueur to the skillet. Bring to boiling; reduce heat to medium. Cook, uncovered, for 6 to 8 minutes or until the liquid is reduced to about 1/4 cup and is the consistency of syrup. Pour the liquid over the citrus slices. Cover and let stand about 30 minutes or until cooled to room temperature.

4 To serve, remove and discard whole cloves. Divide citrus slices and liquid among 4 dessert bowls. Sprinkle each serving with crystallized ginger and garnish with mint.

Make-ahead directions: Prepare as above through step 3. Chill up to 24 hours. Serve as above.

Nutrition Facts per serving:
177 cal., 0 g total fat (0 g sat. fat), 0 mg chol., 10 mg sodium, 42 g carbo., 4 g fiber, 2 g pro.
Daily Values:
15% vit. A, 134% vit. C, 7% calcium, 5% iron
Exchanges:
1 Fruit, 2 Other Carbo.

Nonstick cooking spray

- **6** medium plums
- **1/2** cup unsweetened pineapple juice
- **1/4** cup packed brown sugar
- **1/2** teaspoon ground cinnamon
- **1/4** teaspoon ground cardamom
- **1/8** teaspoon ground cumin
- **1/3** cup light dairy sour cream
- **1** tablespoon packed brown sugar
- **2** tablespoons sliced almonds, toasted

1 Coat a 2-quart rectangular baking dish with nonstick cooking spray. Halve and pit plums. Place plums, cut sides up, in prepared baking dish. Stir together pineapple juice, the 1/4 cup brown sugar, the cinnamon, cardamom, and cumin. Drizzle over plums.

2 Bake in a 450° oven about 20 minutes or until plums are tender. In a small bowl stir together sour cream and the 1 tablespoon brown sugar. To serve, arrange plums in dessert dishes; top with sour cream mixture and almonds.

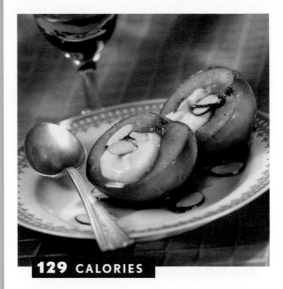

129 CALORIES

Spicy Roasted Plums

Roasting the plums concentrates their flavor and allows the spices to penetrate the fruit. If you prefer, omit the sour cream topper and serve with vanilla frozen yogurt.

Prep: 15 minutes **Bake:** 20 minutes
Oven: 450°F **Makes:** 6 servings

Nutrition Facts per serving:
129 cal., 3 g total fat (1 g sat. fat), 4 mg chol., 14 mg sodium, 25 g carbo., 2 g fiber, 2 g pro.
Daily Values:
6% vit. A, 14% vit. C, 5% calcium, 3% iron
Exchanges:
1 Fruit, 1 Other Carbo.

114 CALORIES

Minted Fruit Compote

In this recipe, winter's best-loved fruits team up with fresh mint, kiwifruit, and pomegranate seeds. This lively dessert doubles as a first-rate brunch item.

Prep: 20 minutes   **Chill:** 2 to 24 hours
Makes: 6 servings

Nutrition Facts per serving:
114 cal., 0 g total fat (0 g sat. fat), 0 mg chol., 1 mg sodium, 29 g carbo., 3 g fiber, 1 g pro.
Daily Values:
7% vit. A, 126% vit. C, 5% calcium, 4% iron
Exchanges:
2 Fruit

1 **15¹/₄-ounce can pineapple chunks (juice pack)**
2 **tablespoons sugar**
2 **tablespoons snipped fresh mint or 1¹/₂ teaspoons dried mint, crushed**
1 **tablespoon finely slivered grapefruit peel**
2 **red grapefruit, peeled, halved lengthwise, and sliced ¹/₄ inch thick**
1 **tablespoon finely slivered orange peel**
2 **oranges, peeled, halved lengthwise, and sliced ¹/₄ inch thick**
1 **kiwifruit, peeled and sliced ¹/₄ inch thick**
¹/₄ **cup pomegranate seeds***
  Thinly sliced orange peel strips (optional)

1 Drain pineapple, reserving juice; add enough water to reserved juice to make 1 cup liquid.

2 In a small saucepan combine reserved juice mixture, sugar, and mint. Bring just to boiling; reduce heat. Simmer, covered, for 5 minutes. Strain, discarding mint. Cool slightly.

3 Meanwhile, in a large serving bowl combine the pineapple chunks, slivered grapefruit peel, grapefruit slices, slivered orange peel, orange slices, and kiwifruit slices. Pour the strained liquid over fruit; cover and chill at least 2 hours or up to 24 hours.

4 To serve, stir in pomegranate seeds. If desired, garnish with orange peel strips.

*Note: To remove pomegranate seeds, cut the fruit in half just through the skin. Remove the peel and break the fruit into sections. Use your fingers or a small spoon to separate the seeds from the membrane. Handle the fruit in a bowl filled with water; this allows the seeds to float to the top and prevents the juice from discoloring your hands. Discard the skin and membrane, and eat only the seeds.

- 2 **egg whites**
- ²/₃ **cup sugar**
- 1 **teaspoon finely shredded orange peel**
- ¹/₄ **teaspoon cream of tartar**
- 4 **teaspoons sugar**
- 1 **tablespoon unsweetened cocoa powder**
- ¹/₃ **cup mascarpone cheese or reduced-fat cream cheese (Neufchâtel), softened (about 3 ounces)**
- ¹/₂ **teaspoon vanilla**
- 2 **to 3 tablespoons milk**
- 1 **cup fresh raspberries**
  Fresh mint sprigs (optional)

1 In a large mixing bowl allow egg whites to stand at room temperature for 30 minutes. Meanwhile, cover a large baking sheet with parchment paper or foil. Draw six 3-inch circles, 3 inches apart, on paper or foil; set aside.

2 For meringues, in a small bowl stir together the ²/₃ cup sugar and the orange peel. Set aside. Add cream of tartar to egg whites. Beat with an electric mixer on medium speed until soft peaks form (tips curl). Add the sugar-orange peel mixture, 1 tablespoon at a time, beating on high speed until stiff peaks form (tips stand straight). Spoon egg white mixture into the circles on the prepared baking sheet, building up sides slightly.

3 Bake in a 300° oven for 35 minutes. Turn off oven. Let meringues dry in oven with door closed for 1 hour. Remove from oven; cool completely on baking sheet.

4 For filling, stir together the 4 teaspoons sugar and the cocoa powder. In a small bowl stir together mascarpone cheese and vanilla. Stir in the cocoa mixture and enough of the milk to make of spreading consistency. Spread cocoa mixture in cooled meringues. Top with raspberries. If desired, garnish with mint.

Make-ahead directions: Prepare as above through step 3. Transfer to an airtight storage container. Store at room temperature up to 1 week. To serve, prepare filling and serve as above.

Chocolate-Filled Orange Meringues

Mascarpone is a buttery rich, extra-creamy cream cheese with a mild flavor that works well in both savory and sweet dishes. Here it's used to enhance a filling of cocoa powder and vanilla, a beguiling match for crisp orange meringue shells.

Prep: 35 minutes
Stand: 30 minutes + 1 hour
Bake: 35 minutes **Oven:** 300°F
Makes: 6 servings

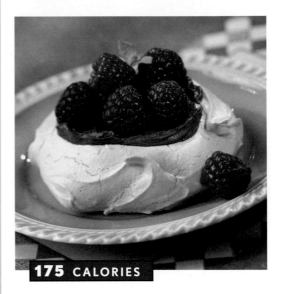

175 CALORIES

Nutrition Facts per serving:
175 cal., 7 g total fat (4 g sat. fat), 18 mg chol., 29 mg sodium, 27 g carbo., 2 g fiber, 5 g pro.
Daily Values:
1% vit. A, 8% vit. C, 2% calcium, 2% iron
Exchanges:
1 Other Carbo., 1 Fat

Granola-Topped Nectarine Gratin

A combination of raspberry applesauce and honey results in a granola topper that's low in fat and high in fruity flavor. Save the leftover granola to munch as a snack or enjoy with milk for breakfast.

Prep: 20 minutes + 15 minutes
Bake: 30 minutes + 7 minutes
Oven: 325°F/450°F   **Makes:** 4 servings

222 CALORIES

Nutrition Facts per serving:
222 cal., 2 g total fat (0 g sat. fat), 0 mg chol., 12 mg sodium, 46 g carbo., 5 g fiber, 4 g pro.
Daily Values:
22% vit. A, 19% vit. C, 4% calcium, 9% iron
Exchanges:
1 Fruit, ½ Other Carbo.

1   **cup Almond-Fruit Granola**
4   **medium nectarines, pitted and sliced**
½   **cup fresh blueberries**
2   **tablespoons orange liqueur (such as Grand Marnier) or orange juice**
2   **tablespoons brown sugar**

1 Prepare Almond-Fruit Granola; set aside.

2 For gratin, in a medium bowl combine nectarines, blueberries, and orange liqueur or orange juice; toss to coat. Spoon fruit into 4 gratin dishes or individual casseroles (12 to 16 ounces each). Sprinkle with brown sugar.

3 Bake in a 450° oven for 7 to 8 minutes or until fruit is warm and most of the sugar is melted. Sprinkle ¼ cup Almond-Fruit Granola over each gratin. Serve immediately.

Almond-Fruit Granola: Lightly coat a 13×9×2-inch baking pan with nonstick cooking spray; set aside. In a medium bowl stir together 1¼ cups rolled oats, ½ cup bran cereal, ¼ cup toasted wheat germ, and 2 tablespoons sliced almonds. In a small bowl stir together ¼ cup raspberry, mixed berry, or plain applesauce (do not use "lite" applesauce); 3 tablespoons honey; and ⅛ teaspoon ground cinnamon. Pour applesauce mixture over cereal mixture. Use a wooden spoon to mix well. Spread granola evenly in prepared pan. Bake in a 325° oven about 25 minutes or until golden, stirring occasionally. Carefully stir in ¼ cup dried berries and cherries. Bake for 5 minutes more. Spread on foil; cool completely. Store in an airtight container up to 2 weeks. Makes 3 cups.

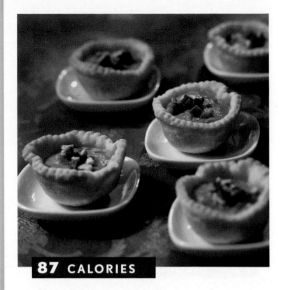

87 CALORIES

Sweet Potato Tarts

These miniature versions of an old-time Southern favorite rely on maple syrup and fat-free half-and-half for an inviting down-home flavor.

Prep: 30 minutes   **Bake:** 15 minutes
Oven: 375°F   **Makes:** 18 tarts

½ of a 15-ounce package folded refrigerated unbaked piecrust (1 crust)

3 tablespoons pure maple syrup or maple-flavored syrup

3 tablespoons refrigerated or frozen egg product, thawed

1 tablespoon brown sugar

½ teaspoon pumpkin pie spice

⅛ teaspoon salt

¾ cup mashed cooked sweet potatoes

3 tablespoons fat-free half-and-half

2 tablespoons finely chopped pecans

Chopped pecans (optional)

1 On a lightly floured surface, roll piecrust into a 12-inch circle. Cut the dough into eighteen 2½-inch circles, rerolling scraps if necessary. Press dough circles onto the bottom and sides of eighteen 1¾-inch muffin cups.

2 In a small bowl stir together maple syrup, egg product, brown sugar, pumpkin pie spice, and salt. Stir in the sweet potatoes and half-and-half. Spoon into piecrust-lined muffin cups. Sprinkle with the 2 tablespoons pecans.

3 Bake in a 375° oven about 15 minutes or until a knife inserted into the center of a tart comes out clean. Cool in muffin cups for 5 minutes. Remove from muffin cups. Serve warm or cover and refrigerate within 2 hours. If desired, garnish with additional pecans.

Nutrition Facts per tart:
87 cal., 4 g total fat (1 g sat. fat), 2 mg chol., 69 mg sodium, 13 g carbo., 0 g fiber, 1 g pro.
Daily Values:
47% vit. A, 4% vit. C, 1% calcium, 1% iron
Exchanges:
1 Other Carbo.

222 CALORIES

Caramelized Apple Tostadas

Crispy tortillas take the place of high-calorie pastry in this enchanting fruit dessert. The caramelized brown sugar and spice combination is equally spectacular with apples or pears.

Prep: 10 minutes   **Bake:** 10 minutes
Oven: 400°F   **Cook:** 30 minutes
Makes: 2 servings

2 6- to 7-inch flour tortillas
   Butter-flavor nonstick cooking spray or nonstick cooking spray
1 teaspoon granulated sugar
⅛ teaspoon pumpkin pie spice
2 apples or pears, peeled, cored, and sliced
1 tablespoon brown sugar
½ teaspoon pumpkin pie spice
1 5½-ounce can apple juice
1 tablespoon dried currants
   Sifted powdered sugar (optional)

1 Place tortillas on a baking sheet. Lightly coat tortillas with nonstick cooking spray. In a small bowl stir together granulated sugar and the ⅛ teaspoon pumpkin pie spice. Sprinkle over tortillas. Bake in a 400° oven about 10 minutes or until crisp. Cool completely on a wire rack.

2 Meanwhile, lightly coat a medium nonstick skillet with nonstick cooking spray. Preheat over medium heat. Add apples or pears, brown sugar, and the ½ teaspoon pumpkin pie spice; cook and stir about 10 minutes or until golden. Add apple juice and currants. Continue cooking, stirring occasionally, about 20 minutes or until the apples caramelize and the liquid evaporates.

3 Spoon apple mixture over tortillas. If desired, sprinkle with powdered sugar. Serve immediately.

Nutrition Facts per serving:
222 cal., 2 g total fat (0 g sat. fat), 0 mg chol., 74 mg sodium, 52 g carbo., 5 g fiber, 2 g pro.
Daily Values:
2% vit. A, 15% vit. C, 5% calcium, 8% iron
Exchanges:
1 Fruit, 1½ Other Carbo.

- ½ **cup dried tart cherries**
- 3 **tablespoons frozen apple juice concentrate, thawed**
- ¼ **teaspoon ground cinnamon**
- ¼ **of an 8-ounce package reduced-fat cream cheese (Neufchâtel)**
- ¼ **cup granulated sugar**
- 2 **tablespoons refrigerated or frozen egg product, thawed**
- 6 **sheets frozen phyllo dough (17×12-inch sheets), thawed**
  Nonstick cooking spray
- ¼ **cup graham cracker crumbs**
  Sifted powdered sugar

1 For filling, in a small saucepan combine cherries, apple juice concentrate, and cinnamon. Bring to boiling; reduce heat. Simmer, covered, about 5 minutes or until liquid is absorbed. Remove from heat. In a small mixing bowl beat cream cheese and 2 tablespoons of the granulated sugar with an electric mixer on medium speed until fluffy. Beat in egg product. Gently stir in cherry mixture. Set aside.

2 Lightly coat both sides of 1 sheet of the phyllo dough with nonstick cooking spray. (To keep remaining sheets of phyllo dough from drying out, place them on a sheet of waxed paper. Cover with a dry kitchen towel; place a damp kitchen towel on top.) Sprinkle with 2 teaspoons of the graham cracker crumbs and 1 teaspoon of the remaining granulated sugar. Repeat layers 2 more times, coating just the top side of each phyllo sheet. Cut phyllo stack crosswise into 6 strips. Place 1 well-rounded teaspoon of the filling about 1 inch from the end of each strip. Bring a corner of the phyllo over the filling so the short edge lines up with the long edge. Continue folding the triangular shape along the strip until the end is reached. Repeat with the remaining strips.

3 Repeat with the remaining phyllo dough, graham cracker crumbs, granulated sugar, and filling. Place on baking sheet. Bake in a 350° oven for 12 to 15 minutes or until lightly browned and crisp. Transfer to a wire rack and let cool. Sprinkle with powdered sugar.

Cherry Cheese Turnovers

These phyllo packets, bursting with cherries and cream cheese, are so fabulous, it's hard to believe that they have only 92 calories and 2 grams of fat each.

Prep: 30 minutes **Bake:** 12 minutes
Oven: 350°F **Makes:** 12 servings

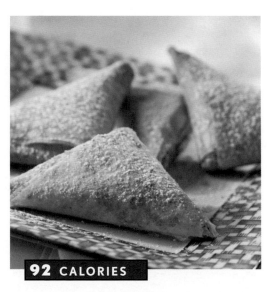

92 CALORIES

Nutrition Facts per serving:
92 cal., 2 g total fat (1 g sat. fat), 4 mg chol., 86 mg sodium, 17 g carbo., 0 g fiber, 2 g pro.
Daily Values:
1% vit. A, 1% calcium, 3% iron
Exchanges:
1 Other Carbo., ½ Fat

Green Tea and Tangerine Sorbet

Citrus flavors mingle with a hint of green tea in this refreshing sorbet, perfect for a hot summer day. Serve the sorbet for dessert, as a snack, or as a palate cleanser between courses.

Prep: 10 minutes   **Stand:** 30 minutes
Freeze: 4 hours + 2 hours
Makes: 6 servings

74 CALORIES

1 stalk lemongrass, cut up
3/4 cup cold water
1 teaspoon green tea leaves or 1 green tea bag
2 cups tangerine juice
1/4 cup light-colored corn syrup
   Tangerine slices, halved (optional)
   Snipped fresh mint (optional)

1 Using the flat side of a meat mallet, lightly pound lemongrass to slightly crush. Place in a small saucepan; add the cold water. Bring just to boiling over medium heat. Remove from heat. Add tea leaves to hot liquid. Steep for 2 minutes.

2 Strain the hot liquid into a medium bowl; discard solids. Let liquid stand about 30 minutes or until cool.

3 Stir tangerine juice and corn syrup into liquid. Pour into a nonmetal freezer container.* Cover and freeze about 4 hours or until nearly firm.

4 Break the mixture into chunks. Transfer to a chilled medium mixing bowl. Beat with an electric mixer on medium speed until smooth. Return to freezer container. Cover and freeze about 2 hours or until firm.

5 To serve, scoop into chilled serving dishes. If desired, garnish with tangerine slices and mint.

*Note: If you prefer, freeze the green tea mixture in a no-ice, no-salt electric ice cream maker according to the manufacturer's directions.

Nutrition Facts per serving:
74 cal., 0 g total fat (0 g sat. fat), 0 mg chol., 18 mg sodium, 19 g carbo., 0 g fiber, 0 g pro.
Daily Values:
7% vit. A, 43% vit. C, 2% calcium, 2% iron
Exchanges:
1 Other Carbo.

1½ **cups sugar**

1 **envelope unflavored gelatin**

3¼ **cups blood orange juice and/or orange juice**

1½ **cups buttermilk**

1 **teaspoon vanilla**

1 In a medium saucepan combine sugar and gelatin. Stir in 2 cups of the orange juice. Cook and stir until sugar and gelatin dissolve. Remove from heat. Stir in the remaining orange juice, the buttermilk, and vanilla.

2 Transfer to a 4-quart ice cream freezer; freeze according to manufacturer's directions. Ripen for 4 hours.*

***Note:** Ripening homemade sherbet is not essential, but it improves the texture and slows down melting. To ripen in a traditional-style ice cream freezer, after churning, remove the lid and dasher and cover the top of the freezer can with waxed paper or foil. Plug the hole in the lid with a small piece of cloth; replace the lid. Pack the outer freezer bucket with enough ice and rock salt to cover the top of the freezer can (use 4 cups ice to 1 cup salt). Let stand about 4 hours. When using an ice cream freezer with an insulated freezer bowl, transfer the ice cream to a covered freezer-proof container and ripen in your regular freezer about 4 hours (or follow the manufacturer's recommendations).

104 CALORIES

Blood Orange Sherbet

This sherbet's appealing pink color and orchard-fresh flavor come straight from the crimson red orange juice.

Prep: 40 minutes **Ripen:** 4 hours
Freeze: According to manufacturer's directions
Makes: 16 servings

Nutrition Facts per serving:
104 cal., 0 g total fat (0 g sat. fat), 1 mg chol., 26 mg sodium, 24 g carbo., 0 g fiber, 1 g pro.
Daily Values:
2% vit. A, 42% vit. C, 3% calcium, 1% iron
Exchanges:
1½ Other Carbo.

Frozen Berry-Orange Bombe

This showy dessert is a dazzling way to end any summer party. Another time, try lemon or pineapple sorbet in place of the strawberry or raspberry flavors suggested here.

Prep: 15 minutes   **Freeze:** 1 hour + 4 hours
Makes: 10 servings

123 CALORIES

3 **cups strawberry or raspberry sorbet, softened**

2 **cups low-fat or light chocolate ice cream**

1 **tablespoon orange liqueur or orange juice**

2 **cups fresh raspberries, blueberries, blackberries, and/or strawberries**

   Fresh mint sprigs (optional)

1 Line a 2-quart bowl with plastic wrap. Press sorbet on bottom and two-thirds up the sides of the bowl to form a shell. Cover and freeze at least 1 hour.

2 Soften chocolate ice cream. Gently stir in orange liqueur or orange juice. Spoon into the center of the sorbet shell, pressing down to remove air bubbles. Cover and freeze for at least 4 hours.

3 Unmold frozen mixture. Remove plastic wrap. Serve with berries. If desired, garnish with mint.

Nutrition Facts per serving:
123 cal., 1 g total fat (1 g sat. fat), 2 mg chol., 17 mg sodium, 27 g carbo., 1 g fiber, 1 g pro.
Daily Values:
1% vit. A, 40% vit. C, 4% calcium, 1% iron
Exchanges:
2 Other Carbo.

M

W–Z

How Recipes are Analyzed

The Better Homes and Gardens® Test Kitchen uses nutrition analysis software to determine the nutritional value of a single serving of a recipe. Here are some factors to keep in mind regarding each analysis:

- Analyses do not include optional ingredients.

- The first serving size listed is analyzed when a range is given. For example, if a recipe makes 4 to 6 servings, the Nutrition Facts are based on 4 servings.

- When ingredient choices (such as butter or margarine) appear in a recipe, the first one mentioned is used for analysis.

- When milk is a recipe ingredient, the analysis is calculated using 2 percent (reduced-fat) milk unless otherwise noted.

- The exchanges, listed for every recipe along with the Nutrition Facts, are based on the exchange list developed by the American Dietetic Association and the American Diabetes Association.

Metric Information

The charts on this page provide a guide for converting measurements from the U.S. customary system, which is used throughout this book, to the metric system.

Product Differences

Most of the ingredients called for in the recipes in this book are available in most countries. However, some are known by different names. Here are some common American ingredients and their possible counterparts:

- Sugar (white) is granulated, fine granulated, or castor sugar.
- Powdered sugar is icing sugar.
- All-purpose flour is enriched, bleached or unbleached white household flour. When self-rising flour is used in place of all-purpose flour in a recipe that calls for leavening, omit the leavening agent (baking soda or baking powder) and salt.
- Light-colored corn syrup is golden syrup.
- Cornstarch is cornflour.
- Baking soda is bicarbonate of soda.
- Vanilla or vanilla extract is vanilla essence.
- Green, red, or yellow sweet peppers are capsicums or bell peppers.
- Golden raisins are sultanas.

Volume and Weight

The United States traditionally uses cup measures for liquid and solid ingredients. The chart below shows the approximate imperial and metric equivalents. If you are accustomed to weighing solid ingredients, the following approximate equivalents will be helpful.

- 1 cup butter, castor sugar, or rice = 8 ounces = $1/2$ pound = 250 grams
- 1 cup flour = 4 ounces = $1/4$ pound = 125 grams
- 1 cup icing sugar = 5 ounces = 150 grams

Canadian and U.S. volume for a cup measure is 8 fluid ounces (237 ml), but the standard metric equivalent is 250 ml.

1 British imperial cup is 10 fluid ounces.

In Australia, 1 tablespoon equals 20 ml, and there are 4 teaspoons in the Australian tablespoon.

Spoon measures are used for smaller amounts of ingredients. Although the size of the tablespoon varies slightly in different countries, for practical purposes and for recipes in this book, a straight substitution is all that's necessary. Measurements made using cups or spoons always should be level unless stated otherwise.

Common Weight Range Replacements

Imperial / U.S.	Metric
$1/2$ ounce	15 g
1 ounce	25 g or 30 g
4 ounces ($1/4$ pound)	115 g or 125 g
8 ounces ($1/2$ pound)	225 g or 250 g
16 ounces (1 pound)	450 g or 500 g
$1 1/4$ pounds	625 g
$1 1/2$ pounds	750 g
2 pounds or $2 1/4$ pounds	1,000 g or 1 Kg

Oven Temperature Equivalents

Fahrenheit Setting	Celsius Setting*	Gas Setting
300°F	150°C	Gas Mark 2 (very low)
325°F	160°C	Gas Mark 3 (low)
350°F	180°C	Gas Mark 4 (moderate)
375°F	190°C	Gas Mark 5 (moderate)
400°F	200°C	Gas Mark 6 (hot)
425°F	220°C	Gas Mark 7 (hot)
450°F	230°C	Gas Mark 8 (very hot)
475°F	240°C	Gas Mark 9 (very hot)
500°F	260°C	Gas Mark 10 (extremely hot)
Broil	Broil	Grill

*Electric and gas ovens may be calibrated using celsius. However, for an electric oven, increase celsius setting 10 to 20 degrees when cooking above 160°C. For convection or forced air ovens (gas or electric) lower the temperature setting 25°F/10°C when cooking at all heat levels.

Baking Pan Sizes

Imperial / U.S.	Metric
$9 \times 1 1/2$-inch round cake pan	22- or 23×4-cm (1.5 L)
$9 \times 1 1/2$-inch pie plate	22- or 23×4-cm (1 L)
$8 \times 8 \times 2$-inch square cake pan	20×5-cm (2 L)
$9 \times 9 \times 2$-inch square cake pan	22- or 23×4.5-cm (2.5 L)
$11 \times 7 \times 1 1/2$-inch baking pan	28×17×4-cm (2 L)
2-quart rectangular baking pan	30×19×4.5-cm (3 L)
$13 \times 9 \times 2$-inch baking pan	34×22×4.5-cm (3.5 L)
$15 \times 10 \times 1$-inch jelly roll pan	40×25×2-cm
$9 \times 5 \times 3$-inch loaf pan	23×13×8-cm (2 L)
2-quart casserole	2 L

U.S. / Standard Metric Equivalents

$1/8$ teaspoon = 0.5 ml

$1/4$ teaspoon = 1 ml

$1/2$ teaspoon = 2 ml

1 teaspoon = 5 ml

1 tablespoon = 15 ml

2 tablespoons = 25 ml

$1/4$ cup = 2 fluid ounces = 50 ml

$1/3$ cup = 3 fluid ounces = 75 ml

$1/2$ cup = 4 fluid ounces = 125 ml

$2/3$ cup = 5 fluid ounces = 150 ml

$3/4$ cup = 6 fluid ounces = 175 ml

1 cup = 8 fluid ounces = 250 ml

2 cups = 1 pint = 500 ml

1 quart = 1 litre

Equivalents

When a recipe calls for a measurement of food or fresh produce and you don't know how much to buy, use these guidelines to help determine what you will need.

Food	Beginning size or amount	Yield and cut
Apple	1 medium	1 cup sliced or $^2/_3$ cup chopped
Apricots	1 pound (8 to 12 whole)	$2^1/_2$ cups sliced
Asparagus	1 pound (18 to 24 spears)	2 to $2^1/_2$ cups 1-inch pieces
Banana	1 medium	$^1/_3$ cup mashed or $^3/_4$ cup sliced
Beans, green	1 pound	3 to $3^1/_2$ cups 1-inch pieces
Blueberries	1 pound	3 cups
Broccoli	1 pound	4 cups florets
Cabbage	1 medium head ($1^1/_2$ pounds)	7 to 10 cups shredded or 6 cups coarsely chopped
Carrot	1 medium	$^1/_2$ cup sliced, chopped, julienned, or finely shredded
Cauliflower	1 medium head ($1^1/_2$ pounds)	6 cups florets
Celery	1 stalk	$^1/_2$ cup sliced or chopped
Cherries	1 pound	3 cups whole or $2^1/_2$ cups halved
Chocolate chips	6 ounces	1 cup
Cranberries	1 pound	4 cups
Cream, whipping	1 cup unwhipped	2 cups whipped
Garlic	1 clove	$^1/_2$ teaspoon minced
Grapes	1 pound	$2^1/_2$ cups
Leek	1 medium	$^1/_3$ cup sliced
Lemon	1 medium	2 teaspoons finely shredded peel 3 tablespoons juice
Lime	1 medium	$1^1/_2$ teaspoons finely shredded peel 2 tablespoons juice
Mango	1 medium	1 cup sliced
Melon		
Cantaloupe	1 medium ($2^1/_2$ pounds)	6 cups cubed or $5^1/_2$ cups balls
Honeydew	1 medium ($2^1/_2$ pounds)	6 cups cubed or $5^1/_2$ cups balls
Mushrooms	8 ounces	3 cups sliced or chopped
Nectarine	1 medium	1 cup sliced or $^3/_4$ cup chopped
Onion	1 medium	$^1/_2$ cup chopped
Onion, green	1 medium	2 tablespoons sliced
Orange	1 medium	1 tablespoon finely shredded peel $^1/_3$ cup juice or $^1/_3$ cup sections
Papaya	1 medium (1 pound)	$1^1/_4$ cups sliced
Parsnip	1 medium	$^3/_4$ to 1 cup sliced or chopped
Peach	1 medium	1 cup sliced or $^3/_4$ cup chopped
Pear	1 medium	1 cup sliced or chopped
Pepper, sweet	1 medium	1 cup strips or $^3/_4$ cup chopped
Potatoes	1 pound	3 cups cubed (unpeeled) or $2^3/_4$ cups cubed (peeled)
Pineapple	1 medium (4 pounds)	$4^1/_2$ cups peeled and cubed
Raspberries	1 pound	4 cups
Rice, long grain	1 cup uncooked	3 cups cooked
Rhubarb	1 pound	4 cups sliced
Shallot	1 medium	2 tablespoons finely chopped
Squash		
Summer (zucchini, yellow)	1 medium	$1^1/_4$ cups sliced
Winter (acorn, butternut)	2 pounds	4 cups chopped or 2 cups mashed
Strawberries	1 pint (about 1 pound)	3 cups whole or $2^1/_2$ cups sliced
Tomato	1 medium	$^1/_2$ cup peeled, seeded, and chopped

Emergency Substitutions

It you don't have:	Substitute:
Baking powder, 1 teaspoon	$1/2$ teaspoon cream of tartar plus $1/4$ teaspoon baking soda
Balsamic vinegar, 1 tablespoon	1 tablespoon cider vinegar or red wine vinegar plus $1/2$ teaspoon sugar
Bread crumbs, fine dry, $1/4$ cup	$3/4$ cup soft bread crumbs, or $1/4$ cup cracker crumbs, or $1/4$ cup cornflake crumbs
Broth, beef or chicken, 1 cup	1 teaspoon or 1 cube instant beef or chicken bouillon plus 1 cup hot water
Buttermilk, 1 cup	1 tablespoon lemon juice or vinegar plus enough milk to make 1 cup (let stand 5 minutes before using) or 1 cup plain yogurt
Chocolate, semisweet, 1 ounce	3 tablespoons semisweet chocolate pieces, or 1 ounce unsweetened chocolate plus 1 tablespoon granulated sugar, or 1 tablespoon unsweetened cocoa powder plus 2 teaspoons sugar and 2 teaspoons shortening
Chocolate, sweet baking, 4 ounces	$1/4$ cup unsweetened cocoa powder plus $1/3$ cup granulated sugar and 3 tablespoons shortening
Chocolate, unsweetened, 1 ounce	3 tablespoons unsweetened cocoa powder plus 1 tablespoon cooking oil or shortening, melted
Cornstarch, 1 tablespoon (for thickening)	2 tablespoons all-purpose flour
Corn syrup (light), 1 cup	1 cup granulated sugar plus $1/4$ cup water
Egg, 1 whole	2 egg whites, or 2 egg yolks, or $1/4$ cup refrigerated or frozen egg product, thawed
Flour, cake, 1 cup	1 cup minus 2 tablespoons all-purpose flour
Flour, self-rising, 1 cup	1 cup all-purpose flour plus 1 teaspoon baking powder, $1/2$ teaspoon salt, and $1/4$ teaspoon baking soda
Garlic, 1 clove	$1/2$ teaspoon bottled minced garlic or $1/8$ teaspoon garlic powder
Ginger, grated fresh, 1 teaspoon	$1/4$ teaspoon ground ginger
Molasses, 1 cup	1 cup honey
Mustard, dry, 1 teaspoon	1 tablespoon prepared (in cooked mixtures)
Mustard, prepared, 1 tablespoon	$1/2$ teaspoon dry mustard plus 2 teaspoons vinegar
Onion, chopped, $1/2$ cup	2 tablespoons dried minced onion or $1/2$ teaspoon onion powder
Sour cream, dairy, 1 cup	1 cup plain yogurt
Sugar, granulated, 1 cup	1 cup packed brown sugar or 2 cups sifted powdered sugar
Sugar, brown, 1 cup packed	1 cup granulated sugar plus 2 tablespoons molasses
Tomato juice, 1 cup	$1/2$ cup tomato sauce plus $1/2$ cup water
Tomato sauce, 2 cups	$3/4$ cup tomato paste plus 1 cup water
Vanilla bean, 1 whole	2 teaspoons vanilla extract
Wine, red, 1 cup	1 cup beef or chicken broth in savory recipes; cranberry juice in desserts
Wine, white, 1 cup	1 cup chicken broth in savory recipes; apple juice or white grape juice in desserts
Yeast, active dry, 1 package	about $2 1/4$ teaspoons active dry yeast

Seasonings

Apple pie spice, 1 teaspoon	$1/2$ teaspoon ground cinnamon plus $1/4$ teaspoon ground nutmeg, $1/8$ teaspoon ground allspice, and dash ground cloves or ginger
Cajun seasoning, 1 tablespoon	$1/2$ teaspoon white pepper, $1/2$ teaspoon garlic powder, $1/2$ teaspoon onion powder, $1/2$ teaspoon ground red pepper, $1/2$ teaspoon paprika, and $1/2$ teaspoon black pepper
Herbs, snipped fresh, 1 tablespoon	$1/2$ to 1 teaspoon dried herb, crushed, or $1/2$ teaspoon ground herb
Poultry seasoning, 1 teaspoon	$3/4$ teaspoon dried sage, crushed, plus $1/4$ teaspoon dried thyme or marjoram, crushed
Pumpkin pie spice, 1 teaspoon	$1/2$ teaspoon ground cinnamon plus $1/4$ teaspoon ground ginger, $1/4$ teaspoon ground allspice, and $1/8$ teaspoon ground nutmeg